UNDERGRADUATE TEXTS IN COMPUTER SCIENCE

Editors

David Gries
Fred Schneider

Springer
New York
Berlin
Heidelberg
Barcelona
Budapest
Hong Kong
London
Milan
Paris
Santa Clara
Singapore
Tokyo

MIGRATING FROM PASCAL TO C++

Susan M. Merritt
Pace University

Allen Stix
Pace University

Springer

Susan M. Merritt
Department of Computer Science
Pace University
1 Martine Avenue
White Plains, NY 10606-1932
USA

Allen Stix
Department of Computer Science
Pace University
1 Martine Avenue
White Plains, NY 10606-1932
USA

Series Editors

David Gries
Department of Computer Science
Cornell University
405 Upson Hall
Ithaca, NY 14853
USA

Fred Schneider
Department of Computer Science
Cornell University
405 Upson Hall
Ithaca, NY 14853
USA

Merritt, Susan M.
    Migrating from Pascal to C++ / Susan M. Merritt, Allen Stix.
        p.   cm. — (Undergraduate texts in computer science)
    Includes bibliographical references and index.
    ISBN 0-387-94730-2 (hard: alk. paper)
    1. C++ (Computer program language) 2. Pascal (Computer program
language) I. Stix, Allen. II. Title. III. Series.
    QA76.73.C153M47   1996
    005.13′3—dc20   96-11796

Printed on acid-free paper.

Production managed by Terry Kornak; manufacturing supervised by Joe Quatela.
Typeset in TEX from author files by The Bartlett Press, Inc.
Printed and bound by R.R. Donnelley & Sons, Harrisonburg, VA.
Printed in the United States of America.

9 8 7 6 5 4 3 2 1

ISBN 0-387-94730-2 Springer-Verlag New York Berlin Heidelberg SPIN 10533267

Preface

This book was written when the authors, who are interested in programming language concepts and systems and the teaching of them, wanted to investigate C++ seriously, and also wanted to assist their colleagues in learning it easily and well. This was in anticipation of a change in the introductory language in the curriculum from Pascal to C++, during which many professors and advanced students would need to make the transition. Towards the latter goal, the authors investigated a couple of books on the market that were allegedly for the Pascal programmer wanting to learn C++. The experience was very interesting and unsatisfactory, because although the book titles referred to Pascal it was clear that the books were originally really written for C programmers. This was obvious because words from C were used without definition, and C ideas were assumed. Moreover, the authors were unable to find a book that in fact took the expertise of the Pascal programmer and used that to teach the important concepts in C++ (not C).

Moreover, as the authors began to learn C++ and read about it and think about it, it became clear that C++ was an extension of procedural programming and was structured along the model of the classic Structured Programming by Dahl, Dijkstra, and Hoare. In *Structured Programming* the authors talk about structured control in the first essay, about structured data types in the second, and about classes and objects in the third; the first two ideas made their way into Pascal, the third into SIMULA. In fact the "better C" part of C++ is more like Pascal than the authors originally suspected, and the object-oriented part of C++ is like SIMULA. The authors wrote a paper that explored this connection between C++ and the origins of structured programming and that became Chapter 1 of this book. The authors then wrote two technical reports that completely described that part of C++ that covers Pascal. That was widely distributed among colleagues at our institution and others, was well received, and has become Chapter 2. Chapter 3 was then developed to complete the conventional or structured part of C++, that is, those features not directly available in Pascal. Chapter 4 explains the big ideas in object-oriented programming including derivation and polymorphism. Finally, the fifth chapter is a comprehensive look at templates that may not be found anywhere else in a comparably readable form. Again the authors did a paper on templates that was widely distributed among colleagues and that paper made its way into the book as Chapter 5.

In summary, the book provides an effective introduction to C++ for the Pascal programmer. It does not assume knowledge of C. It does not teach how to program, but assumes programming expertise and a certain amount of sophistication with programming language ideas. It is very useful for one who wishes to make the transition from Pascal quickly and easily. The exercises extend the text, and new ideas are often presented in both the questions and the answers. It is particularly for those Pascal students, teachers, and programmers who urgently need to learn C++ in a timely way.

We wish to acknowledge our colleagues, many of whom used our materials in preliminary form and gave us very helpful suggestions, corrections, and recommendations. One among them, Dr. Mary Courtney, made a substantial contribution in assisting in the identification of the subset that covers Pascal for the purposes of teaching. Another, Dr. Carol Wolf, read everything in a timely way and commented on it. We would also like to thank our students with whom we used these materials; they gave us many useful insights.

In particular we would like to thank those who assisted us in preparing the manuscript: Jeffrey Coffin, Amanda Markham, Margaret Privitello, Nancy Treuer, and Xiaoyan Wang. Each of these individuals at different times and in different ways went well beyond the call of duty in assisting us when we needed that assistance most. More than anyone else, Jeannie Song tirelessly helped us through three drafts of the manuscript as only someone who is an excellent C++ programmer, skilled in proofreading and editorship from college yearbook days, and a supremely agreeable and giving individual. Jeannie is a special person, and we want to express our gratitude for everything she did.

Susan M. Merritt
Allen Stix

Contents

1

C++ as Structured Programming: An Historical Perspective

1.0   Introduction

C++ can be learned as a structured object-oriented programming language, and can be particularly well learned that way by the Pascal programmer.

To some, the phrase "structured object-oriented programming language" may seem contradictory or inconsistent. There has been a good deal of discussion around the notion that the object-oriented programming paradigm, or style, will supersede the structured programming paradigm. This discussion assumes that the two paradigms are mutually exclusive. This is a confusion, generated in part by another assumption, that the SmallTalk programming language set the standard for object-oriented programming. SmallTalk is a fine object-oriented programming language that is somewhat LOGO-like and somewhat LISP-like; it is not structured and has, in fact, characteristics of a functional programming language. As a result, one can well learn SmallTalk from a LISP or other functional programming language mindset. And one can well learn C++ from a Pascal or other structured programming language mindset.

C++ is also a fine object-oriented programming language that can be viewed as Pascal-like, that is, structured. In Section 1.1, a serious exposition is presented on the invention of structured programming by Dijkstra and Hoare [1], and its continuing meaning. Pascal is shown to be the original realization of structured programming, and the procedural subset of C++ is shown to be structured in the same ways as Pascal. In this sense, it can be argued that Pascal might be a better platform from which to learn C++ than C is. There are some who claim that C++ is an object-oriented extension to C. From a programming language perspective it is more compelling to understand the procedural subset of C++ as a better C, as the inventor of C++, Bjarne Stroustrup, understands it [4]. It is better because like Pascal, it provides stronger type checking, as well as other features that are Pascal-like (e. g., pass by reference, and the keyword *new* for dynamic storage allocation); these are notationally more convenient and provide for more reliability. To learn C++ as the structured language that it is, experience with Pascal can be better than experience with C. C is notorious for the tricks and techniques that can support very low-level, hard to understand programming, and that are not encouraged in C++ (although they are supported).

But C++ is an object-oriented programming language. That means that it includes an extension of the notion of *type* to the notion of *class*. In the same way that types are instantiated in variables in programs, *classes* are instantiated in *objects*. Stroustrup calls his first step toward the development of C++ as having added "Simula-like classes to C." In Section 1.2 is a discussion of Simula-like classes and their relationship to structured programming; a very concise description of what *classes* and *objects* are; and a brief discussion about what functionality they provide.

Finally, in Section 1.3 is a "paradigm discussion." Stroustrup argues that a general-purpose programming language ought to and can support more than one programming paradigm [4]. In fact, C++ can support structured programming and object-oriented programming. (Stroustrup also points out that between the two styles, one can also use C++ as an Ada-like language that supports data abstraction without object-orientation.)

1.1   Structured Programming

The title of this section "Structured Programming" is intentionally chosen to coincide with the title of the classic book *Structured Programming* by Dahl, Dijkstra, and Hoare [1] that introduced the words and the meaning of "structured programming." Here Pascal is shown to be the original realization of a structured programming language and what that means. The procedural subset of C++ is a structured programming language that is very similar to Pascal.

History of Pascal as Structured Programming

In [7] Wirth indicates that early programming was essentially trickery that optimized the running of certain algorithms on certain hardware. (This description might, in fact, apply to some C programming.) The main problem to be solved was the debugging of the trickery to eliminate mistakes. FORTRAN was a significant step forward in that it was a tool that supported the systemization of programming to some extent; FORTRAN was followed by ALGOL 60. Wirth points out that ALGOL 60 extended to the level of statements what FORTRAN had introduced in (arithmetic) expressions: structure.

But the notion of structure, or structured language, did not take hold until Dijkstra first used the term structured programming, and with it introduced a general intellectual approach to be used to tackle problems systematically. In the preface to [9], Wirth attributes the initial outstanding contributions to programming as an academic discipline to Dijkstra and Hoare. The theory and terminology in "Notes on Structured Programming," and "Notes on Data Structuring," both published in 1972 in *Structured Programming* [1] (but distributed earlier) were realized in the programming language Pascal, designed by Niklaus Wirth between 1968 and 1970 and published in 1971 [5]. Although more has been said about structured programming in the two decades since, the fundamental concepts remain unchanged.

Control Structures

In *Structured Programming*, the concatenation, selection, and iteration paradigms that have come to be understood as structured programming were introduced. Concatenation simply refers to the structure of a program segment that can be decomposed into sequential subsegments, such that the cumulative effect of the subsegments equals the desired net effect of the segment. (Although this paradigm is now generally referred to as sequential composition, it was originally called concatenation by Dijkstra.)

In the case of selection, Dijkstra identified two constructs in addition to the **IF . . . THEN** statement of FORTRAN. One is the **if . . . then . . . else** that more explicitly specifies both choices of a selection, and the other is the **case-of**, originally given by Hoare, which provides a choice among more than two possibilities in a selection. With these additions, program segments for selection can always be written so that there is a single entry to the "top" and a single exit from the "bottom." There is thus no need for jumps to labeled points; that is, there is no need for **goto** statements.

In the case of iteration, two distinct loop structures were introduced in addition to the count-driven loop structure of FORTRAN, which is the **for . . . do** in Pascal: the **while . . . do** loop and the **repeat . . . until** loop. With these additions, program segments for iteration can also be written without the **goto** statement.

Dijkstra claimed that all programs could be written and understood in terms of these three constructions: concatenation, selection, and iteration. The resulting program decomposition became the basis of proofs of correctness, thereby increasing the reliability of the programs. C++ provides all these control structures.

	Pascal	*C++*
Concatenation:	Concatenation is either represented by simple juxtaposition of constructions, or by grouping constructions using the following:	
	begin ... end	*{ ... }*
Selection:	**if ... then**	*if ...*
	if ... then ... else	*if ... else*
	case ... of	*switch ... case*
Iteration:	**while ... do**	*while ...*
	repeat ... until	*do ... while*
	for ... do	*for ...*

Data Structures

In *Structured Programming* [1], Hoare introduced the type definition and noted the difference between types and variables. He proposed new kinds of types that could be user-defined such as the symbolic scalar, subrange, generalized array (with the domain of symbolic scalar types, e.g.), and records. These ideas were realized in Pascal in which types can be defined explicitly by the programmer, and include enumerated types (symbolic scalar types), record types, set types, and subrange types. C++ provides user-defined enumerated types and record types (called *structs*, for structures). There are no subrange or set types in C++ (and these are, in fact, rarely used in Pascal). In fact C++ extends the notion of type to *classes*, which are discussed in Section 1.2.

The significance of type in structured programming goes well beyond the particular types available. In Pascal, every variable is said to be of a certain type, either built in or explicitly defined by the programmer. This provides information needed for program verification, which is always at least an implicit goal of structured programming, as well as for efficient compilation. The type of a variable determines suitable storage representation for a variable; it determines the set of operators applicable to a variable; and it excludes information that cannot be determined from a simple textual scan. Pointers are associated with specific types and dynamic data structures are (mostly) homogeneous. In fact, because of these characteristics, Pascal is understood to have static and strong type checking.

C++ also has strong type checking. In his history of C++, Stroustrup [4] indicates that work leading to the development of C++ began in 1979. At that time, Stroustrup developed C With Classes (referring to Simula-like classes, which is discussed in Section 1.3) and which he intended at first to be an extension to the programming language C for expressing modularity and concurrency. Very unlike C, however, the first implementation of C With Classes included static type checking that resulted in stronger type checking. Stroustrup notes that for him strong type checking was a "simple must" in C With Classes. Even stronger type checking made its way into C++, which evolved from C With Classes in 1983.

There are small differences between Pascal and C++ with respect to typing. For example, like Pascal, all variables must be declared in C++; unlike Pascal, C++ allows types of variables to be declared anywhere up to and including their first use; in addition, values may be assigned in type declarations. Like Pascal (and very unlike C) pointers are associated with types, and dynamic data structures are (mostly) homogeneous. Also like Pascal, there is strict checking of function parameter types and return types. Functions must always be declared before use.

There are two extremely important discoveries here for the Pascal programmer. The first is that the strong typing mechanism of Pascal is essential to good structured programming and C++ shares that typing mechanism. (Both Pascal, with the variant record, and C++, with the *union*, have loopholes; these are discussed in subsequent chapters.) The second is that although C++ is still perceived by some to be an extension of C, it is instead a better C. For Pascal programmers, it might be useful to think of C++ as a Pascal-like C. These discoveries underline the implicit assumption of this book, that learning C++ from a Pascal base is not only natural, but also can be preferable to learning C++ from a C base.

Other Characteristics of Structured Programming

Verification of Programs

An explicit goal of the development of the control structures and data structures described here is the development of programming into a systematic methodology. The potential for verification is implicit. Verification rests upon the restriction of control structures to concatenation, selection and iteration, and the structuring and typing of data. C++ is like Pascal in that programs can be written in both disciplines, and are thereby potentially verifiable. (Both Pascal and C++ have the *goto* but it need not be used.) Although pointers are needed in C for such things as simulated pass by reference, they are not needed in procedural C++ except for the building of dynamic data structures, in which case they can be used exactly as pointers in Pascal.

Stepwise Refinement

In *Structured Programming* Dijkstra [1] begins with a model for programming that he calls "stepwise program composition": input, manipulation, and output.

Wirth presents Pascal [7,9] as a language useful for the "stepwise refinement" approach to program construction that decomposes a problem in a top-down way into abstract program segments that can, in turn, be decomposed into successive layers. In general the Pascal **procedure** is used for program composition by stepwise refinement. Pascal also has a **function**, separate from the **procedure**, which always returns a value.

Although C++ provides functions only, each with a return type, there is a return type *void* that effectively and explicitly transforms a function into a procedure. Functions with return type *void* are used for program composition by stepwise refinement. Like Pascal, C++ provides parameter passing by value and by reference. (This is very different from C, which only provides parameter passing by value.) There is another important message here: in the area of parameter passing, C++ is more Pascal-like than it is C-like. C++ also extends the notion of functions in various ways, which are also discussed in subsequent chapters.

Block Structure

In *Structured Programming*, Dijkstra notes that a most significant contribution of ALGOL 60 was the introduction of procedures (rather than FORTRAN subroutines) with local variables. There were some important implications here. The first was the concept of scope, that is, the idea that not all variables are accessible homogeneously throughout the program: local variables of a procedure, for example, may not be accessible outside the procedure body. The second was the concept of recursion, that is, that a procedure can call itself. Recursion is possible when local variables are "created" upon procedure entry and "destroyed" upon exit, that is, when there is automatic control over the lifetime of variables pertaining to a procedure incarnation that permits the use of a stack.

Pascal has nested static scope, where procedures may be nested within other procedures. Variables are local to the procedure in which they are declared, which is the scope of the variable. Because blocks may be nested, so may scopes. Items declared in the main program are global, and accessible throughout the program [2]. Dijkstra notes that a shortcoming of "automatic" or local variables is the inability to transmit information from one instantiation of a procedure to another because of the automatic control of the lifetime of local variables.

C++ also has static scope, but because functions cannot be declared within other functions, there is no nesting. (Thus scope is a simpler issue than it is in Pascal.) Local variables are, in fact, called automatic and are only accessible from within a function block, which constitutes the scope. Variables declared within loop blocks are local to the loop. The *main()* function is handled exactly as any other function, and therefore has its own local variables. Global variables are external, declared outside any function in the program (that means outside *main()*, as well), and are accessible throughout the program. In C++ the notions of scope and lifetime are separated (thus addressing Dijkstra's concern) with something called a *static* automatic variable. Whereas automatic variables have a scope which is the function (or loop) block and a lifetime which is the instantiation of the function (or loop), *static* variables have a scope which is the same as the scope of an automatic variable, but a lifetime which is the instantiation of the program.

Concluding Remarks on Structured Programming

Although there may be a large collection of meanings attributed to the term "structured programming" all that is significant was originally proposed by Dijkstra and Hoare [1], realized in Pascal [5], and realized again in C++ [3]. In fact, the final component of structure, which is presented in "Hierarchical Program Structures" in *Structured Programming*, was not realized in Pascal, but is realized in C++, and may make C++ more completely a structured programming language than Pascal. This is discussed in Section 1.2.

1.2   Algorithms + Data Structures = Objects

The title of this section is intentionally chosen to mimic the title of the first textbook, *Algorithms + Data Structures = Programs*, by Wirth [9], that taught structured programming using the then-new programming language Pascal. The sense of the title of the book is that programs consist of verifiable algorithms (according to Dijkstra) that operate on well-defined and verifiable data structures (according to Hoare). In the third (and final) essay in *Structured Programming*, "Hierarchical Program Structures," the authors Dahl and Hoare claim that data and operations (algorithms) on data are so closely connected in our minds that it takes elements of both kinds to make up any concept useful for understanding computing processes. In the essay they propose the concept of a class, the instances of which are called objects.

Classes and Objects for the Pascal Programmer

Pascal programmers are familiar with two basic abstraction mechanisms: procedural abstraction (procedures and functions) and data abstraction (built-in data types and user-defined types). The *class* is a language abstraction mechanism that allows the grouping of related procedure and data declarations. For the Pascal programmer, a class is like a user-defined type in that it sets up a pattern for data allocation but does not allocate; in this sense it is very similar to the definition of a record type in Pascal. (C++ also includes a record type called a structure.) A class is an extension of the notion of the type in that it might also include one or more functions that operate on the data. An object is an instantiation of a class, that is, an allocation of memory that follows the data pattern given in the class; there may be many objects of a particular class.

Simply put, a class might be understood as a data structure with its own set of procedures, or as a set of functions with their own data (that survive the function calls and returns).

For example, here is the definition of a class called *pair* in C++.

```
class pair
  {
   private:
       int a,b;
   public:
       display();
  };
```

This defines a *class* with a data structure consisting of two integers *a* and *b*, and a function *display( )* that will output the *pair* when it is called. The label *private:* hides the data from anywhere in the program except from the function in the *class* (called the member function). The label *public:* allows the function to be called from other parts of the program. Note that although *display( )* may access *a* and *b*, the lifetime of *a* and *b* are independent of a call to *display( )*. A typical example of a class might, for example, be a stack of integers with member functions push(x), pop(x), empty( ). The stack can then be accessed only through its member functions.

Objects *p* and *q* of the *class pair* can be created with the statement:

```
pair p,q;
```

For *p* there is an allocation of storage for *a* and *b*; and for *q* there is a different allocation of storage for *a* and *b*. The function code is typically stored only once. To apply the function to *p* or to *q*, a dot operator is used: *p.display( )* or *q.display( )*, respectively.

The introduction of a class immediately provides a data abstraction mechanism. There is the notion of encapsulation (the bundling of a data structure with the functions that operate on it) and data hiding (data can be declared private and only accessible to the functions declared in the class). The introduction of the simple class enables a style or paradigm of programming that implements abstract data types.

Simula-Like Classes

The C++ classes and objects are adopted from Simula 67 which, in turn, realized the "hierarchical program structures" proposed by Dahl and Hoare. Simula is a general-purpose programming language, based upon ALGOL 60, that includes the concept of a class and the instantiation of the class called an object. Although the class was originally inspired by the requirements of discrete simulations and concurrency (because the data in a class survive the function calls, there can be several simultaneous instances of a class, or objects, "alive" at the same time), it was later recognized as a general tool for designing large programs organized in levels of abstractions. The classes in Simula 67 provided the conceptual basis for data abstraction mechanisms in languages such as Concurrent Pascal, Clu, Euclid, Modula, and Ada. But none of these languages fully implemented the "hierarchy" of Simula.

Stroustrup intended that classes in C++ be a direct implementation of Simula-like classes, that is, classes with some form of hierarchy (mechanism for expressing variants of concepts), some form of support for concurrency, and static checking of a type system based on classes. These characteristics go further than the encapsulation and data-hiding features of classes that were implemented in other languages for data abstraction.

The Power of Classes and Objects

Class hierarchies are key to what has come to be called object-oriented programming. Again, class hierarchies are used to describe variants of, typically, application-level concepts. For example, different types of shapes (circles, rectangles, triangles) could be derived from a class called shape. Or a *class triple* could be derived from a *class pair* with the following declaration.

```
class triple: public pair
  {
    private:
      int c;
    public:
      display();
  };
```

In this case, the *class triple* inherits all the attributes (data and member functions) of *class pair*, but also appends (or concatenates) an additional integer datum *c*. The function will need to be adjusted, but can use the definition of *display( )* in *pair*, and simply append (concatenate) to it. An important object-oriented feature of C++ is called inheritance, which provides a hierarchical way to derive one class from another. (In Dahl and Hoare it was called concatenation, the meaning of which is implied in the preceding.) The C++ solution for inheritance was adopted directly from Simula.

The key idea here is that often in programming there is no distinction between the general properties of, say, a shape (a shape has a color, it can be drawn, it might have a texture) and the properties of a specific shape (a circle is a shape that has a radius and is drawn by a circle-drawing function rather than a rectangle-drawing function). Expressing this distinction and taking advantage of it defines object-oriented programming. The programming paradigm involves the early identification of the general concept (e.g., a non-specific shape), the definition of a so-called base class for that concept, and the development of the hierarchy that derives the distinct derived classes for the more specific concepts (e.g., circles, rectangles, triangles). That is, the derived classes inherit from the base class. Inheritance is the key way of taking advantage of the distinction between the general and the specific. A further advantage is through a very powerful feature associated with inheritance called a virtual function (meaning "may be redefined later in a class derived from this one"). A virtual function enables the use of a conceptual name (e.g., *draw( )*) for a whole family of functions in derived classes. That is, the function *draw( )* "knows how to draw" circles, rectangles, and triangles, and uses the appropriate derived modification of the virtual function.

Concluding Remarks on Classes and Objects

A class is a direct extension of the Pascal-type statement. An object is an instantiation of a class. A class is a programming language feature that combines data and functions into one structure. In its simplest meaning, it is one additional language feature (that supplements the features provided by Pascal) that supports more explicit data abstraction.

The deeper meaning of a class is that of hierarchy, in which new classes can inherit from a base class; another way to say it is that new classes can be derived from the base class. In this case, general characteristics of a concept can be separated from more specific characteristics. Virtual functions enable the use of conceptual function names for families of functions. This is object-oriented programming.

These ideas of hierarchical data structure were presented in *Structured Programming* [1] along with the introduction of the concepts of structured programming and data structures. Although structured programming and data structures were implemented in Pascal, hierarchical data structures were not;

they were implemented in Simula. Finally these very important ideas are integrated in C++.

1.3   Programming Paradigms

C++ is a language that supports both structured programming and object-oriented programming, at least. The inventor of C++ had the goal of supporting more than one model for programming. But it is also remarkable to note that from the very first publication about structured programming, the idea of Simula-like classes was introduced. It was not until the implementation of C++ that the integration of structured algorithms, data structures, and classes were achieved.

Goals for C++

Stroustrup argues that the fundamental concept of a structured, strongly typed language (providing the facility for structured programming) that includes classes (providing the facility for programming with abstract data types) with virtual functions (providing the facility for object-oriented programming) is sound [4]. The language provides both static type checking and dynamic type identification (e.g., in virtual function calls). This implements two models for programming rather than only one (e.g., the dynamic type-checking mechanisms of SmallTalk). C++ is a large language precisely because it supports more than one way of writing programs and more than one programming paradigm.

Stroustrup suggests that C++ is really three languages in one.

- A C-like language (supporting low-level programming). In this context, Stroustrup mentions that relative to C++, Pascal is roughly equivalent to C.

- An Ada-like language (supporting abstract data type techniques).

- A Simula-like language (supporting object-oriented programming).

Moreover, he advises learning the language "bottom-up," that is, first learning the features C++ provides for procedural programming; then learning to use the data abstraction features; then learning to use class hierarchies to organize sets of related classes.

This book provides the bottom-up approach specifically for the Pascal programmer. Chapter 2 describes, in detail, that subset of C++ which is equivalent to Pascal. Chapter 3 describes the procedural features available in C++ that might be understood as extensions to Pascal. In this context it is interesting to remember that C is a descendent of ALGOL 68, which provided operator overloading. An important set of additional features provided by C++ is operator and function overloading. Chapter 4 gives a comprehensive presentation of classes and objects in C++ and introduces object-oriented programming. Chapter 5 integrates all of C++ through a discussion of templates, an enhancement to the language that provides parameterized functions and objects.

References

1. Dahl, O.-J., Dijkstra, E.W., and Hoare, C.A.R. *Structured Programming.* Academic Press, 1972.
2. Jensen, K. and Wirth, N. *Pascal User Manual and Report.* 4th ed. Springer-Verlag, 1991.
3. Stroustrup, B. *The C++ Programming Language.* 2nd ed. Reading, MA: Addison-Wesley, 1991.
4. Stroustrup, B. *The Design and Evolution of C++.* Reading, MA: Addison-Wesley, 1994.
5. Wirth, N. *"The Programming Language Pascal." Acta Informatica* 1, (1971).
6. Wirth, N. *"Program Development by Stepwise Refinement," Communications of the ACM* 14 (1971).
7. Wirth, N. *"On the Composition of Well Structured Programs." Computing Surveys* 6,4 (1974).
8. Wirth, N. *"An Assessment of the Programming Language Pascal." IEEE Transactions on Software Engineering* SE-1,2 (1975).
9. Wirth, N. *Algorithms + Data Structures = Programs.* Englewood Cliffs, NJ: Prentice-Hall, 1976.

2

The C++ Subset That Covers Pascal

2.0   Introduction

A frustrating part of beginning a new language is struggling to find the data structures, control structures, and embedding syntax required for the level of computational expressiveness to which one is accustomed. The aim of this chapter is to introduce that kernel of C++ which spans Pascal. Because this kernel is Pascal-like, Pascal programmers can learn it quickly and feel comfortable in C++ in short order. Familiarity with C is not required.

Pascal programmers migrating to C++ have two advantages. First, the roots of both languages go back to ALGOL 60 and the work on structured programming by Dahl, Dijkstra, and Hoare. Thus the two languages have similarities—more similarities than do Pascal and SmallTalk. In their syntax, Pascal and C++ are quite alike. Both are free form, allowing statements to appear at any point upon a line (and extend onto two or more lines), allowing blank lines wherever useful for visually grouping logically integral segments of code, and allowing liberties in spacing between tokens along a line. Both use a token to delimit blocks of statements that have the syntactical status of a single compound statement in selection (e.g., within an *if* statement), iteration (e.g., with a *for* statement), and in bracketing the body of a function; but in C++ "{" replaces

begin and "}" replaces **end**. Both use the semicolon in statements, although in Pascal the semicolon separates statements (like the ";" in English), whereas in C++ it ends a statement. The structure of a C++ program is discussed in Section 2.1.

The primitive data types in Pascal are **integer**, **real**, **char**, and **boolean**. In C++, these correspond to *int*, *float* (also *double*), and *char*; there is no **boolean** (any expression that evaluates to 0 is false, and any other expression evaluates to true). Arrays work similarly in the two languages, except that in C++ subscripting always starts at 0. The **record** in Pascal is analogous to the *struct* (for structure) in C++. Dynamically allocated stacks, queues, and trees are contructed as they are in Pascal. Data and data structures are discussed in Section 2.2.

Arithmetic expressions in C++ are essentially the same as in Pascal. C++ has the same six relational operators as Pascal and the same three logical operators. They do not all look alike, even though they are functionally alike. For example, the tests for equality and for nonequality look different, as do conjunction, disjunction, and negation; but they work similarly.

Here is an example of the notations.

Pascal	*C++*
`if ((a = b) and (c <> d))`	`if (a == b && c != d )`

Expressions are discussed in Section 2.3.

C++ provides selection by means of an *if* statement and an *if-else* statement, and C++ provides a switch statement similar to Pascal's **case**. C++ has a *for* loop that is similar to Pascal's **for** loop, although it offers some enhancements. Finally, C++ has a *while* loop, like Pascal's **while** loop, and C++ has a structure analogous to Pascal's **repeat** . . . **until**, called a *do-while*. In C++, *eof* is used in a similar manner to the test for the end of a file in Pascal. Control structures are discussed in Section 2.4.

Procedures and functions in Pascal have equivalents in C++ too, despite the fact that C++ denotes all its subprograms as *functions* whether or not anything is returned. In Pascal, all functions are proper functions, in that a function returns something (e.g., an **integer**, a **real**, a **char**). This is not true in C++. A function in C++ may explicitly return *void*, which is to say nothing.

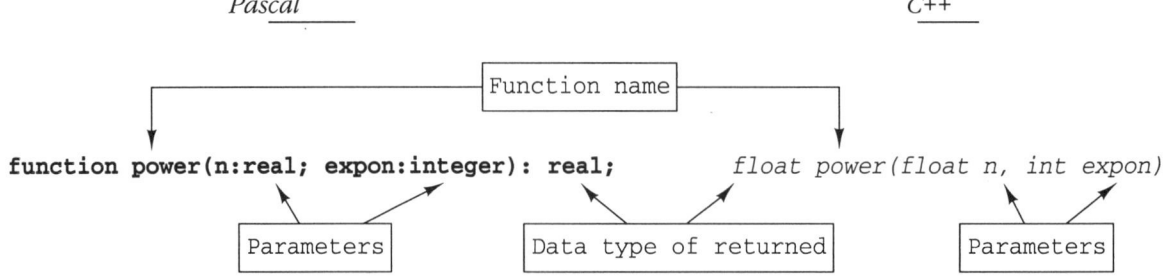

Pascal	*C++*

The keyword **function** is not used in C++. (All subprograms are functions.) Other than that, the information appearing in these headings is identical and its format is similar, with parameters and their data types appearing within parentheses. In both languages, the subprogram's body follows the heading. Now observe how a Pascal procedure is represented in C++.

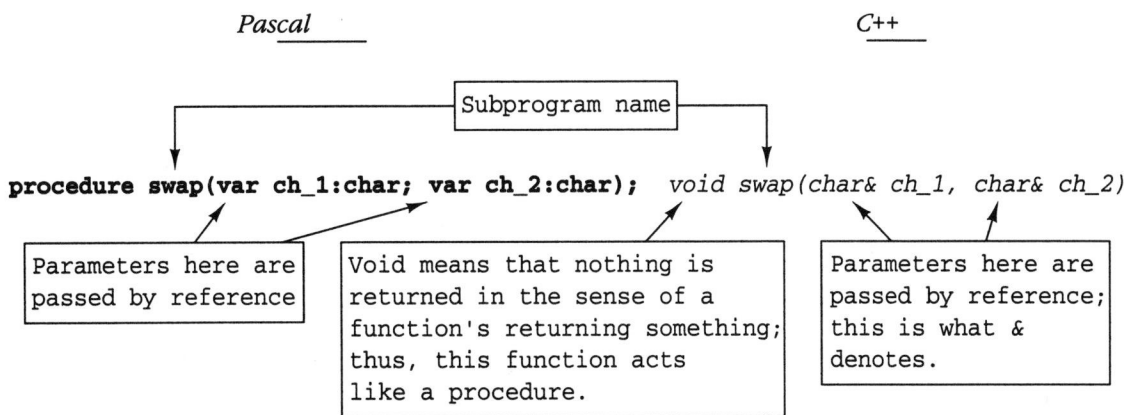

In C++, functions may not be nested (i.e., physically, in the source code) within functions, as they are in Pascal. Therefore, there is very simple static scoping. There is no dynamic scoping; the local variables within a function are not visible from within the function it has called. Functions are discussed in Section 2.5. Dynamic allocation of storage is just as it is in Pascal. This is discussed in Section 2.6. Section 2.7 gives an overview of input and output.

Structured C++ programming does not call for a difference in the way problems are thought about and solved. Both languages have the same functionality. With all this, the migration to C++ from Pascal is straightforward. Section 2.8 includes a comparative summary.

The other piece of good news comes right from Bjarne Stroustrup [1]. C++ is designed so that a user need know only about the subset of the language specifically used to write a program. In other words, says Stroustrup, "What you don't know won't hurt you." This means that a program written in C++ in the style of Pascal is an acceptable C++ program.

2.1   Orientation to C++

Look at the following "hello world" program to examine its structure.

Pascal	*C++*

`{The hello world program in Pascal}`
 	
`program hello_world(input, output);`
`    begin`
`        writeln;`
`        write('hello world');`
`        writeln;`
`    end`
	`// The hello world program in C++.`
	`#include <iostream.h>`
	
	`void main()`
	`    {`
	`    cout << endl;`
	`    cout << "hello world";`
	`    cout << endl;`
	`    }`

Note that object *cout* appears to function like a **write**. It does. For now that is enough to know; *cout* is discussed later in this chapter.

C++ Is in Lower Case

In C++, keywords are in lower case. Identifiers are a different story; they may be in lower case, upper case, or a mixture. Here are examples of identifiers.

`total_amount`	`TOTAL_AMOUNT`	`Total_Amount`
`totalAmount`	`TotalAmount`	

Each identifier is distinct, because upper case characters are distinct from lower case characters. Variable *Total_Amount* is completely different from variable *total_amount*.

Rules for forming identifiers in C++ are the same as in Pascal. This includes names for variables and names for functions. The convention (but not the rule) is to capitalize the first letter of interior words when a name has more than one word:

`totalAmount`	`stackTop`	`depthFirstSearch`

Constants Are in Upper Case

The role of **consts** in Pascal is paralleled by *const* in C++. When a constant name (e.g., *pi*) is associated with a value (e.g., 3.14), the name of the constant is typically given in upper case to enable the reader to differentiate it from a variable. Constants should no more be updated than literals, and C++ will not allow updating.

Pascal	*C++*

`program area_of_circle(input, output);`
`    const`
`        pi = 3.14;`
`    var`
`        radius, area:real`
`    begin`
`        write('Enter radius: ');`
	`// Area of circle.`
	`#include <iostream.h>`
	
	`void main()`
	`    {`
	`    const float PI = 3.14;`
	`    float radius, area;`
	
	`    cout << "Enter radius: ";`

```
    readln(radius);                  cin << radius;

    area := pi * radius * radius;    area = PI * radius * radius;

    writeln;                         cout << endl;
    write('Area is: ', AREA:4:2);    cout << "Area is: " << area;
    writeln;                         cout << endl;
end.                                 }
```

Program Comments

In C++, text following // on a line is treated as a comment. No end delimiter is needed because the end-of-line serves this purpose. This is the preferred way to comment in C++, but there is an alternative. Any text between /* and */ is a comment. The comment may span several lines.

Using Libraries

There is a need, and a way, to copy source code into a program; for example, the directive *#include <iostream.h>*. There are three items here: *#include*, which is a preprocessor directive; *iostream.h*, which is the name of a header file in the C++ language environment that contains code for certain input and output operations (e.g., for facilitating access to the *cout* object); and the angular brackets surrounding the file name.

The extension *.h* on file name *iostream.h* identifies the file as a standard "header." Think of a header file as a "unit" that comes with the programming environment, enabling access to libraries of subprograms. C++ relies heavily on libraries of subprograms. For instance, the standard header file *math.h* must be included to access square root function *sqrt( )*; *iomanip.h* must be included to access the formatting specifications for setting field width *setw( )* and for setting precision, *setprecision( )*; *string.h* must be included to use function *strcpy( )*, which assigns the contents of one string to another.

When a header file of the programmer's own creation is included, its name is placed within quotation marks rather than within the angular brackets, to signify that it is not from among the standard headers. The content of a file can be included at any point within a C++ source program.

```
// Include-ing a programmer's file.
#include <iostream.h>
```

```
void main()
  {
    cout << endl;
    cout << "**************";
    #include "a:MoreCPP";
    cout << "**************";
    cout << endl;
  }
```

Here, the contents of file *A:MORECPP* are

```
cout << endl;
cout << "Printed from a:MoreCPP";
cout << endl;
```

The main( ) *Function*

There is no **program** heading in C++, as there is in Pascal; but just as execution of a Pascal program always starts with the **program** block, also known as the "main procedure," the execution of a C++ program typically starts with the function *main( )*. (Exceptions are given in Chapter 4.) Every C++ program must have a function *main( )*, just as every Pascal program must have a main procedure. Function *main( )* is a genuine function.

A function's first statement, its heading, is known as its declarator. All declarators have the same form. First is the data type of the value returned (which is *void* if the function returns nothing). Next is the function name. Finally, within parentheses, is the list of parameters. Even if the function has no parameters the parentheses must be used.

When writing about C++ code and referring to a function, its name is generally followed by opening and closing parentheses with nothing in between, regardless of whether the function's declarator actually contains parameters. The parentheses communicate to the reader that the identifier represents a function.

Building a C++ Program

The simplest programs are those with only a single function, *main( )*. Function *main( )* is prefaced by any necessary *#include* preprocessor directives, opened with *main( )*'s declarator followed by an opening brace signifying the beginning of the body—the code for the function. It is important not to type a semicolon between *main( )* and the opening brace. The opening brace signifies the beginning of the executable code and *main( )*'s variables are defined after it, not before it. This is a difference in form from Pascal. Finally, the source code is ended with a closing brace. No punctuation follows.

Here is an example.

Pascal	C++

```pascal
program finding_a_square_root;

    var
        num           : real;
        numsqrt       : real;
    begin
        writeln;
        write('Enter a number: ');
        readln(num);

        numsqrt   := sqrt(num);



        write(' Its square root is ');
        write(numsqrt:12:6);
        writeln;
end.
```

```cpp
// Finding a square root.
#include <iostream.h>
#include <math.h>        // For sqrt().

void main()
                    // No semicolon.
    {
     float num;
     float numSqrt;

     cout << endl;
     cout << " Enter a number: ";
     cin  >> num;

     numSqrt = sqrt(num);
                // Function call.

     cout << "Its square root is ";
     cout << numSqrt;
     cout << endl;
    }
```

C++ is more flexible than Pascal when it comes to defining variables. Variables can be defined anywhere within the program before (or at) first use. In the preceding program, for example, *numSqrt*'s definition could have been placed immediately before the assignment *numSqrt = sqrt(num)*,

```cpp
    ⋮
cout << endl;
cout << "Enter a number: ";
cin >> num;

float numSqrt; // The definition of numSqrt.
numSqrt = sqrt(num);
    ⋮
```

or even as late as within the assignment statement itself instead of beforehand.

```cpp
    ⋮
float numSqrt = sqrt(num);
    ⋮
```

In C++ the terms "declaring variables" and "defining variables" have different meanings. A variable is defined at that point where memory is allocated for it. It is declared when the compiler is informed of its existence. Although a variable may be declared and defined at the same time (as has been the case in all the previous examples), it may not be.

All functions follow the *#include* directives and may appear in any order. The first function may be *main( )*, but *main( )* may just as well be the second, the third, or the last. The only requirement is that either the function itself or function prototype precedes the first function call in the source code. The prototype is the function declarator (e.g., the first line of a function definition), standing alone and followed by a semicolon; it corresponds to a **forward** subprogram declaration in Pascal. As mentioned earlier, C++ does not permit a function to contain the source code of another function. Therefore, rules of scope are much simpler in C++ than in Pascal. In C++ all variables defined within every function, including *main( )*, are local: unless passed as arguments, *alpha( )*'s variables are not accessible within *beta( )*, even if *alpha( )* precedes *beta( )* in the source listing. For a variable to be global (i.e., accessible to all functions), it must be defined within the source code ahead of the first function. (Details are given in Chapter 3.)

2.2   Data Types and Data Structures

Pascal's **integer**s, **real**s, and **char**s have analogies in C++ in the data types *int*, *float*, and *char*, respectively. (Others are discussed in Chapter 3.) Also analogous is the way variables are defined. Below, all sets of definitions establish the same collection of variables:

```
int     numStudents;    int     midTerm, final;    char    letterGrade;
int     midTerm;        float   average;           float   average;
int     final;          char    letterGrade;

                                                   int     midTerm, final, numStudents;
float   average;        int     numStudents;
char    letterGrade;
```

Just as in Pascal, more than one *int*, *float*, or *char* can be defined within a single statement, as long as each variable in the list is separated from the previous variable by a comma. Also, there are no restrictions on the number of individual statements defining variables of each type nor on the way these statements may be ordered or mixed.

Constants

Pascal offers constants, user-defined enumerations of constants, and subranges. C++ has constants and enumerations, but no subranges.

The convention in C++ is to define constants with names in upper case.

Pascal	C++

```
const                              const   float   PI       = 3.14;
   pi = 3.14;                      const   char    BLANK       = ' ';
   blank       = ' ';             const   char    TOP_GRADE   = 'A';
   top_grade   = 'A';             const   int     NUM_ROWS    = 24;
   num_rows    = 24;             const   int     NUM_COLS    = 80;
   num_cols    = 80;             const   float   E_TO_THE_PI = 23.141;
   e_to_the_pi = 23.141;        const   float   PI_TO_THE_E = 22.459;
   pi_to_the_e = 22.459;
```

In C++, keyword *const* is used along with the data type of the value being assigned to the identifier. A constant may be defined anywhere a variable may be defined, and the definition of constants may be interspersed with the definition of variables. Definitions of constants are not restricted to any special place.

Enumerated Data Types

Enumerated data types work like their Pascal counterparts. The only difference is that within a C++ program there is no special section (such as Pascal's **type** section) where enumerated data types must be located. The data type is specified and then, at any point thereafter, a variable or variables of that type are defined. The enumeration's specification may appear anywhere within the program. Enumerated types are used in C++ for the same reason they are used in Pascal: to improve the readability of the code. Their implementation and use correspond closely in both languages. Each member within an enumeration is represented by a consecutive integer from 0 upward. When the value of a variable of an enumerated type is displayed, this number appears, not the identifier (i.e., the enumeration's member) within the listing. When values of variables of an enumerated type are compared with relational operators, or used in expressions, the computation uses their integer values. C++ will not allow the same identifier to appear both as a member within an enumeration and to be used as a variable name (or to appear within more than one enumeration). This would cause a syntactic ambiguity because the members of an enumerated listing are indistinguishable from variable names when they appear on the right-hand side of an assignment operator or within expressions.

Here is an example.

```
#include <iostream.h>
void main()
  {
  enum religiousPreference    {Protestant, Catholic, Jewish, other};
  enum politicalAffiliation   {Republican, Democrat, Independent, none};
```

```
enum educationalAttainment {highSchool, baccalaureate, postGraduate};

religiousPreference   motherRel; fatherRel; respondentRel; // Same form as
politicalAffiliation  motherPol; fatherPol; respondentPol; // definitions for
educationalAttainment motherEdu; fatherEdu; respondentEdu; // int, float, and
                                                           // char variables.
int                   i,  j,  k;
float                 f,  g,  h;
 .
 .
 .
if (motherRel == fatherRel && motherPol == fatherPol) ... // Value of variables
                                                          // of enumerated types
                                                          // are tested.

if (respondentEdu > highSchool) ... // Notice how an ambiguity would result if
                                    // there could be a variable named highSchool.


 .
 .
 .


enum Boolean {false, true};   // Notice how an enumerated type can be used to
Boolean  dissonance;          // fashion a datatype analogous to Pascal's BOOLEAN.

if (motherRel != fatherRel && motherPol != fatherPol && motherEdu != fatherEdu)
    dissonance = true;
else
    dissonance = false;


 .
 .
 .


if (dissonance) ... // In the specification of the Boolean enum, false is the first
                    // member and true is the second. Thus their implementing
                    // integers are 0 and 1, respectively. The consequence is that
 .                  // when dissonance is assigned the enumerated value of false,
 .                  // its int value is 0, which is construed by C++ as false in
 .                  // the context of a relational expression.
}
```

The Subrange Type

C++ offers nothing analogous to the subrange type in Pascal.

Pascal	*C++*

type
    test_score : 0..100
 	
var
    mid_term : test_score;
	Nothing corresponds to this.

```
final    : test_score;

caps  : 'A'..'Z';
```

The Struct

The structure is C++'s equivalent of Pascal's record. Each component within a *struct* is called a member, and the section of code that establishes its inventory of members is called its declaration or specification. A *struct* specification may appear anywhere in the code, unlike the requirement in Pascal that declaration be made in a particular section of the program. Naturally a *struct* must be defined before it is used.

Accessing members of particular instantiations of *struct*s is done just as it is in Pascal, with the "dot operator." The dot operator is descriptively called the member access operator. The ordinary assignment operator will copy the values of the entire set of members within one *struct* variable into another *struct* variable.

Consider an example.

Pascal	*C++*

```
                                          #include <iostream.h>
program record_demo (input, output);      void main()
                                          {
                                            enum boolean {false, true};

    type                                    struct sampleStructure  // Struct
                                                                    // specification.
        sample_structure = record           {
            i, j : integer;                  int       i, j;
            f    : real;                     float     f;
            ch   : char;                     char      ch;
            bool : boolean;                  boolean   bool; // Variable of an
        end;                                };              // enumerated type.

    var                                     int    i;   // Okay, even though there
      i : integer;                          float  f;   // are variables of the same
      f : real;                                         // names within the struct.

      s1, s2, s3 : sample_structure;        sampleStructure s1, s2, s3;
                                                        // Struct definitions.
    begin
      s1.i    := 10;    s1.j := 20;
      s1.f    := 1.25;                      s1.i   = 10;      s1.j    = 20;
      s1.ch   := 'A';                       s1.f   = 1.25;
                                            s1.ch  = 'A';  // Char literal in
      s1.bool := true;                                     // apostrophes.
                                            s1.bool = true;
```

```
s2.i    := 11;     s1.j := 21;
s2.f    := 4.75;
s2.ch   := 'B';
s2.bool := false;


s3 := s2;




i := 1000;  f := 0.123;

writeln;

write('Structure 3: ');
write('       i = ', s3.i);
write('       j = ', s3.j);
write('       f = ', s3.f:4:2);
write('      ch = ', s3.ch);
write('    bool = ');

if (s3.bool_ then writeln('true')
    else writeln('false');
end.
```

```
s2.i    = 11;      s1.j      = 21;
s2.f    = 4.75;
s2.ch   = 'B';
s2.bool = true;

                // When one struct is assigned
s3 = s2; // to another, an exact copy of
                // the information in the source
                // is made in the destination.


i = 1000;    f = 0.123;

cout << endl;

cout << "Structure 3: ";
cout << "            i = " << s3.i;
cout << "            j = " << s3.j;
cout << "            f = " << s3.f;
cout << "           ch = " << s3.ch;
cout << "    bool = ";

if (s3.bool) cout << "true" << endl;
   else        cout << "false" << endl;
}
```

Arrays

Arrays in C++ are like arrays in Pascal; they are structures with homogenous, contiguous, subscripted, direct access storage compartments. In C++, the individual compartments are referred to as elements, and a subscript is referred to as an index. C++ allows arrays of *ints*, *floats*, *chars*, enumerated types, *structs*, and, of course, arrays of arrays (as 2-dimensional and higher dimensional arrays). There are, however, important differences between Pascal and C++. First, all arrays in C++ are indexed (i.e., subscripted) starting at 0. Another way of stating this is that the index of the first element is always 0. For example, the subscript range of each and every 10-element array defined in C++ is 0 . . . 9, and 9 is the index of the 10th element. Second, there is no run-time range-checking, so that out-of-bound indices can cause insidious errors.

Here is an example.

Pascal

```
program array_demo (input,output);
   const
      max = 49; {for subscripts 0..49}
```

C++

```
#include <iostream.h>
void main()
   {
     const int MAX = 50; // For 50-cell
```

```
type                                      // arrays index
                                          // range is 0...49.
    data_unit = record            struct dataUnit
        x, y, z : integer;          {
    end;                            int x, y, z;
                                    };

    grades = (a, b, c, d, f, inc);  enum grades {A, B, C, D, F, INC};

var
    int_a : array[0..max] of integer;  int intA[MAX]; // The number of elements
                                                      // in array intA
                                                      // is MAX; the elements'
                                                      // subscripts start at 0
                                                      // and end with MAX-1.

    flo_a : array[0..max] of real;     float floA[MAX]; // Subscript range is
                                                        // 0..MAX-1.

    rec_a : array[0..9] of data_unit;  dataUnit recA[10]; // Subscript range is
                                                          // 0..9 and each
                                                          // element is a
                                                          // dataUnit struct.

    enum_a: array[0..24] of grades;    grades enumA[25]; // Subscript range is
                                                         // 0..24 and each
                                                         // element is a
                                                         // grades enum.

    i     : integer;              int    i;
begin
    for i := 0 to max do          for (i = 0; i < MAX; i = i + 1)
      begin                         {
        int_a[i] := i;              intA[i] = i;
        int_f[i] := 0.0;            floA[i] = 0.0;
      end;                          };

    rec_a[3].x := 15;             recA[3].x = 15;
    rec_a[3].y := 30;             recA[3].y = 30;
    rec_a[3].z := 101 - rec_a[3].y;  recA[3].z = 101 - recA[3].y;

    enum_a[0] := a;               enumA[0] = A;
    enum_a[1] := inc;             enumA[1] = INC;
      .                             .
      .                             .
      .                             .
                                  }
```

Multidimensional Arrays

Arrays in C++ can have any number of dimensions. In the Pascal program segment below, the two dimensional array, is named **two_dim**; in C++, *twoDim*.

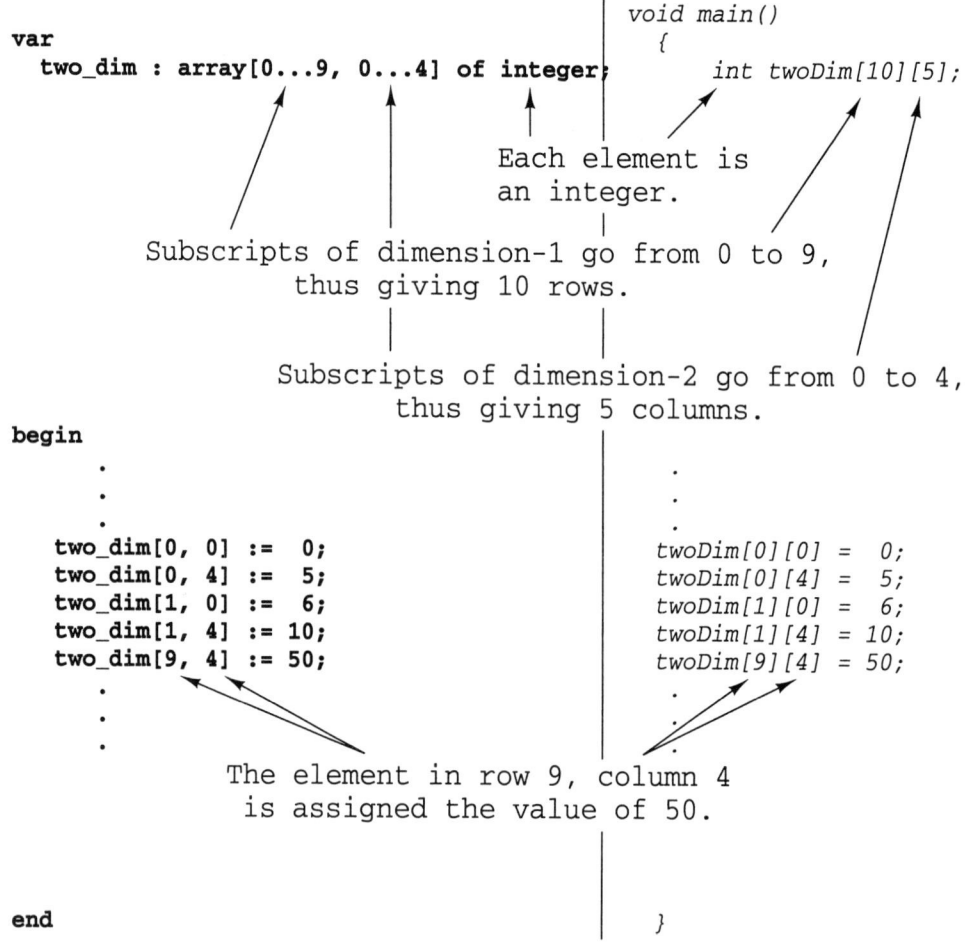

```
var
  two_dim : array[0...9, 0...4] of integer;
```

```
void main()
{
    int twoDim[10][5];
```

Each element is an integer.

Subscripts of dimension-1 go from 0 to 9, thus giving 10 rows.

Subscripts of dimension-2 go from 0 to 4, thus giving 5 columns.

```
begin
    .
    .
    .
  two_dim[0, 0] :=  0;
  two_dim[0, 4] :=  5;
  two_dim[1, 0] :=  6;
  two_dim[1, 4] := 10;
  two_dim[9, 4] := 50;
    .
    .
    .
```

```
    .
    .
    .
  twoDim[0][0] =  0;
  twoDim[0][4] =  5;
  twoDim[1][0] =  6;
  twoDim[1][4] = 10;
  twoDim[9][4] = 50;
    .
    .
    .
```

The element in row 9, column 4 is assigned the value of 50.

```
end
```

```
}
```

Here is the definition of a five-dimensional array of *int*s:

```
int fiveDim[10][5][5][10][2];
```

Its subscript bounds are:

```
dimension 1:  0..9
dimension 2:  0..4
dimension 3:  0..4
dimension 4:  0..9
dimension 5:  0..1
```

It contains $10 * 5 * 5 * 10 * 2 = 5,000$ elements.

Here is a typical assigment.

```
fiveDim[2][1][3][5][0] = 48;
```

Here this element is displayed.

```
cout << fiveDim[2][1][3][5][0];
```

Strings: Char Arrays with a '\0' Delimiter

In Niklaus Wirth's standard Pascal [2], an array of characters is structurally identical to an array of anything else, such as an array of integers. For example, an array of characters must be printed cell-by-cell; it cannot be written out as a unified item the way integers can. In C++, as in standard Pascal, a *char* array may be successfully managed with the same operations that may be applied to arrays of other things, such as *int* arrays.

However, a *char* array is often used to represent a string, i.e., a sequence of *chars*. Because of the mismatch between a string construed as an aggregate item and a *char* array processed as a subscripted succession of solitary elements, C++ systems offer an assortment of library functions, declared in *string.h*, to simplify string processing.

Integral to the provisions for simplified string processing is the delimiter that must be appended to a sequence of *chars* recognized to be a string. This delimiter is ASCII 0. It is sometimes called "the null zero," and it is represented as a *char* literal by the two-symbol sequence \0. For example, the following code stores in *i* the number of non-\0 characters in character array *line*.

```
i = 0;
while (line[i] != '\0')      // Here, line is a char array.
   {
     cout << s[i];
     i := i + 1;
   }
```

The null zero takes up one element in the *char* array, so string "Hello" has six characters. This string may reside in a much longer array, but there is no confusion over its length because all elements beyond the null zero are superfluous. When a *char* array is defined with storage of strings in mind, it is important to provide an element to accommodate the terminating delimiter. For example, strings of up to 80 characters need *char* arrays with 81 elements.

Assume the *char* array and the assignments shown at the start of the following program.

```
#include <iostream.h>
#include <string.h>
void main()
   {
     char str[81];  // This array str has 81 elements, 0..80.
```

```
        char s[10];     // This array s has 10 elements, 0..9.

        str[0] = 'H';
        str[1] = 'e';
        str[2] = 'l';
        str[3] = 'l';
        str[4] = 'o';
        str[5] = '\0';
    }
```

Consider the following.

- A string may be output directly using *cout*, just as an *int, float, char*, or string literal:

```
    cout << endl << "The string is:   **" << str << "**" << endl;
```

Name of the *char* array
holding the string.

The result from execution of this statement will be the line of output:

The string is: **Hello**

The delimiting null zero is not printed.

- A string's length may be found with the function *strlen( )*.

```
    cout << endl << "Length is " << strlen(str) << endl;
```

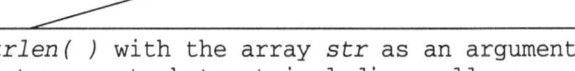

```
This is a call to the function strlen( ) with the array str as an argument.
It returns 5, the number of characters up to but not including null zero.
#include<string.h> must be present for strlen( ) to be accessible.
```

- Although one string may not be copied into another with the assignment operator, the same result may be obtained with the function *strcpy( )*.

```
    //  ILLEGAL:  s = str;
```

instead,

```
    strcpy(s, str);     // Perform this assignment with strcpy().
```

As a result of the preceding function call, *s* now holds a copy of the string "Hello" from *str*. It is the programmer's responsibility to be sure that the receiving *char* array is long enough to hold the string within the source array. Even though *str* is 81 characters long and the array *s* is only 10, this operation is acceptable because the actual string is merely six (the five characters within "Hello" plus the delimiter). Function *strcpy( )* copies the source string up to and including the null zero into the destination string. Notice that the order of the arguments within *strcpy( )*, with the destination array on the left and the source array on the right, is the same as in an assignment. Also notice that though *strcpy( )* is actually a function, it is invoked just like a procedure in Pascal. Finally, notice that the source string may be a literal.

```
                                  // ILLEGAL:  str = "Greetings!";
strcpy(str, "Greetings!");        // Instead, do this with strcpy().
```

- Including the file *string.h* is necessary for access to *strcpy( )*.

- A string may be captured from the input stream and assigned to a *char* array using *cin* (for now, the functional equivalent of a **read** in Pascal), just as an *int*, *float*, or *char*. But just as an *int* being entered from the keyboard is delimited by a character of "white space" such as from striking the enter key or the space bar, so is a string. This code,

```
cout << endl << "Type in a word:   ";
cin >> str;
```

will query the person at the console for a string, capture it, assign it to array *str*, and tack on a null zero. If the user types in the five letters "Hello" and strikes enter, the first six elements of *str* will hold

str	H	e	l	l	o	\0	unknown...
	0	1	2	3	4	5	6 7

If the user had entered "Pretty nifty!", *str* would hold

str	P	r	e	t	t	y	\0	unknown...
	0	1	2	3	4	5	6	7

because the space between the two words acts as an end of string delimiter.

- Function *cin.get( )* can capture a string that includes spaces. It is supplied though header file *iostream.h*. This function takes either two or three arguments. When *cin.get( )* is used with two arguments, the first is the name of the *char* array to receive the entered string and the second is an *int* giving the maximum number of *char*s to accept for assignment. In the two-argument mode, the end of the string is signaled by striking enter (or, in more general terms, when the *newline* character, '\n', is encountered in the input stream).

```
cout << endl << "Type in your name and strike enter:   ";
cin.get(str, 80);
```

If the user types in "Margaret A. Ellis" and strikes enter, *str* will hold

str	M	a	r	g	a	r	e	t		A	.		E	l	l	i	s	\0	unknown...
	0	1	2	3	4	5	6	7	8	9	10	11	12	13	14	15	16	17	18

When used with three arguments, the third is the *char* chosen to serve as an explicit end of input signal. It could be anything, for example, the at sign '@':

```
cout << endl << "Type in your paragraph. At the end, type @" << endl;
cin.get( real_long_char_array, 2000, '@');
```

This allows for multiline strings, since the newline *char*, '\n', is just another ASCII value within the *char* array.

- Two strings may be compared for alphanumeric order (actually, for ordinal value relative to the full collating sequence) with the standard library function *strcmp( )* made available with the inclusion of header file *string.h*.

```
strcmp(string1, string2) returns a negative value if string1 < string2
strcmp(string1, string2) returns zero when string1 is identical to string2
strcmp(string1, string2) returns a positive value if string1 > string2
```

An obvious application of this function is in a sort to alphabetize a roster.

```
if (strcmp(lastName1, lastName2) > 0) swap(lastName1, lastName2);
```

Either or both arguments may be a string literal.

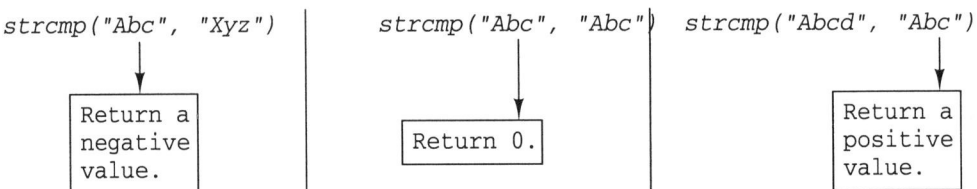

Finally, notice that string literals are delimited by standard quotation marks and *char* literals are delimited by apostrophes.

2.3   Arithmetic, Boolean, and Logical Expressions

In C++ unary minus and plus and the binary operators for addition, subtraction, and multiplication look and work as do those in Pascal. In C++, the operator for division is a forward slash, just as in Pascal, although its operation is a little different. The resulting quotient is a *float* if either or both of the operands are *float*s. It is an *int* when both of the operands are *int*s, the same integer that would be obtained in Pascal with **div**. The modulus operator, represented by the percentage symbol % works just as **mod** does in Pascal. Both operands must be *int*s. In C++, arithmetic expressions are evaluated in accordance with the same precedence hierarchy, the same left-to-right associativity for the binary operators, and right-to-left associativity for unary minus and plus, and the same use of parentheses as in Pascal.

Cast Float

To divide two *int*s and obtain their quotient as a *float*, in other words, to perform a "real" division, requires that at least one operand be a *float*. If necessary, an *int* can be converted to a *float* with a conversion function, called "cast". The term cast refers to a mechanism for remolding or reexpressing a value in a different type, such as recasting an *int* as a *float*. (The term comes from C.) This is done by treating the data type as the name of a function and passing to it the variable or expression to be converted. For instance, *int i* can be cast as a *float* like this:

```
float( i )
```

This function call yields a *float* that is equal to *i*. Here is an example. If a student earns 72 points on an examination with a possible maximum of 83, the score on a percentage basis could be computed in at least three ways.

```
percent = float(72)/83 * 100;    , or
percent = 72/float(83) * 100;    , or
percent = float(72)/float(83) * 100;
```

The Cast int

Conversely, the value of *float f* can be cast as an *int* using:

```
int( f ).
```

Cast *int* performs a truncation. In Pascal, function **trunc** performs the equivalent of the cast *int( )*. Pascal has no function corresponding to the cast *float( )*. C++ provides no function for rounding, but (as usual) one obtains it by adding .5 before the conversion.

Data Conversion with Assignment

C++ allows an *int* value to be assigned to a *float* variable, and it allows a *float* value to be assigned to an *int* variable. In the latter case, the *float* value is truncated.

Char*s and* Ints

In Pascal, the function **ord** is actually a cast for transforming a **char** to an **integer**, and **chr** function is a cast for transforming an **integer** to a **char**.

Pascal	*C++*

```ch := 'a';   {ch is a char}```
```i := ord(ch); {i is an integer}```
	```ch = 'A'; // Here ch is a char.```
	```i = int(ch); // Here i is an int.```

```i := 65;``` ```ch := chr(i);```	```i = 65;``` ```ch = char(i);```
```ch := 'a';``` ```write('ascii of ', ch, ' is ', ord(ch));```	```ch = 'A';``` ```cout<<"ASCII of "<< ch <<" is "<< int(ch);```
```i := 65;``` ```write('ASCII number ',i, ' is ', chr(i));```	```i = 65;``` ```cout<<"ASCII number " << i <<"is"<< char;```

In C++, explicit conversion between *char* and *int* (i.e., casting from *char* to *int*) is only necessary when performing output. This is because C++ recognizes that the only difference between character '*A*' [stored internally within a byte as the binary number 65 (100 0001)] and the integer 65 [stored internally within two bytes as the binary number 65 (100 0001)] is in its presentation for display. C++ allows a variable defined as a *char* to appear in any expression where an *int* can appear, and C++ allows arithmetic values to be assigned to *chars*. For instance, a *char* can be advanced to the next character by adding 1; so that *ch = ch + 1* accomplishes Pascal's **ch := succ(ch)**.

The program that follows displays the characters from 32 (the space bar) through character 255 (which is another blank), with 16 characters per line on 14 lines.

Pascal	*C++*

```/* Print characters 32 to 255 */```
```program see_characters (input, output);```
``` var```
```   line, col : integer;```
```   ch   : char;```
``` begin```
```   writeln;```
```   for line := 1 to 14 do```
```   begin```
```   for col := 1 to 16 do```
```   begin```
```   ch := chr(32+16*(line-1)+col-1);```
```   write(ch, '   ');```
```   end;```
```   writeln;```
```   end;```
```end.```
	```// Print characters to 32 to 255.```
	```#include <iostream.h>```
	```void main()```
	```{```
	``` int line, col;```
	``` char ch;```
	``` cout << endl;```
	``` for (line=1; line<=14; line=line+1)```
	``` {```
	``` for (col=1; col<=16; col=col+1)```
	``` {```
	``` ch = 32 + 16*(line-1) + (col-1);```
	``` cout << ch << " ";```
	``` }```
	``` cout << endl;```
	``` }```
	```}```

Relational and Logical Operators

Pascal and C++ use different symbols for the same relations and logical operators:

Pascal	C++	Pascal	C++
=	==	not	!
<>	!=	and	&&
<	<	or	||
<=	<=		
>	>		
>=	>=		

The C++ symbol that gives everyone the greatest difficulty is the double equal sign, ==. There is no conceptual problem; rather, habit makes it easy to type a single equal sign by mistake. Because this is not a syntax error in C++, the compiler accepts it without warning but performs contrary to intention. Consider this statement for expression in Pascal.

```
if number_left = 0  then  writeln('Sorry, we're sold out.');
```

A correct C++ equivalent in C++ is

```
if (numberLeft == 0)   cout << "Sorry, we're sold out." << endl;
```

In contrast, the statement

```
if (numberLeft = 0)   cout << "Sorry, we're sold out." << endl;
```

does the following:

- Evaluates expression 0.
- Assigns 0 to *numberLeft* and returns 0 as the value of the statement *numberLeft = 0*.
- Since 0 is treated as false, execution of the *if* statement terminates.

Here's why.

- In C++, the assignment $a = e$ performs the usual operation of evaluating expression e and storing the result into variable a. It yields a result, which is the value of e.
- The above definition of the assignment makes it possible to write assignments like

```
x = y = z;
```

Here, "=" is treated associatively from right to left, so that it is equivalent to $x=(y=z)$. Hence execution

1. evaluates z, assigns its value to y, and yields the value as the result of $y=z$.
2. assigns the result of $y=z$ to x and yields this value as a result.

Precedence in Relational Expressions

C++ and Pascal have different precedence for relational and logical operators. In C++, the relational operators have higher precedence than conjunction (&&) and disjunction (||). This means that the order of operations within a Boolean expression is to perform relational tests before and-ing or or-ing their results. In Pascal, the relational operators have a lower precedence than the **and** and **or**.

Pascal	C++

`if ((a=b) and (c=d)) then statement;`
It would be an error not to place the relational tests within parentheses.
	`if ( a==b && c==d ) statement;`
	—— alternatively ——
	
	`if ((a==b) && (c==d)) statement;`

Operator Precedence Table	Operator Precedence Table
`not`	`!`
`*  /  div  mod  and`	`*  /  %  (% stands for mod)`
`+  -  or`	`+  -`

`=  <>  <  <=  >  >=`	`<  <=  >  >=`
	`==  !=`
	`&&`
	`||`

2.4   Control Structures

Pascal and C++ have similar statements controlling the flow of execution. They include the following.

1. a *for* loop for count-controlled iteration; a *while* loop (where a test is performed before each iteration); a *do . . . while* (where a test is performed after each iteration); an *if . . . else* statement; and a *switch* statement for selection among multiple choices; and
2. the same ability to install a sequence of statements within a control statement wherever a *block* exists, which is a sequence of statements delimited by **begin** and **end** (Pascal) or "{" and "}" (C++).

Every selection and every loop that can be coded in Pascal can be coded similarly in C++, but there are differences in detail. In C++, for instance, the *if* statement does not include the word *then*; the *while* loop does not include the word *do*; and the *for* loop requires more programmer direction but provides greater versatility.

The if *and* if . . . else *Statements*

Pascal's **if** statement is as follows.

```
if (a < b)   then   stmt1   else   stmt2;
```

In C++ the equivalent is

```
if (a < b)          stmt1;  else   stmt2;
```

The syntactical distinction is that the semicolon is used to terminate the statement contained by the *if* statement whether or not the *if* statement is followed by an *else* statement.

Note that expression *b* can be any arithmetic or relational expression, since 0 is treated as *false* and anything else as *true*.

Semicolons in Pascal are statement separators whereas in C++ they are statement terminators. Every statement has a terminator. Each extra terminator is construed as sitting at the right-end of a null or "no-op" statement. Line one, with its one extra semicolon is interpreted as

```
cout << endl << "line 1";  noOp;
```

Note that the concluding brace closing off a group of zero, one, or more statements within a control structure is also regarded as a statement terminator. Thus the C++ statement

```
if (a<b)   {stmt1; stmt2; stmt3;}
```

does not need a trailing semicolon following the right-hand brace (the semicolon terminating *stmt3*, however, is necessary). But what if a semicolon had been placed following the brace? If any statement other than an *else* follows it, there is no discernible effect. The semicolon would be construed as terminating a "no-op." The rule for a paired *else* is that it must follow the statement in the *if* clause. Because the semicolon introduces an intervening "no-op", the *else* clause would no longer follow the statement in the *if* clause, and the consequence would be a syntax error. Thus

```
┌─────────────────┐          ┌─────────────────────┐
│ The semicolon   │          │ This semicolon is   │
│ is illegal here.│          │ okay but unnecessary.│
└─────────────────┘          └─────────────────────┘
```

```
if (a<b) {stmt1; stmt2; stmt3;}; else {stmt4; stmt5; stmt6;};
```

The other trap in connection with the *if . . . else* construction is one that seasoned Pascal programmers have faced before: the dangling *else*, which can arise when the *if* part of an *if . . . else* embodies an *if* that has no mated *else*. In C++, like Pascal, an *else* is logically linked to the most recently appearing (i.e., the innermost) unmated *if*. Thus no matter how the following code is formatted on the page, it will not perform as intended.

```
if (a != b)                                    // **mismatched else**
   if (a<b) cout << "a is less than b";   //      This code does not
else  cout << "a and b are equal";        //       perform as intended!
```

The *else*, being associated with the inner *if* statement, is performed when *a* is not equal to *b* and *a* is not less than *b*; in other words, the message "*a and b are equal*" is displayed when *a* is greater than *b*.

When *a* and *b* are equal, this code does nothing. There are two possible corrections: either to cordon off the inner *if* statement using braces or to supply the inner *if* with an "*else no-op*".

```
if (a != b)                                    if (a != b)
  {if (a<b) cout << "a is less than b";}         if (a<b) cout << "a is less than b";
else  cout << "a and b are equal";               else;
                                               else  cout << "a and b are equal";
        ┌──────────────┐
        │ no semicolon │
        └──────────────┘
```

The switch *Statement*

The *switch* statement in C++ is similar to Pascal's **case** statement. Like the **case** statement, the *switch* statement compares the value of an *int* expression, a *char* expression, and an expression of an enumerated type (which is actually an *int*), with a list of values in search of a match. If a match is found, the action associated with it is performed.

```
              Pascal                     |               C++
case  digit  of  {digit is an integer}   | switch (digit)  // Digit is an int.
   0    :  begin stmt1; stmt2 end;        | {
  1,2,3 :  stmt3;                         |   case 0:              stmt1; stmt2; break;
  4,5   :  stmt4;                         |   case 1: case 2: case 3:     stmt3; break;
```

```
  8      :   begin stmt5; stmt6 end;
end.
```

```
case 4: case 5:                stmt4; break;
   case 8:                  stmt5; stmt6; break;
}                // No semicolon needed.
```

The individual cases do not have to be listed in numerical order as they are in the example; and the formatting can be rearranged for clarity or preference. The *break* statements are needed in order to terminate execution of the *switch*. Without it, processing falls through to the action associated with the case or cases next listed. For example, without the break concluding the action to be taken in the case when digit equals 0 (which is the execution of *stmt1* followed by *stmt2*), processing would continue with *stmt3*, the next executable action in the statement.

The switch statement differs from the **case** statement when the value being tested is not listed. It allows processing simply to fall through. For example, if the value of digit were 6 no action would be selected. The keyword *default* can be used to provide an action for all cases except the listed one:

```
switch (digit)   // Digit is an int.
  {
    case 0:                      stmt1; stmt2; break;
    case 1: case 2: case 3:            stmt3; break;
    case 4: case 5:                    stmt4; break;
    case 8:                      stmt5; stmt6; break;
    default:                     stmt7; stmt8;
  }
```

If the value of digit were 6, *stmt7* and *stmt8* would be executed, since these are now denoted as the actions to be taken when "none of the above" applies.

The while *Loop*

The *while* loops in Pascal and C++ perform identically. They look nearly the same too; the only difference is that the *while* loop in C++ omits the word "do."

Pascal	*C++*

``accum := 0;   {accum is a real}``
``i := 0;       {i is an integer}``
	``accum = 0; // accum is a float``
	``i = 0;     // i is an int``

``while (accum <= 5.0) do``
``  begin``
``    i := i + 1;``
``    accum := accum + 1/i;``
``  end;``
	``while (accum <= 5.0)``
	``  {``
	``    i = i + 1;``
	``    accum = accum + 1.0/i;``
	``  };``

The do . . . while *Loop*

C++'s analogue to Pascal's **repeat . . . until** loop is the *do . . . while* loop. Both contain a body, which is executed at least once, and the test for termination is made after each iteration. The difference between them is in the logical polarity of the test that controls termination. The **repeat . . . until** loop expresses a condition that, when true, terminates the loop. Looping continues "until" the condition is met. The *do . . . while* loop expresses a condition that, if met, causes looping to continue.

```
repeat
   game;
   writeln;
   write('Want to play again?  (Y/N) ');
   readln( again );
until ((again = 'N') or (again = 'n'));
```

```
do
   {
   game();
   cout << endl;
   cout << "Want to play again?  (Y/N) ";
   cin  >> again;
   }
while (again=='Y' || again=='y');
```

the *do ... while* statement requires
the parentheses around the expression

The for *Loop*

The heading of the C++ *for* statement contains the three specifications needed to define the execution of the loop:

The initialization of control variable; here, the control variable *i* and is set to 1, but the starting value could have come by way of any arithmetic expression.

The test applied before every iteration, including the first: execution continues if and only if the result is true.

The adjustment to the control variable made following each iteration of the loop. Here, *i* is incremented by 1.

```
for ( i = 1;  i <= 10;  i = i+1 )
   cout << i << "   ";
```

The following loop prints out the integers from 1 to 10 along a line, exactly as this Pascal **for** loop does.

```
for  i := 1  to  10  do
```

```
                         write(i, ' ');
```

Pascal's companion **for** loop that runs in the other direction,

```
        for  i := 10  downto  1  do
            write(i, ' ');
```

is expressed in C++ as

```
    for ( i = 10; i >= 1; i = i-1 )
        cout << i << " ";
```

The body of C++'s *for* loop can consist of a block of statements, some of which may themselves be loops (with the usual, elementary stipulation that the respective control variables be different). The following code displays the contents of a two-dimensional array of characters that represents a screen in text mode. It has 22 rows and 78 columns.

Pascal	*C++*

```
var                                        char screen[22][78];
    screen   : array[0..21, 0..77] of char;
    row, col : integer;                    int row, col;
                 ⋮                                      ⋮
    writeln;                               cout << endl;
    for row := 0  to  21  do               for (row = 0; row < 22; row = row + 1)
      begin                                  {
        for col := 0 to 77 do                  for (col=0; col<78; col=col+1);
          write( screen[row, col] );             cout << screen[row][col];
        writeln;                               cout << endl;
      end;                                   }
```

The Unconditional Branch

Control structures in Pascal and C++ eliminate the need for most *goto* statements. However, for some reason, possibly because some argue that an unconditional branch out from a deeply nested loop can be useful, Niklaus Wirth included the **goto** statement in Pascal. The jump has to be to a labeled statement. Any statement may be labeled by preceding it with a natural number followed by a colon; and its label, which has to be distinct, is this number. C++ also has a *goto*, which works the same way, except that labels are alphanumeric identifiers formed in accordance with the same rules as variable names, function names, and the like.

Pascal	*C++*

```
    53:  stmt;                                t1:  stmt;
         stmt;                                     stmt;
```

```
47:   stmt;                       alternate:   stmt;
      stmt;                                    stmt;
      goto 68;                                 goto fixProblem;
      stmt;                                    stmt;
      if (a > b) goto 53;                      if (a > b) goto t1;
      stmt;                                    stmt;
68:   stmt;                       fixProblem:  stmt;
```

2.5   Functions

Functions such as *sqrt( )*, *strlen( )*, and *strcpy( )* are a standard part of a typical C++ system and are called library functions. Library functions are incorporated into a program by means of header files. Functions with identical effects may be created by the programmer for a particular program and appear explicitly in the program file. Whether a function is a library function or a programmer-defined function, it adheres to the same rules of usage.

Function Basics

- In C++, as in Pascal, a function call yields a single value; the item returned is declared to be an *int*, a *float*, a *char*, an enumerated value, or a *struct*.

- A function call is an expression and may appear wherever an expression may appear.

```
sqrtOfNum = sqrt(num);
curvedMidTerm = sqrt(score) * 10;

if ( sqrt(gradePointAve) > average )
    cout << "Welcome to the Square Root Club!";

    cout << "Square root of "  << n << " is "  << sqrt(n);
```

- A corollary of the preceding point is that there is no limit to the number of function calls an expression may contain, or to their placement:

```
root4  = sqrt( sqrt(num) );
```

- Arguments can be expressions or literals.

```
c = sqrt( a*a + b*b );
sqrtOfe = sqrt(2.718282);
```

- Functions can be written to expect no argument, one argument, two arguments, three arguments, or any other number. (As in Pascal when there are several arguments, they are separated by commas, and the same rule of positional correspondence establishes the actual argument-to-formal parameter association).

- The function construct allows parameters (also called formal arguments) to be defined so that arguments (also called actual arguments) of any type may be transmitted for processing; this includes *structs* and arrays.

- The default mode of information transmission is *pass by value* (except for arrays, which are always passed by reference); and just as in Pascal, if an argument is to be *passed by reference* this is prescribed by an explicit notation accompanying the corresponding parameter's declaration; in Pascal, the notation is the word **var** preceding the identifier; in C++, it is the ampersand following the identifiers. For example, to pass an *int* parameter by reference, use *int&*. The syntax of a call does not require, allow, or offer information on how arguments are passed.

- The source code listing must contain the function itself or a *forward declaration* before its first call (in the case of recursion, the function heading suffices).

Functions and Procedures

A proper function is a function that accepts one or more arguments and returns a resulting value. In C++, functions double as procedures. If a function has a return type of *void*, which is to say that it is constructed so that no value is returned, its call looks and acts like a Pascal procedure call. The difference is that for a function that takes no arguments, such as *heading( )* in the following, C++ requires the empty parentheses. Whenever a no-argument function is invoked, the parentheses are required.

Pascal	C++
`heading;`	`heading(); // Write a page heading.`
`sort( data_array );`	`sort( dataArray );`
`swap(a,b);`	`swap(a,b); // Exchange a and b.`

Even when a function's return type is not *void*, but perhaps a *float* or a *char*, it may be completely disregarded if what the program needs is the function's side effect. For example,

```
if (i>0) sqrt(25);
```

is legal but useless (and is also poor programming).

A different example that uses the side effect as a trick is the use of *getchar( )* or its equivalent as a means for stopping a running program until a key is struck. The standard library function *getchar( )* (declared within header file *stdio.h*) takes no argument. It returns the next character on an input stream from the console. Thus if *ch* is defined to be a *char*, the statement

```
ch = getchar();
```

causes a pause and, when the user strikes a key, for example, the enter key, the assignment of "\n" for *ch*. Note that the input sequence

```
cin >> ch;
```

captures only printable keystrokes. Because '\n,' like an ASCII 32 from the space bar, is white space, no notice is taken of an enter. If the side effect of the function *getchar( )*, namely, the freezing of the output stream, is the desired effect, then the returned value is effectively ignored.

```
getchar();   // Any C++ function can be called in the
             // manner of a Pascal procedure.
```

Constructing Functions

We now consider function definitions. The distinctive feature of *main( )* is that it is generally the point at which C++ programs begin execution. Otherwise, it is an ordinary function. All functions, like *main( )*, consist of a heading (the declarator) followed by a body of statements between a beginning and an ending set of brackets:

```
declarator
   {
      body
   }
```

The body may include variable definitions, the specification and definition of *enum*s and *struct*s, the definition of *enum*s and *struct*s specified externally, function calls, output and input operations, and other C++ system statements. Everything done so far within *main( )* could have been done within any other function. The only prohibition is that no function can incorporate within itself the heading and body of another function; functions are not nested in the source code.

The Declarator

The declarator prescribes the data type of the item returned, the function's name, and the list of parameters. This argument list, just as in Pascal, gives the name, data type, and passing modality (by value or by reference) of each variable participating in information transmission from the call through the explicit interface. (Implicit information transmission may be accomplished by way of global variables, called external variables; this is not good programming practice when explicit transmission is logically preferable.) There are two minor differences in syntax between declarators in C++ and headings in Pascal: in C++, for functions having no parameters, the opening and closing parentheses delimiting the parameter list must still be present, though empty, and there is no semicolon between the declarator and the body. In the declarator, C++ does not allow for the more concise expression of the parameter list, as Pascal does when two or more neighboring parameters have the same description.

The Return

In C++ a value other than *void* (e.g., *int* or *struct*) is returned using the *return* statement. Consider a function that returns the area of a rectangle whose length and width are passed in as arguments. The return statement can take any of the forms illustrated in the following.

Pascal	C++
| ```pascal
function area_of_rect (l, w :real) : real;
   var
      area : real;
   begin
      area := l * w;
      area_of_rect := area;
   end
``` | ```cpp
float areaOfRect (float l, float w)
{
  float area;
  area = l * w;
  return area;
}
``` |

Alternate, equally acceptable returns are as follows.

```cpp
return (area);   // Value may be in parentheses.
return l * w;    // Value may result from the evaluation of an expression.
return (l*w);    // Expression may be in parentheses.
```

An important difference between the return statement in C++ and Pascal's "assignment to the name of the function" is that execution of the return statement in C++ terminates the function call. Returning to the point where the function was invoked includes the dismantling of the current instantiation's referencing environment. In Pascal, this happens only when the function's closing **end** is reached. The following two segments of code are not functionality equivalent.

Pascal	C++
| ```pascal
function letter_grade (score:integer) : char;
  begin
    if (score >= 90) then
      begin
       letter_grade := 'A';
       write('Grade: A');
       if (score = 99 or score = 100) then
``` | ```cpp
char letterGrade (int score)
{
  if (score >= 90)
   {
    return 'A';
    cout << "Grade: A"; // NOT REACHABLE.
    if (score == 99 || score == 100)
``` |

```
        write('+');                        cout << "+";
    end                                }
  else if (score >= 80) then           else if (score >= 80)
        begin                          {
           letter_grade := 'B';          return 'B';
           write('grade: B');            cout << "Grade: B"; // NOT REACHABLE.
              ⋮                              ⋮
end                                    }
```

Suppose this function is passed the score of 100. The Pascal function assigns '**A**' to local variable **letter_grade**, prints '**Grade: A**', prints '+', and then returns the value **letter_grade**, or '*A*'. The C++ function performs the return of the '*A*'. It displays neither the grade nor the plus.

Finally, if a function's declarator proclaims that it returns *void*, it may use the return statement like this

```
return;
```

to transfer control back to the calling function, but it is prohibited from passing back a value. Moreover, when the return type is *void*, a return statement need not be executed. Likewise, if the declarator proclaims that an *int* will be returned, the function must return an *int*. The rule is that a function must return that which its declarator says it will return.

Examples of Functions

To complete the description of the internal structure of functions, here are some samples in C++ alongside their Pascal equivalents.

Pascal	*C++*
```program sample1 (input, output);```	```#include <iostream.h>```
``` var```	
``` arg1, arg2, total: integer;```	```// Print parm1, parm2, parm1+parm2.```
``` { Print parm1, parm2, and parm1+parm2 }```	```// Return parm1+parm2.```
``` { Return parm1+parm2 }```	
``` function echo_and_add (parm1,parm2:integer):```	```int echoAndAdd (int parm1, int parm2)```
``` integer```	
``` var```	```{```
``` sum : integer;```	``` int sum;```
``` begin```	
``` sum := parm1 + parm2;```	``` sum = parm1 + parm2;```
``` writeln;```	``` cout << endl;```
``` write('parm1 = ', parm1);```	``` cout << "parm1 = " << parm1;```
``` write(' parm2 = ', parm2);```	``` cout << " parm2 = " << parm2;```
``` write(' Their sum is: ');```	``` cout << " Their sum is: ";```

```pascal
        writeln(sum);

        echo_and_add := sum;
      end;

  begin


    arg1 := 12;
    arg2 := 34;

    total := echo_and_add( arg1, arg2 );

    total := echo_and_add(1+1, arg2 - 5);
  end.
```

```cpp
    cout << sum << endl;

    return sum;
  }

void main()
  {
    int arg1, arg2, total;

    arg1 = 12;
    arg2 = 34;

    total = echoAndAdd( arg1, arg2 );

    total = echoAndAdd(1+1, arg2 - 5);
  }
```

Pascal

```pascal
program sample2 (input, output);
  var
    arg1, arg2, total: integer;
{ Return total which is passed by reference }
  procedure echo_and_add
    (parm1, parm2:integer; var parm3:integer);
    var
      sum : integer;
    begin
      sum := parm1 + parm2;

      writeln;
      write('parm1 = ', parm1);
      write('   parm2 = ', parm2);
      write('   Their sum is:  ');
      writeln(sum);

      parm3 := sum
    end;

  begin


    arg1 := 12;
    arg2 := 34;

    echo_and_add( arg1, arg2, total );
```

_C++_

```cpp
#include <iostream.h>

// Return total which is passed
// by reference.

void echoAndAdd
    (int parm1, int parm2, int& parm3)
  {
    int sum;

    sum = parm1 + parm2;

    cout << endl;
    cout << "parm1 = " << parm1;
    cout << "   parm2 = " << parm2;
    cout << "   Their sum is:  ";
    cout << sum << endl;

    parm3 = sum;
  }

void main()
  {
    int arg1, arg2, total;

    arg1 = 12;
    arg2 = 34;

    echoAndAdd( arg1, arg2, total );
```

```
      echo_and_add(1+1, arg2 - 5, total)
  end.
```

```
    echoAndAdd(1+1, arg2 - 5, total);
}
```

Pascal

```
program sample3 (input, output);
  var
    arg2, arg3, total: integer;
{ Return parm1 which is passed by reference. }
  procedure echo_and_add
      (var parm1:integer; parm2,parm3:integer);
      var
        sum : integer;

      begin
        sum := parm2 + parm3;

        writeln;
        write('parm2 = ', parm2);
        write('   parm3 = ', parm3);
        write('   Their sum is:  ');
        writeln(sum);

        parm1 := sum;
      end;

      begin


        arg2 := 12;
        arg3 := 34;

        echo_and_add( total, arg2, arg3 );

        echo_and_add(total, 1+1, arg3 - 5)
  end.
```

C++

```
#include <iostream.h>

// Return parm1 which is passed
// by reference.

void echoAndAdd
    (int& parm1, int parm2, int parm3)
  {
    int sum;

    sum = parm2 + parm3;

    cout << endl;
    cout << "parm2 = " << parm2;
    cout << "   parm3 = " << parm3;
    cout << "   Their sum is:  ";
    cout << sum << endl;

    parm1 = sum;
  }

void main()
  {
    int arg2, arg3, total;

    arg2 = 12;
    arg3 = 34;

    echoAndAdd( total, arg2, arg3 );

    echoAndAdd(total, 1+1, arg3 - 5);
  }
```

Pascal

```
program sample4 (input, output);
  var
    x : real;
   { Return 1/f }
   procedure reciprocal (var f : real);
     begin
       f := 1/f
     end;

   begin
```

C++

```
#include <iostream.h>

// Return 1/f.

void reciprocal (float& f)
  {
    f = 1/f;
  }

void main()
```

```
                                           float x;

        x := 3.14;                          x = 3.14;

        writeln;                            cout << endl << "x = "
                                                << x;
        write('x = ', x:12:6);

        reciprocal( x );                    reciprocal( x );

        writeln('   recip = ', x:12:6)      cout << "   recip = "
                                                << x << endl;
    end.                                  }
```

The Prototype

In these samples, the overall structure of a C++ program, with functions positioned ahead of *main( )* in the source listing, looks quite like the overall structure of a Pascal program. In C++, however, the order of functions is arbitrary. Functions, including *main( )*, may appear in the program in any order whatsoever. The only rule is that either the function itself or what plays the part of a forward declaration appear prior to the function's first call. What is called a forward declaration in Pascal is called a prototype in C++.

A function's declarator, followed by a semicolon, may serve as its prototype. So might its declarator without the names of the parameters. When parameters names are shown in the prototype, they do not have to be the actual names used in the function's declarator and within its body. C++ allows these names to be shown in order to make the code self-documenting. The prototype gives the structure of the interface: the number of parameters and their respective types. Consider a function for displaying the time of day; it accepts two arguments, the hour and the minute.

```
void showTime(int hr, int min)          // The apostrophes
   {                                    // around  :  instead of
    cout << endl << hr << ':' << min << endl;   // quotes are okay
   }                                    // because it is a char
                                        // literal, not a string.
```

Each of the following would be an acceptable prototype.

```
void showTime(int hr, int min);          // Prototype identical to function's declarator.

void showTime(int hour, int minute);     // Different parameter names in prototype.

void showTime(int, int);                 // Parameter names omitted.
```

The prototype, like the function itself, may not appear within another function. It must be placed between functions or ahead of them. Each of the following is a workable program.

```cpp
#include <iostream.h>

void showTime(int hr, int min);

void main()
  {
    showTime(10,30);
  }

void showTime(int hr, int min)
  {
    cout<<endl<<hr<<':'<<min<<endl;
  }
```

```cpp
#include <iostream.h>

void showTime(int hr, int min);

void showTime(int hr, int min)
  {
    cout<<endl<<hr<<':'<<min<<endl;
  }

void main()
  {
    showTime(10,30);
  }
```

```cpp
#include <iostream.h>

void showTime(int hr, int min)
  {
    cout<<endl<<hr<<':'<<min<<endl;
  }

void alpha()
  {
    cout<<endl<<"From alpha"<<endl;
  }

void showTime(int hr, int min);
void beta();

void main()
  {
    alpha();
    beta();
    showTime(10,30);
  }

void beta()
  {
    cout<<endl<<"--From beta--"<<endl;
    cout<<endl<<"Time from beta:";
    showTime(9,15);
    cout<<"alpha from beta:";
    alpha();

    cout<<"---end of beta---"<<endl;
  }
```

```cpp
#include <iostream.h>

void showTime(int hr, int min);
void alpha();
void beta();

void main()
  {
    alpha();
    beta();
    showTime(10,30);
  }

void beta()
  {
    cout<<endl<<"--From beta--"<<endl;
    cout<<endl<<"Time from beta:";
    showTime(9,15);
    cout<<"alpha from beta:";
    alpha();
    cout<<"---end of beta---"<<endl;
  }

void alpha()
  {
    cout<<endl<<"From alpha"<<endl;
  }

void showTime(int hr, int min)
  {
    cout<<endl<<hr<<':'<<min<<endl;
  }
```

It is not an error to have several copies of a function's prototype as long as each one is correct.

Scope and Lifetime

In C++, all *const*s, *struct*s, enums, and variables defined within a function have scope that is strictly local to that function. They are not visible (i.e., accessible in any way) within other functions; their lifetime is the lifetime of the function.

External constants, external structure specifications, external enumeration specifications, and external variable declarations are the means through which Pascal's global **const**s, **type**s, and variables are implemented in C++.

- They appear either ahead of all the functions or between functions, which is to say they are apart from any particular function or, synonymously, external.
- They are known within all functions that follow them in the source listing.

Each of these has precisely the same syntactic form whether they appear in the program or within a function. They differ from their internal counterparts only in their scope and lifetime. Here are two examples of their use.

Example 1   Pi as a constant.

Pascal

```
program const_demo (input,output);
  const
    pi = 3.14;
  var
    diameter : real;

    function area (radius:real) : real;
      begin
        area := pi * radius * radius;
      end;

    function circum (radius:real) : real;
      begin
        circum := 2 * pi * radius;
      end;

begin
  diameter := 10;

  writeln;
  write('area = ', area(diameter/2):13:6);
  write('    and circumference = ');
  writeln( circum(diameter/2):13:6 );
  writeln('(pi taken as ', pi:8:6, ')' );
```

C++

```
#include <iostream.h>

const float PI = 3.14;

float area (float radius);    // Prototype.
float circum (float radius); // Prototype.

void main()
 {
   float diameter;
   diameter = 10;

   cout << endl;
   cout << "area = " << area(diameter/2);
   cout << "    and  circumference = ";
   cout << circum(diameter/2) << endl;

   cout<<"(pi taken as "<<PI<<")"<<endl;
 }

float area (float r)
 {
   return (PI * r * r);
 }
```

```
float circum (float r)
{
  return (2 * PI * r);
}
```

end.

Example 2   Database as a global variable.

Pascal

```
program global_array (input,output);
  const
    elements = 5;
  var;
    database : array[1..elements] of integer;

    procedure initialize;
      var
          i : integer;
      begin
        for i := 1 to elements do
          database[i] := 50;
      end;

    procedure print;
      var
        i : integer;
      begin
        writeln;
        for i := 1 to elements do
          write(database[i], '  ');
        writeln;
      end;

  begin
    initialize;
    database[3] := 100;
    print;
  end.
```

C++

```
#include <iostream.h>

const int ELEMENTS = 5;
int database[ELEMENTS]; // 0..4

void initialize(); // Prototype.
void print();      // Prototype.

void main()
{
  initialize();
  database[2] = 100;   // 3rd cell.
  print();
}

void initialize()
{
  int i;
  for (i=0; i<ELEMENTS; i=i+1)
    database[i] = 50;
}

void print()
{
  int i;
  cout << endl;
  for (i=0; i<ELEMENTS; i=i+1)
    cout << database[i] << "  ";
  cout << endl;
}
```

```
The for loop as well as the
other iteration and selection
statements are explained in
detail later in this chapter.
```

Variables defined within a function, with scope restricted to the function, are local variables. In the vernacular of C++ however, they are called automatic variables. When an automatic variable and an external variable have the same name within a local environment, the name references the automatic variable. Just as a global variable is hidden by a local variable of the same name in Pascal, an external variable is hidden by an automatic variable. The double colon, as a prefix operator, allows access to the external variables; *::var* always accesses external variables *var*. Consider the following example.

```
#include <iostream.h>

int var;  // Definition of an external variable, var.

void one()
 {
  cout << endl;
  cout << "From one():  external var (via ::var) = " << ::var << endl;
  cout << "             external var (via   var) = " <<   var; // No automatic named var
  cout << endl << endl;                                        // so this accesses the
 }                                                             // external variable.

void two(int var)
 {
  var   =   var * 2; // Parameter var accessed. (Parameters are automatic variables too.)
  ::var = ::var * 2; // External  var accessed.

  cout << endl;
  cout << "From two():  automatic var (via   var)  = " <<   var << endl;
  cout << "             external  var (via ::var)  = " << ::var;
  cout << endl;
 }

void main()
 {
  int var;

  var   =  6;  // Automatic var accessed.
  ::var = 14;  // External var accessed.

  cout << endl;
  cout << "From main():  automatic var (via   var)  = " <<   var << endl;
  cout << "              external  var (via ::var)  = " << ::var;
  cout << endl;

  one();
  two(var);

  cout << "From main():  automatic var (via   var)  = " <<   var << endl;
  cout << "              external  var (via ::var)  = " << ::var;
  cout << endl;
 }
```

Here is the output.

```
From main():  automatic var (via   var)  = 6
              external  var (via ::var)  = 14
```

```
From one():    external  var (via ::var)  = 14
               external  var (via   var)  = 14

From two():    automatic var (via   var)  = 12
               external  var (via ::var)  = 28

From main():   automatic var (via   var)  = 6
               external  var (via ::var)  = 28
```

Arrays as Parameters

Arrays can be arguments in function calls, just as scalar types can. C++ passes all arrays by reference. It does this without a special token in the declarator, and it does not provide a means for passing them by value. The most significant difference between C++ and Pascal is that C++ does not require anything like a user-defined **type** in order to pass an *int, float,* or *char* array. Passing an array of *struct*s as an argument or an array of enums, just as passing a single *struct* or a single enum, naturally requires that the specification be accessible for defining the corresponding argument in the declarator. This means that the specification for the structure or the enumerated data type must be external. The following program passes a five-element *int* array from *main()* to *print()*.

```
#include <iostream.h>

const int SIZE = 5;

void print(int[]); // Prototype; alternatives are  void print(int a[]);
                //                                  void print(int b[]);
                //                                  void print(int c[size]);

void main()
   {
   int a[SIZE];    // Length of array must be given by a numeric literal or a const.

   a[0]=10; a[1]=11; a[2]=12; a[3]=13; a[4]=14;

   print( a );    // Passing the array to print().
   }

void print(int b[]) // Declarator; alternatives are  void print(int b[SIZE]);
                //                                    void print(int b[4]);
                //                                    void print(int b[3]);
                //              The indicated array length has no effect.
   {
   int i;
```

```
    cout << endl;
    for (i = 0; i < SIZE; i=i+1)  cout << b[i] << "  ";
    cout << endl;
}
```

Two-dimensional arrays (and arrays with more dimensions) are passed to functions just as one-dimensional arrays, which is to say, just by using their name. Variable *twoD* defined

```
    int twoD[3][4];                  // Definition.
```

is an *int* array with 3 rows and 4 columns, 12 elements in all. It could be passed to *twoDimPrint( )* like this:

```
    twoDimPrint( twoD );             // Function call.
```

The prototype for *twoDimPrint( )* has to show that it has one parameter that is a two-dimensional *int* array:

```
    int twoDimPrint( int a[][] );     // Prototype.
    int twoDimPrint( int [][] );      // Alternative prototype.
```

An indication of number of rows and columns, as in the following, is only for the benefit of the reader:

```
    int twoDimPrint( int a[3][4] );   // Yet another prototype.
```

These values are not used. However, in the declarator for the function, the number of columns (i.e., the number of elements in the second dimension) must be given as a numeric literal or a *const*.

The memory location of an element in a one-dimensional array can be computed from its index alone, given the array's basic specifications:

```
location = base_address + (index * amount_of_memory_used_per_element)
```

```
                         ┌─────────────────────────────┐
                         │ Remember, the first element  │
                         │ has an index of 0.           │
                         └─────────────────────────────┘
```

In a two-dimensional array, the address of the third element in the second row depends upon how many elements there are in the first row. In general, the memory location of the element *a[row][col]* is

```
    array's_base_address
    elements_ per_row * amount_of_memory_used_per_element * row
 +  amount_of_memory_used_per_element * col
    ─────────────────────────────────────────────────────────
    memory_location
```

Thus the declarator for *twoDimPrint( )* could assume these forms:

```
int twoDimPrint( a[][4] )    // The 4 is needed for computation.
int twoDimPrint( a[3][4] )   // The 3 is only for documentation.
```

Often, when an array is passed to a function, it is accompanied by information pertaining to the number of elements in use and/or some other information. Certainly the parameter list may include entries that indicate bounds as in:

```
// Sort a [leftEnd ... rightEnd]
void  quickSort( int a[], int leftEnd, int rightEnd )
```

C++ supports recursion, of course. As in Pascal, a recursive function and a recursive function invocation look no different from non-recursive ones.

<table>
<tr><td align="center">Pascal</td><td align="center">C++</td></tr>
<tr><td valign="top">

```
{ Output := input!, for input }
program recursive_fact (input,output);
  var
    i : integer;
  function factorial(n:integer):integer;
    begin
      if (n=0 or n=1) then factorial := 1
      else factorial := n*factorial(n-1);
    end;
begin
  for i:= 0 to 6 do
  writeln(i, 'factorial = ',
                    factorial(i) );
end.
```

</td><td valign="top">

```
#include <iostream.h>
int factorial (int n);
void main()
{
  int i;
  for (i=0; i<=6; i=i+1)
    cout<<i<<" factorial = "<<factorial(i)<<endl;
}
int factorial (int n)
  {
    if (n==0 || n==1)  return 1;
    else return n*factorial(n-1);
  }
```

</td></tr>
</table>

Structs as Parameters

Structures and enumerated types are passed to functions and returned in the same way as *ints*, *floats*, and *chars*. The stage for this is set with external specifications. Consider a program that begins as follows:

```
#include <iostream.h>

enum upOrDown {ascending, descending};

struct itemRec      // External struct specification.
  {
  int     serialNum;
  float   cost;
  int     stockNum;
  char    description[41];
  };
```

Henceforth, *upOrDown* and *itemRec* can be used in all the same places and in all the same ways as built-in data types. For instance, a function may define a 100 element *itemRec* array called inventory:

```
itemRec inventory[100];
```

Consider this function declarator.

```
void sortStock (itemRec piece[], int piecesOnHand, upOrDown direction)
```

The first use of *sortStock( )* may be to put an inventory of 83 items into ascending order.

```
sortStock(inventory, 83, ascending);
```

Within *sortStock( )*, the *stockNum* of the *struct* at index 5 could be accessed like this:

```
piece[5].stockNum.
```

2.6 Dynamically Allocated Structures

Linked lists and, analogously, all data structures built from dynamically allocated *struct*s (records in Pascal terminology), are handled in C++ with language elements that correspond closely to Pascal's. Assume the following list of nodes, each of which has two members (fields in Pascal), a variable called *letter* and a variable called *next*. The first difference is that C++ uses *NULL* instead of Pascal's **nil**. *NULL* is a constant that is set to 0. (It is defined and used in header files *iostream.h* and *alloc.h*.) Because it is a constant, the convention is followed that it be capitalized. Wherever *NULL* appears in a program it may be replaced by 0 (the numeral zero, not within apostrophes, and not preceded by a backslash, and not an ASCII 0).

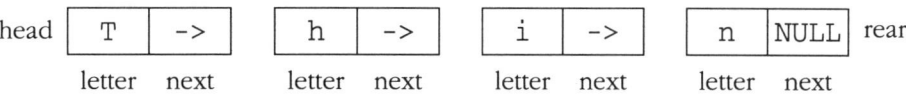

The preparation for this list requires setting forth the configuration of *node* and defining the external pointers *head* and *rear*. Giving the configuration means specifying the members of the *struct* to be used as the *node* data type.

Pascal	*C++*

type
  pointer = ^node;
 	
  node = record
	struct node
	  {
	    char letter;
	    node* next;

```
        letter : char;          |
        next   : pointer;       |
     end;                       |        };
```

Just as identifiers **pointer** and **node** are discretionary names chosen by the programmer of the Pascal fragment, the name of the *struct* is arbitrarily called *node*. The first component of *struct node* has type *char* and name *letter*. Within the *struct*, the first member declared is named *letter*, and it is a *char*. The second member is named *next*. Its data type is "the address of a node" or, more succinctly, a *node pointer*. Like pointers in Pascal, pointers in C++ are typed: a pointer to *structs* of type *node* cannot point to any other kind of *struct* or datum. The asterisk indicates that the data type is a pointer; the identifier to the left of the asterisk indicates what is at the address: a *node struct*. The syntax for defining external pointers (i.e., pointers that are not part of the list) works the same way.

Pascal	*C++*
var	node* head;
head : pointer;	node* rear;
rear : pointer;	node* newNode; // To hold the address of
new_node : pointer;	// a newly allocated node
	// until it is installed
	// within the list.

For *head* and *rear* (along with any other pointer to *node*) to be defined in a single statement, the asterisk must be repeated. Consider the notations:

Pascal	*C++*
var	node* head, * rear, * newNode;
head, rear, new_node : pointer;	
	or
	node * head, * rear, * newNode;
	or
	node *head, *rear, *newNode;

Typedef

C++ offers a mechanism for associating a name with a data type that corresponds to the **type** declaration in Pascal: prefixing a type declaration by the keyword *typedef*. An important use of **type** and *typedef* is to define structures of the same type in different places. In Pascal, the only means for passing a record or an array to a subprogram is to create a data type and to declare the parameter and the prospective arguments to be of this type. This is because two records or two arrays, even if their components are identical, are of distinct types if not defined by way of the same name.

Even though a *typedef* need not be named to implement a dynamically allocated data structure, doing so makes the structure's specification and the definition of external pointers analogous to the customary practice in Pascal.

Pascal	*C++*
| ```
type
  pointer = ^node;

node = record
        letter : char;
        next   : pointer;
       end;
var
  head, rear : pointer;
  new node    : pointer
``` | ```
typedef  struct node*  pointer;

struct node
  {
    char      letter;
    pointer      next;
  };

pointer head,rear;
pointer newNode;
``` |

To append a new node to the list, so that a traversal through the list spells "think," a new *struct* is allocated and then filled with the letter '*k*' and the pointer *NULL* (since it will be the list's rearmost node).

Pascal	*C++*
| ```
new(new_node);




new_node^.letter := 'k';
new_node^.next    := nil;
``` | ```
newNode = new(node);
  // Alternately:  newNode = new node;
  // because new is actually an operator.

newNode -> letter = 'k';
newNode -> next   = NULL;
``` |

Operator new

Pascal and C++ both use a facility called *new* for allocating memory space. In Pascal, the **new** facility may be thought of as a procedure to which the "pointer variable" receiving the address is passed by reference. In C++, the new facility may appear to be a function that returns the address, although technically it is an operator. This operator requires an operand that is the name of the *struct* for which it is to allocate space. It uses the name (1) to determine the size of the memory space that needs to be reserved, and (2) to prescribe the data type of the returned pointer. C++, just like Pascal, is strongly typed with respect to pointers: it will not permit the address of one type of *struct* (e.g., a node *struct*) to be assigned to a pointer variable declared or defined to point to any other type of *struct*.

Member Access

The members within dynamically allocated *struct*s are accessed with the arrow, a two-character operator composed of the dash and the greater than sign. Once again, here is another similarity to Pascal. In Pascal, the dot (.) is used to access fields within records when a variable holds the record itself and the caret-and-dot (^.) to access fields within records when a variable holds a pointer to a record. C++ uses the dot (.) as the member access operator when a variable holds the *struct* itself and the dash and greater than sign (->) as the member access operator when a variable holds a pointer to a *struct*.

Manipulating Dynamic Structures

Linking the new node onto the end of the list involves no additional langauge considerations:

Pascal	C++
| ```
if (rear <> nil)
    then
        rear^.next := new_node
    else
        head := new_node;

rear := new_node;
``` | ```
if (rear != NULL)  // If list not empty.
    rear -> next = newNode;
else
    head = newNode;

rear = newNode;
``` |

Traversing the list is also routine. The mechanics of the operation require an appropriately defined variable (e.g., *movingPtr*) that is repeatedly updated to the address of successive nodes.

Pascal	C++
| ```
var
  moving_ptr : pointer;

         .
         .
         .

moving_ptr := head;
while moving_ptr <> nil do
  begin
    write(moving_ptr^.letter, ' ');
    moving_ptr := moving_ptr^.next
  end;
``` | ```
node*  movingPtr;
       // Alternately:  node * movingPtr;
       //         or:  node  *movingPtr;

    .
    .
    .

movingPtr = head;
while (movingPtr != NULL)
  {
    cout << movingPtr->letter << "  ";
    movingPtr = movingPtr->next;
  }
``` |

Delete

Memory taken with operator *new* is returned (i.e., freed or deallocated) with the operator *delete*. It may be thought of as a function like Pascal's dispose facility, though it is an operator. The following code removes the first two nodes from the list and releases their storage.

Pascal	*C++*
`var` `  old_node : pointer;`	`node*  oldNode;`
⋮	⋮

`old_node := head;`
`head := head^.next;`
`dispose(old_node);`
	`oldNode = head;`
	`head = head -> next;`
	`delete(oldNode);  // Also okay: delete oldNode;`

`old_node := head;`
`head := head^.next;`
`dispose(old_node);`
	`oldNode = head;`
	`head = head -> next;`
	`delete(oldNode);`

Data Structure as Arguments

Data structures are passed to functions by passing the appropriate pointers. A tree may be passed to a preorder traversal function by passing a pointer to its root. A stack may be passed to a pop function by passing a pointer to its top. A queue may be passed to an append function by passing a pointer to its *head* and *rear*. When there is no chance that a pointer will need to be changed, for instance, if the function is a traversal, it may be passed by value. When pointers may need to be updated, such as when a new *struct* is being installed into a priority queue, they must be passed by reference. Functions can also return pointers to *struct*s.

In order for a function's prototype or declarator to declare a pointer to a *struct* as a parameter or as its return type, the *struct* must have been declared earlier. This is also the case for a function to be able to define a pointer to a *struct* as an automatic (local) variable.

Just as a parameter may be declared to receive *struct*s from the call by using the *struct*'s name as its data type, a parameter may be declared to receive pointers to *struct*s by using the *struct*'s name followed by an asterisk. This is syntactically consistent with declarations of a pointer to a *struct* inside the struct (e.g., *node* next*) and with definitions of stand-alone pointer variables such as head and rear (e.g., *node* head*). By default, a pointer argument is passed by value just as an *int, char,* or *float* argument. A pointer argument may be passed by reference by following its data type with an ampersand (e.g., *node*& last*), just as an *int, char,* or *float* argument. A function's return type can be declared to be a pointer to a *struct* by using the *struct*'s name followed by an asterisk. Here are some sample prototypes.

```
int    numOfNodes(node* front);
// Return the number of nodes on list front.

node*  pointerToNodeBeforeIt(char key, node* head);
// Return the point p such that p -> value = key.

void   append(char let, node*& front, node*& rear);
// Allocate a new node, copy character let into its letter member,
// and attaches the node onto the end of the list;
// rear is passed by reference because it is always updated;
// front is changed from NULL when the list's first node is appended.
```

Pointer variables are used as arguments in function calls without any special notation. A pointer argument can be any expression (including a variable) that evaluates to a pointer of the proper data type. For instance, a function that prints segments of a linked list of node *struct*s may have this prototype:

```
void  printList(node* startPlace, node* stopPlace);
```

It may be invoked with the calls

```
printList(head, rear);          // Print full list, from head to rear inclusive.

printList(head->next, rear);   // Print from second node to rear.

printList( head->next, (head->next)->next );   // Print second and third nodes.
```

Finally, the following shows how the complete program for creating and printing the list of nodes depicted at the opening of this section fits together. When it is run, the output is the word "T h i n k".

```
#include <iostream.h>

struct node        // External specification of the node struct
   {               // (node is the name we chose; it is not a keyword).
  char   letter;
  node*  next;                      ┌─────────────────────────────────────────┐
    };                              │ A pointer to structs of type node.        │
                                    └─────────────────────────────────────────┘
                                              ┌─────────────────────┐
                                              │ Passed by reference.  │
                                              └─────────────────────┘
  void  append (char let, node*& front, node*& rear)
   {
  node*  newNode;   // Define a pointer to structs of type node.

  newNode = new(node);           // Get the new node and
                                 // assign its address to newNode.
```

```
newNode -> letter = let;
newNode -> next   = NULL;

if (rear != NULL)            // If list is not empty.
   rear -> next = newNode;
else
   front = newNode;


   rear = newNode;
```

A pointer to structs of type *node*, passed by value (no ampersand).

```
     }

   void  printList (node* startPlace, node* stopPlace)
{
 while (startPlace != NULL  &&  startPlace != stopPlace->next)
   {
     cout << startPlace->letter << "  ";
     startPlace = startPlace->next;    // Parameter startPlace
   }                                   // can be reset without
}                                      // affecting its argument, since
                                       // it is passed by value.
void main()
   {
   node* head;
   node* rear;

   head = NULL;
   rear = NULL;

   append('T', head, rear);
   append('h', head, rear);
   append('i', head, rear);
   append('n', head, rear);
   append('k', head, rear);

   cout << endl;
   printList(head, rear);
   cout << endl;
   }
```

2.7   Output and Input

Header file *iostream.h* provides the interface for accessing the fundamental facilities for entering information into the system's default output stream. These facilities include representation of the output stream itself, *cout*; the insertion operator (into the output stream), << ; and the linefeed and carriage return constant, *endl*. It also provides the fundamental facilities for capturing information from the system's default input stream: the representation of the input stream itself, *cin*; and the extraction operator (from the input stream), >>. The default output stream is often associated with the display screen, the default input stream, with the keyboard.

Using cout *for Output*

The use of *cout* with insertion operator << corresponds functionally to Pascal's **write** and **writeln**. All of the following, in any combination and number, can be an operand for *cout*:

- *int*s, i.e., expressions that evaluate to integers;
- *float*s, i.e., expressions that evaluate to floats;
- *char*s, i.e., expressions that evaluate to characters;
- string literals, i.e., strings enclosed between delimiting quotation marks; and
- strings, i.e., *char* array segments that contain a '\0' to signify the string's end.

New lines with endl

Using *cout* has the effect of a **write**. The operation of the **writeln** is affected when the last item designated for output is the constant *endl*. Suppose that *i* and *j* are *int*s. The following illustrations demonstrate how *cout* may be used.

Pascal	*C++*
`writeln;`	`cout << endl;`
`writeln;`	`cout << endl;`
`writeln;`	`cout << endl;`
`writeln;`	`cout << endl;`
	——alternately——
	`cout << endl << endl << endl;`
`write('i = ', i);`	`cout << "i = " << i;`
`writeln('   and  j = ', j)`	`cout << "   and j = " << j << endl;`

Formatting Output

When items are sent to output without explicit instructions for formatting, defaults are applied. Characters are shown in a field one space wide. String literals and string variables are shown in a field whose width equals the string's length. Integers and floats are similarly printed with neither left nor right padding. Floating point values are printed in standard decimal (not exponential) notation. When a value is fractional, such as .25, it is displayed with a zero to the left of the decimal point. On the right side of the decimal point, trailing zeros are not shown. When a float is an integer value, the default is to display it without the decimal point.

The formatting facilities that obtain the same range of control over output as that offered by Pascal in C++ are *setw( )*, *setprecision( )*, *setiosflags(ios::showpoint)*, *resetiosflags(ios::showpoint)*, *setiosflags(ios::fixed)*, *resetiosflags(ios::fixed)*, and *setiosflags(ios::scientific)*. These are made available with the inclusion of header file *iomanip.h*.

- *setw(e)*.
  Set the width of the field into which the next *int*, *float*, or string will be printed to *e* characters wide, where *e* is any arithmetic expression. When *e* is a *float*, it is truncated; where *e* is negative or zero, the instruction is ignored. Values are displayed right-justified. When the field is not of sufficient length, it is automatically enlarged to the right so that information is not lost.

Pascal	*C++*
`write(' ':25); {gives 25 spaces}`	`cout << setw(25) << " "; // Gives 25 spaces.`
	`cout << setw(25) << ""; // Also gives 25 spaces.`

- *setprecision(e)*.
  Set the maximum number of places to the right of the decimal to be displayed to *e*, where *e* is an arithmetic expression. The literal *e* could have been any other literal, variable, or an expression. A negative or zero spec is ignored to yield the default. This formatting command has no effect on *ints*, *chars*, or strings; and it only shows the indicated number of places for *floats* when these are nonzero and actually present. Once the maximum precision of *floats* has been explicitly set (i.e., once the *setprecision(e)* command has been sent to *cout*), it remains in effect until a subsequent *setprecision( )* command is used with *cout* to change it.

- *setiosflags(ios::showpoint)* and *resetiosflags(ios::showpoint)*.
  Even when *cout* has been sent the command *setprecision(3)*, the value of a *float* will be displayed with only two places to the right of the decimal if that is all it has. If it has only one place, only one will be shown, and if it has no places to the right of decimal point then the point itself will be absent. However, trailing zeros will be shown to pad *floats* to the number of places given by *setprecision( )* after *setiosflags(ios::showpoint)* is sent to *cout*. This directive remains in effect until it is toggled off by *resetiosflags(ios::showpoint)*. Showing the point may be important when printing a report with dollars and cents.

- *setiosflags(ios::fixed), resetiosflags(ios::fixed)*, and *setiosflags(ios::scientific)*.
  To display floating point values in scientific notation, two commands have to be used with *cout*: *resetiosflags(ios::fixed)* followed by *setiosflags (ios::scientific)*. After this, all *floats* will be displayed conventional exponential format (e.g., 1.234e+02) until the fixed notation is reinstated by sending

setiosflags(ios::fixed) to *cout*. The precision of values shown in scientific notation is determined by the most recent *setprecision( )* directive.

```
float   flo;
flo = 123.45678;
cout << setprecision(3);
cout << flo << endl;      // Value displayed is 123.457.
cout << resetiosflags(ios::fixed) << setiosflags(ios::scientific);
cout << flo << endl;      // Value displayed is 1.234e+02.
cout << setiosflags(ios::fixed);
cout << flo << endl;      // Value displayed is 123.457.
```

The following program shows some of these formatting features in action.

```
#include <iostream.h>
#include <iomanip.h>

void main()
  {
  float principal;
  principal = 100;      // One hundred dollars.

  float interestRate;
  interestRate = .04;   // Annual interest rate.

  int compoundingsPerYear;
  compoundingsPerYear = 4;

  int year, collects;

  cout << endl;

  cout << "Principal thru 10 years if the account is otherwise dormant"
       << endl << endl;

  cout << "Annual interest rate:   "
       << setiosflags(ios::showpoint) << setprecision(4) << interestRate
       << setw(5) << " " << "Compoundings per year:   "
       << compoundingsPerYear << endl;

  cout << setw(13) << " " << "Rate per interest period:   "
       << interestRate/compoundingsPerYear << endl << endl;

  cout << setw(51) << "Opening deposit:     $"
       << setprecision(2) << setw(7) << principal << endl;

  for (year = 1;  year <= 10;  year = year + 1)
    {
      for (collects=1; collects<=compoundingsPerYear; collects=collects+1)
        principal = principal + principal * (interestRate/compoundingsPerYear);
```

```
    cout << setw(46) << "at end of year " << setw(2) << year
         << ":   " << setw(7) << principal << endl;
    }
}
```

The output here is as follows.

```
Principal thru 10 years if the account is otherwise dormant

Annual interest rate:  0.0400     Compoundings per year:  4
                Rate per interest period:  0.0100

                              Opening deposit:    $ 100.00
                              at end of year  1:    104.06
                              at end of year  2:    108.29
                              at end of year  3:    112.68
                              at end of year  4:    117.26
                              at end of year  5:    122.02
                              at end of year  6:    126.97
                              at end of year  7:    132.13
                              at end of year  8:    137.49
                              at end of year  9:    143.08
                              at end of year 10:    148.89
```

Using cin *for Input*

The name of the standard input buffer is *cin*. Used in conjunction with extraction operator >>, it corresponds to Pascal's **read**. The extraction operator is used between *cin* and the first variable to receive a captured value as well as ahead of all subsequent variables. The *int* variables i and j, the *float* variables f and g, and the *char* variables c and d can be assigned values from the keyboard with constructions such as:

cin >> i >> j >> f >> g >> c >> d;   cin >> i >> j;
_____   cin >> c;
                                    or
cin >> i >> f >> c >> d >> g >> j;   cin >> f >> d;
                                          cin >> g;

Good programming demands that appropriate prompting be provided with *cout*. Proper integer values and floating point values must be entered where expected. A single mistake, such as typing an 'A' when processing seeks a value for i, or a comma in place of the decimal point in the value for f, will adversely affect that assignment and subsequent assignments.

All leading "white space" input such as key strokes from the space bar, the enter key, and the tab key are ignored by the extraction operator in making these assignments. White space is ignored as trailers, except for the enter key, which causes the value's assignment to the item to be carried out. However, these trailers, including the activating enter, are left on the input stream. Thus when the program pauses in response to *cin* >> *i* >> *j*, the keystrokes:

will cause 123 to be stored in *i* and, continuing without noticable response from the computer,

will cause 456 to be stored in *j*. The final enter will remain on the input stream. Similarly, when the program pauses in response to *cin* >> *c;* the keystrokes

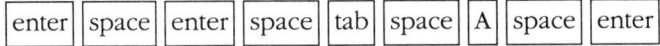

will cause the character *A* to be stored in *c* and leave the trailing space and enter on the input stream. The implication of this latter is that the insertion operator, >>, cannot be used to read-in a space or an enter (also known as a return).

A potentially serious difficulty arises because the enter key must be struck to move the contents of the input stream, including the ASCII representation of the struck enter key, into the processing arena. The insertion operator, although it discards this value with its next input, does not remove it (or any of the other trailing white space) as a clean-up service during the current input. In fact, neither does the statement *cin.get(charVar)*, which is the one used both to rid the input stream of the residual enter character and the other characters left behind. Function *cin.get( )* is provided for by the header file *iostream.h*. Letting *ch1*, *ch2*, *ch3*, *ch4*, and *ch5* be *char* variables and letting *string1* and *string2* both be defined as *char*[81], the following segments of code demonstrate:

```
cin >> ch1; cin.get(ch2);
```

The program awaits a character from the keyboard. User strikes the A key and the enter key. '*A*' is assigned to *ch1* and an "enter" (actually an ASCII 10, which is the new line character represented in C++ code by '\n') is assigned to *ch2*. If the input stream has been holding a residual return from a past input operation, it would have been instantly captured and assigned to *ch1* instead of any character from the keyboard.

```
cin.get(ch1);
```

If the input stream is devoid of characters, the program awaits a character from the keyboard, exactly as it would for *cin>>ch1*. Suppose the user strikes the A key and the enter key. '*A*' is assigned to *ch1* and "enter" is left on the input stream.

```
cin.get(ch1); cin.get(ch2);
```

If the input stream is devoid of characters, the program awaits a character from the keyboard. Suppose the user strikes the A key and the enter key. '*A*' is assigned to *ch1* and without perceptible delay, '\n' is assigned to *ch2*. The input stream is left empty.

```
cin.get(ch1);    cin.get(ch2);    cin.get(ch3);    cin.get(ch4);
cin.get(ch5);
```

If the input stream is devoid of characters, the program awaits a character from the keyboard. Suppose the user strikes these five keys in succession: A B C D enter. They are respectively assigned to *ch1*, *ch2*, and so on; and because the enter is assigned to *ch5*, the input stream is left empty.

```
cin.get(string1,80);    cin.get(ch1);    cin.get(string2,80);
cin.get(ch1);
```

If the input stream is devoid of characters, a string terminated by enter, which may contain spaces, is captured from the keyboard and assigned to *string1*. The function *get( )* automatically appends '\0' to *string1*, but it leaves the terminating "enter" on the input stream. Immediately thereafter the following statement takes it off and assigns it to *ch1*. Next, another such sequence of keystrokes is captured and assigned to *string2*. The final statement clears its terminating return from the input stream.

If the input stream had held a residual return, this sequence of statements would not have performed as intended. Instead, *string1* would have been assigned that which was ahead of the residual return on the input stream, which is to say nothing (so it would equal the null string); *ch1* would get the remaining return; *string2* would receive what was intended for *string1*; and *ch1* would be updated with its delimiting enter.

```
cin.get(string1,80,'@');  cin.get(ch1);  cin.get(string2,80,'~');
cin.get(ch1);
```

This sequence of statements works precisely as those preceding, except that the delimiting character for the first string is the at sign, not the enter, and the delimiting character for the second string is the tilde. For both strings, enters within the captured sequences of characters are stored as an ASCII 10, '\n' character. Following the assignment *string1*, the '@' left behind on the input stream is assigned to *ch1*. Following the assignment to *string2*, *ch1* is assigned its delimiting '~'.

The character on the front of the input stream can be accessed for observation with function *peek( )* that comes with the header file *iostream.h*. Because inputs by way of *cin.get( )* may not work as intended when the input stream holds remaining white spaces, a residual return, or a nonwhite space character that had been used as a sentinel, it can be important to test for these and remove them.

```
while (cin.peek() !=  '\n')  cin.get(ch);        // Remove all chars on
                                                 // the input stream up
```

```
                                                         // to the return.

        if (cin.peek() == '\n') cin.get(ch);            // Remove the return.
```

File I/O

Input can be from disk files as well as from the keyboard and other devices, and output can be to disk files as well as specifically directed to the display screen or the printer. File i/o uses the facilities made available through the header file *fstream.h*.

2.8   Summary and Review

The intent of this chapter was to show that (and how) any process that was expressible in Pascal is expressible in C++. The purpose of the next chapter is to introduce the conventional programming facilities offered by C++ that go beyond those offered by Pascal. Some of these enable familiar operations to be expressed more conveniently (e.g., the unary increment and the various assignment operators such as += and -=). Other facilities enable options that could not be done in Pascal (e.g., function overloading and/or providing default values for parameters).

The chart on pages 70–80 and the following index review the information contained within this chapter in a manner that facilitates reference and use. Recognize that these are only a summary of the C++ "starter subset" for Pascal programmers. They do not form a comprehensive overview of C++.

Index of C++ Symbols, Keywords, Operators, and Library Functions Forming "the Pascal Subset"

//	comment to end of line
/* comment */	
{ }	**begin** and **end**
( )	for grouping terms in expressions
[ ]	to declare/define arrays; accessing subscripted elements of an array
[ ][ ]	to declare/define two-dimensional arrays; accessing elements of 2-dim arrays
\n	escape sequence for newline (ASCII 10)
\0	the null zero string terminator (ASCII 0)
<<	output operator, used with *cout*
>>	input operator, used with *cin*
+ - * / %	arithmetic binary operators
=	assignment operator
++ – –	unary increment and unary decrement
== != < <= > >=	relational operators
&& || !	logical operators
&	to denote parameter is passed by reference
*	declare/define a variable to be a pointer—to hold addresses of dynamically allocated structs
->	member access operator used with pointers to structs
.	member access operator used with a struct directly (e.g., an array of structs)
int	data type ($-32,768 \ldots 32,767$)
int()	cast
float	data type
float()	cast
char	data type
char()	cast
void	denotes that a function returns nothing
long	data type (an extended range *int*: $-2,147,483,648 \ldots 2,147,483,647$)
double	data type (an increased precision float)
const	example: *const float PI = 3.14159;*
enum	to specify an enumerated type
struct	to specify a structure (i.e., "record")
typedef	like **type**, gives a neat definition of pointers to structs
for, while, do-while	loops
break, continue	early exit from a loop
if, else	selection
switch	incorporates keywords like the Pascal **case** statement

This chart is continued on page 80.

Pascal's structures	C++'s structures
comments	comments using the double slash and using the **/* */** pair
data types:	data types:
integer, real, and **char** string literals	*int, float,* and *char*, with variables defined at various points within the program (e.g., variables as they are needed; defining a *for* loop's control variable within the *for* statement) and initialization at the time of variable definition;
	string literals within output statements
write and **writeln** with formatting	*cout,* the extraction operator << and *endl,* optionally with formatting using: *setw(fieldWidth)* *setprecision(places)* *setiosflags(ios::showpoint)* and *resetiosflags(ios::showpoint)* *setiosflags(ios::fixed),* *resetiosflags(ios::fixed),* and *setiosflags(ios::scientific)*
the assignment statement	the assignment statement
the arithmetic operators: addition, subtraction, multiplication, real division (/), integer division (**div**), and modulus (**mod**); the unary minus and plus; **trunc**() and **round**()	the arithmetic operators: addition, subtraction, multiplication; division with two integer operands in contrast to real division; the modulus (integer division remainder) operator, %; the unary minus and plus; cast *int* and cast *float*; the prefix and postfix increment operator ++ and the prefix and postfix decrement operator --

Examples

```
cout << "Hi!";  // Comment.

/* use this for multiline comments
   and to comment-out segments of
   code that include comments to
   end of line that is marked off by //  */


int   age; // To be entered by user.
float seed = 0.45367;
char  yes_or_no = 'y';

int accum = 0;  // To get sum of 1..10.
for (int i = 1, i <= 10, i++)
   accum = accum + i;

cout << "sum = " << accum << endl;

cout << setw(10) << " "; // 10 spaces.

price1 = 12.34;  price2 = 100;
cout << setprecision(2);
cout << setiosflags(ios::showpoint);
cout<<endl<< '$' << setw(8)<< price1;
cout<<endl<< '$' << setw(8)<< price2;


float x = 1.23, y = 100;
cout<<endl<<"x="<<x<<" y="<<y<<endl;
cout<<resetiosflags(ios::fixed)
    << setiosflags(ios::scientific);
cout<<endl<<"x="<<x<<" y="<<y<<endl;
cout<< setiosflags(ios::fixed);
cout<<endl<<"x="<<x<<" y="<<y<<endl;

temp = a;  a = b;  b = temp;



x = a + (b-c)*d;

int   quoti = 12/5; // quoti <- 2
float quotf = 12/5; // quotf <- 2

int   qi=float(12)/5; //qi stores 2
float qf=float(12)/5; //qf stores 2.4

i++;  // means i = i+1;
```

Pascal's structures	C++'s structures
language provided functions (e.g., **sqrt()**); programmer-authored functions and procedures; parameters passed by value and passed by reference	language provided functions (e.g. *sqrt()*); programmer-authored functions, including functions with the return type *void*; parameters passed by value and passed by reference using *&* following the parameter's data type in the function heading (not C's traditional pass by pointer)
char data and the functions **ord()**, **chr()**, **succ()**, and **pred()**	*char* data with the concept of a char as a small integer; the *int* cast for outputting the ordinal value of a *char* and the *char* cast for outputting the character associated with an *int*
control structures:	control structures:
the six relops: **=, <>, <, <=, >, >=**	six relational operators: **==, !=, <, <=, >, >=**
the logical operators: **and, or, not**	the logical operators: *&&, ||, !*; 0 as false
concatenation with **begin** and **end**	concatenation with *{* and *}*
selection with: if . . . then, if . . . then . . . else, and case	selection with: *if*, *if-else*, and *switch* (requires the keyword *case* and *break* statement; use of the *default* option)
iteration with: **for** loops, **while** loops, and **repeat . . . until** loops	iteration with: *for* loops, *while* loops, and *do-while* loops; use of *break* and *continue* to exit from loops
constants and enumerated	defining *const*s and *enum*s

Examples

```
++i;  // means i = i+1;
```

Only headings shown:

```
void printColumnHeadings()

int gcd (int num1, int num2)

void swap (float& a, float& b)
```

```
int digit =  charNumeral + '0';
lowerCase =  upperCaseLetter + 32;

cout << "ASCII of '$' = "
     << int('$');
cout << "ASCII #3 is a heart:  "
     << char(3);
```

```
if (a==b) cout << "They're equal.";
   else cout<<"They're not equal.";

if (grade >= 87 && grade <= 89)
    {
     cout << "B+";
     accumB_Plus = accumB_Plus + 1;
    }
```

```
float sum = 0;
int   i = 0;
while (sum <= 5)
   {
    i++;
    sum = sum + 1.0/i;
   }
cout<<i<<" terms of the harmonic "
   <<"series brings the sum to "<<sum;

const float PI = 3.14159;
```

Pascal's structures	C++'s structures
data types	
type	the *typedef* declaration

read and **readln**	*cin*, insertion operator >>
	  to read an int, float, or
	  nonwhite space char;
	cin.get(ch) to read-in a white space
	  char and to empty the input stream;
	  (the latter requires using *cin.peek()*
	  and using '\n');
	getch( ) to read-in a char, directly
	  from the keyboard (unbuffered);

arrays of **integer, real**,
  and **char**;
  two-dimensional arrays
	arrays of *int, float,* and *char;*
	  two-dimensional arrays;
	  initializing *int* arrays,
	  float arrays, and *char* arrays;
	
	  strings: *char* arrays whose
	  substance is terminated with '\0',
	  the null zero;
	  string output with *cout* and
	  the insertion operator;
	  string input with *cin* and
	  the extraction operator;
	  string input with *cin.get( );* and
	  the string manipulation functions
	  strlen( ), strcmp( ), and *strcpy( )*

Examples

```
enum    boolean {false, true};
boolean keyFound;

typedef int Miles;
Miles   distToPUP, distToPNY;

cout << "Enter number of cases:   ";
cin >> n;

while (cin.peek() != '\n')
   cin.get(ch);
if (cin.peek()=='\n') cin.get(ch);

char ch=getch();// Awaits keystroke.
getch();// Also pauses for keystroke.
        //   The returned character
        //   can be disregarded.

int intArray[10]; // Subscripts: 0..9.

float piPowers[3] = {0, 3.14, 9.86};

char screen[24][80];

char string[] = "Bjarne Stroustrup";
cout<<endl<<'|'<<string<<"|   has "
<< strlen(string) << " letters."
<< endl;

char word1[10], word2[10]; // 9 letter max.
cin >> word1;  // Suppose it is  aaaa.
cin >> word2;  // Suppose it is  bbb.
if ( strcmp(word1, word2) == 0 )
    cout<<"They are the same word.";
else if ( strcmp(word1,word2) < 0 )
    cout<<"Word1 is first."; //It is!
else cout<<"Word2 is first.";

cin.get(charArray, maxNumOfChars);

cin.get(charArray, maxNumOfChars,'@');

strcpy(str, "Hello World!");
```

Pascal's structures	C++'s structures
opening files for output	opening files for output with *ofstream*
opening files for input; the **not eof** construct	opening files for input with *ifstream*; reading input files to their end with the *while (! .eof)* construct
	<< to write-out an *int, float, char,* or string;
	put(ch) to output a *char*
	>> to read-in an *int, float,* or nonwhite space *char*;
	get(ch) to read-in any *char,* including white space *chars*;
	getline( ) to read-in an entire line

Examples

```
ofstream    dataOut("b:proj1cpy.dta");
ofstream    printer("LPT1");
ofstream    screen("CON");

ifstream    dataIn("a:project1.dta");
```

```
// The comments below show what the lines in A:DATA.1 look like:
ifstream data("A:DATA.1");// 65 A
int number = 0;                     // 66 B
char letter = ' ';                  // 67 C

data >> number;

while (! data.eof() )
{
 data >> letter;
 cout << endl << number << "    "
      << letter << endl;
 data >> number;
}

// Copies a file, including white space and end of lines, char by char.
ifstream    termPaper("a:paper");
ofstream    copy("b:paper.cpy");
ofstream    printer("LPT1");
char ch;

termPaper.get(ch);
while (! termPaper.eof() )
{
 copy    <<ch;//or  copy.put(ch);
 printer<<ch;//or printer.put(ch);
 termPaper.get(ch);
}

// Copies a file, line by line (each line is construed as a string).
ifstream    termPaper("a:paper");
ofstream    copy("b:paper.cpy");
ofstream    printer("LPT1");
char line[81].

while (! termPaper.eof() )
   {
```

Pascal's structures	C++'s structures

records:
  arrays of records and
  dynamically allocated
  records
	*struct*s:
	  arrays whose elements are *struct*s,
	  the "dot" operator (member access
	  operator) for accessing members, and
	  passing arrays to functions (arrays
	  are automatically passed by reference);

	dynamically allocated *struct*s:
	  the * for defining a variable as a
	  pointer to a *struct*, the operators
	  new and *delete*, the -> member access
	  operator for use with a pointer to a
	  struct; passing pointers to *struct*s
	  by value and by reference

Examples

```
    termPaper.getline(line,80);
    copy << line << endl;
    printer << line << endl;
   }
```

external

```
Struct sampleStruct
(
  int a, b, c;
);
```

```
void showStruct (sampleStruct triple);
   // Prototype -- structure passed by value.
void showArray (sampleStruct tripleArray[], int n);
   // Prototype -- array passed by reference.

void main()
  {
    int    i;
    sampleStruct s[5];

    for (i=0; i<5; i++)
      {
        s[i].a = i*10 + 1;
        s[i].b = i*10 + 2;
        s[i].c = i*10 + 3;
      }

    showStruct( s[3] );
    showArray( s, 5 );
  }
```

external

```
typedef struct node* nodePtr;

struct node
  {
   char letter;
   nodePtr next;// or node* next;
  };
```

```
void printList (nodePtr front);
          // prototype -- structure passed by value
          // or  void printList (node* front);
void append (nodePtr& front, nodePtr& rear);
```

Examples

```
// prototype -- structure passed by reference
// or   void append (node*& front, node*& rear);

void main()
  {
    nodePtr  head = NULL,  rear = NULL;

    nodePtr  firstNode = new(node);
    firstNode  -> letter = 'a'; firstNode -> next = NULL;
    head = firstNode; rear = firstNode;

    printList( head ); append( head, rear );
  }
```

Chart continued from page 69.

case, break, default

cin	reading *int, float, char* (skips white space)
cin.get()	reading next *char* on input stream (takes white space) also: overloaded to read-in whole strings
cin.peek()	for testing next *char* on input stream
getch()	"pauses until a key is pressed"—entered character is not displayed on the screen
getche()	same as *getch*, except that the entered character is echoed
cout	outputs *int, float, char*, string
endl	linefeed (flushes buffer), used with *cout*
setw()	
setprecision()	
setiosflags(ios::showpoint) and resetiosflags(ios::showpoint)	
setiosflags(ios::fixed), resetiosflags(ios::fixed), and setiosflags(ios::scientific)	
new	create a dynamically allocated *struct*
delete	deallocates memory used by a dynamically allocated *struct*
ifstream	to define and open and input text file
>>	to read-in next *int, float*, nonwhite space *char* from text file
get()	to read-in next *char* from text file
getline()	to read-in entire line from text file
eof()	end of file flag: *while(! dataIn.eof())*
ofstream	to define and open an output text file
<<	to output *int, float, char*, or string to text file
strcpy()	to copy contents of one string into another
strcmp()	to test two strings (such as a relational operator)
strlen()	returns number of *char*s up to the '\0' sentinel
strcat()	to concatenate two strings

References

1. Stroustrup, B. *The C++ Programming Language.* 2nd ed. Reading, MA: Addison-Wesley, 1991.
2. Wirth, N. *Algorithms + Data Structures = Programs.* Englewood Cliffs, NJ: Prentice-Hall, 1976.

3
Procedural C++ That Extends Pascal

3.0 Introduction

Equipped with the C++ subset that covers Pascal, one can write any program in C++ that could have been written in Pascal. Reading code that others have written, however, leads to a discovery of additional operators, the use of dynamic allocation to enable the definition of nonlocal variables (i.e., nonlinked storage with a lifetime exceeding that of the function), and new capabilities of functions beyond those in Pascal. These are the topics discussed in Sections 3.1, 3.2, and 3.3, respectively. The purpose of this chapter is not to provide an exhaustive survey of the entire nonobject part of C++ (which includes C). The aim is to highlight those useful language structures that are characteristic of C++ that lack direct analogues in Pascal.

3.1 Operators

C++ has C's repertoire of operators. Many of the operators are neither found in algebra nor in other widely used languages (e.g., Pascal, PL/1, FORTRAN, and

BASIC), and their presence contributes to C's arcane look. Those who know programming languages, however, recognize some of C's symbology as similar to that of ALGOL 68. Whether familiar or not, nothing is very new here. For example, the modulus operator which is **mod** in Pascal is the percentage sign, %, in C++. Not only does it perform identically, but the same requirement applies that both operands must be integers. The division operator acts differently, however: the familiar forward slash is overloaded in C++ to signify both Pascal's "real divide" and its "integer divide," **div**. When both operands are integers, as in 10 / 3, C++ performs a **div**. This, fortunately, is one of very few operators that look the same but perform differently enough to cause surprises.

Assignment

The assignment operator, =, brings some subtleties. As the assignment operator performs the job of Pascal's assignment **:=**. But its property of resolving to the value of the left operand (in the same manner that the term $a + b$ resolves, within an embedding expression, to a sum) can lead to Boolean expressions that correctly compile, but may be misused. The mistake is not generally made in the context of assignment; it is made in a relational expression, if used incorrectly to test for equality; in C++ the double equal sign, ==, is the relational operator. The correct formulation of the test for whether a equals b is *if (a == b)*. Coding *if (a = b)* will cause b's value to be assigned to a and with the value of a being the value of the assignment expression. Since every non-zero value is contrued as true, the condition resolves to testing for a non-zero value of a.

The Compound Assignment Operators

Using a variable as an accumulator is such a common programming technique that C++ provides an abbreviated notation:

```
accum = accum + amount;   can be expressed as   accum += amount;
```

The operator += is a condensed notation. Four operators like it are -=, *=, /=, and %=.

```
x = x - amount;   can be expressed as   x -= amount;
x = x * amount;   can be expressed as   x *= amount;
x = x / amount;   can be expressed as   x /= amount;
x = x % amount;   can be expressed as   x %= amount;
```

The Unary Increment and Decrement Operators

The unary increment operator, ++, provides an even more concise way of expressing an even more common programming technique, the increment of a variable by one.

`i = i + 1;`   can be expressed as   `i++;`   or as   `++i;`

Likewise, the unary decrement operator, -, provides for the decrement of a variable by one.

`i = i - 1;`   can be expressed as   `i--;`   or as   `--i;`

One place where the unary increment is commonly seen is within *for* loops. It is the operator of choice when the control variable is increased by one at the end of an iteration. The following is the idiom for traversing an n-element array from its first element, at subscript 0, to its nth element, at subscript $n - 1$:

```
for (i = 0; i < n; i++)
{
    cout << setw(2) << i << ".  " << a[i] << endl;
}
```

Note that when i becomes $n - 1$, an iteration is performed. When i becomes n, the test prevents the iteration and causes processing to move to the program statement that immediately follows the loop. Use of the prefix version of the unary increment gives a loop with exactly the same performance.

```
for (i = 0; i < n; ++i)  // Performs identically to the loop above.
{
    cout << setw(2) << i << ".  " << a[i] << endl;
}
```

The control variable, i in the previous case, might not have been defined prior to the *for* loop, it can be defined within it.

```
for (int i = 0; i < n; i++)
{
    cout << setw(2) << i << ".  " << a[i] << endl;
}
```

What is more, the middle expression, the test performed prior to each iteration, can involve terms other than the control variable or in addition to the control variable. In searching for a particular key, looping may halt when either the key has been found or the end of the array is encountered.

```
int searchForKey (int data[], int numOfKeys, int keySought)
{
    int location;  // Will hold the cell number where key is found.

    int found = 0; // Found initialized to 0.
```

```
for (int cell = 0;   found==0  &&  cell<numOfKeys;  cell++)
    if ( data[cell] == keySought )
        {
            found = 1;
            location = cell;
        }

    return location;
}
```

> Parentheses around the individual terms are not needed because the relational operators "bind more tightly" than the logical operators; that is, they have a higher precedence.

The unary increment and decrement can, of course, be part of larger arithmetic expressions. This is the context in which the prefix and postfix versions yield different results. Consider the prefix unary increment. In an expression such as the following, b is incremented before the multiplication is performed.

```
/* 1 */   a = 3;
/* 2 */   b = 5;
/* 3 */   c = 7;

/* 4 */   x = (a * ++b) + c;   // Identical to    x = a * ++b + c;
```

> The prefix unary increment acts before the operand's value is taken for use.

Its value becomes 6. The multiplication of 3*6 yields 18, to which is added 7. Thus the one expression on line 4 both changes the value of b to 6 and the value of x to 25. The prefix increment is completed before the operand's value is used.

The postfix increment is performed after the operand's value is used. Suppose that everything remains the same except for the unary increment.

```
/* 1 */   a = 3;
/* 2 */   b = 5;
/* 3 */   c = 7;

/* 4 */   x = (a * b++) + c;   // Identical to    x = a * b++ + c;
```

> The postfix unary increment acts after the operand's value is taken for use.

The action evoked by line 4 is to multiply a times b's value of 5, yielding a product of 15. Then the value of b is incremented to 6, and the product is added to the value of c, giving 22. As before, b is left storing 6; but here x is left storing 22.

Because the unary increment and the unary decrement modify the value of their operand, they cannot be used where what is actually needed is a temporary sum or difference. For example, suppose that an array holds n elements, each a *struct*. The programmer wants to show the contents of the last one by passing its subscript, $n - 1$, to the *displayBeautifully( )* function. The call *displayBeautifully(–n);* decrements n and passes n's value to the function. The intended *struct* is identified, but the call leaves the value stored by n, the variable that stores the length of the array, reduced by one. This is a fault that later causes a failure. The proper statement is *displayStruct(n-1);*.

The Conditional Expression Operator, ? :

The conditional expression operator is also known as the conditional operator, the arithmetic *if* operator, or the ternary operator; it is the only operator in the language that takes three operands. It is the equivalent of a concise but limited *if . . .else*. The action represented by the *if . . .else* on the left in the display below, is accomplished by the conditional expression on the right.

```
if ( test )                    (test) ? exprWhenTrue; : exprWhenFalse;
    return exprWhenTrue;
else
    return exprWhenFalse;
```

The test can be an expression such as $(x<y)$ or a more complicated formulation. If it evaluates to "true" (nonzero), the expression *exprWhenTrue* is evaluated and the conditional expression resolves to its value. If it evaluates to "false," the expression *exprWhenFalse* is evaluated and the conditional expression resolves to its value. Here are three concrete illustrations. Notice that the conditional expression formed from the two operators and its three terms is itself an expression that may serve as a term within a larger expression.

```
small = (a < b) ? a : b;

small_plus_5 = ((a < b) ? a : b) + 5;

cout << "small = " << ((a < b) ? a : b) ;
```

The parentheses around the test are not required but are recommended for readability. In the second statement, the parentheses around the full expression are needed so that the false alternative is construed as *b*, not as $b + 5$. Without them, the statement would have been parsed as shown in the following because the operator + binds more tightly than the colon, :.

```
small_plus_5 = (a < b)  ? a : (b + 5);
```

In the third statement, the parentheses around the entire expression are needed because the output operator binds more strongly than the question mark, ?. Without them, the statement would have been parsed as the following.

```
( cout << "small = " << (a < b) )  ?  a : b ;
```

The sizeof *Operator*

The *sizeof* operator provides a means for determining the amount of storage that is occupied by a variable of any given data type, language provided (such as *int, float,* or *char*) or user defined (such as a *struct*). To illustrate, suppose that two bytes are allocated to an *int* and one byte to a *char*. The next program shows this as well as the number of bytes that are consumed by each instantiation of the *struct*.

```
void main()
  {
    struct ourRecord
      {
       int  a, b, c;       // Each int requires 2 bytes, so these three will
                           // use 6.
        char string[100];  // Each char requires 1 byte, so this array will
                           // use 100.
      };                   // In total:  each instantiation of the struct will
                           // take up 106 bytes.

    cout << "\n sizeof(int)      = " << sizeof(int)       << " bytes";
    cout << "\n sizeof(char)     = " << sizeof(char)      << " bytes";
    cout << "\n sizeof(ourRecord) = " << sizeof(ourRecord) << " bytes";
  }
```

> Here \n is the "escape sequence" giving a linefeed. Escape sequences are discussed later.

The *sizeof* operator works with variables as it does with data type specifiers. The next program below shows that it can be used to learn the number of bytes occupied by scalars, *structs*, arrays, and arrays of *structs* as well as by the term returned from the evaluation of an expression.

```
#include <iostream.h>

void main()
  {
    int i = 12, j;        //Here, i is initialized; j is not initialized.
    int  intArray[10];

    float  f;
    double d;
    char   c;

    struct ourRecord
      {
        int  a, b, c;
        char string[100];
      };
```

```
ourRecord  oneStruct;
ourRecord  structArray[100];

cout << "\n sizeof( i ) = " << sizeof(i);
cout << "\n sizeof( j ) = " << sizeof(j);
cout << "\n sizeof( intArray ) = " << sizeof(intArray);
cout << "\n sizeof( intArray[3] ) = " << sizeof(intArray[3]);

cout << "\n sizeof( f ) = " << sizeof(f);
cout << "\n sizeof( d ) = " << sizeof(d);
cout << "\n sizeof( c ) = " << sizeof(c);

cout << "\n sizeof( oneStruct ) = " << sizeof(oneStruct) ;
cout << "\n sizeof( structArray ) = " << sizeof(structArray);

cout << "\n sizeof( 1+1 )  = " << sizeof(1+1);      // (1+1) is an int
                                                    // -> 2 bytes.
cout << "\n sizeof( 10/3 ) = " << sizeof (10/3);    // (10/3) is an int
                                                    // -> 2 bytes.
cout << "\n sizeof( 10.0/3 ) = " << sizeof(10.0/3); // (10.0/3) is a double
                                                    // -> 8 bytes.
}
```

Here is the output.

```
sizeof( i ) = 2
sizeof( j ) = 2
sizeof( intArray ) = 20
sizeof( intArray[3] ) = 2
sizeof( f ) = 4
sizeof( d ) = 8
sizeof( c ) = 1
sizeof( oneStruct ) = 106
sizeof( structArray ) = 10600
sizeof( 1+1 )  = 2
sizeof( 10/3 ) = 2
sizeof( 10.0/3 ) = 8
```

The contrasting modes of the division operator are highlighted by taking the size of the temporary variable returned when an integer is divided by an integer, and when a real is divided by an integer. The size of the latter quotient, eight bytes, demonstrates that what results is a *double*. In using the *sizeof* operator, greater clarity can be achieved by surrounding the operand with parentheses. This is a syntactical necessity when the operand is a data type specifier but not when it is a variable or an expression.

Data Type Conversion

The name of a data type can be used as an operator that accepts the value of a variable or expression and returns that value expressed as the operator data type. The data type of the operand is unchanged. Exactly what the returned value is depends on the respective data types. When the transformation is in the direction of a smaller-sized type (e.g., an *int*) to a larger-sized type (e.g., a *float*), there is generally no loss of information. The converse is not true, and C++ does not flag lost information. A type specifier used to coerce a type transformation is known as a cast. In the following output expression, this *char* is cast (performs the part of) as an *int*:

```
char letter = 'A';   // Definition and initialization of a char variable.

cout << "ASCII of " << letter << " is " << int(letter);
```

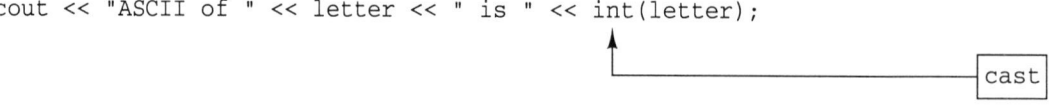

Casts can appear in two forms. As in the preceding, with the operand in parentheses or, as follows, the old way as found in C, with the operator (the type specifier) in parentheses:

```
cout << "ASCII of " << letter << " is " << (int)letter;
```

Both forms signify the same operation, but the former is preferred in C++; it suggests functional notation, which is the correct understanding.

The address-of *Operator and the Indirection Operator*

The ampersand in its role as the address-of operator is serving in a different capacity than when it is used in function declarators to specify that an argument is to be passed by reference. Likewise, the asterisk in its role as the indirection operator has nothing to do with either multiplication or with the definition of pointer variables (as described in the last chapter in connection with a linked list). Standard Pascal offers nothing that corresponds to these.

The address-of *Operator*

The address-of operator returns the address at which a variable is stored in memory. The action of the following definition,

```
int i;
```

is to allocate the memory for an integer (e.g., two bytes) and to record the binding between the variable's name and its location in storage in the symbol table. The symbol table is the database that makes it possible for symbolic variable names to represent addresses. Along with the name-location binding, the symbol table records the variable's data type. The data type is used for determining how large a piece of memory a variable represents as well as how its bit sequence is to be interpreted. Suppose that *i* is situated in the two bytes starting at address 68, and that it currently stores the value 10. Also, suppose there is another *int* named *j*:

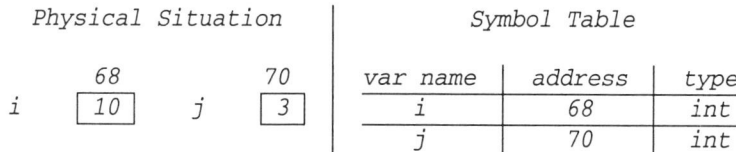

The address of *i* is 68; the value of *i*, which is the value stored at memory location 68, is 10. To display the address of *i*, in contrast to the value of *i*, output &*i*:

```
cout << "\n  Value of i is:     " << i;

cout << "\n  Address of i is:   " << &i;
```

The address-of operator returns the memory location at which the variable is stored.

The output operator is said to be type safe, which means that it takes the responsibility for recognizing the data type of the item being managed and for treating it accordingly. When it receives a *char*, it performs a lookup in the ASCII table and presents the associated symbol. When it receives an *int*, it performs a binary to decimal conversion and presents the digits in the decimal value. When it receives a *float*, it reads the exponent and the mantissa, performs the arithmetic, converts the value to decimal, and presents the character string meaningful to the user. When it receives an address, it presents it in hexadecimal (i.e., in base 16). To have the memory location expressed in base 10, it can be cast as an *unsigned int* or an *unsigned long*. The exact number of bytes allocated to a *long* (e.g., 4) is platform dependent, as it is for an *int*, but it is not incorrect to view a *long* as an ordinary integer with a capacity for a greater number of digits. If the maximum value that can be stored in an *int* is 32767, then an *int* is too small to hold the value of most memory locations.

```
cout << "\n  Address of i is:   " << long(&i);
```

Using a cast to display the address of *i* in base 10.

Suppose that a variable is needed to store the address of *i*. Although it is not wrong to think of an address as a whole number such as an *int* (or a *long*), in the strongly typed view of C++ neither an *int* nor a *long* would be appropriate. Addresses are conceptual commodities to which a different set of operators, and different protective guards for proper treatment, apply. Thus to store the address of an *int* a variable of type *int pointer* is required. Just as a structure pointer is defined by the data type of the *struct* followed by an asterisk, an *int* pointer is defined as follows.

```
int* intPointer; // Or  int *intPointer;  or even  int * intPointer;
```

The asterisk can immediately follow the type specifier, it can immediately precede the variable name, or it can go between them with spaces interspersed on both sides. When two or more *int* pointers are defined in succession, there must be an asterisk for each of them. Here are definitions of five variables. The third is an *int* and the other four are *int* pointers.

```
        int *intPtr1, *intPtr2, anInt, *intPtr3, *intPtr4;

// Same as:   int* intPtr1, *intPtr2, anInt, *intPtr3, *intPtr4;
```

Pointers to *floats*, *chars*, and any other language-provided or user-defined data type are similarly defined and declared. Despite the fact that all pointers are addresses, C++ appropriately considers an *int* pointer to be of a different data type than a *float* pointer. The rule is that if two pointers are defined or declared with different type specifiers, then they are different types. Strongly typing the pointers prevents the indiscriminate mixing of "apples and oranges," thereby affording protection against a whole class of particularly insidious errors.

```
Note: One type of pointer can always be explicitly cast to
      perform as another type of pointer, or even as a pointer
      without a type by casting to (void*).
```

Assuming the following,

```
int   i = 10;
int*  intPointer;
int*  intPtr2;
```

one can assign the address of *i* to *intPointer*,

```
intPointer = &i;
```

and assign the value of *intPointer* to *intPtr2*,

```
intPtr2 = intPointer;
```

As a result of these assignments, *intPointer* stores 68 (the address of *i*, previously given), and *intPtr2* also stores 68. The following three output statements all display the same value (68).

```
cout << "\n i is stored at memory location " << &i;
cout << "\n i is stored at memory location " << intPointer;
cout << "\n i is stored at memory location " << intPtr2;
```

The Indirection Operator, *

Indirection denotes access to one variable by way of a second variable which is storing its address. For instance, the *data* array below seems unsorted. However, it becomes evident that sorting has been performed when accessing the array indirectly by way of the *tag* array:

```
for (i= 0; i<5; i++) cout << data[ tag[i] ]<< "   ";
```

	data		tag
0	11		1
1	3		4
2	14		3
3	6		0
4	4		2

Indirection does not connote "read only." For instance, suppose the intent were to update the largest value in the *data* array with the value -1; the subscript of the largest value, wherever it may be, is stored in *tag[4]*. This update could be done.

```
data[ tag[4] ] = -1;
```

The indirection operator works with memory locations. It enables access of the value stored at the address indicated by an operand. With *intPointer* storing the address of *i*, each of the following statements displays the value of *i* (which is 10).

```
cout << "\n The value of i is "  << i;
cout << "\n The value of i is "  << *intPointer;
cout << "\n The value of i is "  << *(&i);
```

These two statements show alternate ways of assigning the value of *i* to *j*.

```
j = i;
j = *intPointer;    // This, of course, works too:  j = *(&i);
```

In the second statement, the value of *i* is obtained by an indirect reference: the value found at memory location *intPointer* is assigned to *j*.

Access by means of the indirection operator gives full read and write capability. The following two statements show alternate ways of assigning the value of 5 to *i*.

```
i            = 5;
*intPointer = 5;    // This works too:  *(&i) = 5;
```

The second statement works because the indirection operator provides a hold on the content contained at the referenced address. In the previous context, 5 is made the content at the referenced address.

```
      68 ◄─────── intPointer stores 68, i's address

i    5 ◄─────── *intPointer is thus synonymous with i, the variable name
                        Therefore:
                 j = *intPointer; takes the value from the
                 interior of the box and assigns it to j  (just as j = i;)

                 *intPointer = j; copies j's value into the
                 interior of the box  (just as i = j;)
```

3.2   Pointers

To a Pascal programmer pointers are always related to dynamically allocated data structures such as linked lists and trees. Dynamically allocated structures are similarly built in C++ (as shown in Chapter 2). Pointers in C++ also enable a collection of techniques for managing arrays, often *char* arrays serving as strings, and a mechanism for achieving persistence. Persistence refers to defining variables within a function that have a lifetime extending beyond the function's termination. This is seen in Pascal when a dynamically created structure that is built in one function is passed back to another. Pass **root**, initialized to **nil**, to a procedure that builds a binary search tree; it returns not only **root** storing the address of a node at the top, but possibly hundreds of nodes connected to it. Although these nodes were acquired within the procedure, their lifetime extends beyond the procedure's lifetime. This is different from the procedure's local variables. C++ exploits the persistence of dynamically acquired memory much more so than Pascal does.

Four operators are used in connection with pointers: & and *, previously discussed, and *new* and *delete*, introduced in the last chapter. Also there is some terminology. Dynamically allocated memory, which refers to memory acquired by means of the explicit use of *new*, is said to be memory from the heap. Memory bound to variables defined without the use of *new*, such as all those in *someFunction( )*, is said to be memory from the stack. This includes the formal arguments; *a*, *b*, and *c* which, because they are passed by value, will occupy storage captured for the function when it is activated. This includes the scalar *d*. It includes the *float array e*, for which enough storage to hold 100 *floats* is bound (e.g., 100 *floats* * 4 bytes per *float* = 400 bytes) and the *char* array *string*, to which 81 bytes are bound (81 *chars* * 1 byte per *char*). This also includes the *char* pointer, *charPointer*, and the *int* pointer, *intPointer*. That their data types qualify each of them to hold the addresses of dynamically allocated pieces of memory does not mean that they are dynamically allocated. Like all these other variables from the stack, their variable names are attached to memory locations when the function is instantiated.

```
int  someFunction (int a,  float b, char c)
  {
    float d;
    float e[100];
    char string[81];
    char* charPointer;
    int*  intPointer;
      .
      .
      .
  }
```

These variables from the stack are local variables. There is no such thing as a relatively global variable in C++ because one function cannot be nested inside another, as can a subprogram in Pascal. If *someFunction( )* were recursive, the recursive invocation would have its own independent and complete set of name and memory location. No subsequently called function in a succession of invocations, recursive or nonrecursive, can trespass into the memory space of a not yet terminated predecessor. Thus the scope of a function's defined name-space is not an issue that warrants much attention.

On the other hand, the release of memory is a matter that warrants attention. All local variables, which is to say, all a function's memory from the stack, is deallocated automatically when the function returns. This is a service that C++ provides, and it precludes the leak of this memory through the inadvertent failure to return it for reuse. A programmer can do nothing to prevent the deallocation of a local variable, and this makes certain articles unsuitable for return (addresses of local variables). Nor can a programmer deallocate a local variable in advance of the function's return by applying the *delete* operator to it.

Conversely, memory acquired with *new* is never automatically released (except by the operating system when all the resources made available to the program are released). It is the programmer's responsibility to *delete* dynamically acquired storage when there is no longer need for it. Not doing this can be a serious problem for programs that are expected to remain in execution for long periods of time. Repeatedly neglecting to reclaim a tiny parcel of memory in an obscure corner of the program can accumulate "leakage" of memory large enough to cause a failure. The importance of the distinction between automatically deallocated variables and those that persist (and must be explicitly *deleted*) is the reason that variables whose memory comes from the stack are more often referred to as automatic than local in C++.

The stack and the heap may be thought of as two different memory resources made available by the operating system to the program for its use during execution. The stack is the memory resource used by the compiler for allocating space to automatic variables. The heap is the memory resource used when storage is allocated with *new*.

Understanding and Managing Arrays

Imagine a function that displays the values contained within an *int* array. The function's prototype may look like this:

```
void  showIt (int data[], int size);  // Prototype.
```

If the variable names are omitted, as they may be from the prototype, it could look like this:

```
void  showIt (int [], int size);      // Alternate prototype.
```

To indicate that the first argument is an array, a pair of square brackets (called the index operator) is needed even if unaccompanied by an identifier. Within *main( )*, an array to be displayed is defined, some values are installed, and *showIt( )* is called to perform the output.

```
void main()
  {
    int number[5];
    numbers[0] = 16;  number[1] = 12;  number[3] = 15;
    showIt(number, 3 );  // The array may be passed by
             .           // using its name alone, without
             .           // the index operator.
             .
  }
```

The reason for this example is to have a background against which to pose a rhetorical question and then to discuss some syntax and semantics related to the answer. The question is, what exactly does *number*s in the call to *showIt( )* signify? A related question is what is the data type of the formal argument to which it is being passed?

Arrays and Pointers

An automatic variable defined with a pair of square brackets is an array, and an array uses a block of storage. The name of the array is bound to this storage, just as the name of an *int* is associated with the memory location that is allocated for it. The value of an array name may be thought of as the address at which its storage begins or, equivalently, as the address of the array's leading element, &(*number[0]*). As an address, its value behaves very much like a pointer. Unlike a pointer variable, its value cannot be changed. Unlike a pointer, the *sizeof* which is that of all addresses (e.g., two bytes or four bytes, depending upon the platform), the *sizeof* an array (e.g., *sizeof number*) is the number of bytes in its block of memory. The discussion here is intended to examine all this in detail.

An array's name, used without the index operator to pinpoint reference to a particular element, identifies the address at which the array is located in memory; that is, it may be used as a pointer to the array. For instance, if individual *int*s are stored in two bytes and the metaphorical memory location of the array

is 118, *number* may be used as an *int* pointer whose value is 118, *number[0]*
denotes the sequence of bits spanning bytes 118 and 119 interpreted as an *int*
whose value is 16, *number[1]* denotes the *int* occupying bytes 120 and 121,
and so forth.

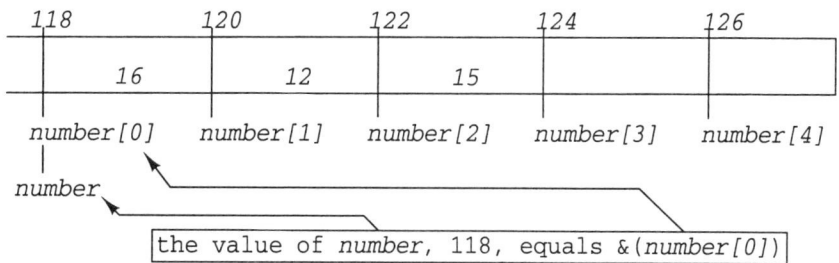

It is important to remember that *number*, because it is the base address of an
automatic array, is a constant. Its value, the address to which it was initially
bound, cannot be changed. This means that *number* cannot be reset so that it
holds an address different from 118.

In the call to *showIt( )*, *number* behaves like any other automatic variable.
Its value, 118, is transmitted to the corresponding formal argument in the function's declarator. To match, the data type of the formal argument must be an *int*
pointer. This is precisely what the first argument, *int data[ ]*, is in the following
function.

```
                                        Despite the bracket pair, data[]
                                        is an int*.  Unlike a true array,
                                        no block of storage is allocated
                                        for it and therefore it is not
void  showIt (int data[], int size)     a const bound to a base address.
  {
    cout << "n The array:   ";
    for (int i = 0; i < size; i++)    cout << data[i] << "  ";
    cout << endl;
  }
```

Furthermore, this is precisely what the first argument, *int* a*, is in this alternate
rendering of the function.

```
                                        Although  a  is declared
                                        as an int*, not as int a[],
                                        it may nonetheless
                                        be accessed with the
void  showIt (int* a, int size)         index operator.
  {
    cout << "n The array:   ";
    for (int i = 0; i < size; i++)    cout << a[i] << "  ";
    cout << endl;
  }
```

```
// The prototype of this function could be
// either of the following:
//
// void showIt (int* a, int size);   or   void showIt(int*, int);
```

Within function declarators, a declaration of an *int* array, using the square brackets, and a declaration of an *int* pointer, using the asterisk, denote variables that are in every way identical. This is true whether or not a number appears between the brackets. Such numbers are disregarded by the compiler (except when given for the number of columns in two-dimensional arrays where they are used for mapping row and column subscripts onto an absolute element number, and similarly for higher-dimensional arrays).

This explains why arrays, unlike scalars, behave as if they had been passed by reference when, in fact, they are passed by value. Even though it is the value of *number* that is copied into the formal argument, this value is the array's address, 118. A "copy" of an address dereferences to the same physical location as the original address. Updates made to the array at location 118 affect the same storage, no matter what variable provides the address. A change in the value of the formal argument (e.g., changing *data* or changing *a* from 118 to something else) will not, of course, affect the value of the actual argument, *number*.

The data type of the variable bound to an automatic *int* array operationalizes as *int* pointer, and the data type of the first formal argument in both versions of *showIt( )* is also *int* pointer. Despite there being no difference in their data type, they are conceptually different kinds of things. The variable bound to an automatic array (e.g., *number*) has an *r-value* consisting of the full width of the array. A variable defined as an *int* pointer is bound to a unit of memory sized to hold an address. On some platforms this is two bytes; on others it is four. When an *int* pointer is assigned the value of the variable bound to an array, it is the base address of the array that is copied. The size of the *int* pointer remains the size of a single address. This is easily illustrated with the *sizeof* operator. Although all addresses have the same size (e.g., two bytes) what is required by a variable to accommodate its value varies from data type to data type (e.g., values of *double*s may use eight bytes). It is easy to see that the address of a node in a linked list, no matter how large the list's nodes are, is always the size of a pointer.

Finally, both *data* and *a* can just as well receive a pointer to an isolated *int* as the base address of an *int* array or the address of any element within an *int* array. The address of the element at subscript 2 may be given as *&(number[2])*. The parentheses are for readability only because the precedence of the array index operator is higher than that of the *address-of* operator. Within the function there is no way of determining from a pointer argument whether the address is that of a detached *int*, that of the leading element within an array (which could be *number* or the functionally equivalent *&number[0]*), or that of some other element. This is why an array is almost invariably passed together with additional information such as its size.

These principles of array management apply to arrays of any type, not just *int* arrays. The following program is intended for exemplification and reinforcement.

```
#include <iostream.h>

void showIt1(int array[], int numOfCells)
  {
    cout << "\n\n From showIt1( ):  contents of array = ";

    for (int i = 0;  i < numOfCells;  i++)  cout << array[i] << " ";

    cout << "\n   memory location of the passed array:   array = " << array;
    cout << "\n   memory location of array's cell 0: &array[0] = " << &array[0];
    cout << "\n   sizeof the formal argument:      sizeof array = " << sizeof array;
    cout << "\n   address of the formal argument:      &array = " << &array;
    cout << endl;

  }

void showIt2(int* array, int numOfCells, int subscriptOfPassedCell)
  {
    cout << "\n\n From showIt2( ):  contents of array = ";

    for (int i = subscriptOfPassedCell;  i < numOfCells;  i++)
       cout << array[i - subscriptOfPassedCell] << " ";

    cout << "\n   memory location of the passed array:   array = " << array;
    cout << "\n   sizeof the formal argument:      sizeof array = " << sizeof array;
    cout << "\n   address of the formal argument:      &array = " << &array;
    cout << endl;
  }

void main( )
  {
    int data[5];  // Defining an int array -- ten bytes are allocated.

    data[0] = 11;  data[1] = 12;  data[2] = 13;  data[3] = 14;  data[4] = 15;

    cout << "\n From main( ):  contents of data = ";

    for (int i = 0;  i < 5;  i++)  cout << data[i] << " ";

    cout << "\n              memory location of the data array = " << data;
    cout << "\n                    memory location of data[0] = " << &data[0];
    cout << "\n                            sizeof data = " << sizeof data;
    cout << "\n        ****  calling showIt1: showIt1(data, 5);  ****";
                                        showIt1(data, 5);
```

```
cout << "\n        ****    calling showIt2: showIt2(data, 5, 0);   ****";
                                        showIt2(data, 5, 0);
cout << "\n        ****    calling showIt2: showIt2( &data[0], 5, 0); ****";
                                        showIt2( &data[0], 5, 0);
cout << "\n        ****    calling showIt2: showIt2( &data[3], 5, 3); ****";
                                        showIt2( &data[3], 5, 3);

int *ptr1;     // Defining an int pointer -- two bytes are allocated.

ptr1 = data;   // Address stored by data is copied into ptr1.

cout << "\n\n From main( ):  ptr1 = data;   contents of ptr1 = ";

for (i = 0;  i < 5;  i++)  cout << ptr1[i] << " ";

cout << "\n     memory location of the data array via ptr1 = " << ptr1;
cout << "\n                   memory location of ptr1[0] = " << &ptr1[0];
cout << "\n                               sizeof ptr1 = " << sizeof ptr1;
cout << "\n\n  *** calling showIt1, passing ptr1:   showIt1(ptr1, 5); ****";
                                        showIt1(ptr1, 5);

int  j;
j = 10;

int  *ptr2;
ptr2 = &j;

cout << "\n\n From main( ):  ptr2 = &j;   contents of ptr2 = ";

for (i = 0;  i < 1;  i++)   cout << ptr2[i] << " ";

cout << "\n     memory location of the data array via ptr2 = " << ptr2;
cout << "\n                   memory location of ptr2[0] = " << &ptr2[0];
cout << "\n                               sizeof ptr2 = " << sizeof ptr2;
cout << "\n\n  *** calling showIt1, passing ptr2:   showIt1(ptr2, 1); ****";
                                        showIt1(ptr2, 1);

// Values of pointers can be changed --  the values of ptr1 and
// ptr2 are swapped.
int*  tempPtr;
tempPtr = ptr1;   ptr1 = ptr2;   ptr2 = tempPtr;

cout << "\n\n ptr2 after the swap:  ";
for (i = 0;  i < 5;  i++)  cout << ptr2[i] << " ";

cout << "\n ptr1 after the swap:  " << *ptr1;  // *ptr1  same as  ptr1[0]

// The value of data cannot be changed because it is an array,
// a constant bound to a block of storage.
}
```

Here is the output:

```
From main( ):  contents of data = 11 12 13 14 15
             memory location of the data array = 0x39b1ffec
                    memory location of data[0] = 0x39b1ffec
                                    sizeof data = 10
        ****    calling showIt1: showIt1(data, 5);   ****

From showIt1( ):  contents of array = 11 12 13 14 15
   memory location of the passed array:    array = 0x39b1ffec
   memory location of array's cell 0:  &array[0] = 0x39b1ffec
   sizeof the formal argument:      sizeof array = 2
   address of the formal argument:        &array = 0x39b1ffde

        ****    calling showIt2: showIt2(data, 5, 0);   ****

From showIt2( ):  contents of array = 11 12 13 14 15
   memory location of the passed array:    array = 0x39b1ffec
   sizeof the formal argument:      sizeof array = 2
   address of the formal argument:        &array = 0x39b1ffdc

        ****    calling showIt2: showIt2( &data[0], 5, 0);  ****

From showIt2( ):  contents of array = 11 12 13 14 15
   memory location of the passed array:    array = 0x39b1ffec
   sizeof the formal argument:      sizeof array = 2
   address of the formal argument:        &array = 0x39b1ffdc

        ****    calling showIt2: showIt2( &data[3], 5, 3);  ****

From showIt2( ):  contents of array = 14 15
   memory location of the passed array:    array = 0x39b1fff2
   sizeof the formal argument:      sizeof array = 2
   address of the formal argument:        &array = 0x39b1ffdc

From main( ):  ptr1 = data;   contents of ptr1 = 11 12 13 14 15
      memory location of the data array via ptr1 = 0x39b1ffec
                    memory location of ptr1[0] = 0x39b1ffec
                                    sizeof ptr1 = 2

    *** calling showIt1, passing ptr1:    showIt1(ptr1, 5);   ****

From showIt1( ):  contents of array = 11 12 13 14 15
   memory location of the passed array:    array = 0x39b1ffec
   memory location of array's cell 0:  &array[0] = 0x39b1ffec
   sizeof the formal argument:      sizeof array = 2
   address of the formal argument:        &array = 0x39b1ffde

From main( ):  ptr2 = &j;   contents of ptr2 = 10
      memory location of the data array via ptr2 = 0x39b1ffe8
```

```
                                    memory location of ptr2[0] = 0x39b1ffe8
                                                   sizeof ptr2 = 2

        *** calling showIt1, passing ptr2:    showIt1(ptr2, 1); ****

     From showIt1( ):  contents of array = 10
        memory location of the passed array:    array = 0x39b1ffe8
        memory location of array's cell 0:  &array[0] = 0x39b1ffe8
        sizeof the formal argument:       sizeof array = 2
        address of the formal argument:       &array = 0x39b1ffde

     ptr2 after the swap:  11 12 13 14 15
     ptr1 after the swap:  10
```

Initializing Arrays

Arrays may be initialized at the same time that they are defined. In the preceding program the *data* array was first defined and then values were installed by way of assignments.

```
int data[5];
data[0]=11;  data[1]=12;  data[2]=13;  data[3]=14;  data[4]=15;
```

A more concise way of achieving the same result is as follows. An array with five elements is defined and the respective elements are set to the values shown within the braces.

```
int data[5] = { 11,   12,   13,   14,   15 };
```

To initialize a 5-element array with the initial element having the value of 11, the next element having the value of 12, and all other elements initialized to 0, the following statement could be used:

```
int data[5] = {11, 12};// Here data[2], data[3], and data[4] are set to 0.
```

The number of elements in the array need not be given in instances where the array will never need to hold a greater number of elements than the number of values in the initialization list. When the array size is omitted, C++ counts the number of initializers and implicitly fills in the blank:

```
int data[] = {11, 12, 13, 14, 15}; // This defines an array sized
                                    // at 5 cells; that is, data[5].
```

The size of an array may be given by an *int* numeric literal, a *const int*, or an expression involving literals and/or constants that evaluates to a positive integer greater than zero. Notably, it may not be given by an *int* that is not a constant nor by an expression containing a nonconstant:

```
const int SIZE = 5;  // SIZE is a constant
int numOfCells = 5;  // Here, numOfCells is not a constant.
```

```
int array1[ SIZE ];        // Okay.
int array2[ numOfCells ];  // Error! -- numOfCells is not a const.
```

Constant Pointers

Just as an *int*, *float*, or *char* may be defined to be a constant, so may a pointer variable. Like any other constant, a *const* pointer must be initialized at the time it is defined because, following definition, a constant becomes read-only. In the following, *ptr* is defined to be a constant and initialized to the address of *abc*. What this means is that the address to which *ptr* points cannot be reset. Although it must always point to the same memory location, the data at that location may be reset.

```
int abc = 25;  // An int is defined and initialized to 25.
int xyz = 50;

int* const ptr = &abc;  // A const int pointer is defined and
                        // initialized to the address-of abc.

cout << "*ptr = " << *ptr;  // Here ptr is dereferenced -- the value
                            // found at the address to which it
                            // points is displayed; the screen
                            // shows  *ptr = 25.

*ptr = 33;  // Here 33 is copied in as the value stored at the
            // address to which ptr points; because this is
            // abc's address, abc's value becomes 33.

ptr = &xyz; // Error! Here, ptr is a constant pointer so
            // its value cannot be reset.
```

Notice the placement of the *const* qualifier, between the data type and the name of the variable. This is required in order to define a constant pointer as described.

Putting the *const* qualifier to the left of the data type provides different properties. The *ptr* can be reset to point from place to place, but it is denied the ability to change the item to which it points. In other words, as far as *ptr* is concerned, the entities to which it points are constants.

```
int abc = 25;
int xyz = 50;

const int* ptr = &abc;  // A pointer to constants is defined and
                        // initialized to the address-of abc.

cout << "*ptr = " << *ptr;  // Here ptr is dereferenced -- the value
                            // found at the address to which it
                            // points is displayed; the screen
                            // shows  *ptr = 25.

ptr = &xyz; // Now okay! Here, ptr's value can be reset.
```

```
cout << "*ptr = " << *ptr;   // Here ptr is dereferenced -- the value
                             // found at the address to which it
                             // points is displayed; the screen
                             // shows  *ptr = 50.

*ptr = 33;   // Error!  ptr now holds the address of xyz, which
             // was not defined to be a const.  Nevertheless,
             // the value of xyz cannot be changed through the
             // auspices of ptr because it is now a pointer to
             // constant ints.
```

It is possible for a pointer to be a pointer constant to constant *ints*, *floats*, or anything else.

```
int abc = 25;

const int* const ptr = &abc;   // Here ptr is a const pointer to
                               // const ints: it cannot be
                               // made to point to any other
                               // location and the value to
                               // which it points cannot be
                               // changed through its auspices.
```

Automatic char *Arrays*

The principles of arrays that have been shown with *int* arrays apply, of course, also to *char* arrays. The factor that complicates them is that they serve as strings. The importance of strings is clear and is underscored by the functionality provided by C++ and the standard library for enabling string manipulation. But the introduction of strings as entities in the language causes some complications.

Character arrays are defined in the same way as any other kind of array, with the data type specifier, an identifier, and a size given between a pair of brackets as on line 3 in the following. A *char* array may be initialized at its point of definition (line 4) and if the size is omitted, it will be tallied and furnished (line 5). Although the number of initializers cannot exceed the array size, if they are fewer, the trailing elements are initialized to 0 (the binary number 0000 0000, which is also the ASCII zero or the null zero, which prints as a blank, and which may be represented in a C++ source code with the escape sequence '\0'). This is shown on line 6.

```
/* 1 */  void main( )

/* 2 */    {
/* 3 */      char a[10];                // A ten-element array
                                        // (ten bytes long).
```

```
/*  4 */      char b[ 2]  = {'H','i'};       // A two-element array,
                                              // both cells initialized.

/*  5 */      char c[  ]  = {'B','y','e'};   // An array whose size is
                                              // found and set to 3.
/*  6 */      char d[ 8]  = {'N','T'};        // Elements 2..7 (the
                          .                    // trailing six) filled
                          .                    // with zeros ('\0').
                          .
          }
```

The initialization of *char* arrays is made less tedious by allowing a succession of characters to be represented as a string literal, which is the sequence delimited on both ends by quotation marks. In the output construction *cout << "Hello world"*; "Hello world" is a string literal. Defining and initializing an array with a string literal is shown at point 3 in the following program. This is a convenience over the character-by-character enumeration of values; but in a way this is where the complications begin. Notice that the initialization is accomplished using the assignment operator. Consistent with the notation for the initialization of scalars, that might easily mislead the unwary into thinking that a string literal may be similarly assigned to a *char* array at other points in the program. Not so! This mistake is shown on line 5. Following initialization, a *char* array can only be updated with the assignment operator in an element-by-element manner (just like an *int* array); or a whole string update can be made using one of the standard library functions such as *strcpy( )* as on line 6.

```
#include <iostream.h>
#include <string.h>     // For strlen() and strcpy().

/*  1 */   void main()
/*  2 */      {
/*  3 */        char e[ ] = "Dog";  // Here, e is made a four-element
                                     // array whose values are
                                     // 'D', 'o', 'g', '\0'.

/*  4 */        cout << "\n /*  4 */  array e = " << e
                     << "    sizeof e = " << sizeof e
                     << "    strlen(e) = " << strlen(e) << endl;

/*  5 */        char g[25];
/*  6 *///      g = "Turkey";        // Error!  strcpy() is needed to
                                     // copy the characters of one string
                                     // into another.  g is an array's
                                     // name, hence not modifiable;
                                     // it is not a pointer variable.
                                     // C++ construes this statement as an
                                     // attempt to update g with address
                                     // of shown string literal. This is
                                     // illegal because g, being
```

```
                                    // bound to an array, is not
                                    // modifiable.

/*  7 */        strcpy(g, "Cat");   // Okay, provided program holds
                                    // #include <string.h>.
                                    // Here strcpy() copies the string
                                    // literal into the first three
                                    // elements of the g array.

/*  8 */        cout << "\n /*  8 */  array g = " << g
                   << "    sizeof g = " << sizeof g
                   << "    strlen(g) = " << strlen(g) << endl;

/*  9 *///      g = e;              // Error!  strcpy() is needed.
                                    // g without the brackets signifies the
                                    // address of the array, its own
                                    // l-value; and l-values are bindings
                                    // between a name and memory location
                                    // that cannot be reset.  Put another
                                    // way, g is the name of an array,
                                    // therefore immutably bound to the
                                    // location of the memory allocated
                                    // for it when it was defined.

/* 10 */        char* f = "Bird";   // Here, f is a pointer, not an array;
                                    // it is initialized with the
                                    // address of a string literal.

/* 11 */        cout << "\n /* 11 */  pointer f = " << f
                   << "    sizeof f = " << sizeof f
                   << "    strlen(f) = " << strlen(f) << endl;

/* 12 */        f = g;              // Okay.  This is an assignment that
                                    // involves pointers.  g in this
                                    // context (without brackets) gives
                                    // its own l-value; hence the address
                                    // of the g array (&g[0]) is made the
                                    // value of f.

/* 13 */        cout << "\n /* 13 */  pointer f = " << f
                   << "    sizeof f = " << sizeof f
                   << "    strlen(f) = " << strlen(f) << endl;

/* 14 */        strcpy(f, "Hi");    // Here, f points to the g array, so
                                    // the g array is overwritten
                                    // by the string 'H', 'i', '\0'.

/* 15 */        cout << "\n /* 15 */  pointer f = " << f
                   << "    sizeof f = " << sizeof f
                   << "    strlen(f) = " << strlen(f) << endl;
```

```
/* 16 */        cout << "\n /* 16 */  array g = " << g
                     << "   sizeof g = " << sizeof g
                     << "   strlen(g) = " << strlen(g) << endl;

/* 17 */        f[0] = 'L';          // Although f is a pointer, not
                f[1] = 'o';          // an array, the elements of the
                f[2] = 'w';          // array to which it points
                f[3] = '\0';         // (the g array) can be accessed
                                     // through it using subscripts.

/* 18 */        cout << "\n /* 18 */  pointer f = " << f
                     << "   sizeof f = " << sizeof f
                     << "   strlen(f) = " << strlen(f) << endl;

/* 19 */        cout << "\n /* 19 */  array g = " << g
                     << "   sizeof g = " << sizeof g
                     << "   strlen(g) = " << strlen(g) << endl;

/* 20 */        f = "Hello";         // Okay.  This is an assignment
                                     // that involves pointers; the
                                     // address of "Hello" is made
                                     // the value of f.

/* 21 */        cout << "\n /* 21 */  pointer f = " << f
                     << "   sizeof f = " << sizeof f
                     << "   strlen(f) = " << strlen(f) << endl;

/* 22 */        cout << "\n /* 22 */  array g = " << g
                     << "   sizeof g = " << sizeof g
                     << "   strlen(g) = " << strlen(g) << endl;

/* 23 *///      strcpy(f, "Bye");    // Error!  f points to a string
                                     // literal.  String literals are
                                     // constants.  The result of this
                                     // action is undefined.
            }
```

Here is the output.

```
/*  4 */  array e = Dog    sizeof e = 4    strlen(e) = 3

/*  8 */  array g = Cat    sizeof g = 25   strlen(g) = 3

/* 11 */  pointer f = Bird    sizeof f = 2    strlen(f) = 4

/* 13 */  pointer f = Cat    sizeof f = 2    strlen(f) = 3

/* 15 */  pointer f = Hi    sizeof f = 2    strlen(f) = 2

/* 16 */  array g = Hi    sizeof g = 25    strlen(g) = 2
```

```
/* 18 */  pointer f = Low    sizeof f = 2   strlen(f) = 3

/* 19 */  array g = Low    sizeof g = 25   strlen(g) = 3

/* 21 */  pointer f = Hello   sizeof f = 2   strlen(f) = 5

/* 22 */  array g = Low    sizeof g = 25   strlen(g) = 3
```

The assignment operator moves the address of a string to a pointer variable (to a *char**, but not to the name of a *char* array). This is shown on lines 10 and 12. When the pointer variable is on the left and a string literal is on the right, the address of the literal (the memory location of its leading element) is copied into the pointer. When the pointer variable is on the left and a character array is on the right, the address of the array is copied into the pointer. When the pointer variable is on the left and another *char* pointer is on the right, the address stored by the latter is copied into the pointer. In each case, what is moved is a scalar: an address, two bytes or four bytes, depending on the platform. The pointer is updated so that it points to another block of memory (i.e., another string). No actual *char* array (string) is physically effected. The names of *char* arrays behave just like *char* pointers when it comes to "reading" their values, such as when on the right-hand side of the assignment operator. However, the name of a *char* array is bound immutably to the address of the block of memory allocated to it; it cannot be reset. The assignment on line 9 does not work because its interpretation is to update the value of *g* with the value of *e*. The value of *e*, where *e* is an array, is the address of *e[0]*. But *g* was defined as an array, so *g*'s address is constant. The assignment on line 12, which appears identical, is fine because the left operand is a character pointer.

A convenience is that character pointers, once assigned to the base address of a *char* array, can be manipulated just as the array itself can. The pointer variable can be used in conjunction with a pair of brackets to access individual elements, as seen on line 17, and it can serve as the argument within string functions such as *strlen( )* and *strcpy( )* as shown on lines 14 and 15. The potential trap is to lose track of which array the *char* pointer references. A change to the content of an array accessed by using a pointer is just as abiding as a change made through the name tied to the array itself, as shown on lines 15 through 19. One way to go wrong is to overwrite an array by writing to the array referenced by a pointer. Another way to go wrong is to forget that the pointer is an alias of a string literal. A string literal, often called a string constant, is not modifiable. The result of mutating such a constant is undefined, thus a potential source of trouble. On line 20 the *char* pointer *f* was assigned the address of the string literal "Hello." By the time the program reaches line 23, the fact that *f* pointed to a constant has apparently been lost. When performing actions on strings by way of variables of type *char**, it is important to be aware of the string's actual identity.

Clearly the delimiting quotation marks around a string literal in the source code are not part of the string as it is stored. Internally, a string literal consists of the characters between the quotation marks followed by a terminating sentinel, the null zero. (The null zero is represented within C++ source code as '\0'. Although two symbols appear, this is an escape sequence signifying a single character. The backslash is a qualifier denoting that the 0 is the eight bits representing a zero in the binary number system: 0000 0000.) The number of characters in a string is, therefore, one more than its displayed contents. This is evident from the action of lines 3 and 4. Array *e* is allocated exactly the number of bytes needed to hold the string literal "Dog" (one byte per character). The array size, as indicated through the application of the *sizeof* operator, is four bytes. The length of the string, as indicated through the *strlen( )* function, is three. The string terminator is present but not counted by *strlen( )*. In lines 5, 7, and 9, notice that the size of array *g* is 25 bytes and the length of its string ("Cat") is three. When copying the contents of one string into another, be mindful that an array must have a size of at least $n + 1$ to accept a string whose length is *n*.

Notice that the size of each variable defined as *char** (i.e., of each *char* pointer) is two bytes. An instructive quiz question is, "How can storage sized at two bytes hold a string whose length is five bytes (as on line 21)?" The answer must explain that a *char** never holds a string of any length. Physically, strings are stored by variables defined as *char* arrays (*char[ ]*) and by unnamed constants (which accommodate string literals). However, the address of a *char* array or string constant can be assigned to a *char* pointer, whereupon the *char* pointer works as an alias. Using *strlen( )* on a *char* pointer gives the length of the string to which it points.

Finally, notice that the content of a string can be displayed using the output operator, <<, just as if it were a scalar. This includes strings literally present within quotation marks, the strings contained within *char* arrays, and the strings to which *char* pointers are pointing.

The name of a *char* array without bracket, in fact, the name of an array of any data type, stands for its l-value, which is its address in memory. This is different from scalars such as *ints*, where the variable's name stands for its r-value. This is why an array name cannot be used on the left-hand side of the assignment operator: l-values can never be changed for arrays or scalars. However, put the name of a *char* array in an output statement and the l-value does not appear. What is output is its r-value: the string it holds. With the names of *char* arrays acting like r-values in output statements, the conclusion that they act like r-values elsewhere is easy to draw. But that is not so. Character arrays are unique in their treatment by the output operator. When the name of an *int* array is displayed you see it as the address that, as an array name, it signifies.

```
void main( )
    {
```

```
int    a[5] = {10, 11, 12, 13, 14};
cout <<"\n        a = " << a     << "            &a = " << &a;

char  string[5] = "abcd";
cout <<"\n  string = " << string << "     &string = " << &string << endl;
}
```

Here is the output.

```
       a = 0x258effec          &a = 0x258effec
  string = abcd        &string = 0x258effe6
```

Treating the address of any *char* pointer as if it were a string and, accordingly, dereferencing it for display, the output operator performs inconsistently on pointer scalars. Displaying a variable of type *int** reveals the address that it holds as its r-value. Displaying a *char** does not. To see the address that is the value of a *char** requires casting it as a pointer of any other kind, such as an *int** or a pointer to *void*.

```
#include <iostream.h>

void main( )
  {
    int  i = 10;
    int *intPtr = &i;

    cout << "\n  intPtr = " << intPtr;

    char  c = 'A';
    char* charPtr = &c;

    cout << "\n charPtr = " << (int*)  charPtr;
    cout << "\n charPtr = " << (void*) charPtr  << endl;
  }
```

Here is the output.

```
  intPtr = 0x257efff4
 charPtr = 0x257efff1
 charPtr = 0x257efff1
```

The library of functions for manipulating strings (e.g., *strlen( )*, *strcpy( )*, *strcmp( )*, *strcat( )*, etc.) is accessed by including the header file *string.h*. These functions are not part of the language, but a core set of functions that invariably accompanies every C++ compiler. This set of functions, their grouping into header files, their interface, and their action (what they do, though not necessarily how they do it) is defined by an ANSI/ISO standard. The definitive reference, at least at this point in time, is *The Draft Standard C++ Library*, by P.J. Plauger [5]. Because functions from the standard C library are also used in C++ programming, Plauger's earlier book, *The Standard C Library* [4], is also a relevant primary resource.

Dynamically Allocated Arrays

The *getName( )* function does not work. The *name* array is properly defined and properly filled with the string captured from the keyboard. The function declarator pledges to return a *char* pointer; and the array identifier, without the brackets, signifies the address of its leading element which, indeed, is the address of a unit of storage that holds a character. Thus in *main( )*, the call to *getName( )* results in the return of *&name[0]*, a *char**, which is assigned to *firstName*. The reason the result is gibberish is that the array to which *first-Name* points was deallocated when *getName( )* returned. In effect, *firstName* is left holding the address of what was once data but is now garbage. All the variables within a function, unless their memory is allocated using the *new* operator, are automatic variables. Automatic variables are so called as a reminder that local variables taken from memory for the use of a function are returned to memory when the function ends. The compiler deallocates storage without regard to whether this leaves a dangling pointer, as it does within this program. It is an error to return the address of (i.e., a pointer to) an automatic variable. The return of an automatic variable is by way of an ephemeral temporary used to carry the value that had been stored by the variable to the point where the function had been called.

```
#include <iostream.h>

char* getName ( )
    {
    char name[40]; // This ought to be long enough to hold any first name!

    cout << "\n Please enter your first name: ";
    cin >> name;
    cout << " name captured from input is =>  " << name << endl;

    return name;    // MISTAKE!  The array is deallocated when the function
                    // ends. What is returned is a pointer to deserted storage.
    }

void main ( )
    {
    char* firstName;  // Will point to the array holding user's name.

    firstName = getName ( );

    cout << " name returned from getName ( ) is => " << firstName << endl;
    }
```

Here is the output.

```
Please enter your first name:  Bjarne
name captured from input is => Bjarne
```

```
name returned from getName( ) is => þM¼ È4
```

The alternative to an automatic variable is a dynamically allocated variable. A dynamically allocated variable is defined using the *new* operator, and it is not returned until it is explicitly discarded by the program using the *delete* operator. It has a physical durability through time referred to as persistence.

Consider the definition of a variable of type *char**, which will be needed to hold the address of the dynamically allocated *char* array.

```
char* addressHolder;    // An automatic variable
                        // for holding values whose
                        // data type is char pointer.
```

Here is how *new* is used to acquire the *char* array with 10 elements.

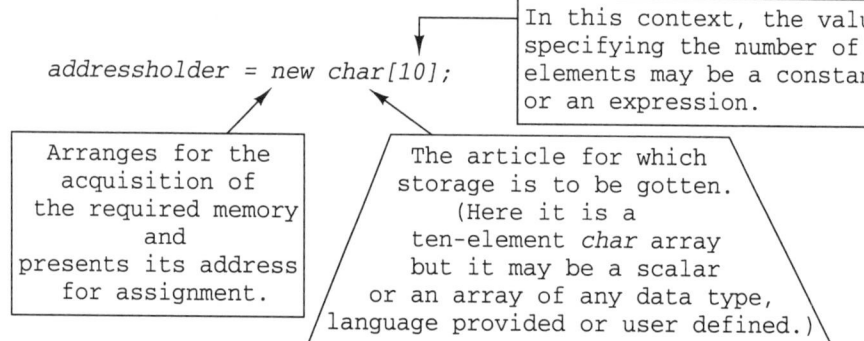

The variable *addressHolder*, now standing for the *char* array, can be used in string functions such as *strcpy( )*, with brackets and subscripts, with the output and input operators, and on the right-hand side of the assignment operator.

The statement for deallocating a dynamically allocated scalar, such as a node that had been on a linked list or within a tree, is

```
delete  oldNode;   // Here oldNode holds the address of a
                   // dynamically allocated struct
                   // from a linked list.
```

The statement for deleting a dynamically allocated array is the same, but with the inclusion of a pair of brackets. Suppose that the *char** variable *ourString* is currently storing the address of the array acquired previously. The array, which is to say, the memory that had been allocated for it with *new*, is deallocated as follows.

```
delete [] ourString;   // The brackets are required for the
                       // proper deletion of a dynamically
                       // allocated array.
```

The deletion of *ourString* does not delete the two bytes of storage bound to *ourString* or in any way detract from this scalar's ability to store addresses of other *char* arrays (or single characters). What becomes defunct is that to which it points. Two of the three general rules for using *delete* are prohibitions: automatic variables (e.g., a *struct* or an array not acquired with *new*) cannot be *deleted*; dynamically acquired memory cannot be *deleted* more than once. The third rule is that applying delete to a variable pointing to *NULL* is acceptable and safe. *NULL* is the symbolic constant standing for the address of zero; literally, it is two bytes or four bytes of zeros, whichever is the size of a pointer variable. The application of *delete*, as shown in the deletion of *oldNode* and *ourString*, does not replace the held address by *NULL*. Each continues to store the address it had been storing, though both are now vacant.

Here is a corrected version of the preceding program.

```
#include <iostream.h>
#include <string.h>  // For strlen().

char* getName()
    {
    char name[40]; // Should be long enough to hold any first name.

    cout << "\n Please enter your first name:   ";
    cin >> name;
    cout << " name captured from input is => " << name << endl;

    int lengthOfName;
    char* addressOfDynamicArray;

    lengthOfName = strlen(name);   // This does not include the null zero.
    addressOfDynamicArray = new char[lengthOfName + 1];  // Get new array.
    strcpy(addressOfDynamicArray, name);

    cout << " name in the dynamically allocated array is => "
         << addressOfDynamicArray << endl;

    return addressOfDynamicArray;
    }

void main()
    {
    char* firstName;  // Will point to the array holding user's name.

    firstName = getName();

    cout << " name returned from getName() is => " << firstName << endl;

    delete [] firstName;
    }
```

Here is the output.

```
Please enter your first name:  Bjarne
name captured from input is => Bjarne
```

```
name in the dynamically allocated array is => Bjarne
name returned from getName() is => Bjarne
```

The variable *addressOfDynamicArray* is an automatic variable, but inasmuch as its data type is *char**, it can hold addresses of character arrays whether automatic or dynamic. It is possible to enter the name directly into a dynamically allocated array as follows.

```
char* addressOfarray = new char[40];          // Get the array.
cout << "\n Please enter your first name:  ";  // Prompt user.
cin >> addressOfarray;                          // Capture and store name.
```

However, because the person's name is likely to be retained for some time (in the hypothetical application), it seems unnecessarily extravagant to tie up 40 bytes for character sequences likely to be considerably shorter (e.g., Sue, Al). Accordingly, *name* is being used as a conduit for taking the string from its point of entry to a precisely sized, dynamically allocated array. Notice that the number of elements in the dynamic array is specified by an expression. The expression could have included the call to *strlen( )*, eliminating the need for *lengthOfName* and making the code more concise.

```
char* getName()
{
    char name[40]; // Should be long enough to hold any first name.

    cout << "\n Please enter your first name:  ";
    cin >> name;
    cout << " name captured from input is => " << name << endl;

    char* addressOfDynamicArray = new char[strlen(name) + 1];
    strcpy(addressOfDynamicArray, name);

    cout << " name in the dynamically allocated array is => "
         << addressOfDynamicArray << endl;

    return addressOfDynamicArray;
}
```

Inside *main( )*, the call to *getName( )* puts the address of the dynamically allocated array into the automatic variable *firstName*. The array persists despite the deallocation of the automatic variable within *getName( )* that had been holding its address. The lifetimes of dynamic commodities and the variables pointing to them are independent. Was it necessary to *delete firstName* at the end of the program? No harm would have come from not deleting it, but as a rule memory acquired with *new* should be *delete*d.

An example in which this is important would be an application where the number of cells within an array may be increased or decreased. The size of an automatic array is fixed when it is defined, and so is the size of a dynamic array. However, the illusion of variability can be created in the case of a dynamic array by allocating a new array of the prescribed size, copying the elements from the old array into the new array, and resetting the pointer serving as the array name to the address of the new array. Imagine that this is done often by a long-running program. If the memory from the old arrays is not recycled, the heap can become exhausted well before the program ends.

3.3 Extending Functions

Functions in C++ have a number of remarkable properties. In this section three of these are described: function name overloading; prescribing default values for trailing arguments; and static variables.

Function-Name Overloading

Function-name overloading, or function overloading, refers to the ability of C++ to attach two or more implementations of a function to one name. One function name, such as *showIt( )*, could serve to display a video clip, a bit-mapped graphic, an ASCII file, an infinite precision integer stored in a linked list (such as a huge prime number), a particular kind of *struct*, an ordinary string, or an *int*. The correct version is selected by matching the data types of the arguments in the call with the data type(s) for the formal argument(s) in the functions. Each version is coded in the standard way; no special notation is needed to designate that a particular function is one of a set that has the same name. Here is a program to exemplify this.

```
#include <iostream.h>

void showSignature( )
    {
      cout << "signature is ( ) ==> no argument was passed\n";
    }

void showSignature(int i)
    {
      cout << "signature is (int) ==> rec'd: " << i << endl;
    }

void showSignature(int i, char c)
    {
      cout << "signature is (int, char) ==> rec'd: " << i << ", " << c << endl;
    }
```

```
void showSignature(char c, int i)
  {
    cout << "signature is (char, int) ==> rec'd: " << c << ", " << i << endl;
  }

int showSignature(int x, int y)
  {
    cout << "signature is (int, int) ==> rec'd: " << x << ", " << y << endl;
    return (x+y);
  }

int showSignature(int x, int y, int z)
  {
    cout << "signature is (int, int, int) ==> rec'd: "<<x<<", "<<y<<", "<<z<<endl;
    return (x+y+z);
  }

void showSignature(char* str)
  {
    cout << "signature is (char*), same as (char[]) ==> rec'd: "<<str<<endl;
  }

void showSignature(char c)
  {
    cout << "signature is (char c) ==> rec'd: " << c <<endl;
  }

int showSignature(double d)
  {
    cout << "signature is (double) ==> rec'd: " << d << endl;
    return int(d);
  }

void main( )
  {
    cout << "\n call 1:  showSignature( ); " << "\n      ";
    showSignature( );

    cout << "\n call 2:  showSignature(3.14159); " << "\n      ";
    showSignature(3.14159);

    cout << "\n call 3:  showSignature(1); " << "\n      ";
    showSignature(1);

    cout << "\n call 4:  showSignature(1,2); " << "\n      ";
    showSignature(1,2);

    cout << "\n call 5:  showSignature(1,2,3); " << "\n      ";
    showSignature(1,2,3);
```

```
cout << "\n call 6:  showSignature(100, 'A'); " << "\n      ";
showSignature(100, 'A');

cout << "\n call 7:  showSignature('A', 100); " << "\n      ";
showSignature('A', 100);

cout << "\n call 8:  showSignature('A'); " << "\n      ";
showSignature('A');

cout << "\n call 9:  showSignature(\"Amazing!\"); " << "\n      ";
showSignature("Amazing!");
}
```

Here is the output.

```
call 1:  showSignature();
    signature is () ==> no argument was passed

call 2:  showSignature(3.14159);
    signature is (double) ==> rec'd: 3.14159

call 3:  showSignature(1);
    signature is (int) ==> rec'd: 1

call 4:  showSignature(1,2);
    signature is (int, int) ==> rec'd: 1, 2

call 5:  showSignature(1,2,3);
    signature is (int, int, int) ==> rec'd: 1, 2, 3

call 6:  showSignature(100, 'A');
    signature is (int, char) ==> rec'd: 100, A

call 7:  showSignature('A', 100);
    signature is (char, int) ==> rec'd: A, 100

call 8:  showSignature('A');
    signature is (char c) ==> rec'd: A

call 9:  showSignature("Amazing!");
    signature is (char*), same as (char[]) ==> rec'd: Amazing!
```

The data types in a function's argument list constitute its signature. Each version of an overloaded function must have a unique signature. A signature is unique if it is different from each of the others. Notice that the *(char)* signature is different from the *(char*)* signature: a data type and a pointer to that data type are two different data types. The *(char*)* signature, however, is equivalent to the *(char[ ])* signature.

Each version of an overloaded function must also be distinguishable by way of the actual arguments in calls. This means two things: it is insufficient for two signatures to differ only in whether one or more of the variables are *passed by value* as opposed to *passed by reference*. Suppose the program has a function with the declarator *int showSignature(int& x, int& y)*. The compiler has no way of determining whether this implementation or the one where the arguments are passed by value is the intended target of an invocation with two *int* variables *m* and *n*, *showSignature(m, n);*. Thus these two versions create ambiguity. It also means that the type of a returned item is of no use in disambiguating the two prospective functions, for example, *void showSignature(int i);* from a possible *int showSignature(int i);*. Characteristics or disposition of the returned entity are not known to the function. In the preceding program, three returned *int*s are simply disregarded. Thus the compiler will not tolerate the coexistence of two functions having the same name and the same sequence of arguments simply because their return types are different.

Default Values for Trailing Arguments

The intent of function overloading is to allow different algorithms for items of different data types to be accessed with the same interface. The intent of default arguments is to allow the general action of a function to be qualified. For instance, a *showIt( )* function for a string argument, in the general mode, might just put the string on the next line of the display screen in whatever text color and text background color happen to be prevalent: *showIt("Hello");*. However, the function may have been written to accept optional second and third arguments specifying the column and row to which the cursor should be moved before the string is written: *showIt("Hello", 20);* would put the string on the next line, indented 20 columns to the right; *showIt("Hello", 20, 5);* would put the string 20 columns to the right on the fifth row. An optional fourth argument might accept a text color, and an optional fifth argument might specify a background color.

Default values may be assigned to formal arguments in one and only one place. If the function has a prototype, this is where they must be assigned:

```
#include    <iostream.h>

void function (int a, int b = 3, int c = 2, int d = 1); // Prototype.
void main()
  {
    function(10, 11, 12, 13);
    function(100);
    function(123, 456);
  }
```

```
void function(int a, int b, int c, int d)
  {
    cout << "\n a = "<< a << "  b = " << b <<
            "  c = "<< c << "  d = " << d  << endl;
}
```

If the function lacks a prototype, then it may be assigned in the declarator accompanying the function's body:

```
#include <iostream.h>

void function(int a, int b = 3, int c = 2, int d = 1)
  {
    cout << "\n a = "<< a <<"  b = "<< b <<
            "  c = "<< c <<"  d = "<< d  << endl;
}

void main()
  {
    function(10, 11, 12, 13);
    function(100);
    function(123, 456);
}
```

Both of these programs result in the output:

```
a = 10    b = 11    c = 12    d = 13
a = 100   b = 3     c = 2     d = 1
a = 123   b = 456   c = 2     d = 1
```

The number of arguments to which default values may be assigned is unlimited, but values must be assigned consecutively starting from the right end of the argument list. If three of the four arguments have default values, these must be the second, third, and fourth.

When calling a function whose arguments have default values, the omitted arguments must be from the right end. The last one may be omitted, or the second to last and the last; or the third to the last, the second to last, and the last and so forth. One cannot provide a first actual argument, skip the second and third (thus accepting the default values), and provide values for the fourth and the fifth: *showIt*("Hello" . . . YELLOW, BLUE);. From the vantage point of the user, the restriction that only trailing arguments may be omitted is a simple syntactical restriction. From the perspective of the function's designer, it is an architectural challenge: to find an ordering of information so that items from left to right become increasingly standard.

The next program shows the construction and use of two functions whose parameters have default values. All arguments of *allHaveDefaults( )* have assigned defaults. Notice that no argument names appear within the prototype, and that it looks as if values are being assigned to type specifiers. Prototypes are not required to show names for the arguments. This is how default values are established when they do not. Two of the *otherFunction( )*'s four arguments have defaults. Which two? The rules state that these must be the last argument and the one before it. Its prototype displays names for the parameters. As always, there is no need to provide a name for each one, and the names provided do not have to match the names that are actually used within the function itself. The prototypes are directly ahead of the functions to underscore that default values, when present, are assigned within the prototype. Prototypes are required to lie ahead of their respective functions, and the functions can follow in the source code at any distance.

To show that the presence of default values does not preclude function overloading, *otherFunction( )* is overloaded. Care must be taken in planning a function that overloads a function having defaults: the signature of an alternate implementation must not match any of the sequences of data types that could satisfy the other. Potential ambiguities do not become compile-time errors unless the source code includes an invocation causing an uncertainty of choice. Thus a set of functions may appear compatible yet have inconsistencies that could cause failures in the future. In the following program, a no-argument version of *allHaveDefaults( )* could have been coded and included; likewise a version having an (*int*) signature. Neither would have caused difficulty until invoked. Should a program attempt to call one of them, for example, *allHaveDefaults(5);*, there would be an ambiguity.

```
#include <iostream.h>

void allHaveDefaults  (int = 1, char = 'A', float = 3.14);  // Prototype.

void allHaveDefaults  (int i,   char c,      float f)
  {
    cout << "from allHaveDefaults(): arg 1 = " << i << "  arg 2 = " << c
         << "  arg 3 = " << f;
  }

void otherFunction (float f, int i, int j = 99, char c = 'Z'); // Prototype.

void otherFunction (float f, int i, int j,      char c)
  {
    cout << "from otherFunction(): arg1 = " <<  f << "  arg 2 = " << i
         << "  arg 3 = " << j << "  art 4 = "  << c;
  }

void otherFunction()                       // Overloading.
  {
    cout << "from otherFunction() -- no-argument version";
  }

void otherFunction(double d)               // More overloading.
  {
```

```
        cout << "from otherFunction() -- (float) version: arg = " << d;
    }

void otherFunction(char message[])       // Still more overloading.
    {
        cout << "from otherFunction() -- (char []) version: "
             << "string = " << message;
    }

void main()
    {
        cout << "\n\n call  1:  allHaveDefaults();" << "\n    ";
        allHaveDefaults();

        cout << "\n\n call  2:  allHaveDefaults(22);" << "\n    ";
        allHaveDefaults(22);

        cout << "\n\n call  3:  allHaveDefaults(333, 'B');" << "\n    ";
        allHaveDefaults(333, 'B');

        cout << "\n\n call  4:  allHaveDefaults(444, 'C', 25.25); " << "\n    ";
        allHaveDefaults(444, 'C', 25.25);

        cout << "\n\n call  5:  otherFunction(75.75, 5555);" << "\n    ";

        otherFunction(75.75, 5555);

        cout << "\n\n call  6:  otherFunction(125.125, 6666, 1234);" << "\n    ";
        otherFunction(125.125, 6666, 1234);

        cout << "\n\n call  7:  otherFunction(77.75, 7777, 5678, '$');" << "\n    ";
        otherFunction(77.75, 7777, 5678, '$');

        cout << "\n\n call  8:  otherFunction();" << "\n    ";
        otherFunction();

        cout << "\n\n call  9:  otherFunction(2.72);" << "\n    ";
        otherFunction(2.72);

        cout << "\n\n call 10:  otherFunction(\"It really works!!\");" << "\n    ";
        otherFunction("It really works!!");
    }
```

Here is the output.

```
call  1:  allHaveDefaults();
  from allHaveDefaults(): arg 1 = 1  arg 2 = A  arg 3 = 3.14

call  2:  allHaveDefaults(22);
  from allHaveDefaults(): arg 1 = 22  arg 2 = A  arg 3 = 3.14
```

```
call  3:  allHaveDefaults(333, 'B');
  from allHaveDefaults(): arg 1 = 333  arg 2 = B  arg 3 = 3.14

call  4:  allHaveDefaults(444, 'C', 25.25);
  from allHaveDefaults(): arg 1 = 444  arg 2 = C  arg 3 = 25.25

call  5:  otherFunction(75.75, 5555);
  from otherFunction(): arg1 = 75.75  arg 2 = 5555  arg 3 = 99  art 4 = Z

call  6:  otherFunction(125.125, 6666, 1234);
  from otherFunction(): arg1 = 125.125  arg 2 = 6666  arg 3 = 1234  art 4 = Z

call  7:  otherFunction(77.75, 7777, 5678, '$');
  from otherFunction(): arg1 = 77.75  arg 2 = 7777  arg 3 = 5678  art 4 = $

call  8:  otherFunction();
  from otherFunction() -- no argument version

call  9:  otherFunction(2.72);
  from otherFunction() -- (float) version: arg = 2.72

call 10:  otherFunction("It really works!!");
  from otherFunction() -- (char []) version: string = It really works!!
```

Static Variables Within Functions

An automatic variable within a function specified as *static* is a local variable that retains its storage, hence its value, from call to call. That is, static variables have local scope but a lifetime beyond the life of the function. Static variables are used when the current call needs to carry on from the point where the function had been when it last ran. They make it unnecessary for the internal state of a function to be kept by external variables, or for functions that call it to be responsible for having and providing information that is beyond their own logic.

For an example, consider a linear pseudorandom generator that must return another random number each time it is called. In a discrete system simulation, it might be called from different points to provide values for entity interarrival times, to set entity attributes, and to determine entity service times. It calculates the current random for return by multiplying the last random times a constant multiplier and stripping off the digits to the left of the decimal point. Randoms spanning the 0 . . 1 range are the most tractable relative to being mapped onto all the discrete and continuous, uniform and nonuniform distributions that an application has to have.

```
If the constant multiplier were 16807
```

and if the initializing pseudorandom value were 0.65549, then

the first pseudo-	*the second pseudo-*	*the third pseudo-*
random generated	*random generated*	*random generated*
would be 0.82043:	*would be 0.96701:*	*would be 0.53707:*

```
        16807                    16807                    16807
     *  0.65549      ⟶       *  0.82043      ⟶       *  0.96701
    11016.82043              13788.96701              16252.53707
```

```
double  getRandom()
  {
    static double random = 0.65549;   // Initialization is performed only once,
                                      // as the variable is defined when the
                                      // function is called for the first time.

    const int MULTIPLIER = 16807;

    double product = MULTIPLIER * random;

    random = product - long(product);   // Subtract off the whole number part.

    return random;
  }
```

Static variables cannot be formal arguments because formal arguments receive values from the outside with each instantiation. The incoming data would replace preserved information before it could be used. Thus updating information is assigned from within the function after the point where the retained value is no longer needed. This implies that for the function's inaugural instantiation an appropriate value is placed in store by way of initialization for use prior to the first update. The coded initialization is performed only once, during the inaugural instantiation. In the absence of an explicit initialization of a static variable, C++ automatically initializes it to 0.

3.4   Summaries

This section summarizes some useful details.

- The data types provided by C++ are listed in the following.

Data type	Comment
char	Usually one byte
short int long	These are three integral types. The number of bytes in each is platform dependent. Often the size of the *int* is the same as either the *short* or the *long*.
float double long double	

These may be qualified in various ways.

- *const*   A variable of any data type may be defined to be a constant.
- *static*   A local automatic variable of any data type may be defined to be *static* so that its value is retained for the function's next instantiation.
- *unsigned* Variables of types *short*, *int*, and *long* may be specified as *unsigned*. If an *int* stored in two bytes had a range of $-32{,}768 . . 32{,}767$, an unsigned bit would have a range $0 . . 65{,}535$.
- *[]*   The index operator may be applied to denote an array.
- ***   The asterisk is the type modifier specifying pointer.

More than one of these may be used at a time.

- This table lists operators in order of decreasing precedence, but the precedence is the same for all operators within a division:

Operator	Descriptive identification
::	scope operator
[]	array subscripting operator
.	member of structure selector
->	member of structure selector via address
( )	function call
sizeof *( )* *new* *delete* & * - + ++ - !	data type conversion operator ("cast") get dynamically allocated memory from the heap return dynamically allocated memory address-of operator indirection operator unary minus (minus sign) unary plus unary increment unary decrement logical not

*	multiplication
/	division
%	modulus
+	addition
-	subtraction
<	less than (relational operator)
<=	less than or equal to
>	greater than
>=	greater than or equal to
==	is equal to ("equality operator")
! =	is not equal to ("inequality operator")
&&	logical and
||	logical or
:	conditional expression operator
=	assignment operator
+=	compound and assignment operator
-=	
*=	
/=	
&=	

- These are the 48 keywords belonging to C++.

asm	*double*	*new*	*switch*
auto	*else*	*operator*	*template*
break	*enum*	*private*	*this*
case	*extern*	*protected*	*throw*
catch	*float*	*public*	*try*
char	*for*	*register*	*typedef*
class	*friend*	*return*	*union*
const	*goto*	*short*	*unsigned*
continue	*if*	*signed*	*virtual*
default	*inline*	*sizeof*	*void*
delete	*int*	*static*	*volatile*
do	*long*	*struct*	*while*

- Escape sequences pair two symbols that stand for a single character that cannot be directly typed. The backslash is a qualifier indicating that the letter immediately following has a special interpretation.

Escape sequence	Meaning
\n	new line
\r	carriage return without a line feed
\f	form feed (new page)
\b	backspace
\a	audible tone ("beep")

\t	horizontal tab
\v	vertical tab
\"	displays double quotes
\\	displays the backslash

- Further references

    An encyclopedic, authoritative, and well written textbook on C++ is Stanley B. Lippman's *C++ Primer* [3]. Although not for beginning programmers, it is accessible and moves along quickly because of the author's explanation and organization. It belongs in your library along with Stroustrup's *The C++ Programming Language* [6] and Ellis and Stroustrup's *The Annotated C++ Reference Manual* [1]. Stroustrup's explanations begin at the beginning and are exceedingly clear. All these volumes exhaustively cover C++ as a conventional programming language. No one should be deluded into thinking that the first step in learning C++ is to learn C. Nonetheless, there is still value in reading what Kernighan and Ritchie have to say in *The C Programming Language* [2], about those features of their language that remain sanctioned within "the better C subset," as the conventional core of C++ is commonly called. To make a study of ANSI C, or to read C code, a good source is Lippman's Appendix C on the "Compatibility of C++ with C."

    P. J. Plauger's two books, *The Standard C Library* [4] and *The Draft Standard C++ Library* [5], are definitive references. The first is needed for those C libraries upon which C++ remains reliant.

References

1. Ellis, M. A. and Stroustrup, B. *The Annotated C++ Reference Manual.* Reading, MA: Addison-Wesley, 1990.
2. Kernighan, B. W. and Ritchie, D. M. *The C Programming Language*, 2nd ed. Englewood Cliffs, NJ: Prentice-Hall, 1988.
3. Lippman, S. B. *C++ Primer*, 2nd ed. Reading, MA: Addison-Wesley, 1991.
4. Plaugher, P. J. *The Standard C Library.* Englewood Cliffs, NJ: Prentice-Hall, 1992.
5. Plaugher, P. J. *The Draft Standard C++ Library.* Englewood Cliffs, NJ: Prentice-Hall, 1995.
6. Stroustrup, B. *The C++ Programming Language*, 2nd ed. Reading, MA: Addison-Wesley, 1991.

4

C++ and Object-Oriented Programming

4.0 Introduction

So far in this book, the programming that has been done is conventional, or procedural, in fact, structured (using "a better C"), and analogous to Pascal with many convenient extensions. As everyone knows, structured programming can accomplish any programming job, and is certainly not obsolete. Structured programming uses both algorithms and data structures; although the programmer attends to both, the focus is probably on the algorithms.

In object-oriented programming the focus is on the data structure, but an enhanced structure that includes algorithmic functionality. A user-defined type in C++ that includes both data members and function members is defined with the keyword class. The word object refers to an instantiation of a class. Once a class is defined, the class name is used to define objects of that class.

An initial and pragmatic characterization of an object-oriented program is one that includes the definition of a class, the declaration of one or more objects of that class, and the use of member functions to manipulate the data in those objects. For example, a class stack might be defined, and member functions push( ), pop( ), and is_empty( ) might be used on the data in the stack. The data and the functions are part of the same structure, defined by the class and instantiated as objects.

It is important to note, however, that this characterization of an object-oriented program really describes a structured program with a new programmer-defined data type. That is, a class extends structured C++ to C++ with data abstraction. Structures are constructed in which data, and functions related to the data, are bound together. This is called encapsulation. Data can be hidden (called data hiding) and access can be restricted to well-defined ways using member functions (the interface).

In *The Design and Evolution of C++* [4], Stroustrup provides his perspective of C++, indicating that as "a better C" it can be used for conventional programming, data abstraction, or objected-oriented programming. A program with classes and objects will be understood from here on to be an object-oriented program. But it is important to note that the extension of structured C++ with classes and objects can really be understood as a structured programming language with abstract data types; in itself this is an important characterization of C++. As such, C++ is a language that provides a more powerful abstraction mechanism than does Pascal. Sections 4.1 through 4.3 develop the concepts of abstraction and their implementation in C++ including classes and objects (4.1), constructors and destructors (4.2), and friends and operator overloading (4.3).

It is only with inheritance and polymorphism that C++ is further extended to a language with the full power of object-orientation. Inheritance and polymorphism are discussed in Section 4.4.

4.1   Classes and Objects

The specification of a class in C++ is very much like the specification of a user-defined data type in Pascal. It provides a pattern with which things of that type, objects, are created. Consider the following simple class and its use in creating objects.

The class is called *Box*, and it is that data type which is used to define a rectangular patch formed with a character. Here are some concrete samples of what instantiations of *Box*, or *Box* objects might be.

```
********
********
********
```
• This is a picture of an instantiation of the *Box* class; it is an object whose length is nine, whose height is three, and whose symbol is the asterisk; call it *box1*.

```
&&
&&
&&
&&
```

- This is a picture of another instantiation of the *Box* class; it is an object whose length is two, whose height is four, and whose symbol is the ampersand; call it *box2*.

```
AAAAA
AAAAA
AAAAA
AAAAA
AAAAA
```

- This is yet another instantiation of the *Box* class; it is a *Box* object whose length is five, whose height is five, and whose symbol is the letter 'A'; call it *box3*.

Each of these three *Box* instantiations or objects is an individual thing having a separate identity. That is, *box1* is an entity apart from and independent of *box2* and *box3*. What is more, the appearance or "attributes" of each box are characterized by three factors: a length, a height, and a symbol. The state of a box is its set of values for its characterizing variables.

In addition to having an identity and a state, all *Box* objects have some functionality or behaviors. For example, they might be able "to become twice as long," or "to become twice as high." To keep things simple, stipulate that the only things these *Box* objects "know how to do" are to set their dimensions and symbol and to display themselves. More specifically, all *Box* objects will have the same behavioral capabilities and these include the ability, on demand, (1) to query a person at a workstation to set or reset their state, and (2) to show themselves in the output, left justified.

Box objects will exist in a program with three state variables and two behavioral capabilities. The state variables, called the data members of *Box*, hold the data pertinent to its condition. The behavioral capabilities are called member functions. Member functions can be invoked only by *Box* objects and are written to enable action on the part of an invoking box. Data members and function members are defined within a "class specifier."

The following program defines a class called *Box* having three data members called *symbol*, *length*, and *height*, and two function members, *showBox( )* and *setSize( )*. The program's *main( )* function declares and uses three objects of this class. The program is followed by an explanation of everything that it contains, but brief annotations accompany the code to provide a quick explanation of the highlighting ideas.

```
#include <iostream.h>

class Box ◄──────────────────────┐ The first letter of a class name,
                                  │ is often, by convention, capitalized.
    {
```

The first letter of a class name, is often, by convention, capitalized.

```
public:

    char symbol; // This is a public data member.

private:

    int length;      // This is a private data member.


    int height;      // This is another private data member.

public:

    void showBox();  // Prototype
    void showBox();  // Prototype.

    void setSize()


    {
      int l, h;
```

If no access specifier is given, the default is *private* for data members and function members.

Private data and function members are accessible only within functions that are members of the class; public data and function members are accessible within *main()* and all other functions, whether member functions belonging to the class or not.

Here *l* and *h* are not data members of this class; they are automatic variables within this function.

```
        cout << "\nEnter a length (an int between 2 and 10):  ";
        cin  >> l;
        if (l >= 2 && l <=10) length = l; // This is the same as
                                          // (*this).length = l; which is also
          else length = 1;                // the same as
                                          // this->length = 1;

        cout << "Enter a height (an int between 2 and 6):  ";

          cin  >> h;
          if (h >= 2 && h <= 6)  height = h;

            else height = 1;


          cout << "\nEnter a symbol:   ";

        cin  >> symbol;

        showBox();  // This is the same as  (*this).showBox();
```

Reference to member functions is for the object whose member function is being executed.

```
                        // and  this->showBox();
       }
};◄ ──────── The class specification ends with a semicolon, just as a structure's specification.
```

> Every function that is part of the class, which is to say,
> every member function, must be declared or defined within the
> class specifier. A function that is defined in full
> inside the class's specification is construed as coming with
> an inline request. A function defined outside the class
> specifier requires the class's name and the scope resolution
> operator to show to which class it belongs.

```
      function's      class's      scope      function's      definition of
      return type     name      resolution      name       formal arguments
       (if any)                  operator
```

```
                              // A member function's definition outside the
    void Box::showBox( )  // class specifier.

    {
      cout << endl;
      for (int i = 1; i <= height; i++)
         {
           for (int j = 1; j <= length; j++)  cout << symbol;
           cout << endl;
         }
    }
```

> The "dot operator" is more formally referred to as
> the member access operator. It is used to access both
> an object's function members and its data members.

```
    void main()
      {
      Box  box1, box2, box3; // Three objects of type Box are defined.

                               // Notice that the class's name is used
                               // as a type specifier, just as int or
                               // float may be.

      box1.setSize();        // Here box1 invokes its member function, setSize().
                             // Accordingly, the person at the terminal is
                             // queried for values for its length, height,
                             // and symbol; then the box is displayed.

    box2.setSize();          // Here box2 invokes its member function, setSize().

    box3.setSize();          // Here box3 invokes its member function, setSize().
```

```
    box1.showBox();        // Here box1 is shown.
    box1.showBox();        // Here box1 is shown again.
    }
```

Classes

Here, again, is the specifier for the *Box* class:

```
class Box
  {
  public:
      char symbol; // This is a public data member.
  private:
      int length;  // This is a private data member.

      int height;  // This is another private data.
                   // member.

  public:
      void showBox();   // Prototype.

      void setSize()
        {
         // Details omitted.
        }
  };
```

All class specifiers open with the keyword *class* in lower case letters followed by the name of the class, which in this case is *Box*. Names for classes are discretionary and formed from the same rules used to form identifiers, including variable names and function names. By convention, the first letter of a class name is capitalized. The data members and function members that are to be part of each object are then declared within braces. Note that the class specifier's closing brace is followed by a semicolon.

Access and Membership

Every data member and every function member has an access status: *public*, *private*, or *protected*. The *public* access status means that the variable or function is accessible in *main( )* and in all other functions in which objects of this class may be present. In other words, the variable or function can be accessed in all parts of a program where the class itself is within scope. The *private* access status means that the variable or function is accessible only within functions that are members of the class. The *protected* access status applies with respect to derived classes. No class or classes are derived from the *Box* class, so a *protected* status would have been operatively identical to *private* throughout this program. The *protected* access status is discussed with inheritance.

The access status specifiers within a class specifier are always followed by a colon. Any number of variables and/or functions may be defined or declared under a single specifier. In specifying the *Box* class, one variable (i.e., one data member), *symbol*, was defined under the first *public* specifier. Two variables (data members) were defined under the following *private* specifier, so both are private. This means they will be accessible in all the class's member functions, but within no other functions. Two functions are given under the next *public* specifier, making them accessible to objects wherever the objects happen to be. The objects may be found among members of the *Box* class, within free functions (i.e., "stand-alone" functions that are not members of any class), or within functions that are members of a different class (if there were another class). One of these functions was declared (not defined); only its prototype appeared. It is defined in full later, but the presence of its declaration is sufficient to make it a member function. The other function is fully defined.

The access specifiers may appear in any order. Any number or mix of data and/or function members may appear under any one. There is no limit on the number of times the access specifiers may be used. If no access specifier appears ahead of a data member or member function, the default is private, in a class.

The functions *setSize( )* and *showBox( )* access the variables *symbol*, *length*, and *height*. One might think that within the class specifier these variables would have to be defined ahead of these functions, but this is not so (though it might reflect good programming practice). Because an object, when it is declared, is created in its entirety, the static layout of its members is immaterial. Even though *setSize( )* calls *showBox( )*, *setSize( )* could have appeared ahead of the other's prototype.

The local variables within these functions (e.g., the *for* loop control variables *i* and *j* in *showBox( )* and the variables *h* and *l* in *setSize( )*) are not data members within objects. They are standard automatic variables that come into existence when their function is invoked to expedite processing. They drop out of existence when the function returns.

Member Functions

In correct C++ terminology, the member function *setSize( )* is defined, not just declared, within the class specifier. The member function *showBox( )* is declared within the class specifier but defined outside it. For a function to be a member function, it must be at least declared within the specifier. More often than not, programmers consider it stylistically preferable to present a list of prototypes within the class specifier rather than obscuring the interface with detail.

There is one technical distinction associated with functions fully defined within the class specifier: an implicit request to the compiler for inline linkage. By placing a function's body within the specifier, the programmer indicates a preference for function invocations to be replaced by code expansions during compilation instead of initiated as calls and returns. Some compilers will issue a warning when the request is denied.

A member function defined beyond the bounds of the class specifier, such as *showBox( )*, must be designated by its "full name" to prevent the possibility of ambiguity. Its full name is the name of the class to which it belongs, the scope resolution operator (which is the double colon), and its name and argument list (i.e., its signature). Its return type is not technically part of its name, but it must nevertheless be present, preceding (i.e., to the immediate left of) its class identification. Without the class identification and scope resolution operator, a function defined outside a class specifier would be construed as a free function, not a member function. There is no reason why a free function and a member function within one or more classes cannot have the same name and argument list. In general, wherever context or usage is insufficient for pinpointing the class to which a member function or data member belongs, its full name is needed. A class member's full name is always formed by attaching the class's name followed by the double colon to the member's identifier.

Objects

Turn now to the action initiated by *main( )*.

```
                    void main()
                    {
/* 1 */                 Box   box1, box2, box3;

/* 2 */                     box1.setSize();
/* 3 */                     box2.setSize();
/* 4 */                     box3.setSize();

/* 5 */                     box1.showBox();
/* 6 */                     box1.showBox();
                    }
```

Objects are created in the same way that *int*s, *float*s, and *char*s are created: the class itself is a data type; the class's name in this context is a data type specifier (like *int*); and the one or more identifiers to its right are instantiations. It is very significant that the class *Box* has become a data type that has a range of properties on a par with the language's built-in data types. This is what is meant by abstraction. Line one creates three *Box* objects, one named *box1*, another named *box2*, and another named *box3*. Each has an identity of its own composed of its own set of data members: *symbol*, *length*, and *height*. With these three definitions, a total of nine memory bindings is established:

```
box1.symbol     box1.length     box1.height
box2.symbol     box2.length     box2.height
box3.symbol     box3.length     box3.height
```

In this manner, an object is like a conventional *struct*. Its data members are accessible with the member access operator (informally called the dot operator). For instance, *main( )* may have included the following statements.

```
    .
    .
    .
box1.symbol = '1';     // Assign to the symbol member of box1.
cout << box1.symbol;   // Display the symbol member of box1.
    .
    .
    .
box2.symbol = '2';     // Assign to the symbol member of box2.
cout << box2.symbol;   // Display the symbol member of box2.
    .
    .
    .
box3.symbol = '3';     // Assign to the symbol member of box3.
cout << box3.symbol;   // Display the symbol member of box3.
    .
    .
    .
```

| object's name | the dot operator (the member access operator) | data member |

Although syntactically acceptable, identical code for either of the other two data members, *length* and *height*, would elicit a fatal compile-time error. Accessing, both "writing" and "reading," of *private* data members (and calling of *private* function members) from *main( )* as well as from all other functions that are not members of the object's class is not possible. Accessing of *symbol* is possible because its access status is *public*.

Line two consists of *box1* accessing its member function *setSize( )*. Member functions are accessed in the same way as data members: the accessing object, followed by the member access operator, followed by the name of the function member. Like any function call, parentheses enclose the argument list and must be present even when no arguments are expected (as is the case here). Just as member functions may have any number and types of arguments, they may return a something of any type, exactly as does a conventional free function.

Member functions such as *setSize( )* and *showBox( )* that belong to a particular class can only be invoked by objects of that class (*Box* objects, in the case of these two functions). These functions cannot be invoked by instantiations of a different class (e.g., by *Triangle* objects if there is a class called *Triangle*) or without an invoking object, as a free function. The scope resolution operator is never necessary when an object invokes a member function because the object's class automatically delineates the referencing environment. Finally, access to function members is governed by the same rules that control access to data members. Member functions specified as *public* may be accessed from *main( )*, from any other free function, from any member function within any other class, and from within other member functions of its same class. Member functions specified as *private* may be accessed only from within other member functions of the same class.

Although an object's function members and data members are characterized as belonging to the object in similar ways, in actuality the code for functions is not replicated for individual objects the way storage for data members is. The invoking object is the object referenced by data members and acted upon by function members when these appear without an accessing object. On line two, the object *box1* invokes its member function *setSize( )*:

```
/* 2 */              box1.setSize();   // This is replicated
                                       // from main().
```

This causes *setSize( )* to run with *box1* as its invoking object.

The *setSize( )* function is replicated in the following.

```
/*  1 */    void setSize()
/*  2 */      {
/*  3 */        int l, h;
/*  4 */
/*  5 */        cout << "\nEnter a length (an int between 2 and 10):  ";
/*  6 */        cin >> l;
/*  7 */        if (l >= 2 && l <=10) length = l;
/*  8 */          else length = 1;
/*  9 */
/* 10 */
/* 11 */        cout << "Enter a height (an int between 2 and 6):  ";
/* 12 */        cin >> h;
/* 13 */        if (h >= 2 && h <= 6)  height = h;
/* 14 */          else height = 1;
/* 15 */
/* 16 */        cout << "\nEnter a symbol:  ";
/* 17 */        cin >> symbol;
/* 18 */
/* 19 */        showBox();
/* 20 */      }
```

On line 7, *length* is assigned the value of *l*; on line 8 *length* is assigned the value of 1. On line 13 *height* is assigned the value of *h*; on line 14 *height* is assigned the value of 1. On line 17 a value from the standard input stream is assigned to *symbol*. Whose data members are these? The answer is whichever *Box* object is the current accessor of the function, which here is *box1*. Values assigned to the accessing object's data members persist beyond the function's return. The changes made extend beyond the function's lifetime. On line 19 there is a call to *showBox( )* to display the updated state of the accessor *Box* object. Because *showBox( )* is a member function, it cannot be invoked without an accessing object. Here again, within a member function (*setSize( )*), a seemingly absent accessor is really the implicit accessor, which is the object that kicked things off with the call.

Consider this part of *main( )*,

```
/* 3 */               box2.setSize();
/* 4 */               box3.setSize();
```

Here *box2* accesses *setSize( )* on line 3. This time, when *setSize( )* runs the implicit accessor within it is *box2*. When *setsize( )* is invoked by *box3*, *box3* becomes the implicit accessor. There is an explicit referent for the accessing object which is *this*. To be precise, *this* is the address of the accessing object or, in different terms, a pointer to it. Dereferencing "the *this* pointer" gives the object itself, **this*. Within the *setSize( )* member function, every "standing alone" (i.e., implicitly accessed) occurrence of

```
length    could be replaced by    (*this).length    or    this->length
```

and

```
height    could be replaced by    (*this).height    or    this->height
```

and

```
symbol    could be replaced by    (*this).symbol    or    this->symbol
```

and the call

```
showBox( );  could be replaced by  (*this).showBox( );  or
this->showBox;
```

The need for an explicit name for the accessing object can arise when it is to be passed back as the item returned, or used as an actual argument in calling another function. In both these cases there are alternate approaches, however, alleviating the need to dereference pointers.

Line 5 of *main( )* shows *showBox( )* called from a nonmember function. The output would confirm that the settings to *box1*'s data members from its invocation of *setSize( )* on line 2 persist. Line 6 underscores the fact that an object and a member function can be used often.

Selectors and Modifiers

It is common for classes to be designed so that at least some *private* data members can be read or written by way of member functions. A function that gets the value of a *private* data member is called a selector. A function that resets or puts a value into a *private* data member is called a modifier. Here is the *Box* class enhanced with a selector function that returns the value of the invoking object's *height* and a modifier function that permits the invoking object's *length* to be updated. If they were not *public*, selectors and modifiers would not be able to serve as interface facilities.

```
class Box
  {
  public:
      char symbol; // This exemplifies a public data member.
  private:
      int length;  // This exemplifies a private data member.
      int height;  // This is another private data member.
  public:
      void showBox();                 // This is a prototype.
      void setSize();                 // This is a prototype.

      int  getHeight();               // This is a prototype
                                      // of a selector.
      void setLength(int newLength);  // This is a prototype
                                      // of a modifier.
  };

int Box::getHeight()   // This returns the height of the accessing
                       // box object.
  {
    return height;
  }
                                    // This resets the length of
void Box::setLength(int newLength)   // the accessing box object.
    {
      if (newLength >= 2 && newLength <= 10)  length = newLength;
    }
```

Overloading Member Functions

The selector and modifier illustrate that member functions are like functions, in general, in that they do information transmission through arguments and returns. Arrays and pointers may be passed as arguments, and arguments may be passed by reference as well as by value. Member functions, like conventional free functions, may have any signature at all and may be overloaded. The following two functions show overloading, an object passed as an argument, and an object returned.

```
class Box
  {
  public:
      char symbol; // This exemplifies a public data member.
  private:
      int length;  // This exemplifies a private data member.
```

```
        int height;   // This is another private data member.
    public:
        void showBox();              // This is a prototype.
        void setSize();              // This is a prototype.

        int  getHeight();            // This prototype is a
                                     // selector.
        void setLength(int newLength); // This prototype is a
                                     // modifier.

        Box  add(int incrementForLengthAndHeight); // This is a
                                     // prototype.
        Box  add(Box boxArgument);   // This is a
                                     // prototype.
    };


Box  Box::add(int incrementForLengthAndHeight)
    {
     Box temp;   // This gets a new box to represent "the sum".

     temp.symbol = symbol; // Symbol of accessing Box copied into
                           // temp.

     temp.length = length + incrementForLengthAndHeight;
     temp.height = height + incrementForLengthAndHeight;

     return temp;
    }


Box  Box::add(Box boxArgument)
    {
     Box temp;

     temp.symbol = symbol;  // Symbol of accessing Box copied into
                            // temp.
     temp.length = length + boxArgument.length;
     temp.height = height + boxArgument.height;

     return temp;
    }
```

Because each of these new functions is a member function, each must be accessed by a *Box* object. In both, *symbol*, *length*, and *height* refer to the data members of the accessing *Box*. Both define a *Box* as an automatic variable, illustrating that a member function may create instantiations of its own class. The second function manages three *Box*es: the accessing *Box*, the automatic variable, *temp*, and the formal argument, *boxArgument*. Members of all *Box*es other than the accessing *Box* have to be accessed using the name of the ad hoc *Box* (e.g., *temp* or *boxArgument*) and the dot operator. *Private* members can be accessed within these functions because these functions are members of the class. It does not matter how an object arrives within a member function—as the accessing object, as an instantiation defined within, or as a formal argument passed by value or by reference. Once there, its *private* members can be read and written freely. Access to *private* members is not limited to the invoking object. Finally, a *Box* as a whole is referenced by its name alone, as in the *return* statement. The assignment operator can also operate on whole objects. Here is an alternate version of the second *add( )* function.

```
                                   // Here is the the first alternate version,
Box  Box::add(Box boxArgument)     // which uses the assignment operator
    {                              // as well as the "this pointer".
      Box temp = *this;

      temp.length += boxArgument.length;
      temp.height += boxArgument.height;

      return temp;
    }
```

The assignment operator performs a member-by-member copy of values from the right operand into the left operand. To refer to the accessing *Box*, we dereferenced the *this* pointer, the variable that holds the address of *Box*.

A variation on this version is to assign the *boxArgument* to *temp*. This is a more straightforward approach that does not involve dereferencing pointers.

```
                                   // The second alternate version, which
Box  Box::add(Box boxArgument)     // uses the assignment operator.
    {
      Box temp = boxArgument;       // Copy symbol of boxArgument into temp.

      temp.symbol = symbol;         // Copy symbol of accessing Box into temp.

      temp.length += length;
      temp.height += height;

      return temp;
    }
```

Free Functions That Have Box Arguments and Return Boxes

Because the name of a class becomes a type specifier, as expected, objects can be defined within any free function just as *Box*es were within *main( )*. Not only can *Box* scalars be defined, but so can *Box* arrays, pointers to *Box*es, arrays of pointers to *Box*es, and so forth.

```
void  someFreeFunction()
```

```
      {
         Box     b1;                // Define a single Box scalar.
         Box     bx1, bx2, bx3;     // Define three Box scalars.

         Box     boxArray[10];      // Define a 10-element array.

         Box*    boxPtr;            // Define a pointer to a Box.
         Box*    boxPtrArray[10];   // Define an array of Box pointers.

         Box**   boxPtrToPtr;       // Define a pointer to a Box pointer.
           .
           .
      }
```

Because a class creates a type specifier, instantiations of that type are available for information transmission into and out of free functions. Here, for example, is a free function that adds two *Box*es, in the manner of the previous *add( )* functions, putting the symbol from the first argument into the *Box* returned.

```
Box  add(Box boxArgument1, Box boxArgument2)
  {
    Box temp;

    temp.symbol = boxArgument1.symbol; // Symbol is a public data member.

    temp.setLength( boxArgument1.getLength() + boxArgument2.getLength() );
    temp.setHeight( boxArgument1.getHeight() + boxArgument2.getHeight() );

    return temp;
  }
```

Free functions are not invoked by an accessing object, therefore there is never an implicit accessor. All data members and function members must appear with the accessing object explicitly shown. *Public* members, including *public* data members such as *symbol* and *public* function members such as *setLength( )*, are accessible. *Private* members, including *private* data members such as *length* and *height*, and *private* function members (there are none in the *Box* class) are not accessible. Any member specified as *private* is only accessible by a free function if interfaces have been engineered into the class by way of selectors and modifiers. The preceding coding presumes that the *getHeight( )* selector has been supplemented with a similar *getLength( )* selector and that the *setLength( )* modifier has been supplemented with a similar *setHeight( )* modifier. Because the *Box* arguments are passed by value, this function may have been coded without defining a *Box temp*.

```
Box  add(Box boxArgument1, Box boxArgument2) //  **ALTERNATE VERSION**
  {
    boxArgument1.setLength( boxArgument1.getLength()
                                + boxArgument2.getLength());
```

```
          boxArgument1.setHeight( boxArgument1.getHeight()
                                  + boxArgument2.getHeight() );

       return boxArgument1;
   }
```

The modifications made to *boxArgument1* have no effect on the actual argument passed to this function because the formal argument, *boxArgument1*, is only a copy. The return operation returns the modified *boxArgument1*, by means of a member-by-member copy, into a temporary variable. Following is a fragment of *main( )* contrasting the difference between the invocation of the *add( )* member function and the *add( )* free function. A member function can be distinguished from a free function by the presence of an accessing object.

```
   ⋮
sumBx = box1.sum(box2);    // This is a member function:
                           // Box Box::add(Box boxArgument).
sumBx = sum(box1, box2);   // This is a free function:
                           // Box add(Box boxArgument1, Box boxArgument2).
   ⋮
```

The following *boxSwap( )* function is a free function to which *Box* objects are passed by reference. The most interesting point to note is that the assignment operator provides an arm's length mechanism for manipulating *private* data members. Even though *length* and *height* are *private*, the assignment operator works within free functions to copy their respective values from the right operand into the left operand.

```
   void  boxSwap(Box& boxA, Box& boxB)
     {
       Box  holder;

       holder = boxA;
       boxA   = boxB;
       boxB   = holder;
     }
```

Abstract Data Types

Consider the bit-string stored in a byte: 0100 0001. What does it represent? Interpreted as a number in binary, it is the integer 65. Interpreted as an ASCII character, it is an 'A.'

Abstraction was introduced into programming languages when memory locations started to be construed as representing specific data types. If a storage location holds an integer, it has a particular universe of values, is treated in a particular way for display, and is allowed to take part in a certain set of processing activities (e.g., arithmetic). If a storage location holds a character, it has a different universe of values, is treated in a different way for display, and can take part in a different set of processing activities. In Pascal, for example, a program cannot add one to the value of a variable defined as a *char*. (This represents an enforcement of data types that is stronger, in this case, than in C++.)

Every programmer knows that integers, characters, floats, and other basic data types in a language have no intrinsic existence within the hardware of the computer. They are conceptual models of items in the problem space, and they are enforced to enable a higher level of thinking, thereby providing more reliability in the programming process. They are abstractions.

Typically, for built-in data types, there is also language-provided functionality. For example, integers and floats can participate in arithmetic activities. High-level languages also provide more powerful data abstraction with structures such as arrays and records, and more powerful procedural abstractions such as functions and procedures. Structural programming languages, such as Pascal, typically offer data abstraction and procedural abstraction. But Pascal, for example, offers no way to create abstract data types like those that are language-provided. It lacks programming language features that both characterize data and have the related ability to manipulate those data through functions. In other words, Pascal does not provide the programmer with the construct that is a data type with its own set of manipulating functions.

Consider abstract data types common to the study of computer science, such as stacks, queues, and binary trees. A queue, for example, is a first-come, first-served waiting line. Besides being constituted of memory, a queue has at least two natural operations: appending an incoming item to the end of the line and delivering the item at the front of the line when it is called. How might a queue be represented in a structured program? In Pascal (or in C++ used like Pascal), a queue might be implemented in a linked list. A node is a record or *struct* that holds each of the enqueued items. Functions manipulate the list as a queue. However, nowhere in the program would there be a type specifier named *Queue* that embraced both the data structures for the node, and the functions that manipulate the queue.

It is now clear that in an object-oriented program, a class named *Queue* can be specified to include both. Here is a *Queue* class. The *head* and the *rear* of each object are *private* data members. The *Queue* class offers the public member functions *initialize( )* to set *head* and *rear* to *NULL*, *append( )*, *empty( )*, and *deliver( )*.

```
class Queue
    {
    private:

        struct node
```

```
            {
               itemRec  entity;     // Here itemRec is the type specifier for a
                                    // struct.
               node*    next;
            }

         node  *head, *rear;    // These are the head and rear of ad hoc
                                // queue.

      public:

         void initialize();              // Sets head and rear to NULL.

         void append(itemRec itemIn);  // Appends a new node holding itemIn
                                       // to the back of the queue.

         int empty();            // Returns 1 if queue is empty, 0 if not
                                 // empty.
         itemRec deliver();      // Returns the itemRec at the front of the
                                 // list and deletes the node that had been
                                 // holding it.
   };
```

In *main( )*, or anywhere else that an instantiation of such a *Queue* were needed, a queue could be declared and used as follows:

```
void main()
   {
      Queue   arrivalQueue;        // No queue like this can be defined in
                                   // Pascal.
      arrivalQueue.initialize();

      Queue   waitForServers;
      waitForServers.initialize();

      Queue   waitForInspectors;
      waitForInspectors.initialize();

      Queue   waitForPackers;
      waitForPackers.initialize();
         .
         .
         .
   }
```

The operations that can be performed upon *Queue* objects are limited to what the class has made possible. No data members are publicly accessible, so the queue itself cannot be touched. All that the class allows for are "telling a queue to append an entity," "telling a queue to deliver an entity," and so forth. A *Queue* has become an abstract data type like *int, float,* and *char.*

Although computer science students and professors are interested in stacks, queues, binary trees, and the like, applications may have banks, ATM machines, customers, accounts, and transactions. Alternatively, they may have users, mail boxes, and messages. It turns out that the kinds of objects comprising a system can be construed as abstract data types just as a stack, queue, or tree. What is more, it turns out that myriad benefits accrue by building classes and programming with objects.

Abstraction refers to defining and using a *Queue* within a program in ways that are natural, that is, with the effect of linear storage structure and applicable operations. A good class will offer precisely these features, and nothing else.

Encapsulation refers to the packaging of a unit of code within a function. Having a computation accessible for nothing but the proper call provides two great benefits. First, it enables anyone who knows how to call a function to do virtually anything. Complicated programming once encapsulated, is tamed. Minimal effort is required to access it, and it is always performed correctly (assuming the function was properly written). Encapsulation is carried to the extreme by program development environments, word processing packages, spread sheets, and the like. In these milieu, one need not even know how to call a function. The function is invoked by clicking on an icon or making a selection from a menu.

A second benefit is that encapsulation is the mechanism that allows classes to offer the right tools for managing objects. For instance, a class allowing the instantiation of stack objects offers functions for pushing and popping. In using a stack object for the evaluation of a postfix expression, pushing and popping by way of function calls eliminates the logical distraction that follows from mingling the stack mechanics with the steps directly pertinent to solving the problem at hand. A string class provides the facilities for making string objects so easy to use that their presence in an application causes no distraction. Encapsulation of functions allows code to be written at the level of the application development.

Information hiding is the means through which encapsulation is enforced. Users are prevented from interacting with any members specified as private, except by means of public member functions that provide the interfacing mechanism. The benefit is that interactions with the class can remain unchanged even if the class undergoes internal modification. Suppose, for instance, that in performing an upgrade of the *Box* class, performance can be improved by changing the data members from *length*, *height*, and *symbol* to *area*, *height*, and *symbol*. A client's functions which doubles the length of a *Box* is unaffected if it uses *Box::getlength( )* and *Box::setLength( )* because these are re-written to work just as if there were a *length* data member. Client's functions that depend on the literal existence of this data member (which is to say functions that use implementation specific details for the *Box* class would be inoperative. Offering explicit interfaces and prohibiting their violations takes care of systems dependent upon the class and makes these systems more reliable.

Concluding Remark on Classes and Objects in C++

The C++ programming language feature, *class*, provides the programmer with abstract data types. This extends C++ beyond its nature as a structured programming language. Finally, it is noteworthy that a program that appears thoroughly conventional, such as the following hello world program and every other C++ program shown so far, incorporates classes, an object, and the invocation of a member function implicitly.

```
#include <iostream.h>
void main()
    {
       cout << endl << "Hello world!" << endl;
    }
```

Class specifications are given within header file *iostream*; *cout* is an object from the *ostream* class; and each use of the insertion operator is a call to a member function defined within the *ostream* class. However, neither this program, nor others that use the facilities of header file *iostream.h*, are what most would think of as object-oriented simply by virtue of output by way of *cout*.

4.2   Constructors and Destructors

Constructors are necessary for the creation of objects. Every time a class is instantiated, that is, every time an object is created, a member function referred to as a constructor, having the name of the class as its name, is invoked and runs. This member function may be programmer-defined; if it is not, the default member function that is a constructor is automatically invoked. Consider the creation of a *Box* object (assuming a *Box* class).

```
void main()
    {
       Box box1;   // The no-argument "Box constructor" runs
         .          // to set-up box1.
         .
         .
    }
```

A special member function of the *Box* class, called *Box( )* is invoked automatically immediately after the memory management process has reserved space for the object and recorded the binding between the memory location and its *box1* identifier. A constructor runs every time memory is allocated for an object.

```
void main()
    {
```

```
Box box1;   // The no-argument constructor, Box(), runs once.

Box b1, b2, b3;     // Box() runs three times.

Box boxArray[10];   // Box() runs ten times.

Box*  boxPtr; // No box constructor runs because no Box is being
              // created;  no memory is being allocated
              // for a Box object because "an address of a Box" is
              // not a Box.

boxPtr = new Box;   // Box() runs once.
    ⋮
}
```

The procedure for creating an object is structured and dependable: a constructor is invoked by the complier. In the *Box* class throughout Section 4.1, a constructor is provided implicitly by the compiler: it is a no-argument constructor. A explicitly programmed no-argument constructor automatically replaces the default function.

An explicit contructor enables the programmer of the class to include object initializations or other preparations for the new object. The *Queue* class can include a no-argument constructor that initializes the *head* and *rear* to *NULL*, relieving the programmer of this responsibility and eliminating the errors that result from oversights. If the designers of the class need to keep count of the number of nodes on the queue, the constructor can perform the increment to a count each time a node is created.

The destructor is the member function that performs activities associated with dismantling an object immediately before the memory holding its data members is deallocated. Each time an object is eliminated from the program, whether it is a local variable automatically deleted at a function return or a dynamically allocated object deallocated with the *delete* operator, the class destructor is invoked. For classes in which no destructor has been explicitly given, a default destructor is provided. The destructor enables the programmer of the class to include processing associated with an object's demise such as decrementing a counter of objects in the system, returning storage the object is associated with, or closing files. The *Queue* class might have a destructor that *delete*s every node on the linked list. The memory manager (which runs after the destructor) will automatically deallocate a *Queue* object's *head* and *rear* of a *Queue* because they are data members defined in the object, but it generally does nothing to any storage that has been acquired in the course of processing with the operator *new*.

Constructors

Like any member function, an explicit constructor is defined in full within the class specifier or declared within the specifier and defined elsewhere. Like any function, it can perform any executable actions. The fact that the role of a constructor is generally to initialize an object or to undertake the housekeeping associated with its creation in no way limits its potential action. Like any function, it may be overloaded; in fact, very often it is. The no-argument constructor is one version.

Constructors differ from ordinary member functions in minor ways. The name of a constructor is always the same as the name of the class. No type specifier is given as the constructor's return type. There is no return statement: the function returns the instantiation of the class; this is understood and implicit. Constructors may have a data member initialization list between the declarator followed by a colon, and the opening brace of the body, to install initial values within the data members of the object being created. These values may be literals, the values copied from formal arguments in the constructor's argument list, or values resulting from an expression. If any of the data members are specified within the class to be *constant*, the list is the only way to initialize them.

An Example with Constructors

Here is the *Box* class, shown with two one-argument constructors, a two-argument constructor, and a three-argument constructor.

```
class Box
   {
    public:
       char symbol;

    private:
       int length;
       int height;

    public:
       Box(int dimension) : length(2*dimension), height(dimension)

          {
            cout << "\nOne argument constructor, Box(int), is running...";
            cout << "\n    length initialized to " << length;
            cout << "\n    height initialized to " << height;
            cout << "\n    --> Please enter symbol for symbol:  ";
          cin >> symbol;
            cout << "\n\nLook at the Box just created:" << endl;
```

> Constructors are functions that have the same name as the class and no type specifier designating the type of that which is returned (which is an object of the class).

```
            showBox();
        }
```

> Data member initializer list is composed of items separated by commas. Each item is a data member followed, in parentheses, by the initializing expression.

```
    Box(char forSymbol) : symbol(forSymbol), length(20), height(4)

    {
        cout << "\nOne argument constructor, Box(char), is running...";
    }
    Box(int dim, char sym) :  length(dim), height(dim), symbol(sym)
    {
        cout << "\nTwo argument constructor is running...";
    }

    Box(char forSymbol, int forLength, int forHeight) :
          symbol(forSymbol), height(forHeight), length(forLength)
    {
        cout << "\nThree argument constructor is running...";
    }
    void showBox()
    {
        // Details omitted.
    }
```

> Constructors never have return statements.

```
    void setSize()
    {
        // Details omitted.
    }
};

void main()
{
    Box   box1;              // COMPILE-TIME ERROR:  NO NO-ARGUMENT
                            // CONSTRUCTOR!
    Box   box2(6);          // Uses one-arg constructor with the int
                            // signature.
    Box   box3('S');        // Uses one-arg constructor with the char
                            // signature.
    Box   box4(7,'#');      // Uses the two-argument constructor.
    Box   box5('*',3,4);    // Uses the three-argument constructor.

    Box* boxPtr;            // No constructor invoked because no object
                            // defined.
```

```
boxPtr = new Box('#',8,2);   // Uses the three-argument constructor.
(*boxPtr).showBox();         // Shows the dynamically allocated Box
boxPtr -> showBox();         // action identical to the statement
                             // above.

Box boxArray1[10];   // COMPILE-TIME ERROR:  ATTEMPTS TO USE THE
                     // NO-ARGUMENT CONSTRUCTOR BUT THERE IS NONE.

Box boxArray2[4] = { Box(9), Box('A'), Box(5,'@'), Box('+',8,6) };
for (int i = 0; i<4; i++)
  {
    cout << endl << "showing boxArray2[" << i << "] below:" << endl;
    boxArray2[i].showBox();
  }

// The new operator cannot be used to allocate an array of Box
// objects or an array of any kind of class instantiations.
  ⋮
}
```

Because the *Box* class contains an explicit constructor (four of them), the no-argument constructor that C++ provides is disabled. Inasmuch as there is no no-argument constructor, any *Box* instantiation that depends upon it will cause an error. This includes the attempted definition of *box1* and the attempted creation of the array of *Box*es, *boxArray1*. Here is the code that can substitute for the default no-argument constructor that C++ disabled.

```
          // Code that exactly replicates the
Box()     // the default no-argument constructor.
  {
  }
```

The constructor does nothing except create an object. Errors stemming from the absence of a no-argument constructor disappear. Here is a constructor that queries the user for values for *length*, *height*, and *symbol*.

```
Box()
  {
    cout << endl << "Enter length for new Box: ";
    cin >> length;

    cout << endl << "Enter height for new Box: ";
    cin >> height;

    cout << endl << "Enter symbol for new Box: ";
    cin >> symbol;
  }
```

An alternative approach is to use the existing *setSize( )* function that queries the user for the same information and even performs some range checking (and gets a value for *symbol* too).

```
Box()
{
  setSize();  // Same as  this -> setSize();  and  (*this).setSize().
}
```

Within a constructor, the new object, the one under construction, is *this and, hence, the implicit accessor. In the preceding code it is the object under construction that is invoking *setSize( )*.

Another option for the no-argument constructor, is to put some values into the data members. One way to do this is with assignment statements.

```
Box()
{
  length = 0;     // Data member length is assigned the value 0.
  height = 0;     // Data member height is assigned the value 0.
  symbol = ' ';   // Data member symbol is assigned the value ' '.
}
```

Initialization and Assignment

Although assignment and initialization may seem to be the same operation, with the nuance that an initialization is a first assignment, they are distinct operations in C++. This becomes relevant when the object holds dynamically allocated memory. For example, consider a *Queue* object, *queueA*, whose data members *head* and *rear* point to 100 dynamically allocated *struct*s. Suppose that *queueB* is a different *Queue* object whose *head* and *rear* point to a different list of *struct*s. Finally, remember that the assignment operator performs by making a member-by-member copy. The assignment

```
queueA = queueB;
```

results in the effective inaccessibility of the 100 nodes that had been held by *queueA*. This phenomenon is sometimes referred to as memory leak. Initialization, on the other hand, need not be concerned about memory leak, or the responsible disposition of resources because the new object holds nothing.

Moreover, constants are read-only variables that are not allowed to be on the left-hand side of an assignment operator (or anywhere else where an update is possible, such as within a function call in the position of an argument passed by reference to a nonconstant, or in the position of an operand to receive input from *cin*). A value must be installed. The solution is to distinguish the initialization, from all later assignments.

Constructors dissociate initialization from assignment by way of the initializer list. The last no-argument constructor is rewritten with such a list because its assignments are really initializations:

```
Box() :  length(0), height(0), symbol(' ')
```

```
    {
    }
```

Initializations may appear in any order on the initialization list; they do not have to appear in the same order in which the data members are declared within the class specifier. To remember whether it is the data member or the value that appears within the parentheses, keep in mind that information travels from right to left in an initialization, just as in an assignment.

The one-argument constructor with the *(int)* signature shows that an argument can be passed to a constructor, that the argument can be used within the data member initializer list (and within arithmetic expressions within the initializer list), and that some data members may be initialized even if all of them are not. The presence of the one-argument constructor with the *(char)* signature and the others demonstrates that constructors can be overloaded. Arguments within constructors can be passed by reference or qualified as *const*.

Constructors do not have to be the first functions to appear within the class specifier. Nor do they have to be fully defined within the specifier; instead they may be declared with prototypes and defined outside. The initializer list is not part of the declarator, therefore it does not appear within prototypes. It accompanies the definition.

A Better Example

Here is a re-do of *Box*'s specifier that includes a no-argument constructor and in which all constructors are defined outside of the specifier.

```
class Box
  {
    public:
      char symbol;

    private:
      int length;
      int height;

    public:
      Box();                    // Prototype; no-argument constructor.
      Box(int dimension);       // Prototype; one-argument constructor.
      Box(char forSymbol);      // Prototype; one-argument constructor.
      Box(int dim, char sym);   // Prototype; two-argument constructor.
      Box(char forSymbol, int forLength, int forHeight);

      void showBox()
        {
          // Details omitted.
        }

      void setSize()
        {
          // Details omitted.
```

```
        }
};
```

```
Box::Box() : length(0), height(0), symbol(' ')
    {
    }

Box::Box(int dimension) : length(2*dimension), height(dimension)
    {
    cout << "\nOne argument constructor, Box(int), is running...";
    cout << "\n    length initialized to " << length;
    cout << "\n    height initialized to " << height;
    cout << "\n    --> Please enter symbol for symbol:   ";
    cin >> symbol;
    cout << "\n\nLook at the Box just created:" << endl;
    showBox();
    }

Box::Box(char forSymbol) : symbol(forSymbol), length(20), height(4)
    {
    cout << "\nOne argument constructor, Box(char), is running...";
    }

Box::Box(int dim, char sym) :  length(dim), height(dim), symbol(sym)
    {
    cout << "\nTwo argument constructor is running...";
    }

Box::Box(char forSymbol, int forLength, int forHeight) :
        symbol(forSymbol), height(forHeight), length(forLength)
    {
    cout << "\nThree argument constructor is running...";
    }
```

Notice that each function definition outside the specifier is identical to the declaration within the specifier except that the class name and the scope operator are attached to the declarator at the left. The constructors' prototypes within the specifier do not need to show the names of the formal arguments. No prototypes must, but these provide a good reminder about what information is placed in each position. Had the declaration of the three-argument constructor appeared without these names, as it could have,

```
    Box(char, int, int);
```

there would not have been as much documentation about the respective arguments.

Declaring Objects in Main( )

Consider *main( )*.

```
void main()
{
    Box  box1;              // Uses the no-argument constructor.
    Box  box2(6);           // Uses one-arg constructor with the int
                            // signature.
    Box  box3('S');         // Uses one-arg constructor with the char
                            // signature.
    Box  box4(7,'#');       // Uses the two-argument constructor.
    Box  box5('*',3,4);     // Uses the three-argument constructor.
      ⋮
}
```

The no-argument constructor is accessed as shown for the definition of *box1*, without an empty pair of parentheses. This is a syntax requirement. Parentheses are used with an object only when arguments are passed to a constructor; the list of actual arguments appears to the right of the identifier for the new object. Because constructors are functions, normal rules apply with respect to the positional correspondence between actual and formal arguments, and with respect to the implementation of that version of the function with a matching signature.

The syntax is slightly different for dynamically allocated objects. Following are two *Box* pointers to hold the addresses of two *Box*es that will be declared using the *new* operator.

```
  ⋮
Box *boxPtrA, *boxPtrB;       // No constructor is used.
boxPtrA  =  new Box;          // Uses the no-argument constructor.
boxPtrB  =  new Box('#',8,2); // Uses the three-argument
                              // constructor.
  ⋮
```

Declaring a *Box* pointer does not cause memory to be allocated for a *Box*; it causes memory to be allocated to a variable that can hold the addresses of *Box*es. Defining a *Box* pointer, therefore, does not invoke a *Box* constructor. Getting the object itself, with *new*, is done as shown in the following: *new* is followed by the class name, the no-argument constructor is invoked when no pair of parentheses follows the class name or another constructor is invoked with the argument list appearing within parentheses to the right of the class name.

  ⋮

```
int intArray1[10];   // Uninitialized array; each element is an int.
Box boxArray1[10];   // No-argument constructor runs 10 times because
                     //   each element is a Box.

int intArray2[4] = { 111, 222, 333, 444 };
Box boxArray2[4] = { Box(9), Box('A'), Box(5,'@'), Box('+',8,6) };
    ⋮
```

Arrays of objects may be defined just as any array is defined without initialization.

Because each element of a array *Box* is a *Box*, a constructor is run for each one; a 10-element *Box* array is defined, and there are 10 constructor invocations. Because no arguments are indicated, the no-argument constructor is the one used throughout. It is also possible to initialize an array of objects. Each initializer is the class name followed by an argument list, within parentheses, that matches a constructor.

It is important to note that a constructor is specified as *public* for it to be accessible in *main( )*, in any function that is not a member of the class, or externally. This implies that a particular constructor that expedites the internal management of the class, but that should not be available to users at large, may be specified to be *private*.

Just as variables of language-provided data types may be created externally, objects may be created outside of functions in order to confer nonlocal status. When an object is defined externally, a constructor runs exactly as it does when an object is defined within a function. This means that if one or more objects are defined externally in the source code ahead of *main( )* as shown in the following, the program execution will start with the actions of the constructors. Although processing usually starts with *main( )* in C++, it does not always.

```
#include <iostream.h>
class Box
  {
    // Details omitted.
  };
                    // Before main() begins, constructors run for both of
                    // these externally defined Boxes:
  Box box1;         // the no-argument constructor runs for box1 followed
  Box box2('J');    // by the one-argument constructor with the (char)
                    // signature for box2.
  void main()
    {
      // Details omitted.
    }
```

The Copy Constuctor

The C++ compiler invokes a function with a default specialized use, called a copy constructor; it is automatically invoked when an object is passed by value to create an object. It is also invoked when an object is returned to create the return object. Just as a default no-argument constructor is supplied when no explicit constructor has been coded, a default copy constructor is likewise provided. The default copy constructor does a member-by-member copy of the actual argument in the call.

The copy constructor assists in preparing a function to run and in terminating it. Consider the following free function, *justForDiscussion( )*. What it does is not important (or known); what is important is the information transmission through its interface. The function *justForDiscussion( )* returns a *Box* and accepts four arguments: an *int* passed by value, two Boxes passed by value, and a *Box* passed by reference.

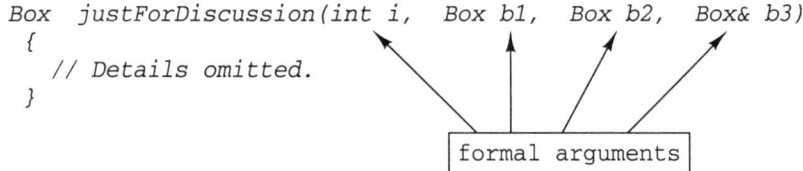

```
Box  justForDiscussion(int i,  Box b1,  Box b2,  Box& b3)
  {
    // Details omitted.
  }
```

formal arguments

Here is a call.

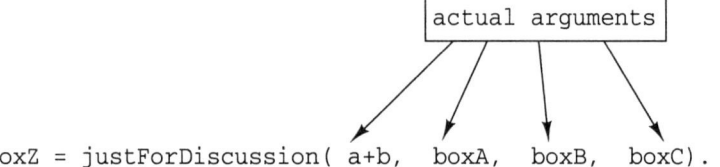

actual arguments

```
boxZ = justForDiscussion( a+b,  boxA,  boxB,  boxC).
```

Passing an argument by value means binding the name of the parameter to a memory location and initializing it with the value of the actual argument. The binding has the same status as that of an automatic variable with a scope local to the function. Passing an argument by reference, denoted by the ampersand, involves attaching the name of the formal argument to the same memory location as the one bound to the actual argument. No new memory or initialization is involved (but only variables, not literals or expressions, can be passed by reference).

The first argument is an arithmetic expression, $a + b$. In preparing to execute the function, it is evaluated. Memory is allocated for i, the parameter is bound to this location, and it is initialized with the value of $a + b$. The operation is like a definition and initialization that may be found within a function.

```
int i = a+b;
```

The second argument is a *Box*, passed by value. The operation here, like the operation for the first argument, amounts to something like the definition and initialization of a *Box*.

```
Box b1 = boxA;
```

Memory for a new *Box* is found and bound to *b1*, and *b1* is initialized to *boxA*. The argument's initialization is not performed by the assignment operator; it is performed by the copy constructor. The object *boxA* is passed to the copy constructor, and the copy constructor initializes and returns the *Box* that becomes *b1*.

A reason for distinguishing between the copy constructor and the assignment operator is that sometimes the two will perform different actions. This is a critical issue for objects with data members that are pointers to data structures. For example, the assignment operator might make a member-by-member copy of a *Queue*, so that the left operand contains the same physical list as the right operand because its *head* and *rear* hold identical addresses. The copy constructor may be written so that the formal argument holds a logical copy of the list, the same content but in an entirely independent location.

The advantage of separating the copy constructor from other constructors, such as the constructor with signature *(Box)*, is that its actions might differ from these too; for example, it may not be appropriate for a counter of *Box* objects to be incremented when a *Box* object is passed from one function to another.

All classes have a default copy constructor so that objects can be passed to (and returned from) functions. It makes a member-by-member copy, just as the default assignment operator does. The default copy constructor for the *Box* class looks like this:

```
// Copy constructor that replicates the implicit default
// as it would appear if coded within the Box specifier.

Box(const Box&  actualArgument)
  {
    length = actualArgument.length;   // Assignment operator for ints.
    height = actualArgument.height;   // Assignment operator for ints.
    symbol = actualArgument.symbol;   // Assignment operator for chars.
  }
```

What differentiates this function as the copy constructor is its formal argument list: one object of the class is passed by reference. Although the *actualArgument* is a constant, this is not necessary. It is quite common, however, for two reasons. It enables the copy constructor to work for both constant and nonconstant *Box* objects in the call; and it ensures that the transmitted object, though it is being passed by reference, will not be modified.

The third argument in *justForDiscussion( )* is another *Box*, passed by value. Accordingly, the argument, *boxB*, is passed to the copy constructor and a *Box* emerges to be bound to *b2*. The data members of the new *Box* are in their own new memory locations, independent of the locations of the data members of *boxB*, which gives them autonomy. Their values are copies of the values of the respective *boxB* data members. Thus *b2.length* equals *boxB.length* when *justForDiscussion( )* starts, but a change in *b2.length* will have no effect on the value held by *boxB.length*.

The third argument, *b3*, is passed by reference. This means that it will be an alias for the argument, *boxC*. Because *b3* is *boxC* (i.e., they reference the same part of memory), no new object is created and the copy constructor is not activated. The observation that the copy constructor is activated only if an object is passed by value suggests why its own formal argument has to be passed by reference: in order to avoid the infinite recursive regress that would result if it had to invoke itself in order to begin.

Finally, *justForDiscussion( )* concludes with the return of a *Box*.

```
return  someBox;   // One plausible "return" -- passing back
                   // a Box defined within the function.
```

or

```
return  boxA;   // Another plausible return -- passing back
                // a selected or refashioned argument Box ;
```

or

```
return  Box('B', 5, 3); // Another plausible return -- passing
                        // back a Box defined at the point of
                        // return.
```

or

```
return  *boxPtr;  // Yet another plausible return -- passing back
                  // a Box obtained by dereferencing a pointer to a
                  // Box.
```

Some actual *Box* object is presented for *return*, and it is the copy constructor that mediates its transmission back to the point at which *justForDiscussion( )* was invoked. The *Box* to be returned is passed to the copy constructor, and the copy constructor returns a new *Box* whose members are bitwise copies. What is done with it depends upon context.

```
// Here, the returned Box is assigned to a preexisting Box.

answerBx = justForDiscussion(n, bxFactor1, bxFactor2, bxFactor3);

// Here, the returned Box invokes a member function of its own.

justForDiscussion(2, square1, square2, rectangle3).showBox();

// Here, the returned Box is displayed via the output operator.
//
//          Section 4.3 will show how to enable
//          the output operator, <<, to handle Boxes.
//
cout << justForDiscussion(5, box1, box2, box3);
```

Other possibilities include its appearance within an expression or as an argument within a function call. In all cases, the *Box* to which the call resolves is a copy of the *Box* that appeared within the *return* statement and was created by the copy constructor.

Power comes from writing an explicit copy constructor. Just because it is a copy constructor does not mean it can only create copies. It can perform range-checking for one or more data members, or test for and trap special information. The ability to write a copy constructor gives the ability to filter. To disallow objects to be passed by value, the copy constructor can be *private*. Forcing users to pass objects by reference might be helpful when the objects are extremely large or when errors would result if changes to data members within formal arguments (e.g., pointers to data structures) are not also made within the actual arguments.

Destructors

The discussion about destructors is shorter than the discussion about constructors. A class can have only one destructor, and it is a no-argument member function that returns nothing. If no destructor is explicitly coded, the compiler provides a default that looks like the following:

```
// Functional equivalent of the destructor automatically provided
// by C++ for the Box class.
```

~Box()	The declarator of a destructor is the tilde (~) followed by the class name, followed by an empty pair of parentheses (no arguments are allowed).
{	
}	

An explicitly programmed destructor automatically replaces the default supplied by C++. No matter what the new destructor does it has the same declarator as the one previously shown. Like the declarator of a constructor, it shows no return type. The destructor name, like that of a constructor, is class name; however, it is preceded by a tilde. It is the tilde that enables both the human reader and the compiler to differentiate the destructor from a no-argument constructor.

The destructor provides the means to perform any kind of housekeeping or system clean-up that might accompany the demise of an object. Often this is the deletion of dynamically allocated memory acquired by the object for its own use (but not information in dynamic storage that existing objects will continue to need). In a graphic application, the destructor might take an object off the display screen. Although a destructor does not have an argument or a return type, there are no restrictions upon the actions that may be coded within it. The data and function members of the invoking object (i.e., the one to be destroyed) remain fully accessible throughout the duration of the destructor's execution. When the destructor ends, the language system's memory manager frees the object.

All objects that are automatically allocated are automatically destroyed. For those objects that are automatic variables within a function, destruction takes place immediately following the end of the function on a last-constructed, first-destroyed basis. If the final action of *main( )* were to display the message "Run Successfully Completed" and the destructor were written to display the *Box* being removed from the system, as shown in the following, visible evidence would reveal that the destructor's processing is undertaken.

```
~Box()
    {                    // The object being destructed is the *this, and
    showBox(); // therefore the implicit accessor of member functions
                         // and data.
    }
```

Included among the automatic variables automatically destructed when a function ends are any objects that had been parameters in the declarator.

The programmer has no discretion over when an automatic object is destroyed. All automatic variables are part of the local referencing environment and are destroyed when the local referencing environment is dismantled. Dynamically allocated objects, that is, objects obtained by using the *new* operator, are different. They are not part of the local referencing environment and are not removed automatically when the function ends. They persist until they are explicitly destroyed with the application of the *delete* operator. This means that the programmer can invoke the destructor to deallocate an object acquired with *new* at any time. However, it also means that if the programmer does not expressly *delete* such an object, the object will continue to exist and to occupy space in memory until the program ends.

An Example with a Destructor

The following program illustrates how the destructor is called to delete dynamically allocated *Box*es. It also shows exactly when a constructor and the destructor operate upon the respective objects. To allow individual *Box*es to be tracked, the symbol within each is a unique identification number.

```
#include <iostream.h>

class Box
    {
    public:
        char symbol;

    private:
        int length;
        int height;

    public:
    // Copy constructor.
    Box (const Box& b)
        {
        length = b.length;
        height = b.height;
```

```
            symbol = b.symbol;
            cout<<"copy constructor  new Box has symbol "<<symbol<<endl;
          }

      // No-argument constructor.
      Box()
        {
          cout << "no-argument constructor" << endl;
        }

      // A one-argument constructor.
      Box(char forSymbol) : length(10), height(2), symbol(forSymbol)
        {
          cout << "onearg (char) constructor  new Box has symbol "
               << symbol << endl;
        }

      // Destructor.
      ~Box()
        {
          cout << "destructor  decommissioned Box has symbol "
               << symbol << endl;
        }
    };

Box*  get_and_return_a_dynamically_allocated_Box()
  {
    Box box('6');  // an "automatic" Box

    Box* boxPtr;
    boxPtr = new Box('7');   // A dynamically allocated Box is created
    delete boxPtr;           // ...and deleted.

    boxPtr = new Box('7');   // A dynamically allocated Box is created
    return boxPtr;           // ...and a pointer to it is returned.
  }

Box  exercising_the_copy_constructor (Box argument1, Box argument2)
  {
    cout << "*** exercising_the_copy_constructor is running ***"
         << endl;
    cout << "     argument1 is Box " << argument1.symbol;
    cout << "     argument2 is Box " << argument2.symbol << endl;

    return Box('8');  // The one-argument constructor creates this Box
  }                   // and the copy constructor makes the copy that
                      // appears at the function's point of call.

void main()
  {
```

```
    Box* boxPtr;  // Box pointer defined no constructor is called.

    // A Box is dynamically allocated:
    boxPtr = new Box('1');  // It is recognizable because its symbol is
                            // '1'.
    delete boxPtr;          // The destructor is invoked for this Box.

    boxPtr = new Box('2');  // This box will need to be deleted - the
                            // destructor will never handle it.

    Box box3('3');     // Here box3 is an automatic variable.
    Box box4('4');     // Here box4 is an automatic variable.

    boxPtr = new Box('5');  // The pointer to box2 is now lost.

    Box box6('6');

    Box* anotherBoxPtr;

    anotherBoxPtr = get_and_return_a_dynamically_allocated_Box();
    delete anotherBoxPtr;

    Box returnedBox;  // The no-argument constructor creates this Box.

    returnedBox = exercising_the_copy_constructor(box3, *boxPtr);

    cout << "from main():  symbol of the returnedBox is "
         << returnedBox.symbol;

    cout << "\n Run Successfully Completed" << endl;
}
```

Here is the output:

```
onearg (char) constructor  new Box has symbol 1
destructor  decommissioned Box has symbol 1
onearg (char) constructor  new Box has symbol 2
onearg (char) constructor  new Box has symbol 3
onearg (char) constructor  new Box has symbol 4
onearg (char) constructor  new Box has symbol 5
onearg (char) constructor  new Box has symbol 6
onearg (char) constructor  new Box has symbol 7
destructor  decommissioned Box has symbol 7
onearg (char) constructor  new Box has symbol 7
destructor  decommissioned Box has symbol 6
destructor  decommissioned Box has symbol 7
noargument constructor
copy constructor  new Box has symbol 5
```

```
copy constructor   new Box has symbol 3
*** exercising_the_copy_constructor is running ***
     argument1 is Box 3     argument2 is Box 5
onearg (char) constructor   new Box has symbol 8
destructor   decommissioned Box has symbol 5
destructor   decommissioned Box has symbol 3
destructor   decommissioned Box has symbol 8
from main():   symbol of the returnedBox is 8
 Run Successfully Completed
destructor   decommissioned Box has symbol 8
destructor   decommissioned Box has symbol 6
destructor   decommissioned Box has symbol 4
destructor   decommissioned Box has symbol 3
```

Static Data and Functions

The data members of the *Box* class are *length, height*, and *symbol*. Each *Box* object will have a *length* variable, a *height* variable, and a *symbol* variable. The memory bound to *bigBox*'s *symbol* variable accessible as *bigBox.symbol* is entirely separate from the memory bound to *smallBox*'s *symbol* variable accessible as *smallBox.symbol* and every other *Box*'s *symbol* variable as well.

A static data member is a data member belonging not to any one object but to all the objects in a class. The binding between its name and its storage is established and its initialization is performed prior to *main( )* and before the first object is created. In fact, its definition and initialization take place apart from the action of a constructor. The static data member endures while specific objects come and go, and even if the number of objects drops to zero. Any object may access a static data member, however, all objects are accessing the same, shared variable that exists apart from any individual object. If a static data member is *private*, then it is directly accessible only within the member functions of the class; if *public*, then it is accessible within all functions where the class's objects may occur.

Static data members are used to keep track of information pertinent to the class as a whole. One property of the class as a whole is the total number of objects that have been so far created, and a static data member can be used as a counter to keep a running total. This might further be used to insert a unique identification number into each new object. Another aggregate property is the current number of objects. A static data member can serve as a counter that is incremented by the constructor and decremented by the destructor. Other pertinent information for objects of a class might be the date or selected settings for the software.

A static function member is a member function that does not require one of the class's objects as an accessor. Static data members may be *private*. In that case *public get* and *set* member functions must be available to make them accessible within the program at large. But because static data members relate to attributes that transcend a particular object, they must be accessible in a broader context.

The intent of a static function member is to enable processing that involves static data members without the need for an accessing object. There is no use of the member access operator (the dot) and reference to *this* (which includes *this).

Implementation of Static Data

A *static* data member is declared within the class specifier exactly as any data member, except that its type specifier is preceded by the keyword *static*. Beyond the class specifier, ahead of *main( )* and outside any function (i.e., externally), it must be defined. This is done by giving its data type specifier followed by its full name, which means that the class scope operator syntax must be used: its identifier prefixed by the class' name followed by the scope resolution operator (the double colon). All *static* data members must be defined in this manner, whether *public* or *private*. If the static data member is to be initialized, it is done at its point of definition in the same way that variables that are not data members are initialized (with the assignment operator). Even if an object is defined externally in the source code ahead of the definition of a *static* data member, the definition (and initialization, if indicated) of the *static* data member is performed first. Within the class's member functions, *static* data members are accessed by their identifier standing alone, just as a data member belonging to the accessing object. If a *static* data member is *public*, it may be accessed in *main( )* or in any other function in which the class is in scope by using the class name, the scope resolution operator, and its name.

Consider the following example.

```
#include <iostream.h>

class Demo
  {
    public:
      static int counter;

    private:
      static char string[11];

    public:
      Demo()    // Constructor.
        {
          counter++;
          cout <<"\nFrom constructor:   " << string << counter;
        }
  };
```

```
Demo object1;    // Object defined externally, ahead of
                 // static data member definitions and initializations.

// Static data member definitions and initializations.
int  Demo::counter = 0;
char Demo::string[11] = "counter = ";
```

> Demo::counter is accessible in *main()* because it is *public*.

```
void main()

    [
      cout << endl << "*** main() is beginning ***";

      cout << "\n       from main() > Demo::counter = " << Demo::counter;

      Demo object2;
      Demo object3;
```

> Objects may access static data members.

```
      cout << endl << endl;

      cout << "   " << object1.counter;
   cout << "   " << object2.counter;
   cout << "   " << object3.counter << endl;
   }
```

Here is the output.

```
From constructor:   counter = 1
*** main() is beginning ***
        from main() > Demo::counter = 1
From constructor:   counter = 2
From constructor:   counter = 3
     3    3    3
```

Implementation of a Static Function

A static function member is defined within the class specifier just as any member function, except that the keyword *static* is put to the left of its return type. *Static* member functions may be *public* or *private*. When a prototype is within the class specifier, the *static* specifier accompanies the prototype but does not accompany the declarator of the subsequent definition. *Static* function members may be invoked within member functions by using their name with an appropriate argument list. If *public*, they may be invoked outside member functions by prefixing their name and argument list with the class name and the scope resolution operator.

The following program stamps each *Box* with an identification number and keeps count of the number of *Box*es within the program. There are two *static* functions, one to report the total number of *Box*es thus far created which is the current value of the *private static* data member *serialNumber* and one to return the number of *Boxes* that are currently on hand which is the value of the *private static* variable *numberOfBoxes*.

```cpp
#include <iostream.h>

class Box
  {
    public:
      char symbol;

    private:
      int length;
      int height;
      int identificationNumber;

      static int serialNumber;   // Stores last serial number assigned.
      static int numberOfBoxes; // Number of Boxes currently in the system.

    public:
      Box() : length(10), height(2), symbol('X')  // Constructor.
        {
          identificationNumber = ++serialNumber;
          ++numberOfBoxes;
        }

      ~Box()                                      // Destructor.
        {
          cout << "\nBox number " << identificationNumber
               << " is being destructed      ";
          cout << numberOfBoxes << " Boxes left in the system";
        }

      static void boxesCreated()       // Static member function.
        {
          cout << "\nTotal number of Boxes so far created = "
               << serialNumber;
        }

      static int boxesInTheSystem();  // Prototype of static member function.
  };

// Defining the static member function that had only been declared within
// the specifier; note the use of the class name and scope resolution operator.

  int Box::boxesInTheSystem()
    {
      return numberOfBoxes;
    }
```

```
// Defining and initializing the static data members; note the use of the
// class name and the scope resolution operator.

   int Box::serialNumber = 0;
   int Box::numberOfBoxes = 0;

void main()
  {
    // Get a Box pointer  and  a dynamically allocated array of 5 Boxes.
         Box* boxPtr;
         boxPtr = new Box[5];

    // Get a report on the number of Boxes created and in the system.
         Box::boxesCreated();
         cout << "\nCurrent number of boxes in the system:  "
              << Box::boxesInTheSystem();

    // Delete all the Boxes in the array pointed to by boxPtr.
    // *** Remember to use the empty brackets when deleting any array ***
    // *** that was dynamically allocated (i.e., allocated with new)  ***
         delete [] boxPtr;

    // Get a static array of Boxes.
         Box  boxArray[3];

    // Get a report on the number of Boxes created and in the system.
         Box::boxesCreated();
         cout << "\nCurrent number of boxes in the system:  "
              << Box::boxesInTheSystem();

    // Program ends; destructor runs afterwards for compile-time array.
         cout << "\n **Run Successfully Completed** " << endl;
  }
```

Here is the output:

```
Total number of Boxes so far created = 5
Current number of boxes in the system:  5
Box number 5 is being destructed     4 Boxes left in the system
Box number 4 is being destructed     3 Boxes left in the system
Box number 3 is being destructed     2 Boxes left in the system
Box number 2 is being destructed     1 Boxes left in the system
Box number 1 is being destructed     0 Boxes left in the system
Total number of Boxes so far created = 8
Current number of boxes in the system:  3
  **Run Successfully Completed**

Box number 8 is being destructed     2 Boxes left in the system
Box number 7 is being destructed     1 Boxes left in the system
Box number 6 is being destructed     0 Boxes left in the system
```

Static Variables in Free
Functions

Within a free function, a *static* variable is a local variable used to retain information from one invocation of the function to the next. *Static* variables are defined like automatic variable but differentiated from automatic variables with the keyword *static* to the left of the data type specifier. *Static* variables may be initialized at their point of definition within the function. If there is no explicit initialization they are automatically set to zero. Initialization is performed only once, with the first function call. Upon the second and subsequent calls the inital assignment is ignored.

It should be noted that a *static* variable does its job even in a recursive function call. (This is a function that uses itself either directly or indirectly.) A *static* variable occupies a fixed memory location that remains throughout the program. A recursive call begins with whatever value the *static* variable currently holds. If its value is changed, the changed value remains in place following the return. Although a *static* variable is only accessible within the function in which it is defined, it is accessible across all activations of the function.

The classic illustration of *static* variables is the counter and the accumulator in a function designed to report a running average.

```
float runningAverage (float  nextValue)    // Free function.
   {
   static float total = 0;  // Running accumulator.
   static   int count = 0;  // Running total of values entered.

   count++; // Count incremented when runningAverage is
            // invoked to entered the nextValue.

   total += nextValue;   // Here nextValue is added to running accum.

   return total/count;   // Return the average as of now.
   }
```

The preorder traversal of a binary tree may increment a *static* variable with each call for a node at a greater depth for the purpose of finding the height of the tree.

```
int preorder (node* root, int level); // Prototype.

int depthOfTree (node* root)
   {
   int depth;

   if (root == NULL)  depth = -1;   // No tree; depth of 0 means a sole root.
   else  depth = preorder(root, 0);

   return depth;
   }

int preorder (node* root, int level)
   {
```

```
    static int maxDepth = 0;

    if (root != NULL)
       {
         if (level > maxDepth)  maxDepth = level;
         preorder(root->left,  level+1);
         preorder(root->right, level+1);
       }

    return maxDepth;
}
```

Constant Objects

An object may be defined to be a *const* (a constant), just as an *int* or a *float* may be.

```
void main()
  {
    const float PI = 3.14159;   // PI is defined as a constant.  Identifiers
                                // for constants are in upper case by
                                // convention.

    const Box   B1('1',1, 1);   // B1, specified to be a constant, is
                                // initialized by the 3-argument constructor.
  }
```

A constant object, like a constant *float*, is initialized at its point of definition. Thereafter, any attempt to modify its data members will fail; this applies to the modification of its *public* data members within nonmember functions as well as to assignments or inputs to *public* or *private* data members within member functions. This means that constructors can assign or input into the data members of a constant object. The values of the data members of a constant object do not become immutable until after the object emerges from the constructor. In this regard the data members of an object defined as constant are different from data members defined within the class specifier to be constant for all objects of the class; these can be initialized only in a constructor's initializer list.

There are three ways for a constant object to arrive in a member function. A constant object may be defined within one of the member functions. Once defined, it is immutable just as if it had been defined within a free function or a member function of another class. Or, a constant object may be an actual argument passed to a formal argument. If the constant is to arrive by means of a pass by reference, then the function's declarator specifies the formal argument to be *const*. This is shown in *function1( )*:

```
void Box::function1(const Box& boxArgument)
  {
```

```
        function2( boxArgument );    // Error -- Attempt to pass a const
                                     // by reference to a nonconstant.

        boxArgument.function3();     // Okay only if there is a const
    }                                // version of function3().

void Box::function2(Box& b)
    {
    // Details omitted.
    }

void Box::function3() const       // Const version -- for accessor
    {                             // objects that are constants (but
                                  // usable by nonconstant accessor
    // Details omitted.           // objects should the mutable version
                                  // not be available.
    }

void Box::function3()             // Regular version for nonconstant
                                  // objects.
    {
    // Details omitted.
    }
```

In this example the *const* specifier ensures that *boxArgument* will not be altered. The compiler prohibits attempts to pass *boxArgument*, which is a constant, to another function with transmission by reference to a formal argument that is not a constant. The call to *function2( )* will fail because *boxArgument* is a constant and *b* is not. Had *b* been passed by value, as shown in the following, then the call to *function2( )* from *function1( )* would be acceptable: although *b's* data members would not be shielded from change, the changes would only be in the copy of the argument made by the copy constructor and for the duration of *function2( )*.

```
void Box::function2(Box b)    // A constant can be passed to b because
    {                         // although changes to its data members are
    // Details omitted.       // permitted for the processing here, the
    }                         // actual argument will be unaffected.
```

A formal argument passed by value can be made immutable, even to changes in the copy, by specifying it to be constant.

```
void Box::function2(const Box b)    // Because b is specified to be a
                                    // constant, actions may not be taken
    {                               // within this function that could result
    // Details omitted.             // in changes to the values held by its
    }                               // data members.
```

Constant Member
Functions

The third way for a constant object to find its way into a member function is to be its accessor. A constant object cannot access just any member function;

it may only access a function specified as *const*. A constant function is a member function that, by definition, will not change the invoking object, and will disallow action that might result in a change to the value of any of its data members. Besides explicit assignment and input, one such action would be the accessing object's attempt to access a nonconstant member function.

The syntax of specifying a function to be constant is demonstrated in *showBox( )*.

```
class Box
   {
     public:
         char symbol;

     private:
         int length;
         int height;

     public:
         Box() : length(15), height(5), symbol('#')   // Constructor.
            {
            }

         void showBox() const          // Constant function.
            {
              cout << "\nFrom the constant showBox() function" << endl;
              // Details omitted.
            }

         void showBox()                // Nonconstant version of showBox().
            {
              cout << "\nFrom the nonconstant version of showBox()" << endl;
            }
   };
```

If the *const* function is defined outside the specifier, its declarator both within the specifier and outside it must include the constant designation.

```
#include <iostream.h>

class Box
   {
     public:
         char symbol;

     private:
         int length;
         int height;

     public:
         Box();  // Prototype for constructor (initializer list does not
```

```
                              // appear).
              void showBox() const;    // Prototype for const version of showBox().
              void showBox();          // Prototype for nonconst version of
                                       // showBox().
    };

       Box::Box() : length(15), height(5), symbol('#')  // Constructor.
          {
          }

       void Box::showBox() const          // Constant function.
          {
             cout << "\nFrom the constant showBox() function" << endl;
             // Details omitted.
          }

       void Box::showBox()                  // Nonconstant version of showBox().
          {
             cout << "\nFrom the nonconstant version of showBox()" << endl;
          }

void main()
   {
      Box b1;
      b1.showBox(); // Invokes the nonconstant version because b1 is not a
                    // constant.

      const Box B2;
      B2.showBox(); // Invokes the constant version because b2 is a constant.
   }
```

Although both versions of *showBox( )* have the same signatures (no arguments), they are different, and there is no ambiguity, because one is *const* and the other is not. Rules for overloading member functions allow for constant and nonconstant variants with the same name and signature. When both variants are present, constant *Box*es automatically access the *const* version and nonconstant *Box*es access the nonconstant version. When there is no nonconstant version, nonconstant *Box*es are given access to the constant version. However, constant versions of all functions to be used by constant objects must be provided because constant objects may not access nonconstant functions.

Here is a summary of the rules applying to constant member functions.

- A *const* member function cannot modify the accessing object's data members.

- A *const* member function cannot call non*const* member functions.

- Although *const* objects cannot access non*const* member functions, *nonconst* objects can access *const* functions.

- There are no special restrictions on a *const* function's return type or arguments.

- The *const* declaration (i.e., the keyword) is not used with constructors or the destructor (they are allowed to assign to the data members of *const* objects).

- In declaring and defining *const* functions, the keyword *const* must be used in all references to the function, in the prototype (if there is one) and in the declarator that accompanies the function body.

- A *const* member function can be overloaded with a non*const* member function having the same signature so that the same call will perform different actions for *const* and non*const* objects.

- A *const* object's *static* data members can be modified (because these are actually variables shared by all the objects of the class).

- Although the values of the pointer data members belonging to a *const* object cannot be modified what is pointed to can be.

Constant Objects in Free Functions

Constant objects may be defined within or passed to any free function for which the class is in scope. The same kinds of restrictions governing their use apply: *public* data members, although accessible for reading, may not be changed; only *const* member functions may be accessed; and argument passing by reference is to a formal argument specified as *const*. If the constant object is passed by reference the formal argument must have a *const* specifier.

4.3   Manipulating Abstractions: Friends and Operator Overloading

Introduction

Once there are classes and objects, their power as abstractions is greatly enhanced if they can be manipulated in the same way as atomic data types. Friend functions and operator overloading make this possible. The dichotomy between the *public* and *private* accessibility status is strong. If a function, *functionX( )*, needs to access *private* function members within two or more classes as well as *private* data members for which no *get* or *set* facilities are provided, respecifying as *public* is possible but may be not desirable. Making *functionX( )* a member of each class might seem a better idea, but it is not technically possible. Inside *class ClassOne* it is really *ClassOne::functionX( )*. Inside *class ClassTwo* it is really *ClassTwo::functionX( )*. These are two different functions, not one. But there is a way. A function from *ClassTwo* or a free function can be declared to be a *friend* by *ClassOne*; this gives the friend the same access to *ClassOne's private* members that its native member functions have.

Put in more general terms, within the class specifier particular free functions, functions that are members of other classes, or other whole classes can be allowed to access the *private* members of a class. This special entitlement is conferred through a citation of the nonmember function or the other class as a *friend*. Friend functions are a way to manipulate different kinds of objects in similar ways.

Consider a different need. In the arithmetic expression $a + b$, there is one operator, the plus, and two operands, the a and the b. The operands might be integers, floats, or even characters. But can they be *Box* objects, or could one be a *Box* and the other either of a language-provided data type (e.g., an *int*) or an object of a different class? This is possible through operator overloading. One of the unique features of C++ is that it allows almost all the language's operators to assume meaning for user-defined objects. This is what is meant by operator overloading, and it is used by viewing an operator as a function. The name of the + function is *operator+( )*. Here *operator* is the keyword designating that the function pertains to the action of an operator. The signature of a free function or a member function determines which of the versions is referenced; that is the case for operator. The data type of the accessing object or of its arguments decides which operator function is used.

An *operator* function having one operand from one class, say, *ClassOne*, and a second operand from a different class, say, *ClassTwo*, may require access to the *private* data or function members of both. If provided as a member function of *ClassOne*, it may be declared as a *friend* within *ClassTwo*. If provided as a member function of *ClassTwo*, it may be declared as a *friend* within *ClassOne*. If provided as a free function, it may be declared as a *friend* within both *ClassOne* and *ClassTwo*. Although these choices each imply somewhat different properties of the operator's action, each enables the *operator* function to access the private sectors of both classes. For example, overloading the inserter (the output operator, <<) so that a statement such as the following works with *Box* objects,

```
cout << "box1: " << box1 << endl;   // Box object displayed with <<
```

requires *friend*ship.

Although most operators (e.g., the arithmetic operators and the relational operators) have no meaning for user-defined objects until their interpretation is given by an explicit *operator* function, certain ones do. Among these are the *sizeof* operator, the *address of* operator &, the *indirection* operator *, the *subscript* operator, [ ], for accessing elements of arrays, *new* and *delete*, and the *assignment operator* =.

The assignment operator requires special consideration for the following reasons. One is that its default action, that of making a bitwise (or shallow) copy of the operand on the right into the operand on the left, may not be appropriate for objects that contain pointers to data. A bitwise copy results in the left operand's pointers holding the same addresses as the right operand's pointers, therefore referencing the identical structures and creating a dependency. A different kind of copy is a conceptual (or deep) copy. The object on the left gets a pointer to newly allocated memory into which has been copied the information from the right object. When the proper action for the assignment operator is a conceptual copy, an *operator=( )* function must be provided giving instructions for everything that is to be done. The explicit function overrides the default.

The second reason the assignment operator requires special consideration is because of its action on different classes of objects and datatypes. When assignment is used between two types, it implicitly contributes a data conversion function. Data conversion is entirely different from making either a bitwise or a conceptual copy of one item into another item of the same type. The coded function must do the conversion as required. The mechanisms for data conversion, and their properties, are considered in this section as these relate to operator overloading.

Friend *Function and* Friend *Classes*

To illustrate the ideas and syntax of friendship, consider these three classes, each of which are identical except for their names and the name of their data member:

```
class A                      class B                      class C
{                            {                            {
   private:                     private:                     private:
      int a;                       int b;                       int c;
   public:                      public:                      public:
      A(int x): a(x)               B(int x): b(x)               C(int x): c(x)
      {                            {                            {
      }                            }                            }
      int getIt()                  int getIt()                  int getIt()
      {                            {                            {
         return a;                    return b;                    return c;
      }                            }                            }
   private:                     private:                     private:
      void doubleIt()              void doubleIt()              void doubleIt()
      {                            {                            {
         a *= 2;                      b *= 2;                      c *= 2;
      }                            }                            }
};                           };                           };
```

Suppose that a free function is needed that squares the data members of an *A* object, a *B* object, and a *C* object each of which is passed by reference.

```
void squareThem(A& aObject, B& bObject, C& cObject)
```

```
        {
          aObject.a = aObject.a * aObject.a;
          bObject.b = bObject.b * bObject.b;
          cObject.c = cObject.c * cObject.c;
        }
```

Notice that this is a perfectly ordinary function and if these data members were *public* instead of private it would work uneventfully. However, being *private* the data members are not accessible within nonmember functions.

If class *A* confers friendship to *squareThem( )*, class *A*'s *private* data and *private* functions will be accessible. This will not make it possible for *squareThem( )* to access the *private* data and functions of other classes, notably *B*'s and *C*'s. But it is possible for a function to be a *friend* of multiple classes, and both class *B* and class *C* may confer friendship. All that needs to be done is to include the prototype of the function to be befriended within the specifier of the classes. To stipulate that the befriended function is a *friend* and not a member, the keyword *friend* is placed to the left of the prototype, before the return type specifier. Unlike a member function, a *friend* is not (and cannot be) accessed by an object of the befriending class. There is no notation within the definition of the befriended function to reflect that friendship was conferred. In other words, there is no change in *squareThem( )*. The *friend* specifier only accompanies the declarator within the class or classes that are actually making it a *friend*. Because the *friend*s of a class are not members of a class, it makes no difference whether their declaration has a *public* or a *private* specifier because this qualification does not apply to them. By convention, declarations of friendship are usually at the top of the class specifier. Here is a program that shows these ideas.

```
#include <iostream.h>
```

```
Class declarations, so that the references to class B and to class C
along squareThem()'s argument list are not unknown commodities within
the declaration inside class A,  and so that the reference to class C
within squareThem()'s prototype is accepted inside class B.
```

```
class B;
class C;

class A
    {
```

```
        friend void squareThem(A& aObject, B& bObject, C& cObject);

    private:
      int a;

    public:
      A(int x): a(x)   // Constructor.
        {
        }

      int getIt()
        {
          return a;
        }

    private:
      void doubleIt()
        {
          a *= 2;
        }
  };
```

Both *class B* and *class C* have yet to be defined; this is why their declarations above are necessary.

Class C is not yet defined, but this is okay because it has been declared.

```
class B
  {
      friend void squareThem(A& aObject, B& bObject, C& cObject);

    private:
      int b;

    public:
      B(int x): b(x)   // Constructor.
        {
        }

      int getIt()
        {
          return b;
        }

    private:
      void doubleIt()
        {
          b *= 2;
        }
  };

class C
  {
      friend void squareThem(A& aObject, B& bObject, C& cObject);
```

```
    private:
      int c;

    // Details omitted.

  };

void squareThem(A& aObject, B& bObject, C& cObject)
  {
    aObject.a = aObject.a * aObject.a;
    bObject.b = bObject.b * bObject.b;
    cObject.c = cObject.c * cObject.c;
  }

void main()
  {
    A   a_object(5);
    B   b_object(6);
    C   c_object(7);

    squareThem( a_object, b_object, c_object );

    cout << "\nThe a_object was 5, now it is " << a_object.getIt();
    cout << "\nThe b_object was 6, now it is " << b_object.getIt();
    cout << "\nThe c_object was 7, now it is " << c_object.getIt();
    cout << endl;
  }
```

Suppose that *class A* is enhanced with a member function that defines objects from the other two classes and needs to double them.

```
//             The New Member Function to be Installed in Class A
// *This, the accessing object, is an A object whose data member is an int
// named a.

void doubling(int numberOfMultiples)
  {
    B b_object( a*a ); // Get a B object initialized to a squared.
    C c_object(a*a*a); // Get a C object initialized to a cubed.

    for (int i = 1; i < numberOfMultiples; i++)
      {
        doubleIt();      // Doubles the data member of the accessing class A
                         // object.
        b_object.doubleIt();   // B::doubleIt() is private.
        c_object.doubleIt();   // C::doubleIt() is private.
      }

    cout << "\n a = " << a;
    cout << "\n b_object.b = " << b_object.b; // The b_object.b is a private
                                              // data member.
```

```
        cout << "\n c_object.getIt() = " << c_object.getIt();

        cout << "\n total = " << a + b_object.b + c_object.getIt() << endl;
    }
```

This might make a perfectly good member function in class *A*, provided that classes *B* and *C* were within scope (which they are because of their forward declarations), except that it attempts to access *private* members of classes: *B::doubleIt( )*, *C::doubleIt( )*, and *b_object.b*. The *private* specifier means that their accessibility is confined to member or friend functions of their own classes. Friendship can be conferred to member functions of different classes just as it can be to free functions. Thus if *A::doubling( )* is declared by *class B* and *class C* to be a *friend*, it will be able to access both classes' data and function members. This is true whether *A::doubling( )* is *public* or *private*.

The only difference in specifying a member function of another class to be a *friend* is that the member function's full name is needed; that is, the name of its class followed by the scope operator must be attached to the left of the function name. This is how *class B* grants friendship to *class A's doubling( )* function.

```
class B
    {
        friend void A::doubling(int numberOfMultiples);
        friend void squareThem(A& aObject, B& bObject, C& cObject);

        private:
          int b;
              .
              .
              .
    };
```

Class C must do the same. Nothing needs to be done to the *doubling( )* function itself. Here is the whole program and the output.

```
#include <iostream.h>

class B;
class C;

class A
  {
    friend void squareThem(A& aObject, B& bObject, C& cObject);

    private:
      int a;

    public:
      A(int x): a(x)   // Constructor.
        {
        }
```

```
    int getIt()
     {
       return a;
     }

    void doubling(int numberOfMultiples)
     {
       B b_object( a*a ); // Get a B object initialized to a squared.
       C c_object(a*a*a); // Get a C object initialized to a cubed.

       for (int i = 1; i < numberOfMultiples; i++)
         {
           doubleIt(); // Doubles the data member of the accessing class A
                       // object.
           b_object.doubleIt();  // B::doubleIt() is private.
           c_object.doubleIt();  // C::doubleIt() is private.
         }

       cout << "\n a = " << a;
       cout << "\n b_object.b = " << b_object.b;  // The b_object.b is
                                                  // private.
       cout << "\n c_object.getIt() = " <<  c_object.getIt();

       cout << "\n total = " << a + b_object.b + c_object.getIt() << endl;
     }

  private:
    void doubleIt()
       {
         a *= 2;
       }
};

class B
  {
    friend void A::doubling(int numberOfMultiples);
    friend void squareThem(A& aObject, B& bObject, C& cObject);

    private:
      int b;

    public:
      B(int x): b(x)  // Constructor.
       {
       }

      int getIt()
       {
         return b;
       }
```

```
     private:
       void doubleIt()
         {
           b *= 2;
         }
};

class C
  {
    friend void squareThem(A&, B&, C&);   // Notice:   names of formal arguments
    friend void A::doubling(int);         //           do not have to appear.

    private:
      int c;

    // Details omitted -- they're the same as in the other two classes.

  };

void squareThem(A& aObject, B& bObject, C& cObject)
  {
    aObject.a = aObject.a * aObject.a;
    bObject.b = bObject.b * bObject.b;
    cObject.c = cObject.c * cObject.c;
  }

void main()
  {
    A   a_object(5);
    B   b_object(6);
    C   c_object(7);

    squareThem( a_object, b_object, c_object );

    cout << "\nThe a_object was 5, now it is " << a_object.getIt();
    cout << "\nThe b_object was 6, now it is " << b_object.getIt();
    cout << "\nThe c_object was 7, now it is " << c_object.getIt();
    cout << endl;

    A   another_a(3);        // Defining another instantiation of class A
    another_a.doubling(1);   // another_a invokes its member function
                             // doubling().
  }
```

Here is the output.

```
The a_object was 5, now it is 25
The b_object was 6, now it is 36
The c_object was 7, now it is 49
```

```
              a = 3
              b_object.b = 9
              c_object.getIt() = 27
              total = 39
```

Suppose that *class A* had more than one member function that accessed *private* data or function members of *class B*. Friendship to each of them individually can be conferred by *class B*. An alternative approach is to befriend all of *class A's* member functions with one specification, by declaring *class A* itself to be a *friend*.

```
class B
   {
      friend class A;   // This confers friendship to each and every function
                        // that is a member of class A.

      friend void squareThem(A& aObject, B& bObject, C& cObject);

      private:
        int b;
           .
           .
           .
   }
```

This confers accessibility to all of *class B's* private sectors including every member function currently within *class A* and any that may be added to *class A* in the future.

Operator Overloading

The idea of operator overloading is already familiar. The division operator, /, performs division in one way for *int*s and in another way when either the numerator object or the denominator object (or both) is a *float*. Thus there are two distinct meanings, and the correct one is chosen based upon the context of the application. Because it has more than one implementation, the operator / is said to be overloaded.

In C++, operators may be enriched with additional meanings so that they apply in some appropriate way to objects of the programmer's own design. For example, consider a class called *String*. The + operator can be overloaded so that if *stringObject1* were "Hello" and *stringObject2* were "World", *stringObject1 + stringObject2* gives the concatenation, "Hello World". Consider a class called *Point* in which each object is a point on a set of Cartesian coordinates. The + operator may be given the meanings such that it adds two *Point* objects:

```
    (a,b)  +  (c,d)  -->  (a+c,  b+d)
```

and allows an *int* to be added to a *Point* or vice versa:

```
5   + (c,d) --> (c+5, d+5)    // A deliberately unconventional
                              // interpretation of addition
(a,b) +   5    --> (a+5, b+5)    // relative to real and complex numbers.
```

Within one program, the + operator might sum numbers, concatenate *String*s, add *Point*s, add *Point*s to *int*s, and signify as many other different operations for objects of user-defined classes as the programmer wants to define.

The technique for defining special meanings to an operator is to write one function for each special meaning. The name of such a function is the keyword *operator* followed by the operator being overloaded. For the + operator, the name of the function is *operator+( )*. (C++ allows a space between the keyword *operator* and the operator; the space makes the operator stand out and easier to see.) Different versions of *operator+( )* are differentiated by their location and their signature, just as overloaded functions are. Functions that overload an operator may be either member functions of a class or free functions. The significance of the fact that *new* is an operator in C++, and not a function, or that the chevrons for output (<<) and input (>>) are operators, is that they can be overloaded to work with any programmer-defined objects.

A Demonstration

For the sake of demonstration, consider the following *Point* class. It has two *public* data members, *x* for the point's abscissa and *y* for its ordinate, and three function members: two constructors that perform data member initializations and a function for displaying an accessing *Point* object, *showPt( )*.

```
class Point
  {
    public:
       int x, y;

    public:
       Point() : x(0), y(0)   // No argument constructor.
         {
         }

       Point(int forX, int forY) : x(forX), y(forY)
         {
         }

       void showPt()
         {
            cout << " (" << x << ", " << y << ") ";
         }
  };
```

Suppose there is a free function that adds two *Point*s and displays their sum.

```
void  showSum  (Point leftPt, Point rightPt)
  {
    Point  sumPt;                          // Temp Point to hold the sum.
```

```
    sumPt.x = leftPt.x + rightPt.x;    // Compute sum of the two abscissas.
    sumPt.y = leftPt.y + rightPt.y;    // Compute sum of the two ordinates.
    sumPt.showPt();                    // Display the resulting Point.
}
```

This function can access the *x* and *y* data members of any *Point* because they are *public*. If the following code appears in *main( )*,

```
Point p1(1,2), p2(3,4); // Two Points are defined and initialized.
cout << endl;
showSum(p1, p2);        // Free function, showSum() displays the sum, p1 + p2
cout << " = ";          //        Note that p1 is the left operand
p1.showPt();            //        and  that p2 is the right operand.
cout << "+"
p2.showPt();
cout << endl;
```

This is the output.

$$(4, 6) = (1, 2) + (3, 4)$$

In the following examples, the same functionality in *showSum( )* is embodied in an overloaded addition operator.

```
void  operator+  (Point leftPt, Point rightPt)
  {
    Point  sumPt;                      // Temp Point to hold the sum.
    sumPt.x = leftPt.x + rightPt.x;    // Compute sum of the two abscissas.
    sumPt.y = leftPt.y + rightPt.y;    // Compute sum of the two ordinates.
    sumPt.showPt();                    // Display the resulting Point.
  }
```

And here is a corresponding fragment of code that uses it and presents the same display.

```
p1 + p2;         // The free function, operator+() displays the sum, p1 + p2.
cout << " = "; //        Note that p1 is the left operand
p1.showPt();   //        and  that p2 is the right operand.
cout << "+"
p2.showPt();
cout << endl;
```

Not only are the function bodies of *showSum( )* and *operator+( )* identical, but parameter transmission to an operator function works in accordance with all the same rules as parameter transmission to any function.

```
            showSum(p1, p2);
            /              \
        passed          passed
          to              to
          ↓                ↘
  void showSum(Point leftPoint, Point rightPoint)
```

The alternative is a call to *operator+( )*:

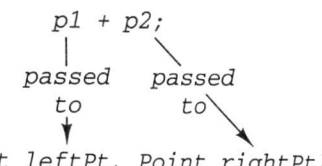

```
void  operator+ (Point leftPt, Point rightPt)
```

In fact, the *operator+( )* function could have been invoked in the traditional manner as well,

```
operator+( p1, p2 );
```

which is the same as

```
p1 + p2;
```

Naming a function with the keyword operator followed by an operator does nothing but provide the ability to call the function in a symbolically concise way.

As previously given, the function *operator+( )* is poorly written. Adding two operands should return the sum, not print it. The sum may be needed as a term within an expression, or it may be assigned to a variable (or an object). The upgrade is easy. In the function declarator, designate that a *Point* will be returned; and, once the sum is ready, return it:

```
Point  operator+  (Point leftPt, Point rightPt)
  {
    Point sumPt;
    sumPt.x = leftPt.x + rightPt.x;
    sumPt.y = leftPt.y + rightPt.y;
    return sumPt;
  }
```

Given the creation of *Points p1, p2, p3*, and *p4*, this function permits the coding of expressions such as

```
p3 = p1 + p2;  // Point p3 is assigned the sum returned by adding p1
               // and p2.
```

and

```
p4 = p1 + p2 + p3;  // The sum returned by adding p1 and p2 is added to
                    // p3.
```

Both the *operator+( )* functions given (the one that returns a *Point* and the one that does not) cannot coexist within the same program because they have the same signature. But either one can coexist with the following two mutually agreeable functions. The function on the left overloads the + operator so that a *Point* may be added to an *int*; the function on the right overloads the + operator so that an *int* may be added to a *Point*.

```
Point  operator+  (Point pt, int i)          Point  operator+  (int i, Point pt)
  {                                             {
    Point sumPt;                                  Point sumPt;
    sumPt.x = pt.x + i;                           sumPt.x = pt.x + i;
    sumPt.y = pt.y + i;                           sumPt.y = pt.y + i;
    return sumPt;                                 return sumPt;
  }                                             }
```

This allows expressions such as: This allows expressions such as:
    p2 = p1 + 5;   p2 = 5 + p1;

If the operation of adding *Point*s and *int*s is to be commutative, both functions are needed. A function call whose first argument is a *Point* and whose second argument is an *int* designates a function with a *(Point, int)* signature. On the other hand, a function call whose first argument is an *int* and whose second argument is a *Point* designates a function with an *(int, Point)* signature. In C++, these are distinctly different.

Operator Access to Private Data

These functions are free functions, not members of the *Point* class, so they can only access a *Point* object's *x* and *y* data members when they are *public*. Most often, there is good reason to specify a class's data members as *private*. How can these *operator+( )* functions work when *x* and *y* are *private*? The answer is to have the *Point* class declare them to be *friend*s. This is done by putting the following three lines within the *Point* class specifier, one for each version of *operator+( )* to which friendship is being conferred.

```
┌──────────────┐                    ┌──────────────────────────────┐
│ the keyword  │                    │ standard function prototypes │
│   friend     │                    └──────────────────────────────┘
└──────────────┘                                   │
        │                                           ▼
        ▼           ┌─────────────────────────────────────────────
    friend  Point  operator+  (Point leftPt, Point rightPt);
    friend  Point  operator+  (Point pt, int i);
    friend  Point  operator+  (int i, Point pt);
```

Being named as a *friend* by the *Point* class does not change these functions. No modifications in their declarators or bodies are needed; and they have not, as a result of the friendship, become member functions of the *Point* class. Everything is just as it had been, except that access to the private sectors of the *Point* class, within these designated functions, is now enabled. This is how *Point*'s specifier might appear.

```
class Point
  {
      friend  Point  operator+  (Point leftPt, Point rightPt);
      friend  Point  operator+  (Point pt, int i);
      friend  Point  operator+  (int i, Point pt);

      private:
          int x, y;
```

```
        public:
            Point() : x(0), y(0)   // No argument constructor.
            {
            }

            Point(int forX, int forY) : x(forX), y(forY)
            {
            }

            void showPt()
            {
                cout << " (" << x << ", " << y << ") ";
            }
    };
```

Another approach to enabling access to x and y when they are private is to install the *operator+( )* functions as members. As member functions there are some differences. The left operand arrives as the function's accessing object; the right operand arrives as the function's argument.

```
class Point
  {
    private:
       int x, y;

    public:
       Point() : x(0), y(0)   // No-argument constructor.
          {
          }

       Point(int forX, int forY) : x(forX), y(forY)
          {
          }

       void showPt()
          {
             cout << " (" << x << ", " << y << ") ";
          }

       Point operator+ (Point rightPt) // Makes possible:  pt1 = pt2 + pt3.
          {
             Point sumPt;
             sumPt.x = x + rightPt.x;     // Here x is the x of the invoking Point,
                                          // pt2
             sumPt.y = y + rightPt.y;     // Here y is the y of the invoking Point,
                                          // pt2.
             return sumPt;
          }

       Point operator+ (int i)           // Makes possible:  pt1 = pt2 + 5.
```

```
    {
      Point sumPt;
      sumPt.x = x + i;              // Here x  is the x of the invoking Point,
                                    // pt2.
      sumPt.y = y + i;             // Here y  is the y of the invoking Point,
                                    // pt2.
      return sumPt;
    }
  };
```

Consider the *operator+( )* function for adding two *Point*s.

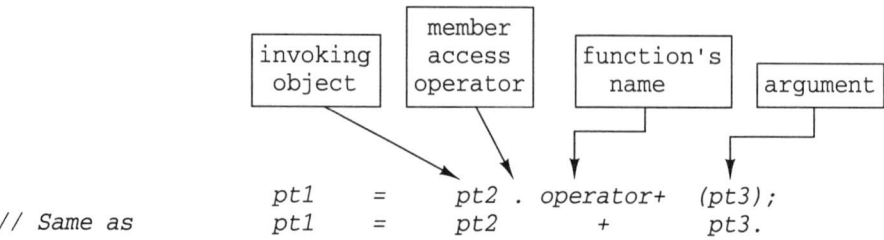

```
Point    operator+ (Point rightPoint) //     leftPt.operator+(rightPt)
  {                                    // and
    Point sumPt;                       //             leftPt + rightPt
    sum.x = x + rightPoint.x;          // are identical in meaning
    sum.y = y + rightPoint.y:          // and actual performance.
                                       //
    return sumPt;                      // The "leftPt" operand is the
  }                                    // class instance which accessed
                                       // the operator.
```

When used as in *pt1 = pt2 + p3*, *pt2* is the *accessing* object and *pt3* is the argument passed to *rightPoint*. The object returned is that to which the addition operation resolves. The returned *Point, sumPt*, is copied into *pt1*. Just as when the *operator+( )* is a free function, it may be invoked by an arithmetic expression involving the + or with the syntax applying to member functions. These two invocations evoke the identical computation:

```
               pt1    =    pt2 . operator+   (pt3);
// Same as     pt1    =    pt2      +          pt3.
```

The situation is the same for the *operator+( )* member function which is accessed by a *Point* and takes as its argument an *int*. But there is no way to install the version where the *int* is on the left as a member function. The left operand is construed by C++ as the accessing object, and only an object of type *Point* can access a member function of the *Point* class.

Overloading the Insertion and Extraction Operators

The use of *cout* to display string literals, *int*s, *float*s, individual *char*s, and *string* variables is familiar:

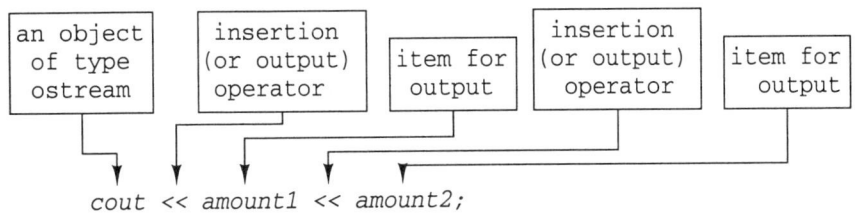

```
cout << amount1 << amount2;
```

Moreover, "tagging" specific devices (e.g., the printer) or files for output and managing them similarly is straightforward:

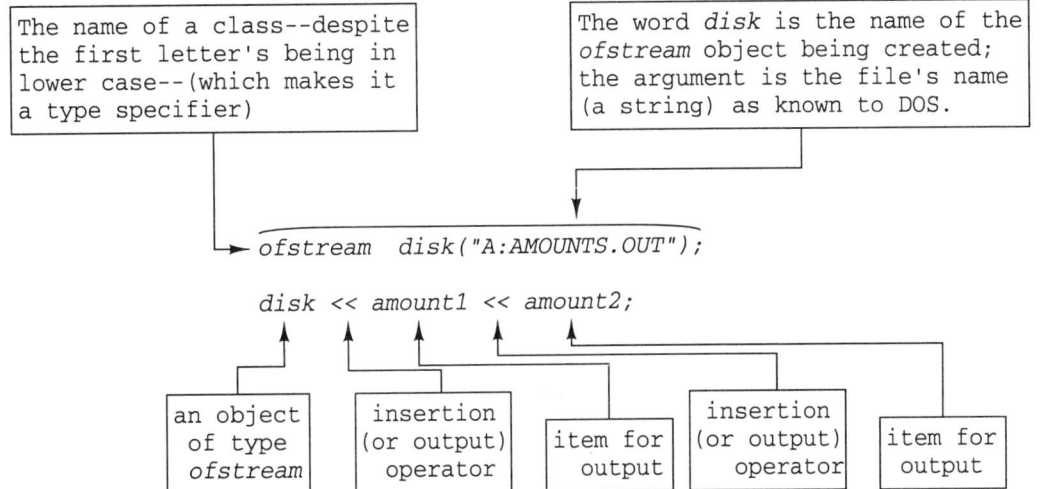

Here is a look-ahead to Section 4.4, on class derivation, in order to clarify the relationship between the *ofstream* ("output file stream") class and the *ostream* ("output stream") class. Because the *ofstream* class is derived from the *ostream* class, every object of type *ofstream* is also of type *ostream*. This means that wherever an *ostream* object may appear, so may an *ofstream* object. An *ofstream* object is an *ostream* object.

For extraction, the *ifstream* ("input file stream") class is derived from the *istream* ("input stream") class. Therefore every instantiation of the *ifstream* class is likewise an instantiation of the *istream* class. In any expression where an *istream* object may appear, so may an *ifstream* object. An *ifstream* object is an *istream* object.

Just as *disk* is declared to be an *ofstream* object and tied to the file on diskette "A:AMOUNTS.OUT", the *iostream.h* header file (and the *fstream.h* header file) defines *cout* as an *ostream* object and ties it to the computer system's "standard output device." In C++, the insertion operator <<, is a binary operator that has as its left operand an *ostream* object and takes as its right operand an object of any data type for which an *operator<<( )* function has been defined. The *ostream* class overloads the inserter with several different versions for which the right operand is an *int*, a *float*, a *char*, a *long*, a *double*, and so on (there are fifteen of these).

With the definition of the *Point* class, *Point* becomes a data type specifier. *Point* as a type specifier is used to declare *Point* objects and is used within function declarators to prescribe the data type of formal arguments. *Point* may therefore be used as a formal argument in functions overloading the inserter. Just as a free function version of *operator+( )* whose left operand was a *Point* and whose right operand was also a *Point* was defined as follows,

```
void  operator+  (Point leftPt, Point rightPt)
  {
    Point  sumPt;                  // Temp Point to hold the sum.
    sumPt.x = leftPt.x + rightPt.x;  // Compute sum of the two abscissas.
    sumPt.y = leftPt.y + rightPt.y;  // Compute sum of the two ordinates.
    sumPt.showPt();                // Display the resulting Point.
  }
```

so can a free function version of *operator<<( )* be defined whose left operand is an *ostream* object and whose right operand is a *Point*.

> The *ostream* object
> has to be passed by reference
> because its copy constructor
> is, by design, inaccessible.

```
void  operator<< (ostream& outputObject, Point pointObject)
  {
    outputObject << " (" << pointObject.x << ", " <<pointObject.y << ") ";
  }
```

A superficial inspection of the *operator<<( )* function may lead to an observation that is at first confusing: the insertion operator is being used within the function to set forth its own definition. In fact, the output of a *Point* is given in terms of the output of string literals (e.g., "(") and integers (e.g., *pointObject.x* is an *int*), which are fundamental operations that have already been defined (using functions in the standard library and incorporated in the program when *iostream.h* or *fstream.h* are *# include*d). Notice that the definition of *operator+( )* for adding two *Points* also makes use of the more primitive + operator upon integers. There is nothing paradoxical or even recursive here. It is simply a case of one function using the services of another function to accomplish the task. The two operators have the same name but different signatures.

Recall that copy constructors mediate the transmission of objects passed by value to and from functions. Like all constructors, copy constructors are member functions within a class and like all member functions, their access status may or may not be *public*. For the preceding function *operator<<( )*, the default copy constructor in the *Point* class creates the *Point* object that is bound to the formal argument *pointObject*. In theory, if the *ostream* object were passed by value, the copy constructor within the *ostream* class would create a new object and bind it to *outputObject*. Because the *ostream* class specifies its copy constructor *private*, however, it is inaccessible. This means that it is not possible to write a function to which an *ostream* object is passed by value. But it can be passed by reference so that the formal argument becomes another name for the argument, with no copy.

The *operator<<( )* function shown has two deficiencies. It does not support the cascading of further operators and arguments to the right of the *Point*'s output. In other words, in *main( )* for two existing *Points, p1* and *p2*,

this would work:

```
cout << "p1 =" << p1;
```

but this would not:

```
cout << "p1 =" << p1 << "   and p2 =" << p2;
```

The latter does not work because *operator<<( )* returns void. The first operation, *cout << "p1 ="*, using the standard library function for strings, returns the left operand, which in this case is *cout*. Because it resolves to *cout*, it leaves within the expression another term that is complete and valid, *cout << p1*. The *operator<<( )* performs the output but resolving to *void* leaves the expression with an erroneous term: *void << " and p2 ="*.

The way to get the *operator<<( )* to replace whatever *ostream* object it received as its left operand back into the expression, is to have it return *outputObject*. Because the copy constructor for *ostream* objects is unavailable, the return must be by reference. Thus the enhancement to enable cascading is as follows.

```
ostream&  operator<< (ostream& outputObject, Point pointObject)
  {
    outputObject << " (" << pointObject.x << ", " <<pointObject.y << ") ";
    return outputObject;
  }
```

Another deficiency lies in the function's possible attempt to access data members of *pointObject* that are likely to be *private*, hence inaccessible. One remedy is to get these values by calls to accessor functions. Such accessors would be *public* member functions within the *Point* class such as *getX( )* and *getY( )* that would return the value of the accessing object's *x* and *y* values, respectively.

Another remedy is to have the *Point* class enable the *operator<<( )* function, though it is not a member, to have the access privileges it needs. This is done by declaring the function *operator<<( )* to be a *friend*: putting its prototype, prefaced by the keyword *friend*, inside the *Point* class specifier. No change is required within the function declarator or body. A strategy that is not an option is to install the *operator<<( )* function as a member of the *Point* class. This would mean that its accessing object had to be a *Point*, but the inserter's left operand is always an *ostream*.

Finally, the idiom for the overloaded inserter is to pass the object bound for output by reference. Not having to create a working copy saves some time and some space.

The extractor operator is overloaded in accordance with all the same principles as the inserter. The obvious difference is that an input stream (e.g., *cin* or a file) is an *istream* object, not an *ostream* object. Here is a program demonstrating the correct, complete, and idiomatic incorporation of functions that overload both the insertion operator and the extraction operator with the facility to handle *Point* objects.

```
#include <iostream.h>

class Point
    {
    private:
        int x, y;

    public:
        Point() : x(0), y(0)   // No-argument constructor.
            {
            }

        Point(int forX, int forY) : x(forX), y(forY)
            {
            }

        friend  Point  operator+  (Point leftPt, Point rightPt);
        friend  Point  operator+  (Point pt, int i);
        friend  Point  operator+  (int i, Point pt);

        friend  ostream&  operator<< (ostream& os, Point& pt);
        friend  istream&  operator>> (istream& is, Point& pt);
    };

ostream&  operator<<  (ostream& os, Point& pt)
    {
      os << " (" << pt.x << ", " << pt.y << ") ";
      return os;
    }
```

```
istream&  operator>>  (istream& is, Point& pt)
  {
    cout << endl;

    cout << "value for x:   ";
    is >> pt.x;

    cout << "value for y:   ";
    is >> pt.y;

    return is;
  }

Point  operator+  (Point leftPt, Point rightPt)
  {
    Point sumPt;
    sumPt.x = leftPt.x + rightPt.x;
    sumPt.y = leftPt.y + rightPt.y;
    return sumPt;
  }

Point  operator+  (Point pt, int i)
  {
    Point sumPt;
    sumPt.x = pt.x + i;
    sumPt.y = pt.y + i;
    return sumPt;
  }

Point  operator+  (int i, Point pt)
  {
    Point sumPt;
    sumPt.x = pt.x + i;
    sumPt.y = pt.y + i;
    return sumPt;
  }

void main()
  {
    Point p1, p2;
    cout << endl << "First enter x and y for point 1, then point 2 ...";
    cin >> p1 >> p2;

    Point sum1;
    sum1 = p1 + p2;
    cout << endl << p1 << "+" << p2 << " gives " << sum1 << endl;

    Point sum2;
    sum2 = p1 + 10;
    cout << endl << p1 << "+ 10   gives " << sum2 << endl;
```

```
Point sum3;
sum3 = 100 + p2;
cout << endl << "100 +" << p2 << " gives " << sum3 << endl;
}
```

Here is the output.

```
First enter x and y for point 1, then point 2 ...
value for x:   1
value for y:   2

value for x:   3
value for y:   4

(1, 2) + (3, 4)  gives  (4, 6)

(1, 2) + 10    gives  (11, 12)

100 + (3, 4)  gives  (103, 104)
```

Overloading the Prefix and Postfix Unary Increment and Decrement

Suppose that *Point pt* holds the value (5,6). In the following expression, because the double plus is to the left of the *pt* operand, 1 should be added to *pt* before *pt* is added to 10.

```
sumPt = ++pt + 10;  // A prefix unary increment applied to pt.
```

By the arbitrary understanding of what it means to add an integer to a *Point* that was used previously, executing this statement should result in *pt*'s holding the value (6,7) and in *sumPt*'s holding (16,17). Here is the *operator++( )* that will do the job, shown as a member function of the *Point* class.

```
Point operator++()  // Preincrement -- return an incremented "temp."
  {
    ++x;  // Increment the invoking Point's  x  data member.
    ++y;  // Increment the invoking Point's  y  data member.

    return *this;  // Replaces the invoking point in the ad hoc expression.
  }                // with a copy of itself after its increment.
```

Because changes made to the data members of the accessing object by a member function persist, the increments made to the invoking *Point*'s *x* and *y* are actual updates. The returned *Point* serves as the intermediary holding the result of the operation just performed for the arithmetic expression underway.

To differentiate the implementation of the unary postincrement from the implementation of the preincrement, the signature is changed.

```
The sole purpose of this int data type
             is to provide
the postincrement operator++() function
    with a different signature than
the preincrement operator++() function.
```

```
Point operator++(int)  // Postincrement -- return an unincremented "temp."

    {
      Point  originalPoint;  // These three statements could have been coded
                             // more concisely as shown right below:
      originalPoint.x = x;   //
      originalPoint.y = y;   //        Point  originalPoint = *this.

      x++;  // Increment the invoking Point's  x  data member.
      y++;  // Increment the invoking Point's  y  data member.

      return originalPoint;  // Replaces the invoking point in the ad hoc
                             // expression with a copy of the Point before
    }                        // it was incremented.
```

If this function is a member of the *Point* class, and *Point pt* again holds the value (5,6), *pt's* unincremented value will be added to 10.

```
sumPt = pt++ + 10;  // A postfix unary increment applied to pt.
```

Executing this statement will result in *sumPt's* holding the value (15,16) and in *pt's* holding (6,7).

Both these functions, because their signatures are different, can exist together. The prefix and postfix versions of the unary minus are constructed in the same manner.

Some Operator Overloading Rules

As a rule, an operator defined by C++ for language-provided data types, can be overloaded. A corollary is that for an operator to apply to instances of a class (e.g., the operator <, to *Point* objects), then it must be overloaded. Like all rules, these come with a number of exceptions, complications, and warnings.

Among the small number of operators that cannot be overloaded are the following:

.   The member access operator.

::   The scope resolution operator.

?:   The conditional expression operator.

sizeof The unary operator returning the bytes taken up by a variable, *struct*, or object.

The preprocessor operator (as in *# include<iostream>*).

The last is not actually an operator belonging to C++, as the preprocessor is not, technically, part of the language. No special symbol or set of special symbols (e.g., ##) beyond those already defined by C++ itself can be "overloaded" because they have no meaning in the first place. Also, when overloading, the binary/unary nature of an operator cannot be changed.

Operators That Perform as Expected

A small number of operators apply not only to language-provided data types but to programmer-created objects as well. These are the operators that are so fundamental that their effect is generally expected. One of these is the assignment operator, =. One might assume that for two *Box* objects, *b1* and *b2*, it is possible to code *b2 = b1*, and that the action will copy the value of each of *b1's* data members into the corresponding member of *b2*. This, in fact, is exactly what happens. C++ provides a default assignment operator that works in this way for any defined classes. The following program illustrates the presence and activity of some of these operators that perform as expected.

```
// Applying the following operators to Box objects:
//
//    sizeof,    &,    *,    new,    delete,    .,    ->, and    =.

#include <iostream.h>

class Box
  {
    public:
       char symbol;

    private:
       int length;
       int height;

    public:
       // No-argument constructor.
       Box()
         {
         }

       // Three-argument constructor.
       Box(int l, int h, char s) : length(l), height(h), symbol(s)
         {
         }

       // One-argument constructor, whose argument is an int.
       Box(int sizer) : length(3*sizer), height(sizer), symbol('I')
         {
         }

       // Destructor.
```

```
        ~Box()
          {
            cout << "box with symbol " << symbol << " is deleted." << endl;
          }

        void showBox()
          {
            for (int h = 1; h <= height; h++)
              {
                cout << endl;
                for (int l = 1; l <= length; l++)  cout << symbol;
              }
            cout << endl;
          }
  };

/*  1 */ void main()
/*  2 */   {
/*  3 */     Box box1(1,1,'1'), box2(2,2,'2'), box3(3,3,'3');
/*  4 */
/*  5 */     Box* boxPointer;
/*  6 */
/*  7 */     // Demonstrating the sizeof operator.
/*  8 */     cout << "sizeof box1 = " << sizeof box1 << endl;
/*  9 */
/* 10 */     // Demonstrating the "address of" operator and the indirection
/* 11 */     // operator.
/* 12 */     cout << "&box1 = " << &box1 << endl;
/* 13 */
/* 14 */     boxPointer = &box1;
/* 15 */     (*boxPointer).showBox(); // Dereferencing boxPointer to display box1.
/* 16 */     // This is the same as  boxPointer>showBox().
/* 17 */
/* 18 */     // Demonstrating new and delete.
/* 19 */     boxPointer = new Box(10, 2, 'N');
/* 20 */     boxPointer > showBox();   // This is the same as
/* 21 */                              // (*boxPointer).showBox().
/* 22 */     delete boxPointer;       // Destructs the Box pointed to by
/* 23 */                              // boxPointer.
/* 24 */     // IMPORTANT:  only objects acquired with new
/* 25 */     //             may be destructed using delete.
/* 26 */
/* 27 */
/* 28 */
/* 29 */     Box box4, box5;   // Get two new Boxes.
/* 30 */
/* 31 */     // Assignment operator applied Box objects.
/* 32 */     box4 = box3;
/* 33 */     box5 = box3;
/* 34 */
```

```
/* 35 */        boxPointer = new Box;
/* 36 */        *boxPointer = box3;
/* 37 */
/* 38 */        cout << "\nbox3, at address, " << &box3 << ", is below:";
/* 39 */        box3.showBox();
/* 40 */
/* 41 */        cout << "\nbox4, at address, " << &box4 << ", is below:";
/* 42 */        box4.showBox();
/* 43 */
/* 44 */        cout << "\nbox5, at address, " << &box5 << ", is below:";
/* 45 */        box5.showBox();
/* 46 */
/* 47 */        cout << "\nthe box pointed to by boxPointer, at address "
/* 48 */             << boxPointer << ", is below:";
/* 49 */        (*boxPointer).showBox();                 // Dereferencing.
/* 50 */        box3 = 3;  // Assignment of an int to a Box exemplifies conversion by
/* 51 */        box4 = 4;  // constructor.  Box(int) is invoked implicitly.
/* 52 */        box5 = 5.5;            // The float is converted by C++ to an int and
/* 53 */        *boxPointer = 6.6;    // Box(int) converts this to a Box.
/* 54 */
/* 55 */        cout << "\n\nbox3, at address, " << &box3 << ", is below:";
/* 56 */        box3.showBox();
/* 57 */
/* 58 */        cout << "\nbox4, at address, " << &box4 << ", is below:";
/* 59 */        box4.showBox();
/* 60 */
/* 61 */        cout << "\nbox5, at address, " << &box5 << ", is below:";
/* 62 */        box5.showBox();
/* 63 */
/* 64 */        cout << "\nthe box pointed to by boxPointer, at address "
/* 65 */             << boxPointer << " is below:";
/* 66 */        (*boxPointer).showBox();
/* 67 */
/* 68 */        cout << "\n\n*** end of main ***" << endl;
/* 69 */    }
```

Here is the output.

```
sizeof box1 = 5
&box1 = 0x39a2fff0

1

NNNNNNNNNN
NNNNNNNNNN
box with symbol N is deleted.

box3, at address, 0x39a2ffe4, is below:
333
333
```

```
333

box4, at address, 0x39a2ffde, is below:
333
333
333

box5, at address, 0x39a2ffd8, is below:
333
333
333

the box pointed to by boxPointer, at address 0x39a2113c, is below:
333
333
333

box3, at address, 0x39a2ffe4, is below:
IIIIIIIII
IIIIIIIII
IIIIIIIII

box4, at address, 0x39a2ffde, is below:
IIIIIIIIIIII
IIIIIIIIIIII
IIIIIIIIIIII
IIIIIIIIIIII

box5, at address, 0x39a2ffd8, is below:
IIIIIIIIIIIIII
IIIIIIIIIIIIII
IIIIIIIIIIIIII
IIIIIIIIIIIIII
IIIIIIIIIIIIII

the box pointed to by boxPointer, at address 0x39a2113c is below:
IIIIIIIIIIIIIIIII
IIIIIIIIIIIIIIIII
IIIIIIIIIIIIIIIII
IIIIIIIIIIIIIIIII
IIIIIIIIIIIIIIIII
IIIIIIIIIIIIIIIII

*** end of main ***
box with symbol I is deleted.
box with symbol I is deleted.
box with symbol I is deleted.
box with symbol I is deleted.
box with symbol I is deleted.
box with symbol I is deleted.
```

```
box with symbol I is deleted.
box with symbol 2 is deleted.
box with symbol 1 is deleted.
```

The Default Assignment Operator

Lines 32 and 33 show that when the assignment operator is used to copy *box3*, in memory at one location, into *box4* and then into *box5*, which are different *Box*es at different locations, memberwise copies are indeed created. This is verified by the output.

```
/* 31 */      // Assignment operator applied Box objects.
/* 32 */      box4 = box3;
/* 33 */      box5 = box3;
```

Assignment works identically to a *Box* accessed by dereferencing a pointer.

```
/* 36 */      *boxPointer = box3;
```

This shows the default activity of the assignment operator, copying the bits in storage within each data member of the right operand into the corresponding data member of the left operand. Public and *private* data members alike are copied.

One-Argument Copy Constructors for Data Conversions

Something entirely different is going on in lines 50 and 51:

```
/* 50 */   box3 = 3;  // Assignment of an int to a Box exemplifies conversion by
/* 51 */   box4 = 4;  // constructor -- Box(int) is invoked implicitly.
```

This may look like another application of the default assignment operator but it is not, because the right and left operands are of different data types. A function that works by making a member-by-member copy would not work when confronted by arguments without coinciding parts. The code, on both lines, calls for the conversion of an *int* to a *Box*. Should the *height* and *length* both be set equal to the integer on the right? What if this integer is very large (e.g., 12345)? What should be used for the *Box*'s *symbol?* The only way to obtain a conversion that is conceptually suitable is to program it. Accordingly, because it is impossible to find an appropriate default, C++ will call a conversion function that has been provided or flag a compile-time error if it cannot find one.

But what will serve as a conversion function? In the case of converting a language-provided data type (such as an *int*) to a *Box* there are two possibilities: the compiler will look for an overloaded assignment operator as a member of the *Box* class having an (*int*) signature and apply it.

```
void  Box::operator= (int i)
  {
    length = i;     // Here length of left operand, the Box,  is set to i.
    height = i/2;   // Here height of left operand, the Box, is set to i/2.
    symbol = '*';   // Here symbol of left operand, the Box, is set to *.
  }
```

Failing to find this, the compiler will look for a one-argument constructor that creates a *Box* from an *int*. It uses the *int* to the right of the equal sign as the argument to the constructor, declares a new *Box*, and copies it into the *Box* on the left. This is "conversion by constructor," and it is the means used by the program:

```
// One-argument constructor, whose argument is an int.
Box::Box(int sizer) : length(3*sizer), height(sizer), symbol('I')
    {
    }
```

Evidence of the intermediary *Box*es may be inferred from the number of *Box*es disengaged by the destructor. Notice that the dynamically allocated *Box* created on line 32 is never *delete*d; this is the *Box* that the destructor does not meet. Above all, observe that conversion by constructor does not replace the *Box* given as the left operand by a new *Box*. That *box3* and *box4* continue to reside at their same locations in memory before and after the type conversions and assignments demonstrates that they are the same *Box*es.

Lines 52 and 53 do similar data conversions of a language-provided type to a user-defined object.

```
/* 52 */ box5 = 5.5;         // The float is converted by C++ to an int and
/* 53 */  *boxPointer = 6.6;  // Box(int) converts this to a Box.
```

The difference is that the conversion is from a *float*, and the program supplies neither an implementation of the operator = (*Box::operator= (float flo);*) nor a one-argument constructor (*Box::Box(float flo);*) with exactly the right signature. Not having a tool of choice, C++ applies the *float* to *int* conversion. Then it enters the resulting *int* for conversion to a *Box* using the *Box(int)* constructor.

Had the program contained a line prescribing an implicit conversion from *char* to *Box*:

```
box3 = 'A';
```

the compiler would have used its predefined standard conversion to transform the character 'A' to the integer 65 (which is its ASCII value) in order to reach the only available route from *char* to *Box*, the *Box(int)* constructor. To get a small box whose symbol was an 'A', the method would be to furnish the *Box* class with either an explicit conversion function in the form of

Box::operator=(char) or an implicit conversion mechanism in the form of the single-argument constructor *Box(char)*.

Resolution of Assignment for Participation in an Expression

The assignment operation, as different from conversion, always involves operands of the same data type. The action of the default assignment operator is evoked within statements such as following.

```
/* statement 1 */    boxB = boxA;
/* statement 2 */    box3 = box2 = box1;   // Mu  iple assignment.
```

Recall that *Boxes* have three data members: *length* and *height*, which are both *ints*, and a *symbol*, which is a *char*. In statement 1, the value of the *length* member of *boxA* is assigned, or copied, into the *length* member of *boxB*. Because *length* is an *int*, this is performed by the language-provided assignment operator. The same is done for *height*. The value of the *height* member of *boxA*, is replicated as the value of the *height* member of *boxB*. Similarly the value of *boxA.symbol* is copied into *boxB.symbol*. The work would be done by the language-provided assignment operator. The default assignment operator for *Boxes* results in a bitwise copy in the left operand *Box* of the right operand *Box*. Here is how this function, as described, may be coded:

```
// This is a member of the Box class.  The Box on the left of the
// assignment operator is the accessing object; the box on the
// right enters the function as its argument.  Single assignments
// as in statement 1 will be properly performed, but this function
// fails when applied to expressions with multiple assignments as
// in statement 2.

void Box::operator= (Box rightOperand)
  {
    length = rightOperand.length;   // Uses assignment for ints.
    height = rightOperand.height;   // Uses assignment for ints.
    symbol = rightOperand.symbol;   // Uses assignment for chars.
  }
```

Several things can be noted. First, it will successfully execute the assignment denoted by statement 1 but not by statement 2. Second, if this function is explicitly coded as a member of the *Box* class, it, not the default, is invoked to perform assignments of one *Box* object to another. Explicitly written routines always override defaults. Third, any other or any alternate processing can be included within the function. Finally, *operator=( )* functions must be situated as member functions; C++ would flag a compile-time error if the function had been installed as a free function. Member functions may be defined in full within the class specifier, or they may be declared with a prototype within the specifier and defined at some further point. The given function is a definition lying beyond the specifier. The scope operator identifies it as a member of the *Box* class. Thus it must have had a prototype within the specifier.

```
class Box
```

```
{
    :
    :
public:
    void operator=(Box rightOperand); // Prototype.
    :
    :
};
```

Statement 2 is intended to show that the default assignment operator that C++ gives to user-defined classes has the same facility for multiple assignment as the assignment operator for language-provided types. C++ views assignment as an expression, like $a + b$, that resolves to something that may subsequently be used. The computed sum of $a + b$ may be part of a larger arithmetic expression (e.g., $(a + b) * (c - d)$), it may be displayed ($cout<<a + b;$), or it may be assigned ($x = a + b;$). All this works because the place where $a + b$ stood is filled by a temporary variable holding the sum, which is able to participate as a term in an embedding expression. The result to which $m = n$ resolves is the value of n. Likewise, the result to which $box2 = box1$ resolves should be the value of $box1$. Resolution to a value is what makes multiple assignment possible. The function $operator=(\ )$ will support multiple assignment, such as in statement 2, if it returns the right operand.

```
Box Box::operator= (Box rightOperand)
{
    // Copy of data members of right operand into the
    // data members of the accessing object, which is
    // the left operand in the assignment expression:

    length = rightOperand.length;  // Uses assignment for ints.
    height = rightOperand.height;  // Uses assignment for ints.
    symbol = rightOperand.symbol;  // Uses assignment for chars.

    // Return the right operand so that the assignment
    // expression being managed resolves to a Box for
    // subsequent use in an embedding expression:

    return rightOperand;   // Just as good would be:  return *this.
}
```

It gives what is called a shallow copy. This now works exactly like the default assignment operator for *Box*es that C++ provides.

Overloading Assignment for Deep Copies

Bitwise or shallow copies may be just what is needed from the assignment operator. For *Box*es it certainly is. But it may not be what is needed for objects that contain a pointer to a dynamically allocated storage structure. This structure could be a stack, a queue, or a tree; or it could be any object or array whose memory was acquired with *new*. The bitwise copy of a variable that holds an address (i.e., a pointer) produces an exact replication of the address.

When the corresponding data members of two different objects hold the same address, these data members are referencing the same entity. The consequence is that neither object is insulated from the changes that might be made to the entity by the other. This could be desirable if the objects are holding the root of a tree serving as a communal database. Storing information in only one place makes for space efficiency, and not having to duplicate updates leads to better performance.

However, this is unsatisfactory if the respective objects stood are players at different tables in a bridge tournament who begin with the same hand. Suppose that the dealt hand of 13 cards is implemented as a linked list, and a player object stores the list's *head* and *rear*. In setting the "north" player at table two equal to the "north" player at table one, the intent is that the list owned by the table two object be a conceptual copy of the list owned by the table one object. Equivalent cards are on the list, but they should not be the same cards in a physical sense. What one player does with the cards should not affect the other's holdings. To make a conceptual copy, also called a deep copy, requires that the contents of the nodes in the right operand's list be copied into new nodes to form the left operand's list. These lists, should they each be printed before either object starts to play, would show the identical hands. But, stored as two physically distinct sets of nodes, their respective external pointers hold different addresses.

For the assignment operator to make a deep copy, the programmer must write an *operator=( )* function. Although creating a shallow copy treats each data member as a simple bit string, making a deep copy requires an understanding of the object's requirements and data structures. For instance, suppose that two of the data members within an object are pointers. Perhaps the requirements stipulate that the assignment operator construct a deep copy for data pointed to by one but not the other. Or suppose that an object holds the *head* and the *rear* of a linked list, but each node within this list contains, among other things, a pointer to a sublist. An example would be the adjacency list that stores a graph. The logic for making a conceptual copy entails making a conceptual copy of the list within each node. Only the programmer knows to provide the customization that is right for the application.

Beyond the issue of whether a bitwise or a conceptual copy is needed of the data members that are pointers, memory leak must be prevented. Memory leak refers to the loss of available memory for dynamic allocation because of neglecting to ensure the deletion of memory acquired with *new*. For instance, suppose that an object contains the *head* and *rear* of a linked list; call it *object2*. Another instantiation of the same class, call it *object1*, contains the same complement of data members. Assignment is said to be destructive because the information held by the left operand is "overwritten" by the information from the right operand. When the assignment operator makes a simple shallow copy, the action of *object2 = object1*; supplants the bit string that comprises *ob-*

ject2.head with the bit string comprising *object1.head* (and likewise for *rear*). The default assignment operator will not, prior to doing this, step through *object2*'s list to *delete* its *struct*s. Because knowledge of the location of the first node (*object2.head*) has been destroyed, this list becomes an inaccessible mass of memory that now defies reuse or deallocation. It is memory effectively lost for the duration of the program.

The same possibility of a leak from the program's memory exists when a deep copy of *object1*'s list supplants *object2*'s list. The memory resources being replaced within an object no matter how they are being replaced, may first have to be released. This extends to other resources as well. For example, if the object undergoing assignment had been writing a file, it may need to be closed. In general, the distinction between assignment and initialization centers upon the disposition of resources controlled by an object. This is a paramount concern when designing an assignment operator; it is not a concern with initialization.

An important practical point is that an application that requires the assignment operator to make a deep copy of one or more data members or to attend to resource disposition will almost invariably require two other things: a copy constructor that makes a deep copy of the same pointer members that the assignment operator copies, and a destructor that explicitly deletes the same dynamically allocated memory that the assignment operator deletes. If the destructor does not free this memory, there is memory leak, which can be damaging for a program that remains in execution for a long time. The destructor, of course, works on the intermediary objects created by the copy constructor. Therefore, if the copy constructor provides only a shallow copy of a pointer, the destructor will deallocate the very structure referenced by the actual argument! Another pitfall is that the deletion of a dynamically acquired object will delete the structure pointed to by the object or objects with which it participated as a term in an assignment statement. To avoid difficulties with objects that contain pointers to anything, from linked lists to strings, write a function *operator=( )* that makes deep copies and accompany it with a suitable copy constructor and destructor.

Here is a program in which *Box*es contain a pointer to a *char* array. Dynamically allocated character arrays are very often used to represent strings for the sake of both economy and flexibility. No object needs to claim more space than its string actually occupies, and the string can be expanded (or shrunk) as the program moves along. Annotations appear with the program and the output.

```
#include <iostream.h>
#include <string.h>

class Box
    {
    private:
        static int boxCounter; // To enable serial numbers.
```

```
private:
    int    length;
    int    height;

public:
    char symbol;
```

Name is the "name of the box" that will be stored by a dynamically allocated *char* array. The definition of this variable does not get the memory for the array, just the memory for a pointer that will hold its address (technically, the address of the element whose subscript is 0).

```
    char*   name; ◄─
```

```
    int serialNumber; // Each Box will have a unique serial number
                      // that we will never change.

public:
    Box(int l, int h, char s) : length(l), height(h), symbol(s)
                            // Constructor.
    {
        char nameHolder[30];
        cout << "\nPlease enter the name for the new box:   ";

        cin.getline(nameHolder, 30); ◄─

        name = new char[ strlen(nameHolder) + 1 ];

        strcpy(name, nameHolder);

        serialNumber = ++boxCounter;
    }
```

Memory for a 30-element array is allocated and bound to a local automatic variable.

Here *getline( )* enables spaces to appear within the captured string.

```
    ~Box()
    {
        delete [] name;
    }
```

The brackets, [] , are needed when deleting an array. Without them, only the memory used by element 0 would be released

```
    Box(const Box& boxBeingPassed) // Copy constructor.
    {
        length = boxBeingPassed.length;
        height = boxBeingPassed.height;
        symbol = boxBeingPassed.symbol;

        name = new char[ strlen(boxBeingPassed.name) + 1 ];
        strcpy(name, boxBeingPassed.name);

        serialNumber = ++boxCounter;
    }
```

```
        Box operator=(Box rightOperand)
          {
              length = rightOperand.length;
              height = rightOperand.height;
              symbol = rightOperand.symbol;

              delete [] name;

              name = new char[ strlen(rightOperand.name) + 1 ];
              strcpy(name, rightOperand.name);

          // Note:  serialNumber  is NOT being assigned to  rightOperand.serialNumber.

              return rightOperand;
          }

        void showBox()
          {
              for (int h = 1; h <= height; h++)
                {
                    cout << endl;
                    for (int l = 1; l <= length; l++)  cout << symbol;
                }
              cout << endl;

              cout << "serialNumber of the box is:  " << serialNumber << endl;
              cout << "name of box is '" << name << "' "<< endl;
              cout << "address of name ===> " << (void*) name << endl;
          }
    };

  // Definition and initialization of the class's static variable.
  int Box::boxCounter = 0;

void function(Box operand)
  {
    cout << "\n...................function begins.....................";
    cout << "\nshowing the operand:";
    operand.showBox();

    cout << "\nResetting the operand's name to OPERAND";
```

Assignment differs from initialization insofar as the object being operated upon holds resources that "new born" objects have not yet acquired (e.g., memory in a dynamically allocated structure). Here the memory currently referenced by *name* must be deallocated so that it is not left dangling and lost to the program.

This cast, *(void*)*, converts *name*, the memory location of a string, to a "pointer to void" so that the output operator will display it as an address.

```
      delete [] operand.name;

      operand.name = new char[ strlen("OPERAND") + 1 ];
      strcpy(operand.name, "OPERAND");

      cout << "\nshowing the operand:";
      operand.showBox();
      cout << "\n....................function ends.......................";
      cout << endl;
    }
```

```
/*  1 */ void main()
/*  2 */ {
/*  3 */    Box box1(10,2,'1'), box2(20,3,'2');
/*  4 */    cout << endl << endl;
/*  5 */
/*  6 */    box1.showBox();
/*  7 */    box2.showBox();
/*  8 */
/*  9 */    box2 = box1;
/* 10 */    box2.showBox();
/* 11 */                                // Here strcpy() stores into the existing memory.
/* 12 */    strcpy(box1.name, "BOX ONE"); // Be careful not to exceed array's length.
/* 13 */
/* 14 */    box2.showBox();
/* 15 */
/* 16 */    function(box1);
/* 17 */    box1.showBox();
/* 18 */    cout << "\n Run Successfully Completed" << endl;
/* 19 */ }
```

Here is the output.

```
      Please enter the name for the new box:   box one
      Please enter the name for the new box:   box two

      1111111111
      1111111111
      serialNumber of the box is:  1
      name of box is 'box one'
      address of name ===> 0x25db1166

      222222222222222222222
      222222222222222222222
      222222222222222222222
      serialNumber of the box is:  2
```

> Longer string replaces shorter string.

> This is *box1* and all the data it received upon initialization.

> This is *box2* and all the data it received upon initialization.

```
address of name ===> 0x25db1172
```

┌───┐
│ This is box2 following the assignment   │
│   box2 = box1;   │

```
1111111111 ◄────────────────────────┤ Its name is stored in a different location
1111111111                          │ from box1's name, even though box2 now
serialNumber of the box is:  2      │ carries the name copied out of box2 as its
name of box is 'box one'            │ own.  That the location of box2.name has
address of name ===> 0x25db1172     │ not changed is fortuitous:  evidently the
                                    │ same memory that was returned to the heap
1111111111                          │ when its original name was deleted was re-
1111111111                          │ allocated to store the newly assigned name.
```

└───┘

```
name of box is 'box one'            ┌──────────────────────────────────────────┐
address of name ===> 0x25db1172 ◄───┤ The change in box1's name has not affected
                                     │ box2's name, which remains "box one."
                                     └──────────────────────────────────────────┘
```

```
..................function begins......................
```

```
   showing the operand:          ┌──────────────────────────────────────────────┐
   1111111111                     │ LOOK!  The formal argument, which is the Box
                            ┌──   │ created by the copy constructor, is box number
                            │     │ 5. Box 3 was the box created by the copy
   1111111111               │     │ constructor in passing box2 to operator=()
   serialNumber of the box is: 5  │ in statement 9, and box 4 was the box created
   name of box is 'BOX ONE'       │ by the copy constructor in mediating the
                            │     │ rightOperand's return.
                            └───  └──────────────────────────────────────────────┘
```

```
address of name ===> 0x25db117e
```

```
Resetting the operand's name to OPERAND
showing the operand:
   1111111111                    ┌──────────────────────────────────────────────┐
   1111111111                    │ Here, operand.name is stored in a different area
   serialNumber of the box is:  5│ from the actual argument's (box1's) name.
   name of box is 'OPERAND'      └──────────────────────────────────────────────┘
   address of name ===> 0x25db117e ◄───┘
```

```
..................function ends......................
```

```
1111111111◄──────────────────────────┐ Here, box1 was not affected by
1111111111                            │ the action of the function.
serialNumber of the box is:  1        └──────────────────────────────────
name of box is 'BOX ONE'
address of name ===> 0x25db1166
```

```
Run Successfully Completed
```

Data Conversions

One kind of data type conversion takes place when an expression holds an operand of one type, say, an *int*, but in its place the operator actually requires an item of another data type, say, a *Box*. For example, suppose the *Box* class contained a member function that enabled the addition of two *Box*es.

```
Box  Box::operator+ (Box rightOperand)
  {
    Box  sumHolder;

    sumHolder.length = length + rightOperand.length;
    sumHolder.height = height + rightOperand.height;
    sumHolder.symbol = 'S';

    return sumHolder;
  }
```

Now suppose in *main( )* the expression appears: *box2 = box1 + 5;*. The data type mismatch between the *int* in the expression, which is the argument in the call to *Box::operator+( )*, and the formal argument in the function, which is a *Box*, will be automatically corrected by C++ provided the programmer has supplied a function for transforming *int*s into *Box*es, as discussed above. Such an automatically performed data type transformation is called an implicit conversion. The data type of the 5 is not actually changed; the conversion function accepts an *int* and returns the *Box* onto which it mapped the 5. This *Box* is then used in the computation.

An explicit conversion refers to a data transformation that takes place because the programmer specifies it by way of a conversion operator called a cast. The following two versions of "casting an *int* as a *Box*" work identically to each other and perform the same operation that previously occurred implicitly:

```
box2 = box1 + Box (5); // The type specifier of the target data type
box2 = box1 + (Box) 5; // (here, Box) serves as the cast operator.
```

One reason for casting is that it enables data conversions that are not made automatically. For example, the addition expression,

```
box2 = 5 + box1; // The +'s left operand must be a Box, otherwise
                 // there is no accessor for Box::operator+().
```

does not invoke the *Box::operator+( )* member function because the left operand must be a *Box* object in order to serve as its accessor. However, a perfectly satisfactory accessor emerges when the *int* is cast as a *Box*. The following would work fine.

```
box2 = Box(5) + box1;
```

What kind of a function does explicit casting from an *int* to a *Box*? The one-argument *Box* constructor whose argument is an *int*. What kind of a function is needed to support implicit conversions from *int* to *Box*? The same one-argument *Box* constructor whose argument is an *int*. The general rule is that data type conversion from any given data type, to that of an object of a class is handled by a single-argument class constructor whose argument's type specifier signifies the data type of the source item.

```
//                 This one-argument Box constructor handles both
//                   implicit and explicit data type conversions
//                             from int to Box.
//
Box::Box(int intValue) : length(3*intValue), height(intValue), s('I')
    {
    }


//                 This one-argument Box constructor handles both
//                   implicit and explicit data type conversions and
//          forms 5 instantiations of the class XYZ (XYZ objects) to Box
//                                 objects.
//
Box::Box(XYZ xyzObj) : length(4 * xyzObj.dataMember1),
                        height(xyzObj.dataMember2),
                            symbol(xyzObj.dataMember3)

    {
    }
```

Although the given one-argument constructor *Box::Box(int)* enables the assignment *box1 = 5;* to be performed in the absence of an appropriately overloaded assignment operator, such as the following,

```
Box Box::operator=(int intValue)
    {
    length = 3 * intValue;
    height = intValue;
    symbol = 'I';
    return *this;  // Here, *this is the accessor, the Box to the left of
                   // the = sign.
    }
```

this assignment operator, in the absence of the one-argument *Box::Box(int)* constructor, would not support implicit data type conversion as needed by other operators within expressions nor the casting of *int*s to *Box*es.

The Cast for Data Conversion

To go in the other direction, from *Box* to *int*, so that *Box*es will be converted implicitly to *int*s as necessary and so that *Box*es may be explicitly transformed into *int*s at the programmer's discretion, requires the installation of a "cast" operator within the *Box* class. This is a function call's standard appearance, *int(box1)* or non-standard appearance *(int)box1*. Thinking about the cast operator in standard form helps to make its declarator more intuitive; it is an *operator* whose function name is *int*. The *Box* being mapped to an *int* is the invoking accessor. Although no return type is shown on the declarator, it is understood to be an *int* by virtue of the function's being an *operator int( )*. Its code must conclude with a return. Here is a sample to show its form.

```
//              This operator int() handles both explicit and implicit
//                    data type conversions from Box to int.
//
Box::operator int()                //Note:  No return type is shown on the
  {                                //       declarator but the code must
    return (length + height)/2;    //       nevertheless conclude with a
  }                                //       return statement denoting the
                                   //       value to be passed back.
```

The need for *operator int( )* is clear: no constructor in the *Box* class, or within any other class that a user defines, can generate an *int*. A constructor can only create objects of the *Box* data type, or objects of whatever kind of class for which it is a constructor. Thus although the programmer may write a single argument constructor for any of these data conversions,

```
                                        int       ==> Box
                                        float     ==> Box
                                        char      ==> Box
/* given a Triangle class */            Triangle  ==> Box
/* given a Hexagon class  */            Hexagon   ==> Box
/* given a Circle class   */            Circle    ==> Box
```

a cast operator is needed to go from the *Box* type, or any user-defined data type, to a built-in data type as follows.

```
Box  ==>  int
Box  ==>  float
Box  ==>  char
```

Its activity is not, however, limited to targets of language-provided types. A cast can be written for mapping *Box*es onto data types of any kind, for example,

```
/* given a Triangle class */   Box  ==>  Triangle
/* given a Hexagon class  */   Box  ==>  Hexagon
/* given a Circle class   */   Box  ==>  Circle
```

Following is a program to illustrate data conversions from built-in types to user-defined types, from user-defined types to built-in types, and from one user-defined type to another user-defined type.

```
#include <iostream.h>

class A
  {
    public:
      int a;

      A() : a(0)    // No-argument constructor.
        {
        }
```

```
    A(int i) : a(i)                              // Here int ==> A.
      {
        cout << "\n  int ==> A     via constructor in class A";
      }

    operator int()                              // Here A ==> int.
      {
        cout << "\n  A ==> int     via A::operator int()";
        return a;
      }

void showA()
      {
        cout << "a = " << a;
      }
  };

class B
  {
    public:
      int b1, b2;

      B() : b1(0), b2(0)  // No-argument constructor.
        {
        }

      B(int i) : b1( i/2 ), b2( i/2 )              // Here int ==> B.
        {
          cout << "\n  int ==> B     via constructor in class B";
        }

      B(A a_object) : b1(a_object.a/2), b2(a_object.a/2) // Here A ==> B.
        {
          cout << "\n  A ==> B     via constructor in class B";
        }

      operator int()                              // Here B ==> int.
        {
          cout << "\n  B ==> int     via B::operator int()";
          return (b1 + b2);
        }

      operator A()                                // Here B ==> A.
        {
          cout << "\n  B ==> A     via B::operator A()";

          A tempA;
          tempA.a = b1 + b2;
          return tempA;
        }
```

```
        void showB()
          {
            cout << "b1 = " << b1 << "     b2 = " << b2;
          }
    };

void main()
  {
    A aObject;

    cout << "\ninteger = 10";                       // Here int ==>  A.
    aObject = 10;
    cout << "\naObject:   ";  aObject.showA();

    cout << "\n\naObject:   ";  aObject.showA();     // Here A  ==> int.
    int i = aObject;
    cout << "\ni = " << i;

    B bObject;

    cout << "\n\ninteger = 100";                     // Here int ==>  B.
    bObject = 100;
    cout << "\nbObject:   "; bObject.showB();

    cout << "\n\nbObject:   "; bObject.showB();      // Here B  ==> int.
    i = bObject;
    cout << "\ni = " << i;

    cout << "\n\naObject:   "; aObject.showA();      // Here A  ==>  B.
    bObject = aObject;
    cout << "\nbObject:   "; bObject.showB();

    cout << "\n\nbObject:   "; bObject.showB();      // Here B  ==>  A.
    aObject = bObject;
    cout << "\naObject:   "; aObject.showA();
  }
```

Here is the output.

```
integer = 10
  int ==> A     via constructor in class A
aObject:  a = 10

aObject:  a = 10
  A ==> int     via A::operator int()
i = 10

integer = 100
  int ==> B     via constructor in class B
bObject:  b1 = 50     b2 = 50
```

```
bObject:  b1 = 50      b2 = 50
  B ==> int     via B::operator int()
i = 100

aObject:  a = 10
  A ==> B         via constructor in class B
bObject:  b1 = 5      b2 = 5

bObject:  b1 = 5      b2 = 5
  B ==> A       via B::operator A()
aObject:  a = 10
```

Surprising possibilities arise when the conversion facilities defined within classes are applied implicitly in conjunction with the standard conversions performed by C++. The following exemplifies the ways in which operands are brought into consonance with operators, given the classes as previously outfitted. Each of these statements is executable.

```
aObject = 3 + 4;       // An int==>A conversion would have been made
                       // by the constructor in class A to allow the
                       // assignment of the sum to aobject.

aObject =  3 + bObject;  // In both, a B==>int conversion via the
aObject =  bObject + 3;  // via B::operator int() would have allowed
                         // the addition by way of the language-
                         // provided + for adding an int to an int;
                         // then an int==>A conversion would have
                         // transformed the integer sum into an
                         // A object.

aObject =  aObject + bObject;  // The A==>int and B==>int conversion
                               // would have enabled the language-
                               // provided + for adding ints to have
                               // to have stood in as a makeshift
                               // operator for adding an object from
                               // class A to an object from class B.
                               //
                               // Similar jury-rigged multiplication,
                               // subtraction, division, and modulus
                               // operations are suddenly possible
                               // too.

char c = aObject + bObject;  // The int sum resulting from the
                             // addition may be implicitly cast
                             // to any other language-provided type.

cout << aObject;  // Although the output operator has not been
                  // overloaded to enable the management of objects
                  // from class A, it can manage ints.  The aObject
                  // is implicitly cast as an int, and it is this
```

```
                                        // integer that is displayed.
```

This last poses a potential ambiguity: How would *cout << aObject;* perform if *class A* included an *operator char( )* function, enabling *B* to *char* conversions, along with the *operator int( )* function that enables conversions from *B* to *int*? The inserter treats *int*s and *char*s with equal agility. Having no rational bias for choosing one conversion over the other, yet needing to perform in a predictable fashion, the compiler flags an error. The ambiguity, hence the error, can be circumvented by casting explicitly to one or the other.

```
    cout << " bObject as an int: " << int(bObject);
```

or

```
    cout << " bObject as a char: " << char(bObject);
```

4.4   Relationships Among Classes: Composition and Derivation

Introduction

The next step in abstraction is to build classes by using other classes. There are two important ways to do this: composition and derivation. Composition denotes the "has-a" relationship. A *Computer* "has-a" *DisplayScreen*; an *Automobile* "has-a" *Engine*; a *Library* "has-a" good number of *Books*. The idea is that a more complex data abstraction may contain another data abstraction as a component. In fact, the data members of a class may include instantiations of other classes. Following is an example that includes a *Point* class and a redesign of a *Box* class so that its data members are *Point* objects.

Derivation, or defining one class to be a subtype or "child" of another, means that the members of the original or "parent" class, called the base class, are "inherited" components of the subordinate class, called the derived class. The inheritance relationship is often shown as a directed graph with boxes representing classes and arrows pointing to classes from which members are inherited.

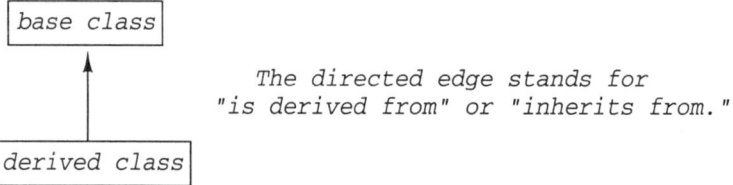

In a derived class, there is typically an inherited part and an incremental part. Not only may the incremental members of a derived class augment the set of inherited member functions, but they may override them. The writer of the derived class can hide an inherited data or function member by adding a variable or function that takes over its name. The effect is that the derived class can be fashioned as a specialization or refinement of the base class through supplementing, reimplementing, renaming, and nullifying its bundle of inherited attributes and behaviors.

The most frequently used form of derivation, *public* derivation (as opposed to *protected* derivation and *private* derivation) models the "is-a" relation. An instantiation of the derived class "is-a" base class object too. An *Automobile* instantiation "is-a" kind of *Vehicle*. A *Vice President* "is-a" kind of *Employee*. A *SmartPhone* "is-a" kind of *Telephone*.

If a derived class can inherit from a base class, can a third class inherit from the derived class? Of course the answer is yes. The inherited part of the "most derived class" will include all the inherited and incremental features of its parent. In fact, very elaborate derivation hierarchies may be designed. The one directly following is a partial model of a library resource management system in which a *Book* "is-a" *CirculatingItem* which "is-a" *OwnedItem*. The incremental part of the *Book* class includes that which is distinctive to books, for example, an author and a form (hardcover or paperback). The class also includes, by inheritance, the characteristics of holdings that may be borrowed (e.g., a function to allow it to be checked out) as well as the characteristics common to every item in the library's depository, whether circulating or noncirculating (e.g., a cost and date of purchase). Besides books, the library owns other kinds of things that may be borrowed such as *Records* and *Cassette* tapes, which are two intrinsically different kinds of *ListeningItems*.

```
class OwnedItem
  {
  protected:
    const char    TITLE[81];
    const float   COST;
          int     condition;
    const char    ISBN[15];
    const char    vendor[51];
          int     numOfCopies;

                    .

                    .

                    .

  }
```

```
class CirculatingItem
  {
   protected:
      int        daysAllowed;
      Date       dateOut, dateDue;
      int        borrowerID;
      int        renewalNumber;
      int        copyNumber;

   public:
      void  borrowIt(int borrowerID);
      float returnIt();
                        .
                        .
                        .
  }
```

```
class Book
  {
  private:
    char authorLast[21];
    char authorFirst[21];
    char authorMidInit;
    int formFlag;
      // Hardcover, paper.
                        .
                        .
                        .
  }
```

```
class ListeningItem
  {
  protected:
    const char content[41];
      // Show, classical, shorthand,
                        .
                        .
                        .
  }
```

```
class Record
  {
    private:
      int speed;
              .
              .
              .
  };
```

```
class Cassette
    {
    };
```

A derivation hierarchy that assumes the structure of a tree, such as this one, is said to be in proper normalized form. There is one base class at the top of the hierarchy; each class may have zero, one, or more subclasses directly derived from it; and each class has only one direct base class (i.e., one "parent" class), except for the base class at the top of the hierarchy which has no parent. To illustrate the terminology used in conjunction with class hierarchies, consider the situation from the standpoint of the *Record* class. Its direct base class is *ListeningItem*. Both *CirculatingItem* and *OwnedItem* are indirect base classes. Speaking in terms of subclasses and superclasses is also widespread. The prefixes sub and super refer to position on the hierarchy, not set-theoretic cardinality. Even though *Record* is a direct subclass of *ListeningItem* (and an indirect subclass of *CirculatingItem* and *OwnedItem*), the composite of its data and function members is very likely a superset inasmuch as it consists of all that it inherited from its ancestors to which are concatenated the zero or more new variables and functions of its own.

Multiple inheritance refers to a derivation hierarchy in which a class is derived from two or more direct base classes. Robert B. Murray [2] describes a *SmartTelephone* that inherits features of telephones from the *Telephone* class and an ability to lookup and dial the number of a vocally specified individual from a *Computer* class:

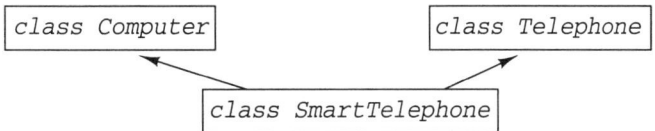

Bjarne Stroustrup [3, p.187] illustrates multiple inheritance with a more built-up derivation hierarchy:

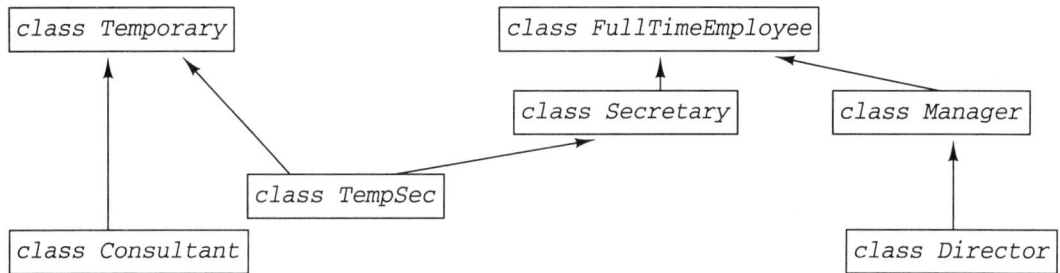

With multiple inheritance, the derivation hierarchy no longer assumes the form of a tree; it is a graph.

The syntax associated with specifying derivation is straightforward. The complicated part, but only at first, is coming to terms with the rules pertaining to where the inherited members belonging to a derived class are accessible. The same set of rules governs the accessibility of data members and function members.

Composition

Composition, from the standpoint of design, refers to using lower-level abstractions in the construction of higher-level abstractions. This is conceptually simple: an abstraction materializes as a class. What this says is that classes may be instantiated (i.e., objects created) within classes just as they may be anywhere else in the program. To show how one class may be built from objects of another class, an object from the *Point* class, given in the following, is used to re-implement the *Box* class.

The data member *col* is interpreted as a horizontal distance, moving to the right, from the vertical boundary. The value of 1 refers to the first column of symbols, the column of symbols to the axis' immediate right. The data member *row* is interpreted as a vertical distance, moving down, from the horizontal boundary. The value of 1 refers to the first row of symbols, the row directly beneath it. An *X* is placed in the point (*col=1, row=1*); a *Y* is at point (*col=6, row=3*).

```
         1   2   3   4   5   6   7   8  . . .
      ┌───┬───┬───┬───┬───┬───┬───┬───┐
    1 │ X │   │   │   │   │   │   │   │
      ├───┼───┼───┼───┼───┼───┼───┼───┤
    2 │   │   │   │   │   │   │   │   │
      ├───┼───┼───┼───┼───┼───┼───┼───┤
    3 │   │   │   │   │ Y │   │   │   │
      ├───┼───┼───┼───┼───┼───┼───┼───┤
    4 │   │   │   │   │   │   │   │   │
      └───┴───┴───┴───┴───┴───┴───┴───┘
    .
    .
    .
```

```
class Point
  {
  private:
    int col, row;

  public:
    Point() : col(0), row(0)                 // No-argument constructor.
      {
      }

    Point(int x, int y) :  col(x), row(y)  // Two-argument constructor.
      {
      }

    void changePoint(int newX, int newY)
      {
      col = newX;
      row = newY;
      }

    int getX()
      {
      return col;
      }

    int getY()
      {
      return row;
```

```
        }
   };
```

> *Box* objects, as given here, are always situated with their leftmost column at the left side of the output page or the screen and their top row on whatever line the cursor lies when they are shown. Because the symbol in the upper left corner is actually placed in column 1 and row 1, it may be thought of as located at point (col=1, row=1). With the upper left point construed as anchored at (col=1, row=1), its lower right point will have the relative placement of (col=length, row=height). This means that the placement and size of a *Box* may be stipulated just as well by its lower right point as by its length and height. The class, re-implemented with a *Point*, is shown in the following.

```
class Box
   {
   private:
       Point lowerRight;   // Exemplifies composition -- an object from
                           // another class is a component of this class.
```

> The *Point(int, int)* constructor is used to initialize the *Box*'s *Point* data member.

```
   public:
       char   symbol;

       Box(int length, int height) : lowerRight(length, height), symbol('$')
          {
          }
```

> *Length* and *height* are local automatic variables, not data members.

```
       void showBox()
          {
           cout << endl;

           for (int height = 1; height <= lowerRight.getY(); height++)
              {
               for (int length = 1; length <= lowerRight.getX(); length++)
                   cout << symbol;
               cout << endl;
              }
          }
   };
```

> Notice the benefit of data hiding. The specifics of how *Box*es are represented along with the internals of the functions responsible for their behavior are not accessible to the users of the class. This forces them to deal with *Box*es through the provided interface, the group of *public* members, and prevents them from becoming dependent upon implementation details. Because these details are completely decoupled from the uses to which *Box*es are put, they may be changed without the danger of untoward effects. This leaves those who support the class free to make upgrades that improve performance and extend functionality.

Inheritance

Derivation of classes from other classes is accomplished in C++ through inheritance. The fundamental ideas of derivation include the syntax needed to construct an "is-a" derivation hierarchy such as the following; an understanding of how to build a hierarchy and how inherited data and function members differ from the incremental data and function members; and transfer of knowledge about C++ language features and how they apply in an inheritance model. These ideas are discussed in this section.

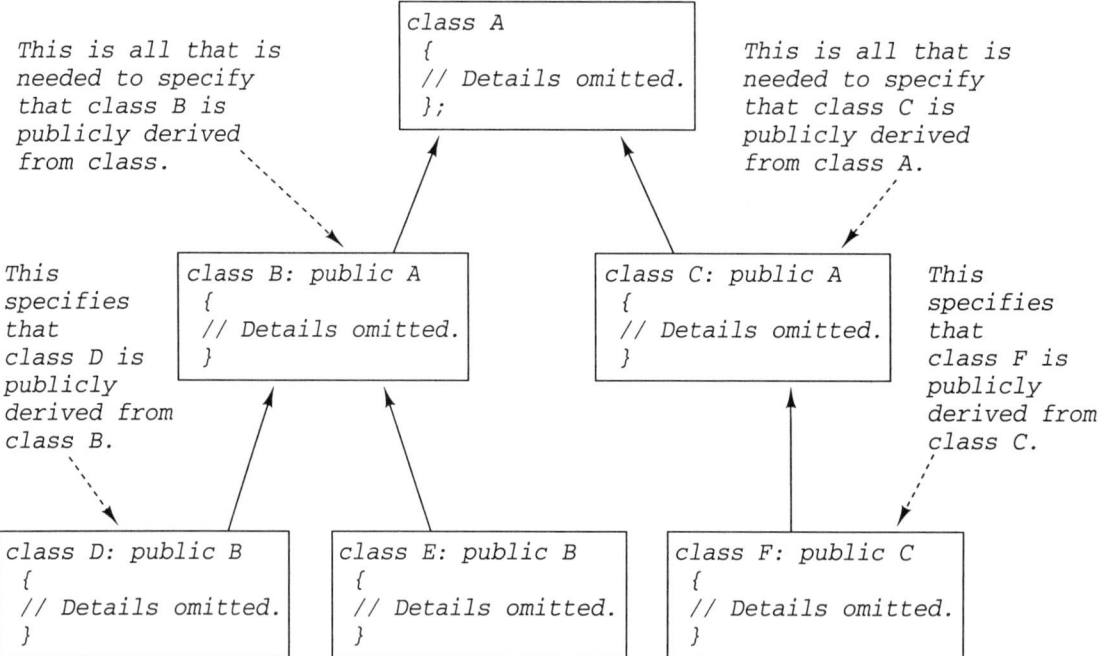

The fundamental ideas do not include multiple inheritance nor polymorphism (including virtual functions, pure virtual functions, and abstract classes), which are discussed later.

As noted, the "is-a" relationship between two classes (e.g., a Limousine "is-a" Car) is modeled by *public* derivation. The other two types of derivation are *private* and *protected*. One of these three keywords appears in the declarator of the derived classes.

Following the discussion of the model, namely, of *public* inheritance, will be a description of the restrictions added by *protected* and *private* derivation. These specify the ways in which inherited members differ from those members that have been explicitly made a part of the class. Ideas of primary importance are: that inheritance is not friendship, and that objects have different accessibility to members when within a member function than when not within a member function. The first is invariably surprising, that an object of a derived class can own variables that it cannot directly write or read (it has to use the *get* and *set* functions provided by the base class). The second relates to how the concept of data hiding unfolds because of the distinction between whether a member is inherited or added. In general, those members specified as *private* are not accessible to objects of that class when they are not within a member function. But in inheritance functions defined by the derived class are not members of the class in which inherited data members are defined. Furthermore, only objects of a class can access the members of that class. Is it appropriate for objects in a derived class, within the action of *main( )*, to be allowed access to members of its base class? The answer is sometimes. C++ uses the *protected* specifier to enable this access.

Building and Using a Basic Hierarchy

Consider two classes, *Upper* and *Lower*, specified as shown.

```
class Upper
  {
    public:
      int upPublic;

    protected:
      int upProtected;

    private:
      int upPrivate;

    public:
      Upper() :  upPublic(100), upProtected(200), upPrivate(300)
        {
        }

      void functionOne()
        {
          cout << "\nFrom Upper::functionOne()";
          cout << "\n    upPublic = " << upPublic
               << "      upProtected = " << upProtected
               << "      upPrivate = " << upPrivate << endl;
        }

      void functionTwo()
        {
          cout << "\n        **Greetings from Upper::functionTwo**"  << endl;
        }
  };

class Lower
  {
    public:
```

```
        int lowPublic;

    protected:
        int lowProtected;

    private:
        int lowPrivate;

    public:
        Lower() :  lowPublic(1), lowProtected(2), lowPrivate(3)
            {
            }

        void functionTwo()
            {
                cout << "\n     **Greetings from Lower::functionTwo**"  << endl;
            }

        void functionThree()
            {
             cout << "\nFrom Lower::functionThree()";
             cout << "\n   lowPublic = " << lowPublic
                  << "     lowProtected = " << lowProtected
                  << "     lowPrivate = " << lowPrivate << endl;
            }
    };

/*  1 */ void main()
/*  2 */    {
/*  3 */       Upper upObject;
/*  4 */       Lower lowObject;
/*  5 */
/*  6 */       upObject.functionOne();
/*  7 */       upObject.functionTwo();    // Invocation of Upper::functionTwo().
/*  8 */
/*  9 */       lowObject.functionTwo();   // Invocation of Lower::functionTwo().
/* 10 */       lowObject.functionThree();
/* 11 */    }
```

Upper and *Lower* are two independent classes. In *main( )*, *upObject*'s invocation of *functionTwo( )* on line 7 is a call to its member function, *Upper::functionTwo( )*, whereas *lowObject*'s invocation of *functionTwo( )*, on line 9, is a call to a completely separate and distinct function, its member function *Lower::functionTwo( )*. None of the following statements are legal additions:

```
    cout << upObject.upPrivate;    // Here upPrivate is a private data
                                   // member and is therefore not accessible
                                   // outside member functions
                                   // belonging to its class.
```

```
cout << lowObject.lowPrivate;  // Here lowPrivate is private.

cout << lowObject.upPublic;    // Here lowObject has no data member
                               // named upPublic -- upPublic is
                               // defined within the Upper class,
                               // but lowObject is an instantia-
                               // tion of the Lower class.

cout << upObject.lowPublic;    // Same kind of problem as above.

lowObject.functionOne();       // Same kind of problem as above,
                               // but exemplified with a function:
                               // lowObject has no function member
                               // named functionOne().

upObject.functionThree();      // Same kind of problem as above.
```

Precisely the same allowances and restrictions that govern the accessibility of *public* data members apply to *public* function members. The same holds true with respect to *private* data members and *private* function members. And all the same rules that pertain to *protected* data members likewise pertain to protected function members. The *protected* access status is new, but when no inheritance is involved it imposes the same exact restrictions as the private specifier: *protected* members are accessible within member functions but not outside member functions.

To transform *Lower* into a class derived from *Upper*,

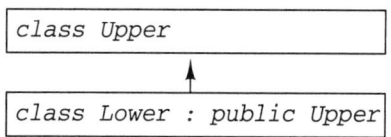

only one syntactical addition is needed, and it is on the first line of the class declaration:

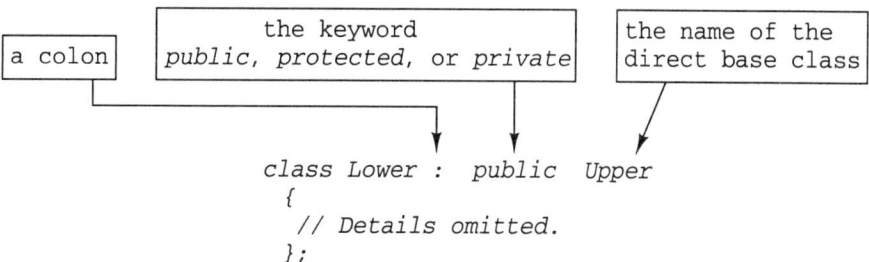

```
class Lower :  public  Upper
{
   // Details omitted.
};
```

No other changes are needed within *Lower*, and no changes are needed within *Upper*. Notice that *Lower* needed no permission from *Upper* to derive from it. Unlike friendship, which is explicitly conferred by the class making access allowances, derivation entails no formal consent. Furthermore, *Upper* is a perfectly ordinary class. No special provision is made within a class to enable it to be a base class, and by the same token there is no way for a class to avoid being a base class. This is why derivation does not convey unrestricted access to the inherited members. A derived class can neither access the *private* data and function members of its base class nor do anything that will affect the way the base class performs. From the standpoint of the base class, the existence of one or more derived classes is inconsequential.

As a result of the (*public*) derivation each object of the *Lower* class has six data members and four function members.

		member's full name
members inherited from Upper	upPublic upProtected upPrivate functionOne() functionTwo()	Upper::upPublic Upper::upProtected Upper::upPrivate Upper::functionOne() Upper::functionTwo()
Lower's own incremental members	lowPublic lowProtected lowPrivate functionTwo() functionThree()	Lower::lowPublic Lower::lowProtected Lower::lowPrivate Lower::functionTwo() Lower::functionThree()

What impact will this have on the previous program (shown again in the following)? There will be no change in its performance.

```
/*  1 */ void main()
/*  2 */    {
/*  3 */       Upper upObject;
/*  4 */       Lower lowObject;
/*  5 */
/*  6 */       upObject.functionOne();
/*  7 */       upObject.functionTwo();      // Invocation of Upper::functionTwo().
/*  8 */
/*  9 */       lowObject.functionTwo();     // Invocation of Lower::functionTwo().
/* 10 */       lowObject.functionThree();
/* 11 */    }
```

The *Upper* object, *upObject*, accesses its members as before, and so does the *Lower* object, *lowObject*. The only questionable statement is on line 9, *lowObject*'s access of *functionTwo()*; and the doubt arises because *lowObject* has two function members that seem to have the same name. In point of fact, however, they do not. The full name of the inherited function is *Upper::functionTwo()*, and the full name of the incremental function is *Lower::functionTwo()*. Reference to a member that is unqualified by the scope operator is to the data or function member defined within the class itself (i.e., the incremental member).

If there is none, then it is to the member with that name in the direct base class. In a deeper hierarchy, the quest to satisfy the access continues up the hierarchy until either an inherited member is found, or the search ends in failure because there is no such member or the encountered member is *private*. A local or more closely derived data member or function member overrides the namesake inherited from a more distant class. Of course, an overridden member that is not *private* may always be accessed by specifying its full name, which is its defined name preceded by the name of its class and the scope resolution operator. For example, in statement 9, *lowObject* could access its inherited *functionTwo( )* like this:

```
/*  9 */      lowObject.Upper::functionTwo();
```

The *protected* access specifier enables access of a data or function member within functions that are members of a derived class, no matter how many levels removed in the hierarchy; but it disables access within functions in classes not along the inheritance path. It offers the refinement of access control that a class needs relative to the prospect of another class inheriting its members. Whereas *public* stipulates "accessible to the object everywhere" and *private* stipulates "accessible to the object only within member functions of the class where the private member is explicitly defined," *protected* stipulates accessibility within member functions of all derived classes (children, grandchildren, great-grandchildren, and so forth.) but no accessibility elsewhere. In short, *protected* stipulates "public" to derived classes "private"; to everything else.

To review the three member access statuses, consider the following function in three contexts: as a member function of *Upper*, as a member function of *Lower*, and as a free function. The function attempts to display every data member in both *Upper* and *Lower*.

First, here is the function as a member function belonging to the *Upper* class.

```
/* 1 */ void  printThem ()  // Upper::printThem().
/* 2 */ {
/* 3 */   cout << upPublic;        // This is okay.
/* 4 */   cout << upProtected;     // This is okay.
/* 5 */   cout << upPrivate;       // This is okay.
/* 6 */   cout << Lower::lowPublic;        //ERROR: Lower::lowPublic is not within
/* 7 */                                    //        scope.
/* 8 */   cout << Lower::lowProtected;     //ERROR: Lower::lowProtected is not within
/* 9 */                                    //        scope.
/*10 */   cout << Lower::lowPrivate;       //ERROR: Lower::lowPrivate is not within
/*11 */ }                                  //        scope.
```

The errors on line 6, 8, and 10 are intended to highlight the fact that members of a derived class are not within the base class. Whether *public*, *protected*, or *private* makes no difference. Inheritance goes down the derivation hierarchy, not up.

As a member of the *Lower* class, this function finds all the referenced members within scope. *upPublic*, *upProtected*, and *upPrivate* are inherited members; and *lowPublic*, *lowProtected*, and *lowPrivate* are incremental members. *upPublic* and *upProtected* are accessible; but *upPrivate* is not. Having an access status of *private*, it is accessible only within member functions of the *Upper* class. Giving its full name will not "un-hide" it. Thus re-coding line 9 as *cout << Upper::upPrivate;* will not get rid of the error. *lowPrivate*, although *private*, is accessible because it is in the class itself.

```
/*  1 */    void  printThem ()  // Lower::printThem().
/*  2 */       {
/*  3 */          cout <<  upPublic;      // This is okay.
/*  4 */          cout <<  upProtected;   // This is okay.
/*  5 */          cout <<  upPrivate;     // ERROR:  access denied.
/*  6 */
/*  7 */          cout <<  lowPublic;
/*  8 */          cout <<  lowProtected;
/*  9 */          cout <<  lowPrivate;
/* 10 */       }
```

A free function is not accessed by an object, so there is no implicit accessor of the data and function members that belong to a class. The accessing object has to be explicitly designated. Aside from that, the only way for an object to appear within the function is to be defined within the function or passed in through a formal argument. For the free function version of *printThem( )*, pass in an *Upper* object and a *Lower* object. Assume that it is called from the *main( )* function shown immediately following.

```
void main()
  {
    Upper upObject;
    Lower lowObject;

    printThem(lowObject, upObject);
  }
```

Within *printThem( )* each object attempts to access every data member of each class. The instantiation of *Upper* is unable to display its data members that are not *publicly* accessible, and its attempts to display the members of *Lower* are futile because no object can access members that are not within its scope. The instantiation of *Lower* is able to access its *public* inherited and incremental members, but not those that are *private* or *protected*.

```
void  printThem (Upper u, Lower l)
  {
    cout <<  u.upPublic;      // This is okay.
    cout <<  u.upProtected;   // ERROR:  not accessible.
    cout <<  u.upPrivate;     // ERROR:  not accessible.
```

```
     cout << u.lowPublic;    // ERROR:  lowPublic is not a member of u.
     cout << u.lowProtected; // ERROR:  lowProtected is not a member of u.
     cout << u.lowPrivate;   // ERROR:  lowPrivate is not a member of u.

     cout << l.upPublic      // This is okay.
     cout << l.upProtected;  // ERROR:  not accessible.
     cout << l.upPrivate;    // ERROR:  not accessible.

     cout << l.lowPublic;    // This is okay.
     cout << l.lowProtected; // ERROR:  not accessible.
     cout << l.lowPrivate;   // ERROR:  not accessible.
   }
```

To see the values of each of the data members within both objects, the following calls to the *public*, and therefore accessible, member functions perform the service.

```
u.functionOne();    // Here functionOne() is a public member of Upper.

l.functionOne();    // Here functionOne() is an inherited public member of
                    // Lower.  Because it is not overridden by a local
                    // function having the same name, this invocation
                    // is fine.  Had Lower had an indigenous function
                    // of the same name, this statement would have had
                    // to have been:    l.Upper::functionOne().

l.functionThree(); // Here functionThree() is a public member of Lower.
```

Private or Protected Derivation

To complete the description of inheritance and the accessibility of inherited members, it is important to look at the differences that would result if *Upper* were a *private* or a *protected* base class instead of a *public* base class. Here *Lower* has been *privately* derived from *Upper*. This is done by changing the keyword describing the mode of inheritance along *Lower's* declarator from *public* to *private*.

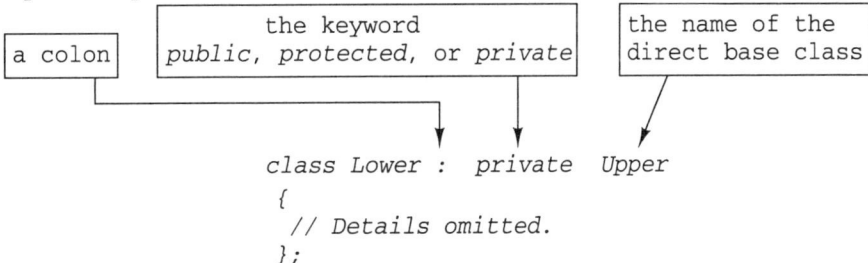

```
class Lower :  private  Upper
{
  // Details omitted.
};
```

Lower still has the same complement of inherited and incremental members as it did previously. Its member functions are still able to access the *public* and *protected* members that it inherited from *Upper*. What is different is that now instantiations of *Lower* within the general program (e.g., in *main( )*, in free functions such as *printThem( )*, and within member functions belonging to other classes) cannot access the inherited members from *Upper* that are *public*. Furthermore, had the hierarchy been deeper, with a class called *Bottom* derived from *Lower*, none of the members derived from *Upper* would be accessible within the member functions of *Bottom*. Private inheritance has the effect of making the original access status prescribed to all inherited members appear to have been, beyond its own confines, *private*. In other words, it will seem to classes derived from *Lower*, and to users of *Lower* objects, that the members inherited from *Upper* that had really been specified to be *public* or *protected* were specified as *private*.

Protected inheritance has the effect of making the inherited *public* members act, beyond the confines of the derived class, as if their original access status had been *protected*. Had *Lower*'s derivation from *Upper* been *protected*, the inherited members whose access status had been *public* (and *protected*) would be accessible in the member functions of a class derived from *Lower* (e.g., *Bottom*) but not to objects of type *Lower* or to objects of type *Bottom* within the general program.

To offer a perspective, *public* inheritance imposes no additional restrictions on top of those stemming from the members' original specifiers. Private inheritance lets the member functions of the derived class take advantage of all the access liberties allowed by the base class, but passes none of these along. Specifically, it blocks out two kinds of things: the ability of its objects to access inherited *public* members within the general program (e.g., *main( )*), and the ability of member functions within any class subsequently derived from it directly or indirectly to access the inherited *public* and *protected* members. Protected inheritance only blocks the first set of these access privileges.

The Utility of Function Overriding

Overriding refers to the mechanism used by C++ to resolve the ambiguity that would otherwise exist when an accessible inherited member and an accessible incremental member have the same name. When two distinct referents would otherwise be indistinguishable, the data member or function member native to the current class prevails over its inherited namesake. When both referents are inherited, the prevailing member will be the native of the nearest ancestor. Should a nondominant member be the one desired, it can be accessed with its class name and the scope operator.

The overriding of inherited functions means to substitute a suitable implementation for an inherited capability that is inappropriate. An inherited function that should be removed completely is voided out by an overriding function that does nothing. To rename an inherited function, it can be overridden by a function that does nothing but be called, using its full name, by the new function with a more fitting name. To extend a useful inherited function and retain its name, an overriding function can call it as part of its code.

If an incremental function in the derived class has the same name as an inherited function, it overrides the inherited function even when their signatures differ. In fact, it overrides all overloaded functions that may exist within the base class. If a function call matches the signature of an overridden function but not the prevailing function, an error is flagged. The only way to correct it is to use the scope operator.

A technicality relating to scope resolution that becomes more relevant in deeper derivation hierarchies is that the actual class in which a desired but overridden member was defined does not have to appear to the left of the scope operator. Any class may serve in which this member is the one that dominates. To illustrate, consider a linear *public* derivation hierarchy in which the uppermost class is named *A* and each successive class is named with the next letter of the alphabet. Suppose there is a function named *target( )* in *class B* that is overridden by a function named *target( )* in *class D*. When an object of *class E* accesses *target( )*, *eObject.target( )*, the reference is to the function defined within *class D*. But class B's *target( )* could be invoked by either *eObject.B::target( )* or *eObject.C::target( )*.

Constructors and Destructors in Class Hierarchies

Consider the following class hierarchy.

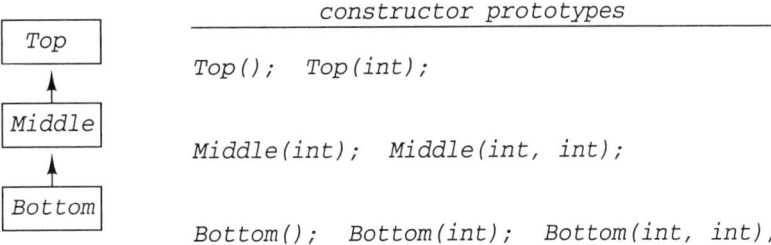

```
                         constructor prototypes
                 ─────────────────────────────────────────────
                 Top();  Top(int);

                 Middle(int);  Middle(int, int);

                 Bottom();  Bottom(int);  Bottom(int, int);
```

The definition of a *Bottom* object, such as within *main( )*,

```
void main()
  {
    Bottom b;
       :
  }
```

initiates the following sequence of events:

• A constructor in the *Bottom* class is called, but it immediately calls a constructor in its direct base class, *Middle*, deferring its own processing, including data member initializations, until the called constructor returns.

• The constructor in the *Middle* class immediately calls a constructor in the *Top* class, its direct base, deferring its own processing until the return.

- The constructor in the *Top* class, being at the top of the derivation hierarchy, expedites the installation of the parts of the object coming from *Top*, initializes the data members, performs all its coded preparatory action, and returns.

- The constructor in the *Middle* class now goes to work; it expedites the installation of the parts of the object coming from *Middle*, initializes the data members, performs all its coded preparatory action, and returns.

- The constructor in the *Bottom* class at last kicks in; it expedites the installation of the parts of the object coming from *Bottom*, initializes the data members, performs all its coded preparatory action, and thereby completes the creation of the object; with its return the object is turned over to the program for use.

A practical consequence of the fact that objects are actually produced from the top of the hierarchy down is that members inherited from an indirect or direct base class are available for use, accessibility permitting, within any given constructor right along with the incremental members. Conversely, members to be added by derived classes are not yet present, therefore simply not available.

Destructors dismantle objects in the opposite direction. This means that inherited members remain allocated and usable within a class's destructor, along with the members that had come from the class at hand. Members from classes at a lower point in the hierarchy have been expunged, leaving nothing to access.

An issue relating to constructors in derivation hierarchies arises because the ostensibly uncomplicated definition of an object in fact starts off a sequence of constructor activations. The initializing arguments in an object's definition determine which of the class constructors is invoked, but how are particular constructors designated for invocation in direct and indirect base classes? The answer is that the selection of the constructor to be invoked within the direct base class has been programmed deterministically into each constructor within the immediate subclass. To declare a *Bottom* object, any of its *publicly* accessible constructors can be chosen; but the chosen constructor takes things from there, with the ultimate effect of following a preestablished succession. This may seem to deprive the programmer of control but it is consistent with a worthy precept that the builder of a derived class should need no implementation knowledge about the classes in a hierarchy beyond the immediate base class.

To illustrate, suppose that the *Top*, *Middle*, and *Bottom* classes have constructors with the signatures that accompanied the diagram of the derivation hierarchy at the opening of this section. The syntax of a constructor's invocation of a particular constructor is shown in the following, with *Bottom(int, int)* designating *Middle(int)*.

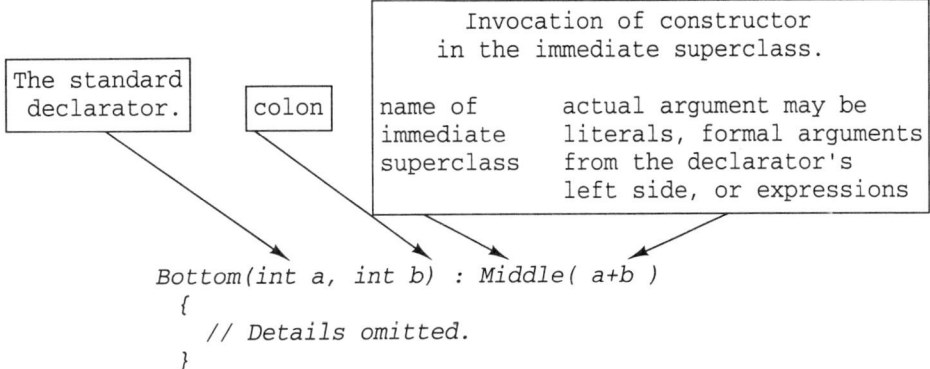

```
Bottom(int a, int b) : Middle( a+b )
{
    // Details omitted.
}
```

The constructor from the direct base class appointed for use is the one whose signature is comprised of a single *int*. The constructor call can appear anywhere along the data member initialization list: before, between, or following member initializations. The use of constructors in a derived class is no different from the use of constructors in a class that stands alone.

```
void main()
{
    Bottom b1;              // No-argument constructor.
    Bottom b2( 5, 10 );    // Two-argument constructor.
    Bottom b3( 20 );       // One-argument constructor.
    Bottom b4( 8, 12 );    // Two-argument constructor.
        ⋮
}
```

If *Middle(int)* intends to use the no-argument constructor in *Top*, the choice is made implicitly by intentionally omitting a constructor call along its initialization list.

```
Middle(int forMember_n) : n(forMember_n)
{
    // Details omitted.
}
```

With *Bottom(int,int)* invoking *Middle(int)* and *Middle(int)* invoking *Top( )*, each time *Bottom's* two-argument constructor is called (as it is twice in the preceding abbreviated *main( )*), the identical process of object-building is followed.

Multiple Inheritance

Multiple inheritance removes the limitation on program design that compels the derivation hierarchy to assume the form of a tree. Here is the syntax for how the class *SmartTelephone* may be derived from both the class *Computer* and the class *Telephone*:

```
class Computer                      class Telephone
   {                                   {
      // Details omitted.                 // Details omitted.
   };                                  };
```

| First base class, with the specification of whether the inheritance is *public* or *private*. | comma | Second base class, with the specification of whether the inheritance is *public* or *private*. |

```
class SmartTelephone :  public Computer, public Telephone

      {
         // Details omitted.
      };
```

A class may be derived from any number of direct base classes simply by listing the names of the base classes with commas between them. In each case, the derivation may be *public*, as shown here, *protected*, or *private*. All the principles of single inheritance continue to hold. The only difference is that they are extended so that the members of both (or all) base classes become parts of the derived class.

Matters become more complicated because there are a greater number of interacting conceptual parts. Consider the constructor and destructor issue. Constructors do their work "on the way down" the inheritance hierarchy. When this hierarchy is a tree, their order of operation is self-evident. But what happens when a class, such as *SmartTelephone*, has two direct base classes? The answer is that constructors from the base classes are invoked in the same order that they are listed in the derived class base list. When an instance of *Smart-Telephone* is defined, first a constructor from the Computer class is called and then a constructor from the Telephone class. Lastly, a *SmartTelephone* constructor performs whatever activity it has been programmed to do. Destructors are activated in the reverse order. In the case of a *SmartTelephone* object, the first destructor to execute would be *SmartTelephone's*, the next would be *Telephone's*, and finally the destructor from the *Computer* class.

Name Ambiguity

Another matter is name ambiguity. This relates to the referential uncertainty that arises if two (or more) base classes have a function member or a data member with the same name and this function (or variable) is not overridden by a local definition in the derived class. To make this concrete, suppose each of two classes, which have a function named *showIt( )*,

```
        class Base1                 class Base2
          {                           {
            public:                     public:
              void showIt()               void showIt()
              {                           {
                // Details omitted.         // Details omitted.
              }                           }

            // More details omitted.    // More details omitted.
          };                          };
```

Following is a class named *Derived*, multiply derived from Base1 and Base2, which inherits both versions of *showIt( )*.

```
class Derived : public Base1, public Base2
  {
    public:
      void display()
        {
          showIt();  // This is ambiguous hence erroneous.
                     // To which of the two inherited showIt()
                     // functions does this call refer?
                     // There is no way to know.  Had a function
                     // named showIt() been declared within
                     // Derived (i.e., this class), the call would
                     // have been unambiguous because locally
                     // defined members override inherited
                     // members.

          // Details omitted.
        }

    // More details omitted.
  };
```

Derived has two distinct, inherited versions of *showIt( )* in its name space. The scope resolution operator is used to distinguish one from the other. The previous call to *showIt( )* should have been:

```
    Base1::showIt();  // Invokes the function inherited
                      // from Base1.
```

or

```
    Base2::showIt();  // Invokes the function inherited
                      // from Base2.
```

or

```
    Base1::showIt();  // Invokes the function from Base1.
    Base2::showIt();  // Invokes the function from Base2.
```

or

```
Base2::showIt();  // Invokes the function from Base2.
Base1::showIt();  // Invokes the function from Base1.
```

or whatever produces the desired result. The rule is that any reference to a
name with more than one referent can be made unambiguous by prepending
the name of a class from which it is inherited followed by the double colon.

This is easy enough, but note the opportunity for an alias to develop when
a member is inherited from an indirect base class. In the following inheritance
hierarchy, the *Bottom* inherits an *int* named *x* indirectly from the *Top* as well
as directly from *LeftMiddle*.

```
class Top
  {
    public:
      int  x;
  }
```

```
class LeftMiddle
  {
    public:
      int  x;
  }
```

```
class RightMiddle:public Top
  {
  // No data member named x
  // is newly defined, so the
  // x inherited from Top is
  // is the only x in the
  // namespace.
  }
```

```
class Bottom : public LeftMiddle, public RightMiddle
  {
  // A data member named x is inherited from LeftMiddle
  // and
  // another data member named x is inherited from RightMiddle.
  }
```

As a result, each *Bottom* object has two distinct data members named *x*. The
x member from *LeftMiddle* is accessible as *LeftMiddle::x*. The other *x* member, inherited directly from *RightMiddle* and indirectly from *Top*, is accessible
both as *RightMiddle::x* and as *Top::x*. *RightMiddle::x* and *Top::x* are alternate
names for the same memory location. The referents may appear to be to distinct
commodities, but they are not.

```
void main()
  {
    Bottom  bObj;
    bObj.RightMiddle::x = 5;    // RightMiddle::x is assigned 5.
    cout << bObj.Top::x;        // The value displayed for Top::x is 5.
  }
```

A subtle but important point of syntax is that had either *Top::x* or *LeftMiddle::x* been specified *private*, access to the *public* alternate would have nevertheless required the scope operator.

This ambiguity ensuing when the same name is inherited from distinct base classes develops into a more formidable problem when it proceeds from inheriting the same base class indirectly through different derivation paths. This arises within a derivation hierarchy incorporating what is colloquially termed "the deadly diamond." Consider a system for a business organization:

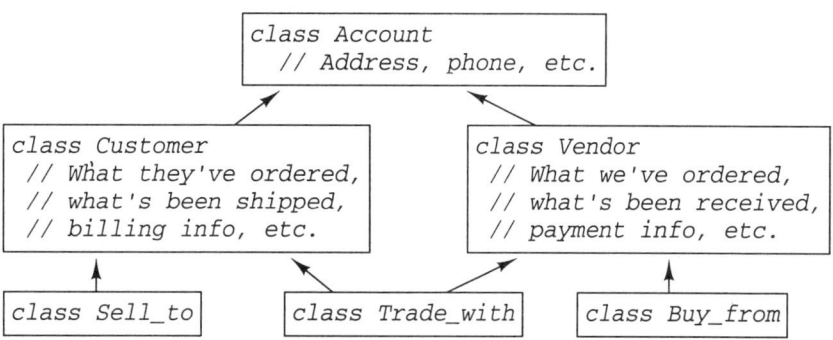

The class *Trade_with*, intended to integrate the attributes of both *Customers* and *Vendors*, inherits from *Account* by way of *Customer* and by way of *Vendor*. If *Account* supplied a *private* data member named *phoneNumber* and public function to enter it named *setPhone( )*, instantiations of *Trade_with* would have two separate copies of each of these: *Customer::phoneNumber* and *Vendor::phoneNumber* as well as *Customer::setPhone( )* and *Vendor::setPhone( )*. The invocation *setPhone( )* would be ambiguous, and *Account::setPhone( )* would not disambiguate it. *Customer::setPhone( )* is needed to set *Customer::phoneNumber* and *Vendor::setPhone( )* is needed to set *Vendor::phoneNumber*. Because there are two distinct, logically independent *phoneNumber* members, nasty surprises may develop. For instance, it might be set only once (e.g., through *Customer::setPhone( )*) and then not be there for an access to *Vendor::getPhone( )*. When multiple copies of members from a base class are not what are sought (although sometimes they are), the multiplicity can be eliminated by specifying the base class to be *virtual* (discussed below). Consider an application wherein each of two intermediate base classes needs its own copy of a database (the data and the management facilities) from a *Database* class. Think of the application as an integrated piece of software for managing franchises; each instantiation of *Franchise* represents a separate store:

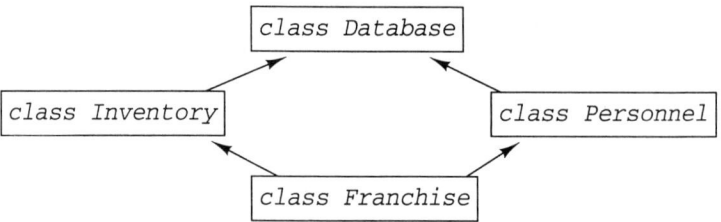

The diamond depicts the physical construction of the software that follows from the static structure of the software's code—there is one *Database* class and both *Inventory* and *Personnel* are derived from it.

```
class Database
  {
    public:
       void enterRec(rec);     // Here rec is an externally declared struct.
       rec  getRec(key);
       void deleteRec(key);

       // Details omitted.
  };

class Inventory : private Database
  {
    // Details omitted.
  };

class Personnel : private Database
  {
    // Details omitted.
  };

class Franchise : public Inventory, public Personnel
  {
    public:
      int storeNumber;

    // Details omitted.
  };
```

> *Inventory* and *Personnel* are privately derived from *Database* because the "uses" or "needs for its implementation" relationship, not the "is-a" relationship, applies. This is the interpretation given to private inheritance in the context of design.

However, the following is more accurate relative to the logical intent of the design and the way in which objects are actually constructed.

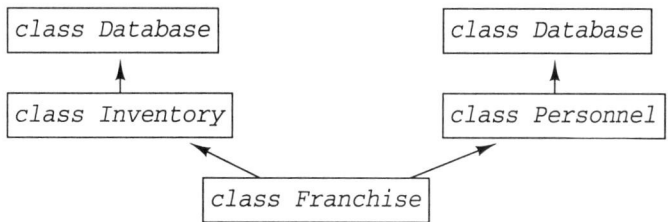

Suppose that within *main( )* a *Franchise* is defined:

```
void main()
  {
    Franchise  newYork(100);  // One-argument constructor called --
                      .        //    the New York store will be
                      .        //    storeNumber 100.
                      .
  }
```

What follows is the resulting action. Imagine that constructors include code to output a message announcing their execution to allow a trace of when each executed:

- A *Franchise* constructor is called from *main( )*, but does not execute yet; it calls an *Inventory* constructor because the *Inventory* class is the first one appearing on its base list.

- The called *Inventory* constructor does not execute yet because there is a class on its base list, *Database*; it calls a *Database* constructor.

- A *Database* constructor runs, displaying: from the Database constructor; the "Inventory part" of the developing object gets the data members and function members of its database; the constructor completes and returns.

- The *Inventory* constructor now runs, displaying: from the Inventory constructor; the developing object receives the members coming from the *Inventory* class; the constructor completes and returns.

- The *Franchise* constructor still has to postpone execution because there is another class on its base list, *Personnel*; a *Personnel* constructor is called.

- The called *Personnel* constructor does not execute yet because there is a class on its base list, *Database*; it calls a *Database* constructor.

- A *Database* constructor runs, displaying: from the Database constructor; the "Personnel part" of the developing object gets the data members and function members of its database; the constructor completes and returns.

- The *Personnel* constructor now runs, displaying: from the Personnel constructor; the developing object receives the members coming from the *Personnel* class; the constructor completes and returns.

- The *Franchise* constructor finally runs, displaying: from the Franchise constructor; its return completes the object's creation.

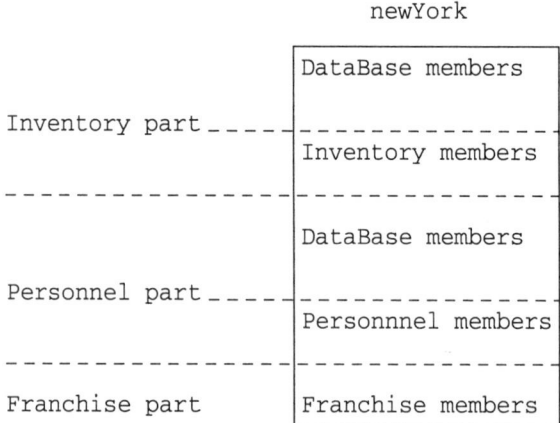

Each store (*Franchise* instantiation) will have one *Database* for its *Inventory* and a distinct *Database*, but with the same look, feel, and mode of operation, for its *Personnel*.

Virtual Base Class

Sometimes the multiple occurrence of a base class is not logically consistent with the design. This is an example Stroustrup gives [3].

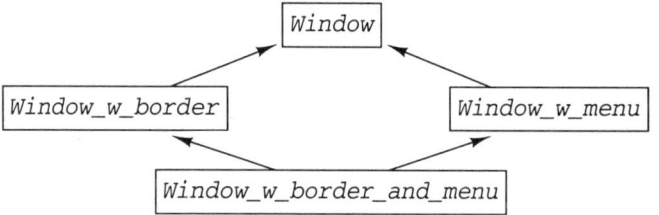

The *Window* class provides for a window's basic attributes and properties, and they are dressed up by the derived classes *Window_w_border* and *Window_w_menu*. To combine the border additions with the menu additions, what is needed is only to derive a class that inherits both sets of enhancements: *Window_w_border_and_menu*. However, an instantiation of *Window_w_border_and_menu* should not have two copies of the window's vital statistics (location, size, background color, etc.). This would be logically inappropriate and wasteful of memory as both the "*Window_w_border part*" and the "*Window_w_menu part*" pertain to the same window. In order that these two sibling base classes share (i.e., inherit) the same members for each instantiation of *Window_w_border_and_menu*, the specifier *virtual* is placed to the left of *Window* on the base list of each. These two changes are all that are needed.

```
class Window
    {
```

```
        // Details omitted.                    Change 1 of 2
    };

class Window_w_border : public virtual Window
    {
      // Details omitted.                    Change 2 of 2
    };

class Window_w_menu : public virtual Window
    {
      // Details omitted.
    };

class Window_w_border_and_menu : public Window_w_border,
         public window_w_menu
    {
      // Details omitted.
    };
```

The keyword *virtual*, in this context, is a directive to every constructor in the named base class that is called from the current class. The directive says: if the members from your class are not yet installed in the developing object, allocate them as usual; otherwise (if they are present) do not allocate another set, but make certain that they will be fully servicable from this class as well.

Polymorphism

Object-oriented programming may mean different things to different constituencies; but in "The Arm" (*The Annotated C++ Reference Manual*), Margaret A. Ellis and Bjarne Stroustrup [1] assert that:

> The use of derived classes and virtual functions is often called *object-oriented programming*. Furthermore, the ability to call a variety of functions using exactly the same interface—as is provided by virtual functions—is sometimes called *polymorphism*.

Polymorphism amounts to a more sophisticated form of function overriding: an object from a derived class, when it accesses a function with a particular name and signature first introduced in the base class and a possible re-implementation of one or more of its subclasses, gets an invocation of the appropriate version (e.g., the version defined or inherited but predominating in its class). Two major extensions differentiate polymorphism from rudimentary function overriding: it affords the builder of the base class the control over whether it will be possible to override a function, and it is dynamic, not static.

Before any confusion results, the keyword *virtual* means something different in the context of polymorphism from its meaning in the context of multiple inheritance. In polymorphism *functions* may be virtual. In multiple inheritance, a base *class* may be virtual.

Control Over Overriding

Within the base class, whether it is actually the class at the top of the hierarchy or a class beneath the top that is serving as departure point for a subhierarchy, a function being declared for the first time may be specified as *virtual*. A function specified to be *virtual* can be overridden in polymorphism. A newly declared function not specified as *virtual* cannot be overridden in polymorphism. A newly declared function specified to be a pure *virtual* function (pure is not a keyword), must be overridden.

The idea behind this last is to have a language-provided mechanism for requiring creators of derived classes to offer functionality that is conceptually understood and operatively needed, but whose implementation is not given in the base class. This is done through a function that has the same name and signature as the pure *virtual* function. A class without such a function predominating over the pure virtual function is not allowed to create objects. A class in which even one pure virtual function predominates (is not overridden) can have no objects. Such classes are said to be abstract classes.

From the standpoint of design, an abstract class is a conceptual common denominator that cannot exist by itself. For instance, in the library resource management system depicted at the beginning of Section 4.4, the class *CirculatingItem* is an abstraction. Suppose someone says, "I want to see an instantiation of a *CirculatingItem*." We hold up a novel. He says, "No, that's a book! I said I want to see a *CirculatingItem*." We show him a cassette tape of shorthand dictation exercises. He says, "No, that's a tape. I want to see a *CirculatingItem* apart from books, tapes, whatever." We cannot oblige because a *CirculatingItem*, apart from any tangible manifestation, cannot exist. It is an abstract generalization. In an object-oriented design such an abstraction is useful because it identifies a distinctive conceptual essence shared by different kinds of real things. There is no reason to instantiate such a class and good reason not to.

Dynamic Function Overriding (Rather than Static Overriding)

Static function overriding refers to the overriding that had been done until now. The function associated with an object's access is evident during compilation, and the compiler actually sets up the call. What makes the exact function inferable is that the invoking object, no matter which one it happens to be, is of a particular type. That is to say that it must be an object of one specific class.

Dynamic function overriding is precisely what is meant by polymorphism. The function associated with an object's access can be any one within the derivation hierarchy that overrides the *virtual* function with the designated name and signature. This is possible because the accessing object can be from any class derived from the class in which the *virtual* function is declared. At different times during the execution of the program the same coded access may be used by different kinds of objects. The association of the function with the call is made in real time, as execution ensues, and is thus dynamic.

The mechanics of achieving polymorphism differ from compile-time overriding in one major way: objects access functions by way of their address stored in a variable whose type is a base class pointer. For instance, in the class hierarchy of the library information system the base class is *OwnedItem*. Three of the classes whose instantiations represent tangible entities are *Book*, *Record*, and *Cassette*. Suppose that a *virtual* function called *lookUp( )* performs the electronic equivalent of an entity's look-up in the card catalogue and displays "the card" on the screen. Naturally, different information, in a different format, is stored and shown for different kinds of resources.

The most literal way of using *lookUp( )* polymorphically, with all pointers explicitly manipulated, is shown in the following.

```
void main()
    {
    OwnedItem* basePtr;   // OwnedItem is the class at the root of
                          // the derivation hierarchy.  OwnedItem*
                          // is therefore the type specifier for a
                          // pointer to the base class.

    // Constructors from three respective classes are used to get
    // three specific objects.  Each object is dynamically allocated.
    //
    //    The address of the   Book   object is stored in bookPtr.
    //    The address of the   Record  object is stored in recPtr.
    //    The address of the Cassette object is stored in tapePtr.

    Book*      bookPtr = new Book("The C++ Programming Language");
    Record*    recPtr  = new Record("Meet the Beatles!");
    Cassette*  tapePtr = new Cassette("Guys and Dolls");

    // Query the user to find which item is to be looked up:

    cout << "\n Which would you like to look up?  b/r/c ";
    char  answer;
    cin >> answer;

    // Which item was chosen, hence which particular lookUp()
    // will be accessed, cannot be known until the program runs.

    //    Assign the address of the chosen object
    //    to the base class pointer.

    if (answer == 'b')       basePtr = bookPtr;
    else if (answer == 'r')  basePtr = recPtr;
    else                     basePtr = tapePtr;  // Our users
                                                 //    *never*
```

```
                                                        // make mistakes.

        //   Polymorphic access of Book::lookUp(), Record::lookUp(),
        //   or Cassette::lookUp() is determined by the kind of object
        //   to which basePtr points:

        basePtr -> lookUp();        // or  (*basePtr).lookUp()
        ⋮
    }
```

Another approach to polymorphism in which the assignment of an object's address to a base class pointer is less overt is through passing a derived object to a base object by reference.

```
// Passing by reference equates the address of the formal argument to
// the address of the actual argument.  Thus if a Book object were
// passed to entity, the Book's address becomes the entity's address.
// Because C++ allows a derived object's address (the Book's) to be
// used as the value of a base pointer (the address of entity) there
// is no data type mismatch.

void  entityProcessor( OwnedItem& entity )
    {
      entity.lookUp();   // Entity's address was assigned the book's
                         // address; but entity itself is an object
                         // (an r-value), not a pointer -- this is why
                         // the dot operator is correct.
    }
void main()
    {
      Book      book("The C++ Programming Language");  // These are
      Record    rec("Meet the Beatles!");             // objects,
      Cassette  tape("Guys and Dolls");               // not pointers
                                                      // to objects.

        // Query the user to find which item is to be looked up:

      cout << "\n Which would you like to look up?  b/r/c ";
      char  answer;
      cin >> answer;

        // Pass the designated object to entityProcessor().

      if (answer == 'b')      entityProcessor(book);
      else if (answer == 'r') entityProcessor(rec);
      else                    entityProcessor(tape);
      ⋮
    }
```

Because of polymorphism, the *entityProcessor( )* function, which exemplifies any function for managing objects from classes derived from the common base, becomes very general and very powerful. Not only can it manage every kind of object in the hierarchy, no matter how diverse, but it can chart any processing procedure. Imagine that a certain algorithm can be decomposed into a succession of high-level actions, each represented by a named function. If each function is a *virtual* function, then a general line of action can be applied in every case, regardless of how differently the different kinds of objects have to be treated.

```
void  algorithm ( nameOfBaseClass*  anyDerivedObject )
  {
    anyDerivedObject.algorithmicAction1();
    anyDerivedObject.algorithmicAction2();
    anyDerivedObject.algorithmicAction3();

         :
         :
  }
```

Syntax for Nonvirtual Functions

There is nothing new to defining functions that are not within the class specifier or their definition outside the specifier. All the functions in previous sections were not virtual.

The tricky part of nonvirtual functions is that they are fully overridable when used "nonpolymorphically" (not by way of base class pointers that hold addresses of derived objects) but not overridable within the polymorphic modality. Nonoverridability gives the designer of a base class a way to enforce the use of a critical facility.

The following program contrasts the behavior of nonvirtual functions used nonpolymorphically and polymorphically. Notice that the nonpolymorphic modality applies when an object directly accesses a member function (i.e., when the access is not through a pointer) as well as when the access is by way of the address held in a pointer variable of the object's own particular type. The polymorphic modality requires that the access be by way of the address held in a pointer variable defined with the name of the base class.

```
#include <iostream.h>

class Base
  {
    public:
      void nonVirtual()
        {
          cout << "\nFrom Base::nonVirtual()";
        }
  };

class Derived : public Base
  {
```

```
       public:
          void nonVirtual()
             {
               cout << "\nFrom Derived::nonVirtual()";
             }
       };

    void main()
       {
       Base      baseObject;
       Derived   derivedObject;

       // Nonpolymorphic overridability.
       baseObject    .nonVirtual();   // Gives:  From Base::nonVirtual().
       derivedObject.nonVirtual();    // Gives:  From Derived::nonVirtual().

       Base*     basePtr    = &baseObject;
       Derived*  derivedPtr = &derivedObject;

       basePtr    > nonVirtual();    // Gives:  From Base::nonVirtual().
       derivedPtr > nonVirtual();    // Gives:  From Derived::nonVirtual().

       // Test of polymorphic overridability -- it fails, as expected.
       Base      *basePtr1,     *basePtr2;

       basePtr1 = &baseObject;
       basePtr2 = &derivedObject;      // Okay  derivedObject "isa" Base object.

       basePtr1 > nonVirtual();     // Gives:  From Base::nonVirtual().
       basePtr2 > nonVirtual();     // Gives:  From Base::nonVirtual().
       }
```

Syntax for Virtual Functions   A function is declared to be *virtual* by placing that keyword to the left of the function return type when it is defined or declared within the class specifier. When only the prototype is given within the class specifier, the *virtual* qualifier appears with it but not with the definition of the function. There are no other differences within the function's coding.

Virtual functions are inherited as *virtual*. They do not need to be redeclared within a derived class. As with a *nonvirtual* function, if a *virtual* function is not re-implemented, the version prevailing within the direct base class serves as the default. An overriding definition may be provided; the keyword *virtual* may, but does not have to, accompany it. However, it is essential that the re-declaration have precisely the same declarator: the same return type, the same name, and the same signature. If there is any discrepancy, the compiler will construe it as an independent function, unrelated to the *virtual* function.

A function not initially specified as *virtual* cannot be transformed into a *virtual* function by a class that inherits it. However, a class at any level within the hierarchy can introduce a new *virtual* function. Then the function cannot be accessed through a pointer or a reference to a base class that is at a higher point.

The next program illustrates the fundamental syntax and properties of *virtual* functions.

```
#include <iostream.h>

class AAA     // Base class.
  {
    public:
      virtual void functionOne()        // Virtual function defined.
        {
          cout << "\nFrom AAA::functionOne()";
        }

      virtual void functionTwo();       // Virtual function is declared here
  };                                    // and defined outside the specifier.

  void AAA::functionTwo()               // The virtual specifier is omitted.
    {
      cout << "\nFrom AAA::functionTwo()";
    }

class BBB : public AAA   // AAA::functionOne() and AAA::functionTwo() are
  {                      // inherited and dominate because they are not overridden.
  };

class CCC : public BBB   // AAA::functionOne() is overridden; the overriding
  {                      // function is virtual despite the absence of the
                         // specifier.
    public:
      void functionOne()
        {
          cout << "\nFrom CCC::functionOne()";
        }
  };

class DDD : public CCC   // Both inherited functions are overridden;
  {                      // the virtual specifier is optional.
    public:
      virtual void functionOne()
        {
          cout << "\nFrom DDD::functionOne()";
        }

      virtual void functionTwo()
        {
          cout << "\nFrom DDD::functionTwo()";
        }
```

```
    };

void callThem(AAA& object)    // AAA is name of the base class.
    {
       object.functionOne();
       object.functionTwo();
    }

void main()
    {
       AAA a;
       BBB b;
       CCC c;
       DDD d;

       cout << "\n object a, from AAA:";  callThem(a);  // Here CallThem() applies
       cout << "\n object b, from BBB:";  callThem(b);  // the customized
       cout << "\n object c, from CCC:";  callThem(c);  // combination of
       cout << "\n object d, from DDD:";  callThem(d);  // functions for each
    }                                                   // kind of object.
```

Here is the output.

```
    object a, from AAA:
From AAA::functionOne()
From AAA::functionTwo()
    object b, from BBB:
From AAA::functionOne()
From AAA::functionTwo()
    object c, from CCC:
From CCC::functionOne()
From AAA::functionTwo()
    object d, from DDD:
From DDD::functionOne()
From DDD::functionTwo()
```

Syntax for Pure Virtual Functions

If a *virtual* function is understood as an interface delineator having a default implementation, then a pure *virtual* function may be thought of as a default implementation that does not provide a default. It is a "pure" placeholder, delineating the return type, name, and signature of a function that at least one class on each descending branch of the inheritance hierarchy must implement.

The pure specifier, $= 0$, is arbitrary symbology that has nothing to do with assignment. Within the class specifier, it is appended to the prototype of a *virtual* function to signify that the function is a pure *virtual* function. No additional definition is needed.

```
                              ┌──────────────┐
                              │ the pure     │
                              │ specifier    │
       class  Sample          └──────┬───────┘
         {                           │
         public:                     ▼
             virtual void displayIt() = 0;   // A pure virtual function.

             virtual void nullFunction()     // Though this is a null function
                {                            // as it has "no body," it is not
                }                            // a pure virtual function.
             ⋮
         };
```

Each derived class that inherits a pure *virtual* function has a choice: either to retain it as a pure *virtual* function or to define it.

The following program illustrates the fundamental syntax and properties of pure *virtual* functions.

```
#include <iostream.h>

class AAA                              // Having a pure virtual function,
  {                                    // this is an abstract class and
    public:                            // so it cannot be instantiated.
        virtual void functionOne() = 0;   // (Attempting to define an A
  };                                   // object would evoke an error.)

class BBB : public AAA                 // AAA::functionOne() is inherited.
  {                                    //
    public:                            // This is an abstract class.
        virtual void functionOne() = 0;
  };

class CCC : public BBB                 // A definition is provided
  {                                    // for the inherited
    public:                            // pure virtual function.
        void functionOne()
  {
    cout << "\nFrom CCC::functionOne()";
  }
  };

class DDD : public CCC                 // CCC::functionOne()
  {                                    // is overridden.
    public:
        virtual void functionOne()
  {
    cout << "\nFrom DDD::functionOne()";
  }
  };

void callIt(AAA& object)
```

```
    {
      object.functionOne();
    }

void main()
    {
      CCC c;
      DDD d;

      cout << "\n object c, from CCC:";   callIt(c);
      cout << "\n object d, from DDD:";   callIt(d);
    }
```

Here is the output.

```
     object c, from CCC:
   From CCC::functionOne()
     object d, from DDD:
   From DDD::functionOne()
```

The Destructor in the Base Class

Suppose that a dynamically allocated object from a derived class is being managed by way of a base class pointer variable. In order for the deallocation of the object to begin with the destructor from its native class, not the destructor in the base class, the destructor in the base class should be specified as *virtual*. This works despite the fact that the succession of destructors down the derivation hierarchy, unlike normal *virtual* functions, do not have the same name. This may be important if memory leak is to be avoided when derived classes include pointers to data structures, including strings. The following program demonstrates the action that results with a virtual destructor.

```
#include <iostream.h>

class AAA
    {
      public:
        virtual ~AAA()
          {
            cout << "\nFrom the AAA destructor";
          }
    };

class BBB : public AAA
    {
      public:
        ~BBB()
          {
            cout << "\nFrom the BBB destructor";
          }
    };
```

```
class CCC : public BBB
  {
    public:
      ~CCC()
        {
          cout << "\nFrom the CCC destructor";
        }
  };

class DDD : public CCC
  {
    public:
      ~DDD()
        {
          cout << "\nFrom the DDD destructor";
        }
  };

void main()
  {
  AAA*  AAAptr = new AAA;
  AAA*  BBBptr = new BBB;
  AAA*  CCCptr = new CCC;
  AAA*  DDDptr = new DDD;

  cout << "\n\ndeleting the AAA object:";  delete AAAptr;
  cout << "\n\ndeleting the BBB object:";  delete BBBptr;
  cout << "\n\ndeleting the CCC object:";  delete CCCptr;
  cout << "\n\ndeleting the DDD object:";  delete DDDptr;
  }
```

Here is the output.

```
deleting the AAA object:
From the AAA destructor

deleting the BBB object:
From the BBB destructor
From the AAA destructor

deleting the CCC object:
From the CCC destructor
From the BBB destructor
From the AAA destructor

deleting the DDD object:
From the DDD destructor
From the CCC destructor
From the BBB destructor
From the AAA destructor
```

References

1. Ellis, M.A. and Stroustrup, B. *The Annotated C++ Reference Manual.* Reading, MA: Addison-Wesley, 1990.
2. Murray, R.B. C++ *Strategies and Tactics.* Reading, MA: Addison-Wesley, 1993.
3. Stroustrup, B. *The C++ Programming Language*, 2nd ed., Reading, MA: Addison-Wesley, 1991.
4. Stroustrup, B. *The Design and Evolution of C++.* Reading, MA: Addison-Wesley, 1994.

5
Templates

5.0 Introduction

Templates enable the construction of parameterized classes and functions. They extend abstraction: procedural and data abstractions can be built without type information; the information is specified by the user.

The template design was first presented by Bjarne Stroustrup in a conference presentation titled *Parameterized Types for C++* in October 1988. Templates are a relatively new addition to the language and there is relatively little written about them. Templates are patterns for defining families of functions or families of classes. Free functions (i.e., stand-alone functions) are created by function templates. Class templates create classes. A free function instantiated by a template is called a template function. A class instantiated by a template is called a template class.

Free function templates make an excellent place to begin the study of templates because they capture the idea of a parameterized type, while being simpler than fully developed class templates. They are discussed in Section 5.1.

A class template, with its member function templates, can be used to form a container class. A container class couples the definition of a data structure, which can store entities of any kind, to a management discipline (e.g., a linear storage structure managed in LIFO manner or a linear storage structure managed in a FIFO manner). Given the class template for a *Queue*, it is possible, on one line, to define queues for any kind of objects in the program. Here are the definitions of four independent queues in a program to simulate student registration at a college. *Queue* is the name of a class template for instantiating individual queues for different objects.

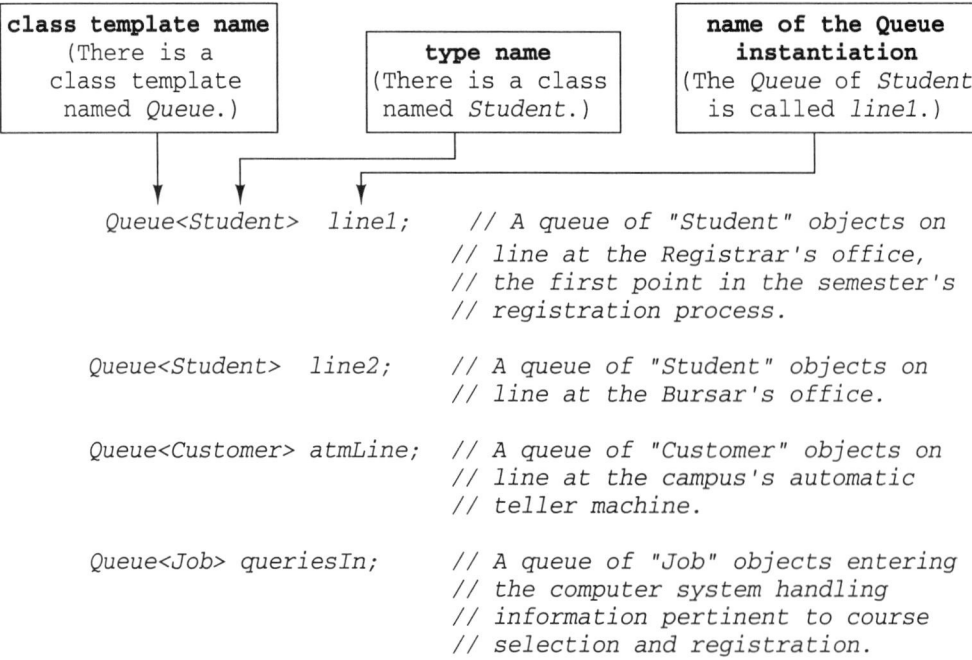

```
Queue<Student>  line1;     // A queue of "Student" objects on
                           // line at the Registrar's office,
                           // the first point in the semester's
                           // registration process.

Queue<Student>  line2;     // A queue of "Student" objects on
                           // line at the Bursar's office.

Queue<Customer> atmLine;   // A queue of "Customer" objects on
                           // line at the campus's automatic
                           // teller machine.

Queue<Job> queriesIn;      // A queue of "Job" objects entering
                           // the computer system handling
                           // information pertinent to course
                           // selection and registration.
```

Similar container classes can be declared for a stack, binary search tree, graph, set, bag, or any other storage structure. The beauty is that, in each case, a single template definition can create cóntainers for as many specific kinds of objects as desired (and as many different containers as needed).

5.1   Function Templates

Function templates are function definitions enhanced so that where an actual argument is customarily transmitted for use, what is passed from the call are both the usual value as well as the actual argument's data type. The function template, or template, might be thought of as a metafunction: instead of being a specialized implementation, called a specialization, such as a *swap( )* written to work for *int*s, it is a pattern for defining a *swap( )* for *int*s, a *swap( )* for *float*s, a *swap( )* for *char*s, or a *swap( )* particularized for any other data type. In all cases, the code is literally the same; but the data types of the variables are different.

Specific implementations of the *template swap( )* are created in accordance with the data type of the items in the call. If *swap( )* is called to exchange the value of two *ints*, a version of *swap( )* is created in which the formal arguments and the "holder" variable defined within the body are *ints*. If the program calls *swap( )* to exchange the value of two *floats*, the template instantiates a version in which these variables are *floats*.

A function instantiated by a template generally adheres to expectations associated with regular functions. As a rule, the calling client needs no idea of whether a function call is being fielded by a regular function or handled by a function instantiated from a template.

The compiler transcribes a function from a template when encountering a call that cannot be resolved by a specialization with a signature that applies (without implicit data type conversion). The function instantiated is not discarded following its use. It is retained as a specialization in the event it may be needed again. Including a function template within a program does not restrict overloading a function name with particular versions. The same function name can be overloaded with multiple templates, provided they have distinctive signatures.

Templates are not intelligent agents that formulate correct code from high-level logical specifications. Templates allow the data type of formal arguments and variables within the function's body to remain unspecified until the function is called. The code within a template is the code that will be repeated within each specialization instantiated. This means that its set of operators, and the function calls it makes, must be appropriate for the data type at hand. For example, suppose two arguments of a free-ranging data type are to be compared with relational operator >= and displayed using the insertion operator:

```
if (argument1 >= argument2)   cout << argument1;
else cout << argument2;
```

A template function in which these arguments are *int* or *float* or *char* will work fine. For *Point* objects [e.g., having an abscissa and an ordinate as data members, such as (4, 3)], an operator >= for *Point* and *cout* for *Point* must be defined.

Motivating Function Templates

The purpose of this section is to demonstrate the utility of template functions. The next section describes how to build them.

Consider the function *fancyPrint( )*.

```
void fancyPrint(int i)
    {
       cout << " ---> " << i << " <---" << endl;
    }
```

A programmer might be tempted to take advantage of automatic type conversion and use the function in a program such as this one.

```
void fancyPrint(int i)
    {
       cout << endl << "  --->  " << i << "  <---" << endl;
    }

void main()
    {
       float f = 0.00098765, g = 1234567.89;
       char c = 'A';

       fancyPrint( f );    // prints  ---> 0 <---
       fancyPrint( g );    // prints  ---> -10617 <---
       fancyPrint( c );    // prints  ---> 65 <---
    }
```

The effect of the argument passing in this program is equivalent to the following assignments (and is an example of poor programming practice).

```
i = f;   // Here, i ends up storing 0.
i = g;   // Overflow; i ends up storing -10617
i = c;   // Here, i ends up holding 65 (ASCII of 'A').
```

There will be no error message here but the programmer may be surprised by the results. The problem, of course, is the type inconsistency between the formal argument and the actual argument.

This example underlines the importance of type consistency. Clearly the correct approach is to overload the function *fancyPrint( )* and to code implementations for each data type. But the code may be exactly the same for *ints*, *floats*, and *chars* as well as for *structs* and for objects of classes. Function templates enable a single representation of this code as an alternative to a set of overloaded functions. Template functions are created for each case from a single function template.

Defining Function Templates

Here is a program in which the function *fancyPrint( )* is coded as a template. As such it is instantiated for the particular data type given in the call, and therefore works correctly for each data type. An explanation follows. The annotations are for concise reference. A full explanation of template definitions follows.

| Template is a keyword | Class is a keyword indicating that the following identifier (here dataType) is a "formal parameter" for holding the type specifier (e.g. int, float, char, whatever) to be passed to the template when it is invoked. |

```
#include <iostream.h>

template <class dataType>
void fancyPrint(dataType i)

{
    cout << endl << "  ---> " << i << " <---" << endl;
}


void main()
{
    float f = 0.00098765, g = 1234567.89;
    char c = 'A';

    fancyPrint( f );    // Prints  ---> 0.000988 <---      .
    fancyPrint( g );    // Prints  ---> 1234567.875 <--- .
    fancyPrint( c );    // Prints  ---> A <---

}
```

DataType is not a keyword; it is the name chosen for the identifier to hold the data type of the actual argument that is to be passed to this template function. Notice how it is used as the data type of the formal argument, i. (Often T or Type is the name chosen.)

Calls to template functions are no different from calls to nontemplate functions. The template mechanism itself reads the data type of the actual argument corresponding to the identifier serving as the type specifier and assigns to the type specifier (i.e., the formal parameter) that type.

Every function template begins with the keyword *template* and a formal parameter list within angle brackets. The keyword *class* signifies that the identifier to follow is a parameterized type (also called a formal parameter), which is to say, a variable to which will be transmitted a data type and will thereafter within the template function be used as a type specifier for that type. Using *class* as the keyword makes sense. The name of any defined class (e.g., *Point, Box*) is a data type specifier (as well as the beginning of a class definition). Thus the word *class* means data type specifier and is appropriate here. It is quite an accomplishment that a language as rich as C++ has so small a list of reserved words (only 48).

A template's formal parameter list is analogous to a function's argument list:

```
template <class Type1,  class Type2,  class Type3>
```
                           parameter list

Here *template* is a keyword announcing that a template's parameter list and
the function's declarator or definition is about to follow. Whereas a function's
argument list is enclosed in parentheses, the template's parameter list is enclosed within angle brackets and *class* is the meta data type of each of its
parameters. Just as a data type precedes each formal argument in a function declarator, the keyword *class* must precedes each formal parameter in
the template's parameter list.

Type1 will be assigned a data type, for instance, an *int*, *float*, or the name of
a class (e.g., *Point*); *Type2* will also be assigned a data type, a type that may be
different from *Type1* or not; and *Type3* will also be assigned a data type. Just as
the values for a function's arguments remain unspecified until the function is
called, the template's formal parameters remain unspecified until the function
template is called to construct a specialization of the function whose heading
lies immediately ahead. Every formal parameter that appears in the parameter
list must be used at least once as a type specifier within the function's declarator. This is because the match between the formal parameter and the type
it stands for is established by mapping the function's call onto the function's
declarator. Only the function's signature, not the return type, is used for this.
The reason is that nothing definite about a function's return type can be inferred from the function's call. An object return can be implicitly transformed,
anonymously used within an expression, or disregarded entirely.

Here is this same formal parameter list in context with the function template
it is helping to define.

```
template <class Type1,  class Type2,  class Type3>     // No semicolon.
int  functionOne  (Type1 x,  Type2 y,  Type3 z)
    {
        int    i,  j;
        Type1  t1Holder;  // Parameter used as a type specifier.
          ⋮
    }
```

The declarator for *functionOne( )* is standard except that it uses the template's
formal parameters as type specifiers. *Type1*, *Type2*, and *Type3* are the data types
of formal arguments *x*, *y*, and *z*. If *Type1* represents an *int*, then *x* is an *int*;
if it holds a *class* called *Box*, then *x* is a *Box* object. *Type2* stands in the same
relationship to the formal argument *y*. Within the body of the function, *Type1*,
Type2, and *Type3* can be used to define local variables of their respective data
types.

The particularizing data types to which the type parameters are bound are
established when the function is called. Suppose that within *main( )* or any
other function, *functionOne( )* is called like this:

```
y = functionOne(25, 2.7, 6);    // A thoroughly ordinary call.
```

The data type of the first actual argument, the 25, is *int*. Accordingly, *Type1* will stand for an *int* because *Type1* represents the parameterized type associated with the first formal argument. The formal argument *x* is created as an *int* and assigned the value of 25. Later, the local variable *t1Holder* is created as an *int* because it becomes whatever data type *Type1* holds. The data type of the second actual argument, the 2.7, is a *float*. Because of positional correspondence between actual arguments and formal arguments, *y* has to become a *float* and so *Type2*, for the duration of function construction under way, becomes a synonym for the type specifier *float*. Finally, by the same reasoning, *Type3* is made to stand for an *int*.

Notice that the call to *functionOne( )* is no different in form from a call to a regular (nontemplate) function. There is no special syntax associated with the invocation of template functions (functions forged from a template). This is consistent with the use of overloaded functions and the use of functions having default arguments. The function's "client" (i.e., caller) need not be aware of how the function is introduced into the program for use. The template's method of operation is straightforward: when the compiler encounters a function call but finds no function with formal arguments whose data types exactly match, it looks for a function template; if an appropriate template is present, the compiler uses it to create the code for a version of the function appropriate to the call. The compiler creates as many different customizations from the template as are needed by the program. Thus the preceding call to *functionOne( )* results in the compiler's installing the following function within the program.

```
int  functionOne  (int x, float y, int z)
    {
      int    i, j;
      int    t1Holder;
      ⋮
    }
```

A subsequent call to *functionOne( )* in which the first argument is again an *int*, the second is again a *float*, and the third is again an *int* would not cause a second copy of the preceding to be turned out. All versions rendered by the template are retained within the program and remain available for future use, just as if they had been specializations written by a programmer. However, each of the following calls would summon the instantiation of a separate specialization.

```
a =  functionOne( 3.14,   10,   1);   // Requires a "float, int, int" specialization.

b =  functionOne(   10, 3.14, 0.2);   // Requires an "int, float, float"
                                      // specialization.
c =  functionOne(  123,    6,  -2);   // Requires an "int, int, int" specialization.
```

```
d =  functionOne(  'A',   'B',   'C'); // Requires a   "char, char, char"
                                       // specialization.
e =  functionOne( 3.14,   'A',   5);  // Requires a   "float, char, int"
                                       // specialization.
```

These calls show how a function template (i.e., a template that creates functions) create a family of functions. The collection of template functions spawned is said to be "a family of functions" that are procedurally the same rather than an "overloaded set of functions."

What if *functionOne( )* had been called with only one argument? Can *Type2* and *Type3*, when arguments corresponding to *y* and *z* are omitted in the call, be expected to assume a data type such as *void*? Definitely not! If the only declaration for *functionOne( )* were the template function, then *functionOne( )* would have to be called with exactly three actual arguments: no fewer and no more. The template would be unable to create a function for the following call, and so this call would elicit an error message from the compiler.

```
x = functionOne( 10 );
```

However, both template functions as well as function templates can be overloaded. Therefore, the call to *functionOne( )* having the signature of a single *int* would be fine if the given template were accompanied by either an explicitly coded specialization such as:

```
int functionOne(int i)    // Function explicitly coded.
  {
   // Details omitted.
  }
```

or the function template:

```
template <class T>       // A template that constructs functions
int  functionOne (T x)   // for calls with one argument.
  {
   // Details omitted.
  }
```

If both of these specifications are given in the program, the explicitly coded function is used in preference to a function created by a template. This is consistent with the way the compiler accumulates a set of template-generated functions. Had no explicitly coded function been available but had it already used the template to forge a version having an *int* signature it would have used that one rather than creating a new one. It is also worth noting that the template:

```
template <class Type1,  class Type2,  class Type3>
int  functionOne (Type1 x,  Type2 y,  Type3 z)
     {
      int    i,  j;
      Type1  t1Holder;  // Formal parameter used as a type specifier.
```

```
       .
       .
       .
  }
```

can coexist in the same program with the following template:

```
template <class Type1>     // A template that constructs functions
int  functionOne (Type1 x)  // for calls with one argument.
  {
   // Details omitted.
  }
```

Both using the identifier *Type1* as a formal parameter. The names of formal parameters, like the names of formal arguments and the names of automatic variables, are local to a function.

Note that any type specifiers can be used in the template function's signature. Any of these may be used as the function's return type. Consider the following function template declarations, overloading *functionTwo( )*. Each has a different signature.

```
//  This template instantiates one-argument specializations of
//  functionTwo() in which the argument can be of any data type.

template <class T>
void  functionTwo(T a);   // Semicolon shows this is a prototype.

// The function defined here requires two arguments.
// The first can be of any data type, the second must be an int.
// The function returns a value of the same class as the first
// argument, whatever that happens to be.

template <class T>
T  functionTwo(T a, int i);

// Specializations to be created here are three-argument versions
// in which the first two arguments in the call have to be ints.
// The third can be of any type.  All the specializations
// constructed from this template will return a float.

template <class T>
float  functionTwo(int i, int j, T a);

// The family of functions denoted for construction take four
// arguments.  The first three can be of any data type, but
// they must all be of the same type.  The fourth argument can
// be of any data type, different from that of the first three
// or the same.  These functions will return an article having
// the same data type as the fourth argument.

template <class T1, class T2>
```

```
T2  functionTwo(T1 a, T1 b, T1 c, T2 d);
```

It is important to note that formal arguments may be passed by reference as well as passed by value. Here is yet another template for *functionTwo( )* that can supplement those above:

```
// The first and the fourth argument in the call have to be of
// the same data type, though the first is passed by value and
// the fourth is passed by reference.  The second argument has
// to be an int.  The third argument can be of any type, and is
// passed by reference. The fifth argument has to be a float.
//  The sixth could be of any type, and it is passed by value.
template <class T1, class T2, class T3>
void functionTwo(T1 arg1, int& arg2, T2& arg3, T1& arg4, float arg5, T3 arg6);
```

Although the preceding is contrived, here is a function template for a swap. It will instantiate specializations that work successfully for *ints*, *floats*, *chars*, and for any objects not needing deep copies. Naturally, it requires that both its arguments be of the same type.

```
template <class T>
void swap(T& a,  T& b)
    {
      T holder;

      holder = a;
      a = b;
      b = holder;
    }
```

Templates play a particularly important role when arguments are passed by reference. This template avoids serious errors resulting from poor programming such as this.

```
void swap (float& a,  float& b)
    {
      float holder;

      holder = a;
      a      = b;
      b      = holder;
    }

int i = 5, j = 10;
swap(i,j);            // Function seems to proceed successfully
                      // as no error is flagged, but the
                      // exchange is not made.
```

When there is a difference in data type between an argument in the call and a formal argument that is passed by reference in the function, a temporary variable is defined for use as an intermediary. The value of the argument is copied into the temporary with data type exactly matching that of the formal argument. Then the temporary, is transmitted to the formal argument. Although updates to the formal argument are made to the temporary these updates are not carried back to the actual argument that appeared in the call. This is an excellent example of the dangers of circumventing strong typing in C++. This would be correct if *swap( )* were appropriately overloaded. But the template is a particularly elegant solution.

Finally, it is worth noting that arguments can be pointers (or arrays). The following is a function template for a linear search through an array of any data type for which the test == for equality is applicable.

```
//   Arguments one and two involve the same data type,
//   but argument one must be a pointer to this type (an l-value)
//   and argument two has to be an r-value.  Argument three must
//   be an int.

template <class Type>
int  find (Type*  array,  Type soughtItem,  int numOfElements)
  {
    int found = 0; // 0 signifies "not found".

    for (int i = 0;  (i < numOfElements) && ( !found );  i++)
        if (array[i] == soughtItem) found = 1;

    return found;  // 0 or 1  ("no" or "yes").

  }
```

5.2 Class Templates

The most common use of *template classes* is for containers, structures designed to hold objects, with mechanisms for storing them, retrieving them, and performing any other tasks that may be needed (e.g., counting them). The mechanisms are implemented with the class member functions. Each member function within a class template is a function template. The class data members provide for the actual storage of the class data (or pointer to them).

Definitions of class *templates* are class definitions headed by a template declaration line that begins with the keyword *template* followed by the template parameter list between angle brackets, analogous to the definition of a template for a function. The formal parameters named within the template parameter list may be used within the class definition anywhere that a type specifier may be. Wherever the formal parameter is used, it stands for the data type passed to the class template at the time it is instantiated. Here is the beginning of a class template for the construction of a generic buffer, which will be a container for information from any source.

```
template <class bufferType>

class Buffer
  {
    private:
                              // Buffer is the base address of an array that
bufferType*  buffer;          // will be acquired using new within the
int          size;            // constructor.
int          nextElement;

    // Details to come a little later.
  };
```

The information stored can be *Point* objects, *Box* objects, or anything else just as readily as *int*s, *float*s, or *char*s. Here are some sample instantiations.

```
Template class name
```

```
Data type for which the class is instantiated; it is passed to the
formal parameter bufferType in the template's template declaration line.
```

```
Buffer<int>      buffer1;            // Buffer1 is a Buffer object to store ints.
Buffer<int>      buffer2, buffer3;   // Buffer2 and buffer3 are additional int
                                     // buffers.
Buffer<Box>      buffer4;            // Buffer4 is a buffer to store Box objects.
Buffer<Point>    buffer5;            // Buffer5 is a buffer to store Point
                                     // objects.
Buffer<Message>  buffer6;
Buffer<Image>    buffer7;
```

This *Buffer* container uses an array and we explore it in detail. We also build a template that provides a first in and first out (FIFO) queue using a linked list. However, the coding for each of these is complicated by considerations that have nothing to do with the syntax or the logic of templates. In the case of the *Buffer* template, the difficulty comes from managing an array that is accessed by way of the data member *bufferType** (a pointer to whatever data type is represented by the template's parameter). The major concerns are: keeping independent copies of a *Buffer* object autonomous by providing a copy constructor and an overloaded assignment operator that install newly allocated duplicates of the array, and preventing memory leaks. In the case of the *Queue* template, there are these same issues as well as the declaration of the nodes from which the list will be formed and the logic for handling the list. After describing a class template in general, a "case study" of template classes is presented through the vehicle of building three different container classes: a container built from two scalars, a container built from an array, and a container built from a linked storage structure.

A Container Built From Two Scalars

Here is a class template called *Couplet*.

```
template <class Type>
class Couplet
  {
    private:
      Type  x, y;     // Couplet classes will contain two scalars of
                      // whatever data type is represented by Type.
    public:
      Couplet(Type forX, Type forY) : x(forX), y(forY)
        {
        }

      Couplet()  // The no-argument constructor is needed by functions
        {          // that must create Couplet objects to facilitate their
        }          // computation, such as a swap or, below, reMatch().

      Type getX()      // The datatype of the template's formal parameter
        {              // is used as a member function's return type.
          return x;
        }

      void setX(Type updateForX)  // The datatype of the template's formal
        {                         // parameter is used as a member function's
          x = updateForX;         // argument type.
        }

                                    // The template class is used as this
                                    // member function's return type
      Couplet reMatch(Couplet c)    // as well as a formal argument type.
        {
          Couplet<Type> tempCouplet;  // Uses the no-arg constructor.
          tempCouplet.x = x;     // New Couplet's x from invoking Couplet.
          tempCouplet.y = c.y;   // New Couplet's y from argument Couplet.
          return tempCouplet;
        }

                          // The insertion operator is applied to the
      void showCouplet()  // invoking object's x and y.  Whatever data type
        {                 // they are, << must be, or have been made, to fit.
          cout << endl;
```

```
            cout << "Couplet:   x = " << x << endl;
            cout << "           y = " << y << endl;
        }
    };
```

Couplet is a container for two objects of any one kind. One of these is held by the data member called *x*, and the other is held by the data member called *y*. It has a two-argument constructor which initializes them. The only noteworthy observation is the use of the template's parameter, *Type*, as the type specifier for the data members and for the constructor's arguments. It is this ability to represent datatypes symbolically, and to be able to set the representation to any type at the time the object of the class is created that characterizes template classes.

The no-argument constructor is familiar. Notice that it leaves the data members of the new object uninitialized. It is not possible to provide a default initialization; that would imply finding a literal that would be suitable for every data type over which *x* and *y* could range. Allowing clients to have objects with uninitialized data members presents vulnerability to errors; yet the programmer may need to forge an object as an intermediary in a computation, such as in a *swap( )* member function.

```
    void swap(Couplet& a, Couplet& b)
        {
            Couplet<Type>  holder;      // Uses the no-arg constructor.
            holder = a;   a = b;   b = holder;
        }
```

An option for the builder of the class is to specify the no-argument constructor as *private*. That would make it available for writing member functions but not for access elsewhere.

The *getX( )* function is a familiar selector or accessor function; it returns the value of the *private* data member *x*. The data type of the object returned is that represented by the template parameter. The *setX( )* function illustrates the use of *Type* as the type specifier for a function argument. The template type parameter can be used in all the same places and in all the same ways as any type specifier. The constructor could have been written with a *const* qualifier, and using pass by reference.

```
    Couplet(const Type& forX, const Type& forY) : x(forX), y(forY)
        {
        }
```

The *setX( )* function, could have been written:

```
    void setX(const Type& updateForX) :
        {
            x = updateForX;
        }
```

To keep the example concise, the selector and modifier for *y* are omitted.

The purpose of the *reMatch( )* function is pedagogical: it shows an object of the template class as a formal argument within a member function; it shows an object of the template class as the function return type; and it shows a member function creating a new object of its own class. The action is depicted in the following.

the invoking Couplet, *this   the argument Couplet, c

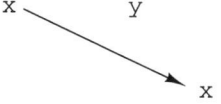   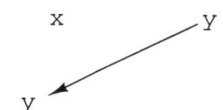

the new Couplet, tempCouplet

Because the function is defined within the class specifier, the references to *Couplet* along the declarator are presumed to stand for an object of the current type. That is:

```
Couplet        reMatch (Couplet        c)
```

has the same effect as:

```
Couplet<Type> reMatch (Couplet<Type> c)
```

In fact, the declarator actually could have been coded like this.
  Within the function, the definition of *tempCouplet*:

```
Couplet<Type> tempCouplet;
```

requires the template argument. Whenever the name of a template class is used within the body of any function to define an object it designates a data type specifier. There are any number of different distinct instantiations of the *Couplet* class: *Couplet<int>*, *Couplet<float>*, *Couplet<Point>*, *Couplet<Line>*, *Couplet<Box>*, and so on. Each has a customized set of data members and a customized set of member functions. It is not enough to define an object to be of type *Couplet*; that is still a generalization. Because an object is concrete, with memory allocated for data members, the object's type must be particularized.
  The *showCouplet( )* function provides a convenient means for displaying an object's data members. It is straightforward, but it hides a potential pitfall. Both data members *x* and *y* are displayed by the *ostream* object, *cout*, and an "inserter." The term "inserter" refers to any one of the overloaded << operators. The *ostream* class supplies inserters with the ability to handle *int*s, *float*s, *char*s, and even strings as the right operand. However, no inserters can be given for all the user-defined types that may be written. Thus there is no native << operator for *Box* objects, *Point* objects, or *Line* objects, three possible classes for which the template class *Couplet* may be instantiated as a container. In order for an instantiation of *Couplet* to compile successfully, every operator used within each of its member functions must be applicable to its operands. This

means that to instantiate *Couplet* for the data type *Line*, the inserter must have been enhanced with the appropriate capability. In other words, *operator<<* must have been overloaded so that *Line* objects can be sent to *cout*.

It is no easier for the builders of the *Couplet* class to anticipate the display requirements of every kind of object than it was for the builders of the *ostream* class. The function that augments the facility of the insertion operator must be provided. Moreover, when the data members to be shown are *private*, which is usually the case, the *operator function* << has to be declared as a *friend* of the contained object class. In practice, therefore, the builders of a class attend to its inserter. By providing the *showCouplet( )* function, the builders have done all that could be done to assist in the couplet's display. Containers, as a rule, do not provide comparable functions because their utility would be limited to classes of objects for which there was an inserter. For maximum utility, containers make minimal assumptions about their content.

The *Couplet* class template would more likely be set forth with its member functions declared within the specifier and defined following it, like this:

```
template <class Type>          // The template's specifier is begun
class Couplet                   // exactly as it was before.
  {
    private:
      Type  x, y;

    public:

      Couplet(Type forX, Type forY);    // The declaration of each
                                        // function, Couplet(); as always,
                                        // may consist of the very line
                                        // opening the function's
      Type getX();                      // definition (i.e., its declarator)
      void setX(Type updateForX);       // followed by a semicolon, as
                                        // here.  Or, it may be presented
      Couplet reMatch(Couplet c);       // without the appearance of
      void showCouplet();               // identifiers representing formal
  };                                    // arguments.

                        // When a general definition is outside the
                        // specifier, it must be preceded, as shown, by
                        // the keyword template followed by the template's
                        // parameter list.

template <class Type>
Couplet<Type>::Couplet(Type forX, Type forY) : x(forX), y(forY)
  {
  }

template <class Type>          // The complete name of a class template, as it
                               // must appear to the left of the scope
```

```
Couplet<Type>::Couplet()  // resolution operator, is the class's name followed
  {                       // by the specializing type specifier, as here,
  }                       // or specifiers.

template <class Type>
Type Couplet<Type>::getX()
  {
    return x;
  }

template <class Type>
void Couplet<Type>::setX(Type updateForX)
  {
    x = updateForX;
  }

template <class Type>
Couplet<Type> Couplet<Type>::reMatch(Couplet<Type> c)
  {
    Couplet<Type> tempCouplet;
    tempCouplet.x = x;
    tempCouplet.y = c.y;
    return tempCouplet;
  }

template <class Type>
void Couplet<Type>::showCouplet()
  {
    cout << endl;
    cout << "Couplet:  x = " << x << endl;
    cout << "          y = " << y << endl;
  }
```

The form of the class template's specifier is no different whether it contains function definitions, declarations, or a mixture. It always opens with the keyword *template* followed by the template parameters within angle brackets. This is followed by the keyword *class* and the class name. Function prototypes are formed in accordance with the usual rules that apply to forming prototypes. The template parameter, *Type*, and the class name, *Couplet*, are used as data type specifiers just as before.

The function definitions look different from typical member functions; but if they look like definitions of function templates, that is because they are. Each one is a class template, member function template, for *Couplet*, a "function factory" owned specifically by *Couplet* for the production of specific instantiations.

Each template function begins with the keyword *template* followed, in angle brackets, by a formal parameter list. Next comes the function's declarator, and it closely resembles the declarator in external definitions of member functions belonging to nontemplate classes. There are three parts to it: the function return type, the function name, and the function argument list. The full name of a member function is its name (e.g., *showBox( )*) preceded by its class name and the scope resolution operator (e.g., *Box::showBox( )*). When the class is a template, the class name requires qualification to show precisely which instantiation within the family of classes is the referent. In each case here, it is the class instantiated for whatever type specifier the template parameter *Type* currently signifies: *Couplet<Type>*. In both meaning and syntax, this is the same construct used in declaring and defining objects: the class name attached to a set of angle brackets that enclose a type specifier.

Such class declarations appear in three places in the *reMatch( )* function; or, more completely in the *Couplet<Type>::reMatch( )* function: as the return type, as an argument type, and as the data type of an automatic variable, *tempCouplet*.

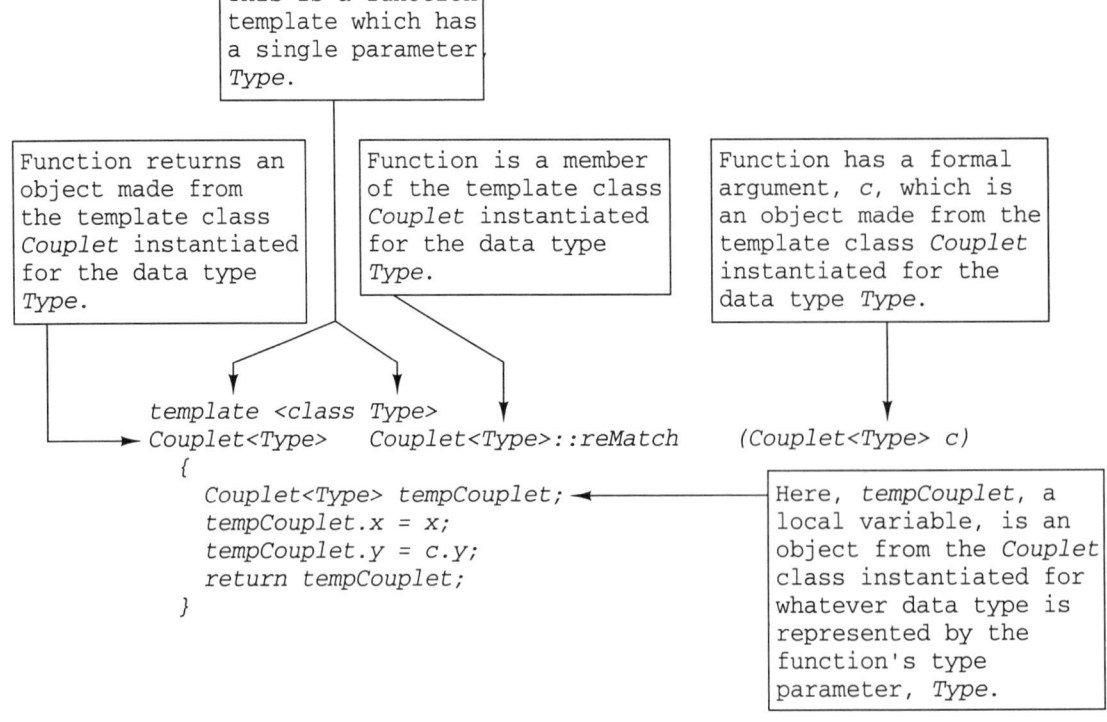

The two places among external member function definitions where the class name is used without the type parameter are within constructor declarators and within destructor declarators. Here the function name, to the right of the scope resolution operator, is the class name, alone.

```
template <class Type>
Couplet<Type>::Couplet (Type forX, Type forY) : x(forX), y(forY)
    {
```

```
                }

            template <class Type>
            ~Couplet<Type>::Couplet()
                {
                }
```

Consider a program that uses the *Couplet template* previously discussed. Notice the definition and use of *Couplet* objects with main( ).

```
#include <iostream.h>

                // A user-defined data type with which to test the
class Line   // Couplet class template that follows.
  {
     private:
       char symbol;
       int  lineLength;

     public:
        Line() : symbol('*'), lineLength(10)    // No-argument constructor.
           {
           }

        Line(int forSym, char forLen) : symbol(forSym), lineLength(forLen)
           {
           }

           // The insertion operator ( << ) will be overloaded
           // so that it can be used with objects of type Line.
        friend ostream& operator<< (ostream& os, Line& line);

  };   // End of class Line's specifier.

ostream& operator<< (ostream& os, Line& line)
  {
    for (int i = 1; i <= line.lineLength; i++)   os << line.symbol;
    return os;
  }

template <class Type>
class Couplet
  {
     private:
       Type x, y;

     public:
        Couplet(Type forX, Type forY) : x(forX), y(forY)
           {
           }
```

```
        Couplet()
          {
          }

        Type getX()
          {
            return x;
          }

        void setX (Type updateForX)
          {
            x = updateForX;
          }

        Couplet reMatch(Couplet c)
          {
            Couplet<Type> tempCouplet;
            tempCouplet.x = x;
            tempCouplet.y = c.y;
            return tempCouplet;
          }

        void showCouplet()
          {
            cout << endl;
            cout << "Couplet:  x = " << x << endl;
            cout << "          y = " << y << endl;
          }

    };  // End of class Couplet's specifier.

void main()
  {
    Couplet<int>  intCoup0;    // IntCoup0 is uninitialized -- DANGEROUS!
    Couplet<int>  intCoup1(1,2);
    Couplet<int>  intCoup2(3,4);

    cout << "\nintCoup1";
    intCoup1.showCouplet();
    cout << "\nintCoup2";
    intCoup2.showCouplet();

    cout <<"\nintCoup1.getX() = " << ( intCoup1.getX() );
    cout <<"\nintCoup2.getX() = " << ( intCoup2.getX() ) << endl;

    cout << "\nintCoup1.setX(111);    gives:";
    intCoup1.setX(111);
    intCoup1.showCouplet();

    cout << "\nintCoup2.setX(222);    gives:";
```

```
      intCoup2.setX(222);
      intCoup2.showCouplet();

      cout << "\nintCoup0 = intCoup1.reMatch(intCoup2);   gives:";
      intCoup0 = intCoup1.reMatch(intCoup2);
      intCoup0.showCouplet();

      // Get some line objects.
      Line  lineA('A',10),  lineB('B',20),  lineC('C',30),  lineD('D', 40);

      // Replicate the processing above with "Couplets of Lines".

      Couplet<Line> lineCoup0;    // LineCoup0 is uninitialized -- DANGEROUS!
      Couplet<Line> lineCoup1(lineA, lineB);
      Couplet<Line> lineCoup2(lineC, lineD);

      cout << "\nlineCoup1";
      lineCoup1.showCouplet();
      cout << "\nintCoup2";
      lineCoup2.showCouplet();

      cout <<"\nlineCoup1.getX() = " << ( lineCoup1.getX() );
      cout <<"\nlineCoup2.getX() = " << ( lineCoup2.getX() ) << endl;

      cout << "\nlineCoup1.setX( Line('@', 50) );    gives:";
      lineCoup1.setX( Line('@', 50) );
      lineCoup1.showCouplet();

      cout << "\nlineCoup2.setX( Line('#', 60) );    gives:";
      lineCoup2.setX( Line('#', 60) );

      lineCoup2.showCouplet();

      cout << "\nlineCoup0 = lineCoup1.reMatch(lineCoup2);   gives:";
      lineCoup0 = lineCoup1.reMatch(lineCoup2);
      lineCoup0.showCouplet();
   }
```

Here is the output.

```
intCoup1
Couplet:  x = 1
          y = 2

intCoup2
Couplet:  x = 3
          y = 4

intCoup1.getX() = 1
intCoup2.getX() = 3
```

```
intCoup1.setX(111);      gives:
Couplet:  x = 111
          y = 2

intCoup2.setX(222);      gives:
Couplet:  x = 222
          y = 4

intCoup0 = intCoup1.reMatch(intCoup2);   gives:
Couplet:  x = 111
          y = 4

lineCoup1
Couplet:  x = AAAAAAAAAA
          y = BBBBBBBBBBBBBBBBBBBB

intCoup2
Couplet:  x = CCCCCCCCCCCCCCCCCCCCCCCCCCCCCC
          y = DDDDDDDDDDDDDDDDDDDDDDDDDDDDDDDDDDDDDDDDDD

lineCoup1.getX() = AAAAAAAAAA
lineCoup2.getX() = CCCCCCCCCCCCCCCCCCCCCCCCCCCCCC

lineCoup1.setX( Line('@', 50) );    gives:
Couplet:  x = @@@@@@@@@@@@@@@@@@@@@@@@@@@@@@@@@@@@@@@@@@@@@@@@@@@@
          y = BBBBBBBBBBBBBBBBBBBB

lineCoup2.setX( Line('#', 60) );    gives:
Couplet:  x = ############################################################
          y = DDDDDDDDDDDDDDDDDDDDDDDDDDDDDDDDDDDDDDDDDD

lineCoup0 = lineCoup1.reMatch(lineCoup2);   gives:
Couplet:  x = @@@@@@@@@@@@@@@@@@@@@@@@@@@@@@@@@@@@@@@@@@@@@@@@@@@@
          y = DDDDDDDDDDDDDDDDDDDDDDDDDDDDDDDDDDDDDDDDDD
```

Note the function that overloads the output operator so that *ostream* objects can deal directly with *Line* objects. It is an ordinary free function that provides a new ability to a binary operator. Being a free function, different from a member function, the invoking object is not the implicit *this*. Rather, the invoking object, the left operand, is passed to the first formal

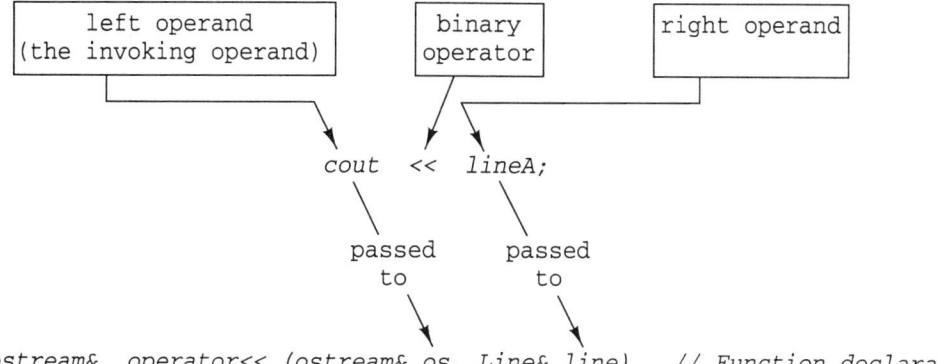

```
ostream&   operator<< (ostream& os, Line& line)     // Function declarator.
```

argument in the function argument list. The left operand, *cout* in the preceding illustration, is an object from the *ostream* class. The right operand, *lineA*, is an object from the class, *Line*. Why is the *ostream* argument passed by reference? C++ forces it to be by not providing a *public* copy constructor for *ostream* objects. Without a copy constructor, there is no means to initialize the parameters in the function with a copy of the argument in the call. Pass by value is thus ruled out. Does the *Line* argument have to be passed by reference too? No, this would be fine:

```
ostream&   operator<< (ostream& os, Line line)   // Function declarator.
```

Does the function have to return an *ostream* object? No, but doing so enables the cascading of operands. The *ostream* object returned is the same one that is passed to the argument *os*. As a result, the function call resolves to the same ostream object that initiated the invocation, be it *cout*, a file, or a printer. If the function had been written as follows,

```
void  operator<< (ostream& os, Line line)
   {
   for (int i = 1; i <= line.lineLength; i++)  os << line.symbol;
   }
```

this would have worked:

```
cout   <<   lineA;
```

but not this:

```
cout   <<   lineA << "<- lineA" << endl;
```

Can the ostream object be returned by value? No, for the same reason that it cannot be passed to the formal argument by value: there is no copy constructor available to mediate the transmission. Does this function have to be declared to be a *friend* of the *Line* class? Yes, because *Line*'s data members *lineLength* and *symbol*, which it accesses, are *private*. Had they been *public*, or had the function obtained their values by way of public accessor functions, friendship would not have been necessary. Instead of being made a *friend*, could this function have been made a member of the *Line* class? No, because when a binary operator is a member function, it is the left operand which is the invoking object. Here, the left operand is an *ostream* object, not a *Line* object.

Specializing Member Functions of Class Templates

Class templates can be neither specialized nor overloaded. The foregoing *Couplet* testing program above could not have included the specification for a second *Couplet* class of any kind: neither a nontemplate class named *Couplet*, nor a class template called *Couplet* specialized for *int*s, nor a class template of a particular data type.

The member functions of a class template that are defined within the class specifier (i.e., whose bodies are given within the class specifier) cannot be specialized. If the following class template had been the specifier for the *Couplet* class, with *showCouplet( )* defined within:

```
template <class Type>
class Couplet
    {
        private:
          Type  x, y;

        public:
          Couplet(Type forX, Type forY);
          Couplet();

          Type getX();
          void setX(Type updateForX);
          Couplet reMatch(Couplet c);

          void showCouplet()
            {
              cout << endl;
              cout << "Couplet:  x = " << x << endl;
              cout << "          y = " << y << endl;
            }
    };
```

a version of *showCouplet( )* especially for *float*s would not be allowed by the compiler. But upon instantiating a float version of the class,

```
Couplet<float>  floatCoup(1.11, 2.22);
```

the *showCouplet( )* definition within the specifier yields the accompanying member. It does not hunt for a specialization or, failing that, resort to creating one by means of a member function template. Later, if the compiler encounters a *float* specialization, it reports a multiple definition error.

The situation is different for member functions that are declared but not defined within the specifier. Suppose this had been the *Couplet* specifier, with *showCouplet( )* declared but not defined.

```
template <class Type>
class Couplet
   {
       private:
          Type  x, y;

       public:
          Couplet(Type forX,  Type forY);
          Couplet();

          Type getX();
          void setX(Type updateForX);
          Couplet reMatch(Couplet c);

          void showCouplet();
   };
```

In this case, no *showCouplet( )* function is defined to the exclusion of specializations. An explicit specialization has to be defined for each *Couplet* object of each data type that will call it (and no version has to be supplied for types of *Couplet* objects that will not call it), or the capability of creating functions when needed has to be provided by way of a template. Consider the following two specializations, one for *float*s and one for *int*s.

```
┌──────────────────┐ ┌──────────────────┐
│This function is  │ │Data type of      │
│a member of the   │ │specialization.   │
│Couplet class     │ └──────────────────┘
│specialized for   │
│floats.           │
└──────────────────┘
```

```
                                        // Not preceded by template <class Type>
void Couplet<float>::showCouplet()  //        or by template <class float>.
   {
      // NOTE:  function uses facilities from the iomanip.h header file.

      cout << setiosflags(ios::showpoint) << setprecision(3);

      cout << endl;
      cout << "float couplet:  x = " << setw(8) << x << endl;
      cout << "                y = " << setw(8) << y << endl;
   }

void Couplet<int>::showCouplet()
   {
      cout << endl;
      cout << "Couplet:  x = " << x << endl;
      cout << "          y = " << y << endl;
   }
```

If *Couplet*s were defined only for *int*s and for *float*s in *main( )*, things would be fine; more support for *showCouplet( )* would be needed. Things would still be fine if the *Couplet* class were instantiated for *char*s and for *Line*s, but those objects never called *showCouplet( )*. The program would fail, though, if a *Couplet* object for any type other than an *int* or a *float* attempted such an invocation. This specialization for *float*s will not serve objects of type *double* nor would a specialization for *double* serve objects of type *float*.

All data types can be accommodated by supplementing the specializations with a member function template.

```
template <class Type>
void Couplet<Type>::showCouplet()
  {
    cout << endl;
    cout << "Couplet:  x = " << x << endl;
    cout << "          y = " << y << endl;
  }
```

With this template, every instantiation of *Couplet* would be complemented with a version of *showCouplet( )* of the matched data type, whether a specialization was supplied or not. No specializations at all would be needed if the code forged from the template were suitable in every case. Of course, there is no guarantee that the code within every instantiated template function will be entirely proper. For example, the insertion operator may not be applicable to all.

A member function of a class template can be overloaded. There can be two or more versions of a nontemplate member function, provided they have different signatures. There can be two or more versions of a specialization for the same class instantiation (e.g., for *Couplet<int>*), as long as they have different signatures. There can be two or more versions of a function template, if being that they have different signatures. There can be specializations for the same class instantiation (e.g., *Couplet<int>*) and template functions. As always when the signatures of a specialization and a template coincide, the specialization is used. A prototype must appear within the specifier for each distinctive signature a member function may have but a single prototype suffices for all the specializations and the template that have the same signature.

As expected the name of the type parameter within member function templates does not have to be the same as the name of the type parameter within the class declaration. For the declaration of *Couplet*,

```
template <class Type>
class Couplet
  {
     // Details omitted.
  };
```

the following member function templates are just as satisfactory as the set in which the type parameter is named *Type* throughout.

```
template <class T>
Couplet<T>::Couplet(T forX, T forY) : x(forX), y(forY)
   {
   }

template <class Type>

Couplet<Type>::Couplet()
   {

   }

template <class TypeParam>
TypeParam  Couplet<TypeParam>::getX()
   {
     return x;
   }

template <class Type>
void Couplet<Type>::setX(Type updateForX)
   {
     x = updateForX;
   }

template <class T>
Couplet<T>  Couplet<T>::reMatch(Couplet<T> c)
   {
     Couplet<T> tempCouplet;
     // Details omitted.
   }

template <class t>
void  Couplet<t>::showCouplet()
   {
    // Details omitted.
   }
```

Class Templates with More Than One Type Parameter

In the discussion so far, the *Couplet* container had only one type parameter. The data type to which it gets instantiated is used as the type for both of "the" class data members.

```
template <class Type>      // One type parameter.
class Couplet
   {
     private:
       Type  x, y;
```

```
                        // Details omitted.
                      };
```

Because the number of individual type parameters in the class template is not restricted, *Couplet* might have been designed to accept two; and these might have been used as the respective data types for *x* and *y*.

```
    template <class T1, class T2>      // Two type parameters.
    class Couplet
      {
        private:
            T1  x;  // Here x is whatever data type T1 stands for.
            T2  y;  // Here y is whatever data type T2 stands for.

          // Details omitted.
        };
```

Note that the keyword *class* precedes both of the type specifier parameters. Had there been three parameters, *class* would have appeared three times. Within the function prototypes (and within the member functions themselves) the parameters are used wherever appropriate. The *getX( )* and *setX( )* functions use *T1*, because that is the data type of *x*. The *getY( )* and *setY( )* functions use *T2*, because that is the data type of *y*. The two-argument constructor uses both.

```
template <class T1, class T2>     // Complete specifier.
class Couplet
  {
    private:
        T1  x;
        T2  y;
    public:
        Couplet(T1 forX, T2 forY);  // Two-argument constructor; uses T1 and T2.
        Couplet();                  // No-argument constructor.

        T1 getX();
        void setX (T1 updateForX);

        T2 getY();
        void setY (T2 updateForY);

        Couplet reMatch(Couplet c);
        void showCouplet();
    };
```

With this *Couplet* class template all the following are allowable definitions of *Couplet* objects.

```
void main()
  {
    Couplet<int, int>     i1(0,0), i2(0,0), i3(0,0); // Three Couplet<int,int> objects
                                                     // defined.
```

```
                                        //
                                        // Both template parameters may be
                                        // of the same data type, but even
                                        // so both still need to be shown.

Couplet<int, float>  intFloat(3, 3.33);   // The class instantiation.
                                          // Couplet<int,float>
Couplet<float, int>  floatInt(4.44, 4);   // is a different class from the
                                          // instantiation Couplet<float,int>.

Couplet<Line, Line>  twoLines;      // Okay if the Line class is within scope.
Couplet<int,  Line>  intLine;

// Details omitted.
}
```

Because there are two formal type parameters in the class template definition, there must be two type specifiers in each instantiation. The same kind of positional correspondence applies here as in parameter passing to functions. The first type specifier is passed to the first template parameter, and the second type specifier is passed to the second. No rule says that the actual data types have to be different, but two distinct entries must appear within the angle brackets because the class has two parameters.

Similarly, two type specifiers have to accompany the class name when it appears within the declarators of member function templates and specializations; also, when these templates are declared, two parameters have to appear directly after the keyword, *template*. Here are some samples.

```
template <class Type1, class Type2>  // Two-argument constructor.
Couplet<Type1, Type2>::Couplet (Type1 forX, Type2 forY) : x(forX), y(forY)
   {
   }

template <class T1, class T2>            // No-argument constructor.
Couplet<T1, T2>::Couplet()
   {
   }

template <class Tp1, class Tp2>
Tp1 Couplet<Tp1, Tp2>::getX()
   {
      return x;
   }

template <class T1, class T2>
T2 Couplet<T1, T2>::getY()
   {
      return y;
   }
```

```
template <class T1, class T2>
Couplet<T1, T2>  Couplet<T1, T2>::reMatch(Couplet<T1, T2>  c)
  {
    Couplet<T1, T2> tempCouplet;
    tempCouplet.x = x;
    tempCouplet.y = c.y;
    return tempCouplet;
  }

template <class T1, class T2>              // Function template.
void Couplet<T1, T2>::showCouplet()
  {
    cout << endl;
    cout << "Couplet:  x = " << x << endl;
    cout << "              y = " << y << endl;
  }

                                          // Specialization of the above
void Couplet<int, int>::showCouplet()     // template; invoked by objects of
  {                                       // type Couplet<int,int>.
    cout << endl;
    cout << "Couplet<int,int>:  x = " << x << endl;
    cout << "                   y = " << y << endl;
  }

                                          // Second specialization of the above
void Couplet<Line,int>::showCouplet()     // template; invoked by objects of
  {                                       // type Couplet<Line,int>.
    cout << endl;
    cout << "Couplet<Line,int>:  x = " << x << endl;
    cout << "                    y = " << y << endl;
}
```

The following is not legal. A member function cannot be part template and part specialization (the second type parameter is a literal type specifier, making this a specialization).

```
template <class T>                        // ILLEGAL!!!
void Couplet<T, int>::showCouplet()
  {
    cout << endl;
    cout << "Couplet<T, int>:  x = " << x << endl;
    cout << "                  y = " << y << endl;
  }
```

Free Functions That Use Objects Instantiated From Template Classes

The free functions to which containers (i.e., objects instantiated from template classes) are passed, and from which containers may be returned, can be either specializations or templates. A function template may be overloaded with one or more specializations, and when this is the case, the specialization is chosen over the template when its formal arguments exactly match the types of the actual arguments in the call, as usual. A function template may even be overloaded by one or more other function templates; the only restriction is that every function call must unambiguously designate a particular one.

Concrete illustrations help. Continuing with the two-parameter version of the *Couplet* container, here is a free function that returns a *Couplet<int,int>* object whose *x* is the sum of the *x* members of two-argument objects of this same type and whose *y* is the is the sum of the objects' *y* members:

```
Couplet<float,float> addThem (Couplet<float,float> augend, Couplet<float,float> addend)
  {
    Couplet<float,float>  sum;

    sum.setX( augend.getX() + addend.getX() );
    sum.setY( augend.getY() + addend.getY() );

    return sum;
  }
```

Because this is an ordinary free function, and not a function template, it is written with respect to a specific kind of *Couplets*. Only templates can use symbolic parameters as type specifiers. The signature of this function qualifies it to handle only those calls to *addThem( )* that have two arguments, each of which is of type *Couplet<float,float>*. C++ enforces the data types of template classes. No automatic conversions are performed; this function would not be invoked if the actual arguments were of type *Couplet<int,int>*. Assuming that this is the only version of *addThem( )* accessible in *main( )*, look at how restricted its usage is.

```
void main()

  {
    Couplet<float,float>   float1(1.11, 2.22),  float2(3.33, 4.44),  floatSum;
    floatSum = addThem(float1, float2);    // Okay.

    Couplet<int,int> int1(1,2), int2(3,4), intSum;
    intSum = addThem(int1, int2);         // Error -- type mismatch both arguments.

    floatSum = addThem(float1, int1);   // Error -- type mismatch in second argument.

    Couplet<int, float>  intFloat(1, 1.11);

    floatSum = addThem(Float1, intFloat);  // Error -- type mismatch in second
                                           // argument.
  }
```

Four versions of *addThem( )* would be needed for the resolution of each of these invocations. Each would need formal arguments of corresponding types;

and the second would have to return an object of type *Couplet<int,int>* for the assignment to succeed.

A function available for objects of one type does not have to have versions available for objects of all types. The compiler will not object to the lack of a version, as long as calls are not made that cannot be resolved.

The *addThem( )* function might have been given as a template, for instance,

```
template <class T>
Couplet<T, T>  addThem  (Couplet<T, T> augend,  Couplet<T, T> addend)
    {
    Couplet<T, T>  sum;

    sum.setX( augend.getX() + addend.getX() );
    sum.setY( augend.getY() + addend.getY() );

    return sum;
    }
```

This is a somewhat restrictive function template; both scalars within all three containers have to be of the same data type, *T*; and all three containers have to be of the same type, *Couplet<T,T>*. Nevertheless, it will return a *Couplet<float,float>* as the sum of two *Couplet<float,float>*s and will return a *Couplet<int,int>* as the sum of two *Couplet<int,int>*s, for example. A danger is that there is nothing to prevent it from swinging into action in attempting to add a *Couplet<Line,Line>* to a *Couplet<Line,Line>* in the absence of an *operator+* defined for *Line*s.

A less restrictive template allows the two scalars within each *Couplet* to be of different types.

```
template <class T1, class T2>
Couplet<T1, T2>  addThem  (Couplet<T1, T2> augend,  Couplet<T1, T2> addend)
    {
    Couplet<T1, T2>  sum;

    sum.setX( augend.getX() + addend.getX() );
    sum.setY( augend.getY() + addend.getY() );

    return sum;
    }
```

This template would facilitate all the additions allowed by the preceding as well as additions such as a *Couplet<int,float>* to a *Couplet<int,float>* to give a *Couplet<int, float>*. Even though the *Couplets*' two data members may hold objects of different data types, the *x* data members of all three *Couplets* must be of the same type and similarly for the *y* data members.

Although either of these two templates could exist with any explicitly given specializations, such as those with the following prototypes,

```
Couplet<int,int>    addThem (Couplet<int,int>  augend, Couplet<int,  int>
```

```
addend);

Couplet<float,float> addThem (Couplet<int,float> augend, Couplet<float,int>
addend);

Couplet<float,float> addThem (Couplet<float,int> augend, Couplet<int,float>
addend);
```

they could not exist with each other. The reason is resolution ambiguity.

Value Semantics and
Reference Semantics

A class template can be instantiated for any data type. Equivalently, a container, such as a *Couplet,* can be defined to hold entities of any kind. This means that a *Couplet* can contain references to objects just as readily as the objects themselves. Nothing about the class needs to be changed, extended, or overloaded.

```
class Line   // Couplet class template that follows
  {
    private:
      char symbol;
      int  lineLength;
    public:
      Line() : symbol('*'), lineLength(10)    // No-argument constructor.
        {
        }

      Line(int forSym, char forLen) : symbol(forSym), lineLength(forLen)
        {
        }

      void resetLine(char newSymbol, int newLength)
        {
          symbol      = newSymbol;
          lineLength = newLength;
        }

      friend ostream& operator<< (ostream& os, Line& line);
  };

ostream& operator<< (ostream& os, Line& line)
  {
    for (int i = 1; i <= line.lineLength; i++)   os << line.symbol;
    return os;
  }

template <class T1, class T2>
class Couplet
  {
    private:
      T1  x;
```

```
         T2  y;
    public:
       Couplet()   // No-argument constructor.
          {
          }

       void setX(T1 updateForX)
          {
            x = updateForX;
          }

       T1 getX()
          {
            return x;
          }

       // Rest of the functions are not shown here.
    };

void main()
   {
     // Get some line objects.
     Line  lineA('A',10),  lineB('B',20),  lineC('C',30),  lineD('D',40);

     Couplet<Line, Line>   lineCouplet;      // Defined to hold Line objects.
     lineCouplet.setX( lineA );   // Here lineCouplet.x holds a copy of lineA.
     lineCouplet.setY( lineB );   // Here lineCouplet.y holds a copy of lineB.

     Couplet<Line*, Line*> linePtrCouplet;  // Defined to hold pointers to Line
                                            // objects.
     linePtrCouplet.setX( &lineC );  // Here linePtrCouplet.x holds the address
                                     // of lineC.
     linePtrCouplet.setY( &lineD );  // Here linePtrCouplet.y holds the address
                                     // of lineD.

     :
     :
   }
```

One of the preceding couplets, *lineCouplet*, holds copies of *lineA* and *lineB*: *lineCouplet.x* contains the value of *lineA*, and *lineCouplet.y* contains the value of *lineB*. This means that the copies within the container will not be affected by subsequent changes. The other couplet, *linePtrCouplet*, holds a reference to addresses of *lineC* and *lineD*: *linePtrCouplet.x* contains a reference to *lineC*, and *linePtrCouplet.y* contains a reference to *lineD*. All changes to *lineC* and to *lineD* will affect the contents of the containers. Whether to enter values or references into a container depends on the application. It is important to be aware of the alternatives and mindful of the implications.

A Container Built From an Array

The reason for using an array is to give a container a collection (and possibly a very large collection) of storage compartments and to enable access to them by way of a subscript. Access by way of a subscript allows for efficient, methodical processing. Subscripts also allow for direct access (which linked structures do not). The drawback to an array over a set of scalars (as in *Couplet*, which had a set of two) is that the elements are homogeneous, that is, the same data type. In practice, this rarely poses a problem. The common technique is to instantiate the class template so that the data type of the array is a pointer to the base class of a derivation hierarchy. This makes it possible for the cells to hold pointers to the entire range of objects from derived "specializations."

There are three ways to set the length of the array. One way is to code it as a fixed literal; but this mandates that the array be the same length for every instantiation of the template and excludes the possibility of a dynamic enlargement. Another way is to allow the array's size, along with its data type, to be given by the user upon the template's instantiation. This is passed to an expression parameter in the template formal type parameter list and explicitly specified as *int*. Thereafter, every reference to a particular template class has to include this number within the angle brackets. Finally, the technique that makes the container the easiest to use, the safest, and the most versatile is to implement the array within the class template as the base address of an array whose memory is acquired, by the constructor, using the *new* operator. This third technique is discussed first, and, afterwards, the other two are illustrated.

A Container Whose Array is Acquired with **new**

Consider this class.

```
template <class bufferType>  // Class template.
class Buffer
  {
    private:               // Buffer will be the base address of an array
      bufferType*  buffer;   // acquired by way of new in the constructor.

      int          size;   // The number of elements within the buffer array.

      int          nextCell; // Subscript of next element to be filled.

    public:
      Buffer(int numOfElements)  // One-argument constructor.
        {
          buffer   = new bufferType[numOfElements];
          size     = numOfElements;
          nextCell = 0;
        }
```

```
Buffer()    // No-argument constructor.
  {
    buffer  = new bufferType[10];  // Default buffer has 10 elements.
    size    = 10;
    nextCell = 0;
  }

~Buffer() // Destructor provided to prevent memory leak.
  {
    delete [] buffer; // Here [] must be used in deleting an array
  }                    // that was acquired with new.

Buffer (Buffer& original)              // Copy constructor --
  {                                    //   makes a deep copy.
    size    = original.size;
    nextCell = original.nextCell;

    buffer  = new bufferType[size];
    for (int i = 0; i < nextCell; i++)
      buffer[i] = original.buffer[i];
  }

Buffer operator= (Buffer rightBuffer)  // Assignment operator --
  {                                    //      makes a deep copy.
    size    = rightBuffer.size;
    nextCell = rightBuffer.nextCell;

    delete [] buffer; // Free the memory that the buffer array
                      // currently occupies.

    buffer  = new bufferType[size];  // Get correct amount of memory.
    for (int i = 0; i < nextCell; i++)
      buffer[i] = rightBuffer.buffer[i];

    return *this;
  }

void append(bufferType  newItem)  // The new item is installed
  {                               // at the end of the buffer.
    if ( roomLeft() )
      buffer[nextCell++] = newItem;    // Here nextCell is
                                       // post-incremented.
    else
      cout << "\n**BUFFER FULL  |"
           << newItem
           << "|  NOT ACCEPTED**"
           << endl;
  }
```

```
int slotsFilled()
  {
     return nextCell;
  }


                 // Returns the number of elements left for storage,
int roomLeft()    // 0 when this is none (remember, 0 is also false).
  {
     return ( size - slotsFilled() );
  }

void reset()
  {                   // The buffer array is not deleted
     nextCell = 0;    // because its space will be reused.
  }

void buffer_Copied_to_Argument (bufferType a[])
  {
     for (int i = 0; i < slotsFilled(); i++)   a[i] = buffer[i];
  }

Buffer  operator+ ( Buffer rightBuffer )
        // This shows how a template class object
        // is passed to a member function  and how
        // a template class object is returned.
  {
     int sizeOfSum = slotsFilled() + rightBuffer.slotsFilled();
     Buffer<bufferType>  combinedBuffer(sizeOfSum);

     for (int i = 0;  i < slotsFilled();  i++)
       combinedBuffer.append( buffer[i] );

     for(i = 0;  i < rightBuffer.slotsFilled(); i++)
       combinedBuffer.append( rightBuffer.buffer[i] );

     return combinedBuffer;
  }

void showIt()  // Displays the contents of the buffer.
  {
     cout << endl;
     for (int i = 0; i < slotsFilled(); i++)
       cout << "       " << buffer[i] << endl;
  }
};
```

The template class opens as expected. It has one formal type parameter, *bufferType*, which will be the data type of the array. The array is the first of the class's data members to be declared: *buffer*. No array is actually allocated and *buffer* is not a *const*ant pointer bound to the base address of a segment of memory. Rather, *buffer* is a variable that can store, as its value, the address at which an object of type *bufferType* is located. As objects of type *Buffer<bufferType>* are defined, a constructor will allocate space for a *bufferType* array dynamically using the *new* operator and assign the address of the leading element to *buffer*. The data member *size* retains the length of the array prescribed for *buffer* as *Buffer* objects are defined. Because these buffer objects will be FIFO queues (e.g., to hold bytes transmitted from the keyboard before they can be processed), the first element of the array to be filled is always cell 0. The next item received for storage is always appended to the end of the queue, which means it goes into the element immediately following the one that became occupied last. The *nextCell* data member holds the subscript at which the succeeding item, when it arrives, will be placed.

Consider the constructors. The argument within the one-argument constructor is the size of the buffer that the current *Buffer<bufferType>* object will have. If 38 is passed to *numOfElements*, the space for storing up to 38 items will be allocated for *buffer*, and 38 will be stored in *size*. Because the buffer holds nothing, the next item to be stored will be its first; it will go into the 0th element of the array. The no-argument constructor works identically, except that because no buffer size is being specified it gives a default size. The programmer has arbitrarily decided that 10 storage locations would make a good default.

The heap is the inventory of memory from which *new* draws when it makes its allocations. Memory leak refers to shrinkage of this inventory caused when allocated memory is not returned following the end of its utilization. Memory becomes lost because it is not formally *delete*d (re-marked as "available for use") before its address is lost track of. In order to avoid memory leak for this *class* when *Buffer<bufferType>* objects are no longer used, a destructor is be provided that explicitly *delete*s the memory comprising the *buffer* array. Just as the automatic allocation of the data member *buffer* does not engage the array to which it will point, *buffer*'s automatic deallocation will not disengage the array. If memory is taken with the two operators *new* and *[ ]* it should be released with the operators *delete* and *[ ]*.

The purpose of the copy constructor is to initialize a new object of type *Buffer<bufferType>* when such an object is passed to a function or returned. For instance, when a *Buffer* object in a function call is passed by value to a formal argument, the copy constructor is the mechanism specifying the exact nature of the information copied into the data members of the formal argument. The default copy constructor, which runs when there is none explicitly provided, makes a member-by-member bitwise copy. The following shows how its action is represented.

```
                              // Representation of the
   Buffer (Buffer& original)  // default copy constructor.
   {
      size    = original.size;    // Bitwise copy.
```

```
        nextCell = original.nextCell;  // Bitwise copy.
        buffer   = original.buffer     // Bitwise copy.
}
```

This is generally acceptable when none of the data members are pointers. When a data member, such as *buffer*, is copied in this way, the new data member *buffer*, being a bitwise copy, is identical to the original. This means that both the actual argument and the formal argument, holding the same address, point to the very same storage structure (e.g., the same array). As the function runs, any changes to the array through the formal argument will be changes in the same array belonging to the actual argument. This is not in itself bad, but it is antithetical to the semantics of pass by value. When an object is passed by value, the understanding is that nothing done to its representation within the function will change it.

So that passing *Buffer<bufferType>* objects by value conforms to the expectations of a user of this container, the copy constructor makes a full independent reproduction of the array. The *buffer* data member in the formal argument holds the base address of a different array from the *buffer* data member in the actual argument, but their respective arrays contain the same information. Such a copy is known as both a conceptual copy and a deep copy.

In C++, assignment (using the assignment operator =) and initialization (using the copy constructor) are considered highly distinctive. The distinction lies in the treatment of pointer data members and relates to the fact that in a pre-existing object something has to be done about the information currently being pointed to. Almost invariably, the action to be taken is the deletion the storage structure currently being pointed to in order to avoid a memory leak. However, this is not something that the default assignment operator automatically does. If it is to be done the programmer must do it in an explicitly coded assignment operator.

The default assignment operator, like the default copy constructor, makes only bitwise copies, also called shallow copies. When objects contain pointers to data structures, a deep copy is needed to make the object on the left of the assignment operator logically autonomous, which it needs to be with few exceptions. Consider an assignment operation that gives a conceptual copy of the arrays A, B, and C, with:

```
A = B = C;
```

A, *B*, and *C* refer to separate and autonomous copies of the contained information. That means that an action

```
A = X;
```

does not affect the information in *B* or *C*. When objects own individual copies of dynamically acquired data structures, these should be deleted before being replaced by an assigned successor. To attain the proper release of resources and the deep copy, it is necessary to provide an assignment operator customized for the class. In certain instances, it may even be necessary to provide specialized customizations (e.g. using *strcpy(buffer[i], rightBuffer.buffer[i])* instead of *buffer[i] = rightBuffer.buffer[i]*).

The only other function that bears special comment is *operator+* which returns a new *Buffer<bufferType>* formed as the concatenation of the *Buffer<bufferType>* constituting the left operand and the *Buffer<bufferType>* constituting the right operand. The size of the array in the new object is set to the sum of the number of slots used by the two operands.

Declaring the Array as an Automatic Variable

If the flexibility obtained by dynamically allocating the array in the preceding class is not needed, a similar class template could be built in which the buffer size is established at the time the code is written, and fixed. Its data members and constructor might be given as shown in the following.

```
template <class bufferType>    // Class template.
class Buffer
   {                            // The array is now a variable automatically
     private:                   // allocated and released with the respective
       bufferType  buffer[16]; // object's construction and destruction.

       const int   size;        // Constants are initialized by the constructor.

       int         nextCell;    // Subscript of next element to be filled.

     public:
       Buffer() : size(16), nextCell(0)  // Here size, a const, must be
                                         // initialized.
          {
          }

     // Details omitted.
   };
```

The salient difference is that *buffer*, an array, is an automatic variable—its 16 elements are allocated automatically upon the object's construction, without use of *new*, and deallocated automatically upon the object's destruction, without use of *delete*. A poignant experiment that dramatizes the difference between a dynamically allocated array and a static array is to display the *sizeof* the variable *buffer*. Here it is reported to have a size of 16 times however many bytes a single *bufferType* occupies. In the previous version, where *buffer* is a pointer to a *bufferType*, it has the size of a pointer variable (e.g., two bytes), regardless of the size of the piece of memory to which it points.

In this version of the *Buffer* class, because *buffer* is an automatic array, the default destructor, the default copy constructor, and the default assignment operator will do (except for those particular data types requiring a specialization). The *operator+*, however, needs some serious rethinking, as the object holding the concatenation cannot have a *buffer* with a greater capacity than either of the operands.

A Class Template with an Expression Parameter

Another design choice, which allows *buffer* to be an automatic array with a size set at the time the class is instantiated, is to pass the desired array length to what is termed "an expression parameter." An expression parameter is a variable of a specified data type appearing within the template's parameter list to which an initialization is passed by value. The value originates as an expression evaluating to the indicated data type within the template class instantiation.

In the following template specification, *bufferType* is a formal parameter that will subsequently serve as a type specifier; and *size*, an *int*, is an expression parameter.

```
template <class bufferType, int size>  // Here size is an expression
                                       // parameter.
class Buffer
  {
    private:                      // The buffer array contains that number
        bufferType buffer[size];  // of elements designated by size.
        int        nextCell;

    public:
        Buffer() : nextCell( 0 )  // Constructor, defined within the
                                  // specifier.
          {
          }

        int roomLeft();                    // Prototype.

        void append(bufferType newItem);  // Prototype.

        void showIt()             // A function defined within the specifier.
          {
            for (int i = 0; i < nextCell; i++)
              cout << endl << buffer[i];
            cout << endl;
          }
  };

template <class bufferType, int size>          // Function template for
                                               // roomLeft().
int Buffer<bufferType, size>::roomLeft()
  {
    return (size - nextCell);  // Expression parameter used in code,
  }                            // is a "read-only" variable.

template <class bufferType, int size>          // Function template for
                                               // append().
void Buffer<bufferType, size>::append(bufferType newItem)
```

```
      {
        if ( roomLeft() )  buffer[nextCell++] = newItem;
        else
          cout << "\n*buffer full!  |" << newItem << "|  not accepted!*" << endl;
      }
```

Here are some sample instantiations.

```
void main()
  {
    Buffer<int, 10>  intBuf1, intBuf2;
    Buffer<int, 25>  intBuf3;
    Buffer<int, 10>  intBuf4;           // From the same class as intBuf1 and
                                        // intBuf2.

    Buffer<Point,6>  hexagon;

    Buffer<float, 25> floatBuf;

    Buffer<float, 'A'> bufferA;         // Error! The second parameter is not an
                                        // int.

    Buffer<int, 10.0> buffer10Point0;   // Error! The second parameter is not an
                                        // int.
         .
         .
         .
  };
```

Three objects, *intBuf1*, *intBuf2*, and *intBuf4*, are instantiations of the same template class instantiation. Although *intBuf3* will hold *int*s, just as the other three *int* Buffers, it is an object from an entirely different template class instantiation. Thus the following would be a type mismatch error, unless a facility has provided for performing the conversion.

```
    intBuf3 = intBuf1;   // Type mismatch.
```

The last two attempts to instantiate the class fail because the expression in each is not an *int*. It matters not that 'A' is ordinarily promoted to an *int* with the value of 65 or that 10.0 is implicitly convertible to 10. An exact correspondence between the data type of the value in the instantiation and the type named in the template parameter is required.

A Container Built From a Linked Storage Structure

A queue is an abstract data type, which means that it is a conceptualization with formal properties that exists apart from its implementation. As an abstract data type, it is a linear storage that appends arriving entities at the back and removes entities from the front. In other words, it is a waiting line.

One implementation is with an array in which the entity occupying element 0 is construed as being at the front of the line. Suppose that the entity at the end of the queue were in element 3. An arriving entity would be stored in element 4. When the next entity is needed, the entity in element 0 is removed. Management of the data structure then requires that each entity in the array be advanced toward the front by one step. The performance of such a data structure is notoriously slow. In the order of 1,000 assignment operations would be needed with a deletion from a queue holding 1,000 entities.

Another implementation construes the queue to be within any contiguous sequence of elements in the array, such as with the head of the line at element 2 and the rear at element 5. An arriving entity would be stored in element 6. When the next entity is called for it is the one that is stored in cell number 2. Then the cursor maintaining the logical front is incremented, making the entity in element 3 the current head of the line. Performance is good because deletion does not require the entities in storage to be moved. The array managed this way holds no less than when the front is anchored at 0 because in this case element 0 is treated as the logical successor of cell n-1 in an n-element array. In an array with 10 elements (subscripted 0..9), a queue with four entities could have its *front* at element 8 and its *rear* at element 1. Elements 8, 9, 0, 1 are logically contiguous.

Still another implementation is through a linked list. A linked list is a logical sequence of nodes that are not necessarily physically contiguous. Each node is typically a dynamically allocated *struct* holding an entity and the address of the node behind it in line. Depicted in the following is a queue with four nodes. The number above each node represents its address in memory.

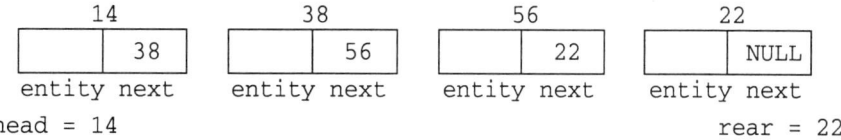

14	38	56	22
38	56	22	NULL
entity next	entity next	entity next	entity next

head = 14   rear = 22

More abstractly (and typically) this is represented:

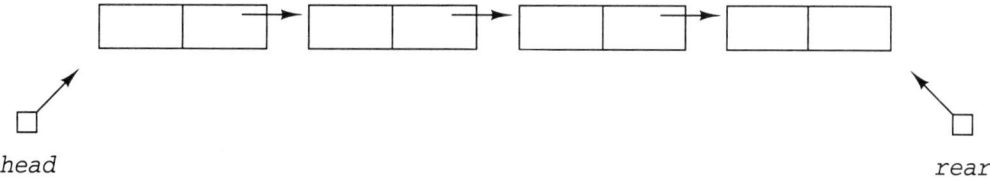

head   rear

The arrival of another entity would require the allocation of a new node to hold it, appending the new node to the end of the list, and updating the external pointer, *rear*. Suppose the *new* operator found space for the new node at memory location 44 (these addresses are metaphorical). The appended list would look like this:

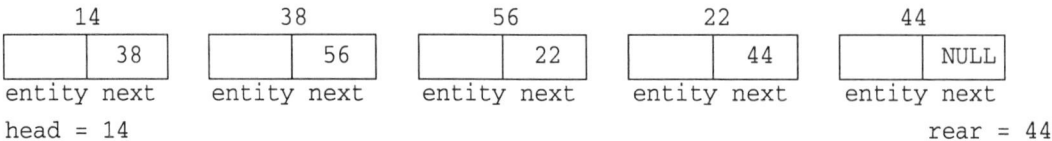

Deleting the front entity from the list puts the entity stored by the node at memory location 38 at the list's head.

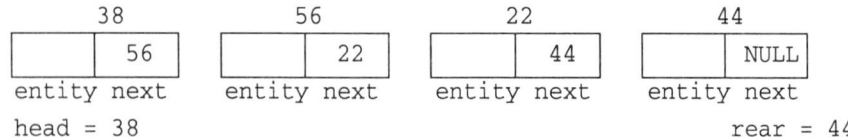

The "queueness" of a queue resides in its first-come, first-served linearity and the fact that the only permissible operations relative to managing the entities are putting arrivals in line at the end of the line and taking departures off the line from the front. The logic of the *append( )* function is independent of the nature of the entities being put in line, and likewise for the logic of a *delete-AndDeliver( )* function. Embodying the list structure and these functions within a class template permits the logic to be expressed once but used for queues of any kind of entity.

A Pascal-Like Queue (Queue Not Implemented as a Class)

No C++ programmer should consider implementing a queue or any other such construct in the following Pascal-like manner. In C++, the data structure and the functions for managing it should be packaged together as a class to provide an abstraction (i.e., a fully encapsulated abstract data type, operationalized through objects whose member functions provide the expected performance capabilities). Nevertheless, a Pascal-like example is given below to begin a discussion of how traditionally scattered definitions and functions can be unified as a class, how a particularized class can be transformed into a template, and how the template can be constructed for greatest flexibility. Four programs are used to illustrate.

What follows is an implementation of a queue for storing integers as a Pascal programmer might have written it (but, of course, the code is C++). In addition to the fundamental functions *appendInt( )* and *deleteAndDeliverInt( )*, the program includes *printQueue( )* as a facility allowing the queue's content to be displayed from head to rear. Also, it includes *deleteAndDeliverNode( )*, which returns the address of the node at the head of the list instead of the *int* that it stores, and *appendNode( )*, which appends a node to the queue. These allow taking a node off one queue and putting it onto another. Because queues are not objects instantiated by a constructor in this program, the initialization of their external pointers *head* and *rear* is performed by *initialize( )*. The function *empty( )* returns 1 if the queue is empty and 0 if it is not. Finally, the *deepCopy( )* function is included as a reminder of the important distinction between a deep and a shallow copy. Documentation within the program explains some of the coding details. It will not take long for a program with this kind of architecture to look antiquated to the C++ programmer.

```cpp
#include <iostream.h>

struct node              // Declaration of the nodes to form the queue.
   {                     //    The "entity" held by each is an int.
     int    entity;
     node*  next;
   };

void initialize(node*& head, node*& rear)  // Here node*& is a node pointer
   {                                        //          passed by reference.
     head = NULL;
     rear = NULL;
   }

int empty(node* head)
   {
    if (head == NULL) return 1;  // True, the queue is empty.
    else return 0;

   }

void append (int value, node*& head, node*& rear)  // An incoming value (an int)
  {                                                 // is appended to the queue.
    node*  newNode = new node;     // Get a new node.

    newNode -> entity = value;     // Put the incoming value into the new node.
    newNode -> next   = NULL;

    if ( empty(head) )    // If the queue is empty, newNode is its first and
        head = newNode;   // only node -- so head (as well as rear) must point
                          // to it.
    else
       rear -> next = newNode;  // If queue is not empty, the new node is
                                // linked onto the end.
    rear = newNode;
  }

void printQueue(node* head)
   {
     node*  rovingPtr = head;
     cout << endl;

     if ( empty(head) ) cout << "+-+-+-+-+-+-+-queue empty-+-+-+-+-+-+-+";

     while (rovingPtr != NULL)
        {
```

```
            cout << "  " << rovingPtr -> entity;   // Output operator must be
                                                   // applicable.
            rovingPtr = rovingPtr -> next;
         }
      cout << endl;
   }

int deleteAndDeliverEntity (node*& head, node*& rear)   //CAUTION!  Must *ONLY*
                                                        //          be called
   {                                                    //          when queue
      int     valueForReturn   = head -> entity;        //          is not
      node*   nodeToBeDeleted  = head;                  //          empty!

      head = head -> next;
      if (head == NULL)  rear = NULL;

      delete  nodeToBeDeleted;
      return  valueForReturn;
   }

void appendNode (node* nodeOn, node*& head, node*& rear) // An incoming node is
   {                                                     // appended to the
                                                         // queue.

      nodeOn -> next = NULL;  // As the end-node, it should "point to" NULL.

      if ( empty(head) )      // If the queue is empty, nodeOn is its first and
         head = nodeOn;       // only node -- so head (as well as rear) must point
                             // to it.
      else
         rear -> next = nodeOn; // If queue is not empty, nodeOn is linked onto
                                // the end.

      rear = nodeOn;
   }

node*  deleteAndDeliverNode (node*& head, node*& rear)
   {
      node*  nodeForReturn = NULL;

      if ( !empty(head) )
         {
           nodeForReturn = head;
           head = head -> next;

           if (head == NULL)  rear = NULL;
         }

      return nodeForReturn;
   }
```

```
void  deepCopy (node* head, node*& headOfCopy, node*& rearOfCopy)
  {
      node*  nodeHolder;                      // Delete the nodes
       while ( !empty(headOfCopy) )           // currently on the
          {                                   // queue which is to
            nodeHolder = headOfCopy;          // be made the copy
            headOfCopy = headOfCopy -> next;  //   --or else--
            delete nodeHolder;                // have a memory leak.
          }
        rearOfCopy = NULL;

     node*  rovingPtr = head;
     while (rovingPtr != NULL)
       {
         append( rovingPtr -> entity,  headOfCopy,  rearOfCopy );
         rovingPtr = rovingPtr -> next;
       }
  }

void main()
  {
     // Define and initialize three independent queues.
        node   *frontQueue1, *rearQueue1;  // Head and rear of queue 1.
        initialize( frontQueue1, rearQueue1 );
        node   *frontQueue2, *rearQueue2;  // Head and rear of queue 2.
        initialize( frontQueue2, rearQueue2 );
        node   *frontQueue3, *rearQueue3;  // Head and rear of queue 3.
        initialize( frontQueue3, rearQueue3 );

     // Put some content into queue 1.
        append( 111, frontQueue1, rearQueue1 );
        append( 222, frontQueue1, rearQueue1 );
        append( 333, frontQueue1, rearQueue1 );

     // Print the queues.
        cout << "\nQueue 1:";
        printQueue( frontQueue1 );
        cout << "\nQueue 2:";
        printQueue( frontQueue2 );
        cout << "\nQueue 3:";
        printQueue( frontQueue3 );

     // Copy Queue 1  into  Queue 3.
        deepCopy( frontQueue1, frontQueue3, rearQueue3 );

     // Move the front node from Queue 1 onto Queue 2.
        node* nodeHolder = deleteAndDeliverNode( frontQueue1, rearQueue1 );
        appendNode (nodeHolder, frontQueue2, rearQueue2 );

     // Display the entity from the current head of Queue 1 and delete it from
```

```
// queue.
    cout << "\n\n...from the front of Queue 1:   "
         << deleteAndDeliverEntity( frontQueue1, rearQueue1 ) << endl;

// Move the front node from Queue 1 onto Queue 2.
    nodeHolder = deleteAndDeliverNode( frontQueue1, rearQueue1 );
    appendNode (nodeHolder, frontQueue2, rearQueue2 );

// Print the queues.
    cout << "\nQueue 1:";
    printQueue( frontQueue1 );
    cout << "\nQueue 2:";
    printQueue( frontQueue2 );
    cout << "\nQueue 3:";
    printQueue( frontQueue3 );

}
```

The Same Queue *Implemented as a* Class

A class is sometimes described as the software analogue to an integrated circuit to connote that it is a complete self-contained product that can be "snapped in place" to provide functionality. Packaged as a class, the facility for a queue can be installed in a program as a unified piece. The variables, from simple scalars (e.g., *head* and *rear*) to complex data structures (whatever may be needed), and the functions are tied together and ready to work. Once the class is snapped in, the program can define queues as objects and use them with no further preparation. Use is by way of queue objects invoking *public* member functions. No supporting variables nor supplemental logic have to be defined.

In the next program notice that the member functions within the class are logically the same as they were in the previous program as free functions. Some of the syntax is different because the invoking object is not an explicit part of the functions' interface. The data members appearing without an accessing object and the function members invoked as a free function belong to *this, the queue object that accessed the function.

The other difference within the class is that the earlier set of free functions is supplemented with a constructor and a destructor. No longer does the client have to worry about initializing a queue's external pointers, *head* and *rear*. The constructor assures that this is always automatically taken care of.

From the client's perspective, queues are now easier to define and use. Not only have the front and rear external pointers passed from view, but a queue can now be defined plainly as a *Queue*. There is no need for the abstruse use of two pointers; and no need to refer to two pointers when, in fact, the reference is to one queue (e.g., in calling the append and delete functions). The *Queue* class makes the program more clear and removes awkward constructs that could cause confusion. Also, with the allusions to the external pointers removed, there is no clue whatsoever as to how the queue is implemented.

This frees the class's vendor to change the class's internals with absolutely no disturbance to clients.

Note that the *deepCopy( )* member function could have been written as an *operator=( )*. Using the assignment operator would offer symbolic convenience to the client, but it could leave a question as to whether "the assignment" were shallow or deep because the equal sign in itself does not signify. Also the *struct node* could have been declared externally to the class (above the class specifier). In this program it is not necessary. Even with the declaration of the *struct node* nested within a class and, under the *private* access specifier, it is still possible to define *node*s and *node* pointers in *main( )*. Only data members (variables, bound to memory) and functions are components of objects, not declarations. The access specifier applies only to components.

```cpp
#include <iostream.h>

class Queue
   {
     private:
                              // The struct serving as the node may be declared,
          struct node         // as shown, within the Queue class's specifier.
             {                // Despite its being nested within the class, it
               int    entity; // can be used as a type specifier in main().  (The
               node*  next;   // private access specifier does not apply to it
             };               // because it is neither a data member nor a
                              // function member.)

          node *head, *rear;  // The storage structure, which is comprised of
                              // two addresses, and the functions for using it
                              // are packaged together as a class.

     public:
          Queue() : head(NULL), rear(NULL)    // Constructor.
             {
             }

          ~Queue()                            // Destructor.
             {
               node*  nodeHolder;       // Delete the nodes
               while ( !empty() )        // on the queue
                  {                      // being destructed
                    nodeHolder = head;   //   -- or else --
                    head = head -> next; // have a memory leak.
                    delete nodeHolder;
                  }
             }

          int empty()
             {
               if (head == NULL) return 1;  // True, the queue is empty.
```

```
           else return 0;
        }

void append (int value) // An incoming value (an int) is appended.
   {
      node*  newNode = new node;    // Get a new node.

      newNode -> entity = value;    // Put the incoming value into the new
                                    // node.
      newNode -> next   = NULL;

      if ( empty() )      // If the queue is empty, newNode is its first
         head = newNode;  // and only node -- so head (and rear) must point
                          // to it.
      else
         rear -> next = newNode;  // If queue is not empty, the new node
                                  // is linked onto the end.
      rear = newNode;
   }

void printQueue()
   {
      node*  rovingPtr = head;
      cout << endl;

      if ( empty() ) cout << "+-+-+-+-+-+-+-queue empty-+-+-+-+-+-+-+";

      while (rovingPtr != NULL)
         {
            cout<<"  "<<rovingPtr -> entity; // Output operator must be
                                             // applicable.
            rovingPtr = rovingPtr -> next;
         }
      cout << endl;
   }

int deleteAndDeliverEntity()                //CAUTION!  Must *ONLY* be
   {                                        //          called when the
      int   valueForReturn  = head -> entity; //        queue is not
      node*  nodeToBeDeleted = head;          //        empty!

      head = head -> next;
      if (head == NULL)  rear = NULL;

      delete nodeToBeDeleted;
      return valueForReturn;
   }

void appendNode (node* nodeOn) // An incoming node is appended.
   {
```

```
            nodeOn -> next = NULL;     // As the end-node, it should "point to"
                                       // NULL.


            if ( empty() )   // If the queue is empty, nodeOn is its first
              head = nodeOn; // and only node -- so head (and rear) must point
                             // to it.
            else
              rear -> next = nodeOn; // If queue is not empty,
                                     // nodeOn is linked onto the end.
            rear = nodeOn;
        }

    node*  deleteAndDeliverNode()
        {
            node*  nodeForReturn = NULL;

            if ( !empty() )
              {
                nodeForReturn = head;
                head = head -> next;

                if (head == NULL)  rear = NULL;
              }
            return nodeForReturn;
        }

    void  deepCopy (Queue& copy)
        {
            node* nodeHolder;                 // Delete the nodes
            while ( !copy.empty() )           // currently on the
              {                               // queue which is to
                nodeHolder = copy.head;       // be made a copy
                copy.head = copy.head -> next; // of the invoking
                delete nodeHolder;            // Queue object
              }                               //   --or else--
            copy.rear = NULL;                 // have a memory leak.

            node*  rovingPtr = head;
            while (rovingPtr != NULL)
              {
                copy.append( rovingPtr -> entity );
                rovingPtr = rovingPtr -> next;
              }
        }
    };

void main()
    {
      // Define and initialize three independent queues.
```

```
                        Queue   queue1, queue2, queue3;

         // Put some content into queue 1.
                queue1.append( 111 );
                queue1.append( 222 );
                queue1.append( 333 );

         // Print the queues.
                cout << "\nQueue 1:";
                queue1.printQueue();
                cout << "\nQueue 2:";
                queue2.printQueue();
                cout << "\nQueue 3:";
                queue3.printQueue();

         // Copy Queue 1  into  Queue 3.
                queue1.deepCopy( queue3 );

         // Move the front node from Queue 1 onto Queue 2.
                node* nodeHolder = queue1.deleteAndDeliverNode();
                queue2.appendNode( nodeHolder );

         // Display the entity from the current head of Queue 1 and delete it from
         // queue.
                cout << "\n\n...from the front of Queue 1:   "
                     << queue1.deleteAndDeliverEntity() << endl;

         // Move the front node from Queue 1 onto Queue 2.
                nodeHolder = queue1.deleteAndDeliverNode();
                queue2.appendNode( nodeHolder );

         // Print the queues.
                cout << "\nQueue 1:";
                queue1.printQueue();
                cout << "\nQueue 2:";
                queue2.printQueue();
                cout << "\nQueue 3:";
                queue3.printQueue();
         }
```

The Same Queue Class Implemented as a Class Template

As improved as the class implementation of the queue seems to be over the free function implementation, it still has one drawback that C++ can overcome. The drawback is that each *Queue* object defined from the preceding class is a queue of *int*s. That its code is not automatically extendible to other built-in and user-defined types poses a severe limitation to its utility. The remedy is to rewrite the class as a class template. That will render the code generic.

Here is the *class redefined* as a *template* with the identical program. The changes are minimal.

- The keyword *template* followed by the formal parameter list precedes the class specifier to form a template declaration.

```
template <class Type>     Type is the formal parameter
class Queue               that will hold a type specifier
   {                      for any built-in or user-defined
                          data type.
```

- The *entity* member of the *node* struct is declared to be of data type *Type*, meaning that the nodes are now capable of being containers for any data type.

```
struct node
   {
    Type    entity;
    node*   next;
   };
```

- The declarator of the *append( )* function is changed so that an object of data type *Type* can be passed to it:

```
void append (Type value)   // An incoming "value" or object
   {                       // of data type Type will be put
                           // into a node and onto the queue.
   }
```

similarly for the *deleteAndDeliverEntity( )* now returns an object of type *Type*.

```
Type deleteAndDeliverEntity()
   {
   }
```

- When defining *Queue* objects, it is now necessary to specify the container's data type.

```
Queue<int>  queue1, queue2, queue3; // This gives three int
                                    // queues, the same as
                                    // before.
```

```
#include <iostream.h>

template <class Type>
class Queue
   {
   private:

   struct node
      {                   // Entities held by nodes in the queue will be of
       Type    entity;    // whatever data type the parameter Type represents.
       node*   next;
      };
```

```
        node *head, *rear;

public:

    Queue() : head(NULL), rear(NULL)    // Constructor.
      {
      }

    ~Queue()                            // Destructor.
      {
        node*  nodeHolder;          // Delete the nodes
        while ( !empty() )          // on the queue
          {                         // being destructed
            nodeHolder = head;      //    -- or else --
            head = head -> next;    // have a memory leak.
            delete nodeHolder;
          }
      }

    int empty()
      {
        if (head == NULL) return 1;  // True, the queue is empty.
        else return 0;
      }

    void append (Type value) // An incoming value (now of type Type) is
                             // appended.
      {
        node*  newNode = new node;   // Get a new node.

        newNode -> entity = value;   // Put the incoming value into the new
                                     // node.
        newNode -> next   = NULL;

        if ( empty() )      // If the queue is empty, newNode is its first
          head = newNode;   // and only node -- so head (and rear) must
                            // point to it.
        else
          rear -> next = newNode;   // If queue is not empty, the new node
                                    // is linked onto the end.
        rear = newNode;
      }

    void printQueue()
      {
        node*  rovingPtr = head;
        cout << endl;

        if ( empty() ) cout << "+-+-+-+-+-+-+-queue empty-+-+-+-+-+-+-+";
```

```
      while (rovingPtr != NULL)
        {
          cout<<"  "<<rovingPtr -> entity; // Output operator must be
                                           // applicable.
          rovingPtr = rovingPtr -> next;
        }
      cout << endl;
    }

Type deleteAndDeliverEntity()            // CAUTION!  Must *ONLY* be
  {                                      // called when the
    int  valueForReturn  = head -> entity; // queue is not
    node*  nodeToBeDeleted = head;         // empty!

    head = head -> next;
    if (head == NULL)  rear = NULL;

    delete nodeToBeDeleted;
    return valueForReturn;
  }

void appendNode (node* nodeOn) // An incoming node is appended.
  {
    nodeOn -> next = NULL;      // As the end-node, it should "point to"
                               // NULL.

    if ( empty() )     // If the queue is empty, nodeOn is its first
      head = nodeOn; // and only node -- so head (and rear) must point
                     // to it.
    else
      rear -> next = nodeOn; // If queue is not empty,
                             // nodeOn is linked onto the end.
    rear = nodeOn;
  }

node*  deleteAndDeliverNode ()
  {
    node*  nodeForReturn = NULL;

    if ( !empty() )
      {
        nodeForReturn = head;
        head = head -> next;

        if (head == NULL)  rear = NULL;
      }

    return nodeForReturn;
  }
```

```
void  deepCopy (Queue& copy)
    {
        node* nodeHolder;                    // Delete the nodes
        while ( !copy.empty() )              // currently on the
            {                                // queue which is to
              nodeHolder = copy.head;        // be made a copy
              copy.head = copy.head -> next; // of the invoking
              delete nodeHolder;             // Queue object
            }                                //    --or else--
        copy.rear = NULL;                    // have a memory leak.

        node*  rovingPtr = head;
        while (rovingPtr != NULL)
            {
              copy.append( rovingPtr -> entity );
              rovingPtr = rovingPtr -> next;
            }
    }
};

void main()
  {
    // Define and initialize three independent queues.
    // The data type of the entities to be held has to be given.
        Queue<int>  queue1, queue2, queue3;

    // Put some content into queue 1.
        queue1.append( 111 );
        queue1.append( 222 );
        queue1.append( 333 );

    // Print the queues.
        cout << "\nQueue 1:";
        queue1.printQueue();
        cout << "\nQueue 2:";
        queue2.printQueue();
        cout << "\nQueue 3:";
        queue3.printQueue();

    // Copy Queue 1  into  Queue 3.
        queue1.deepCopy( queue3 );

    // Move the front node from Queue 1 onto Queue 2.
        node* nodeHolder = queue1.deleteAndDeliverNode();   //DANGEROUS
                                                            //DEFINITION!

        queue2.appendNode( nodeHolder );

    // Display the entity from the current head of Queue 1 and delete it from
    // queue.
        cout << "\n\n...from the front of Queue 1:   "
```

```
        << queue1.deleteAndDeliverEntity() << endl;

// Move the front node from Queue 1 onto Queue 2.
    nodeHolder = queue1.deleteAndDeliverNode();
    queue2.appendNode( nodeHolder );

// Print the queues.
    cout << "\nQueue 1:";
    queue1.printQueue();
    cout << "\nQueue 2:";
    queue2.printQueue();
    cout << "\nQueue 3:";
    queue3.printQueue();
}
```

There is one problematic point in *main( )*, and that is the definition and use of *node**.

```
// Move the front node from Queue 1 onto Queue 2.
    node* nodeHolder = queue1.deleteAndDeliverNode(); // DANGEROUS
                                                      // DEFINITION!
    queue2.appendNode( nodeHolder );
```

This works because there is just one instantiation of the class, hence one kind of *node* (i.e., a *node* whose entity is an *int*). Had the class template been instantiated for any other data type for example,

```
    Queue<float>  queue4;
```

then the definition of *nodeHolder* would have been ambiguous and would therefore have failed. The following would not have constituted a repair because the node's structure is not, itself, declared as a template.

```
    node<int>* nodeHolder = queue1.deleteAndDeliverNode();
```

The ability to have both the class template and to define, beyond the confines of the class [e.g., in *main( )*], any kinds of nodes desired is achieved by specifying the node to be an independent template, outside the class. This enables nodes of any data type to be taken from one queue and put onto another (or processed in any way needed). To show how this is done, the same class template and program is rewritten in the next program. Here are the modifications.

• Both the *node* and the *Queue* are separate templates:

```
template <class T>      // Node is now a struct template.
struct node             //
    {                   // The contained entity will be of
      T       entity;   // whatever data type has been
      node*   next;     // passed to the parameter T.
    };
```

```
template <class Type>           // Queue remains a template.
class Queue                     //
  {                             // The identifier used for its
    private:                    // type parameter, Type, is
      node<Type> *head, *rear;  // different from the
                                // identifier used within the
                                // the struct template; it
                                // could have been the same.

  }
```

- When the node pointers (*head* and *rear*) are defined within an instantiation of *Queue*, the data type of the parameterized member of the associated node is explicitly passed:

  ```
  node<Type> *head, *rear;
  ```

- All other references to node, are qualified with a data type, whether this type is a literal specifier or a parameter representing a specifier; here are some illustrations.

```
// From inside the append() function:

        node<Type>*   newNode = new node<Type>;

// The declarator of the appendNode() function:

        void appendNode (node<Type>* nodeOn)

// The opening of the deleteAndDeliverNode() function:

        node<Type>*   deleteAndDeliverNode()
          {                 node<Type>*  nodeForReturn = NULL;

// From inside main():

    // Move the front node from Queue 1 onto Queue 2.
        node<int>* nodeHolder = queue1.deleteAndDeliverNode();
        queue2.appendNode( nodeHolder );
```

Here is the program.

```
#include <iostream.h>

template <class T>
struct node
  {
    T       entity;
    node*   next;
  };
```

```
template <class Type>
class Queue
  {
    private:
      node<Type> *head, *rear;

    public:
      Queue() : head(NULL), rear(NULL)    // Constructor.
        {
        }

      ~Queue()                            // Destructor.
        {
          node<Type>*  nodeHolder;
          while ( !empty() )
            {
             nodeHolder = head;
             head = head -> next;
             delete nodeHolder;
            }
        }

      int empty()
        {
          if (head == NULL) return 1;  // True, the queue is empty.
          else return 0;
        }

      void append (Type value)
        {
          node<Type>*  newNode = new node<Type>;  // Get a new node.

          newNode -> entity = value;  // Put the incoming value into the new
                                      // node.
          newNode -> next    = NULL;

          if ( empty() )    // If the queue is empty, newNode is its first
            head = newNode; // and only node -- so head (and rear) must point
                            // to it.
          else
            rear -> next = newNode;  // If queue is not empty, the new node
                                     // is linked onto the end.

          rear = newNode;
        }

      void printQueue()
        {
          node<Type>*  rovingPtr = head;
          cout << endl;
```

```
             if ( empty() ) cout << "+-+-+-+-+-+-+-queue empty-+-+-+-+-+-+-+";

          while (rovingPtr != NULL)
            {
              cout<<"  "<<rovingPtr -> entity; // Output operator must be
                                               // applicable.
              rovingPtr = rovingPtr -> next;
            }
          cout << endl;
        }

     Type  deleteAndDeliverEntity()                   //CAUTION!  Must *ONLY* be
        {                                             //          called when the
          int  valueForReturn  = head -> entity;  //          queue is not
          node<Type>* nodeToBeDeleted = head;     //          empty!

          head = head -> next;
          if (head == NULL)  rear = NULL;

          delete nodeToBeDeleted;
          return valueForReturn;
        }

     void appendNode (node<Type>* nodeOn) //An incoming node is appended.
        {
          nodeOn -> next = NULL;  // As the end -- node, it should "point to"
                                  // NULL.
          if ( empty() )     // If the queue is empty, nodeOn is its first and
            head = nodeOn;   // only node -- so head (and rear) must point to
                             // it.
          else
            rear -> next = nodeOn; // If queue is not empty,
                                   // nodeOn is linked onto the end.
          rear = nodeOn;
        }

     node<Type>*  deleteAndDeliverNode ()
        {
          node<Type>*  nodeForReturn = NULL;

          if ( !empty() )
            {
              nodeForReturn = head;
              head = head -> next;

              if (head == NULL)  rear = NULL;
            }

          return nodeForReturn;
        }
```

```
        void  deepCopy (Queue& copy)
          {
            node<Type>* nodeHolder;
            while ( !copy.empty() )
              {
                nodeHolder = copy.head;
                copy.head = copy.head -> next;
                delete nodeHolder;
              }
            copy.rear = NULL;

            node<Type>*  rovingPtr = head;
            while (rovingPtr != NULL)
              {
                copy.append( rovingPtr -> entity );
                rovingPtr = rovingPtr -> next;
              }
          }
      };

  void main()
    {
      // Define and initialize three independent queues.
      //  *** the data type of the entities to be held has to be given ***

          Queue<int>   queue1, queue2, queue3;

      // Put some content into queue 1.
          queue1.append( 111 );
          queue1.append( 222 );
          queue1.append( 333 );

      // Print the queues.
          cout << "\nQueue 1:";
          queue1.printQueue();
          cout << "\nQueue 2:";
          queue2.printQueue();
          cout << "\nQueue 3:";
          queue3.printQueue();

      // Copy Queue 1  into  Queue 3.
          queue1.deepCopy( queue3 );

      // Move the front node from Queue 1 onto Queue 2.
          node<int>* nodeHolder = queue1.deleteAndDeliverNode();
          queue2.appendNode( nodeHolder );

      // Display the entity from the current head of Queue 1 and delete it from
      // queue.
          cout << "\n\n...from the front of Queue 1:   "
```

```
                << queue1.deleteAndDeliverEntity() << endl;

    // Move the front node from Queue 1 onto Queue 2.
        nodeHolder = queue1.deleteAndDeliverNode();
        queue2.appendNode( nodeHolder );

    // Print the queues.
        cout << "\nQueue 1:";
        queue1.printQueue();
        cout << "\nQueue 2:";
        queue2.printQueue();
        cout << "\nQueue 3:";
        queue3.printQueue();
}
```

Reference

1. Ellis, M.A. and Stroustrup, B. *The Annotated C++ Reference Manual*, Reading, MA: Addison-Wesley, 1990.

Exercises

Chapter 1

1.1 Relative to the intellectual history of programming, when was the object-oriented paradigm first described?

1.2 This is a question to consider now but defer answering until you have defined several different classes, and programmed with objects. It presupposes the insights that come from first-hand experience.

A statement often quoted for over a decade following its first appearance in September, 1982 ("Object Oriented Programming," *SIGPLAN Notices* 17, 9; page 51) was Tim Rentsch's observation:

> What is object oriented programming? My guess is that object oriented programming will be in the 1980s what structured programming was in the 1970s. Everyone will be in favor of it. Every manufacturer will promote his products as supporting it. Every manager will pay lip service to it. Every programmer will practice it (differently). And no one will know just what it is.

This may be true because insights into object-oriented programming from the languages then prevalent (Pascal, PL/I, C, FORTRAN, BASIC, and COBOL) were just as difficult to draw as insights into gotoless programming were from assembly languages, FORTRAN-IV, and other languages of the middle 1960s.

Object-oriented programming probably can be characterized by these elements:

(i) abstraction, made possible by "data types" (classes) that unify information and function; and

(ii) inheritance, made possible by programmer-defined data types that are built by augmenting pre-existing programmer-defined data types.

Explain what each of these is and how they will improve the quality of programs.

1.3 Pascal offers procedural abstraction: the ability to build a higher-level language on top of Pascal by defining functions that perform extensive amounts of specialized processing "at the drop of an invocation." Call **sort(data)**; and your data is sorted. Call **append(arrival)**; and a **record** is attached to the end of a queue. Call **newton(5, 634)**; and Newton's method is applied to return the fifth root of 634. Call **getTime(hr, min, sec, hund)**; and the system's clock is read.

1.3.A One definition of abstraction has to do with bundling information and giving the bundle a name. Discuss the two benefits of procedural abstraction: encapsulation and information hiding.

1.3.B Pascal allows a stack to be manipulated with the abstractions *push(datum)*; and *pop*; What protection does Pascal provide to prevent an "append" to the bottom of the stack? (Trick question.)

1.4 An example of a class is the **integer** data type, and an example of three objects are the three **integer** variables *i*, *j*, and *k*. (Classes are data type specifiers, objects are variables.)

How is an **integer** variable a unification of data and function?

To answer, consider:

An **integer** refers to a positive or negative value within a certain range. Is an **integer** intrinsic to the computer, or is it a conceptualization that has been offered?

What properties do **integer**s have? How do they respond when used as operands within a **write** statement? They can be +'ed, -'ed, *'ed, and /'ed, but what results when two of them are /'d? Can we take the successor of an **integer**? Is there a symbolic tool that will allow two **integer**s to be concatenated into one (e.g., so the 1234 is gotten from 12 ≪ 34)?

1.5 Dahl, Dijkstra, and Hoare were visionaries. They described functional abstraction, data abstraction, and "object classes" (i.e., classes, from which objects are defined) along with "concept hierarchies" (inheritance). In short, their teachings presaged both the "structure revolution" of the 1970s and the "object-oriented revolution" of the 1980s and 1990s. Did they see any further fundamental change in the way programs are architected?

1.6 "Concept hierarchies" is the term used by Dahl and Hoare to describe what is now called inheritance. The idea is that new things can often be understood as composites of features from familiar things. One example is the encyclopedia on CD-ROM. It might be intuited in terms of a printed encyclopedia and a diskette. Give another example of how insights into a development, refinement, or specialization are derived from "conceptual predecessors."

1.7 Indicate whether each of the following assertions is true or false.

1.7.A The syntax of C++ may be closer to C than to Pascal, but relative to strong data typing, type safety (i.e., the ability to use operators without having to designate explicitly and correctly their data type), and the canons of structured programming (e.g., loops with one entrance and one exit), C++ is much like Pascal.

1.7.B C++ contains control structures that are very close to each of the following from Pascal:

```
if ... then             for ... do
if ... then ... else    while ... do
case ... of             repeat ... until
```

1.7.C C++, like Pascal, requires that all variables be enumerated at the opening of the referencing environment.

1.7.D Just as in Pascal, variables defined within a function in C++ are not accessible outside that function (i.e., they are local) and have a lifetime that ends when the function ends.

1.7.E C++ provides data types corresponding to Pascal's **integer**, **real**, and **char**.

1.7.F C++ offers both user enumerations and subranges, very similar to Pascal's.

1.7.G In C++, the first compartment of all arrays has the subscript of 0.

1.7.H The *struct* (for structure) is the C++ equivalent of Pascal's **record**, and it is used in exactly the same ways. There is no logical limit to the number and types of components it may contain, including arrays and other *struct*s.

1.7.I C++ affords modularization with subprograms in a manner very similar to Pascal. Its functions work just like Pascal's, and though it does not have procedures per se, its functions that return *void* (nothing) are the operative equivalent.

1.7.J C++ offers argument passing by value and by reference that work precisely as Pascal's pass by value and pass by reference.

1.7.K C++ allows functions to be nested, one inside the other, just as Pascal does.

1.7.L C++ provides for global variables by allowing variables to be defined outside and ahead of all the functions that are to have access.

1.8 Here is another exercise for later.

Write a one or two paragraph essay with the provocative title, "There Is No Such Thing as Object-Oriented Programming." It should argue that even when a program represents its abstract data types as objects, action is accomplished with all the familiar operators and constructs (e.g., selection statements, iteration statements, subprogram calls, etc.). As such, a programmer still must know operator precedence, exercise vigilance in setting up logical expressions, take care with nested *if...else*s that a particular else is the alternative to the intended if, avoid off-by-one errors in looping, and be skilled at translating algorithms into code.

Object-oriented programming remains programming and demands all the skillfulness that programming has always required.

Chapter 2

Although only standard header files and standard library functions are needed, these exercises are framed with reference to Borland's Turbo C++™ for DOS. Files holding source code, which may be augmented to form complete programs or integrated into source code files, have the extension .CPP. In other environments, this extension may have to be changed to .C (an upper case C). Files holding data to be read by programs have the extension .DAT. Programs in answers were compiled and run on an IBM PS/ValuePoint with Borland's Turbo C++™ for DOS, Version 3.0.

2.1 Read the following program.

```
#include <iostream.h>
#include <iomanip.h>     // For the i/o manipulators setw() and setprecision()
                         // and for setting i/o stream flags.

void main()
  {
    // Print column numbers (read vertically):
    cout << endl;
    cout << "          1111111111222222222233333333334444444445" << endl;
    cout << "1234567890123456789012345678901234567890123456789" << endl;

    float float1, float2, float3, float4, float5;  // Five variables defined.

    float1 = 100;         // Integer literal assigned to a float.
    float2 = 1000.0;      // Float literal with an integral value.
    float3 = 12.34567;    // To 2 places, the literal rounds to 12.35.
    float4 = .123456;     // No digit to the left of the decimal.
    float5 = 1234567.5;   // A relatively large value (over a million).

    //  *** Statements for selecting either fixed or scientific notation.  The
    //  *** setting remains in effect within the program until explicitly reset.

    //  cout << setiosflags(ios::fixed);    // Fixed notation.

    //  cout << resetiosflags(ios::fixed) << setiosflags(ios:: scientific);

    //  *** Statements for selecting either to see the decimal point and
    //  *** to pad trailing places to the right of the point (out to the
    //  *** set precision) with zeros or to suppress trailing zeros to the
    //  *** right of the point as well as the point itself when there is
    //  *** no fractional component.  The setting remains in effect within
    //  *** the program until explicitly reset.

    //  cout << setiosflags(ios::showpoint); // Pads trailing places to the right
                                             // of the decimal point with zeros.

    //  cout << resetiosflags(ios::showpoint); // Suppresses trailing filler.

    // *** Statement for setting the maximum number of places displayed to
    // *** the right of the decimal point.  If the i/o stream flag "showpoint"
    // *** is on, the decimal and this number of places is displayed whether
```

```
// *** or not the value to be displayed contains this much precision.

//  cout << setprecision(2); // Displays two places to the right of the
                             // decimal; remains in effect until changed.

                             // Here setw() sets the width of only the
                             // next field to be displayed.
    cout << endl;

    cout << setw(15) << float1 << setw(20) << float1 << endl;
    cout << setw(15) << float2 << setw(20) << float2 << endl;
    cout << setw(15) << float3 << setw(20) << float3 << endl;
    cout << setw(15) << float4 << setw(20) << float4 << endl;
    cout << setw(15) << float5 << setw(20) << float5 << endl;


}
```

Default field widths, number of places to the right of the decimal point, and the like can be overridden with the facilities for i/o manipulation made available with the inclusion of the *iomanip.h* header file.

Among these are *setw( )*, *setprecision( )*, and various others for setting i/o stream flags that affect display formatting.

When the given program is run in its current form this is how the output appears (default formatting applies, except for the two field widths of <u>fifteen</u> and <u>twenty</u>, respectively):

```
              111111 1111222222222233333 3333444444444445
    123456789012345 678901234567890123456 78901234567890

                100                  100
               1000                 1000
           12.34567             12.34567
           0.123456             0.123456
          1234567.5            1234567.5
```

Notice that the precision seen matches the precision of the actual values in storage (i.e., trailing zeros to the right of the decimal point are not shown and the point itself is suppressed when only zeros are stored beyond it) but that decimal points are not vertically aligned.

2.1.A   Make the changes required so that the output appears as shown below:

```
          1111111111222222222233333333334444444445
123456789012345678901234567890123456789012345678901234567890

              100.00                  100.00
             1000.00                 1000.00
               12.35                   12.35
                0.12                    0.12
          1234567.50              1234567.50
```

2.1.B   Revise the program so that the numbers on the second and fourth lines are displayed in scientific notation.

2.1.C   Experiment with the i/o manipulators used in the program to be confident that you can control the appearance of integer and floating point values in C++ with just as much ability as you can in Pascal.

2.2   In Pascal, data conversions from **real** to **integer** must be performed explicitly with either the truncation or the rounding function. C++ performs the conversion on its own by truncation when required to do so by assignment or parameter passing. The same conversion can be performed explicitly with a cast operator, where the cast is the name of the destination data type:

```
#include <iostream.h>

void main()
    {
    float x;
    int   i;

    x = 1.999;

    i = x;          // Implicit float to int data conversion.

    i = int(x);     // Data conversion with a cast.

    i = (int) x;    // Same conversion, different syntax -- with
                    // the cast operator inside the parentheses.
       .
       .
    }
```

The three conversions shown are functionally equivalent. In each case i is assigned a value of one because in each case the decimal portion of the *float* is snipped off and discarded.

Write and test the logic for rounding that entails adding 0.5 to the *float* prior to its truncation.

2.3   In Pascal, the functions **ord( )** and **chr( )** were required to change the internal interpretation of a bit string from character to integer and from integer to character:

65 is **ord('A')**   and   'A' is **chr(65)**

Furthermore, arithmetic could not be performed on characters; **'A' + 1** is not a legal expression.

C++ treats variables defined as *char* as byte-sized integers. The distinction between *int*s and *char*s is that when an integer's value is displayed, the value of its bit string is interpreted as a binary number, then converted to base 10. When a character's value is displayed, it is the symbol in the collating sequence with a number equaling the value of its bit string interpreted as a binary number.

The following program produces this output.

ASCII value --- letter		ASCII value --- letter	
65	A	66	B
67	C	68	D
69	E	70	F
71	G	72	H
73	I	74	J
75	K	76	L
77	M	78	N
79	O	80	P
81	Q	82	R
83	S	84	T
85	U	86	V
87	W	88	X
89	Y	90	Z

Modify it so that the letters A through M are tabulated in the left-hand column and the letters N through Z are tabulated on the right.

```
// Prints the ASCII values of the letters from A to Z.
#include <iostream.h>
#include <iomanip.h>
void main()
{
  char ch;

  cout << endl;
  cout << "ASCII value - letter          ASCII value - letter" << endl;

  for (ch = 'A';  ch <= 'Z';  ch = ch + 2)
    {
      cout<<setw(4)<<" "<<int(ch)  <<setw(10)<<" "<<    ch  <<setw(12)<<" ";
      cout<<setw(4)<<" "<<int(ch+1)<<setw(10)<<" "<<char(ch+1)<<endl;
    }
}
```

2.4   In 1671 the Scottish mathematician James Gregory discovered that *pi*, the ratio of the circumference of a circle to its diameter, could be expressed as the sum of the following convergent (but very slowly convergent) series.

$$pi = 4 * \left(\frac{1}{1} - \frac{1}{3} + \frac{1}{5} - \frac{1}{7} + \frac{1}{9} - \frac{1}{11} + \frac{1}{13} - \frac{1}{15} + \ldots \right)$$

Write a program that gives the value of *pi* obtained with the first thousand terms of this series (i.e., its sum out to and including the term $-1/1999$).

```
Be careful:    remember that    1 / 2 → 0

               and that    float(1/2) → 0.0

               but that    1.0 / 2 → 0.5
               and that    float(1) / 2 → 0.5
               and that    1 / float(2) → 0.5
               and that    float(1) / float(2) → 0.5
```

2.5   Given two positive whole numbers *num1* and *num2*, the largest whole number that divides into each of them, individually, without leaving a remainder is their greatest common divisor. Euclid's algorithm for computing this consists of using a *while* loop that applies these facts:

(i) if *(num1 == num2)*, their greatest common divisor is *num1* (or *num2 —* because they are equal);

(ii) if *(num1 != num2)*, whatever their greatest common divisor is, it is unchanged if the larger of the two values is replaced by the difference between the larger and the smaller.

Write a program that queries the user at the workstation for two positive whole numbers and reports their greatest common divisor; enhance this program by enabling it to continue if the user wishes a replication of the process.

2.6 The sine of an angle given in radians can be approximated as the sum of the following terms:

$$\text{sine(angle in radians)} = \frac{\text{angle}^1}{1!} - \frac{\text{angle}^3}{3!} + \frac{\text{angle}^5}{5!} - \frac{\text{angle}^7}{7!}.$$

Similarly for the cosine of an angle given in radians:

$$\text{cosine(angle in radians)} = \frac{\text{angle}^0}{0!} - \frac{\text{angle}^2}{2!} + \frac{\text{angle}^4}{4!} - \frac{\text{angle}^6}{6!}.$$

The program to be built will output the following table of sines and cosines.

degrees	sine	cosine	degrees	sine	cosine
0	0.000	1.000	45	0.707	0.707
1	0.017	1.000	46	0.719	0.695
2	0.035	0.999	47	0.731	0.682
3	0.052	0.999	48	0.743	0.669
4	0.070	0.998	49	0.755	0.656
5	0.087	0.996	50	0.766	0.643
6	0.105	0.995	51	0.777	0.629
7	0.122	0.993	52	0.788	0.616
8	0.139	0.990	53	0.799	0.602
9	0.156	0.988	54	0.809	0.588
10	0.174	0.985	55	0.819	0.574
11	0.191	0.982	56	0.829	0.559
12	0.208	0.978	57	0.839	0.545
13	0.225	0.974	58	0.848	0.530
14	0.242	0.970	59	0.857	0.515
15	0.259	0.966	60	0.866	0.500
16	0.276	0.961	61	0.875	0.485
17	0.295	0.956	62	0.883	0.469
18	0.309	0.951	63	0.891	0.454
19	0.326	0.946	64	0.899	0.438
20	0.342	0.940	65	0.906	0.423
21	0.358	0.934	66	0.914	0.407
22	0.375	0.927	67	0.920	0.391
23	0.391	0.921	68	0.927	0.375
24	0.407	0.914	69	0.934	0.358
25	0.423	0.906	70	0.940	0.342

26	0.438	0.899	71	0.945	0.325
27	0.454	0.891	72	0.951	0.309
28	0.469	0.883	73	0.956	0.292
29	0.485	0.875	74	0.961	0.275
30	0.500	0.866	75	0.966	0.259
31	0.515	0.857	76	0.970	0.242
32	0.530	0.848	77	0.974	0.225
33	0.545	0.839	78	0.978	0.208
34	0.559	0.829	79	0.982	0.190
35	0.574	0.819	80	0.985	0.173
36	0.588	0.809	81	0.988	0.156
37	0.602	0.799	82	0.990	0.139
38	0.616	0.788	83	0.992	0.121
39	0.629	0.777	84	0.944	0.104
40	0.643	0.766	85	0.996	0.087
41	0.656	0.755	86	0.997	0.069
42	0.669	0.743	87	0.999	0.052
43	0.682	0.731	88	0.999	0.034
44	0.695	0.719	89	1.000	0.017
45	0.707	0.707	90	1.000	-0.000

(The actual cosine of 90° is exactly zero, after which it progresses toward −1. The computed approximation resulted in a very small negative value. Although setting precision to 3 has cropped from view these spurious digits, the fact remains that a stored value of less than zero is being displayed and the minus sign is, dutifully, prepended. There is no logic within the formatting facilities for detecting this and excluding the sign.)

2.6.A Build a function for exponentiating *float*s to *int* powers that has this prototype:

```
float power (float num, int pow);        // Prototype.
        // Returns num raised to the power pow.
```

2.6.B Build a function that returns *n*! (i.e., *n* factorial) where

$$n! = n * (n - 1) * (n - 2)\ldots 2 * 1$$

```
int factorial (int n);                   // Prototype.
        // Returns n!   --   note that  0! = 1  and  1! = 1.
```

2.6.C Build a function called *sineR( )* (the *R* denotes that the argument angle is in radians) that uses the *power( )* and *factorial( )* functions and follows the formula to compute an angle's sine:

```
float sineR (float radians);             // Prototype.
        // Returns the sine of the argument, an angle in radians.
```

2.6.D Build a function called *cosineR( )*, like the preceding function, that returns an angle's cosine:

```
float cosineR (float radians);           // Prototype.
        // Returns the cosine of the argument, an angle in radians.
```

2.6.E Here is a function that accepts an angle expressed in degrees and returns its expression in radians:

```
float degreesToRadians (int degrees)
    // Performs conversion via  radians = (degrees * 3.1416)/180.
    {
        return (degrees * 3.1416)/180;
    }
```

Use this function and *sineR( )* function to build *sineD( )*:

```
float sineD (int degrees);                  // Prototype.
    // Returns the sine of the argument, an angle in degrees.
```

2.6.F Build a similar function for returning the cosine of an angle given in degrees:

```
float cosineD (int degrees);                // Prototype.
    // Returns the cosine of the argument, an angle in degrees.
```

2.6.G The following function calls *sineD( )* and *cosineD( )* to create the table.

```
void displayTable()
    {
        int degreesLeftColumn, degreesRightColumn;
        int line;

        cout << endl << "   degrees  sine   cosine"
             << "             degrees  sine   cosine";

        cout << setprecision(3) << setiosflags(ios::showpoint);

        for (line = 0; line <= 45; line++)
            {
                degreesLeftColumn =  line;
                degreesRightColumn = line+45;

                cout << endl << "        ";
                cout << setw(2) << degreesLeftColumn   << "    " ;
                cout << sineD(degreesLeftColumn)       << "    "
                     << cosineD(degreesLeftColumn)
                     << "           |            ";

                cout << setw(2) << degreesRightColumn << "    ";
                cout << sineD(degreesRightColumn)     << "    "
                     << cosineD(degreesRightColumn);
            }
    }
```

Assemble these modules into a program, and run the program to produce a hardcopy of the table.

If the displayed cosine of 90° strikes you as unaesthetic, install some contrivance in *displayTable( )* that eliminates the minus sign.

2.7 Isaac Newton, in the 17th century, devised a method for computing the rth root (where *r* is a positive whole number) of any value to any degree of precision—for example, the square root of 10 correct to three decimal places or the fifth root of 765 correct to six places.

Newton's method operates by iterating the formula:

$$\text{nextEstimate} = \frac{\text{number} + (\text{root} - 1) * (\text{lastEstimate}^{\text{root}})}{\text{root} * (\text{lastEstimate}^{\text{root}-1})},$$

where:

`nextEstimate` is the estimate of the root currently being computed;

`root`   is the root being sought; for the square root it is 2, for the cube root it is 3, for the tenth root it is 10;

`number`   is the number whose root is to be found; if we wished the fifth root of 765, the number would be 765;

`lastEstimate` was the "nextEstimate" computed during the previous iteration.

If the preceding "equals sign" were construed as the assignment operator, the expression could be written like this:

$$\text{estimate} = \frac{\text{number} + (\text{root} - 1) * (\text{estimate}^{\text{root}})}{\text{root} * (\text{estimate}^{\text{root}-1})}.$$

The computational procedure entails these steps:

(i)   Get an initial estimate of the number's root; a starting point often used is:

$$\text{estimate} = \text{number/root};$$

(ii) Test to determine whether the current estimate is sufficiently precise that computation can stop, or whether another iteration is needed to get a better estimate (with each iteration the estimate improves).

   Continue until the absolute value of the difference between the number and the approximation of the number gotten back when the estimate is raised to the power root is less than one tenth of one percent the magnitude of the number. In other words, continue computing:

$$\text{while} \left(\text{abs} \left(\frac{\text{number} - (\text{estimate}^{\text{root}})}{\text{number}} \right) >= 0.001 \right).$$

   It is advisable to write a function for returning an absolute value because the *abs( )* function in the standard library returns an *int*.

(iii) Use the expression for computing an updated estimate. Then return to step (ii) to test it.

   Write this program.

2.8 The "sieve of Eratosthenes" is the algorithm that identifies primes by "crossing out" composites: all multiples of 2, all multiples of 3, all multiples of 4, all multiples of 5, and so on. The numbers remaining in the array when the crossing out is complete are primes, numbers which are not exact multiples of any smaller positive, whole number (other than 1).

   Implement "the sieve" to find all prime numbers less than 1000.

Step 1: Crossing out multiples of 2 (start with 4)

Step 2: Crossing out multiples of 3 (start with 6)

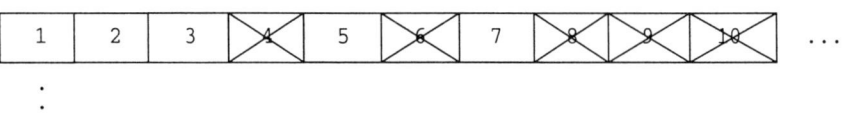

2.9 A two-dimensional *char* array with 21 rows and 73 columns is defined to represent the display screen. Visualize it as a set of Cartesian coordinates in which the middle row (with subscript 10) is the *X*-axis, the row with subscript 20 is the row at the top and corresponds to 1.00, and the row with subscript 0 is the row at the bottom and corresponds to −1.00. The leftmost column (with subscript 0) is the *Y*-axis and corresponds to 0 degrees. The column with subscript 1 stands for 5 degrees; the column with subscript 2 stands for 10 degrees, and each successive column stands for an additional 5 degrees. The column with subscript 72, the rightmost column, stands for 360 degrees. Onto this coordinate system the *X*-axis, the *Y*-axis, and one cycle of the sine curve will be plotted as depicted in the following.

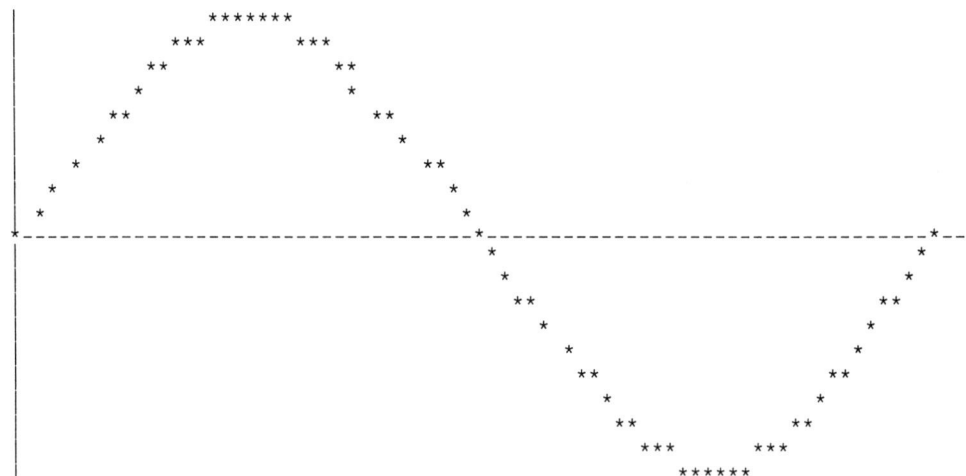

Write a program that will do this.

(i)   Begin by defining the two-dimensional array (suppose that it is called *screen*):

```
char  screen[21][73];   // 21 rows   (0..20)  and
                        // 73 columns (0..72).
```

(ii) Initialize *screen* so that each cell holds a blank space.

(iii) Enter the *X*-axis and enter the *Y*-axis.

(iv) Enter the sine. Values of the sine curve can be obtained from the *sin( )* function (whose argument is an angle in radians), but it must be provided for by including the math library:

```
#include <iostream.h>
#include <math.h>
```

To make a full cycle of the sine curve fit into 73 columns, display its value every 5 degrees. To enlarge its height to fill the vertical expanse of the display, multiply values from the sine function by 10 to get the row corresponding to their height. To map these preliminary rows into actual subscripts, 10 must be added to each:

```
a sine of 0 (0°, 180°, 360°) thus maps into 0*10 + 10 → row 10;
a sine of ½ (30°) maps into  ½*10 + 10 → 15;
a sine of 1 (90°) maps into 1*10 + 10 = 20;
and a sine of -1 (270°) maps into -1*10 + 10 → 0.
```

Array subscripts in C++ must be integers. Thus, the code may look something like this:

```
for (degrees = 0; degrees <= 360; degrees = degrees + 5)
{
  column = degrees/5;  // Quotient is an int.

  radians = (degrees * 3.14159)/180;  // Quotient is a float.

  row = int( 10*sin(radians) + 0.5 ) + 10; // Adding 0.5 makes the cast
                                           // operate as a round instead
                                           // of as a truncation.
    screen[row][column] = '*';
  }
```

```
           Y-value      X-value
```

(v) Print the *screen* array. Keep in mind that the top of the plot, and therefore the first row to be displayed, is the row whose subscript is 20.

2.10 The standard (default) input and output streams, called *cin* and *cout* respectively, relate to the workstation. The extraction operator (as in extracting a value from the input stream) is defined with the abilities to input all the language provided data types in C++, including integer values, float values, individual characters (excluding "white space" characters, which are discarded) as well as strings up to a blank space. Just as a "white space" character (blank, tab, or linefeed) delimits an integer or a float, it also delimits a string. In consequence, no string read-in with the << operator can contain a blank.

2.10.A Here is a program that reads and echoes a succession of integers until a − 1 is entered. Test the program to see how it performs. Enter values, one per line. Try placing several values along the line, separated by blanks and/or the tab key, before striking enter.

```
#include <iostream.h>

const int SENTINEL = -1;  // An externally defined constant.

void main()
{
  int datum;

  do
  {
    cout << "\nEnter datum  (" << SENTINEL<< " to stop):  ";
    cin >> datum;
    cout << "Echo of datum:  |" << datum << "|" << endl;
  }
  while (datum != SENTINEL);
}
```

2.10.B Modify the program so that the data are *float*s and retest it.

2.10.C Modify the program so that the data are *chars*. Be sure to change the definitions of both the *SENTINEL* and the *datum*. Test the program with letters entered individually, with several letters along the line delimited by spaces, and with a succession of letters without delimiting blanks.

2.10.D Modify the program so that the data are strings. Recall that a string is not a basic data type, but a *char* array which has a null zero (an ASCII 0, represented in source code as *\0*) delimiting the elements of data.

The sentinel can be defined like this:
```
const char SENTINEL[5] = "stop";
```

or like this:
```
const char SENTINEL[] = "stop";
```

In the first instance, *SENTINEL* was explicitly defined as a five-element array taking advantage of the fact that we know the string literal "stop" was comprised of four letters and the string delimiter (automatically part of a string literal). The second instance takes advantage of the fact that C++ will count the number of characters in the string literal, including the null zero, and "fill in the blank" with that number.

In both instances, the use of the assignment operator to copy a string into a *char* array is a special allowance made only because this is an initialization (an assignment made at the point of definition). Ordinarily the *strcpy()* function, declared in *<string.h>*, is required for copying either the value of a string literal or a string held by a *char* array into a destination string.

The string library function, *strcmp()*, also from *<string.h>*, is needed for the test to determine whether the value of the entered datum differs from (does not equal) the value of the sentinel. The relational operators that apply for integers, floats, and characters (and the other basic data types to be introduced in the next chapter) cannot be applied to arrays and therefore not to strings.

Test the program with input consisting of one word (e.g. "Hello") and with a line of input consisting of two or more words delimited by spaces. The input operator does not test to prevent more characters than the char array was defined to hold from being extracted and assigned (so do not enter too long a string).

2.11 In order to extract any character that happens to be at the head of the input stream and assign it to the character variable *ch*, instead of this:
```
cin >> ch;
```

use this:
```
cin.get(ch);
```

The *get()* function, from *<iostream.h>*, assigns to the argument character (this is *ch* in the preceding) the next character from the stream being read (this is the standard input stream, *cin*, in the preceding).

Because each call to *get()* picks off only one character from the input stream, a single call is likely not to evacuate it. This means that the next acquisition, no matter how it is performed (by way of a subsequent *get()* or by way of the extraction operator), may be acquiring residual content.

2.11.A Test the following program to see a demonstration of this. When queried to enter data, type in three strings, each one with two or more letters and separated by one or more blanks (e.g., *abcdefg hi jklmonp*):

```
#include <iostream.h>

void main()
{
    char ch;
    char string[50];

    cout << endl << "Enter data:   ";

    cin.get(ch);        // Machine awaits data entry; the first character you
                        // place onto the input stream will be assigned to ch
                        // and the rest of the data (even if they are the sole
                        // linefeed caused by striking enter) remain in
                        // waiting.

    cout << "...first character:  |" << ch << "|" <<  endl << endl;

    cin >> string;   // Bypassing leading white space, data remaining on
                     // the input stream up to the first blank or linefeed
                     // are extracted and assigned to string.

    cout << "...residual:  |" << string << "|" << endl;
}
```

2.11.B Test the following program to see how the *get( )* function may be used to read to the end of the standard input stream (which is delimited by the linefeed transmitted when the enter key is struck).

```
#include <iostream.h>

void main()
{
    char ch;
    cout << endl << "Enter data:   ";

    cin.get(ch);

    while (ch != '\n' )
    {
        cout << "  |" << ch << "|      ASCII value = " << int(ch)  << endl;
        cin.get(ch);  // Get the next character from cin.
    }

    cout<<endl<< "ASCII value of last character ('\n'): " << int(ch) <<endl;
}
```

2.11.C The companion to *get( )* for outputting single characters is *put( )*. Its argument can be a character or an integer, but in either case a character is inserted into the output stream (the ad hoc character or the character having the ASCII value associated with the ad hoc integer). Rewrite the following program, changing *val* from *int* to *char*. Then rewrite the program again replacing *cout.put(val)* with *cout << val* to observe that there is no difference in performance.

```
#include <iostream.h>

void main()
{
    int val;

    for (val = 0;  val <= 126;  val = val + 1)
    {
        if (val % 20 == 0)  cout << endl;   // Linefeed every 20 chars.
```

```
                        if (val != 26)      cout.put(val);   // Character 26 is Ctrl-Z,
                                                             // the end-of-file marker;
                                                             // can't output after that.

                    cout.put(' ');       // Space between characters.
                }
            }
```

2.12 The *getline( )* function from *<iostream.h>* enables a sequences of characters which contains spaces to be read into a character array as a string.

$$cin.getline(\ string, \ 60);$$

```
    WILL TAKE FROM cin
      AND ASSIGN TO THE CHAR ARRAY string
          CHARACTERS UNTIL THE "ENTER" IS ENCOUNTERED OR 60 - 1 = 59
          OF THE ARRAY'S ELEMENTS HAVE BEEN FILLED. THESE 59 CELLS
            INCLUDE THE SUBSTANTIVE CONTENT OF THE LINE. ELEMENT NUMBER
60 WILL BE ASSIGNED THE '\0' WHICH QUALIFIES THE CHAR ARRAY
TO PERFORM AS "A STRING."
```

When *getline( )* is accepting characters from the keyboard, striking the enter key stops the input; blanks do not. When the enter key is struck, '\0', the end of string delimiter, is copied into the element currently at the end of the accepted sequence.

The following program illustrates *getline( )*'s properties. The *strlen( )* function is used to report the number of characters in the entered character sequence—the '\0' is not counted. In contrast, the *sizeof* operator is used to show the number of bytes bound to the *char* array *string*. This, of course, was set when *string* was defined and does not change.

```
#include <iostream.h>
#include <string.h>  // For strlen() and strcmp().

const char SENTINEL[] = 's', 't', 'o', 'p', '\0';
// Here, const char SENTINEL[] = "stop";
// would also be acceptable, since
// the '\0' is automatically appended.

void main()
    {
        char string[60];

        do
          {
            cin.getline(string,60);  // Appends the '\0' but not the '\n' serving
                                     // as getline()'s end of input delimiter.
// --> Call to the function you will write to place a '\n' into string //

            cout << '|' << string << '|' << endl;         // Echo string.

            cout << "Num of chars in string's content = "  // Chars comprising
                 << strlen(string) << endl;                // content of string

            cout << "Num of bytes in string array    = "  // elements in
                 << sizeof(string) << endl;               // string array.
          }
        while ( strcmp(SENTINEL, string) != 0 );
    }
```

Run the program, testing it with a string comprised of several words separated with blanks, a string comprised of just a single letter, and a string comprised of no characters other than an "enter."

2.12.A   Add a function that accepts the string read-in by *getline( )* and appends a '\n' to the end of the string. The '\0' must still follow the rightmost "live character" in the substantive sequence (i.e., the '\n' that you are adding). Therefore, the '\n' cannot be entered into the string if the string already contains 59 character elements (with the 60th element reserved for the '\0'). Test the program again. Notice that now when the string is printed out, the trailing delimiter (' | ') is displayed on the line following the string echo. Also notice that the *strlen( )* function reports an additional character, the '\n' character.

2.12.B   Another form of the *getline( )* function accepts a character as the third parameter and looks for this character as the denotation marking the end of the string for input. With a delimiter other than "the newline default," the entered character sequence may contain any number of "newlines" as the '\n' is accorded the same status as every other nondelimiter.

   Remove the invocation of the function just written to restore the program to its original state. Then, modify the given program to test this variation of *getline( )*; for example:

```
cin.getline(string ,60, '@');
```

   A warning and something to investigate: when a string is entered, followed by the '@' key, followed by the enter key, a '/n' is left on the input stream and will be read with the next input.

2.13   In order to read from an input stream attached to an external source, such as a file on diskette, the *input file stream* must:

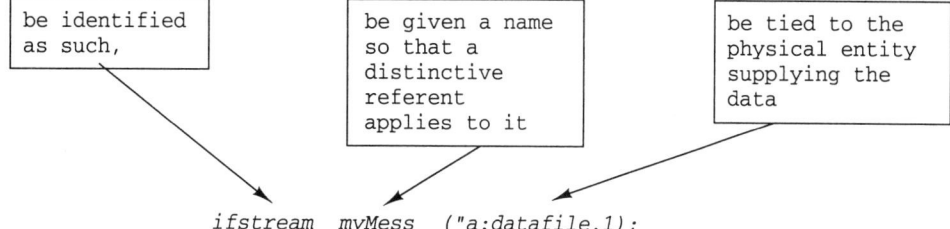

```
ifstream  myMess  ("a:datafile.1);
```

   The preceding statement takes care of all the behind the scenes work entailed in opening the file so that it is ready to be read. The header file *fstream.h* must be included whenever input or output streams are explicitly defined within the program (as shown). When *fstream.h* is included, *iostream.h* is not needed although its inclusion causes no difficulty.

   Data can be extracted from an input stream such as *myMess* just as they are from *cin* (the standard input stream, otherwise known as as the terminal or the keyboard):

(i)   the extraction operator (>>) can extract *ints*, *floats*, *chars*, and strings:

```
myMess >> intVar;
myMess >> floatVar;
myMess >> charVar;
myMess >> string;
```

   When *chars* are sought, white space characters are extracted from the stream and discarded until the first nonwhite space character is encountered. This nonwhite space character is removed from the input stream and assigned to the ad hoc variable.

When strings are sought, white space characters are extracted from the stream and discarded until the first nonwhite space character is encountered. Then the succession of non-white space characters is extracted and returned. A null zero (i.e., a '\0')is gratuitously appended to the end of the captured character sequence.

(ii) *get( )* will extract and return both nonwhite space and white space characters:

```
myMess.get(charVar);
```

(iii) *getline( )* will extract and return strings up to a delimiter, either an "enter" (i.e., a '\n') as the default or the character provided as the third argument:

```
myMess.getline(line, 80);
myMess.getline(transcript, 5000, '@');
```

When an input operation attempts to extract a datum from a file but cannot do so because there is none to be found, the cursor marking the current read position is said to be at the end of the file (at *eof*).

One way to learn whether the read cursor is at the end of file is by testing the value of the input stream with the *eof( )* function. For instance, with the input stream named *myMess* (previously defined):

```
myMess.eof()
```

returns "true" (i.e., a nonzero value) if the last attempted read culled the end of file marker instead of the sought datum. That *myMess.eof( )* does not become true until an input is attempted and fails, such as:

```
myMess >> intVar;
```

or

```
myMess.get(charVar);
```

implies that the test for having encountered the end of the file needs to be performed after the input is tried but before the read or would-have-been-read value is treated. This give rise to logic for going through a file that pseudocodes something like this:

```
first read ( via >> or get() )

while (! myMess.eof() )
    {
    // Processing.
    // Processing.
    // Processing.

    next read ( via >> or get() ) which may find the end of file marker
    }
```

Processing to end-of-file line by line with *getline( )* has to be structured differently because *getline( )*, unlike >> and *get( )*, brings the input cursor through the end-of-file marker when capturing the last line in the file:

```
while (! myMess.eof() )
    {
      myMess.getline(line, 80);
```

```
        // Processing.
        // Processing.
        // Processing.
    }
```

Using any editor, create the following text file with the lines set up exactly as shown:

```
Adams          72     92
Jefferson      73     93
Madison        74     94
Monroe         75     95
Washington     71     91
```

Print the file to confirm its correctness.

2.13.A Construe this file as a roster of unknown length. Each line holds a student's name followed by two scores. Processing with a *while* loop which tests for the end of the file, display each student's name and average (the two scores count equally). Read the name as a string using the extraction operator, and read each score as an integer. The output should look like this:

```
Adams   82
Jefferson   83
Madison   84
Monroe   85
Washington   81
```

2.13.B Display the contents of this file by inputting and outputting character by character. Use the *get( )* function for input, and process with a *while* loop which tests for the end of the file. Note that the newline character, '\n', is extracted and sent to the output device like any other character (in other words, no special testing and action is needed to find and execute the linefeeds).

Re-run the program, replacing *get( )* with >> to see the difference.

2.13.C Display the contents of this file by inputting and outputting line by line. Use the *getline( )* function, and process with a *while* loop which tests for the end of the file. To the left of each line, show a line number so that the output looks like this:

```
1.     Adams          72     92
2.     Jefferson      73     93
3.     Madison        74     94
4.     Monroe         75     95
5.     Washington     71     91
```

2.14 A program can have multiple input and multiple output streams, with each stream attached to a different device or file. Setting things up for output is very much like setting things up for input. An *output file stream* must:

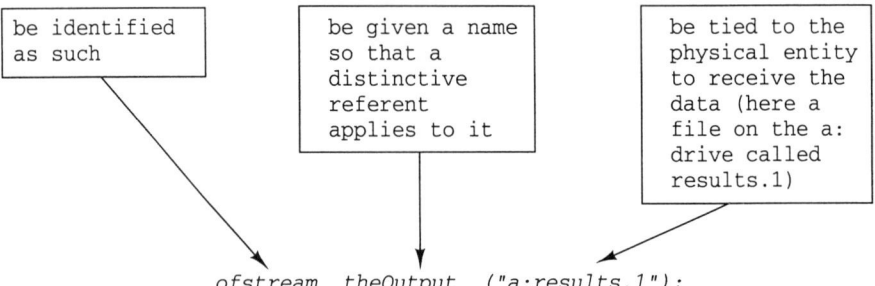

```
ofstream  theOutput  ("a:results.1");
```

The preceding statement takes care of all the behind the scenes work entailed in opening the file so that it is ready for output. If a file with that name currently exits, it will be overwritten; if there is no file with that name, one will be created.

The following statements show how output streams may be explicitly tied to the printer (known to C++ as "LPT1") and the display screen (known to C++ as "CON").

```
ofstream  printerOutput  ("LPT1");
ofstream  consoleOutput  ("CON");
```

Sending the escape sequence '\f' to a printer effects a "formfeed" (page eject):

```
printerOutput << "\nBye now\f";
```

When sending prompting to the console through an attached output stream (an output stream other than the standard output stream, *cout*), be sure to conclude it by flushing the buffer with *endl*. The '\n' escape sequence will cause a linefeed, but its presence does not cause the packet of characters being collected for transport to be transmitted.

2.14.A   The following program prompts the user for the name of an input file. It copies this file to the console, the printer, and to another file (whose name the user also provides).

Modify it so that it tests for '\n' in the input stream and begins each new line with a line number right-justified within a field having a width of three, followed by a period, which is followed by two spaces.

Be careful to enter file names correctly as there is no testing to be sure that they conform to the operating system's specifications nor to warn that an existing file will be written over by the copy.

Inspect the paper output and the created file to confirm that the program ran correctly.

```
#include <fstream.h> // For ifstream, ofstream.

#include <iomanip.h> // For setw().

void main()
    {
    char ch;
    char infname[15], outfname[15];

    ifstream keyboard("CON");
    ofstream screen("CON");
    ofstream printer("LPT1");

    screen << "Enter the name of the input file, "
           << "for example  A:THISPROG.CPP :" << endl;
    keyboard >> infname;
```

```
        screen << "Enter the name of the file to hold the copy:" << endl;
        keyboard >> outfname;

        ifstream sourceFile (infname);
        ofstream destinationFile (outfname);

        sourceFile.get(ch);
        while (! sourceFile.eof())
          {
            screen.put(ch);                 // Or  screen << ch;
            printer.put(ch);                // Or  printer << ch;
            destinationFile.put(ch);        // Or  destinationFile << ch;
            sourceFile.get(ch);
          }

        printer.put('\f');                  // Or  printer << '\f';

      // Files are closed automatically.
    }
```

2.14.B A Vigenere cipher is a method of encryption and decryption in which the letters in a "key" are cyclically used as the additive values (A = 0, B = 1, C = 2, . . . , Z = 25) for shifting plaintext letters into ciphertext letters. When an additive shift takes a plaintext letter beyond the end of the alphabet, the length of the overhang is added to 'A' to wrap the ciphertext letter back into the alphabet: an overhang of 1 maps onto A, an overhang of 2 maps onto B, an overhang of 3 maps onto C, and so on.

```
cipherLetter = shift + plainLetter;

if (cipherLetter > 'Z')
  cipherLetter = (cipherLetter - 'Z') + ('A' - 1);
```

If the key were *BACON*, the given plaintext may be enciphered as shown in the following. Initially, all plain letters are converted to upper case:

```
if (plainLetter >= 'a' && plainLetter <= 'z')
  plainLetter = plainLetter - 32;
```

Only alphabetic characters are transformed (blanks and special symbols are allowed to stand):

```
if (plainLetter >= 'A' && plainLetter <= 'Z')
      cipherLetter = encrypt(plainLetter);
else
      cipherLetter = plainLetter;
```

```
BACONBACONBACONBACONBACONBACONBACONBACONBACONBAC
+++ +++++++++ +++ ++++++++++ +++++++ ++ ++++++++++
FOR REFERENCE: SEE SEDGEWICK'S CHAPTER ON CRYPTOLOGY.
↓↓↓ ↓↓↓↓↓↓↓↓↓  ↓↓↓ ↓↓↓↓↓↓↓↓ ↓ ↓↓↓↓↓↓ ↓↓ ↓↓↓↓↓↓↓↓↓↓
GOT EFFGFROCG: TEG FFDISJJCM'F CJOCUET BO EFLQTQZBHY.
```

The decryption process is the reverse:

```
plainLetter = cipherLetter - shift;
```

```
if (plainLetter < 'A')
    plainLetter = ('Z' + 1) - ('A' - plainLetter);
```

Write a program that encrypts a text file in the manner illustrated. The user should be able to enter these items: (i) the name of the existing plaintext file, (ii) the name of the ciphertext file to be created, and (iii) the encryption key (the *strlen( )* function can be used to find its length).

2.14.C Write a program that decrypts a file that your program encrypted.

2.15 An interpreter takes an instruction, parses it, and causes the indicated processing to be executed. This program is an interpreter. It will read in and perform actions on a linked list comprised of structures containing two members: a letter of the alphabet (a *char*) and the address of the next node (a "pointer").

The list may be depicted as shown in the following. The number in the right-hand compartment (the *next* member) of each *struct* is a metaphorical address in main memory standing for the location of the next *struct* in the list. The number above a *struct* is its location. Locations are used rather than nondescript arrows because having distinct tangible values is helpful in composing and desk-checking code. Dynamically allocated *structs* are invaluable because they dissociate the logical positioning of information from its physical placement.

```
   20          16          12          18          14
 ┌─┬──┐      ┌─┬──┐      ┌─┬──┐      ┌─┬──┐      ┌─┬────┐
 │T│16│      │H│12│      │I│18│      │N│14│      │K│NULL│
 └─┴──┘      └─┴──┘      └─┴──┘      └─┴──┘      └─┴────┘
 head is 20                                      rear is 14
```

The *struct*, named *node*, may be declared like this:

```
struct node
    {
    char  letter;
    node*  next;    // The name of the struct, on the top line,
    };              // becomes a datatype.  The asterisk may be
                    // read as "pointer."  Therefore node*
                    // denotes that the member called next is
                    // a "node pointer" (or a pointer to nodes).
```

Every time a "node pointer" needs to be declared or defined, such as within function declarators or within their body, the data type is *node**. If a formal argument is passed by reference, an ampersand would follow:

```
void append (node*& head, node*& rear, char letter); // Prototype.
```

Some programmers find it neater to create a synonym for *node**. Synonyms are established using the *typedef* statement:

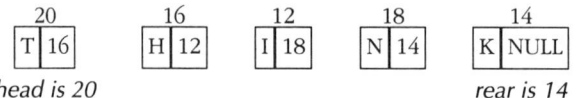

typedef   struct node*   nodePtr;

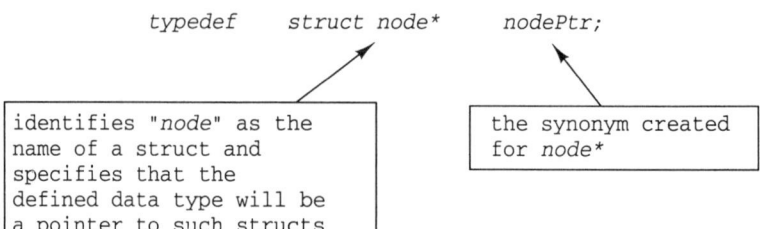

identifies "*node*" as the
name of a struct and
specifies that the
defined data type will be
a pointer to such structs

the synonym created
for *node**

Establishing *nodePtr* as a mnemonic for *node**, the structure may be specified like this:

```
typedef   struct node*   nodePtr;

struct node
    {
    char      letter;
    nodePtr   next;
    };
```

The prototype for the append function may be written like this:

```
void append (nodePtr& head, nodePtr& rear, char letter);
```

The program itself will handle six types of instructions by way of a function for each:

sample instruction	action and function prototype
Az	Appends a new node holding the letter z (of course it could have been any letter) to the rear of the list: *void append (nodePtr& head, nodePtr& rear, char letter);*
Iz3	Inserts a new node holding the letter z as the third node on the list: *void insert (nodePtr& head, nodePtr& rear, char letter, int place);*
D	Deletes the front node from the list (i.e., the node at the list's head); take note: *delete* is a reserved word in C++: *void deleteFront (nodePtr& head, nodePtr& rear);*
R3	Removes the third node from the list: *void remove (nodePtr& head, nodePtr& rear, int nodeNumToGo);*
P	Prints the letters in the list along a horizontal line: *void print (nodePtr& head);*
S	Spacing — a blank line is output: *void spacer();*

The instructions constituting the data are these. Each instruction is on its own line in a data file. The line numbers shown here are not in the file.

line number	instruction	line number	instruction
1	S	31	S
2	AS	32	S
3	AT	33	AH
4	AA	34	AD
5	AR	35	IE2
6	AT	36	IA3
7	AG	37	P
8	IN6	38	R3
9	II6	39	IL3
10	IL6	40	P
11	P	41	R2
12	R5	42	IO2
13	P	43	P
14	R5	44	R1
15	P	45	IF1
16	R3	46	P
17	P	47	R3
18	R3	48	IO3
19	P	49	P
20	R2	50	R4
21	P	51	IT4
22	R4	52	P
23	P	53	S
24	D	54	S
25	P		
26	R2		
27	P		
28	D		
29	S		
30	S		

The program should include the header file *fstream.h* so that the data file can be opened and read. Directly beneath it, ahead of the functions that will be declaring variables which point to *node*s, the *typedef* statement and/or the specification of the node struct should appear:

```
#include <fstream.h>

typedef   struct node*   nodePtr;

struct node
    {
      char      letter;
      nodePtr   next;
    };
```

Here is the *main( )* function that will drive the list management facilities (it is preceded by the *initializeList( )* function which readies the list by setting *head* and *rear* to *NULL*):

```
void initializeList(nodePtr& head, nodePtr& rear)
```

```
        {
            head = NULL;   // NULL must be capitalized in order to be
            rear = NULL;   // the language-provided constant set to 0.
        }

void main()
    {
        nodePtr head, rear;
        initializeList(head,rear);

        char instruction; // The 'A' for append; the 'I' for insert; etc.
        char letter;      // The letter to be appended or inserted.
        int  nodeNum;     // The node number to be removed or the spot
                          // where a new node will be inserted.

        ifstream data("A:LISTDATA");  // Data is in the file A:LISTDATA.

        data >> instruction;
        while (! data.eof())
            {
            switch  (instruction) // Note that instructions are in upper
                                  // case.
                {
                case 'A':  data >> letter;
                           append(head, rear, letter);
                           break;

                case 'I':  data >> letter;
                           data >> nodeNum;
                           insert(head, rear, letter, nodeNum);
                           break;

                case 'D':  deleteFront(head, rear);
                           break;

                case 'R':  data >> nodeNum;
                           remove(head, rear, nodeNum);
                           break;

                case 'P':  print(head);
                           break;

                case 'S':  spacer();
                           break;

                default :  cout << "\n** Error in Data - |" << instruction
                                << "| read as the instruction.**" << endl;

                }    // End of switch statament.

            data >> instruction;

            }    // End of while loop.

        cout << "\n**Run Successfully Completed**" << endl;

    }    // End of main().
```

Write the program.

2.16 This exercise builds a function to sort the *int*s within a given *data* array:

```
void sort(int data[], int numOfValues);   // Prototype.
```

The function will accept an unsorted array and an *int* denoting the number of elements holding "live data." If *numOfValues* were 25, the live data would be in those cells with subscripts from 0 through 24. The values within *data* will be placed into ascending (actually, non-descending) order. Because arrays are always passed by reference, the argument array in the call will be sorted when the function returns.

A sorting routine cannot be tested in isolation. Provision has to be made for supplying the data to sort and for corroborating the routine's proper performace. Accordingly, two methods are offered and explained for data acquisition, and a function is given for displaying the array so that the values in its compartments can be viewed in sequential order.

After this, several instructions are given regarding the construction of the sorting function.

Getting the Data

The data are a series of integers in scrambled numerical order.

One approach to getting the data is by way of a function that loads the array with values that look mixed up even though they have been methodically calculated and placed. Here is such a function:

```
void getData(int mixedUp[], int numOfValues)
    {
    //Remember:  The highest subscript will be numOfValues-1
    //           because the array's first element is number 0.

    int i;  // Subscript for going through the array.

    if (numOfValues % 2  ==  0)    // If numOfValues is even.
      for (i = 0;  i < numOfValues/2;  i = i + 1)
        {
        mixedUp[2*i]                  =  3*(i+1);
        mixedUp[(numOfValues-1) - 2*i] =  3*(i+1) - 1;
        }  // Semicolon here would result in a "MISPLACED ELSE" error.

    else                           // If numOfValues is odd.
      for (i = 0;  i < numOfValues/2 + 1;  i = i + 1)
        {
        if (2*i < numOfValues)
          mixedUp[2*i]   =  3*(i+1);
        if ( (numOfValues - 2*i) < numOfValues )
          mixedUp[numOfValues - 2*i]  =  3*(i+1) - 1;
        }
    }
```

It fills even-numbered compartments, starting with element 0, with multiples of 3: 3, 6, 9, 12, and so on. It fills odd-numbered compartments, working downward from the element having the highest odd-number subscript, with 5, 8, 11, 14, and so on (with each value being 3 more than the last). The reason for its apparent complication, at first blush, is that it will fill an array having any number of compartments. Such sequences give the appearance of being quite unsorted, for example:

```
3   26   6   23   9   20   12   17   15   14   18   11   21   8   24   5
```

Another approach is to use values from a "random" generator. Of course, such a thing as a deterministic process for creating genuinely random numbers is impossible.

The best that can be done algorithmically is to generate pseudorandom numbers that look random and pass statistical tests for randomness (even though they are products of a methodical operation whose replication results in the same sequence).

A simple pseudorandom algorithm entails choosing a whole number multiplier (e.g., 27543) which is used throughout and a "seed" or first random (e.g., 0.3247). The seed and all pseudorandoms are values within the range of 0..1, noninclusive; but these can be appropriately transformed. If, for example, we wished integral values within the 1..99 range, we could multiply the current pseudorandom by 100 and snip off the decimal point and trailing digits; 0.3247 would give 32. The next pseudorandom in an ad hoc sequence is computed by multiplying the constant multiplier times the latest pseudorandom and keeping just that part of the product that includes the decimal point and the digits to its right. With the constant multiplier 27543 and the starting value 0.3247, here are the first several pseudorandoms:

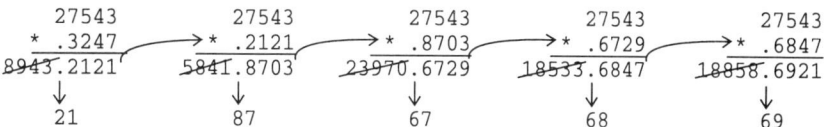

Despite the 67, 68, and 69 (the succeeding value is 51), these values, like snow, fall haphazardly but uniformly over the span.

Different sequences of pseudorandoms can be obtained by using different constant multipliers.

The catch in writing a function that returns the next fractional pseudorandom is that the function requires the pseudorandom it had generated the last time it was called. In Pascal, this could be accomplished by declaring **pseudo_random** to be a global variable so that its lifetime, and hence its ability to store a value, persists from one invocation of the random function to the next. The same mechanism can be used in C++:

Pascal

```
program  sorting (input, output);
  var
    pseudo_random : real;
    .
    .
    .

  function random : real;

    const
      multiplier = 27543;

    begin
      pseudo_random :=
              multiplier * pseudo_random -
          trunc(multiplier * pseudo_random);

      random := pseudo_random;
    end;
    .
    .
    .
```

_C++_

```
#include <iostream.h>

float pseudoRandom; // Global scope.
  .
  .
  .

float random()
  {
    const int MULTIPLIER = 27543;

    pseudoRandom =
            MULTIPLIER * pseudoRandom -
          int(MULTIPLIER * pseudoRandom);

    return pseudoRandom;
  }

void main()
  {
    pseudoRandom = 0.3247;
```

```
begin

      pseudo_random := 0.3247
   .
   .
   .
end.
```

```
   .
   .
   .
}
```

C++ offers features for improving upon this construction that are introduced in the next chapter. One is the ability to initialize variables at the point of their definition; another is the ability to specify that variables within a function are *static*. *Static* variables within a function, like other local variables, are only accessible within the function; but unlike other local variables, their memory is not allocated and released with each call and return. The value stored by a *static* variable at the time a function ends is the value it holds the next time the function begins.

With the preceding random function, a prospective data array for sorting could be filled with random integers within the 1...99 range through the following function:

```
void getRandData(int mixedUp[], int numOfValues)
{
   // Remember:  The highest subscript will be numOfValues-1
   //            because the array's first element is number 0.

   int i;  // Subscript for going through the array.

   for (i = 0; i < numOfValues; i = i + 1)
      mixedUp[i] = 100 * random(); // Randoms are of the form 0.xxxx.
}
```

Printing the Data

The following function will print an array holding data values before sorting, after sorting, and at any intermediate point:

```
void print(int data[], int numOfValues) // Needs iomanip.h for
                                        // setw().
{
   int i;  // Subscript for going through the array.

   for (i = 0; i < numOfValues; i = i + 1)
   {
      if (i % 10 == 0) cout<< endl;  // Linefeed after every ten.
      cout << setw(5) << data[i];
   }
}
```

The *for* loop's construction follows "the idiom" for processing an array: the control variable, which is to be used as the element-by-element subscript (here i) starts at 0; the body of the loop is executed if i is less than *numOfValues*; and i is incremented by 1 after each pass. The loop could have been set up with i starting at 1 and its body run if i were less than or equal to *numOfValues*:

```
for (i = 1;  i <= numOfValues;  i = i + 1)
```

This seems more natural to a Pascal programmer, but in C++ it requires either:

that inside the loop's body, each time the array is accessed, i be decremented by 1: what had been *data[i]* would now be *data[i-1]*

or that the live data run from element 1 to *numOfValues*, and element 0 remain unused (at least to hold data values).

Building the Sorting Function

The process of the straight selection sort may be described as iterating the following three steps:

- determining the subscript of the element which holds the lowest value in the array,
- "copying-out" the value held at that location, and
- filling that location with an inordinately large value (e.g., 32,767 — the greatest possible value of an int implemented in two bytes).

A function is needed that reads through the array and returns the "cell number" at which the smallest datum resides. It should have the prototype:

```
int getSubOfSmallest (int data[], int numOfValues);
```

Its opening actions will be the definitions and assignments:

```
int subOfSmallest; // Here sub of smallest value yet found.
int smallestValue; // Here smallest value yet found.

subOfSmallest = 0;
smallestValue = data[subOfSmallest];
```

Thereafter, a loop will be used to compare each value in the array with *smallestValue* (the smallest value located so far). Each time a *data[i]* is found that is less than *smallestValue*, both *subOfSmallest* and *smallestValue* are updated.

2.16.A Write a "first version" of the sorting function that follows the preceding three steps and uses *getSubOfSmallest( )* to accomplish the sort "on paper"; the "copying-out" operation will be to display the current lowest value. In other words, the function will display the data passed to it in ascending order, but it will not leave the array with these values. Rather, each element in the *data* array will be left holding the number used to obliterate "*smallestValues*" so that the same small value is is not rediscovered on each traversal. The following may be used as the driver.

```
void main()
{
    const DATAVALUES = 25; // Or any number of data values you would like.
    int data[DATAVALUES];
    pseudoRandom = 0.3247; // Starting value for random generator.

    getRandData(data, DATAVALUES); // Or  getData(data, DATAVALUES)
                                   // depending on the set of values
                                   // you would prefer to sort.

    print(data, DATAVALUES);  // View the unsorted data.

    sort(data, DATAVALUES);   // Sort the data.

    print(data, DATAVALUES);  // View the data array after sorting.
}
```

2.16.B Rewrite the sorting function so that *smallestValues* are copied into consecutive cells of a second array instead of being printed. Once the live data have been exhausted, the contents of this holder array should be copied into the argument array so that the "calling client" is passed back the same data, but in sorted order.

2.16.C   Rewrite the sorting function so that the intermediary array is not needed.

When the first *smallestValue* is identified, it can be stored in the first element (the cell with subscript 0), and the value that had been in *data[0]* can be placed in the spot where the *smallestValue* had been, *data[subOfSmallest]*; the search for the next *smallestValue* should start with *data[1]*.

When the second *smallestValue* is identified, it can be stored in the second element (the cell with subscript 1) by swapping the contents of *data[1]* with *data[subOfSmallest]*; the search for the next *smallestValue* should start with *data[2]*.

Write and use a *swap( )* function within *sort( )* so that the logic of sorting is not jumbled up with the logic of swapping.

```
void swap(int& a, int& b);    // Prototype.
```

2.16.D   Create a file holding the last names of the presidents of the United States of America in the order in which they held office, one name per line. (Data is in the table following the next item.)

```
Washington
Adams
Jefferson
  .
  .
  .
```

Read this file into an array of strings:

```
char presidents[42][11];
```

Rebuild the culminating sorting function so that it accepts a *data* array such as *presidents* and passes it back alphabetically ordered. Use *strcmp( )*, from the *<string.h>* library, for the relational test of two names.

The program should perform as the previous program: the unsorted *data* array should be displayed, it should be sorted, and then displayed again.

2.16.E   Create a file which holds for each president of the United States of America. The *data* is supplied by the table that follow; age at inaguration is the number within parentheses.

```
the last name

the first letter of the first name

presidency number

age when inaugurated
```

(Grover Cleveland was elected as the 22nd and as the 24th president. His non-consecutive terms cause no end of confusion to schoolchildren trying to assign ordinal numbers to presidents from the 24th onward: was William McKinley, elected after Cleveland's second term, the 24th or the 25th president? Cleveland is counted as both the 22nd and the 24th, and McKinley as the 25th.)

The file should begin as follows, formatted in either manner (or another — any number of spaces may be placed where one space appears).

format 1	format 2	
Washington G 1 57	Washington	G 1 57
Adams J 2 61	Adams	J 2 61
Jefferson T 3 57	Jefferson	T 3 57
Madison J 4 57	Madison	J 4 57
Monroe J 5 58	Monroe	J 5 58
.	.	
.	.	

The objective is to read the file into an array of structures, print the array, sort it by age at inauguration, and then print it again. The structure may be declared and the data array defined like this:

```
struct presRec
{
    char name[11];
    char firstInit;
    int  presNum;
    int  age;
};
presRec presData[42];
```

The individual members of a *struct* held within the array at subscript *i* can be accessed with "the dot operator" (more descriptively called the "member access operator" inasmuch as the variables within a structure are called its members); for example:

```
cout << presData[0].name << " was " << presData[0].age
     << " years old when he took office.";
```

Print the array, one *struct* per line, formatted more or less like this:

```
G. Washington    (57)    1
J. Adams         (61)    2
T. Jefferson     (57)    3
J. Madison       (57)    4
    .
    .
```

G. Washington	(57)	1	G. Cleveland	(47)	22
J. Adams	(61)	2	B. Harrison	(55)	23
T. Jefferson	(57)	3	G. Cleveland	(55)	24
J. Madison	(57)	4	W. McKinley	(54)	25
J. Monroe	(58)	5	T. Roosevelt	(42)	26
J. Adams	(57)	6	W. Taft	(51)	27
A. Jackson	(61)	7	W. Wilson	(56)	28
M. vanBuren	(54)	8	W. Harding	(55)	29
W. Harrison	(68)	9	C. Coolidge	(51)	30
J. Tyler	(51)	10	H. Hoover	(54)	31
J. Polk	(49)	11	F. Roosevelt	(51)	32
Z. Taylor	(64)	12	H. Truman	(60)	33
M. Fillmore	(50)	13	D. Eisenhower	(62)	34
F. Pierce	(48)	14	J. Kennedy	(43)	35
J. Buchanan	(65)	15	L. Johnson	(55)	36
A. Lincoln	(52)	16	R. Nixon	(56)	37
A. Johnson	(56)	17	G. Ford	(61)	38
U. Grant	(46)	18	J. Carter	(52)	39
R. Hayes	(54)	19	R. Reagan	(69)	40
J. Garfield	(49)	20	G. Bush	(64)	41
C. Arthur	(50)	21	B. Clinton	(46)	42

Chapter 3

Throughout these exercises and those in the following chapters, make an effort to use the unary increment wherever you would have coded $i = i + 1$ (whatever the variable), to use the $+ =$ compound assignment operator wherever you would have coded $i = i + n$ (regardless of the variable names), and to use the other abbreviated forms whenever applicable.

3.1 Euler's method offers a quick and easy way of getting an approximate numerical solution to ordinary differential equations, including nonlinear differential equations.

The procedure is to take a differential equation, such as Newton's law of cooling, applied to a cup of coffee:

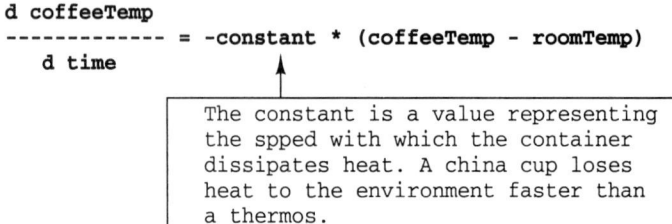

```
d coffeeTemp
------------ = -constant * (coffeeTemp - roomTemp)
   d time
```

The constant is a value representing the spped with which the container dissipates heat. A china cup loses heat to the environment faster than a thermos.

The equation reads; the rate at which *coffeeTemp* changes with respect to time is proportional to the difference between its temperature and the room's temperature. What it means is that the hotter the coffee, the faster it will lose temperature.

Re-express it as a difference equation:

$$\Delta \text{ coffeeTemp}_t \quad = \quad \text{-constant * (coffeeTemp}_t \text{ - roomTemp)}$$

This equation is interpreted as saying that the change in the coffee's temperature during some finite interval of time is equal to the difference between its temperature and the room's temperature times some negative constant.

Convert the delta to the literal difference between the coffee's temperature at the end of the time interval minus its temperature at the start of the interval:

$$\text{coffeeTemp}_{t+1} \text{ - coffeeTemp}_t = \text{-constant * (coffeeTemp}_t \text{ - roomTemp)}$$

The rationale is that a "change" during an interval of time, such as the change in a child's height over the course of a year, is her height on January 1 of year $i + 1$ minus her height on January 1 of year i.

Finally, do the tiny bit of algebra needed to express the value of the coffee's temperature at time $t + 1$ in terms of its value at time t:

$$\text{coffeeTemp}_{t+1} = \text{coffeeTemp}_t \text{ - constant*(coffeeTemp}_t \text{ - roomTemp)}$$

This is an equation that can use the starting value of *coffeeTemp* to yield the coffee's temperature at the beginning of the next interval of time. Then this can be plugged into the equation to get its temperature at the following point. And so it continues. The plot of the resulting temperatures delineates the function constituting the solution to the original differential equation.

As a practical addendum, the constant for a coffee cup can be determined experimentally. Suppose that a minute is adopted as the unit interval of time. Take the coffee's temperature and then, exactly a minute later, take it again. Put the former into the equation as *coffeeTemp$_t$* and the latter into the equation as *coffeeTemp$_{t+1}$*. Solve for the constant.

Given the preceding, write a program that uses a for loop to determine the temperature of a cup of coffee, initially at 135 degrees, after being in a refrigerator at 38 degrees for 10 minutes. Use 0.06 as the value of the cup's constant and a minute as the interval between computed temperatures. Take every opportunity when coding to apply the unary increment, the unary decrement and the compound assignment operators.

3.2 The law of radioactive disintegration posits that the rate of disintegration of a radioactive substance is proportional, at any instant, to the amount of substance which is present. Letting A stand for the amount present and t stand for time, this is represented by the differential equation:

```
dA
-- = -k * A        The value of k represents
dt                 the substance's half-life.
```

Euler's method can be used to fashion a recursive equation allowing the decay of a quantity of radioactive iodine to be simulated:

$$\Delta_t A = -k \cdot {}_t A$$

$$A_{t+1} - A_t = -k * A_t$$

$$A_{t+1} = A_t - k * A_t$$

Given that the half-life of radioactive iodine is eight days and the fact that we want our simulation to run in time units of a day, the value of k is 0.087. Start with 10 grams. Use a for loop to display how much of the isotope remains on each of the next 16 days. Apply the unary increment operator, the unary decrement operator and the compound assignment operator wherever they may be exercised.

3.3   The address-of operator can be used to get the location in memory of any variable of any type, and the *sizeof* operator can be used to ascertain how much memory the variable possesses.

3.3.A   Write a program that defines and initializes a variable of each of the types shown in the following, then for each one display its value, the bytes occupied, and the location in memory to which it is bound. The number of bytes a variable spans depends upon its data type, not upon the value it happens to hold at any particular point in time. A *long*, for instance, will be bound to four bytes whether it holds eight or eight million. The number of bytes allocated for the various types is implementation dependent. In some implementations an *int* has the same number of bytes as a *short*; in others it has the same number of bytes as a *long*.

char	short	float
	int	double
	long	long double

When running this program, a problem will occur: the address-of the *char* variable prints its value, not the memory location to which it is anchored. Here this is a bothersome inconsistency in the way the output operator handles "addresses of characters." In the vast majority of applications, however, this proves to be a convenience because it allows character arrays (used to hold strings) to be displayed simply by using the name of the array.

To display the *char*'s address, its address will have to be cast to another type of address. An *int** signifies the address of an *int*; a *void** signifies an untyped address.

First cast the address-of the *char* to an *int** and then to a *void** to see where it is bound. (Both will show the same location.) In performing this casting, use the "older form" to insure that the asterisk left-associates to qualify the type specifier:

```
(int*) charVar    and    (void*) charVar
```

Cast the *char* to a long and display the *sizeof* the temporary operand that results. If *c* were the *char* variable, try:

```
cout << sizeof c;
cout << sizeof long( c );
cout << sizeof c;
```

A cast does not change its operand; it is a function call which resolves to a value of the ad hoc data type.

3.3.B   Suppose that the *int* had been named *i*. Displaying &*i* reveals its address. This is the location in memory to which *i* had been bound by the compiler; it is *i*'s *l*-value. Can it be changed? For instance, if *j* is another *int*, can one code:

```
&i = &j;  // To make i's address the same as j's.
```

Try this out to see the error message. The fault is that the memory location to which a variable is statically bound (i.e., bound when defined) is set for the duration. The compiler's binding cannot be broken by giving *i*, or any other variable, a new address.

3.3.C   Memory is bound to arrays the same way it is bound to scalars (i.e. variables which are not arrays). For instance, an array of ten *int*s such as *a*, defined below:

```
int a[10];
```

Displaying &*a* will show the memory location to which it is bound, and displaying the *sizeof a* will show it possesses an expanse of memory having a width 10 times that of a single *int*.

Write a program that defines such an array and displays both its address (using the address-of operator) and its size.

The address of *a* is said to be the array's base address because that is the point of departure for the locations of its elements. Display &*a[0]* to see that the address of the array's initial element is on its baseline. (This is a truism for arrays of all data types: the base address, which is the address of its name, is the location of its 0th element.) Also display the addresses of elements with subscripts 1, 2, and 3 to see how each begins "the *sizeof* one *int*" after its predecessor. Each of these addresses is, of course, immutable as each represents a binding established by the compiler.

An important fact to recognize and remember is that for all arrays, the address accessed by using the address-of operator with its name is identical to the address accessed by way of its name alone. The name of an array, used without a subscript to denote a particular element, is a synonym for its base address. Confirm this by displaying *a* and &*a*.

3.3.D   Define an array of characters initialized to "Hello":

```
      char string[] =  'H', 'e', 'l', 'l', 'o', '\0' ;
//
//    char string[] = "Hello"; // Produces the identical initializtion.
//
```

Confirm that the *sizeof string* is six bytes.

The address to which this array is bound is signified by both &*string* and *string*, which is the same as &*string[0]*.

Confirm this with these displays:

```
cout << "\n    (void*) &string = " << (void*) &string;
cout << "\n    (void*) string = " << (void*) string;
cout << "\n (void*) &string[0] = " << (void*) &string[0];
```

Confirm that both of the following, owing to the way the output operator has been defined to operate, display the full string, and not just the contents of its leading element:

```
cout << "\n    string = " << string;
cout << "\n &string[0] = " << &string[0];
```

3.3.E   Given the two definitions:

```
char  hi[10] = "Hello";
char bye[10] = "Good bye";
```

explain how the compiler interpets the following statement and why it flags it as an error:

```
hi = bye;
```

3.3.F   Define the following structure ahead of *main( )*:

```
struct twoInts
{
    int intOne;
    int intTwo;
};
```

Within *main( )* define two of these and make the shown assignments:

```
twoInts  x;
x.intOne =    1;      x.intTwo =    2;

twoInts  y;
y.intOne = 1111;      y.intTwo = 2222;
```

Display the *sizeof* and the address of both *x* and *y* in addition to the values, sizes of, and addresses of their respective members.

After this, perform the assignment: *x = y;*

Confirm that this results in a "memberwise copy" but does not affect the placement in memory of either structure or its data members.

Structures work like ordinary scalars: assigning to *&x* would be illegal because that would be an attempt to change the address at which the *struct* was installed by C++ (i.e., its binding); however, assigning to *x* updates that which is held in storage at *&x*. This is different from the case of an array, where, if the array's name were *a*, *a = something;* actually means *&a = something;*.

3.3.G   This is a repetition of the preceding, but here the *struct* is defined as holding only one member, a *char* array, which is to say, a string:

```
struct stringHolder
{
    char str[25];
};
```

Within *main( )* define two of these *structs* and make the shown "assignments" via *strcpy( )* (remember to *#include<string.h>*):

```
stringHolder s1;
strcpy(s1.str, "Hello");

stringHolder s2;
strcpy(s2.str, "Good bye");
```

Display the *sizeof* and the address of both *s1* and *s2* in addition to the values, the string lengths, sizes of, and the addresses of their respective members.

After this, perform the assignment: *s1 = s2;*

Confirm that this results in a "memberwise copy" but does not affect the placement in memory of either structure or its data members.

Notice that the structure offered a mechanism for copying the contents of one string into another without the use of string copy. This is because two structures of the same type have precisely the same size. The assignment operator, applied to structures, simply copies values of the bits in the right operand into the bits in the left operand. It does not look at the nature of the member(s) within. The name of a structure, *s1* is not a synonym for its address, *&s1*; so the assignment statement is not interpreted as a faulty attempt to change an immutable binding.

3.4 The asterisk is used to define variables that can hold addresses as their value. Colloquially, such variables are called pointer variables or pointers. For instance *int**, as shown in the following, defines a variable that can hold addresses of *int* variables. The *float* specifier, used in conjunction with an asterisk, defines a variable that can hold addresses of *float* variables. The *char* specifier with the asterisk defines a variable that can hold addresses of *char* variables.

```
int*    intPtr;     // Identical to    int   *intPtr;
float*  floatPtr;   // Identical to    float *floatPtr;
char*   charPtr;    // Identical to    char  *charPtr;
```

Even though all addresses are stored in the same number of bytes and with the same format, the address of variables of only one certain type can be stored in a pointer variable of that type. For instance, the address of a *float* can be stored in a variable of type *float** but not in a variable of type *int**.

3.4.A Define an *int* initialized to 10, a *float* initialized to 1.5, and a *char* initialized to 'A'.

Next, define *intPtr*, *floatPtr*, and *charPtr* as shown previously.

Assign to *intPtr* the address of your *int* variable; assign to *floatPtr* the address of your *float* variable, and assign to *charPtr* the address of your *char* variable.

Display the value of your *int* variable, display its address, and display its size. On the next line, display the value of *intPtr*, display its address, and display its size. Notice that the value (the *r*-value) of *intPtr* is an address (the *int*'s address), and that this is different from *&intPtr*, the address at which it stores its values.

Do the same for your *float* variable and for *floatPtr*.

Do the same for your *char* variable and for *charPtr*. Notice that the output operator displays the value of *charPtr* not as the address which it is but as the character stored at that address. It does this same thing when the char's address is presented by way of the address-of operator applied to the *char* variable itself. The address of *charPtr*, however, displays as its memory location because the *r*-value of a *char** is not a character; it is a pointer.

Replicate the preceding, but casting both representations of the *char* variable's address to *void**.

Once you have run the program and studied the output, add a final line that assigns the address of the *float* to *intPtr*. The compiler will alert you to a type mismatch error. C++ is strongly typed with respect to pointers.

3.4.B In a new program, define three "*int* pointers" with a single type specifier in a manner similar to the the way you can define three *int*s (e.g., *int i, j, k;*). The syntactical catch is that an asterisk is needed for each and every pointer variable:

```
int *ptrA, *ptrB, *holder;
```

Without their asterisks, the second and third variables would be *int*s, not *int**s.

Define two *int* variables named *a* and *b*.

Assign the address of *a* to *ptrA* and the address of *b* to *ptrB*. Display the values *ptrA* and *ptrB*. To convince yourself that addresses (the values of pointer variables) are manipulated in the same manner as ordinary integers, write a swap that exchanges their values. Print out the values of *ptrA* and *ptrB* again to confirm the exchange.

3.4.C   Pointers can be passed to functions. Define two *ints*, *a* and *b*, and two *int* pointers, *aPtr* and *bPtr*. Assign the address of *a* to *aPtr* and the address of *b* to *bPtr*. Display the values of *aPtr* and *bPtr* as well as their addresses.

Pass *aPtr* to *ptr1* and *bPtr* to *ptr2* in the function whose prototype is given in the following:

```
void  receivePointers (int* ptr1, int* ptr2);
```

The function should display the values of both its formal arguments as well as their addresses. Examine the output to confirm that the value of *aPtr* was passed to *ptr1*, but that the two variables are indeed distinct (that is, bound to different memory locations). Likewise, examine the output to confirm that the value of *bPtr* was passed to *ptr2* and that these two variables are distinct.

Change the function so that both pointers are passed by reference:

```
void  receivePointers (int*& ptr1, int*& ptr2);
```

The output will now confirm that *aPtr* and *ptr1* are different names bound to the same memory location (the address of the actual argument, *aPtr*); likewise for *bPtr* and *ptr2*. This should serve as a concrete and vivid demonstration of the difference between the two modes of argument transmission.

In pass by value, the actual argument and the formal argument are entirely independent variables. When the function starts, the the value of the actual argument is copied into its corresponding formal argument.

In pass by reference, the actual argument itself is used by the function. However, within the function it goes by the name of the formal argument. This is why a change in the value of the formal argument is later seen as a change in the actual argument — they are one and the same.

Add a function that will accept two *int* pointers as arguments and swap their values. Call it from *main( )*, displaying the values of *aPtr* and *bPtr* both before and after the call in order to observe that the exchange was performed. Re-run the program after changing the arguments' transmission to pass by value (which, of course, is wrong when the objective is a swap). The exchange of values between *aPtr* and *bPtr* will not have been made.

3.4.D   Suppose we have an array named *array*. This is possible in C++, unlike Pascal, because in C++ array is not a keyword. The base address of the array; whether given as *array*, as *&array*, or as *&array[0]*; is a pointer to whatever data type constitutes each element. If array had been defined to hold *ints* (e.g., *int array[10]*), *array* would be an *int**. If *array* had been defined to hold *chars*, *array* would be a *char**. That the leading *int* (or the leading char) just happens to be the first *int* (or the first *char*) in a succession of *ints* (or *chars*) that had been allocated as an array in no way affects either its data type as an individual element nor the data type of its address. This program uses an *int** to hold the address of an *int* array and a *char** to hold the address of a *char* array.

Begin the *main( )* by setting the stage with the following definitions:

```
int*    intPtr1;
int*    intPtr2;

int     intArray1[5]  = {0, 1, 2, 3, 4};
int     intArray2[5]  = {5, 6, 7, 8, 9};
```

```
char*   charPtr;
char    charArray1[8] = "ABCDEFG";
char    charArray2[]  = "Bye now";
```

Assign *intArray1* to *intPtr1*. Display the *sizeof* each. This should portray the very crucial difference between an array and a pointer variable. The array's size equals the number of bytes allocated when the array was defined. The pointer's size is the size of an address.

Despite this difference, once a pointer variable holds the base address of an array, the pointer may be used with subscripts to access the array exactly like the name of the array actually bound to the expanse of memory. In other words, if the value of *intPtr1* equals the value of *intArray1* (which they do, by virtue of your assignment statement, and which can be seen by displaying them), then *intPtr1[i]* can be used wherever *intArray1[i]* is used and with precisely the same effects. Show this by displaying the values within *intArray1* by displaying *intPtr1[0]*, *intPtr1[1]*, *intPtr1[2]*, *intPtr1[3]*, and *intPtr1[4]* (feel free to use a loop).

Reassign *intPtr1* to the address of *intArray1[2]* and display *intPtr1[0]*, *intPtr1[1]*, and *intPtr1[2]*. This will demonstrate that an *int** can be set to the address of any element within an array, and that the element to which it is set acts as a base address relative to the pointer variable.

Reassign *intPtr1* to *intArray1*. Because the base address of *intArray1* is "being saved," can *intArray1* be updated with another address, such as either of the following?

```
intArray1 = &intArray1[2];
intArray1 = intArray2;
```

No. The true base address of an array, the symbolic name in the array's definition to which the address of the expanse of memory is bound by C++, can never be changed. Remember, *intArray1* actually stands for *&intArray1*. The compiler's assignment of an address to a name is immutable. Pointer variables, on the other hand, are variables that store addresses as their values. When a pointer variable, like *intPtr1*, is assigned the address of *intArray1[2]* or the address of *intArray2*, this address is accepted as its value, not an attempt to change its binding (i.e., not an attempt to change *&intPtr1*).

Can two pointer variables both point to the same array? Positively. Assign to *intPtr2 intArray1*. Install the following loop and then display the values in the array first using *intArray1* and next using *intPtr1*.

```
for (int k = 0; k < 5; k++)  intPtr2[k] += 10;
```

This will demonstrate that the contents of an array can be altered by way of a pointer holding the array's address. Also, any other pointer pointing to that array will have had its values updated too.

To see that *char*s relate to *char* arrays in a corresponding manner, examine the output produced by the following code.

```
charPtr = charArray1;
cout << "\n charArray1 = " << charArray1
     << "          charPtr = " << charPtr;

charPtr = &charArray1[3];
cout << "\n charPtr after assignment to &charArray1[3] = "
     << charPtr;

strcpy(charPtr, "XYZ");
cout << "\n        charPtr after  strcpy(charPtr, \"XYZ)  = "
     << charPtr;
cout << "\n                              and charArray1 = "
     << charArray1;
```

```
charPtr = charArray2;
cout << "\n   charPtr after assignment to charArray2 = "
     << charPtr << endl;
```

Notice the difference between *strcpy( )*ing into *charPtr* and assignments to *charPtr*. *strcpy(charPtr, 'XYZ');* copies the *'X'* into the memory location referenced by *charPtr* and the rest of the string appearing as the right argument into the succeeding locations. *charPtr = charArray2;* updates the value of *charPtr* with another address, *charArray2*, so that it points elsewhere.

Replace the call to *strcpy( )* with the following four assignments and rerun the program to confirm that this replicates its effect:

```
charPtr[0] = 'X';
charPtr[1] = 'Y';
charPtr[2] = 'Z';
charPtr[3] = '\0';   // '\0' is part of the string literal.
```

3.4.E The technique for passing arrays to and from functions is to pass their base address. This series of demonstrations shows: (i) that arrays as formal arguments within declarators are synonyms for pointer variables; (ii) why it is that passing a pointer by value achieves the effect of passing the array by reference; and that (iii) the return type of a pointer may (and often does) stand for a whole array.

Begin by typing *main( )*, as given in the following, preceded with the two function prototypes.

```
void showArray(int   a[], int size); // Prototype.
void showArray(char c[]);            // Prototype.

void main()
{
    int*    intPtr1;
    int*    intPtr2;

    int     intArray1[5]  =  {0, 1, 2, 3, 4};
    int     intArray2[8]  =  {5, 6, 7, 8, 9, 10, 11, 12};

    char*   charPtr;
    char    charArray[25] = "ABCDEFG";

    cout << "\n &intArray1 = " << intArray1
         << "     sizeof intArray1 = " << sizeof intArray1;
    showArray(intArray1, 5);

    cout << "\n &intArray2 = " << intArray2
         << "     sizeof intArray2 = " << sizeof intArray2;
    showArray(intArray2, 8);

    cout << "\n &charArray = " << (void*) charArray
         << "     sizeof charArray = " << sizeof charArray;
    showArray(charArray);
}
```

Write the functions that will: display the address of the formal argument to which the array is transmitted, display the value passed to this formal argument (which will be the array's address), display the size of this formal argument (which will be the size of a pointer), and display the contents of the array. Assume that the character array will be a string terminated by a *NULL* zero, therefore displayable directly by way of *cout* and the output operator.

Run the program and observe the results.

Without changing your function, change the prototypes so that they appear as shown in the following. The program should run just as it did before. Variable names do not have to appear within prototypes, but brackets do to indicate when variables are arrays.

```
void showArray(int   [], int);      // Prototype.
void showArray(char []);            // Prototype.
```

Now change the prototypes, so that pointers replace the arrays. The program should continue to work just as it had:

```
void showArray(int*   a, int size); // Prototype.
void showArray(char* c);            // Prototype.
```

Change the declarator accompanying the functions' bodies so that they are exactly the same as within the prototypes (do not copy the semicolon). The program should continue to run with the same results.

Finally, get rid of the variable names within the prototypes and run the program again. You will get the same results.

```
void showArray(int*,   int);        // Prototype.
void showArray(char*);              // Prototype.
```

Change *main( )* so that instead of passing the arrays themselves to the functions you pass pointers:

assign *intArray1* to *intPtr2* and make the call *showArray(intPtr1, 5);*

assign *&intArray[5]* to *intPtr2* and make the call *showArray(intPtr2, 3);*

assign *charArray* to *charPtr* and make the call *showArray(charPtr);*

These calls would work just as well had the formal arguments matching the pointers been declared with the brackets, as they had been at first.

One of the noteworthy features of the output is the evidence that the formal argument to which an array is passed is a variable entirely independent of the array itself. It is a pointer situated at a different location in memory, not an alias. However, because the formal argument is initialized to the value of the actual argument, and because each is a pointer they both point to the same place. In other words, their *l*-values differ but their *r*-values are the same. Because it is the *r*-value (where a pointer points) that applies in accessing array elements, both access the same locations. Modify both functions so that they put a distinctive value into the 0th element of their arrays. Display the arrays following the function calls to show that the changes stuck.

A way to communicate to a code reader that a function will not change a formal argument passed by reference, an array, or a pointer is to specify the argument as constant. More than an idle pledge, the compiler enforces the proscription. Any attempt, inadvertent or otherwise, to change the value of an argument designated as *const* will be flagged. Because the prototype has to agree with the declarator accompanying the function, change the pointer to *const* in both places for each function and attempt to rerun the program:

```
void showArray(const int*,   int);  // Prototype.
void showArray(const char*);        // Prototype.
```

Write a function with the prototype:

```
int* returnArray(const int* a, const int* b); // Prototype.
```

to which you will pass *intArray1* and *intArray2* to *a* and *b*, respectively. The function will ask the user whether to return *a* or to return *b* and will do as directed.

To receive the returned array, an *int** such as *intPtr1* or *intPtr2* will be needed. The address of an authentic array, bound to an allocated chunk of memory, cannot be used because it cannot be updated. Test your function by calling it and displaying the first five elements of the returned array.

3.5 In addition to its use as the multiplication operator and its use to signify that a type specifier denotes a pointer, the asterisk is used to reference the variable stored at the location designated by an address. Given the definitions:

```
int  a    = 10;
int* aPtr = &a;
```

*aPtr is a synonym for the variable bound to the memory address held by *aPtr*. Here **aPtr* is a synonym for *a* because *aPtr* holds *a*'s address. Thus

```
cout << a;            and            cout << *aPtr;
```

both display the value of *a*, and

```
a = 5;               and          *aPtr = 5;
```

both assign 5 to the location signified by *a*. Where the use of *a* evokes its *r*-value, **aPtr* supplies the value held at the location stored by *aPtr*. Where the use of *a* evokes its *l*-value, **aPtr* supplies the *aPtr*'s value (i.e., the location it stores).

Given the following program, add the code needed to swap the values of *a* and *b* but done by manipulating *aPtr* and *bPtr*.

```
void main()
{
   int a = 5, b = 10;

   int *aPtr = &a,   *bPtr = &b, *holder;

   cout << "\n Before swap:  a = "  << *aPtr << ",    b = " << *bPtr;

   // Place answer here.

   cout << "\n  After swap:  a = "  << *aPtr << ",    b = " << *bPtr;
   cout << endl;
}
```

3.6 The following exercises, on the address-of operator, should offer insight into the way your compiler manages the stack. Recall that the stack refers to the segment of memory allocated to the program by the operating system that the program uses for the function's automatic (or "local") variables. This memory, allocated when the function is activated, is referred to as *static* memory allocation.

3.6.A Given the following program, complete the output statements so that they display the address of the prescribed variable and bytes of storage its values may occupy:

```
#include <iostream.h>

void main()
{
   double r;
   cout << "\n Address of r is: " <<        ;
   cout << "    bytes of storage occupied is:  " <<      ;

   double s;
   cout << "\n Address of s is: " <<        ;
   cout << "    bytes of storage occupied is:  " <<      ;
```

```
        double t;
        cout << "\n Address of t is: " <<        ;
        cout << "      bytes of storage occupied is:  " <<     ;

        cout << endl;
    }
```

3.6.B This replicates the preceding with the purpose of examining where the automatic variables within a function called by *main( )* reside relative to those within *main( )* itself. Once again, complete the output statements and study the results.

```
    #include <iostream.h>

    void function(double a, double& b)
    {
        cout << endl;
        // Formal arguments passed by value are automatic
        // variables with a location different from that
        // of their corresponding actual argument.
        cout << "\n Address of a is: " <<        ;
        cout << "      bytes of storage occupied is:  " <<     ;

        // Formal arguments passed by reference are bound
        // to the same location as that of their corresponding
        // actual argument.
        cout << "\n Address of b is: " <<        ;
        cout << "      bytes of storage occupied is:  " <<     ;

        // This variable named r has nothing to do with the
        // variable of the same name in main().
        double r;
        cout << "\n Address of function's r is: " <<       ;
        cout << "      bytes of storage occupied is:  " <<      ;

        double z;
        cout << "\n Address of z is: " <<        ;
        cout << "      bytes of storage occupied is:  " <<     ;

        cout << endl;
    }

    void main()
    {
        double r;
        cout << "\n Address of main's r is: " <<        ;
        cout << "      bytes of storage occupied is:  " <<     ;

        double s;
        cout << "\n Address of s is: " <<        ;
        cout << "      bytes of storage occupied is:  " <<     ;

        double t;
        cout << "\n Address of t is: " <<        ;
        cout << "      bytes of storage occupied is:  " <<     ;

        function(s, t);

        // Has the memory allocated for u been used elsewhere?
        double u;
        cout << "\n Address of u is: " <<        ;
        cout << "      bytes of storage occupied is:  " <<     ;

        double v;
        cout << "\n Address of v is: " <<        ;
        cout << "      bytes of storage occupied is:  " <<     ;

        cout << endl;
    }
```

3.7 These exercises parallel those of Exercise 3.6. They should offer insight into the way your compiler manages the free store, often called the heap. Recall that the heap refers to the segment of memory allocated to the program by the operating system that the program uses for dynamically allocated memory. Dynamically allocated memory is acquired at run time as needs arise.

If memory is acquired for a variable by way of the *new* operator, the memory is said to be dynamically allocated and is from the heap. If a variable is not defined with the *new* operator, its memory is not dynamically allocated and comes from the stack.

3.7.A Given the following program, complete the output statements so that they display the address of the prescribed variable and bytes of storage its values may occupy.

Often the stack and the heap are based at opposite ends of the same segment of memory. The stack "grows" toward the heap's end, and the heap "grows" toward the stack's end. Does the output suggest that this may be so in the case of your compiler?

```
#include <iostream.h>

void main()
{

    double* pointer1;   // Here pointer1 is not defined with new.
                        // This means that its memory is acquired
                        // from the stack.

    cout << "\n Address of pointer1 is: " <<      ;
    cout << "      bytes of storage occupied is:   " <<      ;

    double* pointer2;
    cout << "\n Address of pointer2 is: " <<      ;
    cout << "      bytes of storage occupied is:   " <<      ;

    double* pointer3;
    cout << "\n Address of pointer3 is: " <<      ;
    cout << "      bytes of storage occupied is:   " <<      ;

    cout << endl;

    pointer1 = new double;   // Here pointer1 is assigned the address
                             // of a dynamically acquired double.

    *pointer1 = 1.0; // Assigns 1.0 not to pointer1 but
                     // to the memory location
                     // to which pointer 1 points.

    cout << "\n Address of the first double from the heap is: "
         <<      ;
    cout << "\n     It stores the value: " << *pointer1 ;
    cout << "\n     It occupies "  <<
         << " bytes of storage.";

    pointer2 = new double;

    *pointer2 = 2.0;

    cout << "\n Address of the second double from the heap is: "
         <<      ;
    cout << "\n     It stores the value: " << *pointer2 ;
    cout << "\n     It occupies "  <<
         << " bytes of storage.";

    pointer3 = new double;
```

```
      *pointer3 = 3.0;
      cout << "\n Address of the third double from the heap is: "
           <<              ;
      cout << "\n    It stores the value: " << *pointer3 ;
      cout << "\n    It occupies " <<
           << " bytes of storage.";

      cout << endl;

      // The delete operator releases the dynamically allocated
      // memory at the address stored by a pointer variable; it
      // does not deallocate the pointer variable itself.

      delete pointer1;
      delete pointer2;
      delete pointer3;
  }
```

3.7.B An automatic variable is *static. Static* denotes that its memory is acquired and bound to the variable when the referencing environment is activated. This memory cannot be "unbound" and recycled as the program runs. In contrast, dynamically acquired memory is allocated as the program runs, not when the function begins. What is more, it can be released and reused. A chunk of memory can be allocated to hold an *int* at one point then released and reused to hold a *float* (or, more accurately, to be part of the memory used to hold a *float — floats* require more bytes than *ints*).

This program demonstrates that the amount of memory allocated dynamically can be dependent upon events that take place at run time (and not knowable in advance).

A *char* is stored in one byte. The user is asked how many bytes should be taken from the heap. A *for* loop iterates this number of times. Within each iteration another *char* is allocated, but without deallocating one acquired on the previous iteration. The program prints the address of the initially allocated *char* and the address of the last one acquired. Fill in the missing pieces so that the program runs.

```
#include <iostream.h>

void main()
  {
    cout << "\n How many bytes would you like to take from the heap?"
    cout << "\n Enter an integer between 1 and 1000:  ==> "

    int numOfBytes;
    cin >> numOfBytes;

    char*  pointer = new char;  // A char takes up a byte.

    cout << "\n\n   Address of byte 1 is:  " <<              ;

    for (int i = 2; i <= numOfBytes; i++)
      {
        // Allocation of the next char.

      }

    cout << "\n   Address of byte " << numOfBytes << " is:  " <<         ;
  }
```

3.7.C Modify the preceding program so that the same byte of memory is reused for each successive allocation.

Check the output to confirm that your modification did the job.

3.7.D   The following program will literally use a dynamically allocated chunk of memory for an *int* and then reuse it to store a *float*. Provide the code to perform the described actions.

```
#include <iostream.h>

void main()
{
    // Define an int pointer.

    // Define a float pointer.

    // Get an int from the heap, and
    // store its address in the int pointer.

    // Display the address of the dynamically allocated int.

    // Return this memory to the heap for reuse.

    // Get a float from the heap, and
    // store its address in the float pointer.

    // Display the address of the dynamically allocated float.

}
```

3.8   This item is on the confusion that may be caused by the terminology "*l*-value" and "*r*-value" when they are used to describe the action of the operators & and *.

It concludes by asking a multiple choice question and for a sentence or two to reconcile the seeming inconsistency.

The *int* variable *a* is located at the metaphorical memory location 2194 and stores the value 9. The *int* variable *b* is located at the metaphorical memory location 3806:

```
        2194                3806
      ┌───────┐          ┌───────┐
      │   9   │          │       │
  a   └───────┘      b   └───────┘
```

What does the identifier *a* stand for? In the output statement:

```
cout << a;   // Displays 9, the value of variable a.
```

it stands for the value stored at the memory location symbolically referred to as *a*. This is also what it stands for in the assignment statement:

```
b = a;   // The value of variable a is copied into the
         // memory location designated by b.
```

b, being the variable into which *a*'s value will be copied, stands for a location memory; specifically, it represents *b*'s address.

Sometimes a variable stands for the value held at a symbolic location, and sometimes it stands for the location itself. Context determines which. Using the assignment statement as the point of reference, the value in storage is called the variable's right value or *r*-value. When *a* is on the right-hand side of the assignment operator, it signifies a 9. The address of a unit of memory is called its left value or *l*-value. When *b* is on the left-hand side of the assignment operator it signifies the address to be used as the target for an assembler store.

In Pascal, this was all there was to it. The idea of an *l*-value and an *r*-value was clear and did not require a closer look. C++, however, permits the ability to access and manipuiate *l*-values and *r*-values through its address-of operator, &, and its indirect reference operator, *. To explore their properties, we define two "*int* pointer" variables. Notice that in the context of variable definition and variable declaration, the * is a qualifier for a data type specifier meaning "pointer"; it is neither the indirection operator nor, for that matter, the multiplication operator.

```
int*  aPtr;  // Here aPtr may store "int pointers," which is to say
             // the addresses at which int variables are held
             // in memory.
int*  bPtr;

// These two definitions may have been coded, with the same
// results, like this:   int *aPtr, *bPtr;
```

Having the two pointer variables, we may assign the address-of *a* to *aPtr* and the address-of *b* to *bPtr*.

```
aPtr = &a;   // Here aPtr will hold the address of a, 2194.
bPtr = &b;   // Here bPtr will hold the address of b, 3806.
```

Displaying the value of *bPtr* shows *b*'s address (or *l*-value):

```
cout << bPtr;  // Here 3806 is shown, b's l-value.
```

The indirect reference operator enables access to the value in storage at a designated address. Therefore, displaying **aPtr* shows the value in store at the memory location held by *aPtr*.

```
cout << *aPtr;  // Here 9 is shown, which is a's r-value,
                // the value in store at 2194.
```

Finally, here is the question: which of these statements will accomplish the assignment of *a*'s value to *b*?

```
choice    i)     bPtr  = *aPtr;
choice   ii)     &b    = *aPtr;
choice  iii)     &b    = a;
choice   iv)    *bPtr = *aPtr;
```

Pinpoint a seeming symbolic inconsistency and try to account for it.

3.9   There are three aims of this exercise: (i) to examine how arrays are stored in memory; (ii) to examine how a pointer to a scalar (e.g., a pointer to a single *int*; i.e., a variable of type *int**) can serve as the base address of a pre-existing array; and (iii) to examine how arrays are passed to functions. You will see how it comes to be that arrays are operatively passed by reference.

Complete the missing parts of the program and examine the results of its run.

```
#include <iostream.h>

void arrayReceiver(int array[]);  // Same as   void arrayReceiver(int []);

void main()
 {
    // Define an int array:  the array will have 10
    // elements, each one an int.

    int a[10];  // Memory allocated for the array.

    //  Demonstrate that the sizeof the array equals
    //  the sizeof 10 ints:

    cout <<    "\n          sizeof an int = " <<                    ;
```

```
cout << "\n\n            sizeof a[0] = " <<              ;
cout <<     "\n            sizeof a[1] = " <<              ;
cout <<     "\n            ...and so on... ";
```

```
// Notice in the statement beneath that a, the array's name
// used without a subscript, signifies the entire array:
```

```
cout << "\n\n sizeof the whole array = " << sizeof a    ;
```

```
// Display the memory locations of a's first three elements:
```

```
cout << "\n\n  location of a[0] is: " <<              ;
cout <<     "\n  location of a[1] is: " <<              ;
cout <<     "\n  location of a[2] is: " <<              ;
```

```
// Notice in the statement beneath that a, the array's name
// used without a subscript, signifies the array's address,
// which is the same as the address of a[0].  Also, notice
// that &a represents the same value as a -- they are synonyms
// for the array's location:
```

```
cout << "\n\n  the location of the array is  a: " <<  a   ;
cout <<     "\n          which is the same as &a[0]: " << &a[0];
cout <<     "\n          which is the same as   &a : " << &a   ;
```

```
// Define an int pointer:
```

```
int* ptr;
```

```
// Set the pointer equal to the address of the array.
```

```
ptr = a;    // This is legal because a, the array's name, which
            // is the array's base address, is the same as the
            // address of the array's 0th element, &a[0], which
            // is a pointer to an int.
```

```
// What is the sizeof ptr?
```

```
cout <<   "\n            sizeof an int ptr = " <<              ;
```

```
// Can ptr be treated as the base address of the a array?
// Test to determine whether ptr[0], ptr[1], and ptr[2] are
// syntactical realities and see if the output shows their
// addresses coincide with a[0], a[1], and a[2] :
```

```
cout << "\n\n  location of ptr[0] is: " <<              ;
cout <<     "\n  location of ptr[1] is: " <<              ;
cout <<     "\n  location of ptr[2] is: " <<              ;
```

```
// Recall that a, construed as the base address of the allocated
// array, is identical to &a, the location in memory at which a
// is situated.  This latter is a reflection of the activation-time
// binding of the allocated array to the name a.
//
// Confirm that it is ptr's value that equals a, but that ptr
// is situated elsewhere.
```

```
cout<<"\n\n  base address of the allocated array is: " <<    ;
cout<<  "\n                   value stored by ptr is: " <<    ;
cout<<  "\n the location in memory of ptr (&ptr) is: " <<    ;
```

```
int b[10];  // Another array is defined.  Which of the
            // assignments below is an error and why?
            // Comment out the error so that the program can run.
```

```
ptr = b;  // Base address of array b assigned to ptr.
```

```
    a    = b;   // Base address of array b assigned to a.

    // Pass the a array to the function arrayReceiver().

    arrayReceiver( a );

    // Rewrite the declarator of arrayReceiver() so that the
    // int array in the call is passed to an int* formal argument.
    // Rerun the program to confirm that the function performs
    // in exactly the same way.

    cout << "\n\n\n*****Run Completed*****" << endl;
}

void arrayReceiver(int array[])
{
    cout << "\n\n **From arrayReceived()**";

    // Use the sizeof operator to see how many bytes of memory
    // are allocated the formal argument, array:

    cout << "\n  sizeof array =  " <<                 ;

    // Use the address-of operator to see array's location in
    // memory.

    cout << "\n  array is bound to memory location:  " <<          ;

    // Display the value transmitted to array (which is an int*):

    cout << "\n  the value stored by array is:  " << array;

    // Display the addresses of the element 0, 1, and 2
    // when array is accessed with subscripts and the
    // array subscripting operator (the square brackets):

    cout << "\n\n  location of array[0] is:  " <<              ;
    cout <<    "\n  location of array[1] is:  " <<              ;
    cout <<    "\n  location of array[2] is:  " <<              ;

    // Notice the implication of the above.  The formal argument
    // array is an int* stored at a different memory location from
    // the actual argument a.  Because a is an array (bound to a
    // set of individual elements), it is a pointer too but special
    // in that both its value (r-value) and its address (l-value or
    // binding) are the same.  The value of a is passed by value
    // to array, which means that both array and a point to the
    // same place in memory (which is the array's element 0).
    // The result is that array[i] is an alias for a[i].

}
```

3.10   Test this program to examine dynamically allocated arrays.

```
#include <iostream.h>

void main()
{
    // Define two variables that will be used to hold the
    // addresses of two dynamically allocated int arrays:

    int*  a;
    int*  b;
```

```
// Allocate an int array with three elements and assign
// its base address to a:

a = new int[3];

// Allocate an int array with six elements and assign
// its base address to b:

// Are the sizes of these respective arrays attainable by
// taking the sizeof a and the sizeof b?  Test to find out:

cout << "\n sizeof a = " <<              ;
cout << "\n sizeof b = " <<              ;

// What is the memory location to which a is bound, and
// where are the elements in the array to which it points?

cout << "\n\n  address of a is:   " <<              ;

cout << "\n\n  address of a[0] is:  " <<              ;
cout <<    "\n  address of a[1] is:  " <<              ;
cout <<    "\n  address of a[2] is:  " <<              ;

// What is the memory location to which b is bound, and where are
// the first three elements in the array to which it points?

cout << "\n\n  address of b is:   " <<              ;

cout << "\n\n  address of b[0] is:  " <<              ;
cout <<    "\n  address of b[1] is:  " <<              ;
cout <<    "\n  address of b[2] is:  " <<              ;

// Swap the arrays pointed to by a and b (so that a points to
// the array b is currently pointing to, and b points to a's).

int* holder;

// To corroborate the successful exchange, once again display a's
// memory location and the address of the first three elements of
// its array:

cout << "\n\n  address of a is:   " <<              ;

cout << "\n\n  address of a[0] is:  " <<              ;
cout <<    "\n  address of a[1] is:  " <<              ;
cout <<    "\n  address of a[2] is:  " <<              ;

// Also, once again display b's memory location and the addresses
// of the three elements of its array:

cout << "\n\n  address of b is:   " <<              ;

cout << "\n\n  address of b[0] is:  " <<              ;
cout <<    "\n  address of b[1] is:  " <<              ;
cout <<    "\n  address of b[2] is:  " <<              ;

// Allocate another six-element array and assign it to a
// but without first deleting a's current array.  You will
// see that the compiler has no objection to this.

// delete [] a;

// Allocate another three-element array and assign it to b
// without first deleting b's current array.
```

```
// delete [] b;

// Once again display a's memory location and the addresses of
// the first three elements of the array to which it now points:

cout << "\n\n  address of a is:  " <<                    ;

cout << "\n\n  address of a[0] is:  " <<                  ;
cout <<   "\n  address of a[1] is:  " <<                  ;
cout <<   "\n  address of a[2] is:  " <<                  ;

// Once again display b's memory location and the addresses
// of the three elements of the array to which it now points:

cout << "\n\n  address of b is:  " <<                    ;

cout << "\n\n  address of b[0] is:  " <<                  ;
cout <<   "\n  address of b[1] is:  " <<                  ;
cout <<   "\n  address of b[2] is:  " <<                  ;

// Once the address of a dynamically allocated unit of memory
// (an array, scalar, or struct) is lost, this memory remains
// allocated but cannot be either accessed or deleted.

// Activate the commented-out statements deleting []a and []b,
// and rerun the program.  Inspect the output to see if the
// two newly allocated arrays make use of the returned memory.
}
```

3.11 This exercise looks at some of the traps associated with dynamically allocated arrays: surprises that may occur when two variables point to the same array (when you change one, you change the other), and that it is an error to delete one array more than once (but it is not an error to delete a pointer to NULL). Complete the program, run it, and examine the output.

By the way, it is always an error to delete an automatic variable of any kind.

```
#include <iostream.h>

void main()
{
    // Define a dynamically allocated array and assign values to it:

    int* a = new int[3];
    a[0] = 111;   a[2] = 222;   a[3] = 333;

    // Define two additional int* variables:

    int *b, *c;

    // Perform the assignments so that b points to the same address
    // as a,  and so that c points to the same address as b:

    // Assign  888 to b[1]  and  999 to c[1]:

    // Display the three respective arrays:
    cout<<"\n a[0]  = "<<a[0]<<"   a[1] = "<<a[1]<<"   a[2]  ="<<a[2];
    cout<<"\n b[0]  = "<<b[0]<<"   b[1] = "<<b[1]<<"   b[2]  ="<<b[2];
    cout<<"\n c[0]  = "<<c[0]<<"   c[1] = "<<c[1]<<"   c[2]  ="<<a[2];

    //  Delete these three arrays.  But be vigilant, deleting any one
    //  deletes them all.  Run the program to see the result of the
    //  mistake of deleting a single chunk of dynamically allocated
    //  memory more than once.  Comment out the first deletion and
```

```
//   run the program again.  There will still be an abnormal end
//   because there remains an attempt to delete the same memory
//   twice.  Leave the first deletion commented out, comment out
//   the second, and run the program for a third time.  It will
//   then run without flaw.

delete [] a;
delete [] b;
delete [] c;

//   Set a and b equal to NULL.  To show that it is not an
//   error to delete a pointer NULL, delete each of them.
//   Delete a as if it were a scalar and delete b as if it
//   were an array:

a = b = NULL;

delete a;
delete [] b;

//   After the program has successfully run, activate the
//   code below to see the result of deleting an automatic
//   scalar:

//   int x;     delete x;

//   Deactivate the code directly above and run the program
//   one more time to see the result of the following:

//   int y[5];  delete [] y;
}
```

3.12 A chief use of dynamically allocated arrays is to enable functions to return "more storage" than they received.

Suppose a programmer is writing an exercise on sorting. One function that would print the data array is needed. (It could be used to display the values before and after sorting as well as at any time during the course of the sort for the purpose of viewing the action or for debugging.) Naturally a function to perform the sort itself is also needed. Finally, the exercise would need a function that generates data in a scrambled order.

The strategy used in Pascal, and also usable in C++, would be to define the data array and pass it to *getData( )* to be loaded:

```
void main()
{
  int data[];
  getData( data );   // Remember, arrays are effectively
                     // passed by reference.

     .
     .
     .
}
```

Another strategy would be to define the array within *getData( )* and return its base address (i.e., a pointer to it) so that *main( )* would look like this:

```
void main()
{
  int* data;
  data = getData(); // We may wish to design getData() to
     .              // accept n, the number of ints to be
     .              // loaded into the data set, as an
     .              // argument.
                    //
                    // Or, getData() could place a sentinel
                    // in the final element of an array of
                    // an unspecified size.
                    //
```

```
                                               // Or SIZE could be a global constant.
    }
```

The array returned has to have been dynamically allocated within *getData( )* because dynamically allocated blocks of memory, unlike automatic variables whose deletion upon the conclusion of the function we are powerless to prevent, will persist indefinitely. Thus, *getData( )* may be written along these lines:

```
int*  getData()
    {
        int* dataArray = new int[3]; // Small dataset of 3 elements.
           :
        return dataArray;
    }
```

Write an implementation of *getData( )* in which the three elements of *dataArray* are loaded with the three values 123, 456, 789 and returned. Write *main( )* as a driver to confirm that the array allocated and loaded within *getData( )* is received in working condition. Notice that the program ends normally whether, in *main( )*, the dynamically allocated array is deleted or not.

In order to see what happens, modify *getData( )* so that what is returned is the address of an automatic array that had been loaded with the same data. This is always a serious fault (i.e., error, bug, mistake); never attempt to return an automatic array.

3.13 Here we shall work with an array of pointers. This leads to a program that accepts and echoes arguments from the command line.

An *int** can hold the address of a dynamically allocated array. Provide what the following program needs to display the array's three values:

```
void main()
    {
        int* base;  // Base is a scalar, but it may point to an array.
        base = new int[3];
        base[0] = 11;      base[1] = 12;      base[2] = 13;

        int col;
        for (col = 0; col < 3; col++)
            {

            }

    }
```

The same syntax that enables the *int* type specifier to define an *int* array (i.e., following the variable's name with a pair of brackets: *int a[ ]*), can be used to define an *int** array. Provide what the following progam needs to display the five arrays whose base addresses are held in the pointer array *baseArr*:

```
void main()
    {
        int* baseArr[5];  // Here baseArr is an array of five int pointers.

        baseArr[0] = new int[3];
        baseArr[1] = new int[3];
        baseArr[2] = new int[3];
        baseArr[3] = new int[3];
        baseArr[4] = new int[3];

        baseArr[0][0] = 11;    baseArr[0][1] = 12;    baseArr[0][2] = 13;
        baseArr[1][0] = 21;    baseArr[1][1] = 22;    baseArr[1][2] = 23;
        baseArr[2][0] = 31;    baseArr[2][1] = 32;    baseArr[2][2] = 33;
        baseArr[3][0] = 41;    baseArr[3][1] = 42;    baseArr[3][2] = 43;
        baseArr[4][0] = 51;    baseArr[4][1] = 52;    baseArr[4][2] = 53;
```

```
int row, col;
for (row = 0; row < 5; row++)
    {
    cout << endl;
    for (col = 0; col < 4; col++)
        {

        }
    }
}
```

There is no logical difference between a *char* array and an *int* array. However, because *char* arrays are often used to represent strings, and because it can be more convenient to think of strings as integral entities than as a succession of elements, C++ makes certain allowances when it comes to manipulating them. One of these allowances is the ease with which strings may be displayed:

```
char* string;
string = new char[ strlen("What a snap!")  + 1 ];
strcpy( string, "What a snap!");

cout << string; // A string may be displayed as readily as an int.
```

Provide what the following progam needs to display the three strings held by the array of *char* pointers *strPtrs*. Be certain to *#include <string.h>* for *strcpy( )*.

```
void main()
    {
    char* strPtrs[3]; // An array of three char pointers.

    strPtrs[0] = "Line one.";    // Here strPtrs[0] holds the address of a
                                 // string literal.

    strPtrs[1] = new char[10];   // Here strPtrs[1] holds the address of a
                                 // dynamically allocated char array.

    strcpy(strPtrs[1], "Line two.");   // The shown string literal is
                                       // copied into the array to
                                       // which strPtrs[1] points.

    strPtrs[2] = strPtrs[1];     // Here strPtrs[2] is assigned the same
                                 // address as the one stored by
                                 // strPtrs[1].

    for (int line = 0; line < 3; line++)
        {
        cout << endl;

        }
    }
```

Command line arguments are the arguments that, in DOS, appear to the right of the name of a .EXE file. For instance, the XCOPY copy program, used as follows, has three arguments:

```
XCOPY  c:*.cpp   a:   /s
                           └─A third argument   (will be in argv[3] )
                      └─A second argument   (will be in argv[2] )
                └─A first argument   (will be in argv[1])
       └─A name of the file being run   (will be in argv[0])
```

A program in C++ can intercept the pieces along a command line by way of two arguments in *main( )*:

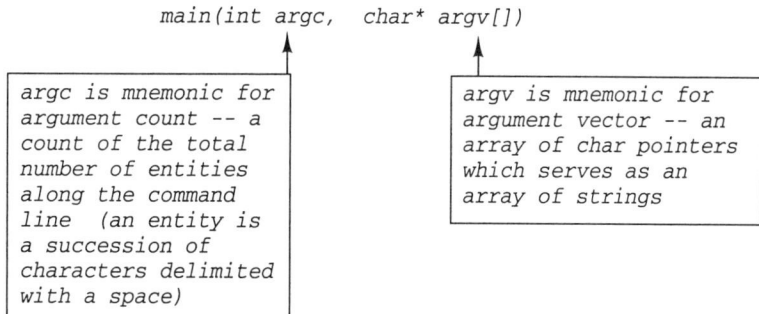

```
main(int argc,  char* argv[])
```

argc is mnemonic for argument count -- a count of the total number of entities along the command line (an entity is a succession of characters delimited with a space)

argv is mnemonic for argument vector -- an array of char pointers which serves as an array of strings

If XCOPY (preceding) was the name of an executable file holding the runnable version of a C++ program whose *main( )* included the arguments *argc* and *argv* as shown, *argc* would equal 4 because there are four items along the command line. As for the array of strings:

```
argv[0] would point to the string "C:\DOS\XCOPY"

argv[1] would point to the string "c:*.cpp"

argv[2] would point to the string "a:"

argv[3] would point to the string "/s"
```

Although the first argument in *main( )* must be an int and the second must be a *char*[ ]*, their names do not have to be *argc* and *argv*. These names, however, are traditional, going back to the appearance of the first edition of *The C Programming Language* in 1978.

Write a program that displays all the strings found along a command line. Test it with a run that contains no arguments other than the program's file name. Test it again with a command line holding the arguments:

```
MARY HAD A LITTLE LAMB ITS FLEECE WAS WHITE AS SNOW
```

3.14 This group of exercises expands upon the idea of a constant. Recall that the *const* specifier can be applied to protect the value of an *int* or a *float* from modification:

```
const float PI = 3.14159;  // The value of PI is immutable.
```

The value to which a pointer points is similarly protected by specifying the *float**, *int**, or *char** as being const:

```
const int*  IMMUTABLE_INT;
const char* IMMUTABLE_STRING;
```

However, although the *int* or string to which either *IMMUTABLE_INT* or *IM-MUTABLE_STRING* points cannot be changed through the auspices of these pointers, these pointers can be reset. Debug and run the following program to see *IMMUTABLE_INT* in action.

```
void main()
   {
   const float PI = 3.14;
   PI = 3.14159;

   const int*  IMMUTABLE_INT;  // The int it points to cannot be reset
                               // through its auspices.
```

```
int* ptrArray[3];
ptrArray[0] = new int(100);   // A dynamically allocated int is
                              // initialized to 100.
ptrArray[1] = new int(200);
ptrArray[2] = new int(300);

// This loop assigns each value in the ptrArray to IMMUTABLE_INT
// and prints, via IMMUTABLE_INT, the value of the int to which it
// points.  IMMUTABLE_INT is not const; it is being reset:
cout << endl;
for (int i = 0; i < 3; i++)
    {
    IMMUTABLE_INT =  ptrArray[i];
    cout << *IMMUTABLE_INT << "  ";
    }

// Changing the ints to which ptrArray points (the ints themselves
// are not const):
for (i = 0; i < 3; i++)
    {
    *ptrArray[i] += i+1; // 100 becomes 101, 200 becomes 202,
    }                    // and 300 becomes 303.

// Observe and remove the error in the loop below:
cout << endl;
for (i = 0; i < 3; i++)
    {
    IMMUTABLE_INT =  ptrArray[i];
    *IMMUTABLE_INT += 696;
    cout << *IMMUTABLE_INT << "   ";
    }
}
```

Alternately, a pointer may be immutably set to a memory location to which it points, even though what is stored at that location may be changed, using it as the means of reference.

```
int*  const  IMMUTABLE_INT_LOCATION    = new int;
char* const  IMMUTABLE_STRING_LOCATION = new char[25]
```

Because the address to which each of these pointers is fixed cannot be changed following their definition, they have to be initialized when defined.

Debug and run the following program to see *IMMUTABLE_INT_LOCATION* in action.

```
void main()
{
  int*  const  IMMUTABLE_INT_LOCATION  =  new int;

  // Note that this location could have been initialized with 12345:
  //    int*  const  IMMUTABLE_INT_LOCATION  =  new int(12345);
  //
  // Because it was not, put 12345 into the memory location pointed to
  // IMMUTABLE_INT_LOCATION with an assignment statement.

  *IMMUTABLE_INT_LOCATION = 12345;

  // Display the value held that the location pointed to by
  // IMMUTABLE_INT_LOCATION:

  cout << *IMMUTABLE_INT_LOCATION;

  // This loop demonstrates that the value in storage at the
  // location pointed to by IMMUTABLE_INT_LOCATION can be reset:
  cout << endl;
  for (int i = 0; i < 3; i++)
    {
    *IMMUTABLE_INT_LOCATION = 111 * (i+1);
    cout <<  *IMMUTABLE_INT_LOCATION << "  ";
    }
```

```
int* ptrArray[3];
ptrArray[0] = new int(100);
ptrArray[1] = new int(200);
ptrArray[2] = new int(300);

// IMMUTABLE_INT_LOCATION is reset to the address of each element
// in ptrArray, and the value at that location is displayed:
cout << endl;
for (i = 0; i < 3; i++)
    {
    IMMUTABLE_INT_LOCATION = ptrArray[i];
    cout << *IMMUTABLE_INT_LOCATION << " ";
    }
}
```

It is of course possible to define a variable like the following *K_PTR*. The *int* to which it points cannot be changed through its auspices nor can it be reset to point elsewhere.

```
const int* const K_PTR = new int(1024);
```

Write a program to test whether this renders the 1024 at the location to which *K_PTR* points inviolable. (Hint: define another *int**, assign to it the value of *K_PTR*; and see if through this other pointer the number can be changed.)

3.15 Write and test a function called *avePurchase( )* that accepts the amount of the current purchase and returns the amount of the average purchase as of the current time:

```
float averagePurchase(float amtOfCurrentPurchase);
```

It will need two *static* variables: one to keep a count of the number of purchases and another to accumulate the total amount spent.

3.16 The following program runs because calls to all the missing versions of *printLine( )* have been deactivated as comments.

3.16.A Run the program as it is to observe that the no-argument version of *printLine( )*, which is supplied, displays a line of 40 characters: 20 "+-" pairs.

```
void printLine();  // Prototype.

void main()
    {
        printLine();              // +-+-+-+-+-+-+-+-+-+-+-+-+-+-+-+-+-+-+-+-
//      printLine(10);            // +-+-+-+-+-+-+-+-+-
//      printLine('#');           // ########################################
//      printLine(15, '^');       // ^^^^^^^^^^^^^^^
//      printLine('^', 15);       // ^^^^^^^^^^^^^^^
    }


void printLine()
    {
        cout << endl;
        for (int i = 0; i < 20; i++)  cout << "+-";
        cout << endl;
    }
```

3.16.B Overload *printLine( )* with a version having a signature of one *int*, so that its prototype looks like this:

```
void printLine(int numOfpairs);  // Prototype.
```

This function should print the designated number of "+-" pairs beginning at the left end of a new line.

Activate the function call within *main( )* that will test this function and rerun the program.

3.16.C Create an additional implementation of *printLine( )* with a signature of one *char*:

```
void printLine(char symbolShown);  // Prototype.
```

The transmitted character should be displayed 40 times beginning at the left end of a new line.

Activate the function call within *main( )* that will test this function and rerun the program.

3.16.D To enable hypothetical users to specify both the length of the displayed sequence as well as the character shown, provide a version of *printLine( )* having an (*int, char*) signature:

```
void printLine(int repetitions, char symbolShown);
```

Once again, the generated line should start at the left end of the display.

Activate the function call within *main( )* that will test this function and run the program.

3.16.E The preceding function gives users the ability to control the appearance of these horizontal separators, but it requires them to know and remember that "the number" is the first argument and "the symbol" is the second. We want our software to be more friendly than that. Instead of generating a bad line when the user juxtaposes the order of the arguments, the program should perform just as it does in the previous case.

Accordingly, provide an additional version of *printLine( )* having the (*char, int*) signature. Test it as before.

3.17 For the purpose of this exercise on prescribing default values for a function's formal arguments, a box will be construed as an item created on the fly for display. Each will have a length and a height and will be presented by showing its perimeter using a particular character. Here are some samples. The annotations are not part of the boxes as the program will draw them.

```
symbol =  '*'                        symbol =  '+'
******                               ++++++++
*      *                             +      +
*      *  height = 5                 +      +  height = 5
*      *                             +      +
******                               ++++++++
length = 6                           length = 8

                    symbol = '~'
~~~~~~~~~~~~~~~~~~~~~~~~~~~~~~~~
~                            ~      height = 3
~~~~~~~~~~~~~~~~~~~~~~~~~~~~~~~~
                length = 30
```

3.17.A Complete the program for displaying boxes by writing the *drawBox( )* function and by supplying, within *main( )*, the calls for testing it. All boxes are depicted in the output "left justified"; that is, with their left side at the far left end of the display.

```
// Prototype for the drawBox() function;  notice the default values
// for the arguments (argument names, here, are optional but helpful).
```

```
void drawBox(char symbol = '*', int length = 6, int height = 4);

void main()
{
    // Call drawBox(), having it display the default box:

    // Call drawBox(), having it use a '#' to display
    // a box of default size:

    // Call drawBox(), having it use a '+' to display a box
    // with a length of 25 but having the default height:

    // Call drawBox(), having it use the default character
    // but with a length of 40 and a height of 6:

}
```

3.17.B Upgrade *drawBox( )* so that users may specify the distance (the number of spaces) that the box will be set off from the left margin. Do this by adding a fourth argument whose default value is 0 so that preexisting calls will continue to elicit the same action they had before.

Test the calls used in Exercise 3.17.A, and supplement them with calls that will exercise the enhancement.

Chapter 4

Bjarne Stroustrup, in The *Design and Evolution of C++* (page 171), writes that " . . . the safest bet is to learn C++ bottom-up, that is, first learn the features C++ provides for traditional procedural programming, the better-C subset, then learn to use and appreciate the data abstraction features, and then learn to use class hierarchies to organize sets of related classes." Chapters 2 and 3 focused on procedural programming. These exercises focus upon data abstraction and derivation.

4.1 This is a series of exercises which reviews many of the fundamentals pertinent to object-oriented programming in C++.

Please begin entering the following program and testing it to confirm that it is entirely correct:

```
#include <iostream.h>

class Box
{
    public:
        char symbol;

    private:
        int  length, height;

    public:
        void showBox();  // Prototype.

        void setSize()
        {
            int l, h;
```

```
                              cout << "\nEnter a length (an int between 2 and 10):  ";
                              cin >> l;

                              if (l >= 2  && l <= 10)  length = l;
                              else  length = 1;

                              cout << "\nEnter a height (an int between 2 and 6):   ";
                              cin >> h;

                              if (h >= 2  && h <= 6)   height = h;
                              else  height = 1;

                              cout << "\nEnter a symbol:  ";
                              cin >> symbol;

                              showBox();
                          }

                  };  // End of Box's class specifier.

              void Box::showBox()
                  {
                     cout << endl;
                     for (int i = 1;  i <= height;  i++)
                        {
                           for (int j = 1;  j <= length;  j++)  cout << symbol;
                           cout << endl;
                        }
                  }

              void main()
                  {
                     Box box;
                     box.setSize();
                     box.showBox();
                  }
```

4.1.A   Delete the three statements within *main( )* and re-write it according to the following instructions:

Create a large *Box* with the symbol 'A' and a small *Box* with the *symbol* 'B'.

```
For each:    display it (use showBox())
             display its size in bytes (use sizeof)
             display its address (use &, the address-of operator)
```

Within *main( )*, write the code to swap them (so that the 'A' *Box* assumes the dimensions and *symbol* of the 'B' *Box* and vice versa). Display the two boxes to confirm the exchange.

Notice that the assignment operator creates a full member-by-member copy (i.e., a bitwise copy of the whole object) duplicating both *public* and *private* data members.

4.1.B   Write a free function which swaps two Boxes:

```
void swapBoxes(Box& box1,  Box& box2);  // Prototype.
```

Test it by creating two *Box* objects in *main( )* and displaying them, swapping them via a function call to *swapBoxes( )*, and then redisplaying them.

4.1.C Write and similarly test a member function which swaps the invoking *Box* with the argument *Box* using the same three logical steps that were used by free function. (Hint: Use *this* as a referent for the accessing *Box*.)

4.1.D Write and test a *friend* free function called *shift( )* which exchanges the argument *Box's length* and *height* so that it transforms a *Box* object that looks like this:

into one that looks like this:

shift( ) had to be declared a *friend* function within the *Box* class specifier so that it could access the private data members of the argument.
Remove the declaration of friendship and attempt to run the program again in order to observe the error messages.

4.1.E Remove the *shift( )* function from the program written in part D so that both its declaration as a *friend* and the function are no longer present.
Write and test a member function called *rotate( )* which exchanges the invoking *Box's length* and *height* in the same manner that the *shift( )* function had — so that it transforms a *Box* object that looks like this:

into one that looks like this:

4.1.F Remove the *Box::rotate( )* function from the program written in in part E.
Install within the *Box* class "get" functions which return the invoking *Box's length* and *height*:

```
int Box::getLength();  // Prototype.
int Box::getHeight();  // Prototype.
```

Install within the *Box* class "set" functions which allow the invoking *Box's length* and *height* to be updated:

```
void Box::setLength(int newLength); // Prototype.
void Box::setHeight(int newHeight); // Prototype.
```

Use these to write a free function called *shift( )*, which is not a *friend*, that exchanges the *length* and *height* of the argument *Box* to offer the same service and interface supplied by the *shift( )* function from part D.
Test the function.

4.1.G Write and test a free function which accepts a *Box* and returns another *Box* which is twice as high and twice as long as the argument *Box*. (This function will use the selector and modifier functions with which you equipped the class in the previous item.)

4.1.H Write and test a free function which accepts a *Box* and returns another *Box* which is twice times as high and three as long as the argument *Box*. Unlike the function written for the item above, do not use the *get* and *set* functions you wrote in part G. Have the *Box* class confer friendship to make *length* and *height*, although *private*, accessible.

4.1.I   If the privacy of *private* data members is maintained (by not granting friendship) so that only functions written by the purveyors of the class can modify their values, it becomes very much less likely that they will ever be assigned insane values (e.g., a negative value for a *length*). Our functions can test prospective settings before they are initiated. This is valuable.

Another valuable property of data hiding is that changes within the class can be made without impacting on its clients. Imagine that the *Box* class were reworked so that dimensions of *Boxes* were represented by an area and a *height*. In other words, the three data members were changed to be area, *height*, and *symbol*; and *length*, as a data member, were eliminated. Corresponding changes could be made to *setSize( )*, *showBox( )*, *getLength( )*, *getHeight( )*, *setLength( )*, and *setHeight( )* (that is, all the member functions) so that they continued to work as before. With the existing interfaces preserved, there should be no reason why any non-member function should be affected. *Friends* however, may not fare so well as "strangers".

Write, but do not actually run, the code for the superseding *getLength( )* and *setLength( )* functions.

Software must undergo continual change if it is to retain utility in a changing problem-space. Explain why friendship may be hazardous to the integrity of a system that uses a class undergoing regular upgrade and how it may hamper the class's evolution.

4.1.J   Write and test a free function which accepts two *Boxes* and returns "their sum" — a *Box* whose *length* is the sum of their *lengths* and whose height is the sum of their *heights*. The symbol of the "sum" *Box* should be a '+'.

```
Box  plus (Box box1, Box box2);  // Prototype.
```

Following a successful test, change the function's name from *plus( )* to *operator+( )*; that is, change its declarator to:

```
Box  operator+ (Box box1, Box2);  // Prototype.
```

Its name change must be reflected in its invocations. A call that had been:

```
sumBox = plus(boxA, boxB);
```

will now be:

```
sumBox = operator+(boxA, boxB);
```

Test these modifications.

Named *operator+( )*, this function has overloaded the + operator so that it can be used in the conventional symbolic manner with *Box* operands. Confirm this is so by replacing the invocation as it stands:

```
sumBox = operator+(boxA, boxB);
```

with:

```
sumBox = boxA + boxB
```

4.1.K   Re-write and test the *operator+( )* from part J as a member function.

4.1.L   Decide what it means to add an *int* to a *Box* and to add a *Box* to an *int*. Then overload the + operator so that it accomplishes these operations in the standard symbolic manner. Confirm the operator's abilities with tests such as:

```
Box b = 10 + boxC;
b.showBox();
Box c = boxC + 10;
c.showBox();
```

4.1.M   Add the following free function to your program.

```
ostream& operator<< (ostream& outputStream, Box b)
{
    outputStream << endl;
    for (int i = 1; i <= b.getHeight(); i++)
    {
        for (int j = 1; j<= b.getLength(); j++)
        {
            outputStream << b.symbol;
        }
        outputStream << endl;
    }
    return outputStream;
}
```

Test it with a statement such as:

```
cout << box1 << "Box 1 is above" << endl;
```

and

```
cout << box1 << box2 << box3;
```

Change the declarator so that function returns *void*, and comment out the return statement. Rerun the tests.

Restore the function to its original form. Now test the ability of the output operator to direct boxes to the printer as well as to a file.

4.1.N   Install and test a no-argument constructor which initializes *length* to 12, *height* to 3, and *symbol* to '*'. This constructor should not display the *Box*.

Install and test a one-argument constuctor which initializes the *length* and the *height* to the value arriving in the *int* argument. The *symbol* data member is initialized to '*'. This constructor should not display the *Box*.

Install and test a one-argument constructor which initializes symbol to the value of an arriving in the char argument. The length data member should be initialized to 10 and height to 5. The *Box* should not be displayed.

Install and test a three-argument constructor which initializes length to the value of the first argument, height to the value of the second, and symbol to the value of the third. The *Box* should not be displayed.

4.1.O   One-argument constructors, such as *Box::Box(int)* and *Box::Box(char)* written in part N, also serve as data conversion functions. Test their abilities with the following code in *main( )* (or code like it of your own design):

```
Box x;
cout << x << "Address of Box x = " << &x << endl;

x = 3;
cout << x << "Address of Box x = " << &x << endl;
```

```
x = '!';  // ASCII value of '!' is 33
cout << x << "Address of Box x = " << &x << endl;
```

Displaying *x*'s address after each assignment confirms that *x* remains the same *Box* despite the involvement of a constructor.

Remove the one-argument constructor having the *char* signature from *Box*. Re-run the program to test the effect of assigning the character '!' to *x*. (C++ will convert '!' to an *int*, its ASCII value, in order to apply the only possible means for facilitating the assignment.)

Without re-activating the *Box(char)* constructor attempt the following. (C++ will convert the 5.6 to an *int* and use the *Box(int)* constructor to execute the assignment statement.)

```
x = 5.6;
cout << x << "Address of Box = " << &x << endl;
```

4.1.P All *Box* constructors output *Box*es. All one-argument *Box* constructors serve as implicitly invoked data conversion fucntions, mapping an object of the argument's data type onto a *Box*. These same one-argument constructors enable explicit data conversion, otherwise known as casting. For instance, the one-argument constructor having the *int* signature, *Box::Box(int)*, allows for the following (with our overloaded output operator from part M):

```
cout << Box(5);  // Operates identicaly to:  cout << (Box)5;
                 // Uses the overloaded output operator from M.

Box b1;
b1 = Box(3);     // Operates identically to:  b1 = (Box)3;
                 //                    and to:  b1 = 3;
```

How do we accomplish data transformation going in the other direction, for example to convert a *Box* into an *int*? Because a *Box* constructor cannot output an *int*, a different mechanism is needed — an overloaded cast operator, such as the following, must be installed as a member function of *Box*:

```
Box::operator int()
  {
    return (length + height)/2;
  }
```

Install this function and test its ability for both implicit and explicit "*Box* to *int*" conversion in *main( )*. These three statements, for instance, perform identically (*i* is an *int*, and *BoxA* exists and is initialized):

```
i = BoxA;        i = int(BoxA);        i = (int)BoxA;
```

4.1.Q Clean-up the *Box* class so that its specifier appears as:

```
class Box
  {
    public:
       char symbol;

    private:
       int  length, height;
```

```
public:
    void showBox();                    // Prototype.
    void setSize();                    // Prototype.
    void setLength(int newLength);     // Prototype.
    void setHeight(int newHeight);     // Prototype.
    int  getLength();                  // Prototype.
    int  getHeight();                  // Prototype.
};
```

Be sure that the code for each function is present following the specifier. Notice that the constructors have been removed.

Install a *private static* data member called *total* which will be an *int* accumulator keeping a count of the total number of *Box* objects created.

Install a no-argument constructor which increments *total* by 1, initializes *length* to 3, *height* to 3, and *symbol* to '*'.

Install a constructor with an int argument, *Box::Box(int)*, which increments *total* by 1, initializes *length* and *height* to the value of the argument, and initializes *symbol* to '*'.

Install a *public static* function member called *reportTotal( )* which displays the value of *total*:

```
cout << "\ntotal number of Box objects created = "<< total;
cout << endl;
```

Test these functions from *main( )*:

```
void main()
{
    Box::reportTotal();       // Should see 0.

    Box box1, box2, box3;
    box1.showBox();
    Box::reportTotal();       // Should see 3.

    Box box4(4), box5(5);
    box4.showBox();
    Box::reportTotal();       // Should see 5.
}
```

4.1.R   Initialize *total* to 10, so that the three reports display 10, 13, and 15.
Remove this initialization so that *total* once again starts at 0.

4.1.S   Install a *private* data member called *serialNumber* which will uniquely identify each *Box* object by storing the value in *total* (counting itself) at the time it is instantiated. The *serialNumber* of the first *Box* will be 1.

Modify both constructors so that they assign the value to the new *Box*'s *serialNumber* data member and display:

```
cout << "\nBox number " << serialNumber;
cout << " is being created" << endl;
```

Install a destructor which displays the *serialNumber* of the *Box* being deallocated:

```
cout << "\nBox number " << serialNumber;
cout << " is being deleted" << endl;
```

Test these functions with the following program, which includes an externally defined *Box*:

```
Box  box0;      // Externally defined Box.

void main()
{
    cout << endl << "-----main beginning-----" << endl;
```

```
    box0.showBox();
    Box::reportTotal();      // Should see 1.

    Box box1, box2, box3;
    box1.showBox();
    Box::reportTotal();      // Should see 4.

    Box box4(4), box5(5);
    box4.showBox();
    Box::reportTotal();      // Should see 6.

    cout << endl << "-------main ending-------" << endl;
}
```

Examine the output. Notice that constructors run prior to the beginning of *main( )* for externally defined objects. Notice that automatic objects are deallocated in a last-created, first-deleted order.

4.1.T In the program for part S, remove the externally defined *Box* and *main( )*, replacing it with what follows:

```
Box*  boxPtr1 = new Box;

void main()
{
    cout << endl << "-----main beginning-----" << endl;

    boxPtr1 -> showBox();
    Box::reportTotal();      // Should see 1.

    Box *boxPtr2, *boxPtr3, *boxPtr4;  // A Box pointer
                                       // is not a Box.

    Box::reportTotal();      // Should see 1.

    boxPtr2 = new Box;       // No-argument constructor used.
    boxPtr3 = new Box(4);    // One-argument constructor used.

    boxPtr4 = boxPtr3;

    boxPtr4 -> showBox();

    Box::reportTotal();      // Should see 3.

    delete boxPtr1;
    delete boxPtr4;

    boxPtr4 = new Box(5);
    boxPtr4 -> symbol = 'd'; // Here, 'd' stands for dynamic.

    boxPtr4 -> showBox();
    Box::reportTotal();      // Should see 4.

    cout << endl << "-------main ending-------" << endl;
}
```

Examine the output. Notice that the destructor runs when dynamically allocated objects are explicitly *deleted*, which may be at any point the programmer deems appropriate. Notice that dynamically allocated objects are not automatically *deleted* at the close of the function in which they are acquired.

4.1.U Automatic and dynamically allocated objects may exist within the same function. Continuing with the same *Box* class, write a *main( )* function which exemplifies.

4.1.V It is a fault (i.e. an error) to *delete* an automatic object as if it had been dynamically allocated, although the failure may not occur until the function ends.

It is an error to *delete* the same dynamically allocated object more than once, but the *delete* operator may be applied to the same pointer variable any number of times so long as it points to a non-deleted object or to *NULL* each time. (It is not an error to apply *delete* to a pointer variable whose value is *NULL*.)

It is an error to treat a *deleted* object as if it still existed (e.g., to access one of its data members, to use it on either side of an assignment operator, or to use it as an argument in a function call).

Continuing with the same *Box* class specified in part Q and enhanced in part S, write and run either one program or three short programs (i.e., three separate *main( )*s) that illustrate each of these errors. In each case, observe the result then correct the error and re-run the program.

4.1.W The following is a listing of the *Box* class that has been used for parts S, T, U, and V. In this exercise and those that follow it will be the base class from which a new class named *Square* will be derived.

```
#include <iostream.h>

class Box
{
    public:
        char symbol;

    private:
        int  length, height, serialNumber;
        static int total;

    public:
        Box();          // No-argument constructor, prototype.
        Box(int);       // One-argument constructor, prototype.
        ~Box();         // Destructor, prototype.
        static void reportTotal();      // Prototype.
        void showBox();                 // Prototype.
        void setSize();                 // Prototype.
        void setLength(int newLength);  // Prototype.
        void setHeight(int newHeight);  // Prototype.
        int  getLength();               // Prototype.
        int  getHeight();               // Prototype.
};

int Box::total = 0;

Box::Box() : length(3), height(3), symbol('*')
{
    serialNumber = ++total;

    cout << "\nBox number " << serialNumber << " is being created";
    cout << endl;
}

Box::Box(int side) : length(side), height(side), symbol('*')
{
    serialNumber = ++total;

    cout << "\nBox number " << serialNumber << " is being created";
    cout << endl;
}

Box::~Box()
{
    cout << "\nBox number " << serialNumber << " is being deleted";
```

```
            cout << endl;
    }

void Box::reportTotal()
    {
        cout << "\ntotal number of Box objects created = " << total;
        cout << endl;
    }

void Box::setSize()
    {
        int l, h;

        cout << "\nEnter a length (an int between 2 and 10):   ";
        cin >> l;

        if (l >= 2  &&  l <= 10)  length = l;
        else  length = 1;

        cout << "\nEnter a height (an int between 2 and 6):   ";
        cin >> h;

        if (h >= 2  &&  h <= 6)   height = h;
        else  height = 1;

        cout << "\nEnter a symbol:   ";
        cin >> symbol;

        showBox();
    }

void Box::showBox()
    {
        cout << endl;
        for (int i = 1;  i <= height;  i++)
            {
                for (int j = 1;  j <= length;  j++)  cout << symbol;
                cout << endl;
            }
    }

void Box::setLength(int newLength)
    {
        if (newLength > 0  &&  newLength <= 70)  length = newLength;
    }

void Box::setHeight(int newHeight)
    {
        if (newHeight > 0  &&  newHeight <= 10)  height = newHeight;
    }

int  Box::getLength()
    {
        return length;
    }

int  Box::getHeight()
    {
        return height;
    }
```

Add the following specifier for the *Square* class and test it by running the given *main( )* function:

```
class Square : public Box
    {

    };
```

```
void main()
{
  Square square1;
  square1.showBox();
  Square::reportTotal();
}
```

Examine the output, noticing that although the *Square* class may appear vacant, functionality is inherited from *Box* and *Square* objects have all the data members that *Box* objects have. That each *Square* object "IS-A" *Box* is evident the fact that a *Box* constructor ran in the process of creating the *square1*, from the output issued by *reportTotal( )* that 1 *Box* object had been created, and from the notification displayed by *Box*'s destructor.

4.1.X This item builds upon the classes in the previous item.

The values of *square1.length* and *square1.height* were assigned by *Box*'s no-argument constructor which was called implicitly, as the default, by *Square*'s default, no-argument constructor.

Supply the *Square* class with two constructors of its own:

Square::Square( );	which will use *Box::Box(int)* to set the sides to 5 and to set *serialNumber* and which will, itself, set *symbol* to 's' (lower case s); also, this constructor should output a message indicating that it has run
Square::Square(int);	which will use *Box::Box(int)* to set the sides to the value passed to its own argument and to set *serialNumber* and which will, itself, set symbol to 'S' (upper case S); also, this constructor should output a message indicating that it has run.

Supply the *Square* class with a destructor that outputs a message indicating that it has run.

Test the program and notice that when a *Square* object is created the *Box* constructor runs ahead of the *Square* constructor. Notice that for destructors the situation is reversed; the destructor in the derived class runs before the destructor in the base class.

4.1.Y This item builds upon the classes in the previous item.

The *Square* class inherits two functions from *Box* which are not appropriate for *Square* objects, *setLength( )* and *setHeight( )*. With these a square's *length* and *height* could become unequal.

Arrange so that these functions are rendered inoperative members of the *Square* class (i.e., so that nothing happens should a square object invoke them). Add a new *public* function to the *Square* class called *setSide( )* which uses *Box::setLength( )* and *Box::setHeight( )*, with their tests, to reset the invoking square's length and height to the integer passed to *setSide( )*.

Provide the *Square* class with its own version of *setSize( )* that performs similarly to the version within *Box* but does not allow the possibility of *length* and *height* becoming unequal.

Write a driver which tests these modifications to *Square*. Test to be sure that a *Square* object's attempt to *setLength( )* or to *setHeight( )* is ignored. Test *setSide( )*. Test the new version of *setSize( )*.

Create a *Box* object and have it attempt to call *Square's setSide( )*. This should confirm that inheritance only works down the derivation hierarchy.

4.1.Z This item focuses upon how the access status specifiers *public, protected*, and *private* used within the declaration of the *Box* class effect the accessibility of *Box's* members (same rules apply to both data members and function members) within *Box* objects and within *Square* objects.

For this exercise use the *Box* class and the *Square* class given in part W, but modify *Box's* class specifier so that *length* is *protected* as shown below:

```
class Box
{
  public:
      char symbol;

  protected:
      int  length;

  private:
      int  height, serialNumber;
      static int total;

  // The rest of the class is the same as given in part W.
};
```

(i) Install the function below as a public member within the of the *Box* class. Create two *Box* objects in *main( )*. Have one of these invoke this function, and use the other as the argument. You will see that *public, protected*, and *private* members of *Box* objects are accessible within it because it is a member function of *Box*; and this is so regardless of how a *Box* found its way into the function (i.e., as the invoking object, as an argument, or as a local instantiation).

```
void Box::accessDataMembers(Box argument)
{
  cout << endl;
  cout << "Re. the invoking object:            ";
  cout << "    length = " << length;
  cout << "    height = " << height;
  cout << "    symbol = " << symbol;
  cout << endl;

  cout << "Re. the argument object:            ";
  cout << "    length = " << argument.length;
  cout << "    height = " << argument.height;
  cout << "    symbol = " << argument.symbol;
  cout << endl;

  Box newBox;
  cout << "Re. a newly defined Box object: ";
  cout << "    length = " << newBox.length;
  cout << "    height = " << newBox.height;
  cout << "    symbol = " << newBox.symbol;
  cout << endl;
}
```

(ii) Remove this function from the *Box* class. Install it as a *public* member within the *Square* class. Create a *Square* object in *main( )* and have this object invoke this function. (A *Box* object cannot access a member function belonging to a derived class.) Create a *Box* object to be used as the argument. Here is its current prototype:

```
void Square::accessDataMembers(Box argument)
```

You will see that the function's accessing *Square* object can reference the *public* and *protected* members it inherited from *Box* but not the inherited member prescribed as *private, height*. A derived object, within a member function belonging to its own class, can access any inherited members originally defined as *protected* or *public* (as well as all of its own incremental members).

The *Box* objects on the other hand (the argument object and the *Box* defined within the function), are not within a member function of their own class. Therefore, only the *public* members are accessibile, just as if these were *Box*es in *main( )*.

Revise the *Square::accessDataMembers( )* function so its argument is a *Square* and so that the object defined within it is a *Square*. Rerun the program. You will see that regardless of how a *Square* gets into a member function, inherited *public* and and *protected* members are accessible while inherited *private* members are not.

(iii) Write *main( )* so that it defines a *Box* and a *Square* and performs the same set of attempted accesses:

```
void main()
{
    Box b;
    Square s;

    cout << endl;
    cout << "Re. the Box object:          ";
    cout << "    length = " << b.length;
    cout << "    height = " << b.height;
    cout << "    symbol = " << b.symbol;
    cout << endl;

    cout << "Re. the Square object:       ";
    cout << "    length = " << s.length;
    cout << "    height = " << s.height;
    cout << "    symbol = " << s.symbol;
    cout << endl;
}
```

In the case of the *Box* object, its own (incremental) members specified as *public* are accessible in non-member functions, but not those specified as *private* or *protected*. Non-member functions include free functions, like *main( )*, as well as functions which are members of different classes (including those classes derived from *Box*).

In the case of the *Square* object, its inherited *private* and *protected* members are not accessible in non-member functions (i.e., functions which are not members of the *Square* class). Its inherited *public* members are accessible, but this is not always true. It is true here because *Square* is *publicly* derived from *Box*; it would not have been true if *Square* had been *privately* derived from *Box*.

4.2 Given is the specifier for a simple *Queue* class. Each instantiation is a first-in, first-out linear storage structure for characters. Also given is a *main( )* function that uses it. Provide the member functions of *Queue*.

Once the program runs, overload the + operator so that the statement:

```
q1.append('V'); // Appends the letter 'V' to the end of q1.
```

can be coded like this:

```
q1 = q1 + 'V';  // Left operand is a Queue object; right operand
                // a char; returns the invoking Queue, *this.
```

Hint: The function's signature will be:

```
Queue Queue::operator+ (char incomingChar);
```

Overload the unary predecrement operator, - -, so that the statement:

```
charFromFront = q1.deliver(); // Deletes the front node from q1
                              // and hands over the stored char.
```

can be coded like this:

```
charFromFront = --q1;  // Unary predecrement operator performs
                       // the same operation as deliver().
```

Hint: The function's signature will be:

```
char Queue::operator--();

class Queue
{
    struct node
    {
        char  letter;
        node* next;
    };

    private:
        node *head;     // Data member.
        node *rear;     // Data member.

    public:
        Queue();        // Constructor, initializes head and read to NULL.

        int Empty(); // Returns 0 if queue is empty; 1 if it is not.

        void append(char letterToAdd);   // Gets a new node; installs
                                         // letterToAdd; attaches node
                                         // to the rear of the queue.

        char deliver(); // Gets the letter stored in the front node;
                        // deletes the node; returns the letter.
};

// Version of main() for the first test of the class.
// Notice how parsimoniously queues are managed as objects.

void  main()
{
    Queue   q1, q2, q3;

    q1.append('V');
    q1.append('Y');
    q1.append('O');

    q2.append('E');
    q2.append(' ');
    q2.append('O');

    q3.append('R');
    q3.append('G');
    q3.append('D');

    char charFromFront;
```

```
        Queue message;

        for (int i = 0; i < 3; i++)
            {
            charFromFront = q1.deliver();
            message.append(charFromFront);

            charFromFront = q2.deliver();
            message.append(charFromFront);

            charFromFront = q3.deliver();
            message.append(charFromFront);
            }

        cout << endl;
        while (! message.Empty() )
            {
            cout << message.deliver();
            }
        cout << endl;
        }

    // Version of main() for testing the operloaded operators.

    void  main()
        {
        Queue  q1, q2, q3;

        q1 = q1 + 'V';
        q1 = q1 + 'Y';
        q1 = q1 + 'O';

        q2 = q2 + 'E';
        q2 = q2 + ' ';
        q2 = q2 + 'O';

        q3 = q3 + 'R';
        q3 = q3 + 'G';
        q3 = q3 + 'D';

        char charFromFront;
        Queue message;

        for (int i = 0; i < 3; i++)
            {
            charFromFront = --q1;
            message = message + charFromFront;

            charFromFront = --q2;
            message = message + charFromFront;

            charFromFront = --q3;
            message = message + charFromFront;
            }

        cout << endl;
        while (! message.Empty() )
            {
            cout << --message;
            }
        cout << endl;
        }
```

4.3   Here is a program implementing both a queue and a stack, coded in the same manner as it would be in Pascal (i.e., no use is made of classes). The queue allows nodes to be appended to the rear and returned from the front. The stack allows nodes holding the same kind of content to be pushed and popped. The problem addressed is to take a list such as depicted in the following (held by a queue):

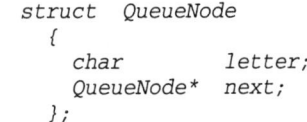

```
struct   QueueNode
    {
      char          letter;
      QueueNode*   next;
    };
```

A	→		B	→		C	→		D	→		E	NULL
letter	next		letter	next		letter	next		letter	next		letter	next

head   rear

and "reverse the direction of the pointers" (which also transforms the *head* to the *rear* and the *rear* to the *head*):

A	NULL		B	←		C	←		D	←		E	←
letter	next		letter	next		letter	next		letter	next		letter	next

rear   head

The computational strategy is:

(i)   to load the queue with nodes;

(ii) while the queue is not empty, to take the node from the front of the queue and push it onto the stack; and

(iii) while the stack is not empty, pop the top node and append it to the rear of the queue.

The complete program follows.

```
#include <iostream.h>

// Nodes for the queue.
struct queueNode
    {
      char    letter;
      queueNode*  next;
    };

// Nodes for the stack.
struct stackNode
    {
      char    letter;
      stackNode*  next;
    };

// Prototypes of functions for managing the queue.

void  initializeQueue(queueNode*& head, queueNode*& rear);
    // Here head and rear are set to NULL.

void  append(queueNode*& head, queueNode*& rear, char  letterToAdd);
    // Attaches a new node, holding letterToAdd; updates rear (if necessary, head).

char takeOff_and_return(queueNode*& head, queueNode*& rear);
    // Takes front node off list and returns its letter; updates head (if necessary,    // rear).

int   queueEmpty(queueNode* head);
    // Returns "true" if the queue is empty, "false" if it is not.
```

```
void  showQueue(queueNode* head);
   // A utility for displaying the letters on the queue.

// Prototypes for managing the stack.

void  initializeStack(stackNode*& stackTop);
   // Here stackTop is set to NULL.

void  push(stackNode*& stackTop,  char letterToAdd);
   // Pushes new node, holding letterToAdd, onto top of stack; updates stackTop.

char  pop(stackNode*& stackTop);
   // Pops node from the top of the stack and returns the letter it held; updates
   // stackTop.

int   stackEmpty(stackNode* stackTop);
   // Returns "true" if stack is empty, "false" if it is not.

void main()
   {
     // Define head and rear for the stack; initialize them.
     queueNode  *head,  *rear;
     initializeQueue(head, rear);

     // Define top for the stack; initialize it.
     stackNode* top;
     initializeStack(top);

     // Load the queue.
     char letter;
     for (letter = 'A'; letter <= 'E'; letter++)  append(head, rear, letter);

     // Display the queue.
     cout << endl << "The loaded list:     ";
     showQueue( head );
     cout << endl;

     // Flip the pointers.

        // Step 1:  tranfer the nodes from the queue to the stack.
        while ( !queueEmpty(head) )
           {
           letter = takeOff_and_return(head, rear);
           push(top, letter);
           }

        // Step 2:  transfer the nodes from the stack to the queue.
        while ( !stackEmpty(top) )
           {
           letter = pop(top);
           append(head, rear, letter);
           }

     // Display the queue.
     cout << endl << "The reversed list:  ";
     showQueue( head );
     cout << endl;

   }     // End of main().

// Functions for managing the queue.

void  initializeQueue(queueNode*& head, queueNode*& rear)
   {
     head = rear = NULL;
   }
```

```
void  append(queueNode*& head, queueNode*& rear, char letterToAdd)
  {
    queueNode* newNode = new  queueNode;
    newNode->letter = letterToAdd;
    newNode->next   = NULL;

    if ( queueEmpty(head) )
      {
       head = newNode;
       rear = newNode;
      }
    else
      {
       rear->next = newNode;
       rear = newNode;
      }
  }

char takeOff_and_return(queueNode*& head, queueNode*& rear)
  {
    char forReturn;
    queueNode* oldNode;  // To enable removed node to be deleted.

    if ( !queueEmpty(head) )  // Only works if queue is not empty.
      {
       forReturn = head->letter;
       oldNode = head;

       if (head->next == NULL) // If the head node is the only node on queue.
         {
          head = NULL;
          rear = NULL;
         }
       else head = head->next;
      }
    else forReturn = '\0';  // If list is empty, return the null zero.

    delete oldNode;
    return forReturn;
  }

int   queueEmpty(queueNode* head)
  {
    if (head == NULL) return 1;  // Yes, queue is empty.
    else  return 0;
  }

void  showQueue(queueNode* rovingPtr)
  {
    while (rovingPtr != NULL)
      {
       cout << rovingPtr->letter;
       rovingPtr = rovingPtr -> next;
      }
  }

// Functions for managing the stack.

void  initializeStack(stackNode*& stackTop)
  {
    stackTop = NULL;
  }

void  push(stackNode*& stackTop,  char letterToAdd)
  {
    stackNode* newNode = new stackNode;
    newNode->letter = letterToAdd;

    if ( stackEmpty(stackTop) )  newNode->next = NULL;
    else  newNode ->next = stackTop;

    stackTop = newNode;
  }
```

```
char pop(stackNode*& stackTop)
  {
    char forReturn;
    stackNode* oldNode;

    if (! stackEmpty(stackTop) ) // Only works if stack is not empty.
      {
        forReturn = stackTop->letter;
        oldNode = stackTop;
        stackTop = stackTop -> next;
      }
    else  forReturn = '\0';  // If stack is empty, return null zero.

    delete oldNode;
    return forReturn;
  }

int  stackEmpty(stackNode* stackTop)
  {
    if (stackTop == NULL) return 1;  // Yes, stack is empty.
    else return 0;
  }
```

4.3.A The following function, which converts inches to centimeters, is a typical example of abstraction.

```
float  centimeters(float inches)
  {
    return inches*2.54;
  }
```

It is not easy to see why writing the function and calling it:

```
cout << "Radius = " << centimeters(inches);
```

is preferable to multiplying in line whenever a number of *inches* needs to be represented as *centimeters*:

```
cout << "Radius = " << 2.54*inches;
```

In what sense is this better? Think in terms of expressing an action with respect to its meaning, and not having to know it might be performed or having any involvement with its operationalization.

4.3.B The preceding program contains implementations of two constructs touted as "abstract data types." Explain what makes a queue and what makes a stack an abstract data type. The preceding program contains a queue and a stack, but where are they?

4.3.C The epitome of abstraction comes when queues, stacks, or anything else that might be construed as an abstract data type may be instantiated as palpable entities. For instance, once a *Queue* class is specified, queue objects can be defined, hence named, then seen and manipulated as items within the program just as concrete and seemingly intrinsic as the ints *i, j,* and *k.*

Rewrite the given program so that it contains a *Queue* class and a *Stack* class. The queue and the stack should be defined as instances of these respective classes.

The best way to organize your program is like this:

The specifier for each class lies ahead of *main( )*, and all the bodies of the functions from both classes should follow *main( )*.

The class specifier for the *Queue* class contains the *struct* specifying the nodes from which queues (i.e., queue objects) are composed, the declaration of *head* and *rear* as data members, and the prototypes for the class's function members.

The specifier for the *Stack* class contains the *struct* specifying the nodes for stack objects, the declaration of *stackTop* as a data member, and the member function prototypes.

In case you did not organize your program this way, re-architect it. If you are programming "in the large," the specifier for the *Queue* class is placed in a header file as would be the specifier for the *Stack* class.

4.3.D   With a *Queue* class, the class's name becomes a data type specifier. As with any data type specifier, it can be used to define as many instantiations as needed. Each *Queue* object will have its own set of data members (in this case, its own head and its own rear) and be an autonomous entity.

Modify your program from Exercise 4.3.C. (or the following one) so that at the end of the program there are five queues:

queue1, which will display as ABCDE;

queue2, which will be the computed reversal of queue1;

queue3, which will display as 123456789;

queue4, which will be the computed reversal of queue3; and

queue5, which will display as SCRUNCHED

(according to Martin Gardner, the longest word of one syllable in the English language).

Display each of these.

```
#include <iostream.h>

class Queue
   {
   private:
      struct queueNode
         {
         char  letter;
         queueNode* next;
         };

      queueNode  *head, *rear;

   public:
      void  initializeQueue();

      void  append(char  letterToAdd);
   // Attaches new node, holding letterToAdd.

      char  takeOff_and_return();
   // Takes front node off list and returns its letter.

      int  queueEmpty();
   // Returns "true" if the queue is empty, "false" if it is not.

      void  showQueue();
   // A utility for displaying the letters on the queue.
   };

class Stack
   {
   private:
      struct stackNode
         {
         char   letter;
         stackNode*  next;
         };

      stackNode* stackTop;
```

```
    public:
        void  initializeStack();

        void  push(char letterToAdd);
    // Pushes new node, holding letterToAdd, onto top of stack.

        char  pop();
    // Pops node from the top of the stack and returns the letter it held.

        int   stackEmpty();
    // Returns "true" is stack is empty, "false" if it is not.
    };

void main()
    {
    // Define a Queue.
    Queue queue;
    queue.initializeQueue();

    // Define a Stack.
    Stack stack;
    stack.initializeStack();

    // Load the queue.
    char letter;
    for (letter = 'A'; letter <= 'E'; letter++)  queue.append(letter);

    // Display the queue.
    cout << endl << "The loaded list:    ";
    queue.showQueue();
    cout << endl;

    // Flip the pointers.

        // Step 1:  tranfer the letters from the queue to the stack.
        while ( !queue.queueEmpty() )
            {
            letter = queue.takeOff_and_return();
            stack.push(letter);
            }

        // Step 2:  transfer the letters from the stack to the queue.
        while ( !stack.stackEmpty() )
            {
            letter = stack.pop();
            queue.append(letter);
            }

    // Display the queue.
    cout << endl << "The reversed list:  ";
    queue.showQueue();
    cout << endl;
    }

// Functions for managing the queue (Queue's member functions).

void  Queue::initializeQueue()
    {
    head = rear = NULL;
    }

void  Queue::append(char letterToAdd)
    {
    queueNode* newNode = new  queueNode;
    newNode->letter = letterToAdd;
    newNode->next   = NULL;

    if ( queueEmpty() )
        {
        head = newNode;
```

```
                rear = newNode;
            }
    else
        {
            rear->next = newNode;
            rear = newNode;
        }
    }

char Queue::takeOff_and_return()
    {
        char forReturn;
        queueNode* oldNode;

        if ( !queueEmpty() )  // Only works if queue is not empty.
            {
                forReturn = head->letter;
                oldNode = head;
                if (head->next == NULL) // If the head node is the only node on queue.
                    {
                        head = NULL;
                        rear = NULL;
                    }
                else head = head->next;
            }
        else forReturn = '\0';  // If list is empty, return the null zero.

        delete oldNode;
        return forReturn;
    }

int   Queue::queueEmpty()
        {
            if (head == NULL) return 1;  // Yes, queue is empty.
            else   return 0;
        }

void  Queue::showQueue()
    {
        queueNode*  rovingPtr;
        rovingPtr = head;

        while (rovingPtr != NULL)
            {
               cout << rovingPtr->letter;
               rovingPtr = rovingPtr -> next;
            }
    }

// Function for managing the stack (Stack's member functions).

void  Stack::initializeStack()
    {
       stackTop = NULL;
    }

void  Stack::push(char letterToAdd)
    {
       stackNode* newNode = new stackNode;
       newNode->letter = letterToAdd;

       if ( stackEmpty() )  newNode->next = NULL;
       else  newNode ->next = stackTop;

       stackTop = newNode;
    }

   char Stack::pop()
       {
           char forReturn;
           stackNode* oldNode;
```

```
        if (! stackEmpty() ) // Only works if stack is not empty.
          {
             oldNode = stackTop;
             forReturn = stackTop->letter;
             stackTop = stackTop -> next;
          }
        else  forReturn = '\0';  // If stack is empty, return null zero.
        delete oldNode;
        return forReturn;
    }

int   Stack::stackEmpty()
    {
     if (stackTop == NULL) return 1;  // Yes, stack is empty.
     else return 0;
    }
```

4.3.E   There are certain correctable shortcomings in the preceding program:

The responsibility for initializing each defined *Queue* and *Stack* is foist upon "the user" of these classes. Failing to do this is a fatal omission.

No provision is made for releasing the memory consumed by instantiations of *Queues* and *Stacks*.

The former can be rectified by writing a constructor that does this, for the user, automatically. The latter can be rectified with a destructor that deletes each *struct* on the list. Write these four functions.

For the purpose of testing, have both constructors (*Queue::Queue( )* and *Stack::Stack( )*) display an enunciation when they run. Have both destructors (*Queue:: Queue( )* and *Stack:: Stack( )*) enunciate themselves and display the letters in the structs that are being deleted. Remember to remove the calls to the initialization functions.

Rebuild program 4.3.D so that all the processing that had been done within *main( )* is now done by the function:

```
void  allProcessing();  // Prototype.
```

which is called by *main( )*:

```
void main()
    {
      cout <<"\n** main() invoking allProcessing() **\n";
      allProcessing();
      cout <<"\n** main() concluding **\n";
    }
```

4.3.F   If the constructors shoulder the responsibility for initializing the *Queues* and *Stacks*, what should be done with the *Queue::initializeQueue( )* and *Stack::initializeStack( )*? One choice is to leave them so users can "reset" or "clear" existing objects in accordance with the requirements of their applications. In this case these functions must be modified to prevent memory leak. Make this modification.

4.3.G   In completing Exercise 4.3.D, which asked for one *Queue* to hold "ABCDE" and another to be loaded with the same "ABCDE" and then reversed, one might have been tempted to code it like this:

```
Queue  queue1;

Queue  queue2;
```

```
// Load queue1.
char letter;
for (letter = 'A'; letter <= 'E'; letter++)
    queue.append(letter);

queue2 = queue1;
```

Displaying *queue2* would confirm that the assignment had worked, however reversing *queue2* would have resulted in the demolition of *queue1*. This is because the language-provided assignment operator makes a shallow copy.

If you wish to test the default assignment operator, be sure first to comment-out the fragment of the destructor that deletes the nodes on the defunct *Queue*. Because the default assignment operator causes the *head* and the *rear* of the left operand to equal the *head* and the *rear* of the right operand, the left *Queue* is composed of the same physical list as the right *Queue*. Deleting the nodes on either one does away with the nodes on the other. Because it is an error to reference a member of a deleted node and an error to code the deletion of a chunk of deleted memory, a destructor that releases the memory for one of these *Queues* would cause a failure when it handles the other.

Provide the *Queue* class with an assignment operator that makes deep copies. Test it with the preceding code (or code like it) to corroborate that:

(a) the content of the two queues is the same (e.g., *queue2* displays the same as *queue1*), and

(b) that changing the content of either queue has no effect on the content of the other.

If your assignment operator requires a copy constructor either for the creation of the formal argument or for the creation of the *Queue* to which the action of the assignment operator resolves (so that your *operator=()* supports multiple assignment) and you do not provide one of your own, your program will use the default. The default copy constructor, like the default assignment operator, supplies a shallow copy, which means that the replicated *Queue* is physically one and the same as the source. All of a class's objects are dismantled by the same destructor, including those objects created by the copy constructor. Thus, if your destructor is deleting nodes, as it ought to be, and you are using the default copy constructor, your program will malfunction. The remedy is to write a copy constructor that produces a deep copy. (You will need such a copy constructor for Exercise 4.3.H too.)

4.3.H C++ tries to give user-defined data types all the same symbolic capabilities it gives to entities defined from type specifiers built into the langauge (e.g., *ints* and *floats*). Just as the + operator is applied to invoke a function to add two integers, C++ will allow it to stand for functions that manipulate *Stacks* and *Queues*.

Build a free function with the prototype:

```
Queue operator + (Queue q, char letter);
```

that will enable statements such as:

```
for (letter = 'A'; letter <= 'E'; letter++)
    queue.append(letter);
```

to be replaced with:

```
for (letter = 'A'; letter <= 'E'; letter++)
 ,    queue = queue + letter;
```

```
[Hint:   The operator+() function may encapsulate the
         append() function.]
```

Build a free function with the prototype:

```
Stack operator + (char letter, Stack s);
```

that will enable statements such as:

```
stack.push(letter);
```

to be replaced with:

```
stack = letter + stack;
```

Build a free function with the prototype:

```
ostream& operator << (ostream& outputStream, Queue q);
```

that would enable calls to *showQueue( )*, such as:

```
// Display the queue.
cout << endl << "The loaded list:     ";
queue.showQueue();
cout << endl;
```

to be replaced with:

```
       // Display the queue.
       cout << endl << "The loaded list:     " << queue << endl;
```

```
[Hint:   The operator<<() function should not encapsulate the
         showQueue() function because showQueue(), writing only
         to the standard output stream, is insufficiently
         versatile.   In order to step through the Queue, the
         Queue class will have to confer friendship to
         operator<<().]
```

Replace all calls to *append( )*, *push( )*, and *showQueue( )* with these newly defined operators in the most recent version of this program in order to test them. Rerun the program by defining an alternate output stream to corroborate the general utility of *Queue::operator<<( )*:

```
// Remember to #include <fstream.h>.
ofstream printer("LPT1"); // Or whatever.
```

4.4 Consider the following piece of code. First make the changes needed to remove all invocations of the assignment operator. Then make the changes needed to remove all invocations of the copy constructor. It will not be possible to make these changes without the loss of some processing activities, but the spirit of the endeavor is to retain as much of these as possible.

```
#include <iostream.h>

class Point
{
    private:
        int  x, y;

    public:
        friend  Point operator+ (Point leftPt, Point rightPt);
        friend  ostream& operator<< (ostream& output, Point& p);

        Point()
        {
            cout << "\nFrom the no-argument constructor\n";
        }
```

```
            Point (int abcissa, int ordinate) : x(abcissa), y(ordinate)
              {
                cout << "\nFrom the two-argument constructor\n";
              }

            Point (Point& sourcePoint)
              {
                cout << "\nFrom the copy constructor\n";
                x = sourcePoint.x;
                y = sourcePoint.y;
              }

            Point operator =  (Point rightPoint)
              {
                cout << "\nFrom the assignment operator\n";
                x = rightPoint.x;
                y = rightPoint.y;
                return *this;
              }

      };  // End of Point specifier.

ostream& operator<< (ostream& output, Point& p)
  {
    output << " (" << p.x << ", " << p.y << ") ";
    return output;
  }

Point operator + (Point leftPoint, Point rightPoint)
  {
      Point sum;
      sum.x = leftPoint.x + rightPoint.x;
      sum.y = leftPoint.y + rightPoint.y;
      return sum;
  }

Point supplyPoint()
  {
    cout << "\nFrom supplyPoint() -- no-argument version\n";
    Point p(11, 22);
    return p;
  }

Point supplyPoint(Point p)
  {
     cout <<"\nFrom supplyPoint(Point)\n";
     return p;
  }

void main()
  {
     Point p1(1,2);
     Point p2(0,0);
     cout << "\nFrom main():  p1 = " << p1 << "  and p2 = " << p2 << endl;

     cout << "\nFrom main(), coding:  p2 = p1  \n";
     p2 = p1;

     cout << "\nFrom main():  p1 = " << p1 << "  and p2 = " << p2 << endl;

     Point p3(33, 333);
     Point p4(44, 444);
     cout << "\nFrom main():  p3 = " << p3 << "  and p4 = " << p4 << endl;

     cout << "\nFrom main(), coding:  cout <<¨ p3 + p4  = ¨  p3 + p4; \n";
     cout << "\n p3 + p4 = " <<  p3 + p4 << endl;

     cout << "\nFrom main(), coding:  supplyPoint();  \n";
     supplyPoint();
```

```
        cout << "\nFrom main(), coding:  p1 = supplyPoint(); \n";
        p1 = supplyPoint();

        cout << "\nFrom main(), coding:  supplyPoint(p2); \n";
        supplyPoint(p2);

        cout << "\nFrom main(), coding:  p1 = supplyPoint(p2); \n";
        p1 = supplyPoint(p2);

        cout << "\n        ********* end of main() *********" << endl;
}
```

Here is the output.

```
From the two-argument constructor

From the two-argument constructor

From main():  p1 =  (1, 2)    and p2 =  (0, 0)

From main(), coding:  p2 = p1

From the copy constructor

From the assignment operator

From the copy constructor

From main():  p1 =  (1, 2)    and p2 =  (1, 2)

From the two-argument constructor

From the two-argument constructor

From main():  p3 =  (33, 333)    and p4 =  (44, 444)

From main(), coding:  cout <<" p3 + p4  = "  p3 + p4;

From the copy constructor

From the copy constructor

From the no-argument constructor

From the copy constructor

p3 + p4 =  (77, 777)

From main(), coding:  supplyPoint();

From supplyPoint() -- no-argument version

From the two-argument constructor

From the copy constructor

From main(), coding:  p1 = supplyPoint();

From supplyPoint() -- no-argument version

From the two-argument constructor

From the copy constructor
```

```
From the copy constructor

From the assignment operator

From the copy constructor

From main( ), coding:  supplyPoint(p2);

From the copy constructor

From supplyPoint(Point)

From the copy constructor

From main( ), coding:  p1 = supplyPoint(p2);

From the copy constructor

From supplyPoint(Point)

From the copy constructor

From the copy constructor

From the assignment operator

From the copy constructor

         ********* end of main() *********
```

4.5.A Consider the following classes. Establish the derivation relationship shown by adding the necessary syntax. All derivation is public.

```
class Adder
  {
    public:
      char*  getType() { return "Adder"; }
      int  add(int a, int b)) { return a+b; }
  };




class Subtracter
  {
    public:
      char*  getType()  { return "Subtracter"; }
    private:
      int addInverse(int a)  { return 0 - a;  }


  public:
      int  sub(int a, int b)
        {
          return add(a, addInverse(b));  // Uses inherited function.
        }
  };
```

```
       ┌──────────────┐
       │    Adder     │
       └──────────────┘
              ▲  public
       ┌──────────────┐
       │  Subtracter  │
       └──────────────┘
              ▲  public
       ┌──────────────┐
       │  Multiplier  │
       └──────────────┘
              ▲  public
       ┌──────────────┐
       │   Divider    │
       └──────────────┘
```

```
class Multiplier
  {
    public:
      char*  getType()  return "Multiplier";
      int  mult(int a, int b);                           // Prototype.
  };

class Divider
  {
    public:
      char*  getType()  return "Divider";
      int  div(int a, int b);                            // Prototype.
  };

int Multiplier::mult(int a, int b)
  {
    // Multiplies a*b  for  b >= 0.
    int accum = 0;
    int loopCounter = 0;
    while(loopCounter < b)
      {
        accum = add(accum, a);              // Uses inherited function.
        loopCounter = add(loopCounter,1);
      }
    return accum;
  }

int Divider::div(int a, int b)
  {
    // Performs an integer divide, a/b,  for  a >= 0  and  b > 0.
    int accum = 0;
    while(a >= 0)
      {
        accum = add(accum, 1);           // Uses inherited function.
        a     = sub(a, b);               // Uses inherited function.
      }
    accum = sub(accum, 1);               // Uses inherited function.
    return accum;
  }
```

4.5.B Write a *main( )* function that:

statically defines an *Adder* object and tests its *getType( )* and *add( )* functions;

statically defines a *Subtracter* object and tests its *getType( )* and *sub( )* functions;

statically defines a *Multiplier* object and tests its *getType( )* and *mult( )* functions; and

statically defines a *Divider* object and tests its *getType( )* and *div( )* functions.

Test to confirm that the *Divider* object has the ability to *add( )*, *sub( )*, and *mult( )*. Notice that its incremental *getType( )* function overrides the versions it inherited. Confirm that these remain accessible with the use of the scope operator.

Replicate the preceding tests for a dynamically defined instantiation of each kind of object.

4.5.C Test this statement in *main( )*:

```
cout << "123 + 321 = " << Adder().add(123, 321) << endl;
```

If this elicits a syntax error, install within the *Adder* class a no-argument constructor that explicitly performs the same processing performed by the default no-argument constructor which is:

```
Adder()
  {
```

```
       }
```

Retry the program.

4.5.D Build a free function called *exponentiate( )* having the following prototype and which performs its arithmetic by way of the *Multiplier* object supplied by the calling function. If should return the vaue base^power (i.e., base to the exponent power) where power is a whole, positive number.

```
int  exponentiate(Multiplier* m, int base, int power);
```

Test it with the invocation in *main( )*:

```
cout<<"2**10 = "<<exponentiate( new Multiplier, 2, 10 ) << endl;
```

Also try:

```
cout<<"2**10 = "<<exponentiate( new Multiplier(), 2, 10 ) << endl;
```

4.5.E Make a copy of the code containing the class hierarchy. Using the copy, install within *Multiplier* these three constructors:

```
Multiplier()
{
    cout << "\n from Multiplier's no-argument constructor \n";
}

Multiplier(int a, int b)
{
    cout << "\n from Multiplier's (int,int) constructor:   ";
    cout << "rec'd:  " << a << "  and   " << b << endl;
}

Multiplier(char* string)
{
    cout << "\n from Multiplier's (char*) constructor:   ";
    cout << "rec'd:  " << string << endl;
}
```

Install within *Divider* the following three constructors, supplemented in accordance with the stated instructions:
Have this constructor invoke *Multiplier*'s no-argument constructor:

```
Divider()
{
    cout << "\n from Divider's no-argument constructor \n";
}
```

Have this constructor invoke *Multiplier*'s *(int,int)* constructor, passing $i + j + k$ to its first argument and 100 to its second argument:

```
Divider(int i, int j, int k)
{
    cout<< "\n from Divider's (int,int,int) constructor:   ";
    cout<<"rec'd: "<< i <<",  " << j <<" and,  " << k << endl;
}
```

Have this constructor invoke *Multiplier*'s (char*) constructor, passing it the received string

```
Divider(char* string)
{
    cout << "\n from Divider's (char*) constructor:   ";
    cout << "rec'd:  " << string << endl;
}
```

main( ) should be comprised of three static instantiations of *Divider*, one to test each constructor, and three dynamic instantiations of *Divider* for similar tests.

4.5.F   Starting once again with the initial class hierarchy:
Install within each class an explicit no argument constructor having the access status of *protected*. The one within *Adder* will look like this:

```
protected:
    Adder() { }
```

This will make it impossible to instantiate an object of any of these kinds within *main( )* or any other function not within the derivation hierarchy. Test to see that within *main( )* objects of types *Adder*, *Subtracter*, *Multiplier*, and *Divider* cannot be defined.

*public*ly Derive a new class from *Divider* called *Arithmetic* that will use its inherited functionality to define the four functions:

```
plus()    which is built on  add()
minus()   which is built on  sub()
times()   which is built on  mult()
slash()   which is built on  div()
```

and that "voids out" *getType( )*. Within *main( )*, statically define and test one *Arithmetic* object and dynamically define and test another.

4.6   Begin by going back once again to the stripped-down class hierarchy given for the previous exercise. Be sure to remove everything that was added in doing all parts of Exercise 4.5.

4.6.A   Write the following two free functions, each of which displays the class to which the "argument object" belongs. In one case the argument is actually a pointer to an object; in the other case it is the object itself. Their signatures are different so this overloading does not create an ambiguity. (Both functions work by calling *getType( )*.)

```
void displayType(Adder* baseClassPtr);  // Prototype.

void displayType(Adder& baseClass);     // Prototype.
```

Test both these functions with a battery of calls from *main( )* given as follows.

```
void main()
{
    Adder       a;   displayType(a);
    Subtracter  s;   displayType(s);
    Multiplier  m;   displayType(m);
    Divider     d;   displayType(d);
```

```
            Adder*       aPtr;  aPtr = new Adder;       displayType(aPtr);
            Multiplier* mPtr;   mPtr = new Multiplier; displayType(mPtr);
            Subtracter* sPtr;   sPtr = new Subtracter; displayType(sPtr);
            Divider*    dPtr;   dPtr = new Divider;     displayType(dPtr);
        }
```

4.6.B   In the base class, which is *Adder*, specify *getType( )* to be a *virtual* function:

```
class Adder
{
    public:
        virtual char*  getType() { return "Adder"; }
        int   add(int a, int b) { return a+b; }
};
```

Or

```
class Adder
{
    public:
        virtual char*  getType();                 // Prototype.
        int   add(int a, int b) { return a+b; }
};

    char* Adder::getType() // Virtual specifier is not used here.
    {
        return "Adder";
    }
```

Rerun the program from Exercise 4.6.A. This time the *getType( )* functions specific for the particular types of objects were called.

4.6.C   Supplement the *Adder* class with the following definitions of three pure virtual functions:

```
class Adder
{
    public:
        virtual sub (int a, int b) = 0;  // Here = 0  is the pure specifier.
        virtual mult(int a, int b) = 0;
        virtual div (int a, int b) = 0;

        virtual char*  getType() { return "Adder"; }
        int   add(int a, int b) { return a+b; }
};
```

Rerun the program from Exercise 4.6.B. Remove the errors by commenting-out the definitions from the classes which are now abstract. Test the *Divider* objects to see if they can *add( )*, *sub( )*, *mult( )*, and *div( )*.

4.7   The following five true or false questions refer to the derivation depicted here.

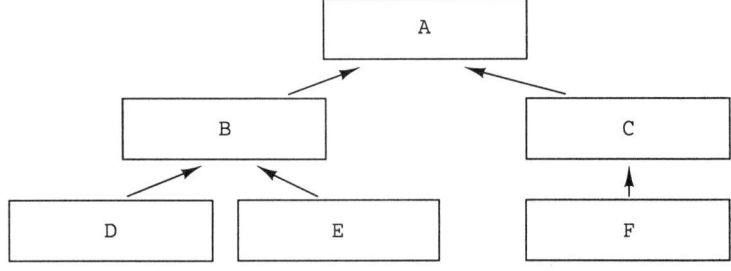

4.7.A If a function is first defined in class B, it may be specified to be virtual and serve as a *virtual* function in classes D and E. True or false?

4.7.B If a *virtual* function is first defined as *virtual* in class A, it may be reimplemented in class D, as well as in classes C and F without having to be reimplemented also in classes B and E. True or false?

4.7.C A reimplementation of a *virtual* function is *virtual* whether or not the *virtual* specifier accompanies its declaration. True or false?

4.7.D A reimplementation of a virtual function (i.e., a specialized overriding version) must have the same name and signature as the base version, but it may have a different return type. True or false?

4.7.E Suppose that objects are defined only from classes D, E, and F; and suppose that virtual functions $v1()$, $v2()$, and $v3()$ are defined in class A and reimplemented in each of the other classes to provide the necessary refinements. Is the following assertion true of false?

What the "*virtual*" feature makes possible, and which is not possible without it, is the ability to write one function such as:

> Base class type specifier, object passed by reference.

```
void  aFunction(A& object)
    {
    object.v1();
    object.v2();
    object.v3();
    }
```

That will perform in the correctly specialized manner for instantiations of classes D, E, and F (and will work for instantions of classes to be added to the hierarchy in the future that we cannot even imagine at present).

4.8 The organization of classes given in Exercise 4.5 is weak. The *Divider* class needs the functionality inherited from the *Subtracter* class, and the *Subtracter* class needs the functionality from the *Adder* class. But the *Multiplier* class does not need functionality from the *Subtracter* class, and the *Divider* class does not need functionality from the *Multiplier* class.

Thus, a more appropriate structure would be the following:

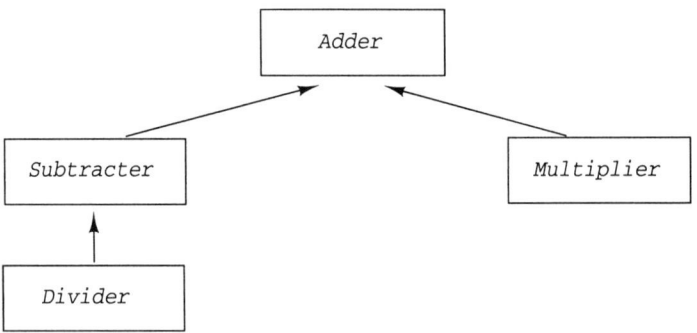

4.8.A Redefine the class specifications from the opening of Exercise 4.5.A so that this is the resulting hierarchy. Suppose we want a "full featured" class called *Arithmetic* that can *add( )*, *sub( )*, *mult( )*, and *div( )*. The only way to arrange this is to have *Arithmetic* inherit functionality both from *Divider* and from *Multiplier*. Fortunately, C++ allows a class to have two base classes:

```
class Arithmetic : public Divider, public Multiplier
{

};
```

Within *main( )*, define an Arithmetic object and test it to confirm that it can *sub( )*, *div( )*, and *mult( )*. Do not test its ability to *add( )*.

4.8.B There is a subtlety here: each *Arithmetic* object will have two independent incremental parts inherited from *Adder*: an *add( )* function(and an *Adder::getType( )* function) installed by way of its derivation from *Divider* and another *add( )* (and another *Adder::getType( )*) installed by way of its derivation from *Multiplier*.

To see that an instantiation of an *Arithmetic* object causes the *Adder* constructor to run twice, once down each derivation path, install a no-argument constructor within each class that annunciates its invocation. For instance, the one in *Adder* might look like this:

```
Adder()
{
    cout << "\n Adder constructor is running";
}
```

Rerun the program from Exercise 4.8.A.

4.8.C With two copies of the *add( )* function, an *Arithmetic* object such as *arith* will encounter an ambiguity when it calls it unless it explicitly denotes one or the other using the scope resolution operator:

```
arith.Divider::add(1,1);      // Here add() function is inherited
                              // via Subtracter and Divider.

arith.Subtracter::add(2,2);   // Same add() function as
                              // above.

arith.Multiplier::add(3,3);   // Here add() function is inherited
                              // via Multiplier.

arith.add(4,4);         // Which add()?  AMBIGUOUS!   ERROR!
```

arith.Adder::add(5,5); // Which Adder? AMBIGUOUS! ERROR!

Install each of these attempts by arith to use *add( )* within *main( )* to confirm their acceptability or unacceptability.

4.8.D   There is a way to eliminate the multiple inclusion of the same incremental segments within objects and the possibility of the errors that these may cause. This, however, must be done when the class hierarchy is being built in anticipation of multiple inheritance.

The technique is to specify that those classes derived directly from the class subject to multiple inclusion be virtually derived. In this case *Subtracter* and *Multiplier* would be *virtually* derived from *Adder*.

```
class Adder
    {
        // Details omitted.
    };

class Subtracter : public virtual Adder
    {
        // Details omitted.
    };

class Multiplier : public virtual Adder
    {
        // Details omitted.
    };

class Divider : public Subtracter
    {
        // Details omitted.
    };

class Arithmetic : public Divider, public Multiplier
    {
        // Details omitted.
    };
```

The data and function members from a *virtual* base class are only installed within a derived object once. The *virtual* specifier means that if the ad hoc components have not yet been incorporated into the object being formed, put them in; if already present, do not install another set of them.

Change the program so that *virtual* inheritance is used for *Subtracter* and for *Multiplier*.

Run it now, with the annunciating constructors, to confirm that *Adder's* constructor runs only once. Also, test to see that the calls to *add( )* which had been ambiguous now execute properly (as do those that had worked properly before).

4.9   Consider the following hierarchy. All inheritance is *public*.

```
Class Shape
  {
   protected:
       int   dimensional;
       char symbol;
       const char* kind; //object's class

   public:
       void whichAreYou();
       virtual   void newSymbol(char s);
       virtual   void show() = 0;
       virtual   void grow(int change) = 0;
       virtual   -Shape();
     Shape(char forKind[]);
     };
```

```
class Flat
  {
   public;
     Flat(char* forKind);
     void grow(int change);
  };
```

```
class Spatial
  {
   public;
     Spatial(char* forKind);
  };
```

```
class Horizontal
 {
  public:
    void show();
    Horizontal();
};
```

```
class Vertical
  {
   public:
     void show();
     Vertical();
  };
```

```
class OneDimen
  {
   public:
     void grow(int amount);
     OneDimen(char* );
  };
```

```
class TwoDimen
  {
   protected:
     int dimensional2;
   public:
     void grow(int amount);
     TwoDimen(char* );
  };
```

```
class Square
 {
  public:
    void show();
    Square();
};
```

```
class RightTri
  {
   public:
     void show();
     RightTri();
  };
```

```
class Diamond
  {
   public:
     void show();
     Diamond();
  };
```

```
class Rectangle
  {
   public:
     void show();
     Rectangle();
  };
```

4.9.A The *Shape* class, the *Flat* class, and the *Spatial* class, the *OneDimen* class, and the *TwoDimen* class are abstract classes because each contains at least one pure *virtual* function. (*Flat*, and *Spatial*, contain theirs by inheritance.)

In *main( )*, attempt to define an object from each of these classes to see that the compiler will not allow it.

4.9.B The function *whichAreYou( )*, defined in the *Shape* class, is a nonvirtual function. Install distinctive versions of it in the *Horizontal* class and in the *Rectangle* class that have the same declarator as the version within *Shape*. Run the program to convince yourself that nonvirtual functions cannot be polymorphically overridden. Leave these functions in the program.

4.9.C Specify *whichAreYou( )* to be *virtual* and rerun the program. This time the functions you added will be accessed.

4.9.D Specify *whichAreYou( )* to be a pure virtual function, but retain its implementation. Attempt to run the program. You will see that other implementations are now required even though the pure *virtual* function has a body (and you will see that pure *virtual* functions are allowed to have a body). Install distinctive versions of *whichAreYou( )* in the other leaf classes: *Vertical, Square, RightTri,* and *Diamond*. The program will now run with the versions in the most derived classes overriding.

From a member function of one of these leaf classes (e.g., Rectangle's constructor) test to confirm that the pure virtual version in *Shape* is accessible by adding the call *Shape::whichAreYou( )*; Also, test to see if *Shape::whichAreYou( )* is accessible to a *Rectangle* object in *main( )*.

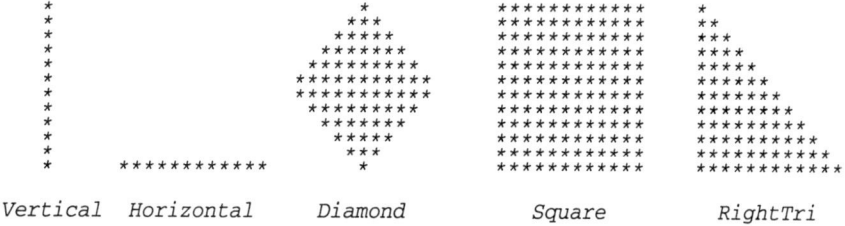

```
          Vertical   Horizontal      Diamond          Square           RightTri
```

```
#include <iostream.h>

class Shape                                  // Abstract class.
    {
    protected:
        int   dimension1;
        char symbol;
        const char* kind;

    public.:
        void whichAreYou();                  // Prototype: nonvirtual function
        virtual void newSymbol(char s);      // Prototype: virtual function.
        virtual void show() = 0;             // Prototype: pure virtual function.
        virtual void grow(int change) = 0;   // Prototype: pure virtual function.
        virtual ~Shape();                    // Prototype: virtual destructor.
        Shape(char* forKind);                // Prototype: constructor.
    };
```

```
class Flat : public Shape
  {
    public:
      void grow(int change);            // Prototype: virtual function.
      Flat(char* forKind);              // Prototype: constructor.
  };

class Spatial : public Shape
  {
    public:
      Spatial(char* forKind);          // Prototype: constructor.
  };

class Horizontal : public Flat
  {
    public:
      void show();                     // Prototype: virtual function.
      Horizontal();                    // Prototype: constructor.
  };

class Vertical : public Flat
  {
    public:
      void show();                     // Prototype: virtual function.
      Vertical();                      // Prototype: constructor.
  };

class OneDimen : public Spatial
  {
    public:
      void grow(int amount);           // Prototype: virtual function.
      OneDimen(char* forKind);         // Prototype: constructor.
  };

class TwoDimen : public Spatial
  {
    protected:
      int   dimension2;
    public:
      void grow(int amount);           // Prototype: virtual function.
      TwoDimen(char* forKind);         // Prototype: constructor.
  };

class Square : public OneDimen
  {
    public:
      void show();                     // Prototype: virtual function.
      Square();                        // Prototype: constructor.
  };

class RightTri : public OneDimen
  {
    public:
      void show();                     // Prototype: virtual function.
      RightTri();                      // Prototype: constructor.
  };

class Diamond : public OneDimen
  {
    public:
      void show();                     // Prototype: virtual function.
      Diamond();                       // Prototype: constructor.
  };

class Rectangle : public TwoDimen
  {
    public:
      void show();                     // Prototype: virtual function.
      Rectangle();                     // Prototype: constructor.
  };
```

```
    };

Shape::Shape(char* forKind) : dimension1(3), symbol('*'), kind(forKind)
    {

    }

Shape::~Shape()
    {
    cout << "\n...deleting a " << kind << endl;
    }

void Shape::whichAreYou()
    {
    cout << "\n==>" << kind << "<==";
    }

void Shape::newSymbol(char s)
    {
    symbol = s;
    }

Flat::Flat(char* forKind) : Shape(forKind)
    {

    }

void Flat::grow(int change)
    {
    dimension1 += change;
    }

Spatial::Spatial(char* forKind) : Shape(forKind)
    {

    }
Horizontal::Horizontal() : Flat("Horizontal")
    {
    whichAreYou();
    show();
    }

void Horizontal::show()
    {
    cout << endl;
    for(int i = 1; i <= dimension1; i++)  cout << symbol;
    cout << endl << endl;
    }

Vertical::Vertical() : Flat("Vertical")
    {
    whichAreYou();
    show();
    }

void Vertical::show()
    {
    for(int i = 1; i <= dimension1; i++)  cout << "\n    " << symbol;
    cout << endl << endl;
    }

OneDimen::OneDimen(char* forKind) : Spatial(forKind)
    {

    }

void OneDimen::grow(int amount)
    {
    dimension1 += amount;
```

```
        }

TwoDimen::TwoDimen(char* forKind) : Spatial(forKind), dimension2(3)
    {

    }

void TwoDimen::grow(int amount)
    {
       dimension1 += amount;
       dimension2 += amount;
    }

Square::Square() : OneDimen("Square")
    {
       whichAreYou();
       show();
    }

void Square::show()
    {
       for (int row = 1; row <= dimension1; row++)
         {
           cout << endl;
           for (int col = 1; col <= dimension1; col++)  cout << symbol;
         }
       cout << endl;
    }

RightTri::RightTri() : OneDimen("RightTri")
    {
       whichAreYou();
       show();
    }

void RightTri::show()
    {
       for (int row = 1 ; row <= dimension1; row++)
         {
           cout << endl;
           for (int col = 1; col <= row; col++)  cout << symbol;
         }
       cout << endl;
    }

Diamond::Diamond(): OneDimen("Diamond")
    {
       whichAreYou();
       show();
    }

void Diamond::show()
    {
       int tempDimension = dimension1;

       if (tempDimension % 2  != 1)  tempDimension++;  // Make it odd.

       // Show the top half.
       for (int row = 1 ; row <= tempDimension/2 + 1; row++)
         {
           cout << endl;
           for (int col=1; col <= tempDimension/2 - (row-1); col++) cout << ' ';
           for (col=1; col <= 2*row - 1; col++)  cout << symbol;
         }

       // Show the bottom half.
       for( row = tempDimension/2 + 1; row <= tempDimension; row++)
         {
           cout << endl;
           for (int col=1; col <= (row-1) - tempDimension/2; col++) cout << ' ';
```

```
        for (col=1; col <= 2*(tempDimension-(row-1)) - 1; col++) cout << symbol;
      }

    cout << endl;
  }

Rectangle::Rectangle() : TwoDimen("Rectangle")
  {
    whichAreYou();
    show();
  }

void Rectangle::show()
  {
    for (int row = 1 ; row <= dimension1; row++)
      {
      cout << endl;
      for (int col = 1; col <= dimension2; col++)  cout << symbol;
      }
    cout << endl;
  }

void main()
  {
    Shape* shapes[10];

    shapes[0] = new Horizontal;
    shapes[1] = new Vertical;
    shapes[2] = new Square;
    shapes[3] = new Square;
    shapes[4] = new RightTri;
    shapes[5] = new Diamond;
    shapes[6] = new Rectangle;
    shapes[7] = new RightTri;
    shapes[8] = new Diamond;
    shapes[9] = new Square;

    for (int i = 0; i < 10; i++)
      {
      cout << "Printing shape[ " << i << "]   ";
      shapes[i] -> show();
      }

    for (i = 0; i < 10; i++)
      {
      shapes[i] -> grow(i);
      }

    for (i = 0; i < 10; i++)
      {
      shapes[i] -> show();
      }

    for (i = 0; i < 10; i++)
      {
      delete shapes[i];
      }
  }
```

Chapter 5

5.1.A   The following function will faithfully display the value of any kind of integer: *int* variables, *int* literals, and numerical expressions that evaluate to *int*.

```
void fancyPrint(int i)
{
    cout << "  ---> " << i << " <---" << endl;
}
```

However, it will not do so for *floats*, *chars*, or strings. In the program that follows, use comments to inactivate both it and its prototype. Replace these with a function template and its prototype capable of creating instantiations that will.

```
#include <iostream.h>

void fancyPrint(int i);    // Prototype.

void main()
{
    cout << endl;

    // Passing int, float, char, and string literals.
    cout << " 1:   " ;   fancyPrint(12);
    cout << " 2:   " ;   fancyPrint(3.14159);
    cout << " 3:   " ;   fancyPrint('A');
    cout << " 4:   " ;   fancyPrint("Wow!  It's Working!!");

    // Passing variables and pointers.
    int     i = 123;
    float   f = 2.71828;
    char    c = 'Z';
    char    string[] = "Greetings";

    cout << " 5:   " ;   fancyPrint( i );
    cout << " 6:   " ;   fancyPrint( f );
    cout << " 7:   " ;   fancyPrint( c );
    cout << " 8:   " ;   fancyPrint( string );
    cout << " 9:   " ;   fancyPrint( &i );

    // Passing expressions.
    cout << "10:   " ;   fancyPrint( 1+1 );
    cout << "11:   " ;   fancyPrint( 2*i );
    cout << "12:   " ;   fancyPrint( (int) ('z' - c) );
}

void fancyPrint(int i)
{
    cout << "     ---> " << i << " <---" << endl;
}
```

5.1.B   Reinstall the original version of *fancyPrint()* as a specialization for *ints*. On the line for output, add the message "int specialization" so that when the program runs there will be evidence that it ran when expected. Rerun the program and inspect the output.

5.1.C   Overload the *fancyPrint()* template and *int* specialization with a *template* that will accept two arguments of any type, *provided they are both of the same type*.

Add the calls to test this *template* (by removing the comment slashes from the tests given in the following).

```
#include <iostream.h>

void fancyPrint(int i)      // An int specialization.
    {
    cout << "      --->  " << i << " <--- "
         << "(via int specialization)" << endl;
    }

template <class Type>       // Function template definition.
void fancyPrint(Type t)
    {
    cout << "      --->  " << t << " <---" << endl;
    }

// template <            ****COMPLETE THIS LINE****
// void fancyPrint(      ****COMPLETE THIS LINE****
//    {
//    cout << "argument 1: " << arg1;
//    cout << endl << "      argument 2: " << arg2 << endl;
//    }

void main()
    {
    cout << endl;

    // Passing int, float, char, and string literals.
    cout << " 1:   " ;  fancyPrint(12);
    cout << " 2:   " ;  fancyPrint(3.14159);
    cout << " 3:   " ;  fancyPrint('A');
    cout << " 4:   " ;  fancyPrint("Wow!  It's Working!!");

    // Passing variables and pointers.
    int     i = 123;
    float   f = 2.71828;
    char    c = 'Z';
    char    string[] = "Greetings";

    cout << " 5:   " ;  fancyPrint( i );
    cout << " 6:   " ;  fancyPrint( f );
    cout << " 7:   " ;  fancyPrint( c );
    cout << " 8:   " ;  fancyPrint( string );
    cout << " 9:   " ;  fancyPrint( &i );

    // Passing expressions.
    cout << "10:   " ;  fancyPrint( 1+1 );
    cout << "11:   " ;  fancyPrint( 2*i );
    cout << "12:   " ;  fancyPrint( (int) ('z' - c) );

    // Testing the two-argument function template.
    //  cout << "13:   "; fancyPrint(i, 456);
    //  cout << "14:   "; fancyPrint(f, 10*f);
    //  cout << "15:   "; fancyPrint('A', c);
    //  cout << "16:   "; fancyPrint("Seasons", string);
    }
```

5.1.D Overload the two existing *fancyPrint( )* templates and *int* specialization with a *template* that will accept three arguments of any type and in any combination.
Add the calls to test this *template*.

```
#include <iostream.h>

void fancyPrint(int i)      // An int specialization.
    {
    cout << "      --->  " << i << " <--- "
         << "(via int specialization)" << endl;
    }
```

```
template <class Type>        // Function template definition.
void fancyPrint(Type t)
    {
    cout << "      ---> " << t << " <---" << endl;
    }

template <class Type>
void fancyPrint(Type arg1, Type arg2)
    {
    cout << "argument 1: " << arg1;
    cout << endl << "      argument 2: " << arg2 << endl;
    }

// template <          ****COMPLETE THIS LINE****
// void fancyPrint(    ****COMPLETE THIS LINE****
//    {
//      cout << "argument 1: " << arg1;
//      cout << endl << "      argument 2: " << arg2;
//      cout << endl << "      argument 3: " << arg3 << endl;
//    }

void main()
    {
    cout << endl;

    // Passing int, float, char, and string literals.
    cout << " 1:  " ;  fancyPrint(12);
    cout << " 2:  " ;  fancyPrint(3.14159);
    cout << " 3:  " ;  fancyPrint('A');
    cout << " 4:  " ;  fancyPrint("Wow!  It's Working!!");

    // Passing variables and pointers.
    int     i = 123;
    float   f = 2.71828;
    char    c = 'Z';
    char    string[] = "Greetings";

    cout << " 5:  " ;  fancyPrint( i );
    cout << " 6:  " ;  fancyPrint( f );
    cout << " 7:  " ;  fancyPrint( c );
    cout << " 8:  " ;  fancyPrint( string );
    cout << " 9:  " ;  fancyPrint( &i );

    // Passing expressions.
    cout << "10:  " ;  fancyPrint( 1+1 );
    cout << "11:  " ;  fancyPrint( 2*i );
    cout << "12:  " ;  fancyPrint( (int) ('z' - c) );

    // Testing the two-argument function template.
    cout << "13:  "; fancyPrint(i, 456);
    cout << "14:  "; fancyPrint(f, 10*f);
    cout << "15:  "; fancyPrint('A', c);
    cout << "16:  "; fancyPrint("Seasons", string);

    // Testing the three-argument function template
    //  cout << "17:  "; fancyPrint(i, 456, 789);
    //  cout << "18:  "; fancyPrint(i,    f,    c);
    //  cout << "19:  "; fancyPrint(c,    i,    f);
    //  cout << "20:  "; fancyPrint(string, 3*60/45, "All");
    }
```

5.1.E The following program is a replication of the answer to Exercise 5.1.B to which has been added a *Point* class and a *Box* class. A point is a pair of values representing an abscissa and an ordinate. A box is a rectangular shape with a *height* and a *length* formed from some printable character.

As it stands, the program will not run. Although the invocations of *fancyPrint( )* will accept *Point* objects and *Box* objects, the output operator (which all versions of it use) will not. Overload the output operator so that it will.

```
#include <iostream.h>

class Point
{
    private:
        int x; // Point's abscissa.
        int y; // Point's ordinate.

    public:
        Point(int abscissa, int ordinate) : x(abscissa), y(ordinate)
        {

        }
        Point() : x(0), y(0)
        {

        }
        Point(int x_and_y) : x(x_and_y),  y(x_and_y)
        {

        }
        // friend ostream& operator<< (ostream& os, Point& p);
};

class Box
{
    private:
        int  height;
        int  length;
        char symbol;

    public:
        Box(int h, int l, char s) : height(h), length(l), symbol(s)
        {

        }
        Box(int h_and_l) : height(h_and_l), length(h_and_l), symbol('*')
        {

        }
        Box() : height(3), length(10), symbol('X')
        {

        }
        // friend ostream& operator<< (ostream& os, Box& b);
};

void fancyPrint(int i);    // Prototype for int specialization.

template <class Type>      // Prototype for function template.
void fancyPrint(Type t);

void main()
{
    cout << endl;

    // Passing int, float, char, and string literals.
    cout << " 1:  " ;  fancyPrint(12);
    cout << " 2:  " ;  fancyPrint(3.14159);
    cout << " 3:  " ;  fancyPrint('A');
    cout << " 4:  " ;  fancyPrint("Wow!  It's Working!!");
```

```
                   // Passing variables and pointers.
                   int        i = 123;
                   float      f = 2.71828;
                   char       c = 'Z';
                   char string[] = "Greetings";

                   cout << " 5:  " ;  fancyPrint( i );
                   cout << " 6:  " ;  fancyPrint( f );
                   cout << " 7:  " ;  fancyPrint( c );
                   cout << " 8:  " ;  fancyPrint( string );
                   cout << " 9:  " ;  fancyPrint( &i );

                   // Passing expressions.
                   cout << "10:  " ;  fancyPrint( 1+1 );
                   cout << "11:  " ;  fancyPrint( 2*i );
                   cout << "12:  " ;  fancyPrint( (int) ('z' - c) );

                   // Passing Boxes.
                   Box box1(5, 25);
                   Box box2;
                   Box box3(3);

                   cout << "13:  " ;  fancyPrint( box1 );
                   cout << "14:  " ;  fancyPrint( box2 );
                   cout << "15:  " ;  fancyPrint( box3 );

                   // Passing Points.
                   Point point1(18, 5, 'B');
                   Point point2;
                   Point point3(3);

                   cout << "16:  " ;  fancyPrint( point1 );
                   cout << "17:  " ;  fancyPrint( point2 );
                   cout << "18:  " ;  fancyPrint( point3 );

               }

void fancyPrint(int i)     // An int specialization.
   {
       cout << "      ---> " << i << " <--- "
            << "(via int specialization)" << endl;
   }

template <class Type>        // Function template definition.
void fancyPrint(Type t)
   {
       cout << "     ---> " << t << " <---" << endl;
   }

ostream& operator<< (ostream& os, Box& b)
     {
       os << endl;
       for (int height = 1; height <= b.height; height++)
         {
           os << "          ";
           for (int length = 1; length <= b.length; length++)
             os << b.symbol;
           os << endl;
         }
       return os;
     }

ostream& operator<< (ostream& os, Point& p)
 // Install code so that a point will appear like this:  ( 3, 4 ).
```

5.2 Run the following program, noticing that the addresses reported by the function templates and those reported by *main( )* are not the same. Determine why there is a discrepancy and remove it.

```
#include <iostream.h>

class Point
{
    private:
        int x; // Point's abscissa.
        int y; // Point's ordinate.

    public:
        Point(int abscissa, int ordinate) : x(abscissa), y(ordinate)
        {

        }
        Point() : x(0), y(0)
        {

        }
        Point(int x_and_y) : x(x_and_y),  y(x_and_y)
        {

        }

        friend ostream& operator<< (ostream& os, Point& p);
};

class Box
{
    private:
        int  height;
        int  length;
        char symbol;

    public:
        Box(int h, int l, char s) : height(h), length(l), symbol(s)
        {

        }
        Box(int h_and_l) : height(h_and_l), length(h_and_l), symbol('*')
        {

        }
        Box() : height(3), length(10), symbol('X')
        {

        }

        friend ostream& operator<< (ostream& os, Box& b);
};

struct memUser
{
    int array[100];
};

template <class Type>
void reportSizeAndAddress(Type thing)
{
    cout << "size = " << sizeof(thing) << "bytes;  "
         << "location = " << &thing;
}

void main()
{
    char    c;      char*  pc;      char**   ppc;
```

```
int      i;        int*     pi;        int**     ppi;
long     l;        long*    pl;        long**    ppl;
float    f;        float*   pf;        float**   ppf;
double   d;        double*  pd;        double**  ppd;

Point    p;        Point*   pp;        Point**   ppp;
Box      b;        Box*     pb;        Box**     ppb;

memUser  m;        memUser* pm;        memUser** ppm;

// Size and location of char c:
cout << "\n char c      -- main():  ";
cout <<  "size = " << sizeof(c) << "bytes;   "
     << "location = " << &c;
cout << "\n            from template:   ";
reportSizeAndAddress(c);

// Size and location of int i:
cout << "\n int i       -- main():  ";
cout <<  "size = " << sizeof(i) << "bytes;   "
     << "location = " << &i;
cout << "\n            from template:   ";
reportSizeAndAddress(i);

// Size and location of long l:
cout << "\n long l      -- main():  ";
cout <<  "size = " << sizeof(l) << "bytes;   "
     << "location = " << &l;
cout << "\n            from template:   ";
reportSizeAndAddress(l);

// Size and location of float f:
cout << "\n float f     -- main():  ";
cout <<  "size = " << sizeof(f) << "bytes;   "
     << "location = " << &f;
cout << "\n            from template:   ";
reportSizeAndAddress(f);

// Size and location of double d:
cout << "\n double d    -- main():  ";
cout <<  "size = " << sizeof(d) << "bytes;   "
     << "location = " << &d;
cout << "\n            from template:   ";
reportSizeAndAddress(d);

// Size and location of Point p:
cout << "\n Point p     -- main():  ";
cout <<  "size = " << sizeof(p) << "bytes;   "
     << "location = " << &p;
cout << "\n            from template:   ";
reportSizeAndAddress(p);

// Size and location of Box b:
cout << "\n Box b       -- main():  ";
cout <<  "size = " << sizeof(b) << "bytes;   "
     << "location = " << &b;
cout << "\n            from template:   ";
reportSizeAndAddress(b);

// Size and location of memUser m:
cout << "\n memUser m  -- main():  ";
cout <<  "size = " << sizeof(m) << "bytes;   "
     << "location = " << &m;
cout << "\n       from template:   ";
reportSizeAndAddress(m);
}
```

5.3 In the following program, convert the sorting function, and all supporting functions as well as *print( )*, into *templates* and perform the necessary operator overloading so that all calls in *main( )* are successfully completed.

```
#include <iostream.h>

enum boolean {false, true};

void swap(int& a, int& b)
{
    int holder;

    holder = a;
    a      = b;
    b      = holder;
}

void print(int array[], int numOfItems)
{
    cout << endl;

    for (int i = 0;  i < numOfItems;  i++)   cout << array[i] << endl;

    cout << endl;
}

int getSubOfSmallest(int a[], int startSub, int size)
{
    int sub = startSub;
    for (int i = startSub+1; i < size; I++)
        if (a[i] < a[sub])  sub = i;
    return sub;
}

void sort(int array[], int numOfItems)
{
    int subOfSmallest;
    for(int i = 0;  i < (numOfItems-1);  i++)
    {
        subOfSmallest = getSubOfSmallest( array, i, numOfItems );
        swap( array[i], array[subOfSmallest] );
    }
}

class Point
{
    private:
        int x; // Point's abscissa.
        int y; // Point's ordinate.

    public:
        Point() : x(0), y(0)
        {

        }
        Point(int x_and_y) : x(x_and_y),  y(x_and_y)
        {

        }

        Point(int abscissa, int ordinate) : x(abscissa), y(ordinate)
        {

        }

        friend ostream& operator<< (ostream& os, Point& p);

        // Here point1 < point2  if it is closer to the origin.
```

```
                };

ostream& operator<< (ostream& os, Point& p)
    {
      cout << "( " << p.x << ", " << p.y << " )";
      return os;
    }

class Box
   {
     private:
        int  height;
        int  length;
        char symbol;

     public:
        Box() : height(3), length(10), symbol('X')
           {

           }

        Box(int h, int l, char s) : height(h), length(l), symbol(s)
           {

           }

        Box(int h_and_l) : height(h_and_l), length(h_and_l), symbol('*')
           {

           }

        friend ostream& operator<< (ostream& os, Box& b);

        // Here box1 < box2  if its length is less.

   };

ostream& operator<< (ostream& os, Box& b)
    {
      os << endl;
      for (int height = 1; height <= b.height; height++)
         {
           os << "           ";
           for (int length = 1; length <= b.length; length++)
              os << b.symbol;
           os << endl;
         }
      return os;
    }

void main()
   {
     cout << endl;

     int    ia[6]  = { 6, 4, 3, 2, 5, 1 };

     float  fa[5]  = { .2, .1, .7, .6, .5 };

     Box    b[4]   = { Box(4,12,'&'), Box(2,6,'#'),
                       Box(4,10,'+'), Box(3,5,'*') };

     Point  p[3]   = { Point(6,1), Point(4,5), Point(2,1) };

     // print(ia, 6);  sort(ia, 6);  print(ia, 6);
     // print(fa, 5);  sort(fa, 5);  print(fa, 5);
     // print( b, 4);  sort( b, 4);  print( b, 4);
     // print( p, 3);  sort( p, 3);  print( p, 3);
   }
```

5.4 In the following, supplement the member function *template showCouplet( )* with an *int* specialization. All it should do above and beyond the family of *template* functions is print a distinctive annunciation so it is clear, when observing the output, that the specialization was the one which showed objects of type *Couplet<int, int>*.

```
#include <iostream.h>

class Line
   {
   private:
     char symbol;
     int  lineLength;

   public:
     Line() : symbol('*'), lineLength(10)
       {

       }

       Line(int forSym, char forLen) : symbol(forSym), lineLength(forLen)
         {

         }

       friend ostream& operator<< (ostream& os, Line& line);
   };

ostream& operator<< (ostream& os, Line& line)
   {
   for (int i = 1; i <= line.lineLength; i++)   os << line.symbol;
   return os;
   }

template <class T1, class T2>
class Couplet
   {
   private:
     T1  x;
     T2  y;

   public:
     Couplet(T1 forX, T2 forY);  // Constructor's prototype.

     void showCouplet();
   };

template <class T1, class T2>
Couplet<T1, T2>::Couplet(T1 forX, T2 forY) : x(forX), y(forY)
   {

   }

template <class T1, class T2>
void Couplet<T1, T2>::showCouplet()
   {
   cout << endl;
   cout << "Couplet:  x = " << x << endl;
   cout << "          y = " << y << endl;
   }

void main()
   {
   Couplet<int, int>  intCoup1(1,2);
   Couplet<int, int>  intCoup2(3,4);

   cout << "\nintCoup1:" << endl;
   intCoup1.showCouplet();
```

```
cout << "\nintCoup2:" << endl;
intCoup2.showCouplet();

// Get some Line objects.

Line lineA('A',10), lineB('B',20), lineC('C',30), lineD('D', 40);

// Replicate the processing above with "Couplets of Lines."

Couplet<Line, Line> lineCoup1(lineA, lineB);
Couplet<Line, Line> lineCoup2(lineC, lineD);

cout << "\nlineCoup1:" << endl;
lineCoup1.showCouplet();
cout << "\nlineCoup2:" << endl;
lineCoup2.showCouplet();

// Replicate the processing above with "Couplets of <int and Line>."

Couplet<int, Line> intLineCoup1(11, lineA);
Couplet<int, Line> intLineCoup2(22, lineB);

cout << "\nintLineCoup1:" << endl;
intLineCoup1.showCouplet();
cout << "\nintLineCoup2:" << endl;
intLineCoup2.showCouplet();
}
```

5.5 The following program is similar to the the program in 5.4, except that the function *template* for *showCouplet( )* has been removed. It runs nonetheless because the *Couplet<int,int>::showCouplet( )* specialization is present, and the only objects created are of type *Couplet<int,int>*.

5.5.A In *main( )*, define an object of type *Couplet<int,char>*, an object of type *Couplet<int,float>*, and an object of type *Couplet<float, float>*. You'll know the constructor ran because it now annunciates itself. Do not have these objects attempt to access *showCouplet( )*. Run the program to convince yourself that member functions do not have to be provided for objects of every template class instantiated.

5.5.B Next, try to show each of these objects with *showCouplet( )*. You will see that the compiler will not perform any data type conversions in an attempt to apply the only facility that might possibly work (the *showCouplet( )* function).

5.5.C Remove the comment slashes from the *showCouplet( )* function template to demonstrate that its presence repairs the fault.

```
#include <iostream.h>

template <class T1, class T2>
class Couplet
    {
    private:
        T1   x;
        T2   y;

    public:
        Couplet(T1 forX, T2 forY);   // Constructor's prototype.
```

```
                void showCouplet();
        };

        template <class T1, class T2>
        Couplet<T1, T2>::Couplet(T1 forX, T2 forY) : x(forX), y(forY)
            {
            cout<<endl<<"***constructing a Couplet<T1, T2> object***"<<endl;
            }

        void Couplet<int, int>::showCouplet()
            {
            cout << endl;
            cout << "From  Couplet<int,int>::showCouplet()  Specialization";
            cout << endl;
            cout << "Couplet:   x = " << x << endl;
            cout << "           y = " << y << endl;
            cout << "int==int==int==int==int==int==int==int==int==int";
            cout << endl;
            }

        // For Part C:   remove the comment slashes
        // template <class T1, class T2>
        // void Couplet<T1, T2>::showCouplet()
        //    {
        //     cout << endl;
        //     cout << "Couplet:   x = " << x << endl;
        //     cout << "           y = " << y << endl;
        //    }

        void main()
            {
            Couplet<int, int>  intCoup1(1,2);
            Couplet<int, int>  intCoup2(3,4);

            cout << "\nintCoup1:" << endl;
            intCoup1.showCouplet();
            cout << "\nintCoup2:" << endl;
            intCoup2.showCouplet();

            // For Part A:   remove the comment slashes
            // Couplet<int,   char>   intCharCouplet(100, 'A');
            // Couplet<int,   float>  intFloatCouplet(200, 1.75);
            // Couplet<float, float>  floatFloatCouplet(1.111, 2.222);

            // For Part B:   remove the comment slashes
            // intCharCouplet.showCouplet();
            // intFloatCouplet.showCouplet();
            // floatFloatCouplet.showCouplet();
            }
```

5.6   A *static* data member declared within a class *template*, such as *counter* in the following program, may be used to keep track of the number of objects defined from each distinct *template* class.

5.6.A   Run the following program to observe how *static* data members work within *template* classes: each class of a different type has a separate *counter* of its own. The *counter* of objects defined from *Couplet<int,int>* is a different variable from the *counter* dedicated to the *Couplet<int,float>* class.

5.6.B   Notice that there are two approaches to initializing the *counter*: either a general initialization which initializes it as a *static* data member within any class that may come to be instantiated from the *template*:

```
// The general initialization, for any instantiation of the template.
```

```
template<class T1, class T2>  int Couplet<T1, T2>::counter = 0;
```

or a series of specialized initializations for particularly identified classes:

```
// A list of specialized initializations.
int Couplet<int, int>    ::counter = 100;
int Couplet<int, char>   ::counter = 200;
int Couplet<int, float>  ::counter = 300;
int Couplet<float, float>::counter = 400;
```

Both approaches cannot be used in the same program. If any one initializiation is specialized, all initializations must be specialized. Rerun the program from Exercise 5.6.A, commenting-out the general initialization and activating the particularized ones.

```
#include <iostream.h>

template <class T1, class T2>
class Couplet
    {
      private:
        T1  x;
        T2  y;

      public:                    // A static variable is declared for the
        static int counter;      // template class.  Each instantiation will
                                 // have an independent one of its own.

        Couplet(T1 forX, T2 forY);  // Constructor's prototype.

        void showCouplet();  // Note:  This function is declared but not
                             // defined for any instantiation.  This is
    };                       // okay because it is never called.

// The general initialization of all instantiations of count.
template<class T1, class T2>  int Couplet<T1, T2>::counter = 0;

// A list of specialized initializations.
//    int Couplet<int,int>     ::counter = 100;
//    int Couplet<int,char>    ::counter = 200;
//    int Couplet<int,float>   ::counter = 300;
//    int Couplet<float,float>::counter = 400;

template <class T1, class T2>
Couplet<T1, T2>::Couplet(T1 forX, T2 forY) : x(forX), y(forY)
    {
      counter++;        // The static variable is incremented with the
    }                   // definition of each object

void main()
    {
      cout<<"\nCouplet<int,int>::counter     = " << Couplet<int,int>::counter;
      cout<<"\nCouplet<int,char>::counter    = " << Couplet<int,char>::counter;
      cout<<"\nCouplet<int,float>::counter   = " << Couplet<int,float>::counter;
      cout<<"\nCouplet<float,float>::counter = " << Couplet<float,float>::counter;

      cout<<endl;

      Couplet<int, int>  intCoup1(1,2);
      Couplet<int, int>  intCoup2(3,4);
      Couplet<int, int>  intCoup3(5,6);
      Couplet<int, int>  intCoup4(7,8);

      Couplet<int, char>   intCharCouplet1(65, 'A');
      Couplet<int, char>   intCharCouplet2(66, 'B');
      Couplet<int, char>   intCharCouplet3(67, 'C');
```

```
Couplet<int, float>   intFloatCouplet1(15, 1.5);
Couplet<int, float>   intFloatCouplet2(25, 2.5);

Couplet<float, float>   floatFloatCouplet1(1.111, 2.222);

cout<<"\nCouplet<int,int>::counter     = " << Couplet<int,int>::counter;
cout<<"\nCouplet<int,char>::counter    = " << Couplet<int,char>::counter;
cout<<"\nCouplet<int,float>::counter   = " << Couplet<int,float>::counter;
cout<<"\nCouplet<float,float>::counter = " << Couplet<float,float>::counter;

cout<<endl;
}
```

5.6.C Suppose we had wanted a cumulative tally kept of the number of Couplet objects created, regardless of their particular type. In other words, suppose we had wanted a
variable such as *totalCount* to be incremented by a constructor whenever any kind of
a Couplet object was defined. In the preceding program, with four *Couplet<int,int>*
objects, three *Couplet<int,char>* objects, two *Couplet<int,float>* objects, and one object
in the *Couplet<float,float>* class; this variable should indicate that a total of ten *Couplet*
objects had been instantiated.

The technique for defining one variable that spans the whole open-ended set of *Couplet* classes lies in defining a *static* variable within a nontemplate base class from which
the class template is derived. That the class *template Couplet* is coded as derived from
Base means that every instantiation of *Couplet* will be a subclass of *Base*:

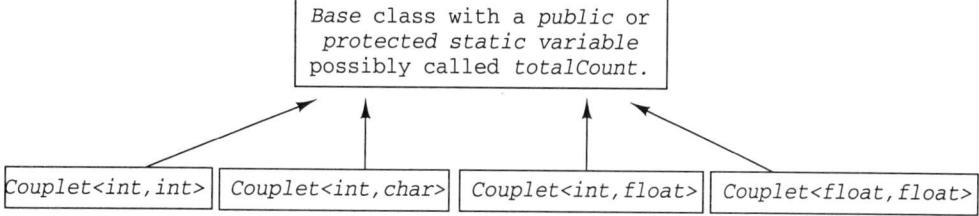

The result is that each and every object defined from each and every different Couplet class will have a derived part, from the base class, and an incremental part, from its
particular instantiation of the class *template*. Now, recalling that a *static* data member is
a single variable (i.e., a single storage location) shared in common by each object endowed with the class's ensemble of data members, it is apparent that the derived part of
every *Couplet* object will include the variable named, say, *totalCount* but that in every
instance it is bound to the same address in memory. Apply these ideas to the program
from Exercise 5.6.A, in which *counter* was initialized to 0, so that the following *main()*
function runs to show the number of objects defined from each different instantiation
of *Couplet* (as before) as well as the total number of *Couplet* objects defined from all
template instantiations (which will be stored by the variable *Base::totalCount*).

```
void main()
{
    cout<<"\nCouplet<int,int>::counter     = " << Couplet<int,int>::counter;
    cout<<"\nCouplet<int,char>::counter    = " << Couplet<int,char>::counter;
    cout<<"\nCouplet<int,float>::counter   = " << Couplet<int,float>::counter;
    cout<<"\nCouplet<float,float>::counter = " <<
            Couplet<float,float>::counter;
    cout<<"\nBase::totalCount              = " << Base::totalCount;
    cout<<endl;
```

```
Couplet<int, int>  intCoup1(1,2);
Couplet<int, int>  intCoup2(3,4);
Couplet<int, int>  intCoup3(5,6);
Couplet<int, int>  intCoup4(7,8);

Couplet<int, char>   intCharCouplet1(65, 'A');
Couplet<int, char>   intCharCouplet2(66, 'B');
Couplet<int, char>   intCharCouplet3(67, 'C');

Couplet<int, float>  intFloatCouplet1(15, 1.5);
Couplet<int, float>  intFloatCouplet2(25, 2.5);

Couplet<float, float>  floatFloatCouplet1(1.111, 2.222);

cout<<"\nCouplet<int,int>::counter      = " << Couplet<int,int>::counter;
cout<<"\nCouplet<int,char>::counter     = " << Couplet<int,char>::counter;
cout<<"\nCouplet<int,float>::counter    = " << Couplet<int,float>::counter;
cout<<"\nCouplet<float,float>::counter = " <<
        Couplet<float,float>::counter;
cout<<"\nBase::totalCount               = " << Base::totalCount;
cout<<endl;
}
```

5.7 Given the following program, read the code and predict what it will output.

```
#include <iostream.h>

class Line
{
    private:
        char symbol;
        int  lineLength;

    public:
        Line(int forSym, char forLen) : symbol(forSym), lineLength(forLen)
        {

        }

        void resetLine(char newSymbol, int newLength)
        {
            symbol    = newSymbol;
            lineLength = newLength;
        }

        friend ostream& operator<< (ostream& os, Line& line);
};

ostream& operator<< (ostream& os, Line& line)
{
    for (int i = 1; i <= line.lineLength; i++)   os << line.symbol;
    return os;
}

template <class T1, class T2>
class Couplet
{
    private:
        T1  x;
        T2  y;

    public:
        Couplet(T1 forX, T2 forY) : x(forX), y(forY)
        {

        }
```

```
            void showCouplet();
    };

    template<class T1, class T2>
    void Couplet<T1, T2>::showCouplet()
        {
            cout << endl;
            cout << "Couplet:  x = " << x << endl;
            cout << "          y = " << y << endl;
        }

    void Couplet<Line*, Line*>::showCouplet()
        {
            cout << endl;
            cout << "Couplet:  x = " << (*x) << endl;
            cout << "          y = " << (*y) << endl;
        }

    void main()
        {
            // Get some line objects.
            Line  lineA('A',10),  lineB('B',20),  lineC('C',30),  lineD('D',40);

            Couplet<Line, Line>   lineCoup1( lineA,  lineB);
            Couplet<Line*, Line*> lineCoup2(&lineC, &lineD);

            cout << "\nlineCoup1";
            lineCoup1.showCouplet();
            cout << "\nlineCoup2";
            lineCoup2.showCouplet();

            lineA.resetLine('Z', 40);
            lineB.resetLine('Y', 30);
            lineC.resetLine('X', 20);
            lineD.resetLine('W', 10);

            cout << "\nlineCoup1";
            lineCoup1.showCouplet();
            cout << "\nlineCoup2";
            lineCoup2.showCouplet();
        }
```

5.8.A   Given the following program, install the function *showIt_N_times( )* within *Couplet's* specifier; install its tests, in *main( )*, which are currently commented-out; and run the program to verify that that the function works.

```
void showIt_N_times(int n)
    {
        cout << endl << "++++++showIt " << n << " times++++++" << endl;
        for (int i = 1; i <= n; i++) showCouplet();
        cout << "++++++++++++++++++++++++++" << endl;
    }

#include <iostream.h>

class Line
    {
        private:
            char symbol;
            int  lineLength;

        public:

            Line(int forSym, char forLen) : symbol(forSym), lineLength(forLen)
                {

                }
```

```
                    friend ostream& operator<< (ostream& os, Line& line);
        };

ostream&  operator<<  (ostream& os, Line& line)
    {
        for (int i = 1; i <= line.lineLength; i++)   os << line.symbol;
        return os;
    }

template <class T1, class T2>
class Couplet
    {
      private:
        T1   x;
        T2   y;
      public:
        Couplet(T1 forX, T2 forY);  // Constructor's prototype.

        void showCouplet();
    };

template <class T1, class T2>
Couplet<T1, T2>::Couplet(T1 forX, T2 forY) : x(forX), y(forY)
    {

    }

void Couplet<int, int>::showCouplet()  // Specialization for Couplet<int,int>.
    {
      cout << endl;
      cout << "From  Couplet<int,int>::showCouplet()  Specialization";
      cout << endl;
      cout << "Couplet:  x = " << x << endl;
      cout << "          y = " << y << endl;
      cout << "int==int==int==int==int==int==int==int==int==int";
      cout << endl;
    }

template <class T1, class T2>
void Couplet<T1, T2>::showCouplet()
    {
      cout << endl;
      cout << "Couplet:  x = " << x << endl;
      cout << "          y = " << y << endl;
    }

void main()
    {
      Couplet<int, int>  intCoup1(1,2);
      Couplet<int, int>  intCoup2(3,4);

//    cout << "\nintCoup1 -- shown 2 times:" << endl;
//    intCoup1.showIt_N_times(2);
//    cout << "\nintCoup2 -- shown 3 times:" << endl;
//    intCoup2.showIt_N_times(3);

      // Get some Line objects.
      Line  lineA('A',10),  lineB('B',20),  lineC('C',30),  lineD('D', 40);

      // Replicate the processing above with "Couplets of Lines."

      Couplet<Line, Line> lineCoup1(lineA, lineB);
      Couplet<Line, Line> lineCoup2(lineC, lineD);

//    cout << "\nlineCoup1 -- shown 2 times:" << endl;
//    lineCoup1.showIt_N_times(2);
//    cout << "\nlineCoup2 -- shown 3 times:" << endl;
//    lineCoup2.showIt_N_times(3);

      // Replicate the processing above with "Couplets of <int and Line>."
```

```
        Couplet<int, Line> intLineCoup1(11, lineA);
        Couplet<int, Line> intLineCoup2(22, lineB);

//      cout << "\nintLineCoup1 -- shown 2 times:" << endl;
//      intLineCoup1.showIt_N_times(2);
//      cout << "\nintLineCoup2 -- shown 3 times:" << endl;
//      intLineCoup2.showIt_N_times(3);
    }
```

5.8.B   In the program you just completed, replace the *showIt_N_times( )* function within *Couplet's* specifier by its prototype and install it beneath the specifier as a function template. Run the program to confirm that the same output is produced now as was produced before this change.

5.8.C   Supplement the program completed for Exercise 5.8.B with a *Couplet<int,int>* specialization of *showIt_N_times( )*. The only special action it should take is to output an annunciation so that we can see that it was invoked, and not an *<int,int>* version instantiated by the *function template*.

5.8.D   Finally, make the program from Exercise 5.8.C run with the following addition at the end of *main( )*:

```
        :
        // Get some Point objects.
        Point  topLeft(1,3),  bottomRight(8,27);

        // Replicate the processing above with a "Couplet of Points."

        Couplet<Point, Point> menuWindow(topLeft, bottomRight);

        cout << "\nmenuWindow -- shown 2 times:" << endl;
        menuWindow.showIt_N_times(2);

        // Replicate the processing above with "Couplets of <Point and Line>".

        Couplet<Point, Line> pointLineCoup1(topLeft, lineA);
        Couplet<Point, Line> pointLineCoup2(bottomRight, lineB);

        cout << "\npointLineCoup1 -- shown 2 times:" << endl;
        pointLineCoup1.showIt_N_times(2);
        cout << "\npointLineCoup2 -- shown 3 times:" << endl;
        pointLineCoup2.showIt_N_times(3);
    }
```

The *Point* class will of course have to be installed:

```
        class Point
        {
            private:
                int x, y;
            public:
                Point(int forX, int forY) : x(forX), y(forY)
                {

                }
```

```
                    void showPoint()
                    {
                        cout << " (" << x << ", " << y << ") ";
                    }
            };
```

Don't forget that the output operator will have to be overloaded in order for *showCouplet( )* to be applicable to *Couplets* containing *Points*.

5.9   Recode the following program, so that each of the member functions defined within *Buffer's* specifier, including the constructors and the destructor, is defined as a function template outside the specifier.

```
#include <iostream.h>

template <class bufferType>
class Buffer
{
    private:
        bufferType*  buffer;
        int          size;
        int          nextCell;

    public:

        Buffer(int numOfElements)  // One-argument constructor.
        {
            buffer  = new bufferType[numOfElements];
            size    = numOfElements;
            nextCell = 0;
        }

        Buffer()   // No-argument constructor.
        {
            buffer  = new bufferType[10];  // Default buffer has 10
                                           // elements.
            size    = 10;
            nextCell = 0;
        }

        ~Buffer()  // Destructor.
        {
            delete [] buffer;
        }

        Buffer (Buffer& original)  // Copy constructor.
        {
            size    = original.size;
            nextCell = original.nextCell;

            buffer  = new bufferType[size];
            for (int i = 0; i < nextCell; i++)
                buffer[i] = original.buffer[i];
        }

        Buffer operator= (Buffer rightBuffer)
        {
            size    = rightBuffer.size;
            nextCell = rightBuffer.nextCell;

            delete [] buffer;

            buffer  = new bufferType[size];
            for (int i = 0; i < nextCell; i++)
                buffer[i] = rightBuffer.buffer[i];

            return *this;
        }
```

```
    void append(bufferType  newItem)   // The new item is installed
        {                              // at the end of the buffer.
          if ( roomLeft() )
              buffer[nextCell++]  = newItem;   // Here nextCell is
                                               // post-incremented.
          else
              cout << "\n**BUFFER FULL  |"
                   << newItem
                   << "|  NOT ACCEPTED**"
                   << endl;
        }

    int slotsFilled()
        {
          return nextCell;
        }


                      // Returns the number of elements left for
                      // storage, 0 when this is done
    int roomLeft()    // (remember, 0 is also false).
        {
          return ( size - slotsFilled() );
        }

    void reset()
        {                // The buffer array is not deleted
          nextCell = 0;  // because its space will be reused.
        }

    void buffer_Copied_to_Argument (bufferType a[])
        {
          for (int i = 0; i < slotsFilled(); i++)   a[i] = buffer[i];
        }

    Buffer  operator+ (Buffer rightBuffer)
        {
          int sizeOfSum = slotsFilled() + rightBuffer.slotsFilled();
          Buffer<bufferType>  combinedBuffer(sizeOfSum);

          for (int i = 0;  i < slotsFilled();  i++)
              combinedBuffer.append( buffer[i] );

          for (i = 0;  i < rightBuffer.slotsFilled(); i++)
              combinedBuffer.append( rightBuffer.buffer[i] );

          return combinedBuffer;
        }

    void showIt()   // Displays the contents of the buffer.
        {
          cout << endl;
          for (int i = 0; i < slotsFilled(); i++)
              cout << "     " << buffer[i] << endl;
        }
};

class Point
{
  private:
    int x, y;

  public:
    Point() : x(0), y(0)                        // Constructor.
        {

        }

    Point(int forX, int forY) : x(forX), y(forY)  // Constructor.
        {
```

```
                    }

            friend  ostream&  operator<< (ostream& outputStream, Point& point);
        };

    ostream&  operator<< (ostream& outputStream, Point& point)
        {
        outputStream << "  ( " << point.x << ", " << point.y << " )   ";
        return outputStream;
        }

    void main()
        {
        Buffer<int>  intBuf1(3), intBuf2(3), intBuf3;

        intBuf1.append( 100 );
        intBuf1.append( 200 );
        intBuf1.append( 300 );
        intBuf1.append( 400 );
        cout << "\nShowing intBuf1:";
        intBuf1.showIt();

        intBuf2.append( 500 );
        intBuf2.append( 600 );
        cout << "\nShowing intBuf2:";
        intBuf2.showIt();

        intBuf3 = intBuf1 + intBuf2;
        cout << "\nShowing intBuf3:";
        intBuf3.showIt();

        intBuf3 = intBuf2 + intBuf1;
        cout << "\nShowing intBuf3:";
        intBuf3.showIt();

        intBuf1.reset();
        intBuf2.reset();
        cout << "\nShowing intBuf1:";
        intBuf1.showIt();
        cout << "\nShowing intBuf2:";
        intBuf2.showIt();
        cout << "\nShowing intBuf3:";
        intBuf3.showIt();

        //  Here are some Points:
        Point  p0, p1(1,1), p2(2,2), p3(3,3), p4(4,4), p5(55,55), p6(66,66);

        Buffer<Point> pointBuf1(3), pointBuf2(3), pointBuf3;

        pointBuf1.append( p0 );
        pointBuf1.append( p1 );
        pointBuf1.append( p2 );
        pointBuf1.append( p3 );
        pointBuf1.append( p4 );
        cout << "\nShowing pointBuf1:";

        pointBuf1.showIt();
        pointBuf2.append( p5 );
        pointBuf2.append( p6 );
        cout << "\nShowing pointBuf2:";
        pointBuf2.showIt();

        pointBuf3 = pointBuf1 + pointBuf2;
        cout << "\nShowing pointBuf3:";
        pointBuf3.showIt();

        pointBuf3 = pointBuf2 + pointBuf1;
```

```
        cout << "\nShowing pointBuf3:";
        pointBuf3.showIt();

        pointBuf1.reset();
        pointBuf2.reset();
        cout << "\nShowing pointBuf1:";
        pointBuf1.showIt();
        cout << "\nShowing pointBuf2:";
        pointBuf2.showIt();
        cout << "\nShowing pointBuf3:";
        pointBuf3.showIt();
    }
```

5.10 Perform the following three tests using the preceding program. Begin by making a backup of the program so that you will always be able to get a fresh copy.

5.10.A Within *main( )*, at the bottom, add the following:

```
    Buffer<int> a(3), b(6); // This defines two int Buffers.

    a.append( 11 );          // Put some integers into Buffer.
    a.append( 22 );
    a.append( 33 );

    b = a;                   // Assignment:  b <- a.

    cout << "\nShowing buffer a:";   // Show that a and b
    a.showIt();                      // hold the same content.
    cout << "\nShowing buffer b:";
    b.showIt();
```

Then *reset( )* buffer *a* and fill it with different integers. Replicate the code to show the contents of buffers *a* and *b* to confirm that they are independent, that the change in *a*'s substance did not affect *b*'s.

5.10.B The only relational and equality operators provided by the language are those for built-in data types. This means that in order to use the == operator to test whether two buffers are conceptually equal (i.e., hold the same content), we first have to define its "Buffer-pertinent" operation.

Begin by removing the code you just installed that *reset( ) a* and *b* (i.e., the code beyond what is given).

Next comment-out the definition and subsequent reference to all *Buffer<Point>* objects. We do not want a *Buffer* class instantiated for *Points*. For the present, the only kind of *Buffer* instantiations we want to think about are instantiations of basic types (so the buffer array holds *ints*, *floats*, *chars*, or some such).

Now install the following code at the end of the program:

```
    if ( a == b )
        cout << "\n   a == b " << endl;
    else
        cout << "\n   **** a != b **** " << endl;
```

Finally, supply the *Buffer* template with an overloaded *operator==* which provides the test for conceptual equality that we want. Then rerun the program to confirm that the buffers *a* and *b* are recognized as operatively equal.

5.10.C At the end of the program, define two additional *Buffers*:

```
    Buffer<int>  fiveSlots(5),  tenSlots(10);
```

display the both the

```
sizeof (fiveSlots.buffer)
```

and the

```
sizeof (tenSlots.buffer)
```

to confirm that *buffer* is the size of a single pointer in each case. Make a mental note of this result because we shall be replicating this measurement when *buffer* is defined explicitly as an array.

5.10.D   Rewrite the *Buffer<bufferType>::append( )* function so that the storage array is enlarged by five compartments each time an append would have otherwise failed because its space had been exhausted. Do this by allocating a new storage array, copying into it the contents from the filled array, and "*delete [ ] ing*" the array which is now defunct.
Test this function by defining a *Buffer<int>* and overfilling it.

5.11   What follows is the code for a *Buffer<dataType>* class template similar to the one in Exercises 5.9 and 5.10. The difference is that its data member *buffer* is implemented not as a pointer to *dataType* but as a veritable array, with storage automatically allocated as each object is defined.

5.11.A   Write a *main( )* that confirms: (i) that the *sizeof* the *buffer* data member shows it be an array (please — no hair splitting about constant pointers!), (ii) that changes made to a *Buffer* object passed by value to a function will not corrupt the actual argument, and (iii) that when *buf2* is assigned to *buf1* (i.e., *buf2 = buf1;*) subsequent changes in *buf1* do not affect *buf2* and vice versa.

```
template <class bufferType>
class Buffer
    {                                    // The array is now a variable automatically
    private:                             // allocated and released with the respective
        bufferType   buffer[16]; // object's construction and destruction.
        int          size;
        int          nextCell;

    public:
        Buffer() : size(16), nextCell(0)
            {

            }

        void append(bufferType  newItem)  // The new item is installed
            {                             // at the end of the buffer.
                if ( roomLeft() )
                    buffer[nextCell++] = newItem;
                else
                    cout << "\n**BUFFER FULL  |"
                         << newItem
                         << "|  NOT ACCEPTED**"
                         << endl;
            }

        int slotsFilled()
            {
                return nextCell;
            }
```

```
int roomLeft()          // Returns the number of elements left for storage,
{                       // 0 when this is none (remember, 0 is also false).
    return ( size - slotsFilled() );
}

void reset()
{
    nextCell = 0;
}

void buffer_Copied_to_Argument (bufferType a[])
{
    for (int i = 0; i < slotsFilled(); i++)    a[i] = buffer[i];
}

void showIt()   // Displays the contents of the buffer.
{
    cout << endl;
    for (int i = 0; i < slotsFilled(); i++)
        cout << "      " << buffer[i] << endl;
}
};
```

5.11.B You may have noticed that the data member *size*, which stores the number of elements comprising the *buffer* array, was not defined as a constant despite the fact that the *buffer's length* cannot be changed (and changing *size* would usher in serious errors).

Had size been specified a constant, attempting to use the default assignment operator would have evoked an error because it works by making a bit-wise, member-by-member copy, but copying into *const* is strictly prohibited.

Redefine *size* as a *const* (one change on one line) and try the program again. It will fail because of the assignment. Install an *operator=* that is compatible with a constant *size* and performs the required updates of the left operand's other data members.

5.11.C Can a container, such as the *Buffer<dataType>* container, hold, as its stored entities, other containers, such as *Couplet<int>*s? Well, is *Couplet<int>* a type specifier? A container can be defined to hold objects of any data type for which there exists a valid type specifier. There are no logical problems in defining a *Buffer* to hold *Couplet*s:

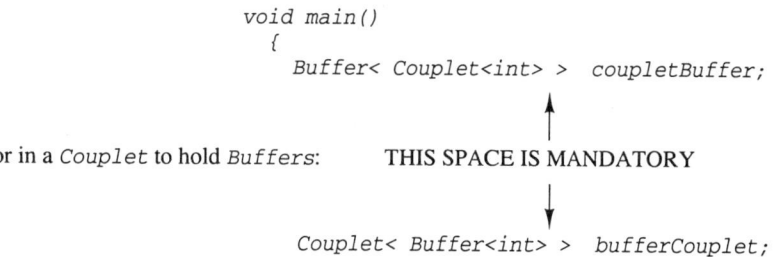

```
void main()
{
    Buffer< Couplet<int> >  coupletBuffer;
```

or in a *Couplet* to hold *Buffers*:   THIS SPACE IS MANDATORY

```
    Couplet< Buffer<int> >  bufferCouplet;
```

The only catch is a matter of syntax: that a space is necessary where indicated in the preceding.

Given the abbreviated *Buffer<dataType>* and *Couplet<dataType>* classes on the following pages and the test of a Buffer that holds *Couplet<int>*s, run the program to see it work. Code a similarly concise test of a *Couplet* that holds *Buffer<int>*s.

```
#include <iostream.h>
```

```
template <class bufferType>
class Buffer
{
    private:
        bufferType  buffer[16];
        const   int  size;
        int         nextCell;

    public:
        Buffer() : size(16), nextCell(0)
            {

            }

        void append(bufferType  newItem)
            {
                if ( roomLeft() )
                    buffer[nextCell++]  = newItem;
                else
                    cout << "\n**BUFFER FULL  |"
                         << newItem
                         << "|  NOT ACCEPTED**"
                         << endl;
            }

        int slotsFilled()
            {
                return nextCell;
            }

        int roomLeft()
            {
                return ( size - slotsFilled() );
            }

        void reset()
            {
                nextCell = 0;
            }

        void showIt()
            {
                cout << endl;
                for (int i = 0; i < slotsFilled(); i++)
                    cout << "     " << buffer[i] << endl;
            }
};

template <class Type>
class Couplet
{
    private:
        Type  x, y;

    public:
        Couplet()
            {

            }

        Couplet(Type forX, Type forY) : x(forX), y(forY)
            {

            }

        friend ostream& operator<< (ostream& os, Couplet<Type>& c);

        void showBuffers(); // Prototype -- specializations will be needed.
};
```

```
// Couplet<int> specialization.
ostream& operator<< (ostream& os, Couplet<int>& c)
   {
     os << endl;
     os << "Couplet:  x = " << c.x << endl;
     os << "          y = " << c.y << endl;

     return os;
   }

// Couplet<Buffer<int> > specialization.
void  Couplet<Buffer<int> >::showBuffers()
   {
     cout << "\nBuffer in compartment 1:" << endl;
     x.showIt();
     cout << "\nBuffer in compartment 2:" << endl;
     y.showIt();
   }

void main()
   {
     Couplet<int>  c1(1,2);
     Couplet<int>  c2(3,4);
     Couplet<int>  c3(5,6);

     Buffer< Couplet<int> > coupletBuffer;
     coupletBuffer.append(c1);
     coupletBuffer.append(c2);
     coupletBuffer.append(c3);

     coupletBuffer.showIt();
   }
```

Our addition:

```
Buffer<int> b1, b2;              // Get two buffers.

for (int i = 0; i < 5; i++)      // Fill the buffers with ints.
   {
     b1.append(i + 11);
     b2.append(i + 21);
   }

b2.append(26);
                                         // Put the buffers
Couplet< Buffer<int> > bufferCouplet(b1, b2);  // into a couplet.

bufferCouplet.showBuffers();    // View the couplet.
```

5.12 Given the following program featuring a *class template* serving as a generalized queue container.

```
#include <iostream.h>

template <class T>
struct node
   {
     T       entity;
     node*   next;
   };

template <class Type>
class Queue
   {
     private:
       node<Type> *head, *rear;
```

```
public:
    Queue() : head(NULL), rear(NULL)    // Constructor.
    {

    }

    ~Queue()                            // Destructor.
    {
        node<Type>*  nodeHolder;
        while ( !empty() )
        {
            nodeHolder = head;
            head = head -> next;
            delete nodeHolder;
        }
    }

    int empty()
    {
        if (head == NULL) return 1;  // True, the queue is empty.
        else return 0;
    }

    void append (Type value)
    {
        node<Type>* newNode = new node<Type>;   // Get a new node.

        newNode -> entity = value;   // Put the incoming value into the new node.
        newNode -> next   = NULL;

        if ( empty() )      // If the queue is empty, newNode is its first and.
            head = newNode;  // only node - so head (and rear) must point to it
        else
            rear -> next = newNode;   // If queue is not empty, the new node
                                      // is linked onto the end.
        rear = newNode;
    }

    void printQueue()
    {
        node<Type>*  rovingPtr = head;
        cout << endl;

        if ( empty() ) cout << "+-+-+-+-+-+-+-+-queue empty-+-+-+-+-+-+-+-+";

        while (rovingPtr != NULL)
        {
            cout<<"  "<<rovingPtr -> entity; // Output operator must be applicable.
            rovingPtr = rovingPtr -> next;
        }
        cout << endl;
    }

    Type  deleteAndDeliverEntity()              //CAUTION!  Must *ONLY* be
    {                                           //          called when the
        int  valueForReturn  = head -> entity;  //          queue is not
        node<Type>* nodeToBeDeleted = head;     //          empty!

        head = head -> next;
        if (head == NULL)  rear = NULL;

        delete nodeToBeDeleted;
        return valueForReturn;
    }

    void appendNode (node<Type>* nodeOn) // An incoming node is appended.
    {
        nodeOn -> next = NULL;    // As the end-node, it should "point to" NULL.
```

```
        if ( empty() )    // if the queue is empty, nodeOn is its first and
          head = nodeOn;   // only node - so head (and rear) must point to it
        else
          rear -> next = nodeOn; // If queue is not empty,
                                  // nodeOn is linked onto the end.
        rear = nodeOn;
    }

  node<Type>*  deleteAndDeliverNode ()
    {
      node<Type>*  nodeForReturn = NULL;

      if ( !empty() )
        {
          nodeForReturn = head;
          head = head -> next;

          if (head == NULL)  rear = NULL;
        }

      return nodeForReturn;
    }

  void  deepCopy (Queue& copy)
    {
      node<Type>* nodeHolder;
      while ( !copy.empty() )
        {
          nodeHolder = copy.head;
          copy.head = copy.head -> next;
          delete nodeHolder;
        }
      copy.rear = NULL;

      node<Type>*  rovingPtr = head;
      while (rovingPtr != NULL)
        {
          copy.append( rovingPtr -> entity );
          rovingPtr = rovingPtr -> next;
        }
    }
};

void main()
  {
  // Define and initialize three independent queues.
  //  *** the data type of the entities to be held has to be given ***

      Queue<int>  queue1, queue2, queue3;

  // Put some content into queue 1.
      queue1.append( 111 );
      queue1.append( 222 );
      queue1.append( 333 );

  // Print the queues.
      cout << "\nQueue 1:";
      queue1.printQueue();
      cout << "\nQueue 2:";
      queue2.printQueue();
      cout << "\nQueue 3:";
      queue3.printQueue();

  // Copy Queue 1  into  Queue 3.
      queue1.deepCopy( queue3 );

  // Move the front node from Queue 1 onto Queue 2.
      node<int>* nodeHolder = queue1.deleteAndDeliverNode();
      queue2.appendNode( nodeHolder );
```

```
// Display the entity from the current head of Queue 1 and delete it from queue.
    cout << "\n\n...from the front of Queue 1:   "
            << queue1.deleteAndDeliverEntity() << endl;

// Move the front node from Queue 1 onto Queue 2.
    nodeHolder = queue1.deleteAndDeliverNode();
    queue2.appendNode( nodeHolder );

// Print the queues.
    cout << "\nQueue 1:";
    queue1.printQueue();
    cout << "\nQueue 2:";
    queue2.printQueue();
    cout << "\nQueue 3:";
    queue3.printQueue();
}
```

5.12.A   Rewrite this final version of the program with the member functions belonging to the class *template* defined outside the class's specifier.

5.12.B   Test the program with three different kinds of queues: a queue of *int*, a queue of *Point* objects, and a queue of strings (i.e., *char*s*).

5.13   In Exercise 5.12.B, the *Queue* class template was used to forge three independent queues of three distinctly different kinds of entities: *ints, Points*, and strings. A queue of type *Queue<int>* held int *ints*; a queue of type *Queue<Point>* held the *Points*, and a queue of type *Queue<char*>* held the strings (in truth, the addresses of *NULL*-terminated *char* arrays.

How is a *Queue* template class instantiated that will hold all of these in the same queue? Since a single queue can contain objects of only a single type (i.e., the type denoted by the specifier in its instantiation), a subsuming type specifier has to be created. The mechanism is to set-up a class hierarchy in which all the different kinds of entities are derived from a common base class, and then to instantiate the container as holding "pointers to base objects." This works because any the address of any object from derived class can be stored in a pointer to a base class object.

A difficulty in the problem at hand is the absence of a means for placing language-provided data types (e.g., *int* and *char**) within a user-constructed hierarchy. Our contrivance is to fabricate two classes: a class called *Integer* whose only data member is an *int* and a class called *String*, whose only data member is a *char**. The derivation heirarchy will look like this:

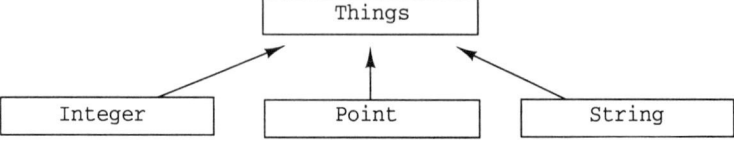

The less a container template expects of the objects it contains the better. This is why a container, as a rule, offers no services beyond storage. Our *Queue* class, however, will offer a function, *showQueue( )*, which displays the entities to which it holds pointers by way of a call to a function expected to be, for all entities, applicable, *showIt( )*. Thus, the *Integer, Point*, and *String* classes will each need a customized version of the virtual *showIt( )* defined in *Things*. As protection against ever having a class derived from

Things which yields objects unable to respond to a "*showIt()* message," *Things::showIt()* is declared to be a pure virtual function.

Study and run the following program. Modify the *showQueue()* function so that the queue is displayed vertically instead of horizontally. Then, enhance the program so that the same queue can hold "floats" and "Boxes." Rerun the program after activating the lines in *main()* provided for testing.

```cpp
#include <iostream.h>

class Things
  {
    public:
      virtual void showIt() = 0;
  };

class Integer : public Things
  {
    private:
      int value;

    public:
      Integer(int forValue) : value(forValue)
        {

        }
      void showIt()
        {
          cout << " " << value << " ";
        }
  };

class Point : public Things
  {
    private:
      int x, y;

    public:
      Point(int abscissa, int ordinate) : x(abscissa), y(ordinate)
        {

        }
      Point() : x(0), y(0)
        {

        }
      void showIt()
        {
          cout << " (" << x << ", " << y << ") ";
        }
  };

class String : public Things
  {
    public:
      char* stringPtr;

      String(char* ptr) : stringPtr(ptr)
        {

        }
      void showIt()
        {
          cout << " " << stringPtr << " ";
        }
  };

template <class Type>
```

```
struct node
  {
    Type    entity;
    node*   next;
  };

template <class T>
class Queue
  {
    private:
      node<T> *head, *rear;

      public:
        Queue();
        ~Queue();
        int empty();
        void append (T value);
        void showQueue();
  };

template <class T>
Queue<T>::Queue() : head(NULL), rear(NULL)
  {
  }

template <class T>
Queue<T>::~Queue()
  {
    node<T>*  nodeHolder;
    while ( !empty() )
      {
        nodeHolder = head;
        head = head -> next;
        delete nodeHolder;
      {
  }

template <class T>
int Queue<T>::empty()
  {
    if (head == NULL) return 1;  // True, the queue is empty
    else return 0;
  }

template <class T>
void Queue<T>::append (T value)
  {
    node<T>*  newNode = new node<T>;

    newNode -> entity = value;
    newNode -> next   = NULL;

    if ( empty() )
      head = newNode;
    else
      rear -> next - newNode;

    rear = newNode;
  }

template <class T>
void Queue<T>::showQueue()
  {
    node<T>*  rovingPtr = head;
    cout << endl;

    if ( empty() ) cout << "+-+-+-+-+-+-+-queue empty-+-+-+-+-+-+-+";

    while (rovingPtr != NULL)
      {
```

```
                    (rovingPtr -> entity) -> showIt(); // Not via the output operator, <<.
                    cout << endl;
                    rovingPtr = rovingPtr -> next;
            }
        cout << endl;
    }

    void main()
    {
        // Define and exercise a Queue of Things.
        Queue<Things*> thingQ;

        // Get some "Things".
        Integer *int1 = new Integer(1),    *int2 = new Integer(2);
        Point   *pnt1 = new Point(1,11),   *pnt2 = new Point(2,22);
        String  *str1 = new String("one"), *str2 = new String("two");

        // Put our "Things" on the thingQ.
        thingQ.append( int1 ); thingQ.append( int2 );
        thingQ.append( pnt1 ); thingQ.append( pnt2 );
        thingQ.append( str1 ); thingQ.append( str2 );

        // Print the thingQ.
        thingQ.showQueue();

        // Print the thingQ.
        thingQ.showQueue();

        // Get two Float objects, append them onto the thingQ, show the queue.
        // Float *flo1 = new Float(1.1111111), *flo2 = new Float(2.2222222);
        // thingQ.append( flo1 );  thingQ.append( flo2 );
        // thingQ.showQueue();

        // Get two Box objects, append them onto the thingQ, show the queue.
        // Box *box1 = new Box(5,3,'1'), *box2 = new Box(8,4,'2');
        // thingQ.append( box1 );  thingQ.append( box2 );
        // thingQ.showQueue();
    }
```

5.14 A traditional application in which multiple queues are needed is the radix sort, the procedure used on mechanical sorting machines to order punched cards on the basis of an identification "key" within the group columns constituting that field. From the standpoint of the study of algorithms, the radix sort is interesting because its time complexity is $O(N)$, it works without comparing keys, and it is stable (meaning the relative order of "records" that have the same key is preserved).

We describe how the sort was performed on punched card sorters in order to convey the action of the algorithm. Then we give a full implementation in which queues replace the machine's input bin and distribution bins. The exercise is to rewrite the *Queue* class as a *template* so that it can be used in conjunction with radix sorts of *struct*s of any kind, which contain an *int* member named *key*. (Sorting is with respect to values of *key*.)

Background on the hardware

Input on a sorting (or "tabulating") machine is by way of a bin on the top right end of the machine into which is placed the collection of cards comprising the file to be sorted. Cards pass from the input bin, through a "reader" that recognizes the value of the punch on a pre-set column, and are conveyed to the bin where cards with the respective punch are deposited. There is a separate bin for each numerical digit (0, 1, 2, . . . , 9). For instance, suppose cards (physical analogues for records or structs) had identification numbers punched into columns 1 through 3, and that the read brush were positioned over column 3. If a card had an 8 punched into column 3, it would be dropped into the 8 bin. A card behind this one in the data set which also had an 8 punched into column 3 would be dropped on top of it. To help you visualize this, here is a picture of a punch card and a sorter:

The punch card was invented by Herman Hollerith in the 1880s. The set of perforations and their interpretation as alphabetic characters (note, only capitals), numerals, and special symbols is known as the Hollerith code.

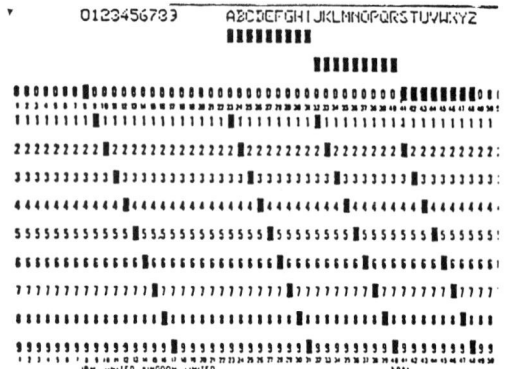

An early mechanical sorting machine:

distribution bins

Action of the "Least-Significant Digit First" Radix Sort

Keys in this example (and the following program) are three-digit *ints*.

Step 1:   Pass 1, Distribution Phase

The *struct*s to be sorted are place in the machine's input bin. The "read brush" is anchored over the the column holding the key's least significant digit.

The machine is turned on, and for each *struct* the least significant digit of its key is read

and the *struct* is coveyed to the bin for collecting *struct*s with that numeral.

The results of this distribution are shown in the following.

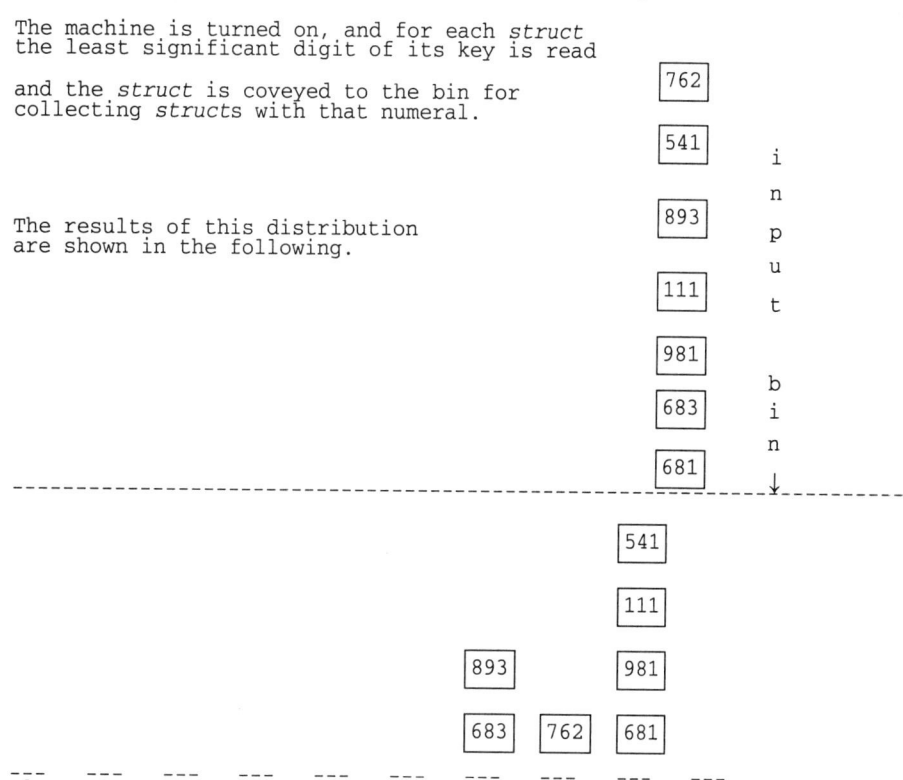

```
                                  762
                                  541      i
                                           n
                                  893      p
                                           u
                                  111      t
                                  981
                                  683      b
                                           i
                                  681      n
                                           ↓
  ----------------------------------------------

                          541
                          111
                  893     981
                  683 762 681
  --- --- --- --- --- --- --- --- --- ---
   9   8   7   6   5   4   3   2   1   0
  bin bin bin bin bin bin bin bin bin bin

              collection bins
```

Step 2: Pass, Collection Phase

Collect the cards from the bins, removing the cards (if any) from bin 0, placing on top of them the cards (if any) from bin 1, placing on top of them the cards (if any) from bin 2, and so on through bin 9.

The data set is reordered so that it now appears as shown to the right. Notice that keys are sorted on the least significant digit (the units digit).

```
893 |
    |--from bin 3
683 |
762 |--from bin 2
541 |
111 |
    |--from bin 1
981 |
681 |
```

Another pass is taken through the data set, replicating the distribution phase and collection phase of the last pass, for the key's next digit to the left, which is the 10s' place. The data set as it emerged from the last pass is put into the sorter's input bin.

Step 3: Pass 2, Distribution Phase

Read the 10s' digit of each key
and drop the *struct* into the bin

for collecting *structs* with that
numeral. (Same action as Step~1.)

The results of this distribution
are shown in the following.

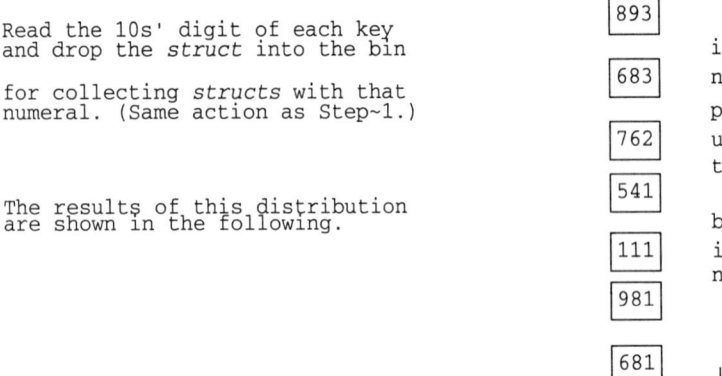

```
 683

 981

893  681      762      541      111
---  ---  ---  ---  ---  ---  ---  ---  ---  ---
 9    8    7    6    5    4    3    2    1    0
bin  bin  bin  bin  bin  bin  bin  bin  bin  bin
                  collection bins
```

Step 4: Pass 2, Collection Phase

Collect the cards from the bins, removing
the cards (if any) from bin 0, placing on top
of them the cards (if any) from bin 1,
placing on top of them the cards (if any)
from bin 2, and so on through bin 9.
(This is the same action as in Step 2.)

The data set is repermuted set so that
it now appears as shown to the right.
Notice that keys are sorted with respect
to their rightmost digits.

```
893|--from bin 9

683|

981|--from bin 8

681|

762|--from bin 6

541|--from bin 4

111|--from bin 1
```

Because keys have three places, a third pass is needed to complete the sort. Once again, the data set as it emerged from the last pass constitutes the input for the present pass. The collected cards are put in the input bin:

Step 5: Pass 3, Distribution Phase

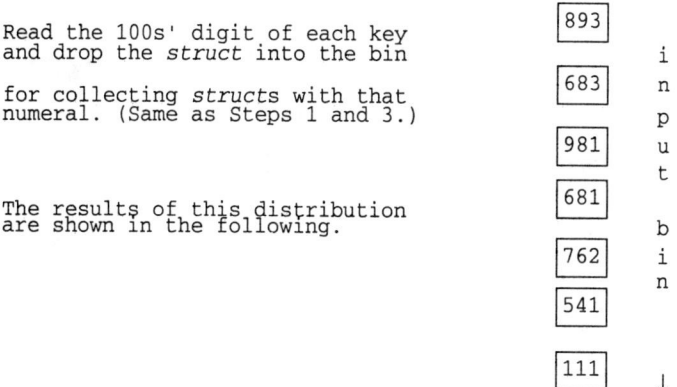

Read the 100s' digit of each key and drop the *struct* into the bin

for collecting *structs* with that numeral. (Same as Steps 1 and 3.)

The results of this distribution are shown in the following.

```
                    683

  981  893  762  681  541                    111
  ---  ---  ---  ---  ---  ---  ---  ---  ---  ---
   9    8    7    6    5    4    3    2    1    0
  bin  bin  bin  bin  bin  bin  bin  bin  bin  bin
                  collection bins
```

Step 6: Pass 3, Collection Phase

Collect the cards from the bins, removing the cards (in any) from bin 0, placing on top of them the cards (if any) from bin 1, placing on top of them the cards (if any) from bin 2, and so on through bin 9. (This is the same action as in Steps 2 and 4.)

The data set, shown to the right, is now sorted with respect to the keys' three rightmost digits. Thus these *structs*, having three-numeral keys, are fully sorted.

```
981|--from bin 9

893|--from bin 8

762|--from bin 7

683|
    |--from bin 6
681|

541|--from bin 5

111|--from bin 1
```

Implementing the Radix Sort in C++

A queue is a linear storage structure in which items are removed only from the front and added only to the back.

The data set, as it sits in the input bin, can be thought of as a queue because structs are taken for processing form the front.

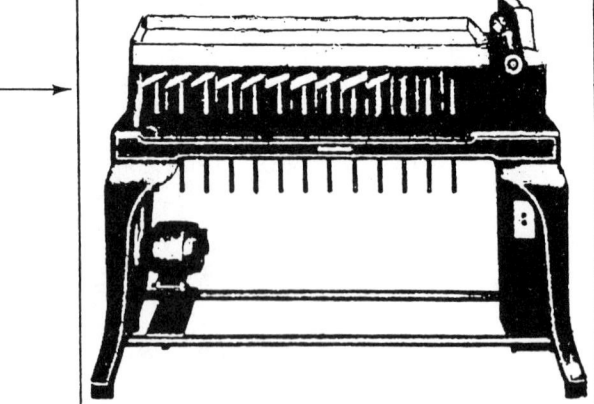

Each bin can be thought of as a queue because deposited structs are being dropped onto the end of the set already present.

Although a queue as an abstract data type (a formal construct) can be implemented in a variety of ways, a particularly good realization for this application is as a linked list of *structs*. A *struct*, as a unit of memory, can be thought of just like a card-stock record that can be moved from a master data set into a bin. Moving a card-stock record from the data set into a bin is accomplished by:

- copying the address of the node at the head of the data set queue into a variable
  (e.g., *currentRec = head; //pseudo code, is head probably private*);

- updating the *head* of the data set queue with the address of the next *struct* in line
  (e.g., *head = head -> next; //pseudo code*);

- reading the needed numeral from the *key* of the *currentRec*
  (e.g., *binNum = extractDigit(currentRec->key, place);*);

- appending the *currentRec* onto the end of the queue of *structs* representing bin number *binNum*
  (e.g., *bin[binNum].appendNode(currentRec);*).

Individual *structs* may be conceptualized as if they were things, just like punch cards, that can be picked up, examined, and moved from place to place. This is productive because dynamically allocated *structs* are logically mobile: their logical position is totally independent of their physical residence in memory.

In writing our program, we visualized the sorting machine's bank of bins as an array of queues. Each bin is an independent queue, with its own head and rear; but being elements in an array, each queue can be directly accessed by way of a subscript. Subscripts represent bin numbers. If we have an appropriate class called *Queue*, we may define the 10 bins like this:

```
Queue bin[10];  // Subscript range is 0..9, just what we need.
```

Here is our actual implementation of the algorithm for the radix sort. You should be able to see how directly it follows from the visualization of the process.

```
    void radixSort(Queue& data, int placesInKey)
    {
        Queue  bin[10];

        node*  currentRec;
        int    key;
        int    binNum;

        for (int place = 1; place <= placesInKey; place++)
        {
            while( ! data.empty() )                        // Distribution phase.
            {
                currentRec = data.deleteAndDeliverNode();
                key        = currentRec -> key;
                binNum     = extractDigit(key, place);
                bin[binNum].appendNode(currentRec);
            }

            for (binNum = 0; binNum < 10; binNum++)        // Collection phase.
                data.appendQueue( bin[binNum] );
        }
    }
```

The full program follows. Notice that the *Queue* class is specialized: an instantiation can only be a queue of *node* structures, and the node structure was designed specifically with the possibility in mind of being on a queue (i.e., its specification included a *node** member to hold the address of the *struct* behind it).

```
    struct node
    {
        int    key;            // Record identification number.

        char   substance[2];   // Represents any number of satellite
                               // members holding substantive info

        node* next;            // to enable these nodes to be linked.
    };
```

Reengineer the *Queue* class as a container (i.e., as a *template*) so that it is capable of supplying queues for holding any kind of struct — in particular, *struct*s that do not have a "next" pointer member (this is a piece of low-level mechanics that should be hidden from the user's data). You may, however, presume that all *struct*s have an *int* member named *key*, and that sorting is performed with respect to it.

```
#include <iostream.h>
#include <iomanip.h>   // For setw().

struct node
{
    int    key;           // Record identification number.
    char   substance[2];  // Represents content of the record.
    node* next;           // A link.
};

class Queue
{
    private:
        node *head, *rear;

    public:
        Queue() : head(NULL), rear(NULL)   // Constructor.
        {
        }

        ~Queue()                            // Destructor.
        {
            node*  nodeHolder;              // Delete the nodes
            while ( !empty() )              // on the queue
```

```
            {                              // being destructed
                nodeHolder = head;        //    --or else--
                head = head -> next;      // have a memory leak.
                delete nodeHolder;
            }
    }

int empty()
    {
        if (head == NULL) return 1;  // True, the queue is empty.
        else return 0;
    }

void append (int value)
    {
        node*  newNode = new node;

        newNode -> key   = value;
        newNode -> next  = NULL;

        if ( empty() )
            head = newNode;
        else
            rear -> next = newNode;

        rear = newNode;
    }

void appendNode (node* nodeOn)
    {
        nodeOn -> next = NULL;

        if ( empty() )
            head = nodeOn;
        else
            rear -> next = nodeOn;

        rear = nodeOn;
    }

void appendQueue(Queue& q)
    {
        if (q.head != NULL)
        {
            if (head == NULL)
            {
                head = q.head;
                rear = q.rear;
            }
            else
            {
                rear -> next = q.head;
                rear = q.rear;
            }

            q.head = NULL;
            q.rear = NULL;
        }
    }

int deleteAndDeliverKey ()
    {
        int    valueForReturn  = head -> key;
        node*  nodeToBeDeleted = head;
        head = head -> next;
        if (head == NULL)  rear = NULL;

        delete nodeToBeDeleted;
        return valueForReturn;
    }
```

```
            node*  deleteAndDeliverNode ()
            {
                node*  nodeForReturn = NULL;

                if ( !empty() )
                {
                    nodeForReturn = head;
                    head = head -> next;

                    if (head == NULL)  rear = NULL;
                }

                return nodeForReturn;
            }

        void printQueue()
        {                               // If the queue is empty,
            node*  rovingPtr = head; // rovingPtr will equal NULL.
            cout << endl;

            if ( empty() )
                cout << "+-+-+-+-+-+-+-queue empty-+-+-+-+-+-+-+";

            while (rovingPtr != NULL)
            {
                cout << endl;
                for (int i = 0; (i < 10  &&  rovingPtr != NULL); i++)
                {
                    cout<< setw(5) << rovingPtr -> key;
                    rovingPtr = rovingPtr -> next;
                }
            }

            cout << endl;
        }
};    // End of class Queue.

                    // Returns a value between 0 and 1, noninclusive
double getRandom() // (i.e., a value from the standard uniform
                    // distribution).
{
    static double random      = 0.319999876777;
    const  long    multiplier = 711237237;

    double product = multiplier * random;

    random = product - long(product);

    return random;
}

void getData(Queue& q, int n, int placesInKey)
{
    double random;
    int    id;
    long   powOf10 = 1;

    for (int i = 1; i <= placesInKey; i++)  powOf10 *= 10;

    for (i = 0; i < n; i++)
    {
        random = getRandom();  // Random is between 0 and 1,
                                // noninclusive.
        id = int(powOf10 * random);
        q.append(id);
    }
}
```

```
int  extractDigit(int key, int place)
{
    int returnDigit;
    int tenThousands, thousands, hundreds, tens, ones;

    tenThousands = key / 10000;    // Integer divide.

    key = key - tenThousands * 10000;
    thousands = key / 1000;

    key = key - thousands * 1000;
    hundreds = key / 100;

    key = key - hundreds * 100;
    tens = key / 10;

    key = key - tens * 10;
    ones = key;

    switch (place)
    {
        case 5 : returnDigit = tenThousands; break;
        case 4 : returnDigit = thousands;    break;
        case 3 : returnDigit = hundreds;     break;
        case 2 : returnDigit = tens;         break;
        case 1 : returnDigit = ones;         break;
        default: returnDigit = 0;
    }

    return returnDigit;
}
// There is a much more concise way to extract this numeral.
// Given a function:
//
//              int tenToTheP(int p); // Prototype.
//
// that returns the value of 10 raised to the power p
// (if passed 3 it would return 1000), the digit for return
// may be directly computed with:
//
//      (key % tenToTheP(place) ) / tenToTheP(place-1)

void testNonDecreasingOrder (Queue& q)
{
    int okay = 1;   // So far everything is okay.

    int leftKey = q.deleteAndDeliverKey();
    int rightKey;

    while (!q.empty() && okay)
    {
        rightKey = q.deleteAndDeliverKey();
        if (leftKey > rightKey)  okay = 0;
        leftKey = rightKey;
    }

    if (okay)  cout << endl << "**Successful Sort**" << endl;
    else cout<<endl<< "----> Sorting Function is Faulty <----" <<endl;
}

void radixSort(Queue& data, int placesInKey)
{
    Queue  bin[10];

    node*  currentRec;
    int    key;
    int    binNum;
```

```
    for (int place = 1; place <= placesInKey; place++)
    {
        while( ! data.empty() )                    // Distribution phase.
        {
            currentRec = data.deleteAndDeliverNode();
            key        = currentRec -> key;
            binNum     = extractDigit(key, place);
            bin[binNum].appendNode(currentRec);
        }

        for (binNum = 0; binNum < 10; binNum++)   // Collection phase.
            data.appendQueue( bin[binNum] );
    }
}

void main()
{
    // Set the number of places in the key:
    int placesInKey = 3;

    // Set number of "records" in the "datafile":
    int size = 1000;

    // Define and initialize a queue to hold the data set.
    Queue  data;

    // Put 1000 structs with random values as keys into the data queue.
    //  **    Values for keys range from 0 through 999 inclusive;
    //  **    duplicate values are permitted.

    getData( data, size, placesInKey );

    // Display the unsorted data set to see what the values look like.
    cout << endl << "                       unsorted data";
    data.printQueue();

    // Sort the data with a radix sort.
    radixSort( data, placesInKey );

    // Display the data set, in case you want to see the results.
    data.printQueue();

    // Test the data set to be certain it is in nondescending order.
    testNonDecreasingOrder( data );
}
```

Answers to Odd-Numbered — Exercises

Chapter 1

1.1 It was described in 1972 in *Structured Programming* by Dahl, Dijkstra, and Hoare.

1.3.A See answer to Exercise 4.1.A.

1.3.B None.

1.5 No.

1.7.A True.

1.7.B True.

1.7.C False.

1.7.D True.

1.7.E True.

1.7.F   False (No subranges).

1.7.G   True.

1.7.H   True.

1.7.I   True.

1.7.J   True.

1.7.K   False.

1.7.L   True.

Chapter 2

2.1.A
```
#include <iostream.h>
#include <iomanip.h>    // For the i/o manipulators setw() and setprecision()
          // and for setting i/o stream flags.

void main()
    {
    //Print column numbers (read vertically):
    cout << endl;
    cout << "         1111111111222222222233333333334444444444445" << endl;
    cout << "123456789012345678901234567890123456789012345678901234567890" << endl;

    float float1, float2, float3, float4, float5;  // Five variables defined.

    float1 = 100;        // Integer literal assigned to a float.
    float2 = 1000.0;     // Float literal with an integral value.
    float3 = 12.34567;   // To 2 places, the literal rounds to 12.35.
    float4 = .123456;    // No digit to the left of the decimal.
    float5 = 1234567.5;  // A relatively large value (over a million).

    //* Statements for selecting either fixed or scientific notation.  The
    //* setting remains in effect within the program until explicitly reset.

    cout << setiosflags(ios::fixed);   // Fixed notation.

    //  cout << resetiosflags(ios::fixed) << setiosflags(ios:: scientific);

    //* Statements for selecting either to see the decimal point and
    //* to pad trailing places to the right of the point (out to the
    //* set precision) with zeros or to suppress trailing zeros to the
    //* right of the point as well as the point itself when there is
    //* no fractional component.  The setting remains in effect within
    //* the program until explicitly reset.

    cout << setiosflags(ios::showpoint); // Pads trailing places to the right
                                         // of the decimal point with zeros.

    //   cout << resetiosflags(ios::showpoint); //Suppresses trailing filler.
```

```
//* Statement for setting the maximum number of places displayed to
//* the right of the decimal point.  If the i/o stream flag "showpoint"
//* is on, the decimal and this number of places is displayed whether
//* or not the value to be displayed contains this much precision.

cout << setprecision(2); // Displays two places to the right of the decimal.

      // Here setw() sets the width of only the
      // the next field to be displayed.
cout << endl;

cout << setw(15) << float1 << setw(20) << float1 << endl;
cout << setw(15) << float2 << setw(20) << float2 << endl;
cout << setw(15) << float3 << setw(20) << float3 << endl;
cout << setw(15) << float4 << setw(20) << float4 << endl;
cout << setw(15) << float5 << setw(20) << float5 << endl;
}
```

2.1.B
```
#include <iostream.h>
#include <iomanip.h>     // For the i/o manipulators setw() and setprecision()
                         // and for setting i/o stream flags.

void main()
   {
   // Print column numbers (read vertically):
   cout << endl;
   cout << "          1111111111222222222233333333334444444445" << endl;
   cout << "123456789012345678901234567890123456789012345678901234567890" << endl;

   float float1, float2, float3, float4, float5; // Five variables defined.

   float1 = 100;          // Integer literal assigned to a float.
   float2 = 1000.0;       // Float literal with an integral value.
   float3 = 12.34567;     // To 2 places, the literal rounds to 12.35.
   float4 = .123456;      // No digit to the left of the decimal.
   float5 = 1234567.5;    // A relatively large value (over a million).

   //* Statements for selecting either fixed or scientific notation.  The
   //* setting remains in effect within the program until explicitly reset.

   cout << setiosflags(ios::fixed);    // Fixed notation.

   //  cout << resetiosflags(ios::fixed) << setiosflags(ios:: scientific);

   //* Statements for selecting either to see the decimal point and
   //* to pad trailing places to the right of the point (out to the
   //* set precision) with zeros or to suppress trailing zeros to the
   //* right of the point as well as the point itself when there is
   //* no fractional component.  The setting remains in effect within
   //* the program until explicitly reset.

   cout << setiosflags(ios::showpoint); // Pads trailing places to the right
                                        // of the decimal point with zeros.

   //   cout << resetiosflags(ios::showpoint); //Suppresses trailing filler.

   //* Statement for setting the maximum number of places displayed to
   //* the right of the decimal point.  If the i/o stream flag "showpoint"
   //* is on, the decimal and this number of places is displayed whether
   //* or not the value to be displayed contains this much precision.

   cout << setprecision(2); // Displays two places to the right of the decimal
                            // setw() sets the width of only the
                            // the next field to be displayed.
```

```
    cout << endl;

    cout << setw(15) << float1 << setw(20) << float1 << endl;

    cout << resetiosflags(ios::fixed) << setiosflags(ios::scientific);
    cout << setw(15) << float2 << setw(20) << float2 << endl;

    cout << resetiosflags(ios::scientific) << setiosflags(ios::fixed);
    cout << setw(15) << float3 << setw(20) << float3 << endl;

    cout << resetiosflags(ios::fixed) << setiosflags(ios::scientific);
    cout << setw(15) << float4 << setw(20) << float4 << endl;

    cout << resetiosflags(ios::scientific) << setiosflags(ios::fixed);
    cout << setw(15) << float5 << setw(20) << float5 << endl;
}
```

2.3

```
// Prints the ASCII values of the letters from A to Z.

#include <iostream.h>
#include <iomanip.h>

void main()
{
    char ch;

    cout << endl;
    cout << "ASCII value - letter        ASCII value - letter" << endl;

    for (ch = 'A';  ch <= 'M';  ch = ch + 1)
    {
        cout<<setw(4) <<" "<<int(ch)    <<setw(10)<<" "<<      ch;
        cout<<setw(16)<<" "<<int(ch+13)<<setw(10)<<" "<<char(ch+13)<<endl;
    }
}
```

2.5

```
#include <iostream.h>

void main()
{
    int num1, num2;
    char test = 'y';   // For holding the user's indicating of whether or
                       // not to run the algorithm again;  the 'y'
                       // initialization guarantees it will run once
                       // (A do..while loop would avoid the necessity for
                       // this initialization.)

    while (test == 'y' || test == 'Y')
    {
        cout << "Please enter a positive, whole number:   ";
        cin  >> num1;
        cout << "Enter another positive, whole number:     ";
        cin  >> num2;

        while (num1 != num2) // Condition under which GCD has not been found.
        {
            if (num1 > num2)
                num1 = num1 - num2; // Larger num replaced by the difference.
            else
                num2 = num2 - num1;
        }

        cout<<endl<<"Their greatest common divisor is:   "<<num1<<endl;
```

```
        cout<<"Do you want to try again with two more numbers (Y or N)?   ";
        cin >> test;

        while (test != 'y' && test != 'Y' && test != 'n' && test != 'N')
            {
            cout << endl << "Invalid Entry.  Try again (Y or N)?   ";
            cin  >> test;
            }
        cout << endl; //Flushes output buffer; necessary for some printers.
        }
    }
```

2.7

```
#include <iostream.h>
#include <iomanip.h>

float getRoot(float num, int root);     // Function prototype.
    // Returns the ith root of num.

float absVal(float argument);           // Function prototype.
    // Returns the absolute value of the argument.

float power(float num, int exponent);  // Function prototype.
    // Returns num raised to the exponent.

void main()
    {
    float number;   // Number whose root will be found.
    int   root;
    char  YorN;     // Algorithm repetition.

    do
        {
        cout << endl;
        cout << "****Finding the Nth root of a given number****" << endl;
        cout << "Please enter the number whose root you want:   ";
        cin  >> number;
        cout << endl<<"Please enter the root (a whole, positive number):   ";
        cin  >> root;

        cout << endl << "The " << root << " root of " << number << " is ";
        cout << setprecision(3) << setiosflags(ios::showpoint);
        cout << getRoot(number, root) << endl << endl;

        do
            {
            cout<<"Do you want to find the root of another number (Y/N)?   ";
            cin >> YorN;
            }
        while (YorN != 'y' && YorN != 'Y' && YorN != 'n' && YorN != 'N');
        }
    while (YorN == 'y' || YorN == 'Y');
    }

float getRoot(float num, int root)
    {
    float estimate = num/root;

    while ( absVal( (num - power(estimate,root))/num ) >= 0.001 )
        {
        estimate = (num + (root-1)*power(estimate,root) )  /
        ( root*power(estimate, root-1) );
        }

    return estimate;
    }
```

```
float absVal (float argument)
    {
    if (argument >= 0)   return argument;
    else return -1 * argument;
    }

float power (float num, int exponent)
    {
    int i;
    float accum = 1;
    for (i = 1; i <= exponent; i = i+1)   accum = accum * num;
    return accum;
    }
```

2.9

```
#include <iostream.h>
#include <math.h>      // For sin().

void main()
    {
    char screen[21][73];   // 21 rows (0..20) and 73 columns (0..72).

    float radians;
    int   degrees;
    int   row, column;

    // The screen array is initialized to "blank".
    for (row = 0; row < 21; row = row + 1)
        {
        for (column = 0; column < 73; column = column + 1)
            {
            screen[row][column] = ' ';
            }
        }

    // The X-axis is installed at row 10, the middle of the screen array.
    for (column = 0; column < 73; column = column + 1)
        {
        screen[10][column] = '-';
        }

    // The Y-axis is installed in column 0, the far left of the screen array.
    for (row = 0; row < 21; row = row + 1)
        {
        screen[row][0] = '|';
        }

    // The sine function is plotted; to make it fit, take every 5th degree.
    for (degrees = 0; degrees <= 360; degrees = degrees + 5)
        {
        column = degrees/5;    //this gets us from column 0 to column 72

        radians = (degrees * 3.14159)/180;   // Here, sin() function require the
                                             // argument angle in radians.

        row = int( 10*sin(radians) + 0.5) + 10;
        // Multiplying times 10 gives a vertical expanse of 10..-10;
        // adding .5 makes the cast's truncation perform as a round;
        // adding 10 transforms the expanse to 20..0 to fit the array.

        screen[row][column] = '*';
        }

    // Display the screen array.
    for (row = 20; row > -1; row = row -1)
        {
```

```
        for (column = 0; column < 73; column++)
          {
           cout << screen[row][column];    // Displays one row.
          }
        cout << endl;                      // Linefeed between rows.
      }
  }
```

2.11.C

```
    #include <iostream.h>

    void main()
      {
        char val;

        for (val = 0; val <= 126; val = val + 1)
          {
           if (val % 20 == 0)  cout << endl;    // Linefeed every 20 chars.

           if (val != 26)        cout << val;    // Character 26 is Ctrl-Z,
                                                 // the end-of-file marker;
                                                 // cannot output after that.

           cout.put(' ');                        // Space between characters.
          }
      }
```

2.13.A

```
    #include <fstream.h>

    void main()
      {
        ifstream  roster ("a:data2-13.dat");   // CRUCIAL:  BE SURE THAT THIS
                                               //           FILE EXISTS AND
                                               //           IS ON THE DEVICE
                                               //           INDICATED!

        char name[10];                // to hold student's name
        int score1, score2, average;  // for averaging calculations

        roster >> name;               // gets the first name

        while ( ! roster.eof() )
          {
           roster >> score1;                // gets the first number
           roster >> score2;                // gets the second number
           average = (score1 + score2) / 2;
           cout << name << "   " << average << endl;
```

2.13.B

```
#include <fstream.h>

void main()
  {
    ifstream  roster ("a:data2-13.dat");

    char singleChar; // To store the value obtained with the get() function.

    roster.get(singleChar);
```

```
    while ( ! roster.eof() )
      {
        cout << singleChar;
        roster.get(singleChar);
      }

    cout << endl;    // Remember, it is not a bad idea to end your
                     // output with an endl to ensure a buffer flush.
  }
```

2.13.C

```
#include <fstream.h>

void main()
  {
    ifstream  roster ("a:data-13.dat");

    char lineOfChar[50];  // To store value obtained with getline() function.
    int j = 1;            // To provide line numbers.

    while ( ! roster.eof() )
      {
        roster.getline(lineOfChar,50);

        cout << j << ".    " << lineOfChar << endl; // Here the linefeeds are
        j = j + 1;                                  // the disposed of sentinel.
      }
  }
```

2.15

```
#include <fstream.h>

typedef   struct node*   nodePtr;

struct node
  {
    char      letter;
    nodePtr   next;
  };

void initializeList(nodePtr& head, nodePtr& rear)
  {
    head = NULL;  // Could just as well have been:  head = 0;
    rear = NULL;  // Could just as well have been:  rear = 0;
  }

///////////////////////////// prototypes

void append (nodePtr& head, nodePtr& rear, char letter);
void insert (nodePtr& head, nodePtr& rear, char letter, int place);
void deleteFront (nodePtr& head, nodePtr& rear);
void remove (nodePtr& head, nodePtr& rear, int nodeNumToGo);
void spacer();
void print(nodePtr head);

///////////////////////////// main()

void main()
  {
    nodePtr head, rear;
    initializeList(head,rear);

    char instruction; // The 'A' for append; the 'I' for insert; etc.
```

```
        char letter;        // The letter to be appended or inserted.

        int  nodeNum;       // The spot in the list where a node will be
                            // inserted (e.g. insert as node number 3) or
                            // deleted.

        ifstream data("A:DATA2-15.DAT");   // Data is in file A:DATA2-15.DAT

        data >> instruction;
        while (! data.eof())
          {
            switch (instruction)  // Instructions are all in upper case.
              {
                case 'A':  data >> letter;
                append(head, rear, letter);
                break;

                case 'D':  deleteFront(head,rear);
                break;

                case 'I' : data >> letter;
                data >> nodeNum;
                insert(head, rear, letter, nodeNum);
                break;

                case 'R':  data >> nodeNum;
                remove(head, rear, nodeNum);
                break;

                case 'P':  print(head);
                break;

                case 'S':  spacer();
                break;

                default  : cout << "\n** Error in Data - " << instruction
                                << " read as the instruction.\n";

              }     // End of switch statement.

          data >> instruction;

          }     // End of while loop.

      cout << "\n**Run Successfully Completed**" << endl;

  }     // End of main().

void append (nodePtr& head, nodePtr& rear, char letter)
  {
    nodePtr  newNode;

    newNode = new node;
    newNode -> letter = letter;
    newNode -> next   = NULL;

    if (head == NULL)  head = newNode;
    else   rear -> next = newNode;

    rear = newNode;
  }

void deleteFront (nodePtr& head, nodePtr& rear)
  {
    nodePtr  oldNode;

    oldNode = head;
```

```
            if (head != NULL) head = head -> next;  // If the list is not empty,
                                                     // then move the head along.
            if (head == NULL) rear = NULL;

            delete oldNode;    // This is okay, even if oldNode equals NULL.
        }

    void insert (nodePtr& head, nodePtr& rear, char letter, int place)
        {
        nodePtr  newNode;

        newNode = new node;
        newNode -> letter = letter;

        if ( head == NULL )    // If there are no nodes currently on the list.
            {
            head = newNode;
            rear = newNode;
            newNode -> next = NULL;
            }

        else
        if ( place == 1 )
            {
            newNode -> next = head;
            head = newNode;
            }

        else
            {
            nodePtr leftRovingPtr  = head;
            nodePtr rightRovingPtr = head -> next;
            int     currentPosition = 2;  // We're set to insert at spot 2.

            while ( (currentPosition < place) && (rightRovingPtr != NULL) )
                {
                leftRovingPtr  = rightRovingPtr;
                rightRovingPtr = rightRovingPtr -> next;
                currentPosition = currentPosition + 1;
                }

            leftRovingPtr -> next = newNode;
            newNode -> next       = rightRovingPtr;
            }
        }

    void remove (nodePtr& head, nodePtr& rear, int nodeNumToGo)
        {
        nodePtr  oldNode;

        if (head != NULL) // Don't try to remove anything if the list is empty.
            {
            if (nodeNumToGo == 1)
                {
                oldNode = head;
                head = head -> next;
                if (head == NULL)  rear = NULL;  // If list held this node only.
                delete oldNode;
                }
            else
                {
                nodePtr  leftRovingPtr   = head;
                nodePtr  middleRovingPtr = leftRovingPtr   -> next;
                nodePtr  rightRovingPtr  = middleRovingPtr -> next;

                int      currentNodeToGo = 2;
                while (currentNodeToGo<nodeNumToGo  &&  rightRovingPtr != NULL)
                    {
                    leftRovingPtr   = middleRovingPtr;
                    middleRovingPtr = rightRovingPtr;   // Node to get deleted.
                    rightRovingPtr  = rightRovingPtr -> next;
```

```
                        currentNodeToGo = currentNodeToGo + 1;
                    }

                oldNode = middleRovingPtr;
                leftRovingPtr -> next = rightRovingPtr;
                if (rightRovingPtr == NULL)  rear = leftRovingPtr;
                delete oldNode;
                }
            }
    }

void print(nodePtr head)
    {
    while (head != NULL)
        {
        cout << head -> letter;
        head = head -> next;
        }

    cout << endl;
    }

void spacer()
    {
    cout << endl;
    }
```

Chapter 3

Many of the exercises are demonstrations that illustrate syntax or explore semantics. Because they are not "problems," they have no answers.

3.1

```
#include <iostream.h>
#include <iomanip.h>

void main()
    {
    int temp = 135;

    cout << endl << "        starting temperature = " << temp;

    for (int minute = 1; minute <= 10; minute++)
        {
        temp -= 0.06*(temp - 38);
        cout << endl << " temperature after minute "
             << setw(2) << minute << ":   " << temp;
        }
    cout << endl;
    }
```

Here is the output.

```
        starting temperature = 135
temperature after minute  1:  129
temperature after minute  2:  123
temperature after minute  3:  117
temperature after minute  4:  112
temperature after minute  5:  107
temperature after minute  6:  102
```

```
temperature after minute  7:   98
temperature after minute  8:   94
temperature after minute  9:   90
temperature after minute 10:   86
```

3.3.E Used apart from the subscript operator, the name of an array designates the address to which the array is bound when it is defined; this is the memory location to which element 0 is cemented.

The compiler interprets the shown assignment as an attempt to update, with the address of *bye*, the address of *hi*. This latter cannot be updated because it is the base of address of an array, hence a constant.

3.5 Here is the typical WRONG answer. The fault is in the assignment statement marked ERROR. The variable *holder* can store addresses of *int*s, and the *int* whose address it stores can be updated with code as given; but because *holder* has not been loaded with an *int*'s address (it is uninitialized), its value is garbage and so it is pointing to garbage. Before we can assign to **holder*, *holder* must be given the address of a defined *int*.

```
/***   ERRONEOUS CODE   *   BE SURE YOU UNDERSTAND WHAT'S THE MATTER WITH IT    *
#include <iostream.h>                                                           *
void main()                                                                    *
{                                                                              *
    int a = 5, b = 10;                                                        *
                                                                              *
    int *aPtr = &a,  *bPtr = &b,  *holder;                                    *
                                                                              *
    cout << "\n before swap:  a = "  << *aPtr << ",   b = " << *bPtr;         *
                                                                              *
    *holder = *aPtr;  // the value of a is made the value of holder - ERROR*
    *aPtr   = *bPtr;  // the value of b is made the value of a               *
    *bPtr   = *holder; // the value of holder is made the value of b         *
                                                                              *
    cout << "\n after swap:  a = "  << *aPtr << ",   b = " << *bPtr;          *
    cout << endl;                                                            *
}                                                                           *
************************************************************************************/

// Correct answer.

#include <iostream.h>
void main()
{
    int a = 5, b = 10;

    int *aPtr = &a,  *bPtr = &b,  *holder;

    cout << "\n before swap:  a = "  << *aPtr << ",   b = " << *bPtr;

    // Get an int for holder to point to and
    // assign its address to holder.
    int temp;
    holder = &temp;     // Now holder points to a location we can use.

    *holder = *aPtr;  // The value of a is made the value of temp.
    *aPtr   = *bPtr;  // The value of b is made the value of a.
    *bPtr   = *holder; // The value of holder is made the value of b.

    cout << "\n after swap:  a = "  << *aPtr << ",   b = " << *bPtr;
    cout << endl;
}
```

3.13 This is the program that, when compiled and run as an executable file, displays all the strings found along the command line.

```cpp
#include <iostream.h>
#include <iomanip.h>  // For setw().

void main(int argc, char* argv[])
    {
    cout << "\n number of arguments, "
        << "including name of program's .EXE file:  "
        << argc;

    // Here argv[0] is the name of the program's .EXE file.
    // Here argv[1] is the first command line argument.
    // Here argv[2] is the second command line argument.
    //      .
    //      .
    //      .
    // Here argv[argc-1] is the last of the command line arguments.

    cout << "\n\n These are:";

    for (int i = 0; i < argc; i++)
        {
        cout << "\n" << setw(12) << " "
            << setw(2) << i << ".  " <<argv[i];
        }

    cout << endl;
    }
```

3.15

```cpp
#include <iostream.h>
#include <iomanip.h>

float averagePurchase (float amtOfCurrentPurchase)
    {
    static int   numOfPurchases = 0;
    static float totalAmount = 0;

    numOfPurchases++;
    totalAmount += amtOfCurrentPurchase;

    return  totalAmount/numOfPurchases;
    }

void main()
    {
    int    purchaseNum;
    float amount = 0;

    cout << setiosflags(ios::showpoint) << setprecision(2);

    for (purchaseNum = 1; purchaseNum <= 5; purchaseNum++)
        {
        amount += 10;
        cout << "\n current amt: " << amount
            << "    average amount: "
            << setw(6) << averagePurchase(amount);
        }

    cout << endl;
    }
```

Here is the output.

```
current amt: 10.00     average amount:  10.00
current amt: 20.00     average amount:  15.00
current amt: 30.00     average amount:  20.00
current amt: 40.00     average amount:  25.00
current amt: 50.00     average amount:  30.00
```

3.17.A

```
#include <iostream.h>

// Prototype for the drawBox() function; notice the default values
// for the arguments (argument names, here, are optional but helpful).

void drawBox(char symbol = '*', int length = 6, int height = 4);

void main()
   {
    // Calling drawBox(), displaying the default box.
    drawBox();
    cout << endl;

    // Replace default character with '#' in a box of the default size.
    drawBox('#');
    cout << endl;

    // Here '+' as the character, 25 as the length, default height.
    drawBox('+', 25);
    cout << endl;

    // Arguments to the left of a given actual argument must be provided;
    // this would have been an error:  drawBox( , 40, 6);
    drawBox('*', 40, 6);   // Default character must be explicitly given.
    cout << endl;
   }

void drawBox(char symbol, int length, int height)
   {
    const leftMargin = 25;

    if (length < 2)  length  = 2;
    if (height < 2)  height = 2;

    cout << endl << endl;

    // Top line.
    for (int i = 1; i <= leftMargin; i++) cout << " ";   // Top line.
    for (int j = 1; j <= length; j++) cout << symbol;
    cout << endl;

    // Left and right sides of middle lines.
    for (j = 1; j <= height-2; j++)
       {
        for (i = 1; i<= leftMargin; i++) cout << " ";
        cout << symbol;
        for (int k = 1; k <= length-2; k++) cout << " ";
        cout << symbol << endl;
       }

    // Bottom line.
    for (i = 1; i <= leftMargin; i++) cout << " ";
    for (j = 1; j <= length; j++) cout << symbol;
   }
```

Here is the output.

```
******
*    *
*    *
******

#####
#   #
#   #
#####

++++++++++++++++++++++++
+                      +
+                      +
++++++++++++++++++++++++

*****************************************
*                                       *
*                                       *
*                                       *
*****************************************
```

3.17.B

```
#include <iostream.h>

// Here leftMargin has been made a formal argument with a default value;
// when a corresponding actual argument is omitted in the call, the
// function will perform as before.

void drawBox(char symbol='*', int length=6, int height=4, int leftMargin=25);

void main()
{
    // Calling drawBox(), displaying the default box.
    drawBox();
    cout << endl;

    // Replace default character with '#' in a box of the default size.
    drawBox('#');
    cout << endl;

    // Here '+' as the character, 25 as the length, default height.
    drawBox('+', 25);
    cout << endl;

    // Arguments to the left of any given actual argument must be provided;
    // this would have been an error:  drawBox( , 40, 6);
    drawBox('*', 40, 6);   // default character must be explicitly given.
    cout << endl;

    // Print a box repeatedly with increasing left margins.
    for (int i = 1; i <= 5; i++)
    {
        drawBox('!', 25, 3, i*7);
    }

}

void drawBox(char symbol, int length, int height, int leftMargin)
{
    if (leftMargin < 2)  leftMargin = 2;
    if (length < 2)      length  = 2;
    if (height < 2)      height  = 2;

    cout << endl << endl;

    // Top line.
    for (int i = 1; i <= leftMargin; i++) cout << " ";  // top line
    for (int j = 1; j <= length; j++) cout << symbol;
    cout << endl;
```

```
        // Left and right sides of middle lines.
        for (j = 1; j <= height-2; j++)
          {
              for (i = 1; i<= leftMargin; i++) cout << " ";
              cout << symbol;
              for (int k = 1; k <= length-2; k++) cout << " ";
              cout << symbol << endl;
          }

        // Bottom line.
        for (i = 1; i <= leftMargin; i++) cout << " ";
        for (j = 1; j <= length; j++) cout << symbol;
    }
```

Here is the output.

```
                               ******
                               *    *
                               *    *
                               ******

                               ######
                               #    #
                               #    #
                               ######

                 +++++++++++++++++++++++++++
                 +                         +
                 +                         +
                 +++++++++++++++++++++++++++

          *********************************************
          *                                           *
          *                                           *
          *                                           *
          *                                           *
          *********************************************


       !!!!!!!!!!!!!!!!!!!!!!!!!!
       !!!!!!!!!!!!!!!!!!!!!!!!!!

          !!!!!!!!!!!!!!!!!!!!!!!!!!
          !!!!!!!!!!!!!!!!!!!!!!!!!!

             !!!!!!!!!!!!!!!!!!!!!!!!!!
             !!!!!!!!!!!!!!!!!!!!!!!!!!

                !!!!!!!!!!!!!!!!!!!!!!!!!!
                !!!!!!!!!!!!!!!!!!!!!!!!!!

                   !!!!!!!!!!!!!!!!!!!!!!!!!!
                   !!!!!!!!!!!!!!!!!!!!!!!!!!
```

Chapter 4

Many of the exercises are demonstrations that illustrate syntax or explore semantics.
Because they are not "problems," they have no answers.

4.1.A

```
#include <iostream.h>
```

```
class Box
{
    public:
        char symbol;

    private:
        int  length, height;

    public:
        void showBox();  // Prototype.

        void setSize()
        {
            int l, h;

            cout << "\nEnter a length (an int between 2 and 10):  ";
            cin >> l;

            if (l >= 2  &&  l <= 10)  length = l;
            else  length = 1;

            cout << "\nEnter a height (an int between 2 and 6):   ";
            cin >> h;

            if (h >= 2  &&  h <= 6)   height = h;
            else  height = 1;

            cout << "\nEnter a symbol:  ";
            cin >> symbol;

            showBox();
        }
};   // End of Box's class specifier.

void Box::showBox()
{
    cout << endl;
    for (int i = 1;  i <= height;  i++)
    {
        for (int j = 1;  j <= length;  j++)  cout << symbol;
        cout << endl;
    }
}

void main()
{
    Box large;
    cout << "\nPlease provide the specs for the large box:";
    large.setSize();  // length, height, and symbol (to be 'A') set here

    Box small;
    cout << "\n\nPlease provide the specs for the small box:";
    small.setSize();  // length, height, and symbol (to be 'B') set here

    cout << "\n\nDisplay of large:  stored at memory location "
         << &large << " in " << sizeof large << " bytes " << endl;
    large.showBox();

    cout << "\n\nDisplay of small:  stored at memory location "
         << &small << " in " << sizeof small << " bytes " << endl;
    small.showBox();

    //  Swapping the large and small.
    cout << "\n\n ** swap of large and small in progress " << endl;

    Box holder;
    holder = large;
    large  = small;
```

```
        small  = holder;

        cout << "\n\nDisplay of large:  stored at memory location "
             << &large << " in " << sizeof large << " bytes " << endl;
        large.showBox();

        cout << "\n\n Display of small:  stored at memory location "
             << &small << " in " << sizeof small << " bytes " << endl;
        small.showBox();
    }
```

4.1.B

```
    #include <iostream.h>

    class Box
        {
        public:
            char symbol;

        private:
            int  length, height;

        public:
            void showBox();   // Prototype.

            void setSize()
                {
                int l, h;

                cout << "\nEnter a length (an int between 2 and 10):  ";
                cin >> l;

                if (l >= 2  && l <= 10)  length = l;
                else  length = 1;

                cout << "\nEnter a height (an int between 2 and 6):    ";
                cin >> h;

                if (h >= 2  && h <= 6)   height = h;
                else  height = 1;

                cout << "\nEnter a symbol:  ";
                cin >> symbol;

                showBox();
                }

        };  // End of Box's class specifier.

    void swapBoxes(Box& box1, Box& box2)
        {
        Box holder;
        holder = box1;
        box1   = box2;
        box2   = holder;
        }

    void Box::showBox()
        {
        cout << endl;
        for (int i = 1;  i <= height;  i++)
            {
            for (int j = 1;  j <= length;  j++)  cout << symbol;
            cout << endl;
            }
        }
```

```
void main()
{
    Box large;
    cout << "\nPlease provide the specs for the large box:";
    large.setSize();  // length, height, and symbol (to be 'A') set here

    Box small;
    cout << "\n\nPlease provide the specs for the small box:";
    small.setSize();  // length, height, and symbol (to be 'B') set here

    cout << "\n\nDisplay of large:  stored at memory location "
         << &large << " in " << sizeof large << " bytes " << endl;
    large.showBox();

    cout << "\n\n Display of small:  stored at memory location "
         << &small << " in " << sizeof small << " bytes " << endl;
    small.showBox();

    //  Swapping the large and small.
    cout << "\n\n ** swap of large and small in progress " << endl;
    swapBoxes(large, small);

    cout << "\n\nDisplay of large:  stored at memory location "
         << &large << " in " << sizeof large << " bytes " << endl;
    large.showBox();

    cout << "\n\nDisplay of small:  stored at memory location "
         << &small << " in " << sizeof small << " bytes " << endl;
    small.showBox();
}
```

4.1.C

```
#include <iostream.h>

class Box
{
    public:
        char symbol;

    private:
        int   length, height;

    public:
        void swapBoxes(Box& argumentBox)
        {
            Box holder;
            holder = *this; // *this is the referent for the accessing object.
            *this = argumentBox;
            argumentBox = holder;
        }

        void showBox();  // Prototype.

        void setSize()
        {
            int l, h;

            cout << "\nEnter a length (an int between 2 and 10):  ";
            cin >> l;

            if (l >= 2  &&  l <= 10)  length = l;
            else  length = l;

            cout << "\nEnter a height (an int between 2 and 6):   ";
            cin >> h;
```

```
                    if (h >= 2 && h <= 6)    height = h;
                    else   height = 1;

                    cout << "\nEnter a symbol:   ";
                    cin >> symbol;

                    showBox();
            }
    };   // End of Box's class specifier.
```

4.1.D

```
    #include <iostream.h>

    class Box
    {
        public:
            char symbol;

        private:
            int  length, height;

        public:
            friend  void shift(Box& argumentBox);  // Not a member function.

            void showBox();   // Prototype.

            void setSize()
            {
                int l, h;

                cout << "\nEnter a length (an int between 2 and 10):   ";
                cin >> l;

                if (l >= 2  &&  l <= 10)   length = l;
                else   length = 1;

                cout << "\nEnter a height (an int between 2 and 6):    ";
                cin >> h;

                if (h >= 2  &&  h <= 6)    height = h;
                else   height = 1;

                cout << "\nEnter a symbol:   ";
                cin >> symbol;

                showBox();
            }
    };   // End of Box's class specifier.

    void Box::showBox()
    {
        cout << endl;
        for (int i = 1;  i <= height;  i++)
        {
            for (int j = 1;  j <= length;  j++)   cout << symbol;
            cout << endl;
        }
    }

    void shift(Box& argumentBox)
    {
        int holder;
        holder            = argumentBox.length; // Access of private data.
```

```
        argumentBox.length = argumentBox.height; // Access of private data.
        argumentBox.height = holder;             // Access of private data.
    }

    void main()
    {
        Box box;
        box.setSize();

        cout << "\n\n * Box's length and height are being exchanged" << endl;
        shift(box);

        box.showBox();
    }
```

4.1.E

```
        #include <iostream.h>

        class Box
        {
            public:
                char symbol;

            private:
                int  length, height;

            public:
                void rotate()
                {
                    int holder;
                    holder = length;
                    length = height;
                    height = holder;
                }

                void showBox();   // Prototype.

                void setSize()
                {
                    int l, h;

                    cout << "\nEnter a length (an int between 2 and 10):   ";
                    cin >> l;

                    if (l >= 2  &&  l <= 10)  length = l;
                    else  length = 1;

                    cout << "\nEnter a height (an int between 2 and 6):    ";
                    cin >> h;

                    if (h >= 2  &&  h <= 6)   height = h;
                    else   height = 1;

                    cout << "\nEnter a symbol:   ";
                    cin >> symbol;

                    showBox();
                }

        };   // End of Box's class specifier.

        void Box::showBox()
        {
            cout << endl;
            for (int i = 1;  i <= height;  i++)
            {
```

```
                          for (int j = 1;  j <= length;  j++)  cout << symbol;
                          cout << endl;
                      }
              }

         void main()
             {
               Box box;
               box.setSize();

               cout << "\n\n * Box is being stood on its side" << endl;
               box.rotate();

               box.showBox();
             }
```

4.1.F

```
#include <iostream.h>

class Box
    {
      public:
         char symbol;

      private:
         int  length, height;

      public:
         int getLength()
             {
               return length;
             }

         int getHeight()
             {
               return height;
             }

         void setLength(int newLength)
             {
               length = newLength;
             }

         void setHeight(int newHeight)
             {
               height = newHeight;
             }

         void showBox();   // Prototype.

         void setSize()
             {
               int l, h;

               cout << "\nEnter a length (an int between 2 and 10):  ";
               cin >> l;

               if (l >= 2  &&  l <= 10)  length = l;
               else  length = 1;

               cout << "\nEnter a height (an int between 2 and 6):   ";
               cin >> h;

               if (h >= 2  &&  h <= 6)   height = h;
               else  height = 1;
```

```
                        cout << "\nEnter a symbol:   ";
                        cin >> symbol;

                        showBox();
                }

        };   // End of Box's class specifier.

    void Box::showBox()
        {
            cout << endl;
            for (int i = 1;  i <= height;  i++)
                {
                    for (int j = 1;  j <= length;  j++)  cout << symbol;
                    cout << endl;
                }
        }

    void shift(Box& argumentBox)
        {
            int holder;

            holder = argumentBox.getLength();
            argumentBox.setLength( argumentBox.getHeight() );
            argumentBox.setHeight( holder );
        }

    void main()
        {
            Box box;
            box.setSize();

            cout << "\n\n * Box's length and height are being exchanged" << endl;
            shift(box);

            box.showBox();
        }
```

4.1.G

```
    #include <iostream.h>

    class Box
        {
            public:
                char symbol;

            private:
                int  length, height;

            public:
                int getLength()
                    {
                        return length;
                    }

                int getHeight()
                    {
                        return height;
                    }

                void setLength(int newLength)
                    {
                        length = newLength;
                    }
```

```
            void setHeight(int newHeight)
              {
                height = newHeight;
              }

            void showBox();   // Prototype.

            void setSize()
              {
                int l, h;

                cout << "\nEnter a length (an int between 2 and 10):   ";
                cin >> l;

                if (l >= 2  &&  l <= 10)  length = l;
                else  length = 1;

                cout << "\nEnter a height (an int between 2 and 6):    ";
                cin >> h;

                if (h >= 2  &&  h <= 6)   height = h;
                else  height = 1;

                cout << "\nEnter a symbol:  ";
                cin >> symbol;

                showBox();
              }

       };   // End of Box's class specifier.

   void Box::showBox()
     {
       cout << endl;
       for (int i = 1;  i <= height;  i++)
         {
           for (int j = 1;  j <= length;  j++)  cout << symbol;
           cout << endl;
         }
     }

   Box enlarge(Box argumentBox)
     {
       Box localBox;

       localBox.setLength( 2 * argumentBox.getLength() );
       localBox.setHeight( 2 * argumentBox.getHeight() );
       localBox.symbol = argumentBox.symbol;

       return localBox;
     }

   void main()
     {
       Box box;
       box.setSize();

       cout << "\n * an enlargement of this box is being created" << endl;
       Box enlargement;
       enlargement = enlarge(box);

       enlargement.showBox();
     }
```

4.1.H

```
   #include <iostream.h>
```

```
class Box
  {
    public:
      char symbol;

    private:
      int  length, height;

    public:
      friend Box expandIt(Box argumentBox);

      void showBox();  // Prototype.

      void setSize()
        {
          int l, h;

          cout << "\nEnter a length (an int between 2 and 10):  ";
          cin >> l;

          if (l >= 2  &&  l <= 10)  length = l;
          else  length = 1;

          cout << "\nEnter a height (an int between 2 and 6):  ";
          cin >> h;

          if (h >= 2  &&  h <= 6)   height = h;
          else  height = 1;

          cout << "\nEnter a symbol:  ";
          cin >> symbol;

          showBox();
        }

  };  // End of Box's class specifier.

void Box::showBox()
  {
    cout << endl;
    for (int i = 1;  i <= height;  i++)
      {
        for (int j = 1;  j <= length;  j++)  cout << symbol;
        cout << endl;
      }
  }

Box expandIt(Box argumentBox)
  {
    Box localBox;

    localBox.length = 2 * argumentBox.length;
    localBox.height = 2 * argumentBox.height;
    localBox.symbol = argumentBox.symbol;

    return localBox;
  }

void main()
  {
    Box box;
    box.setSize();

    cout << "\n * an expansion of this box is being created" << endl;
    Box expansion;
    expansion = expandIt(box);
```

```
        expansion.showBox();
}
```

4.1.I   Even if the data member *length* were physically absent, the class could maintain a facade to enable users to program as if it were present. For instance, the following member functions would support users' functions that required a *Box*'s *length* to be ascertained and reset:

```
int getLength()
{
    return area/height;
}

void setLength(int newLength)
{
    area = newLength * height;
}
```

In a system that has corrupted a class with many friends, nonmember functions are dependent upon private members. Because the list of *friend* functions is explicit, the places upon which a change in the class's implementation may impact is known. Still, it is possible inadvertently to miss a compensatory adjustment.

Upgrades in functionality or performance may be discouraged if the number of modules (i.e., *friend* functions or classes) that must be scrutinized is large.

4.1.J

```
#include <iostream.h>

class Box
{
    public:
        char symbol;

    private:
        int  length, height;

    public:
        int getLength()
        {
            return length;
        }

        int getHeight()
        {
            return height;
        }

        void setLength(int newLength)
        {
            length = newLength;
        }

        void setHeight(int newHeight)
        {
            height = newHeight;
        }

        void showBox();   // Prototype.

        void setSize()
        {
            int l, h;
```

```
                    cout << "\nEnter a length (an int between 2 and 10):   ";
                    cin >> l;

                    if (l >= 2  &&  l <= 10)  length = l;
                    else  length = 1;

                    cout << "\nEnter a height (an int between 2 and 6):    ";
                    cin >> h;

                    if (h >= 2  &&  h <= 6)   height = h;
                    else  height = 1;

                    cout << "\nEnter a symbol:  ";
                    cin >> symbol;

                    showBox();
                }
        };  // End of Box's class specifier.

    void Box::showBox()
        {
        cout << endl;
        for (int i = 1;  i <= height;  i++)
            {
            for (int j = 1;  j <= length;  j++)  cout << symbol;
            cout << endl;
            }
        }

//  For part i.
//
  Box plus (Box box1, Box box2)
        {
        Box sumBox;

        sumBox.setLength( box1.getLength() + box2.getLength() );
        sumBox.setHeight( box1.getHeight() + box2.getHeight() );
        sumBox.symbol = '+';

        return sumBox;
        }

//   For parts ii and iii.
//
//Box operator+ (Box box1, Box box2)
//  {
//    Box sumBox;
//
//    sumBox.setLength( box1.getLength() + box2.getLength() );
//    sumBox.setHeight( box1.getHeight() + box2.getHeight() );
//    sumBox.symbol = '+';
//
//    return sumBox;
//  }

void main()
    {
    Box boxA, boxB, boxC;

    cout << "\n\nPlease provide the specs for boxA:";
    boxA.setSize();

    cout << "\n\nPlease provide the specs for boxB:";
    boxB.setSize();

//   For part i.
//
    cout<<"\n\n * Getting the sum of boxA and boxB via  plus()"<<endl;
```

```
            boxC = plus(boxA, boxB);
            boxC.showBox();

    //    For part ii.
    //
    //    cout<<"\n\n * Getting sum of boxA and boxB via  operator+()"<<endl;
    //    boxC = operator+(boxA, boxB);
    //    boxC.showBox();

    //    For part iii.
    //
    //    cout<<"\n\n * Getting sum of boxA and boxB via  boxA + boxB"<<endl;
    //    boxC = boxA + boxB;
    //    boxC.showBox();

      }
```

4.1.K

```
        #include <iostream.h>

        class Box
          {
            public:
              char symbol;

            private:
              int  length, height;

            public:
              Box operator+ (Box rightOperand);   // Prototype.

              void showBox();  // Prototype.

              void setSize()
                {
                  int l, h;

                  cout << "\nEnter a length (an int between 2 and 10):  ";
                  cin >> l;

                  if (l >= 2  &&  l <= 10)  length = l;
                  else  length = 1;

                  cout << "\nEnter a height (an int between 2 and 6):   ";
                  cin >> h;

                  if (h >= 2  &&  h <= 6)   height = h;
                  else  height = 1;

                  cout << "\nEnter a symbol:   ";
                  cin >> symbol;

                  showBox();
                }

          };  // End of Box's class specifier.

        void Box::showBox()
          {
            cout << endl;
            for (int i = 1;  i <= height;  i++)
              {
                for (int j = 1;  j <= length;  j++)  cout << symbol;
                cout << endl;
              }
          }
```

```
Box Box::operator+ (Box rightOperand)
  {
    Box sumBox;

    sumBox.length = length + rightOperand.length;
    sumBox.height = height + rightOperand.height;
    sumBox.symbol = '+';

    return sumBox;
  }

void main()
  {
    Box boxA, boxB, boxC;

    cout << "\n\nPlease provide the specs for boxA:";
    boxA.setSize();

    cout << "\n\nPlease provide the specs for boxB:";
    boxB.setSize();

    cout<<"\n\n * Getting the sum of boxA and boxB via  boxA + boxB"
        <<endl;
    boxC = boxA + boxB;
    boxC.showBox();
  }
```

4.1.L

```
#include <iostream.h>

class Box
  {
    public:
      char symbol;

    private:
      int  length, height;

    public:
      int getLength()
        {
          return length;
        }

      int getHeight()
        {
          return height;
        }

      void setLength(int newLength)
        {
          length = newLength;
        }

      void setHeight(int newHeight)
        {
          height = newHeight;
        }

      void showBox();  // Prototype.

      void setSize()
        {
          int l, h;

          cout << "\nEnter a length (an int between 2 and 10):  ";
          cin >> l;
```

```
                       if (1 >= 2  &&  1 <= 10)   length = 1;
                       else   length = 1;

                       cout << "\nEnter a height (an int between 2 and 6):    ";
                       cin >> h;

                       if (h >= 2  &&  h <= 6)    height = h;
                       else   height = 1;

                       cout << "\nEnter a symbol:  ";
                       cin >> symbol;

                       showBox();
                   }

            };   // End of Box's class specifier.

      void Box::showBox()
        {
           cout << endl;
           for (int i = 1;  i <= height;  i++)
             {
                for (int j = 1;  j <= length;  j++)  cout << symbol;
                cout << endl;
             }
        }

      //   Adds  an int  to  a Box    to enable:  "Box b = 10 + boxC;".
      //
      Box operator+ (int leftOperand, Box rightOperand)
        {
           Box sumBox;

           sumBox.setLength( leftOperand + rightOperand.getLength() );
           sumBox.setHeight( leftOperand + rightOperand.getHeight() );
           sumBox.symbol = '+';

           return sumBox;
        }

      //   Adds  a Box  to  an int   to enable:  "Box c =  boxC + 10;".
      //
      Box operator+ (Box leftOperand, int rightOperand)
        {
           Box sumBox;

           sumBox.setLength( leftOperand.getLength() + rightOperand );
           sumBox.setHeight( leftOperand.getHeight() + rightOperand );
           sumBox.symbol = '+';

           return sumBox;
        }

      void main()
        {
           Box  boxC;

           cout << "\n\nPlease provide the specs for boxC:";
           boxC.setSize();

           cout<<"\n\n * Getting the sum of 10 + boxC"<<endl;
           Box b = 10 + boxC;
           b.showBox();

           cout<<"\n\n * Getting the sum of boxC + 10"<<endl;
           Box c = boxC + 10;
           b.showBox();
        }
```

4.1.M

```
#include <iostream.h>
#include <fstream.h>   // To allow writing to an output file on diskette
                       // and writing to the printer as if it were a file.
class Box
  {
    public:
       char symbol;

    private:
       int  length, height;

    public:
       int getLength()
         {
           return length;
         }

       int getHeight()
         {
           return height;
         }

       void setLength(int newLength)
         {
           length = newLength;
         }

       void setHeight(int newHeight)
         {
           height = newHeight;
         }

       void showBox();  // Prototype.

       void setSize()
         {
           int l, h;

           cout << "\nEnter a length (an int between 2 and 10):  ";
           cin >> l;

           if (l >= 2  &&  l <= 10)  length = l;
           else  length = 1;

           cout << "\nEnter a height (an int between 2 and 6):   ";
           cin >> h;

           if (h >= 2  &&  h <= 6)   height = h;
           else  height = 1;

           cout << "\nEnter a symbol:  ";
           cin >> symbol;

           showBox();
         }
  };  // End of Box's class specifier.

void Box::showBox()
  {
    cout << endl;
    for (int i = 1;  i <= height;  i++)
      {
        for (int j = 1;  j <= length;  j++)  cout << symbol;
        cout << endl;
      }
  }
```

```
//   Adds  an  int  to  a  Box   to enable:  "Box b = 10 + boxC;".
//
Box operator+ (int leftOperand, Box rightOperand)
  {
    Box sumBox;

    sumBox.setLength( leftOperand + rightOperand.getLength() );
    sumBox.setHeight( leftOperand + rightOperand.getHeight() );
    sumBox.symbol = '+';

    return sumBox;
  }

//   Adds  a  Box  to  an  int   to enable:  "Box c = boxC + 10;".
//
Box operator+ (Box leftOperand, int rightOperand)
  {
    Box sumBox;

    sumBox.setLength( leftOperand.getLength() + rightOperand );
    sumBox.setHeight( leftOperand.getHeight() + rightOperand );
    sumBox.symbol = '+';

    return sumBox;
  }

ostream&  operator<< (ostream& outputStream, Box b)
  {
    outputStream << endl;
    for (int i = 1; i <= b.getHeight(); i++)
      {
        for (int j = 1; j<= b.getLength(); j++)
          {
            outputStream << b.symbol;
          }
        outputStream << endl;
      }
    return outputStream;
  }

void main()
  {
    Box  boxC;

    cout << "\n\nPlease provide the specs for boxC:";
    boxC.setSize();

    cout<<"\n\n * Getting the sum of 10 + boxC"<<endl;
    Box b = 10 + boxC;
    cout << endl << b << "Box b is above, which is (10 + boxC)" << endl;

    cout<<"\n\n * Getting the sum of boxC + 10"<<endl;
    Box c = boxC + 10;
    cout << endl << b << "Box b is above, which is (boxC + 10)" << endl;

    // Directing Boxes to the printer (which is "LPT1" on our system).
    //             Program requires printer to be ready.

    ofstream  printer("LPT1");
    printer<<endl<<boxC<<"boxC, entered from the terminal, is above"
          <<endl;
    printer << endl << b << "Box b is above, which is (10 + boxC)"
          << endl;
    printer << endl << b << "Box b is above, which is (boxC + 10)"
          << endl;
    printer << "\f";  // Escape sequence designating a form feed
                      // (page eject).

    // Directing Boxes to a file on diskette ("A:4-1-M.OUT").
```

```
//              Program requires a diskette in drive A:
//
//    A string literal to designate a file in a subdirectory must
//    use a double backslash (the escape sequence for a backslash)
//         This file:    C:\CPP\4-1-M.OUT     is represented by
//         this string: "C:\\CPP\\4-1-M.OUT"

ofstream  diskette("A:4-1-M.OUT");
diskette<<endl<<boxC<<"boxC, entered from the terminal, is above"
        <<endl;
diskette<<endl << b << "Box b is above, which is (10 + boxC)"
        <<endl;
diskette<<endl << b << "Box b is above, which is (boxC + 10)"
        <<endl;
}
```

4.1.N

```
#include <iostream.h>

class Box
{
    public:
      char symbol;

    private:
      int  length, height;

    public:
      Box() : length(12), height(3), symbol('*')
      {
      }

      Box(int forSides) : length(forSides), height(forSides),
        symbol('*')
      {
      }

      Box(char forSymbol) : length(10), height(5), symbol(forSymbol)
      {
      }

      Box(int forLength, int forHeight, char forSymbol) :
        length(forLength), height(forHeight), symbol(forSymbol)
      {
      }

      int getLength()
      {
        return length;
      }

      int getHeight()
      {
        return height;
      }

      void setLength(int newLength)
      {
        length = newLength;
      }

      void setHeight(int newHeight)
      {
        height = newHeight;
      }

      void showBox();  // Prototype.
```

```
            void setSize()
            {
                int l, h;

                cout << "\nEnter a length (an int between 2 and 10):   ";
                cin >> l;

                if (l >= 2  &&  l <= 10)   length = l;
                else   length = 1;

                cout << "\nEnter a height (an int between 2 and 6):    ";
                cin >> h;

                if (h >= 2  &&  h <= 6)    height = h;
                else   height = 1;

                cout << "\nEnter a symbol:   ";
                cin >> symbol;

                showBox();
            }

    };   // End of Box's class specifier.

void Box::showBox()
{
    cout << endl;
    for (int i = 1;  i <= height;  i++)
    {
        for (int j = 1;  j <= length;  j++)   cout << symbol;
        cout << endl;
    }
}

ostream&  operator<< (ostream& outputStream, Box b)
{
    outputStream << endl;
    for (int i = 1; i <= b.getHeight(); i++)
    {
        for (int j = 1; j<= b.getLength(); j++)
        {
            outputStream << b.symbol;
        }
        outputStream << endl;
    }
    return outputStream;
}

void main()
{
    // Testing the no-argument constructor.
    Box  b1;  //Note:  no parentheses --> this would be wrong:  Box b1();
    cout<<b1<<"b1 is above, via Box(), the no argument constructor"
        <<endl;

    // Testing the Box(int) constructor.
    Box  b2(5);
    cout<<b2<<"b2 is above, via Box(int) with sides designated as 5"
        <<endl;

    // Testing the Box(char) constructor.
    Box  b3('A');
    cout<<b3<<"b3 is above, via Box(char) with the symbol 'A'"<<endl;

    // Testing the three-argument constructor.
    Box  b4(30, 2, 'X');
    cout<<b4<<"b4 is above, via Box(int,int,char) with 30, 2, 'X'"<<endl;
}
```

4.1.0

```
#include <iostream.h>

class Box
{
    public:
        char symbol;

    private:
        int   length, height;

    public:
        Box() : length(12), height(3), symbol('*')
        {

        }

        Box(int forSides) : length(forSides), height(forSides),
            symbol('*')
        {

        }

        Box(char forSymbol) : length(10), height(5), symbol(forSymbol)
        {

        }

        Box(int forLength, int forHeight, char forSymbol) :
            length(forLength), height(forHeight), symbol(forSymbol)
        {

        }

    int getLength()
        {
            return length;
        }

    int getHeight()
        {
            return height;
        }

    void setLength(int newLength)
        {
            length = newLength;
        }

    void setHeight(int newHeight)
        {
            height = newHeight;
        }

    void showBox();   // Prototype.

    void setSize()
        {
            int l, h;

            cout << "\nEnter a length (an int between 2 and 10):   ";
            cin >> l;

            if (l >= 2  &&  l <= 10)  length = l;
            else  length = l;

            cout << "\nEnter a height (an int between 2 and 6):    ";
```

```
            cin >> h;

            if (h >= 2  &&  h <= 6)    height = h;
            else   height = 1;

            cout << "\nEnter a symbol:   ";
            cin >> symbol;

            showBox();
        }

    };  // End of Box's class specifier.

void Box::showBox()
{
    cout << endl;
    for (int i = 1;  i <= height;  i++)
    {
        for (int j = 1;  j <= length;  j++)  cout << symbol;
        cout << endl;
    }
}

ostream&  operator<< (ostream& outputStream, Box b)
{
    outputStream << endl;
    for (int i = 1; i <= b.getHeight(); i++)
    {
        for (int j = 1; j<= b.getLength(); j++)
        {
            outputStream << b.symbol;
        }
        outputStream << endl;
    }
    return outputStream;
}

void main()
{
    Box x;
    cout << x << "Address of Box x = " << &x << endl;

    x = 3;
    cout << x << "Address of Box x = " << &x << endl;

    x = '!';  // ASCII value of '!' is 33
    cout << x << "Address of Box x = " << &x << endl;

    // Comment-out the Box(char) constructor, activate the following,
    // and re-run the program.
    //
    //   x = 5.6;
    //   cout << x << "Address of Box x = " << &x << endl;
}
```

4.1.P

```
#include <iostream.h>

class Box
{
    public:
        char symbol;

    private:
        int  length, height;
```

```
public:
   operator int()
     {
       return (length + height)/2;
     }

   Box() : length(12), height(3), symbol('*')
     {

     }

   Box(int forSides) : length(forSides), height(forSides),
     symbol('*')
       {

       }

   Box(char forSymbol) : length(10), height(5), symbol(forSymbol)
     {

     }

   Box(int forLength, int forHeight, char forSymbol) :
     length(forLength), height(forHeight), symbol(forSymbol)
       {

       }

   int getLength()
     {
       return length;
     }

   int getHeight()
     {
       return height;
     }

   void setLength(int newLength)
     {
       length = newLength;
     }

   void setHeight(int newHeight)
     {
       height = newHeight;
     }

   void showBox();   // Prototype.

   void setSize()
     {
       int l, h;

       cout << "\nEnter a length (an int between 2 and 10):   ";
       cin >> l;

       if (l >= 2  &&  l <= 10)   length = l;
       else   length = 1;

       cout << "\nEnter a height (an int between 2 and 6):    ";
       cin >> h;

       if (h >= 2  &&  h <= 6)    height = h;
       else   height = 1;

       cout << "\nEnter a symbol:   ";
```

```
                                cin >> symbol;

                                showBox();
                         }

                  };   // End of Box's class specifier.

            void Box::showBox()
                  {
                     cout << endl;
                     for (int i = 1;  i <= height;  i++)
                         {
                            for (int j = 1;  j <= length;  j++)  cout << symbol;
                            cout << endl;
                         }
                  }

            ostream&  operator<< (ostream& outputStream, Box b)
                  {
                     outputStream << endl;
                     for (int i = 1; i <= b.getHeight(); i++)
                         {
                            for (int j = 1; j<= b.getLength(); j++)
                                {
                                   outputStream << b.symbol;
                                }
                            outputStream << endl;
                         }
                     return outputStream;
                  }

            void main()
                  {
                     Box x;
                     cout << x << "Address of Box x = " << &x << endl;

                     x = Box(5);            // Cast, uses the Box(int) constructor.
                     cout << x << "Address of Box x = " << &x << endl;

                     x = (Box)4;            // Cast, uses the Box(int) constructor.
                     cout << x << "Address of Box x = " << &x << endl;

                     cout << Box(2);        // Cast, uses the Box(int) constructor.

                     Box BoxA(8,2,'A');  // Uses the Box(int, int, char) constructor.
                     int i;
                     i = BoxA;
                     cout << "\n\nFollowing the assignment i = BoxA,     i = " << i
                          << endl;

                     i = int(BoxA);         // Cast, uses Box::operator int().
                     cout << "Following the test of i = int(BoxA),  i = " << i << endl;

                     i = (int)BoxA;         // Cast, uses Box::operator int().
                     cout << "Following the test of i = (int)BoxA,  i = " << i << endl;
                  }
```

4.1.Q

```
#include <iostream.h>

class Box
    {
       public:
          char symbol;

       private:
          int  length, height;
```

```cpp
        static int total; // In addition to their declaration,
                          // static data members must be defined
                          // following the specifier.

    public:
      Box() : length(3), height(3), symbol('*')
        {
          total++;
        }

      Box(int forSides):length(forSides), height(forSides), symbol('*')
        {
          total++;
        }

      static void reportTotal()
        {
          cout << "\ntotal number of Box objects created = " << total;
          cout << endl;
        }

      void showBox();                 // Prototype.
      void setSize();                 // Prototype.
      void setLength(int newLength);  // Prototype.
      void setHeight(int newHeight);  // Prototype.
      int  getLength();               // Prototype.
      int  getHeight();               // Prototype.
  };

int Box::total; // C++ automatically initializes static data members to 0,
                // but this could have been coded as  int Box::total = 0;

void Box::showBox()
  {
    cout << endl;
    for (int i = 1;  i <= height;  i++)
      {
        for (int j = 1;  j <= length;  j++)  cout << symbol;
        cout << endl;
      }
  }

void Box::setSize()
  {
    int l, h;

    cout << "\nEnter a length (an int between 2 and 10):  ";
    cin >> l;

    if (l >= 2  &&  l <= 10)  length = l;
    else   length = 1;

    cout << "\nEnter a height (an int between 2 and 6):   ";
    cin >> h;

    if (h >= 2  &&  h <= 6)   height = h;
    else   height = 1;

    cout << "\nEnter a symbol:  ";
    cin >> symbol;

    showBox();
  }

void Box::setLength(int newLength)
  {
    length = newLength;
  }
```

```
void Box::setHeight(int newHeight)
  {
    height = newHeight;
  }

int Box::getLength()
  {
    return length;
  }

int Box::getHeight()
  {
    return height;
  }

void main()
  {
    Box::reportTotal();      // Should see 0.

    Box box1, box2, box3;
    box1.showBox();
    Box::reportTotal();      // Should see 3.

    Box box4(4), box5(5);
    box4.showBox();
    Box::reportTotal();      // Should see 5.
  }
```

4.1.R

```
#include <iostream.h>

class Box
  {
    public:
      char symbol;

    private:
      int  length, height;
      static int total;       // Static data members are initialized where
                              // defined, which is following the specifier.

    public:
      Box() : length(3), height(3), symbol('*')
        {
          total++;
        }

      Box(int forSides):length(forSides), height(forSides), symbol('*')
        {
          total++;
        }

      static void reportTotal()
        {
          cout << "\ntotal number of Box objects created = " << total;
          cout << endl;
        }

      void showBox();                      // Prototype.
      void setSize();                      // Prototype.
      void setLength(int newLength);  // Prototype.
      void setHeight(int newHeight);  // Prototype.
      int  getLength();                    // Prototype.
      int  getHeight();                    // Prototype.
  };

int Box::total = 10;  // Static data member initialized to 10.
```

```
void Box::showBox()
    {
    cout << endl;
    for (int i = 1;  i <= height;  i++)
        {
        for (int j = 1;  j <= length;  j++)  cout << symbol;
        cout << endl;
        }
    }

void Box::setSize()
    {
    int l, h;

    cout << "\nEnter a length (an int between 2 and 10):  ";
    cin >> l;

    if (l >= 2  &&  l <= 10)  length = l;
    else  length = 1;

    cout << "\nEnter a height (an int between 2 and 6):  ";
    cin >> h;

    if (h >= 2  &&  h <= 6)  height = h;
    else  height = 1;

    cout << "\nEnter a symbol:  ";
    cin >> symbol;

    showBox();
    }

void Box::setLength(int newLength)
    {
    length = newLength;
    }

void Box::setHeight(int newHeight)
    {
    height = newHeight;
    }

int Box::getLength()
    {
    return length;
    }

int Box::getHeight()
    {
    return height;
    }

void main()
    {
    Box::reportTotal();     // Should see 10.

    Box box1, box2, box3;
    box1.showBox();
    Box::reportTotal();     // Should see 13.

    Box box4(4), box5(5);
    box4.showBox();
    Box::reportTotal();     // Should see 15.
    }
```

4.1.S

```
#include <iostream.h>
```

```
class Box
{
    public:
        char symbol;

    private:
        int   length, height, serialNumber;
        static int total;

    public:
        Box() : length(3), height(3), symbol('*')
        {
            serialNumber = ++total;
            cout << "\nBox number " << serialNumber;
            cout << " is being created" << endl;
        }

        Box(int forSides):length(forSides), height(forSides), symbol('*')
        {
            serialNumber = ++total;
            cout << "\nBox number " << serialNumber;
            cout << " is being created" << endl;
        }

        ~Box()
        {
            cout << "\nBox number " << serialNumber;
            cout << " is being deleted" << endl;
        }

        static void reportTotal()
        {
            cout << "\ntotal number of Box objects created = " << total;
            cout << endl;
        }

        void showBox();                      // Prototype.
        void setSize();                      // Prototype.
        void setLength(int newLength);       // Prototype.
        void setHeight(int newHeight);       // Prototype.
        int  getLength();                    // Prototype.
        int  getHeight();                    // Prototype.
};

int Box::total = 0;

void Box::showBox()
{
    cout << endl;
    for (int i = 1;  i <= height;  i++)
    {
        for (int j = 1;  j <= length;  j++)  cout << symbol;
        cout << endl;
    }
}

void Box::setSize()
{
    int l, h;

    cout << "\nEnter a length (an int between 2 and 10):  ";
    cin >> l;

    if (l >= 2  &&  l <= 10)  length = l;
    else  length = l;

    cout << "\nEnter a height (an int between 2 and 6):   ";
    cin >> h;
```

```
            if (h >= 2  &&  h <= 6)    height = h;
            else   height = 1;

            cout << "\nEnter a symbol:   ";
            cin >> symbol;

            showBox();
        }

    void Box::setLength(int newLength)
        {
            length = newLength;
        }

    void Box::setHeight(int newHeight)
        {
            height = newHeight;
        }

    int Box::getLength()
        {
            return length;
        }

    int Box::getHeight()
        {
            return height;
        }

    Box box0; // Externally defined Box;
              // Its constructor runs before main() starts.

    void main()
        {
            cout << endl << "-----main beginning-----" << endl;

            box0.showBox();
            Box::reportTotal();    // Should see 1.

            Box box1, box2, box3;
            box1.showBox();
            Box::reportTotal();    // Should see 4.

            Box box4(4), box5(5);
            box4.showBox();
            Box::reportTotal();    // Should see 6.

            cout << endl << "-------main ending-------" << endl;
        }
```

4.1.T

```
    #include <iostream.h>

    class Box
        {
        public:
            char symbol;

        private:
            int  length, height, serialNumber;
            static int total;

        public:
            Box() : length(3), height(3), symbol('*')
                {
                    serialNumber = ++total;
```

```
            cout << "\nBox number " << serialNumber;
            cout << " is being created" << endl;
        }

    Box(int forSides):length(forSides), height(forSides), symbol('*')
        {
            serialNumber = ++total;
            cout << "\nBox number " << serialNumber;
            cout << " is being created" << endl;
        }

    ~Box()
        {
            cout << "\nBox number " << serialNumber;
            cout << " is being deleted" << endl;
        }

    static void reportTotal()
        {
            cout << "\ntotal number of Box objects created = " << total;
            cout << endl;
        }

    void showBox();                     // Prototype.
    void setSize();                     // Prototype.
    void setLength(int newLength);      // Prototype.
    void setHeight(int newHeight);      // Prototype.
    int  getLength();                   // Prototype.
    int  getHeight();                   // Prototype.
};

int Box::total = 0;

void Box::showBox()
{
    cout << endl;
    for (int i = 1;  i <= height;  i++)
    {
        for (int j = 1;  j <= length;  j++)  cout << symbol;
        cout << endl;
    }
}

void Box::setSize()
{
    int l, h;

    cout << "\nEnter a length (an int between 2 and 10):  ";
    cin >> l;

    if (l >= 2  &&  l <= 10)  length = l;
    else  length = 1;

    cout << "\nEnter a height (an int between 2 and 6):   ";
    cin >> h;

    if (h >= 2  &&  h <= 6)   height = h;
    else  height = 1;

    cout << "\nEnter a symbol:  ";
    cin >> symbol;

    showBox();
}

void Box::setLength(int newLength)
{
    length = newLength;
```

```
            }

    void Box::setHeight(int newHeight)
        {
        height = newHeight;
        }

    int Box::getLength()
        {
        return length;
        }

    int Box::getHeight()
        {
        return height;
        }

Box*  boxPtr1 = new Box;

void main()
    {
    cout << endl << "-----main beginning-----" << endl;

    boxPtr1 -> showBox();
    Box::reportTotal();          // Should see 1.

    Box *boxPtr2, *boxPtr3, *boxPtr4;  // a Box pointer
        // is not a Box

    Box::reportTotal();          // Should see 1.

    boxPtr2 = new Box;           // No-argument constructor used.
    boxPtr3 = new Box(4);        // One-argument constructor used.

    boxPtr4 = boxPtr3;

    boxPtr4 -> showBox();

    Box::reportTotal();          // Should see 3.

    delete boxPtr1;
    delete boxPtr4;

    boxPtr4 = new Box(5);
    boxPtr4 -> symbol = 'd';  // Here 'd' stands for dynamic.

    boxPtr4 -> showBox();
    Box::reportTotal();          // Should see 4.

    cout << endl << "-------main ending-------" << endl;
    }
```

4.1.U

```
#include <iostream.h>

class Box
    {
    public:
        char symbol;

    private:
        int  length, height, serialNumber;
        static int total;
```

```
public:
  int getSerialNumber()
    {
      return serialNumber;
    }

  Box() : length(3), height(3), symbol('*')
    {
      serialNumber = ++total;
      cout << "\nBox number " << serialNumber;
      cout << " is being created" << endl;
    }

  Box(int forSides):length(forSides), height(forSides), symbol('*')
    {
      serialNumber = ++total;
      cout << "\nBox number " << serialNumber;
      cout << " is being created" << endl;
    }

  ~Box()
    {
      cout << "\nBox number " << serialNumber;
      cout << " is being deleted" << endl;
    }

  static void reportTotal()
    {
      cout << "\ntotal number of Box objects created = " << total;
      cout << endl;
    }

  void showBox();                  // Prototype.
  void setSize();                  // Prototype.
  void setLength(int newLength);   // Prototype.
  void setHeight(int newHeight);   // Prototype.
  int  getLength();                // Prototype.
  int  getHeight();                // Prototype.
};

int Box::total = 0;

void Box::showBox()
{
  cout << endl;
  for (int i = 1;  i <= height;  i++)
    {
      for (int j = 1;  j <= length;  j++)  cout << symbol;
      cout << endl;
    }
}

void Box::setSize()
{
  int l, h;

  cout << "\nEnter a length (an int between 2 and 10):  ";
  cin >> l;

  if (l >= 2  &&  l <= 10)  length = l;
  else  length = 1;

  cout << "\nEnter a height (an int between 2 and 6):   ";
  cin >> h;

  if (h >= 2  &&  h <= 6)   height = h;
  else  height = 1;

  cout << "\nEnter a symbol:  ";
```

```
      cin >> symbol;

      showBox();
   }

void Box::setLength(int newLength)
   {
   length = newLength;
   }

void Box::setHeight(int newHeight)
   {
   height = newHeight;
   }

int Box::getLength()
   {
   return length;
   }

int Box::getHeight()
   {
   return height;
   }

Box*  boxPtr1 = new Box;
Box   box2(4);

void main()
   {
   cout << endl << "-----main beginning-----" << endl;

   Box* boxPtr1 = new Box(5);
   Box  box2(6);

   Box::reportTotal();     // Should see 4.

   ::boxPtr1->showBox();   // The scope operator is used to access an
                           // external variable having the same name
                           // as a local variable.

   cout << "Box above is the external, "
        << "dynamically allocated Box, Box number "
        << ::boxPtr1 -> getSerialNumber() << endl;

   ::box2.showBox();       // The scope operator is used to access an
                           // external variable having the same name
                           // as a local variable.

   cout << "Box above is the external static Box, Box number "
        << ::box2.getSerialNumber() << endl;

   boxPtr1->showBox();
   cout<<"Box above is the local dynamically allocated Box, Box number "
        << boxPtr1 -> getSerialNumber() << endl;

   box2.showBox();
   cout<<"Box above is the local static Box, Box number "
        << box2.getSerialNumber() << endl;

   delete ::boxPtr1;     // External dynamically allocated Box deleted.

   delete boxPtr1;       // Local dynamically allocated Box deleted.

   cout << endl << "-------main ending-------" << endl;
   }
```

4.1.V

```
#include <iostream.h>

class Box
{
   public:
      char symbol;

   private:
      int  length, height, serialNumber;
      static int total;

   public:
      Box() : length(3), height(3), symbol('*')
      {
         serialNumber = ++total;
         cout << "\nBox number " << serialNumber;
         cout << " is being created" << endl;
      }

      Box(int forSides):length(forSides), height(forSides), symbol('*')
      {
         serialNumber = ++total;
         cout << "\nBox number " << serialNumber;
         cout << " is being created" << endl;
      }

      ~Box()
      {
         cout << "\nBox number " << serialNumber;
         cout << " is being deleted" << endl;
      }

      static void reportTotal()
      {
         cout << "\ntotal number of Box objects created = " << total;
         cout << endl;
      }

      void showBox();                      // Prototype.
      void setSize();                      // Prototype.
      void setLength(int newLength);       // Prototype.
      void setHeight(int newHeight);       // Prototype.
      int  getLength();                    // Prototype.
      int  getHeight();                    // Prototype.
};

int Box::total = 0;

void Box::showBox()
{
   cout << endl;
   for (int i = 1;  i <= height;  i++)
   {
      for (int j = 1;  j <= length;  j++)  cout << symbol;
      cout << endl;
   }
}

void Box::setSize()
{
   int l, h;

   cout << "\nEnter a length (an int between 2 and 10):  ";
   cin >> l;

   if (l >= 2  &&  l <= 10)  length = l;
   else  length = 1;
```

```
    cout << "\nEnter a height (an int between 2 and 6):    ";
    cin >> h;

    if (h >= 2  &&  h <= 6)    height = h;
    else   height = 1;

    cout << "\nEnter a symbol:  ";
    cin >> symbol;

    showBox();
}

void Box::setLength(int newLength)
{
    length = newLength;
}

void Box::setHeight(int newHeight)
{
    height = newHeight;
}

int Box::getLength()
{
    return length;
}

int Box::getHeight()
{
    return height;
}

void main()
{
    cout << endl << "-----main beginning-----" << endl;

    Box* boxPtr1 = new Box;
    Box* boxPtr2 = new Box(4);

    Box box3(5);
    Box box4(6);

    // Part One-----------------------------------------------------------
    // deleting a statically allocated object:  AN ERROR
    Box* boxPtrX;              // Okay.
    boxPtrX = &box4;           // Okay.
    boxPtrX -> showBox(); // Okay.
    cout<<"Above is a statically allocated Box, shown via pointer it.";
    cout << endl;
    //delete boxPtrX;     // Deleting a statically allocated object!  ERROR!

    // Part Two -----------------------------------------------------------
    // deleting a dynamically allocated object more than once:  AN ERROR
    delete boxPtr2;
    //delete boxPtr2;           // Deleting a deleted object!  ERROR!
    //delete boxPtr2;           // Deleting a deleted object!  ERROR!

    // The following is okay:
    boxPtr2 = NULL;    // Equivalent statement:  boxPtr2 = 0;
    delete boxPtr2;    // Okay to apply the delete operator to a pointer
    delete boxPtr2;    // variable which equals NULL any number of times.

    // Part Three ---------------------------------------------------------
    // using an object following its deletion:  AN ERROR
    boxPtr1 -> showBox();
    cout<<"Above is the dynamally allocated Box pointed to by boxPtr1.";
    cout << endl;
    delete boxPtr1;          // Okay.
    //boxPtr1->showBox();    //Accessing a deleted object!  ERROR!
```

```
        cout << endl << "-------main ending-------" << endl;
    }
```

4-1-W

```
#include <iostream.h>

class Box
{
    public:
        char symbol;

    private:
        int  length, height, serialNumber;
        static int total;

    public:
        Box();          // No-argument constructor, prototype.
        Box(int);       // One-argument constructor, prototype.
        ~Box();         // Destructor, prototype.
        static void reportTotal();      // Prototype.
        void showBox();                 // Prototype.
        void setSize();                 // Prototype.
        void setLength(int newLength);  // Prototype.
        void setHeight(int newHeight);  // Prototype.
        int  getLength();               // Prototype.
        int  getHeight();               // Prototype.
};

int Box::total = 0;

Box::Box() : length(3), height(3), symbol('*')
{
    serialNumber = ++total;

    cout << "\nBox number " << serialNumber << " is being created";
    cout << endl;
}

Box::Box(int side) : length(side), height(side), symbol('*')
{
    serialNumber = ++total;

    cout << "\nBox number " << serialNumber << " is being created";
    cout << endl;
}

Box::~Box()
{
    cout << "\nBox number " << serialNumber << " is being deleted";
    cout << endl;
}

void Box::reportTotal()
{
    cout << "\ntotal number of Box objects created = " << total;
    cout << endl;
}

void Box::setSize()
{
    int l, h;

    cout << "\nEnter a length (an int between 2 and 10):  ";
    cin >> l;

    if (l >= 2  &&  l <= 10)  length = l;
    else   length = 1;
```

```
            cout << "\nEnter a height (an int between 2 and 6):    ";
            cin >> h;

            if (h >= 2  &&  h <= 6)    height = h;
            else   height = 1;

            cout << "\nEnter a symbol:  ";
            cin >> symbol;

            showBox();
        }

    void Box::showBox()
        {
            cout << endl;
            for (int i = 1;  i <= height;  i++)
                {
                    for (int j = 1;  j <= length;  j++)  cout << symbol;
                    cout << endl;
                }
        }

    void Box::setLength(int newLength)
        {
            if (newLength > 0  &&  newLength <= 70)  length = newLength;
        }

    void Box::setHeight(int newHeight)
        {
            if (newHeight > 0  &&  newHeight <= 10)  height = newHeight;
        }

    int  Box::getLength()
        {
            return length;
        }

    int  Box::getHeight()
        {
            return height;
        }

    class Square : public Box
        {
        };

    void main()
        {
            Square square1;
            square1.showBox();
            Square::reportTotal();
        }
```

4.1.X

```
#include <iostream.h>

class Box
    {
    public:
        char symbol;

    private:
        int  length, height, serialNumber;
        static int total;

    public:
        Box();        // No-argument constructor, prototype.
```

```
        Box(int);      // One-argument constructor, prototype.
        ~Box();        // Destructor, prototype.
        static void reportTotal();       // Prototype.
        void showBox();                  // Prototype.
        void setSize();                  // Prototype.
        void setLength(int newLength);   // Prototype.
        void setHeight(int newHeight);   // Prototype.
        int  getLength();                // Prototype.
        int  getHeight();                // Prototype.
    };

int Box::total = 0;

Box::Box() : length(3), height(3), symbol('*')
    {
        serialNumber = ++total;

        cout << "\nBox number " << serialNumber << " is being created";
        cout << endl;
    }

Box::Box(int side) : length(side), height(side), symbol('*')
    {
        serialNumber = ++total;

        cout << "\nBox number " << serialNumber << " is being created";
        cout << endl;
    }

Box::~Box()
    {
        cout << "\nBox number " << serialNumber << " is being deleted";
        cout << endl;
    }

void Box::reportTotal()
    {
        cout << "\ntotal number of Box objects created = " << total;
        cout << endl;
    }

void Box::setSize()
    {
        int l, h;

        cout << "\nEnter a length (an int between 2 and 10):  ";
        cin >> l;

        if (l >= 2  &&  l <= 10)  length = l;
        else  length = 1;

        cout << "\nEnter a height (an int between 2 and 6):   ";
        cin >> h;

        if (h >= 2  &&  h <= 6)   height = h;
        else  height = 1;

        cout << "\nEnter a symbol:  ";
        cin >> symbol;

        showBox();
    }

void Box::showBox()
    {
        cout << endl;
        for (int i = 1;  i <= height;  i++)
            {
```

```
                      for (int j = 1;   j <= length;   j++)   cout << symbol;
                      cout << endl;
                }
        }

    void Box::setLength(int newLength)
        {
            if (newLength > 0  &&  newLength <= 70)  length = newLength;
        }

    void Box::setHeight(int newHeight)
        {
            if (newHeight > 0  &&  newHeight <= 10)   height = newHeight;
        }

    int  Box::getLength()
        {
            return length;
        }

    int  Box::getHeight()
        {
            return height;
        }

    class Square : public Box
        {
          public:
                                        // Only data members declared within an ad hoc
                Square() :  Box(5)  // class can be initialized on a constructor's
                    {                   // initialization list.  This excludes symbol.
                      symbol = 's';
                      cout<<"\nSquare's no-argument constructor is running."<<endl;
                    }

                Square(int forSides) : Box(forSides)
                    {
                      symbol = 'S';
                      cout<<"\nSquare's one-argument constructor is running."<<endl;
                    }

                ~Square()
                    {
                      cout << "\nSquare's destructor is running." << endl;
                    }
        };

    void main()
        {
            Square square1;
            square1.showBox();
            Square::reportTotal();

            Square square2(8);
            square2.showBox();
            Square::reportTotal();
        }
```

4.1.Y

```
    #include <iostream.h>

    class Box
        {
          public:
            char symbol;
```

```
        private:
          int  length, height, serialNumber;
          static int total;

        public:
          Box();         // No-argument constructor, prototype.
          Box(int);      // One-argument constructor, prototype.
          ~Box();        // Destructor, prototype.
          static void reportTotal();      // Prototype.
          void showBox();                 // Prototype.
          void setSize();                 // Prototype.
          void setLength(int newLength);  // Prototype.
          void setHeight(int newHeight);  // Prototype.
          int  getLength();               // Prototype.
          int  getHeight();               // Prototype.
    };

int Box::total = 0;

Box::Box() : length(3), height(3), symbol('*')
    {
        serialNumber = ++total;

        cout << "\nBox number " << serialNumber << " is being created";
        cout << endl;
    }

Box::Box(int side) : length(side), height(side), symbol('*')
    {
        serialNumber = ++total;

        cout << "\nBox number " << serialNumber << " is being created";
        cout << endl;
    }

Box::~Box()
    {
        cout << "\nBox number " << serialNumber << " is being deleted";
        cout << endl;
    }

void Box::reportTotal()
    {
        cout << "\ntotal number of Box objects created = " << total;
        cout << endl;
    }

void Box::setSize()
    {
        int l, h;

        cout << "\nEnter a length (an int between 2 and 10):  ";
        cin >> l;

        if (l >= 2  &&  l <= 10)  length = l;
        else  length = 1;

        cout << "\nEnter a height (an int between 2 and 6):   ";
        cin >> h;

        if (h >= 2  &&  h <= 6)   height = h;
        else  height = 1;

        cout << "\nEnter a symbol:  ";
        cin >> symbol;

        showBox();
    }
```

```cpp
void Box::showBox()
{
    cout << endl;
    for (int i = 1;  i <= height;  i++)
    {
        for (int j = 1;  j <= length;  j++)  cout << symbol;
        cout << endl;
    }
}

void Box::setLength(int newLength)
{
    if (newLength > 0  &&  newLength <= 70)  length = newLength;
}

void Box::setHeight(int newHeight)
{
    if (newHeight > 0  &&  newHeight <= 10)  height = newHeight;
}

int  Box::getLength()
{
    return length;
}

int  Box::getHeight()
{
    return height;
}

class Square : public Box
{
    public:
        Square()  :  Box(5)
        {
            symbol = 's';
            cout<<"\nSquare's no-argument constructor is running."<< endl;
        }

        Square(int forSides) : Box(forSides)
        {
            symbol = 'S';
            cout<<"\nSquare's one-argument constructor is running."<<endl;
        }

        ~Square()
        {
            cout << "\nSquare's destructor is running." << endl;
        }

        void setLength(int)     // A function in the derived class overrides
        {                       // a function of the same name in the base
        }                       // class even when these functions have
                                // have different signatures.  However, we
                                // have made the signatures the same so that
        void setHeight(int)     // a call to either of these in the derived
                                // class with an argument will not cause a
        {                       // syntax error.  When a formal argument will
                                // not actually be used, it need not be
        }                       // defined.

        void setSide(int sideLength)
        {
            Box::setLength(sideLength);      // Invocations of overridden
            Box::setHeight(sideLength);      // functions inherited from
        }                                    // the base class.

        void setSize()
        {
            int sideLength;
```

```
                              cout << "\nEnter a length for the Square's side:   ";
                              cin >> sideLength;

                              if (sideLength >= 2  &&  sideLength <= 6)
                                 setSide(sideLength);
                              else  setSide(1);

                              cout << "\nEnter a symbol:   ";
                              cin >> symbol;

                              showBox();
                        }

                  };

            void main()
               {
                  Square s;
                  s.showBox();
                  cout << "Square s, above, has sides of length "
                       << s.getLength() << endl;

                  // confirm that setLength() and setHeight() are inactive for Squares
                  s.setLength(21);
                  s.setHeight(7);
                  s.showBox();
                  cout << "Square s, above, has sides of length "
                       << s.getLength() << endl;

                  // testing Square::setSide()
                  s.setSide(9);
                  s.showBox();
                  cout << "Square s, above, has sides of length "
                       << s.getLength()<<endl;

                  // testing Square::setSize()
                  s.setSize();       // Here setSize() displays the re-set Square.
                  cout << "Square s, above, has sides of length "
                       << s.getLength() << endl;

                  // confirm that inheritance works only down the derivation hierarchy
                  Box b;
                  b.showBox();
                  cout << "Box b, created with Box(), is above" << endl;

            // b.setSize(6);        // Box::setSize() takes no argument,    //ERROR!
                                    // It is Square::setSize() that takes an int.

            // b.Square::setSize(6);  // Explicit attempt to invoke         //ERROR!
                                    // Square::setSize(), but this
                                    // is not a member function
                                    // for Box objects.

               }
```

4.1.Z   part i

```
            #include <iostream.h>

            class Box
               {
                  public:
                     char symbol;

                  protected:
                     int length;
```

```
      private:
        int   height, serialNumber;
        static int total;

      public:
        Box();          // No-argument constructor, prototype.
        Box(int);       // One-argument constructor, prototype.
        ~Box();         // Destructor, prototype.
        static void reportTotal();                  // Prototype.
        void showBox();                             // Prototype.
        void setSize();                             // Prototype.
        void setLength(int newLength);              // Prototype.
        void setHeight(int newHeight);             // Prototype.
        int  getLength();                           // Prototype.
        int  getHeight();                           // Prototype.
        void accessDataMembers(Box argument);       // Prototype.
  };

void Box::accessDataMembers(Box argument)
  {
      cout << endl;
      cout << "Re. the invoking object:         ";
      cout << "    length = " << length;
      cout << "    height = " << height;
      cout << "    symbol = " << symbol;
      cout << endl;

      cout << "Re. the argument object:         ";
      cout << "    length = " << argument.length;
      cout << "    height = " << argument.height;
      cout << "    symbol = " << argument.symbol;
      cout << endl;

      Box newBox;
      cout << "Re. a newly defined Box object: ";
      cout << "    length = " << newBox.length;
      cout << "    height = " << newBox.height;
      cout << "    symbol = " << newBox.symbol;
      cout << endl;
  }

int Box::total = 0;

Box::Box() : length(3), height(3), symbol('*')
  {
      serialNumber = ++total;

      cout << "\nBox number " << serialNumber << " is being created";
      cout << endl;
  }

Box::Box(int side) : length(side), height(side), symbol('*')
  {
      serialNumber = ++total;

      cout << "\nBox number " << serialNumber << " is being created";
      cout << endl;
  }

Box::~Box()
  {
      cout << "\nBox number " << serialNumber << " is being deleted";
      cout << endl;
  }

void Box::reportTotal()
  {
      cout << "\ntotal number of Box objects created = " << total;
      cout << endl;
```

```
        }
void Box::setSize()
    {
        int l, h;

        cout << "\nEnter a length (an int between 2 and 10):  ";
        cin >> l;

        if (l >= 2  &&  l <= 10)  length = l;
        else  length = 1;

        cout << "\nEnter a height (an int between 2 and 6):   ";
        cin >> h;

        if (h >= 2  &&  h <= 6)   height = h;
        else  height = 1;

        cout << "\nEnter a symbol:  ";
        cin >> symbol;

        showBox();
    }
void Box::showBox()
    {
        cout << endl;
        for (int i = 1;  i <= height;  i++)
            {
                for (int j = 1;  j <= length;  j++)  cout << symbol;
                cout << endl;
            }
    }
void Box::setLength(int newLength)
    {
        if (newLength > 0  &&  newLength <= 70)  length = newLength;
    }

void Box::setHeight(int newHeight)
    {
        if (newHeight > 0  &&  newHeight <= 10)  height = newHeight;
    }

int  Box::getLength()
    {
        return length;
    }

int  Box::getHeight()
    {
        return height;
    }

class Square : public Box
    {
    };

void main()
    {
        Box b1(5);
        Box b2(7);
        b1.accessDataMembers(b2);
    }
```

4.1.Z part ii

```
#include <iostream.h>
```

```
class Box
    {
      public:
        char symbol;

      protected:
        int length;

      private:
        int  height, serialNumber;
        static int total;

      public:
        Box();          // No-argument constructor, prototype.
        Box(int);       // One-argument constructor, prototype.
        ~Box();         // Destructor, prototype.
        static void reportTotal();          // Prototype.
        void showBox();                     // Prototype.
        void setSize();                     // Prototype.
        void setLength(int newLength);      // Prototype.
        void setHeight(int newHeight);      // Prototype.
        int  getLength();                   // Prototype.
        int  getHeight();                   // Prototype.
    };

int Box::total = 0;

Box::Box() : length(3), height(3), symbol('*')
    {
      serialNumber = ++total;

      cout << "\nBox number " << serialNumber << " is being created";
      cout << endl;
    }

Box::Box(int side) : length(side), height(side), symbol('*')
    {
      serialNumber = ++total;

      cout << "\nBox number " << serialNumber << " is being created";
      cout << endl;
    }

Box::~Box()
    {
      cout << "\nBox number " << serialNumber << " is being deleted";
      cout << endl;
    }

void Box::reportTotal()
    {
      cout << "\ntotal number of Box objects created = " << total;
      cout << endl;
    }

void Box::setSize()
    {
      int l, h;

      cout << "\nEnter a length (an int between 2 and 10):   ";
      cin >> l;

      if (l >= 2  &&  l <= 10)  length = l;
      else  length = l;

      cout << "\nEnter a height (an int between 2 and 6):    ";
      cin >> h;
```

```
        if (h >= 2  &&  h <= 6)    height = h;
        else  height = 1;

        cout << "\nEnter a symbol:  ";
        cin >> symbol;

        showBox();
    }

void Box::showBox()
    {
        cout << endl;
        for (int i = 1;  i <= height;  i++)
        {
            for (int j = 1;  j <= length;  j++)  cout << symbol;
            cout << endl;
        }
    }

void Box::setLength(int newLength)
    {
        if (newLength > 0  &&  newLength <= 70)  length = newLength;
    }

void Box::setHeight(int newHeight)
    {
        if (newHeight > 0  &&  newHeight <= 10)  height = newHeight;
    }

int  Box::getLength()
    {
        return length;
    }

int  Box::getHeight()
    {
        return height;
    }

class Square : public Box
    {
      public:
        void accessDataMembers(Box argument);     // Prototype of version 1.
        void accessDataMembers(Square argument); // Prototype of version 2.
    };

// ***** The First Version that the Exercise Has Us to Test ******
void Square::accessDataMembers(Box argument)
    {
        cout << endl;
        cout << "Re. the invoking object:          ";
        cout << "    length = " << length;
//      cout << "    height = " << height;                // Not accessible => ERROR.
        cout << "    symbol = " << symbol;
        cout << endl;

        cout << "Re. the argument object:          ";
//      cout << "    length = " << argument.length; // Not accessible => ERROR.
//      cout << "    height = " << argument.height; // Not accessible => ERROR.
        cout << "    symbol = " << argument.symbol;
        cout << endl;

        Box newBox;
        cout << "Re. a newly defined Box object: ";
//      cout << "    length = " << newBox.length;   // Not accessible => ERROR.
//      cout << "    height = " << newBox.height;   // Not accessible => ERROR.
        cout << "    symbol = " << newBox.symbol;
        cout << endl;
    }
```

```
// ***** The Second Version that the Exercise Has Us to Test ******
void Square::accessDataMembers(Square argument)
   {
      cout << endl;
      cout << "Re. the invoking object:        ";
      cout << "    length = " << length;
//    cout << "    height = " << height;              // Not accessible => ERROR.
      cout << "    symbol = " << symbol;
      cout << endl;

      cout << "Re. the argument object:         ";
      cout<< "    length = "<<argument.length;
//    cout<< "    height = "<<argument.height;    // Not accessible => ERROR.
      cout << "    symbol = " << argument.symbol;
      cout << endl;

      Square newSquare;
      cout << "Re. a newly defined Square object:";
      cout<< " length = "<<newSquare.length;
//    cout<< "    height = "<<newSquare.height;   // Not accessible => ERROR.
      cout << "    symbol = " << newSquare.symbol;
      cout << endl;
   }

void main()
   {
   Box     b(7);
   Square  s;

   //test of function's version 1
   cout << endl << "Test of accessDataMembers() -- Version 1" << endl;
   s.accessDataMembers(b);

   cout << endl << endl;

   //test of function's version 2
   cout<<endl<<endl<< "Test of accessDataMembers() -- Version 2" << endl;
   Square s2;
   s.accessDataMembers(s2);
   }
```

4.1.Z   part iii

```
#include <iostream.h>

class Box
   {
      public:
        char symbol;

      protected:
        int length;

      private:
        int  height, serialNumber;
        static int total;

      public:
        Box();          // No-argument constructor, prototype.
        Box(int);       // One-argument constructor, prototype.
        ~Box();         // Destructor, prototype.
        static void reportTotal();              // Prototype.
        void showBox();                         // Prototype.
        void setSize();                         // Prototype.
        void setLength(int newLength);          // Prototype.
        void setHeight(int newHeight);          // Prototype.
        int  getLength();                       // Prototype.
        int  getHeight();                       // Prototype.
   };
```

```
int Box::total = 0;

Box::Box() : length(3), height(3), symbol('*')
{
    serialNumber = ++total;

    cout << "\nBox number " << serialNumber << " is being created";
    cout << endl;
}

Box::Box(int side) : length(side), height(side), symbol('*')
{
    serialNumber = ++total;

    cout << "\nBox number " << serialNumber << " is being created";
    cout << endl;
}

Box::~Box()
{
    cout << "\nBox number " << serialNumber << " is being deleted";
    cout << endl;
}

void Box::reportTotal()
{
    cout << "\ntotal number of Box objects created = " << total;
    cout << endl;
}

void Box::setSize()
{
    int l, h;

    cout << "\nEnter a length (an int between 2 and 10):   ";
    cin >> l;

    if (l >= 2  &&  l <= 10)   length = l;
    else   length = 1;

    cout << "\nEnter a height (an int between 2 and 6):    ";
    cin >> h;

    if (h >= 2  &&  h <= 6)    height = h;
    else   height = 1;

    cout << "\nEnter a symbol:   ";
    cin >> symbol;

    showBox();
}

void Box::showBox()
{
    cout << endl;
    for (int i = 1;  i <= height;  i++)
    {
        for (int j = 1;  j <= length;  j++)  cout << symbol;
        cout << endl;
    }
}

void Box::setLength(int newLength)
{
    if (newLength > 0  &&  newLength <= 70)   length = newLength;
}

void Box::setHeight(int newHeight)
```

```
        {
            if (newHeight > 0  &&  newHeight <= 10)  height = newHeight;
        }

    int  Box::getLength()
        {
            return length;
        }

    int  Box::getHeight()
        {
            return height;
        }

    class Square : public Box
        {
        };

    void main()
        {
            Box b;
            Square s;

            cout << endl;
            cout << "Re. the Box object:        ";
            //cout << "   length = " << b.length;    // Access denied => ERROR.
            //cout << "   height = " << b.height;    // Access denied => ERROR.
            cout << "   symbol = " << b.symbol;
            cout << endl;

            cout << "Re. the Square object:        ";
            //cout << "   length = " << s.length;    // Access denied => ERROR.
            //cout << "   height = " << s.height;    // Access denied => ERROR.
            cout << "   symbol = " << s.symbol;
            cout << endl;
        }
```

4.3.A Well worth reading is George A. Miller's seminal paper entitled "The Magical Number Seven, Plus or Minus Two: Some Limits on Our Capacity for Processing Information" in the March 1956 issue of *The Psychological Review*. Among his illustrations of the power of abstraction, which he spoke of as the recoding of data or facts into chunks, is how much more information we can handle, and more reliably, when bit strings are expressed in hex (e.g., the advantage of ABC over 101010111100). Spoken languages offer simple subsuming names for things it would be inefficient to reference by enumerating their components and structure (e.g., a bicycle as opposed to a vehicle propelled by pedaling consisting of two wheels, in tandem, connected by a tubular frame upon which is mounted a saddle seat . . .).

Programming students see the advantage of abstraction when given the problem of using a stack to evaluate a postfix expression. It is a boon to be able to code "push" and "pop" when we want these actions performed, rather than to digress from the focus of the postfix evaluation to the stack's mechanics. Similarly, it is a boon to be able to refer to a data composite by way of the struct's name.

Abstraction designates this kind of information chunking, and it enables programs that are easier to follow and more likely to be correct. It works against logical clutter and thereby promotes clean, incisive, problem-solving.

If abstraction refers to the bundling of functionality and/or data, encapsulation denotes abstraction with the connotation that what is bundled up is something we might not be able to do for ourselves. For instance, a beginner may know how to call functions but not know how to drop back into assembler to read the system's clock. Encapsulation confers this ability. Alternately, "encapsulation" may connote a list of the activities embodied within an abstraction: "function X encapsulates this, that, and the other thing."

Encapsulation stresses access to operations we might be unable to do or find difficult to do ourselves or an enumeration of the embodied parts.

Information hiding connotes the enforcement of provided abstraction. If the parts within a structure are concealed, they cannot be directly manipulated and their implementation becomes irrelevant. This leads to exceedingly weak coupling and thus promotes maintainability. (See exercise 4.1.I.)

4.3.B.i An abstract data type is traditionally described as an information storage structure coupled to a set of operations for the information's management.

A queue is any linear storage structure managed with the operations of appending incoming information to the rear and removing information from the front.

A stack is any linear storage structure managed by entering and removing information from the same end. Being a well-known abstract data type, its operations have agreed-upon names: push and pop. These are abstractions inasmuch as they have a definite semantic content but do not denote operative detail. Beginning students sometimes observe that it is, in fact, possible to provide programming support for entering new information at the stack's other end. This, of course, is true; but violating the management discipline destroys the formal properties of the abstract data type.

What makes the queue and the stack abstract data types is that they may be implemented in any number of ways and that the specifics of the construction have no bearing on their formal properties. A stack may be implemented as an array, or it may be implemented with dynamically allocated nodes. To the application pushing and popping operands in order to evaluate a postfix expression, the operationalization is of no relevance.

Those of us in the trade of writing programs such as operating systems or compilers find that we often need queues and stacks. But those who design applications for different realms deal with other kinds of objects, such as a savings account. If these are viewed as an information repository, where the information represents its "vital statistics" or state, and viewed as requiring management in accordance with a particular set of constraints; then they are abstract data types in the same sense as a queue or a stack.

4.3.B.ii Pascal has no ability to realize an operative analogue of a queue, a stack, a bank account, a television set, or any other abstract data type. It is impossible to put our pencil on the point where the queue or the stack is defined in the given program, or to put a circle around an appearance of the queue or the stack on any line of code because these are simply not there.

At best, the queue's existence is shadowy. There is a head and a rear, but two pointers are not the same thing as a queue. Nothing about the sequence of nodes that we construe as the queue governs the operations that may be applied to it. We are on our honor not to push a node onto the front.

4.3.C This answer (a program) is given in Exercise 4.3.D.

4.3.D

```
#include <iostream.h>
```

```
class Queue
  {
    private:
      struct queueNode
        {
          char  letter;
          queueNode* next;
        };

      queueNode  *head, *rear;

    public:
      void  initializeQueue();

      void  append(char  letterToAdd);
      // Attaches new node, holding letterToAdd.

      char  takeOff_and_return();
      // Takes front node off list and returns its letter.

      int  queueEmpty();
      // Returns "true" if the queue is empty, "false" if it is not.

      void  showQueue();
      // A utility for displaying the letters on the queue.
  };

class Stack
  {
    private:
      struct stackNode
        {
          char  letter;
          stackNode*  next;
        };

      stackNode* stackTop;

    public:
      void  initializeStack();

      void  push(char letterToAdd);
      // Pushes new node, holding letterToAdd, onto top of stack.

      char  pop();
      // Pops node from the top of the stack and
      // returns the letter it held.

      int  stackEmpty();
      // Returns "true" is stack is empty, "false" if it is not.
  };

void main()
  {
    // Define the five queues:
    Queue queue1, queue2, queue3, queue4, queue5;

    // Initialize the queues:
    queue1.initializeQueue();
    queue2.initializeQueue();
    queue3.initializeQueue();
    queue4.initializeQueue();
    queue5.initializeQueue();

    // Define a Stack.
    Stack stack;
    stack.initializeStack();
```

```
// Load queue1.
char letter;
for (letter = 'A'; letter <= 'E'; letter++)
   queue1.append(letter);

// Load queue2.
for (letter = 'A'; letter <= 'E'; letter++)
   queue2.append(letter);

// Reverse the letters on queue2.

   // Step 1:  tranfers the letters from the queue to the stack.
   while ( !queue2.queueEmpty() )
      {
        letter = queue2.takeOff_and_return();
        stack.push(letter);
      }

   // Step 2:  transfers the letters from the stack to the queue.
   while ( !stack.stackEmpty() )
      {
        letter = stack.pop();
        queue2.append(letter);
      }

// Load queue3.
char numeral;
for (numeral = '1'; numeral <= '9'; numeral++)
   queue3.append(numeral);

// Load queue4.
for (numeral = '1'; numeral <= '9'; numeral++)
   queue4.append(numeral);

// Reverse the numerals on queue4.

   // Step 1:  tranfers the numerals from the queue to the stack.
   while ( !queue4.queueEmpty() )
      {
        letter = queue4.takeOff_and_return();
        stack.push(letter);
      }

   // Step 2:  transfers the numerals from the stack to the queue.
   while ( !stack.stackEmpty() )
      {
        letter = stack.pop();
        queue4.append(letter);
      }

// Load queue5.
queue5.append('S');
queue5.append('C');
queue5.append('R');
queue5.append('U');
queue5.append('N');
queue5.append('C');
queue5.append('H');
queue5.append('E');
queue5.append('D');

// Display the queues.
cout << endl << "queue1:    ";  queue1.showQueue();
cout << endl << "queue2:    ";  queue2.showQueue();
cout << endl << "queue3:    ";  queue3.showQueue();
cout << endl << "queue4:    ";  queue4.showQueue();
cout << endl << "queue5:    ";  queue5.showQueue();
}  // main()

// Functions for managing the queue (Queue's member functions).
```

```
void  Queue::initializeQueue()
  {
    head = rear = NULL;
  }

void  Queue::append(char letterToAdd)
  {
    queueNode* newNode = new  queueNode;
    newNode->letter = letterToAdd;
    newNode->next   = NULL;

    if ( queueEmpty() )
      {
        head = newNode;
        rear = newNode;
      }
    else
      {
        rear->next = newNode;
        rear = newNode;
      }
  }

char Queue::takeOff_and_return()
  {
    char forReturn;
    queueNode* oldNode = NULL;

    if ( !queueEmpty() )  // Only works if the queue is not empty.
      {
        forReturn = head->letter;
        oldNode = head;
        if (head->next == NULL) // Here head node is the only node.
          {
            head = NULL;
            rear = NULL;
          }
        else head = head->next;
      }
    else forReturn = '\0';     // List is empty; return null 0.

    delete oldNode;
    return forReturn;
  }

int  Queue::queueEmpty()
  {
    if (head == NULL) return 1;  // Yes, queue is empty.
    else  return 0;
  }

void  Queue::showQueue()
  {
    queueNode*  rovingPtr;
    rovingPtr = head;

    while (rovingPtr != NULL)
      {
        cout << rovingPtr->letter;
        rovingPtr = rovingPtr -> next;
      }
  }

// function for managing the stack (Stack's member functions)

void  Stack::initializeStack()
  {
    stackTop = NULL;
  }

void  Stack::push(char letterToAdd)
```

```
      {
        stackNode* newNode = new stackNode;
        newNode->letter = letterToAdd;

        if ( stackEmpty() )  newNode->next = NULL;
        else  newNode ->next = stackTop;

        stackTop = newNode;
      }

  char Stack::pop()
      {
        char forReturn;
        stackNode* oldNode = NULL;

        if (! stackEmpty() ) // Only works if stack is not empty.
          {
            oldNode = stackTop;
            forReturn = stackTop->letter;
            stackTop = stackTop -> next;
          }
        else  forReturn = '\0';  // If stack empty, return null zero.

        delete oldNode;
        return forReturn;
      }

  int   Stack::stackEmpty()
      {
        if (stackTop == NULL) return 1;  // Yes, stack is empty.
        else return 0;
      }
```

4.3.E

```
  #include <iostream.h>

  class Queue
      {
      private:
        struct queueNode
          {
            char  letter;
            queueNode* next;
          };

        queueNode  *head, *rear;

      public:
        Queue();   // Constructor -- sets head and rear to NULL.

        ~Queue();  // Destructor  -- deletes the nodes on the queue.

        void  initializeQueue();

        void  append(char  letterToAdd);
         // Attaches new node, holding letterToAdd.

        char  takeOff_and_return();
        // Takes front node off list and returns its letter.

        int   queueEmpty();
        // Returns "true" if the queue is empty, "false" if it is not.

        void  showQueue();
        // A utility for displaying the letters on the queue.
      };
```

```
class Stack
{
  private:
    struct stackNode
      {
        char   letter;
        stackNode*  next;
      };

    stackNode* stackTop;

  public:
    Stack();     // Constructor  -- sets stackTop to NULL.

    ~Stack();    // Destructor   -- deletes nodes on the stack.

    void  initializeStack();

    void  push(char letterToAdd);
     // Pushes new node, holding letterToAdd, onto top of stack.

    char  pop();
    // Pops node from the top of the stack and
    // returns the letter it held.

     int   stackEmpty();
     // Returns "true" if stack is empty, "false" if it is not.
};

void allProcessing()
{
    // Define the five queues:
    Queue queue1, queue2, queue3, queue4, queue5;

    // Define a Stack.
    Stack stack;

    // Load queue1.
    char letter;
    for (letter = 'A'; letter <= 'E'; letter++)
       queue1.append(letter);

    // Load queue2.
    for (letter = 'A'; letter <= 'E'; letter++)
       queue2.append(letter);

    // Reverse the letters on queue2.

      // Step 1:  tranfers the letters from the queue to the stack.
      while ( !queue2.queueEmpty() )
        {
          letter = queue2.takeOff_and_return();
          stack.push(letter);
        }

      // Step 2:  transfers the letters from the stack to the queue.
      while ( !stack.stackEmpty() )
        {
          letter = stack.pop();
          queue2.append(letter);
        }

    // Load queue3.
    char numeral;
    for (numeral = '1'; numeral <= '9'; numeral++)
       queue3.append(numeral);

    // Load queue4.
    for (numeral = '1'; numeral <= '9'; numeral++)
```

```
          queue4.append(numeral);

       // Reverse the numerals on queue4.

          // Step 1:   tranfers the numerals from the queue to the stack.
          while ( !queue4.queueEmpty() )
             {
               letter = queue4.takeOff_and_return();
               stack.push(letter);
             }

          // Step 2:   transfers the numerals from the stack to the queue.
          while ( !stack.stackEmpty() )
             {
               letter = stack.pop();
               queue4.append(letter);
             }

       // Load queue5.
       queue5.append('S');
       queue5.append('C');
       queue5.append('R');
       queue5.append('U');
       queue5.append('N');
       queue5.append('C');
       queue5.append('H');
       queue5.append('E');
       queue5.append('D');

       // Display the queues.
       cout << endl << "queue1:     ";   queue1.showQueue();
       cout << endl << "queue2:     ";   queue2.showQueue();
       cout << endl << "queue3:     ";   queue3.showQueue();
       cout << endl << "queue4:     ";   queue4.showQueue();
       cout << endl << "queue5:     ";   queue5.showQueue();
    }   // allProcessing()

void main()
    {
       cout << "\n** main() invoking allProcessing() **\n";
       allProcessing();
       cout << "\n** main() concluding **\n";
    }

// functions for managing the queue (Queue's member functions)

Queue::Queue() : head(NULL), rear(NULL)
    {
       cout << "\n** Queue constructor initializing head and rear **\n";
    }

Queue::~Queue()
    {
       cout << "\n** Queue destructor deleting nodes on queue:   ";
       showQueue();
       cout << " **\n";

       queueNode* oldNode;
       while (head != NULL)
          {
            oldNode = head;
            head = head -> next;
            delete oldNode;
          }
    }

void  Queue::initializeQueue()
    {
      head = rear = NULL;
    }
```

```
void  Queue::append(char letterToAdd)
{
    queueNode* newNode = new  queueNode;
    newNode->letter = letterToAdd;
    newNode->next   = NULL;

    if ( queueEmpty() )
    {
        head = newNode;
        rear = newNode;
    }
    else
    {
        rear->next = newNode;
        rear = newNode;
    }
}

char Queue::takeOff_and_return()
{
    char forReturn;
    queueNode* oldNode = NULL;

    if ( !queueEmpty() )  // Only works if the queue is not empty.
    {
        forReturn = head->letter;
        oldNode = head;
        if (head->next == NULL) // Here head node is the only node.
        {
            head = NULL;
            rear = NULL;
        }
        else head = head->next;
    }
    else forReturn = '\0';  // If list empty, return the null zero.

    delete oldNode;
    return forReturn;
}

int  Queue::queueEmpty()
{
    if (head == NULL) return 1;  // Yes, queue is empty.
    else  return 0;
}

void  Queue::showQueue()
{
    queueNode*  rovingPtr;
    rovingPtr = head;

    while (rovingPtr != NULL)
    {
        cout << rovingPtr->letter;
        rovingPtr = rovingPtr -> next;
    }
}

// Function for managing the stack (Stack's member functions).

Stack::Stack() : stackTop(NULL)
{
    cout << "\n** Stack constructor initializing stackTop **\n";
}

Stack::~Stack()
{
    cout << "\n** Stack destructor running **\n";

    stackNode* oldNode;
    while (stackTop != NULL)
```

```
                                {
                                    oldNode = stackTop;
                                    stackTop = stackTop -> next;
                                    delete oldNode;
                                }
                        }

                void  Stack::initializeStack()
                        {
                            stackTop = NULL;
                        }

                void  Stack::push(char letterToAdd)
                        {
                            stackNode* newNode = new stackNode;
                            newNode->letter = letterToAdd;

                            if ( stackEmpty() )  newNode->next = NULL;
                            else  newNode ->next = stackTop;

                            stackTop = newNode;
                        }

                    char Stack::pop()
                        {
                            char forReturn;
                            stackNode* oldNode = NULL;

                            if (! stackEmpty() ) // Only works if stack is not empty.
                                {
                                    oldNode = stackTop;
                                    forReturn = stackTop->letter;
                                    stackTop = stackTop -> next;
                                }
                            else  forReturn = '\0';  // If stack empty, return null zero.

                            delete oldNode;
                            return forReturn;
                        }

                int   Stack::stackEmpty()
                        {
                            if (stackTop == NULL) return 1;  // Yes, stack is empty.
                            else return 0;
                        }
```

4.3.F The program for this answer is the same as for Exercise 4.3.E. except for the two
functions shown in the following.

The function prototypes, as they appear within their respective class specifiers:

```
void  initializeQueue();
// Deletes nodes on the queue; sets head and rear to NULL.

void  initializeStack();
// Deletes nodes on the stack; sets stackTop to NULL.
```

The function definitions:

```
void  Queue::initializeQueue()
    {
        queueNode* oldNode;
        while (head != NULL)
            {
                oldNode = head;
                head = head -> next;
                delete oldNode;
            }
```

```
      rear = NULL;
}

void  Stack::initializeStack()
    {
    stackNode* oldNode;
    while (stackTop != NULL)
        {
        oldNode = stackTop;
        stackTop = stackTop -> next;
        delete oldNode;
        }
    }
```

4.3.G. The exercises asked for an assignment operator, *Queue::operator =( )*, which makes deep copies.

In order to contrast the action of the language-provided assignment operator to the one being written (as well as to allow the right operand *Queue* passed to *Queue::operator =( )* and the returned *Queue* to be transmitted by value), a copy constructor that furnishes deep copies was also needed.

Following is the assignment operator, the copy constructor, and some code to test these.

The function declarations (prototypes), appearing within *Queue* class specifier:

```
Queue(Queue&); // Copy constructor -- makes a deep copy
               //  of the Queue in transmitted arguments.

Queue operator= (Queue rightQueue);
// Provides deep copies, supports multiple assignment.
```

The definitions of these functions:

```
// Copy constructor.
Queue::Queue(Queue& q)  : head(NULL), rear(NULL)
    {
    cout << "\n** Queue's copy constructor is running **\n";

    queueNode* traversingPtr;
    traversingPtr = q.head;

    while (traversingPtr != NULL)
        {
        append(traversingPtr -> letter);
        traversingPtr = traversingPtr -> next;
        }
    }

// Assignment operator, makes deep copies.
Queue Queue::operator= (Queue rightQueue)
    {
    cout << "operator= is running" << endl;
    initializeQueue();  // deletes nodes (if any)
                        // on left operand

    queueNode* traversingPtr;
    traversingPtr = rightQueue.head;
    while (traversingPtr != NULL)
        {
        append(traversingPtr -> letter);
        traversingPtr = traversingPtr -> next;
        }

    return rightQueue;
    }
```

```
                              // Code to test these functions.

                              void allProcessing()
                                  {
                                  // Define three queues:
                                  Queue queue1, queue2, queue3;

                                  // Load queue1.
                                  char letter;
                                  for (letter = 'A'; letter <= 'E'; letter++)
                                      queue1.append(letter);

                                  queue3 = queue2 = queue1;

                                  // display the queues
                                  cout << endl << "queue1:     ";  queue1.showQueue();
                                  cout << endl << "queue2:     ";  queue2.showQueue();
                                  cout << endl << "queue3:     ";  queue3.showQueue();

                                  // Append to queue1.
                                  queue1.append('X'); queue1.append('Y'); queue1.append('Z');

                                  // Reverse queue2.
                                  Stack stack;
                                  while (! queue2.queueEmpty() )
                                      {
                                      letter = queue2.takeOff_and_return();
                                      stack.push(letter);
                                      }
                                  while (! stack.stackEmpty() )
                                      {
                                      letter = stack.pop();
                                      queue2.append(letter);
                                      }

                                  // display the queues
                                  cout << endl << "queue1:     ";  queue1.showQueue();
                                  cout << endl << "queue2:     ";  queue2.showQueue();
                                  cout << endl << "queue3:     ";  queue3.showQueue();
                                  }  // allProcessing()

                          void main()
                              {
                              cout << "\n** main() invoking allProcessing() **\n";
                              allProcessing();
                              cout << "\n** main() concluding **\n";
                              }
```

4.3.H

```
        #include <iostream.h>

        class Queue
            {
            private:
                struct queueNode
                    {
                    char  letter;
                    queueNode* next;
                    };

                queueNode  *head, *rear;

            public:
                Queue();   // constructor -- sets head and rear to NULL

                Queue(Queue&); // copy constructor -- makes a deep copy
                // of the Queue in transmitted arguments
```

```
~Queue();  // destructor -- deletes the nodes on the queue

Queue operator= (Queue rightQueue);
// provides deep copies, supports multiple assignment

friend ostream& operator<< (ostream& outStream, Queue q);
// friendship grants access to the private data member, head

void  initializeQueue();
// deletes nodes on the queue; sets head and rear to NULL

void  append(char  letterToAdd);
// attaches new node, holding letterToAdd

char  takeOff_and_return();
// takes front node off list and returns its letter

int   queueEmpty();
// returns "true" if the queue is empty, "false" if it is not

void  showQueue();
// a utility for displaying the letters on the queue
    };

class Stack
    {
    private:
        struct stackNode
            {
            char   letter;
            stackNode*  next;
            };

        stackNode* stackTop;

    public:
        Stack();          // Constructor -- sets stackTop to NULL.

        Stack(Stack&);  // Copy constructor -- makes a deep copy
        // of the stack in transmitted arguments.

        ~Stack();          // Destructor -- deletes nodes on the stack.

        Stack operator= (Stack rightStack);
        // Provides deep copies, supports multiple assignment.

        void  initializeStack();
        // Deletes nodes on the stack; sets stackTop to NULL.

        void  push(char letterToAdd);
        // Pushes new node, holding letterToAdd, onto top of stack.

        char  pop();
        // Pops node from the top of the stack and
        // returns the letter it held.

         int   stackEmpty();
         // Returns "true" is stack is empty, "false" if it is not.
    };

Queue operator+ (Queue q, char letter)
    {
    Queue newQ;
    newQ = q;        // Uses our operator=() which provides a deep copy.
    newQ.append(letter);
    return newQ;
    }
```

```
Stack operator+ (char letter, Stack s)
{
    Stack newS;
    newS = s;
    newS.push(letter);
    return newS;
}

ostream& operator<< (ostream& outStream, Queue q)
{
    queueNode*  rovingPtr;
    rovingPtr = q.head;

    while (rovingPtr != NULL)
    {
        outStream << rovingPtr->letter;
        rovingPtr = rovingPtr -> next;
    }

    return outStream;
}

void allProcessing()
{
    // Define three queues:
    Queue queue1, queue2, queue3;

    // Load queue1.
    char letter;
    for (letter = 'A'; letter <= 'E'; letter++)
        queue1.append(letter);

    queue3 = queue2 = queue1;

    // Display the queues.
    cout << endl << "queue1:     " << queue1;
    cout << endl << "queue2:     " << queue2;
    cout << endl << "queue3:     " << queue3;

    // Append to queue1.
    queue1 = queue1 + 'X';
    queue1 = queue1 + 'Y';
    queue1 = queue1 + 'Z';

    // Reverse queue2.
    Stack stack;
    while (! queue2.queueEmpty() )
    {
        letter = queue2.takeOff_and_return();
        stack = letter + stack;
    }
    while (! stack.stackEmpty() )
    {
        letter = stack.pop();
        queue2 = queue2 + letter;
    }

    // display the queues
    cout << endl << "queue1:     " << queue1;
    cout << endl << "queue2:     " << queue2;
    cout << endl << "queue3:     " << queue3;
}   // allProcessing()

void main()
{
    cout << "\n** main() invoking allProcessing() **\n";
    allProcessing();
    cout << "\n** main() concluding **\n";
}
```

```
// Functions for managing the queue (Queue's member functions).

Queue::Queue() : head(NULL), rear(NULL)
  {
    cout << "\n** Queue constructor initializing head and rear **\n";
  }

Queue::Queue(Queue& q) : head(NULL), rear(NULL)
  {
    cout << "\n** Queue's copy constructor is running **\n";

    queueNode* traversingPtr;
    traversingPtr = q.head;

    while (traversingPtr != NULL)
      {
        append(traversingPtr -> letter);
        traversingPtr = traversingPtr -> next;
      }
  }

Queue::~Queue()
  {
    cout << "\n** Queue destructor deleting nodes on queue:   ";
    showQueue();
    cout << " **\n";

    queueNode* oldNode;
    while (head != NULL)
      {
        oldNode = head;
        head = head -> next;
        delete oldNode;
      }
  }

Queue Queue::operator= (Queue rightQueue)
  {
    cout << "Queue's operator=() is running" << endl;
    initializeQueue();  // deletes nodes (if any) on left operand

    queueNode* traversingPtr;
    traversingPtr = rightQueue.head;
    while (traversingPtr != NULL)
      {
        append(traversingPtr -> letter);
        traversingPtr = traversingPtr -> next;
      }

    return rightQueue;
  }

void  Queue::initializeQueue()
  {
    queueNode* oldNode;
    while (head != NULL)
      {
        oldNode = head;
        head = head -> next;
        delete oldNode;
      }
    rear = NULL;
  }

void  Queue::append(char letterToAdd)
  {
    queueNode* newNode = new  queueNode;
    newNode->letter = letterToAdd;
    newNode->next   = NULL;
```

```
            if ( queueEmpty() )
              {
                head = newNode;
                rear = newNode;
              }
            else
              {
                rear->next = newNode;
                rear = newNode;
              }
        }

char Queue::takeOff_and_return()
  {
    char forReturn;
    queueNode* oldNode = NULL;

    if ( !queueEmpty() )  // Only works if queue is not empty.
      {
        forReturn = head->letter;
        oldNode = head;
        if (head->next == NULL) // Here head node is the only node.
          {
            head = NULL;
            rear = NULL;
          }
        else head = head->next;
      }
    else forReturn = '\0';  // If list empty, return the null zero.

    delete oldNode;
    return forReturn;
  }

int  Queue::queueEmpty()
  {
    if (head == NULL) return 1;  // Yes, queue is empty.
    else  return 0;
  }

void  Queue::showQueue()
  {
    queueNode*  rovingPtr;
    rovingPtr = head;

    while (rovingPtr != NULL)
      {
        cout << rovingPtr->letter;
        rovingPtr = rovingPtr -> next;
      }
  }

// Function for managing the stack (Stack's member functions).

Stack::Stack() : stackTop(NULL)
  {
    cout << "\n** Stack constructor initializing stackTop **\n";
  }

Stack::Stack(Stack& s) : stackTop(NULL)
  {
    cout << "\n** Stack's copy constructor is running **\n";

    Stack holder;

    stackNode* traversingPtr;
    traversingPtr = s.stackTop;

    while (traversingPtr != NULL)
      {
```

```
            holder.push(traversingPtr -> letter);
            traversingPtr = traversingPtr -> next;
        }

    traversingPtr = holder.stackTop;
    while (traversingPtr != NULL)
        {
            push(traversingPtr -> letter);
            traversingPtr = traversingPtr -> next;
        }
}

Stack::~Stack()
    {
    cout << "\n** Stack destructor running **\n";

    stackNode* oldNode;
    while (stackTop != NULL)
        {
            oldNode = stackTop;
            stackTop = stackTop -> next;
            delete oldNode;
        }
    }

Stack Stack::operator= (Stack rightStack)
    {
    cout << "Stack's operator=() is running" << endl;
    initializeStack();  // deletes nodes (if any) on left operand

    Stack holder;

    stackNode* traversingPtr;
    traversingPtr = rightStack.stackTop;

    while (traversingPtr != NULL)
        {
            holder.push(traversingPtr -> letter);
            traversingPtr = traversingPtr -> next;
        }

    traversingPtr = holder.stackTop;
    while (traversingPtr != NULL)
        {
            push(traversingPtr -> letter);
            traversingPtr = traversingPtr -> next;
        }

    return rightStack;
    }

void  Stack::initializeStack()
    {
    stackNode* oldNode;
    while (stackTop != NULL)
        {
            oldNode = stackTop;
            stackTop = stackTop -> next;
            delete oldNode;
        }
    }

void  Stack::push(char letterToAdd)
    {
    stackNode* newNode = new stackNode;
    newNode->letter = letterToAdd;

    if ( stackEmpty() )  newNode->next = NULL;
    else  newNode ->next = stackTop;
```

```
        stackTop = newNode;
    }

    char Stack::pop()
    {
        char forReturn;
        stackNode* oldNode = NULL;

        if (! stackEmpty() ) // Only works if stack is not empty.
        {
            oldNode = stackTop;
            forReturn = stackTop->letter;
            stackTop = stackTop -> next;
        }
        else  forReturn = '\0';  // If stack empty, return null zero.

        delete oldNode;
        return forReturn;
    }

int    Stack::stackEmpty()
{
    if (stackTop == NULL) return 1;  // Yes, stack is empty.
    else return 0;
}
```

4.5.A The name of a class's immediate base class (or classes) appears on the opening line of its specifier. That the Subtracter class is derived from Adder class is shown by:

```
class Subtracter : public Adder
{
    // ...
};
```

that the Multiplier class is derived from the Subtracter class is shown by:

```
class Multiplier : public Subtracter
{
    // ...
};
```

and that the Divider class is derived from the Multiplier class is shown by:

```
class Divider   :   public Multiplier
{
    // ...
};
```

4.5.B

```
#include <iostream.h>

class Adder
{
    public:
        char*  getType() { return "Adder"; }
        int  add(int a, int b) { return a+b; }
};

class Subtracter : public Adder
{
    public:
        char*  getType()  { return "Subtracter"; }

    private:
        int addInverse(int a)  { return 0 - a; }
```

```
    public:
       int  sub(int a, int b)
          {
            return add(a, addInverse(b));   // Uses inherited function.
          }
  };

class Multiplier : public Subtracter
  {
    public:
       char*  getType() { return "Multiplier"; }
       int  mult(int a, int b);                          // Prototype.
  };

class Divider : public Multiplier
  {
    public:
       char*  getType() { return "Divider"; }
       int  div(int a, int b);                           // Prototype.
  };

  int Multiplier::mult(int a, int b)
    {
      // multiplies a*b  for  b >= 0

      int accum = 0;

      int loopCounter = 0;
      while (loopCounter < b)
         {
           accum       = add(accum, a);      // Uses inherited function.
           loopCounter = add(loopCounter, 1);
         }
      return accum;
    }

  int Divider::div(int a, int b)
    {
      // performs an integer divide, a/b,  for  a >= 0  and  b > 0
      int accum = 0;
      while (a >= 0)
         {
           accum = add(accum, 1);            // Uses inherited function.
           a     = sub(a, b);                // Uses inherited function.
         }
      accum = sub(accum, 1);                 // Uses inherited function.
      return accum;
    }

  void main()
    {
      cout << endl;

      // Definition and test of a statically defined Adder.
      Adder  adder;
      cout << "\nTest of adder.getType(): " << adder.getType();
      cout << "\nTest of adder.add(3,4):  " << adder.add(3,4);

      // Definition and test of a statically defined Subtracter.
      Subtracter subtracter;
      cout << "\nTest of subtracter.getType(): "
              << subtracter.getType();
      cout << "\nTest of subtacter.sub(10,4):   "
              << subtracter.sub(10,4);

      // Definition and test of a statically defined Multiplier.
      Multiplier multiplier;
      cout << "\nTest of multipler.getType():  "
              << multiplier.getType();
      cout << "\nTest of multipler.mult(7,3):  "
```

```
                                     << multiplier.mult(7,3);

            // Definition and test of a statically defined Divider.
            Divider divider;
            cout << "\nTest of divider.getType():  "
                 << divider.getType();
            cout << "\nTest of divider.div(54,6):  "
                 << divider.div(54,6);

            // Testing the inherited functionality of the Divider object.
            cout <<endl;

            cout << "\nTest of divider.add(12,8):  "  << divider.add(12,8);
            cout << "\nTest of divider.sub(12,8):  "  << divider.sub(12,8);
            cout << "\nTest of divider.mult(2,3):  "  << divider.mult(2,3);

            cout << "\nTest of divider.Adder::getType():       "
                 << divider.Adder::getType();
            cout << "\nTest of divider.Subtracter::getType():  "
                 << divider.Subtracter::getType();
            cout << "\nTest of divider.Multiplier::getType():  "
                 << divider.Multiplier::getType();
            cout << "\nTest of divider.Divider::getType():  "
                 << divider.Divider::getType();
            cout << endl;

            // Definition and test of a dynamically defined Adder.
            Adder*  addPtr;
            addPtr = new Adder;
            cout << "\nTest of addPtr->getType():  " << addPtr->getType();
            cout << "\nTest of addPtr->add(3,4):   " << addPtr->add(3,4);

            // Definition and test of a dynamically defined Subtracter.
            Subtracter* subPtr;
            subPtr = new Subtracter;
            cout << "\nTest of subPtr->getType():   " << subPtr->getType();
            cout << "\nTest of subPtr->sub(10,4):   " << subPtr->sub(10,4);

            // Definition and test of a dynamically defined Multiplier.
            Multiplier* multPtr;
            multPtr = new Multiplier;
            cout << "\nTest of multPtr->getType():  "
                 << multPtr->getType();
            cout << "\nTest of multPtr->mult(7,3):  "
                 << multPtr->mult(7,3);

            // Definition and test of a dynamically defined Divider.
            Divider* divPtr;
            divPtr = new Divider;
            cout << "\nTest of divPtr->getType():  " << divPtr->getType();
            cout << "\nTest of divPtr->div(54,6):  " << divPtr->div(54,6);
            cout << endl;

            // Testing the inherited functionality of the dynamic Divider.

            cout << "\nTest of divPtr->add(12,8):  "  << divPtr->add(12,8);
            cout << "\nTest of divPtr->sub(12,8):  "  << divPtr->sub(12,8);
            cout << "\nTest of divPtr->mult(2,3):  "  << divPtr->mult(2,3);

            cout << "\nTest of divPtr->Adder::getType():       "
                 << divPtr->Adder::getType();
            cout << "\nTest of divPtr->Subtracter::getType():  "
                 << divPtr->Subtracter::getType();
            cout << "\nTest of divPtr->Multiplier::getType():  "
                 << divPtr->Multiplier::getType();
            cout << "\nTest of divPtr->Divider::getType():  "
                 << divPtr->Divider::getType();
```

```
        cout << endl;
    }
```

4.5.D We installed the following function just ahead of main( ):

```
int exponentiate(Multiplier* m, int base, int power)
{
    int accum = 1;
    while (power > 0)
    {
        accum = m->mult(base, accum);
        power = m->sub(power, 1);
    }
    return accum;
}
```

Within *main( )* we tested with this:

```
void main()
{
    cout << endl << "2**10 = "
         << exponentiate(new Multiplier, 2, 10) << endl;

    cout << endl << "2**10 = "
         << exponentiate(new Multiplier(), 2, 10) << endl;
}
```

4.5.E The three *Multiplier* constructors and the three *Divider* constructors are shown in the following.

```
class Multiplier : public Subtracter
{
  public:
    Multiplier()
    {
        cout << "\nfrom Multiplier's no-argument constructor \n";
    }

    Multiplier(int a, int b)
    {
        cout << "\nfrom Multiplier's (int,int) constructor:   ";
        cout << "rec'd:  " << a << "  and  " << b << endl;
    }

    Multiplier(char* string)
    {
        cout << "\nfrom Multiplier's (char*) constructor:   ";
        cout << "rec'd:  " << string << endl;
    }

    char* getType() { return "Multiplier"; }
    int  mult(int a, int b);                              // Prototype.
};

class Divider : public Multiplier
{
  public:
    Divider()
    {
        cout << " from Divider's no-argument constructor \n";
    }

    Divider(int i, int j, int k) : Multiplier(i+j+k, 100)
    {
        cout << " from Divider's (int,int,int) constructor:   ";
        cout << "rec'd:  "<< i <<",  " << j <<", and  " << k << endl;
    }
```

```
            Divider(char* string) : Multiplier(string)
                {
                    cout << " from Divider's (char*) constructor:  ";
                    cout << "rec'd:  " << string << endl;
                }

            char*  getType() { return "Divider"; }
            int  div(int a, int b);                          // Prototype.
        };
```

Following is their test.

```
    void main()
        {
            Divider    d_noArg;
            Divider    d_threeInt(1,2,3);
            Divider    d_string("Test string one.");

            Divider*   ptrD_noArg     = new Divider();
            Divider*   ptrD_ThreeInt  = new Divider(4,5,6);
            Divider*   ptrD_string    = new Divider("Test string two.");
        }
```

4.5.F

```
#include <iostream.h>

class Adder
    {
    protected:
        Adder()
            {
            }

    public:
        char*  getType() { return "Adder"; }
        int  add(int a, int b) { return a+b; }
    };

class Subtracter : public Adder
    {
    protected:
        Subtracter()
            {
            }

    public:
        char*  getType()  { return "Subtracter"; }

    private:
        int addInverse(int a)  { return 0 - a; }

    public:
        int  sub(int a, int b)
            {
                return add(a, addInverse(b));   // Uses inherited function.
            }
    };

class Multiplier : public Subtracter
    {
    protected:
        Multiplier()
            {

            }
```

```
    public:
      char*  getType() { return "Multiplier"; }
      int  mult(int a, int b);                           // Prototype.
  };

class Divider : public Multiplier
  {
    protected:
      Divider()
        {

        }

    public:
      char*  getType() { return "Divider"; }
      int  div(int a, int b);                            // Prototype.
  };

class Arithmetic : public Divider
  {
    public:
      int plus(int operand1, int operand2)
        {
          return  add(operand1, operand2);
        }

      int minus(int operand1, int operand2)
        {
          return sub(operand1, operand2);
        }

      int times(int operand1, int operand2)
        {
          return mult(operand1, operand2);
        }

      int slash(int operand1, int operand2)
        {
          return div(operand1, operand2);
        }

      char* getType()
        {
          return "";
        }
  };

  int Multiplier::mult(int a, int b)
    {
      // Multiplies a*b  for  b >= 0.

      int accum = 0;

      int loopCounter = 0;
      while (loopCounter < b)
        {
          accum       = add(accum, a);          // Uses inherited function.
          loopCounter = add(loopCounter, 1);    // Uses inherited function.
        }
      return accum;
    }

  int Divider::div(int a, int b)
    {
      // Performs an integer divide, a/b,  for  a >= 0  and  b > 0.
      int accum = 0;
      while (a >= 0)
        {
          accum = add(accum, 1);                // Uses inherited function.
          a     = sub(a, b);                    // Uses inherited function.
```

```
                }
            accum = sub(accum, 1);              // Uses inherited function.
            return accum;
        }

    void main()
        {
        //Definition and test of a statically defined Arithmetic object.
        Arithmetic arithmetic;
        cout << "\n arithmetic.plus(6, 7)    = " << arithmetic.plus(6,7);
        cout << "\n arithmetic.minus(19, 4) = " << arithmetic.minus(19,4);
        cout << "\n arithmetic.times(6, 8)   = " << arithmetic.times(6,8);
        cout << "\n arithmetic.slash(28,7)   = " << arithmetic.slash(28,7);
        cout << "\n arithmetic.getType()   ==> " << arithmetic.getType();
        cout << endl;

        //Definition and test of a dynamically defined Arithmetic object.
        Arithmetic*  arithPtr = new Arithmetic;
        cout << "\n arithPtr->plus(6, 7)    = " << arithPtr->plus(6,7);
        cout << "\n arithPtr->minus(19, 4) = " << arithPtr->minus(19,4);
        cout << "\n arithPtr->times(6, 8)   = " << arithPtr->times(6,8);
        cout << "\n arithPtr->slash(28,7)   = " << arithPtr->slash(28,7);
        cout << "\n arithPtr->getType()   ==> " << arithPtr->getType();
        cout << endl;
        }
```

4.7.A   True.

4.7.B   True.

4.7.C   True.

4.7.D   False. Its return type must be the same as well.

4.7.E   True.

Chapter 5

5.1.A

```
#include <iostream.h>

// void fancyPrint(int i);    // Prototype.

template <class Type>          // Prototype for function template.
void fancyPrint(Type t);

void main()
    {
    cout << endl;

    // Passing int, float, char, and string literals.
    cout << " 1:   " ;  fancyPrint(12);
    cout << " 2:   " ;  fancyPrint(3.14159);
    cout << " 3:  " ;   fancyPrint('A');
    cout << " 4:   " ;  fancyPrint("Wow!  It's Working!!");
```

```
// Passing variables and pointers.
int     i = 123;
float   f = 2.71828;
char    c = 'Z';
char    string[] = "Greetings";

cout << " 5:   " ;  fancyPrint( i );
cout << " 6:   " ;  fancyPrint( f );
cout << " 7:   " ;  fancyPrint( c );
cout << " 8:   " ;  fancyPrint( string );
cout << " 9:   " ;  fancyPrint( &i );

// Passing expressions.
cout << "10:   " ;  fancyPrint( 1+1 );
cout << "11:   " ;  fancyPrint( 2*i );
cout << "12:   " ;  fancyPrint( (int) ('z' - c) );
}

//   void fancyPrint(int i)
//      {
//         cout << "    ---> " << i << " <---" << endl;
//      }

template <class Type>        // Function template definition.
void fancyPrint(Type t)
   {
      cout << "    ---> " << t << " <---" << endl;
   }
```

5.1.B

```
#include <iostream.h>

void fancyPrint(int i);     // Prototype for int specialization.

template <class Type>        // Prototype for function template.
void fancyPrint(Type t);

void main()
   {
      cout << endl;

      // Passing int, float, char, and string literals.
      cout << " 1:   " ;  fancyPrint(12);
      cout << " 2:   " ;  fancyPrint(3.14159);
      cout << " 3:   " ;  fancyPrint('A');
      cout << " 4:   " ;  fancyPrint("Wow!  It's Working!!");

      // Passing variables and pointers.
      int     i = 123;
      float   f = 2.71828;
      char    c = 'Z';
      char    string[] = "Greetings";

      cout << " 5:   " ;  fancyPrint( i );
      cout << " 6:   " ;  fancyPrint( f );
      cout << " 7:   " ;  fancyPrint( c );
      cout << " 8:   " ;  fancyPrint( string );
      cout << " 9:   " ;  fancyPrint( &i );

      // Passing expressions.
      cout << "10:   " ;  fancyPrint( 1+1 );
      cout << "11:   " ;  fancyPrint( 2*i );
      cout << "12:   " ;  fancyPrint( (int) ('z' - c) );
   }
```

```
void fancyPrint(int i)     // An int specialization.
{
    cout << "    ---> " << i << " <--- "
         << "(via int specialization)" << endl;
}

template <class Type>       // Function template definition.
void fancyPrint(Type t)
{
    cout << "     ---> " << t << " <---" << endl;
}
```

5.1.C

```
#include <iostream.h>

void fancyPrint(int i)     // An int specialization.
{
    cout << "    ---> " << i << " <--- "
         << "(via int specialization)" << endl;
}

template <class Type>       // Function template definition.
void fancyPrint(Type t)
{
    cout << "     ---> " << t << " <---" << endl;
}

template <class Type>
void fancyPrint(Type arg1, Type arg2)
{
    cout << "argument 1: " << arg1;
    cout << endl << "     argument 2: " << arg2 << endl;
}

void main()
{
    cout << endl;

    // Passing int, float, char, and string literals.
    cout << " 1:   " ;  fancyPrint(12);
    cout << " 2:   " ;  fancyPrint(3.14159);
    cout << " 3:   " ;  fancyPrint('A');
    cout << " 4:   " ;  fancyPrint("Wow!  It's Working!!");

    // Passing variables and pointers.
    int     i = 123;
    float   f = 2.71828;
    char    c = 'Z';
    char    string[] = "Greetings";

    cout << " 5:   " ;  fancyPrint( i );
    cout << " 6:   " ;  fancyPrint( f );
    cout << " 7:   " ;  fancyPrint( c );
    cout << " 8:   " ;  fancyPrint( string );
    cout << " 9:   " ;  fancyPrint( &i );

    // Passing expressions.
    cout << "10:   " ;  fancyPrint( 1+1 );
    cout << "11:   " ;  fancyPrint( 2*i );
    cout << "12:   " ;  fancyPrint( (int) ('z' - c) );

    // Testing the two-argument function template.
    cout << "13:   "; fancyPrint(i, 456);
    cout << "14:   "; fancyPrint(f, 10*f);
    cout << "15:   "; fancyPrint('A', c);
    cout << "16:   "; fancyPrint("Seasons", string);
}
```

5.1.D The additional template may be coded like this:

```
template <class T1,  class T2,  class T3>
void fancyPrint(T1 arg1,  T2 arg2,  T3 arg3)
{
  cout << "argument 1: " << arg1;
  cout << endl << "       argument 2: " << arg2;
  cout << endl << "       argument 3: " << arg3 << endl;
}
```

5.1.E

```
#include <iostream.h>

class Point
{
    private:
        int x; // Point's abscissa.
        int y; // Point's ordinate.

    public:
        Point(int abscissa, int ordinate) : x(abscissa), y(ordinate)
        {

        }
        Point() : x(0), y(0)
        {

        }
        Point(int x_and_y) : x(x_and_y),  y(x_and_y)
        {

        }

        friend ostream& operator<< (ostream& os, Point& p);
};

class Box
{
    private:
        int  height;
        int  length;
        char symbol;

    public:
        Box(int h, int l, char s) : height(h), length(l), symbol(s)
        {

        }
        Box(int h_and_l) : height(h_and_l), length(h_and_l), symbol('*')
        {

        }
        Box() : height(3), length(10), symbol('X')
        {

        }

        friend ostream& operator<< (ostream& os, Box& b);
};

void fancyPrint(int i);   // Prototype for int specialization.

template <class Type>      // Prototype for function template.
void fancyPrint(Type t);
```

```
void main()
{
  cout << endl;

  // Passing int, float, char, and string literals.
  cout << " 1:   " ;   fancyPrint(12);
  cout << " 2:   " ;   fancyPrint(3.14159);
  cout << " 3:   " ;   fancyPrint('A');
  cout << " 4:   " ;   fancyPrint("Wow!  It's Working!!");

  // Passing variables and pointers.
  int         i = 123;
  float       f = 2.71828;
  char        c = 'Z';
  char string[] = "Greetings";

  cout << " 5:   " ;   fancyPrint( i );
  cout << " 6:   " ;   fancyPrint( f );
  cout << " 7:   " ;   fancyPrint( c );
  cout << " 8:   " ;   fancyPrint( string );
  cout << " 9:   " ;   fancyPrint( &i );

  // Passing expressions.
  cout << "10:   " ;   fancyPrint( 1+1 );
  cout << "11:   " ;   fancyPrint( 2*i );
  cout << "12:   " ;   fancyPrint( (int) ('z' - c) );

  // Passing Boxes.
  Box box1(5, 25, 'B');
  Box box2;
  Box box3(3);

  cout << "13:   " ;   fancyPrint( box1 );
  cout << "14:   " ;   fancyPrint( box2 );
  cout << "15:   " ;   fancyPrint( box3 );

  // Passing Points
  Point point1(18, 5);
  Point point2;
  Point point3(3);

  cout << "16:   " ;   fancyPrint( point1 );
  cout << "17:   " ;   fancyPrint( point2 );
  cout << "18:   " ;   fancyPrint( point3 );

}

void fancyPrint(int i)      // An int specialization.
{
  cout << "    ---> " << i << " <--- "
       << "(via int specialization)" << endl;
}

template <class Type>       // Function template definition.
void fancyPrint(Type t)
{
  cout << "    ---> " << t << " <---" << endl;
}

ostream& operator<< (ostream& os, Box& b)
{
  os << endl;
  for (int height = 1; height <= b.height; height++)
  {
    os << "         ";
    for (int length = 1; length <= b.length; length++)
      os << b.symbol;
    os << endl;
  }
```

```
        return os;
    }

ostream& operator<< (ostream& os, Point& p)
    {
        os << "( " << p.x << ", " << p.y << " )";
        return os;
    }
```

5.3

```
#include <iostream.h>

enum boolean {false, true};

template <class typeOfEntity>
void swap(typeOfEntity& a, typeOfEntity& b)
    {
        typeOfEntity holder;

        holder = a;
        a      = b;
        b      = holder;
    }

template <class T>   // Output operator << must manage items of data type
                     // T.
void print(T array[], int numOfItems)
    {
        cout << endl;
        for (int i = 0;  i < numOfItems;  i++)   cout << array[i] << endl;
        cout << endl;
    }

template <class T>
int getSubOfSmallest(T a[], int startSub, int size)
    {
        int sub = startSub;
        for (int i = startSub+1; i < size; i++)
            if (a[i] < a[sub])  sub = i;
        return sub;
    }

template <class Type>
void sort(Type array[], int numOfItems)
    {
        int subOfSmallest;
        for(int i = 0;  i < (numOfItems-1);  i++)
            {
                subOfSmallest = getSubOfSmallest( array, i, numOfItems );
                swap( array[i], array[subOfSmallest] );
            }
    }

class Point
    {
        private:
            int x; // Point's abscissa.
            int y; // Point's ordinate.

        public:
            Point() : x(0), y(0)
                {

                }
            Point(int x_and_y) : x(x_and_y), y(x_and_y)
                {
```

```
        }
        Point(int abscissa, int ordinate) : x(abscissa), y(ordinate)
        {

        }

        friend ostream& operator<< (ostream& os, Point& p);

        // Here point1 < point2  if it is closer to the origin.
        boolean  operator< (Point p)
        {
            // Left point.
            float squareOfDistance1 = x*x + y*y;

            // Right point.
            float squareOfDistance2 = (p.x * p.x) + (p.y * p.y);

        return (squareOfDistance1 < squareOfDistance2) ? true : false;

        }
    };

ostream& operator<< (ostream& os, Point& p)
    {
        os << "( " << p.x << ", " << p.y << " )";
        return os;
    }

class Box
{
    private:
        int  height;
        int  length;
        char symbol;

    public:
        Box() : height(3), length(10), symbol('X')
        {

        }
        Box(int h, int l, char s) : height(h), length(l), symbol(s)
        {

        }
        Box(int h_and_l) : height(h_and_l), length(h_and_l), symbol('*')
        {

        }

        friend ostream& operator<< (ostream& os, Box& b);

        // Here box1 < box2  if its length is less.
        boolean  operator< (Box b)
        {
            return (length < b.length ? true : false);
        }
    };

ostream& operator<< (ostream& os, Box& b)
    {
        os << endl;
        for (int height = 1; height <= b.height; height++)
        {
            os << "             ";
            for (int length = 1; length <= b.length; length++)
                os << b.symbol;
            os << endl;
        }
        return os;
```

```
    }

void main()
  {
    cout << endl;

    int     ia[6] = { 6, 4, 3, 2, 5, 1 };

    float   fa[5] = { .2, .1, .7, .6, .5 };

    Box     b[4]  = { Box(4,12,'&'), Box(2,6,'#'),
                      Box(4,10,'+'), Box(3,5,'*') };

    Point   p[3]  = { Point(6,1), Point(4,5), Point(2,1) };

    print(ia, 6);  sort(ia, 6);  print(ia, 6);
    print(fa, 5);  sort(fa, 5);  print(fa, 5);
    print( b, 4);  sort( b, 4);  print( b, 4);
    print( p, 3);  sort( p, 3);  print( p, 3);
  }
```

5.5 No answer; the exercise was a demonstration.

5.7 The following is the result of the program's execution.

```
lineCoup1
Couplet:  x = AAAAAAAAAA
          y = BBBBBBBBBBBBBBBBBBBB

lineCoup2
Couplet:  x = CCCCCCCCCCCCCCCCCCCCCCCCCCCCCC
          y = DDDDDDDDDDDDDDDDDDDDDDDDDDDDDDDDDDDDDDDD

lineCoup1
Couplet:  x = AAAAAAAAAA
          y = BBBBBBBBBBBBBBBBBBBB

lineCoup2
Couplet:  x = XXXXXXXXXXXXXXXXXXXX
          y = WWWWWWWWWW
```

5.9

```
#include <iostream.h>

template <class bufferType>
class Buffer
  {
    private:
      bufferType*  buffer;
      int          size;
      int          nextCell;

    public:

      Buffer(int numOfElements);
      Buffer();
      ~Buffer();
      Buffer (Buffer& original);
      Buffer operator= (Buffer rightBuffer);
      void append(bufferType  newItem);
      int slotsFilled();
      int roomLeft();
      void reset();
      void buffer_Copied_to_Argument (bufferType a[]);
```

```
                              Buffer  operator+ (Buffer rightBuffer);
                              void showIt();
                      };

              template <class bufferType>        // Constructor.
              Buffer<bufferType>::Buffer(int numOfElements)
                      {
                          buffer   = new bufferType[numOfElements];
                          size     = numOfElements;
                          nextCell = 0;
                      }

              template <class bufferType>        // Constructor.
              Buffer<bufferType>::Buffer()
                      {
                          buffer   = new bufferType[10];   // Default buffer has 10 elements.
                          size     = 10;
                          nextCell = 0;
                      }

              template <class bufferType>        // Destructor.
              Buffer<bufferType>::~Buffer()
                      {
                          delete [] buffer;
                      }

              template <class Type>              // Copy constructor.
              Buffer<Type>  Buffer<Type>::Buffer (Buffer<Type>& original)
                      {
                          size     = original.size;
                          nextCell = original.nextCell;

                          buffer   = new bufferType[size];
                          for (int i = 0; i < nextCell; i++)
                              buffer[i] = original.buffer[i];
                      }

              template <class Type>
              Buffer<Type>  Buffer<Type>::operator=  (Buffer<Type> rightBuffer)
                      {
                          size     = rightBuffer.size;
                          nextCell = rightBuffer.nextCell;

                          delete [] buffer;

                          buffer   = new bufferType[size];
                          for (int i = 0; i < nextCell; i++)
                              buffer[i] = rightBuffer.buffer[i];

                          return *this;
                      }

              template <class Type>
              void Buffer<Type>::append(Type  newItem)
                      {
                          if ( roomLeft() )
                              buffer[nextCell++]  = newItem;        // Here nextCell is
                                                                    // post-incremented.
                          else
                              cout << "\n**BUFFER FULL    "
                                   << newItem
                                   << "    NOT ACCEPTED**"
                                   << endl;
                      }

              template <class Type>
              int Buffer<Type>::slotsFilled()
                      {
                          return nextCell;
                      }
```

```
template <class Type>
int Buffer<Type>::roomLeft()
    {
    return ( size - slotsFilled() );
    }

template <class Type>
void Buffer<Type>::reset()
    {
    nextCell = 0;
    }

template <class Type>
void Buffer<Type>::buffer_Copied_to_Argument (Type a[])
    {
    for (int i = 0; i < slotsFilled(); i++)   a[i] = buffer[i];
    }

template <class Type>
Buffer<Type>  Buffer<Type>::operator+  (Buffer<Type> rightBuffer)
    {
    int sizeOfSum = slotsFilled() + rightBuffer.slotsFilled();
    Buffer<Type>  combinedBuffer(sizeOfSum);

    for (int i = 0;  i < slotsFilled();  i++)
       combinedBuffer.append( buffer[i] );

    for (i = 0;  i < rightBuffer.slotsFilled(); i++)
       combinedBuffer.append( rightBuffer.buffer[i] );

    return combinedBuffer;
    }

template <class Type>
void Buffer<Type>::showIt()
    {
    cout << endl;
    for (int i = 0; i < slotsFilled(); i++)
       cout << "      " << buffer[i] << endl;
    }

// ***Rest of the program, from the Point class onward, is the same***
```

5.11.A

```
#include <iostream.h>

template <class bufferType>
class Buffer
    {                              // The array is now a variable automatically
    private:                       // allocated and released with the respective
       bufferType  buffer[16];    // object's construction and destruction.
       int  size;
       int  nextCell;

    public:
       Buffer() : size(16), nextCell(0)
           {

           }

       void append(bufferType  newItem)  // The new item is installed
           {                              // at the end of the buffer.
           if ( roomLeft() )
              buffer[nextCell++]  = newItem;
           else
              cout << "\n**BUFFER FULL  |"
                   << newItem
```

```
                               << "|  NOT ACCEPTED**"
                               << endl;
                }

        int slotsFilled()
            {
                return nextCell;
            }

                               // Returns the number of elements left for storage,
        int roomLeft()         // 0 when this is none (remember, 0 is also false).
            {
                return ( size - slotsFilled() );
            }

        void reset()
            {
                nextCell = 0;
            }

        void buffer_Copied_to_Argument (bufferType a[])
            {
                for (int i = 0; i < slotsFilled(); i++)  a[i] = buffer[i];
            }

        void showIt()
            {
                cout << endl;
                for (int i = 0; i < slotsFilled(); i++)
                    cout << "      " << buffer[i] << endl;
            }

        // Added for answer 5.11.A.
        int getSizeofBuffer()
            {
                return sizeof buffer;
            }
    };

// This function is part of the answer to exercise 5.11.A, part ii.
void modifyArgument(Buffer<int> arg)
    {
        cout << "\nfrom modifyArgument() ... below is the incoming argument:";
        arg.showIt();

        arg.reset();
        for (int i = 0; i < 5; i++)  arg.append( 1111 * (i+1) );

        cout << "\nfrom modifyArgument() ... the argument after modification:";
        arg.showIt();
    }

void main()
    {
        // Part i:  Investigating the sizeof the buffer data member.
        Buffer<int>  intBuf;
        cout << "\n sizeof intBuf = " << sizeof intBuf << " bytes";
        cout << "\n sizeof intBuf.buffer = "
             << intBuf.getSizeofBuffer() << " bytes" << endl;

        Buffer<double> doubleBuf;
        cout << "\n sizeof doubleBuf = " << sizeof doubleBuf << " bytes";
        cout << "\n sizeof doubleBuf.buffer = "
             << doubleBuf.getSizeofBuffer() << " bytes" << endl;

        // Part ii:
        intBuf.reset();
        for (int i = 0; i < 10; i++) intBuf.append(i);
```

```
cout << "\n\n the intBuf before call to modifyArgument():";
intBuf.showIt();
modifyArgument(intBuf);
cout << "\n the intBuf after call to modifyArgument()";
intBuf.showIt();

// Part iii:
Buffer<int> buf1, buf2;
buf1.reset();
buf1.append(123); buf1.append(456); buf1.append(789);

buf2 = buf1;

cout << "\n\nbuf1 is displayed below:";
buf1.showIt();
cout << "\nbuf2 is displayed below:";
buf2.showIt();

buf1.append(1); buf1.append(2); buf1.append(3);
buf2.append(9); buf2.append(8); buf2.append(7);

cout << "\n\nbuf1 is displayed below:";
buf1.showIt();
cout << "\nbuf2 is displayed below:";
buf2.showIt();
}
```

5.11.B

```
template <class bufferType>
class Buffer
    {
    private:
      bufferType  buffer[16];
      const int  size;           // Now a const.
      int         nextCell;

    public:

      Buffer operator= (const Buffer rightBuffer)
          {
          // Update the left operand.
          reset();
          for (int i = 0; i < rightBuffer.slotsFilled(); i++)
            append(rightBuffer.buffer[i]);

          return *this;
          }

      // All the rest is as it was.
    };
```

5.11.C

```
void main()
    {
    Couplet<int>  c1(1,2);
    Couplet<int>  c2(3,4);
    Couplet<int>  c3(5,6);

    Buffer< Couplet<int> > coupletBuffer;
    coupletBuffer.append(c1);
    coupletBuffer.append(c2);
    coupletBuffer.append(c3);

    coupletBuffer.showIt();
```

```
                    // Answer for 5.11.C.

                    Buffer<int> b1, b2;                  // Get two buffers.

                    for (int i = 0; i < 5; i++)     // Fill the buffers with ints.
                        {
                        b1.append(i + 11);
                        b2.append(i + 21);
                        }

                    b2.append(26);
                                                                // Put the buffers
                    Couplet< Buffer<int> > bufferCouplet(b1, b2);  // into a couplet.

                    bufferCouplet.showBuffers();   // View the couplet.
                    }
```

5.13

```
#include <iostream.h>

class Things
    {
    public:
        virtual void showIt() = 0;
    };

class Box : public Things
    {
    private:
        int  length, height;

    public:
        char symbol;

        Box(int forLength, int forHeight, char forSymbol) :
                length(forLength), height(forHeight), symbol(forSymbol)
            {

            }

        void showIt()
            {
            for (int h = 0; h < height; h++)
                {
                cout << endl;
                for (int l = 0; l < length; l++) cout << symbol;
                }
            }
    };

class Float : public Things
    {
    private:
        float value;

    public:
        Float(float forValue) : value(forValue)
            {
            }

        void showIt()
            {
            cout << " " << value << " ";
            }
    };
```

```
class Integer : public Things
  {
    private:
      int value;

    public:
      Integer(int forValue) : value(forValue)
        {
        }

      void showIt()
        {
          cout << " " << value << " ";
        }
  };

class Point : public Things
  {
    private:
      int x, y;

    public:
      Point(int abscissa, int ordinate) : x(abscissa), y(ordinate)
        {

        }

      Point() : x(0), y(0)
        {

        }

      void showIt()
        {
          cout << " (" << x << ", " << y << ") ";
        }
  };

class String : public Things
  {
    public:
      char* stringPtr;

      String(char* ptr) : stringPtr(ptr)
        {

        }

      void showIt()
        {
          cout << " " << stringPtr << " ";
        }

  };

template <class Type>
struct node
  {
    Type   entity;
    node*  next;
  };

template <class T>
class Queue
  {
    private:
      node<T> *head, *rear;

    public:
```

```
            Queue();
            ~Queue();
            int empty();
            void append (T value);
            void showQueue();
    };

    template <class T>
    Queue<T>::Queue() : head(NULL), rear(NULL)
        {
        }

    template <class T>
    Queue<T>::~Queue()
        {
        node<T>*  nodeHolder;
        while ( !empty() )
            {
            nodeHolder = head;
            head = head -> next;
            delete nodeHolder;
            }
        }

    template <class T>
    int Queue<T>::empty()
        {
        if (head == NULL) return 1;  // True, the queue is empty.
        else return 0;
        }

    template <class T>
    void Queue<T>::append (T value)
        {
        node<T>*  newNode = new node<T>;

        newNode -> entity = value;
        newNode -> next   = NULL;

        if ( empty() )
            head = newNode;
        else
            rear -> next = newNode;

        rear = newNode;
        }

    template <class T>
    void Queue<T>::showQueue()
        {
        node<T>*  rovingPtr = head;
        cout << endl;

        if ( empty() ) cout << "+-+-+-+-+-+-+-queue empty-+-+-+-+-+-+-+";

        while (rovingPtr != NULL)
            {
            (rovingPtr -> entity) -> showIt(); // Not via the output operator, <<.
            cout << endl;
            rovingPtr = rovingPtr -> next;
            }
        cout << endl;
        }

    void main()
        {
        // Define and exercise a Queue of Things.
        Queue<Things*> thingQ;

        // Get some "Things".
```

```
    Integer *int1 = new Integer(1),     *int2 = new Integer(2);
    Point   *pnt1 = new Point(1,11),    *pnt2 = new Point(2,22);
    String  *str1 = new String("one"), *str2 = new String("two");

    // Put our "Things" on the thingQ.
    thingQ.append( int1 );   thingQ.append( int2 );
    thingQ.append( pnt1 );   thingQ.append( pnt2 );
    thingQ.append( str1 );   thingQ.append( str2 );

    // Print the thingQ.
    thingQ.showQueue();

    // Get two Float objects, append them onto the thingQ, show the queue.
    Float *flo1 = new Float(1.1111111), *flo2 = new Float(2.2222222);
    thingQ.append( flo1 );   thingQ.append( flo2 );
    thingQ.showQueue();

    // Get two Box objects, append them onto the thingQ, show the queue.
    Box *box1 = new Box(5,3,'1'), *box2 = new Box(8,4,'2');
    thingQ.append( box1 );   thingQ.append( box2 );
    thingQ.showQueue();
}
```

Index